Contents

First published 1980 by Octopus Books Limited
59 Grosvenor Street London W1

© 1980 Octopus Books Limited

ISBN 7064 0995 7

Produced by Mandarin Publishers Limited
22a Westlands Road
Quarry Bay, Hong Kong

Printed in Czechoslovakia
50401

Introduction

'Let no one think that real gardening is a bucolic and meditative occupation. It is an insatiable passion . . .' Some of you will have already discovered the truth of this statement by the Czech writer Karel Capek. On the other hand, you may have yet to experience the satisfaction that comes from eating your own home-grown food, which you have nursed from the seedling stage through to harvesting, or the pride and pleasure that come from having grown a prize-winning rose or carnation. Gardening has so many sides to it that there is bound to be something in it to interest everyone.

Gardening is the number one hobby in Britain; a recent conservative estimate suggested that there are over nine million amateur gardeners in these islands, and about 150,000 new greenhouses are sold every year. Britain is in fact the garden of the world; our climate, in spite of our constant and often bitter grumbles about it, does enable us to grow a particularly wide range of plants, and we can extend this still further by using cloches, frames and greenhouses.

Growing garden plants brings another very important benefit in addition to giving you pleasure and relaxation and beautifying your surroundings. In these days of increasing urbanization and industrialization, it is essential to try and help redress the balance and to improve the quality of our environment, and gardening can have a profound effect in this direction. Not only do the plants improve the atmosphere, help to prevent soil erosion and maintain soil fertility, but also our gardens provide a home for a great variety of wild animals. Although a few of these may cause damage to your plants, others are welcome allies that consume large quantities of pests, and the vast majority neither help nor hinder your efforts. To a considerable extent, the network of gardens throughout the country has helped maintain the numbers of a wide range of birds and other animals, and you can aid their survival in your garden by avoiding the use of possibly harmful pesticides and other chemicals as much as possible.

Food in the form of fruit and vegetables is another major contribution by the gardener; growing them yourself will result in a large saving in your shopping bill each week. Moreover, the food you grow will be more nutritious and better flavoured, being inevitably fresher and consequently richer in vitamins than shop-bought crops, if eaten soon after harvest. Also you can choose from a wide range of varieties, bred for superb flavour rather than for size, ease in processing and long shelf life. Finally, if you wish, you can make sure that neither inorganic fertilizers nor pesticides or weedkillers have been used in producing your crops.

Our aim in this book is to inspire in you an enthusiasm for a hobby which will be with you all your life, and to help you all, whether you are beginners or not, to get as much pleasure as possible out of your garden. The team of writers we have gathered together is made up of experienced, practising gardeners; they are all experts in the subjects on which they have written, and know exactly what pitfalls you will be likely to come across, as well as the tips and short cuts which produce first-class results.

We have arranged the book in five main parts. You will find that it starts with practicalities such as the effects of the weather, the nature of

soil, plant health and plant foods, and includes the basic techniques of digging, sowing, potting, applying manures and fertilizers, dealing with pests and diseases, and propagation (increasing your stock), so that you become familiar with the theory of cultivation. Putting the theory into practice will inevitably result in some mistakes and failures, but how else will you become experienced and more successful unless you try?

In order to include as much relevant information as possible, we have tried to avoid repetition of various routine jobs. For instance, the section on seedbed preparation in the first part of the book will apply to all the different kinds of vegetables and ornamental plants, so it is not discussed in detail again in either of the later sections dealing with these two major groups of plants. General points regarding plant health, too, are given in the first section, and should be referred to when dealing with individual plants, and similarly with the other features common to many plants. The cross references will help you to do this.

In the second part, we deal with the ornamental garden, and you will find here information on its arrangement and planning; the use of trees, shrubs, herbaceous perennials, annuals and biennials, bulbs and rock plants, with details of how and where to grow them and ways of cutting down on work or filling difficult sites by using the right plants; choosing and growing roses, with a clear but comprehensive explanation of pruning; the best ways of growing superb dahlias and chrysanthemums; imaginative hedges; the correct way to make and maintain a lawn; the use of climbing and trailing plants; making a pool and growing water plants; and a whole section on choosing and making the most of a greenhouse. You will find recommendations for suitable plants in the various categories, and details of their individual requirements. We have also given you an indication of some of the best modern varieties and hybrids, because we know that it is difficult when faced with a catalogue listing many huhdreds of varieties to pick out those which are the most suitable for your garden, especially if you are a beginner.

The third part is devoted to the kitchen garden: vegetables, fruits and culinary herbs. Plans for fruit gardens and rotations of vegetables are given; suitable fruit tree pollinators, harvesting times and storage methods are all included, as well as full details of cultivation and clear accounts of pruning methods. The way to grow each vegetable, fruit and herb is given in straightforward, alphabetical sections, and again we have felt it important to give you a guide to varieties. Sowing or planting times, sowing or planting depths, germination times and thinning or transplanting distances, are all given.

The fifth part contains information on establishing the 'bones' of the garden, showing you the right way to construct paths, steps, patios, walls, fences, and pergolas and how to erect a ready-made garden shed. Finally, a monthly diary provides a quick check of what to do when, a glossary explains the technical words, and there is a detailed index.

As we began with Karel Capek, it seems appropriate to end this introduction with him and, at the same time, wish you all the success possible in your gardening ventures.

'We gardeners live somehow for the future; if roses are in flower, we think that next year they will flower better; and in some few years this little spruce will become a tree – if only those few years were behind me! I should like to see what these birches will be like in fifty years. The right, the best is in front of us. Each successive year will add growth and beauty. Thank God that again we shall be one year further on!'

PRACTICALITIES

Weather

A garden requires adequate sunshine and rainfall if it is to thrive, but it also needs protection against extremes of weather. It is the gardener's task to make use of the weather as much as possible, and also to achieve by artificial means what our climate fails to achieve naturally.

How Heat is Transmitted

Heat always moves from a warmer to a cooler substance. Two ways in which this happens are by CONDUCTION (within one substance or between two surfaces in contact) and by RADIATION of electromagnetic waves.

Air itself is not warmed appreciably by direct radiation and it is a very poor conductor of heat, but it does heat up by the process known as CONVECTION. Every thin layer of air in contact with a warmer surface becomes hotter and therefore less dense. It rises and is replaced by colder and denser air from above or alongside, which then takes its turn upon the warming surface. As each tiny parcel of air warms and then moves upwards, the whole environment – for example, living room, greenhouse or garden – gradually fills with warmed air (see diagram).

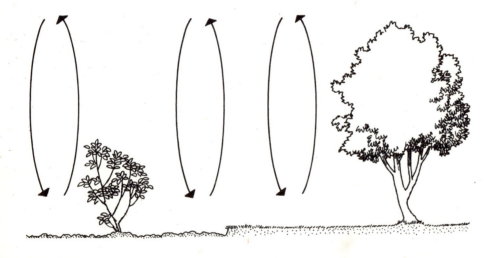

Left: the principle of convection, whereby air rises from contact with a warming surface (in this case the ground), to be replaced by colder air, which in turn moves upwards. The movement of air is illustrated by the arrows.

Day-time Temperatures

The sun is the principal natural radiator of heat. The higher the sun rises in the sky the greater is the concentration of its rays on each unit of ground. Surface temperatures are therefore greater at midday than in early morning, greater in summer than in winter, and greater at the equator than at the poles. These factors cannot themselves be changed, of course, but some effective increase in sunshine can be obtained by planting carefully to avoid undue shading from nearby houses or trees.

Every surface on Earth re-radiates heat, each material reacting differently to a given dose of sunshine. Some examples are given below.

Brick absorbs heat readily, so the ripening of fruit on a south-facing brick wall is assisted not only by direct radiation from the sun but also by re-radiation from the wall.

Water warms up very slowly in sunshine, but it is an excellent conductor of heat, so that the warmth spreads throughout a considerable volume of the water. The surface temperature of deep water therefore rises hardly at all during a single day and appreciably only after a whole summer.

Soil, which consists of millions of particles of rock interspersed with air, warms rapidly in direct sunshine. If the soil is dry, the insulating air pockets prevent heat from being conducted down to the subsoil, so that it boosts the temperature of the surface instead. Wet soil, by contrast, permits easier conduction of heat down into the subsoil and so the surface temperature rises less than it does if the soil is dry.

Glass is transparent to short wavelength radiation from the sun and so the temperatures of surfaces under enclosed glass, such as cloches or a greenhouse, rise rapidly in sunshine. Re-radiation of heat from these surfaces, however, is of long wavelength, to which glass is less transparent. Hence on a sunny day more heat enters through glass than can leave (this is called the 'Greenhouse Effect'), and the accumulated heat can cause dangerous scorching and excessively high temperatures. For this reason, blinds or whitewash on greenhouse roofs may often be necessary in high summer.

Night-time Temperatures

The Earth is the principal radiator at night, so whenever there is no cloud cover to intercept the radiation and redirect it back to the ground, surface temperatures fall quickly, according to the length of night and the particular surface concerned.

The surface temperature of DEEP WATER falls very little during any one night and only appreciably during a whole winter; every time the top layer cools by radiation it becomes more dense and sinks, being replaced at the surface by warmer and less dense water from below.

Glass, being moderately transparent to long-wave radiation, offers a little protection to plants beneath, but not enough on cloudless winter nights. This can be remedied by giving the glass an opaque covering, such as sacking or blinds.

Soil cools rapidly, but heat will be conducted through any water in the soil, right up from the deeper sub-soil layer, thus counteracting heat lost by radiation at the surface. The air temperature at night is therefore usually higher over wet soil than over dry soil.

Grass and weeds, having air pockets between them, are insulated from any heat retained in the sub-soil. Seedlings or other small plants therefore have the best chance of surviving a short sharp frost if they stand in weed-free soil. They will be safer too, if the soil has been watered to assist conducted heat from below, and if they are covered by sacking, a cardboard box, or even a wig-wam of twigs to prevent heat loss by radiation.

Air in contact with cooling surfaces becomes colder and therefore heavier. It remains on level ground when there is no wind, continuing to cool in the same manner as the surface on which it rests. Thus the air temperature near the ground on a still, cloudless night is always considerably lower than it is a metre or so above the ground. This may mean escape for fruit blossom when the soil is hard with frost.

When the ground slopes, dense cold air moves downhill to collect and cool even further at the lowest point, so it is folly to plant frost-shy plants in hollows. You should try to ensure easy drainage of cold air through a garden by keeping hedge bottoms free of dead leaves and by leaving gaps beneath close-boarded fences and gates.

If the wind is too fresh to permit light coverings to stay in place without damaging plants, then the risk of frost on a cloudless night is diminished anyhow. The wind stirs up air near the ground ensuring that every layer takes its turn at being cooled, so that the overall temperature falls less.

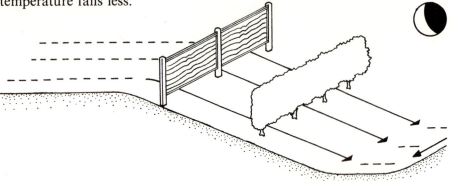

Left: cold air squats on level ground but slides downhill to collect in hollows, on calm, cloudless nights. Ensure good drainage of air through your garden by leaving gaps beneath fences and hedges.

The Effects of Wind

Wind is moving air and has already been warmed or cooled in distant places. Whatever the season, air is relatively cold when it comes from the Arctic, and relatively warm when it has travelled from sub-tropical regions. Wind from the heart of Europe is usually cold in winter, because the land mass cools drastically during long winter nights, but it is frequently very warm in summer when the temperature of the land often soars. Wind from the south-west is consistently mild throughout the year because of the warming effect of the North Atlantic Drift and because the surface temperature of the sea changes so little. All coastal areas have a more equable climate than inland areas for the latter reason.

Cold winter winds from Europe are rarely more than a few degrees below freezing point after their passage across the relatively warm North Sea. However, the wind often brings cloud as well, which prevents the sun raising temperatures the next day. Such an imported **air frost** may persist day and night for long periods and do more damage to a garden than a much colder, but temporary, frost on a still night. Unheated greenhouses and sheds are no protection against persistent air frost, so bring frost-shy plant stores, such as dahlia tubers, indoors.

Dealing with wind in the garden

Wind cannot stop; it eddies round corners and over walls, and it funnels between obstacles with increased speed, rather like water forced through the nozzle of a hose pipe. Avoid siting tender plants at the end of narrow passageways and provide barriers to break the battering power of strong winds.

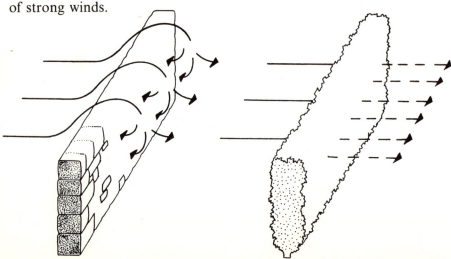

Left: solid walls cause especially strong wind to flow over them and eddies to leeward, whenever the wind is blowing hard. Semi-permeable barriers, such as hedges or wattle fencing, filter the wind without eddies or gusts.

Brick walls are not the best barriers (unless heat storage is also a prime consideration) because eddies in their lee can be as vicious as the open wind. Semi-permeable barriers break the power of the wind by filtering. Wattle or slatted fences require maintenance, but do not compete for water with the plants they are protecting; hedges are more decorative, but make demands upon soil moisture.

Site wind barriers with care, balancing the need for wind protection against possible loss of light. Fully exposed coastal gardens may need several barriers – trees, hedges and bushes – against strong off-sea winds.

What Happens When it Rains?

Water is produced from air. Absolutely dry air is a mixture of gases in fixed proportions, but in the atmosphere, air also acts as host to another gas, water vapour, which it accommodates, like a guest house, according to capacity. If air cools, it is like knocking down rooms in the guest house – there is no need to worry about decreasing capacity until the building has shrunk so that the number of guests equals the maximum capacity. Any further demolition means that guests must be turned out into the streets. In terms of weather, when air temperature falls below dew point, which is the temperature at which the actual vapour content is the maximum possible, some vapour condenses out as dew, fog, cloud or rain. If dew point is below 0°C (32°F), then condensation occurs directly as ice crystals, in the form of hoar frost or snow.

Drying Winds

Air acquires vapour from any water surface over which it journeys. The main sources are the oceans, but every single plant also contributes by 'breathing out', or transpiring, water vapour. When air has been starved of vapour by a long land journey or when its temperature has risen, it absorbs large amounts from foliage and soil. A strong wind, which is a lot of air passing quickly, may therefore make particularly heavy demands upon the garden water supply. Fresh easterly winds in spring are often dry and liable to deprive young plants of essential water.

Water clings by surface tension to soil particles and only percolates downwards when forced by the persistent pressure of more water from above. If you poured a bucketful of water onto dry ground much of it would be wasted in run-off, and what was left would not penetrate far into the soil. This would do harm by encouraging the plant roots to curl upwards towards the water at the surface, thus exposing themselves to the wind. Slow but thorough watering is the only effective way to get water down to root level where it is required. Mulch *after* the ground has been watered if you wish to prevent further evaporation; however, this may hinder warmth from sunshine getting into the soil.

Dew, Mist and Fog

The capacity of air for vapour shrinks when temperature decreases. If the air is fairly dry, i.e. well below vapour saturation capacity, then air temperature may fall far, perhaps to frost level, before condensation occurs. But if the air is moist, its temperature need fall only a little before condensation occurs.

Dew forms first on grass where transpiration by the leaves creates a specially moist micro-environment. The tiny droplets spread along the grass blades are dew, but the large drops which hang from the tips are transpired water (guttation) which cannot evaporate into the air because it is already saturated and consequently it is incapable of holding any more moisture.

Mist and fog form later as the cooling spreads through a greater thickness of air, and this acts as a blanket to prevent further heat loss by radiation. Fog is therefore a friend rather than a foe to the gardener, and some fruit growers actually create fog (by means of overhead mist sprinklers) to give frost protection. Beware, however, the sudden transition from fog to bright sunshine on a spring morning. Greenhouses which have been closed tight against fog must be ventilated again before air temperature builds up too much under the glass.

Dealing with Floods and Snowstorms

Cloud produces rain and snow when air is lifted into regions of lower atmospheric pressure – over mountains, in thermal upcurrents or at confrontations with air masses of greater density. The air expands, cools and condenses and, within the cloud, ice crystals or drops amalgamate until they are heavy enough to fall as rain or snow. There is nothing any gardener can do about excessive rainfall except to minimize the consequences by ensuring adequate land drainage. Be sure to keep all water channels free from blockage, because weeds, dead leaves and so on can create floods in an alarmingly short time.

After fresh-water floods have receded, you can start cultivating the garden again as soon as the soil is workable. If a garden is flooded by sea water after a tidal surge, do not dig or even tread on the soil until you have obtained expert advice. Salt displaces valuable cohesive materials in the soil so that its structure breaks down, and gypsum is usually required to counteract the damage.

Snow is an excellent insulator because of the air particles between the ice crystals, and is therefore a good protection against cold winds, particularly if it falls early in the season when there is still some residual warmth in the soil. However, snow is heavy and can break overloaded branches of young trees and bushes. An occasional shake may avert such permanent damage.

The British Climate

Average figures for temperature, rainfall and so on for an area are not of much use to the gardener except as a broad guide; as we have seen in this chapter, it is not the average rainfall or temperature that harms plants, but extremes of either. The extremes that matter most are frost, drought and strong winds.

In Britain, the prevailing south-westerly winds often bring us warm, rather wet weather, mild in winter for a country so far north, because of the influence of the warm North Atlantic Drift. This warming effect is particularly marked along the western and southern edges of the British Isles. Along this narrow coastal strip, extending from West Sussex, along the coasts of the West Country and those of Wales, and right up to the extreme north-west of Scotland, and including much of the coast of Ireland, it is possible to grow many tender plants, such as some sub-tropical trees and shrubs, without protection.

However, when the wind blows from the north, north-east or east, we can expect bitterly cold weather. This can be a problem particularly in spring, after south-west winds have brought mild weather which lulls the gardener and his newly set-out plants into a false sense of security. This may be followed very rapidly by a cold easterly, bringing frost, the

Above: protect tender young shrubs from frost with polythene sheeting or sacking attached to a frame.

effects of which on the plants will be even worse if subsequent nights are still and clear.

As to rainfall, the eastern side of Britain is much drier than the west, but drought is still possible in western areas.

Using the Dates Given in this Book
From the above, it is obvious that the dates given throughout this book for sowing, planting and other gardening operations cannot possibly be correct for all parts of the country. Unless otherwise stated, they apply to the warmer southern and extreme western parts of Britain.

A very rough rule of thumb is to add one week to the date for every 160km (100 miles) north of the south coast of England, bearing in mind that coastal areas are generally milder than inland ones, that the extreme west may be as warm as the south coast, and that the higher up you are above sea level, the harsher the climate. Even within a single garden, climatic conditions can vary considerably from one area to another – these are known collectively as the 'microclimate' of the garden.

We have been able to give you only very general rules, and with our extremely variable weather, the best course is to get to know your local climate and the microclimate of your garden as well as you can, and to ask experienced gardeners in the area for advice if you need it.

Soil and Composts

Soil
Soil is a living thing which must be very carefully looked after if you are to grow plants successfully. Once a soil is badly treated, it rapidly deteriorates, and is then extremely difficult to get back into a suitable state for growing plants.

To care for the soil properly it is necessary to know something of its physical and chemical nature – what gardeners call its 'structure'.

The Structure of Soil Soils consist mainly of particles of weathered rock with tiny air spaces between them, the original or 'parent' rock having been broken up on the surface by the action of frost, snow, rain and wind. This of course has taken place over thousands of years. Generally the parent rock may still be found beneath the soil; often this is very deep, but in some areas it may be only a few feet below the surface. The particles of weathered rock may be fairly large, as in sandy and gravelly soils; or they may be extremely fine or small, as in clay soils.

The Nature of Humus The second, vital ingredient of soil is humus. This is organic matter – decomposed plant and animal remains. A point of confusion here is that many gardeners talk of adding humus to the soil when in fact they are adding partially decomposed organic matter such as garden compost or farmyard manure. Humus is fully decomposed organic matter and it is really only formed in the soil. Humus gives the surface layer of fertile soil its rich, dark colour. Some soils, such as peaty and woodland soils, are naturally rich in humus. In others, the humus content has to be built up.

Life in the Soil A fertile soil contains countless millions of microscopic bacteria, and these, together with soil fungi and certain soil animals, work on the organic matter to produce humus. In so doing, they break down the complex organic substances into simple, soluble mineral salts that plants can absorb. Humus absorbs the reservoir of these mineral nutrients and prevents them from being washed, or leached, out of the soil. The soil organisms must have enough organic matter to live on, so it is important to add this in the form of manure, garden compost or leafmould. The soil organisms also need sufficient oxygen and moisture, so the soil must be well-drained.

The most important soil animals are the earthworms which, by their tunnelling action, help to aerate and drain the soil. They also pull down organic matter, such as dead leaves, into the soil from the surface, and by passing this through their bodies, help to mix it thoroughly with the soil. There will be many thousands of earthworms in an average-sized garden with fertile soil.

The more thoroughly and regularly you cultivate your soil, the faster the soil organisms break down the organic matter, and the sooner it will become depleted; accordingly, you should manure more generously.

Soil Layers Soil is usually made up of two distinct layers. The top layer of soil is known as the topsoil, and its depth may vary from about 5cm (2in) to as much as 60cm (2ft). The average depth in most cultivated gardens is about 30cm (1ft). The topsoil is the most fertile layer and it is in this that you sow your seeds and set out plants. The gardener can increase the depth of topsoil over the years by regularly adding organic matter such as garden compost, manure, leafmould or peat.

Below the topsoil lies the less fertile subsoil. You should aim to improve this layer as much as possible by adding organic matter to it during planting, especially for deep planting of permanent subjects like trees, shrubs and hedges. Finally, beneath the subsoil lies the parent rock from which the soil was formed.

In gardening, it is essential that you keep these layers in their correct places – on no account during cultivation should you mix the topsoil and subsoil together.

Soil Texture This is the 'feel of the soil'. You can easily determine the texture of your soil by taking a small sample and rubbing it between your fingers.

Clay soils have a dense, fine texture because they consist of very fine rock particles. When wet, these soils feel sticky and can be moulded easily with the fingers.

Sandy soils, by contrast, have a coarse or gritty texture because they are made up of larger rock particles. Their texture is said to be more 'open', and when wet, they will not stick together.

Soils rich in organic matter, such as peaty soils, have a spongy texture. These hold a lot of moisture, just like a sponge.

Chalky soils are thin because their organic matter is broken down quickly. Like clay soils, they become sticky when wet, and dry into hard lumps.

So the texture of soil is governed by its ingredients. Try not to confuse texture with soil structure: the structure is really the way the soil is made up by the combination of various ingredients. It is the balance of these ingredients that governs the texture.

Drainage A soil can hold only so much water – whether the water is applied in the form of rain or as artificial irrigation from your hose. It is essential that a garden soil will allow excess water to drain away to the lower levels, otherwise it will become waterlogged. In this condition it is impossible to grow plants. Firstly, the plants' roots will rot. Also, all the air will be driven out of the soil and therefore both the plants and the soil organisms will be starved of oxygen. In a healthy soil there is a good balance between moisture and oxygen.

Sometimes the drainage of excess water is impeded by a hard layer of soil, or 'hard pan', in the subsoil. This may be formed naturally, particularly in sandy acid soils which contain a lot of the mineral iron. Over the years the iron seeps down into the subsoil where it forms into a hard layer of 'ironstone', known as an 'iron pan'.

Most gardeners, however, are more likely to encounter a 'cultivation pan', formed as a result of cultivating the soil to the same depth over many years. This results in severe compaction of the subsoil so that drainage is impeded.

These pans have to be broken up by deep digging to improve the drainage. Cultivation pans can be avoided by varying the depth of cultivation each year. Rotary cultivators are notorious for producing cultivation pans, because the blades pound the lower soil into a hard layer.

Soils vary in their ability to hold water and release the excess. Clay soils, with their very fine, close texture, are able to hold on to a large quantity of water and these often remain very wet, though not necessarily waterlogged, over the winter. This is what makes them very sticky and difficult to cultivate, and it is necessary to wait until they dry out somewhat before carrying out soil cultivation.

A peaty soil, as we have seen, acts like a sponge. In low-lying peaty areas, excess water is unable to escape and therefore waterlogging occurs in winter.

Sandy soils, on the other hand, are unable to hold onto much water because of their very open texture. Chalky soils, too, are usually quick-draining, because chalk is very porous. So in summer, these two types of soil often dry out very quickly and plants rapidly become short of moisture. In extreme cases, when you water them, the water simply runs straight through into the lower layers.

Different Types of Soil and How to Treat Them

The basic features of different soil types have been described above. Let us now consider how they require different treatment. Soils can be classified in many different ways, but the main types of concern to the gardener are clay, sand, loam, chalk, marl and peat. These are not rigid divisions, but grade into one another. Do not worry if your soil does not fit perfectly into one or other of the categories; simply decide which type it most resembles. It is not unusual for a large garden to contain many different types of soil.

Clay soils, because they hold a lot of moisture, are slow to warm up in the spring and are therefore known as 'cold' soils. Wet clay is difficult to dig and so it is also commonly referred to as a 'heavy' soil. When a clay soil dries out after being wet the surface often cracks. The sun can bake the surface rock-hard so that planting and cultivation in summer may be difficult or impossible.

However, it is generally possible to grow most plants well in a clay soil, as it usually contains enough moisture in the summer and often has large natural reserves of plant foods. Because of the latter, clays may not need such heavy applications of manures or fertilizers as some other soils.

Clay soils are often yellowish or bluish in colour and they have a very solid appearance.

Sandy soils, with their free drainage, warm up quickly in the spring so it is possible to make an early start with sowing. However, sands often lack plant foods and humus because these are quickly washed through the soil to the lower layers. A sandy soil is very easy to dig and is therefore known as a 'light' soil. Sands are also often light in colour – pale yellow or buff, or silvery.

Loam is a mixture of clay and sand and it also contains a good quantity of humus. It is the most suitable soil for the majority of plants: it is well drained, but without the problem of rapid drying out, and it is highly fertile as it contains an excellent balance of plant foods in the right quantities. Loam is easy to cultivate and is generally dark in colour.

There are various types of loam – heavy loam which contains more clay than sand; light loam which has more sand than clay; and medium loam which has an equal balance of clay and sand. The latter is the finest soil, and gardeners who have it are extremely fortunate.

Chalk or limestone soils, like sands, unfortunately have their problems too. Plants may be unable to obtain all the iron or other minerals they need because much of the iron combines with the lime and becomes 'locked away' so that the lack of iron, for example, causes them to become stunted and the leaves yellowish – a condition known as chlorosis. Chlorotic fruit and vegetables will give low yields of poor-quality crops.

Very often, chalks have very little topsoil in which to grow plants, as the natural chalk rock is just below the surface. Because chalk soils are generally unable to hold much moisture, there may be problems with drought in the summer. Chalk soils may be hard to dig, and are often lacking in plant foods. They are usually whitish in colour, especially when dry. Lumps of chalk and large flints are often visible on and below the surface. Marl is a mixture of clay and chalk and is generally a fertile soil.

Peat soils are formed from partly decayed sedges or sphagnum moss, which gives them their high humus content. However, they do not usually contain much plant food in a readily assimilable form, so a complete fertilizer may have to be applied before you can start growing plants. Because they occur in low-lying regions or areas of high rainfall, they are generally badly drained. Peats are very dark brown in colour and light in weight. Their lightness makes them easy to cultivate, but it also means that they cannot normally provide enough anchorage for large fruit trees. Apart from their poor drainage, the major problem with peat soils is that they are very acid. This is ideal for growing lime-hating plants such as rhododendrons, azaleas and ericas, but for most plants you must lime a peat soil, as described below.

Ways of Improving Soils

Most soils, except for peats, benefit from having organic matter added regularly, usually during digging. Organic matter provides humus, thus helping to conserve moisture in freely-draining soils and to open up and improve the drainage of water in clay soils. You can reduce the stickiness of clay soils by giving annual applications of horticultural gypsum. Apply 540gm per sq m (1lb per sq yd) after digging and work it into the surface.

If your soil is prone to waterlogging, then first of all check to see if there is a hard pan in the lower soil. If there is, then break it up by double digging (see chapter on TECHNIQUES). On a waterlogged clay soil, the addition of large quantities of fine gravel or coarse sand will greatly help to improve the drainage.

If these measures do not cure the problem, then you will have to lay a drainage system in the lower soil, consisting of land drain pipes in a system of trenches. The pipes are laid end to end, with gaps of about 1.25cm (½in) between each one to let the water in, on a 5cm (2in) bed of clinker, stones, gravel or rubble, then covered with similar material to within 45cm (1½ft) of the surface; and finally with topsoil to the surface. When digging the trenches, which should be about 90 cm (3ft) deep and 30cm (1ft) wide, always remember to keep the topsoil and subsoil separate.

There should be a main drain sloping down, at a gradient of at least 1 in 100 or 10cm in 10m (4in in 11yd), to a soakaway at the lowest edge of the site, with lateral 'feeder' drains on either side joining the main one. The main drain should be of 10cm (4in) diameter pipes and the feeder drains of 7.5cm (3in) pipes. The feeder drains should be about 4.5m (5yd) apart for a heavy clay soil or as much as 9m (10yd) apart for a light sandy soil, and those of each side should not meet the main drain directly opposite each other, but should be staggered. The whole system forms a herringbone pattern when viewed from above.

The soakaway should be at least 90cm (3ft) wide and deep enough to reach a naturally-draining layer beneath the subsoil; this may be 3m (10ft) or more down. Fill the pit with stones and rubble to within 90cm (3ft) of the surface, then cover this with a 45cm (1½ft) deep layer of small stones and finally fill in with topsoil and firm.

If you have a ditch at the bottom of your garden, you may be able to run your drains into this, but if it is not on your land, you must first consult the owner and your local water authority.

If your drainage problem is not too serious, you may need only a soakaway, or a soakaway with drainage trenches lined with a 30cm (1ft) layer of brushwood or rubble.

Soil pH

In this country, an alkaline soil is one which contains chalk or lime, while an acid soil has very little of either. The acidity and alkalinity are measured on a logarithmic scale known as the pH scale, pH 7 being neutral, figures above this indicating increasing alkalinity and figures below it indicating increasing acidity.

Many garden plants grow well in soil with a pH of 6.5 to 7. Acid-loving kinds prefer a pH of 4 to 6.5, while chalk-lovers thrive in soil of pH 7.5 to 8. Examples are given below under pH Preferences of Plants. Just as cultivated plants have preferences, so do wild ones; your soil is likely to be acid if there is much moss on the surface, or sheep's sorrel, sow thistle, corn spurrey or woodrush are among the weeds growing in it.

To ascertain the pH of your soil accurately, you will need to test it with a reliable soil-testing kit, available from any good garden shop or centre, following the instructions given with it. The results will indicate whether or not you will need to apply lime to raise the alkalinity of your soil, and, if so, how much to apply.

It is unlikely that you will need to make your soil more acid, but if you have a strongly alkaline soil, the best way to reduce its pH is by digging in large amounts of well-rotted manure, garden compost or peat. This organic matter is converted into humus as already described, and humus is largely acid. For a very alkaline soil, an alternative is to fork in flowers of sulphur at 70g per sq m (2oz per sq yd).

An important point to remember when testing soil is that the pH may vary in different parts of the garden.

pH Preferences of Plants

Lime-haters, which need a somewhat acid soil, include the following ornamental plants: *Arctostaphylos*, azaleas, camellias, gaultherias, grevilleas, heaths and heathers (all ericas except *E. carnea*, callunas, daboecias and phyllodoces), kalmias, some lilies and lupins, pernettyas, *Pieris* and *Skimmia reevesiana*. Potatoes should be grown without lime, or they are likely to get scab disease. Among fruit, bilberries, cranberries and blueberries (*Vaccinium*) need markedly acid soil, while most other fruit prefer slightly acid soil.

Lime-lovers, which tolerate alkaline soils, include the following ornamental plants: aubrietas, buddleias, most clematis, *Dianthus* (carnations and pinks), gypsophilas, saxifragas and many trees, including beeches, box, hornbeams, junipers and yews. The brassica group of vegetables (including cabbages, cauliflowers, Brussels sprouts and turnips) should have lime in the soil, as this helps to discourage clubroot disease. Many herbs also do well in alkaline soils.

The great majority of garden plants, however, including most trees, shrubs, annuals, biennials, perennials, fruit and vegetables, thrive in a soil that is slightly acid to neutral – pH 6.5 to 7. This is principally because the nutrients essential for their healthy growth are easily available to them.

In a strongly acid soil, by contrast, some of these nutrients become 'locked up' while others may become so concentrated that they damage the plants. Also, bacteria, earthworms and other soil organisms cannot flourish in acid soils, so that the soil structure and humus content deteriorate. In this country, soil is most likely to become over-acid in wet areas, because the lime in it is continually being washed out by rain, in urban or industrial regions where the large amounts of acids in the air speed up this process, and in light, sandy soils.

Lime and Liming

If the results of a soil test indicate that your soil is acid and lime is needed to raise its pH, then ideally you should apply it in late autumn or winter, forking it into the top 10cm (4in) of soil. As a general rule, unless you have a very acid soil, you should apply subsequent dressings of lime only every three to four years at the most. The heaviest dressings will be needed for a clay soil, lighter applications for loams, and the lightest of all for sandy soils, which are easy to overlime. Remember that overliming can be very harmful. Never add lime to chalky soils, or to plots where you want to grow acid-loving plants or potatoes. Lime is especially useful on clay soils, as it not only alters the pH, but helps to make them less sticky and more workable.

The exact amounts of lime you should apply for different plants will be given as they are described throughout the book.

You should never add lime at the same time as manures, garden compost or fertilizers, or chemical reactions will occur which will ruin the effects of both. Apply lime at least one month before or three months after manuring, or one month after adding fertilizers.

Different Types of Lime

There are a number of different types of lime available to the gardener.
Ground chalk, ground limestone and magnesium (Dolomite) limestone,
which contain calcium carbonate, and are granular, are the safest and
easiest types to apply and store well. They are slow-acting, continuing to
release lime over several years.

Hydrated or slaked lime, containing calcium hydroxide, is also safe and
easy to use. It is a fine, dry powder, more concentrated than the last
type, and quicker-acting, so that if you did not lime in autumn or
winter, you could apply hydrated lime in early spring.

Quicklime or burnt lime, containing calcium oxide, is not recommended
for the average gardener as it is very caustic and dangerous to handle.
Gypsum or sulphate of lime (calcium sulphate) is a very good soil
conditioner, particularly for a heavy clay.

Seed and Potting Composts

In gardening, the word 'compost' has two completely different
meanings. It is used to describe the humus-rich manure substitute made
by rotting down vegetable matter in a compost heap. In this book we
shall always refer to this as 'garden compost' to distinguish it from the
compost being discussed here. This compost is a mixture of ingredients
specially 'composed' to form a growing medium in which plants can be
raised in pots or seeds sown in trays.

Ingredients Traditional composts consist of loam, peat and coarse
horticultural sand. Fertilizers are also included to supply plant foods,
and also chalk, unless an acid compost is required.

Many modern composts consist of peat, or a mixture of peat and
sand, with fertilizers added, plus chalk if required. These are often
termed soilless or loamless composts.

Apart from the ingredients, what are the main differences between
loam-based and soilless types? Loam-based types dry out less quickly
than soilless types and they can hold on to their plant foods for a longer
period. Loam-based composts are easily remoistened if they dry out,
while soilless kinds are often very difficult to wet when dry. Also, there
is more risk of overwatering the soilless types.

Loam-based composts are far heavier than all-peat types so that
potted plants are less prone to falling over or being blown over by the
wind. Also, the former have to be firmed during potting or seed-tray
preparation, whereas soilless types generally do not need to be firmed.

What is a Good Compost? A compost must be of such a texture that air
can circulate within it freely. It must also be well drained, yet at the
same time hold enough moisture for the plants' needs. It must release
plant foods in just the right amounts over a long period of time –
maybe as much as a year – and it must allow the roots to obtain a firm
anchorage. Finally, it should also be partially sterilized, to kill all weed
seeds and soil pests or diseases while allowing beneficial soil organisms
to survive. All composts which can be bought today in bags from garden
centres, etc., whether loam-based or soilless, comply with these
standards.

Of course, buying composts is far easier, although more expensive,
than mixing your own. It is not advisable for the average gardener to
mix his or her own soilless composts, because this calls for considerable
skill to achieve a 'well-balanced' mix. However, it is a lot easier to mix
your own loam-based types and therefore the formulae for these are

given below. Make sure you use partially sterilized medium loam, moist sphagnum peat and washed coarse horticultural sand for these mixes. You can buy all the ingredients from garden centres.

Mixing Your Own Composts

JOHN INNES POTTING COMPOST NO. 1

7 parts loam
3 parts fine peat ⎱ parts by volume
2 parts sand ⎰
To each bushel (36 litres) of the mixture add:
   113gm (4oz) John Innes base fertilizer
   21gm ($\frac{3}{4}$oz) ground chalk

JOHN INNES POTTING COMPOST NO. 2

To each bushel (36 litres) of the mixture add double the amount of fertilizer and chalk.

JOHN INNES POTTING COMPOST NO. 3

To each bushel (36 litres) of the mixture add treble the amount of fertilizer and chalk.

JOHN INNES SEED COMPOST

2 parts loam
1 part medium peat ⎱ parts by volume
1 part sand ⎰
To each bushel (36 litres) of the mixture add:
   42 gm (1$\frac{1}{2}$oz) super-phosphate of lime
   21gm ($\frac{3}{4}$oz) ground chalk
To make acid potting or seed composts use an acid loam and omit the ground chalk.

CUTTING COMPOST

For rooting cuttings use the following mixture:
   50 per cent peat
   50 per cent sand

Plant Food

Gardeners generally grow a great many plants in the available space, particularly on the fruit or vegetable plot. This 'intensive cropping' can quickly exhaust the soil of plant foods or nutrients which plants must have for growth. Therefore fertilizers and manures have to be applied to the soil to maintain the supply of these foods. The soil should contain some for immediate use by the plants and also a reserve of foods available over a fairly long period of time.

If too little food is supplied, the plants will make very poor growth and may start to show various deficiency symptoms, such as stunted growth, reduced cropping and discoloured foliage. Also they will be more prone to diseases.

One point which must be made clear is the difference between 'feeding the soil' and 'feeding plants'. FEEDING THE SOIL means applying bulky organic matter, such as garden compost and farmyard manure. Such materials often help to provide plant foods which are made available over a long period of time, as well as helping to improve the soil structure. Most important, these bulky substances encourage a large population of beneficial humus-forming bacteria in the soil. Most manures and some fertilizers do not contain the foods in a form which can readily be taken up by the plants, but the bacteria convert these into a suitable form.

FEEDING PLANTS means applying fertilizers which contain concentrations of nutrients which are immediately available to the plants, or which can be changed into a readily absorbed form relatively quickly. To give an example, a dried blood or nitrate of soda solution watered around plants will be immediately taken up by the plants and the effects will be apparent within a matter of three or four days – growth will increase and the leaves will take on a deeper green colour. Some organic fertilizers supply plant foods steadily but slowly over a long period.

Mineral Nutrients and Plant Needs
The foods that are needed by plants are often referred to as mineral nutrients. Those needed in the largest amounts are nitrogen, phosphorus (phosphate) and potassium (potash). Calcium, magnesium and sulphur are also needed in smaller quantities. You will most likely need to apply the first four, as these are the ones generally deficient in the soil. Other nutrients that are essential to plants, but needed only in tiny amounts, include iron, boron, manganese, copper, zinc and molybdenum. These are known as 'trace elements', and you should not usually need to supply these as they will be available in the soil if it is kept fertile by regular applications of farmyard manure, garden compost and the like.

Let us now consider in more detail the ways in which plants use the most important mineral nutrients and the effects on plants of a deficiency or an excess of each one. It is a general rule that an excess of one nutrient in the soil causes a deficiency of others. For example, there must be sufficient potash in the soil in relation to nitrogen – if you increase the nitrogen content of your soil then you must also increase the potash content, otherwise your plants are likely to exhibit symptoms of potash deficiency.

Nitrogen This nutrient affects the rate of growth and development of plants and the colour of the leaves. Nitrogen makes plants grow vigorously and produce large, lush, deep green leaves. Plants starved of nitrogen will show the following symptoms: stunted growth; small leaves and shoots; pale-coloured or bluish leaves, which may become yellow, orange, red or purple, and premature leaf fall. All plants need adequate nitrogen, particularly lawns, foliage plants, such as many shrubs, hedges and trees, and green vegetable crops, such as cabbages, Brussels sprouts, kale, lettuce and so on. An excess of nitrogen leads to overlush soft stems and leaves at the expense of flower or fruit formation, and lowered disease-resistance.

Phosphorus (Phosphate) This nutrient, absorbed as phosphates, is essential for good root growth which in turn ensures vigorous healthy plants. Phosphorus also helps to ripen seeds and fruits. As with nitrogen, phosphorus is essential for all plants, especially lawns and also fruiting trees and shrubs, and root vegetables such as carrots and swedes. If this nutrient is deficient in the soil, then plants will display similar symptoms to nitrogen deficiency, as well as purplish or scorched leaves, stunted roots and poor ripening of fruits and seeds. Too much phosphorus causes premature fruit ripening.

Potassium (Potash) Potash helps to form and ripen flowers, seeds and fruits, but is again needed by all plants, especially the fruiting kinds, from fruit trees to tomatoes. Potash deficiency symptoms are as follows: fruits are poorly coloured and small, and leaves have 'scorched' or bronzed edges.

Calcium This again is needed by plants and it is also essential for the soil. Usually applied in the form of lime, it keeps the soil fertile and corrects acidity, as described on page 22. Calcium deficiency results in generally poor growth and the dieback of shoot tips.

Magnesium This nutrient is essential as it is used by the plant to make chlorophyll. This is the green pigment or colouring matter in leaves. When magnesium is deficient in the soil, chlorophyll is only partially formed and the leaves have bright yellow patches. Premature loss of leaves is another symptom of magnesium deficiency. Older leaves are affected first. All plants need magnesium, but especially roses, hydrangeas, apples, cherries and tomatoes. Excess potash and shortage of humus can cause magnesium deficiency.

Sulphur All plants require a constant supply for healthy growth, but a deficiency is very unlikely in this country.

Iron All plants need a constant supply of minute amounts of this trace element. A deficiency of iron results in young leaves turning yellow at their tips, stunted and weak growth, loss of foliage and eventual death of the plant. Acid-loving plants such as rhododendrons, azaleas, camellias and heathers are especially susceptible to a shortage of iron. If these plants are grown in a chalky soil then they will suffer from an iron deficiency as iron is made unavailable in such a soil.

Lack of the other nutrients mentioned earlier (the trace elements) results in various symptoms according to the type of plant, but in a soil kept well supplied with manures or garden compost, they are not generally deficient. They are needed in very small quantities and therefore it is almost impossible for amateur gardeners to apply them to the soil. An overdose could do more harm than good.

How Plants Absorb Food

Plants absorb their foods in solution – they are unable to take in solid particles. The nutrients must therefore be dissolved in water before they can be taken up by the plants' roots. It is therefore essential to keep the soil moist in dry weather, otherwise the plants, apart from suffering from lack of moisture, will be unable to feed. It is pointless applying fertilizers to dry soil if it is not watered thoroughly afterwards.

The plants take in the nutrient solution through minute 'root hairs' which are found at the tips of all main roots. It is important, when planting or transplanting, not to damage the root tips or allow the roots to dry out, otherwise the root hairs will be killed or damaged, so that the plant will be unable to absorb nutrients for some time – new root hairs will have to be produced and in the meantime the plant will suffer from lack of food and moisture. With organic fertilizers and manures, the nutrients are released by the action of soil bacteria and fungi close to the root hairs and this is a particular good and efficient way of providing food.

Plants can also take in some food as nutrient solutions through their leaves and in this instance the foods are immediately circulated in the sap stream. Gardeners can feed plants in this way by applying what are known as 'foliar feeds', which are really diluted liquid fertilizers. They can either be sprayed onto the foliage or watered on using a fine rose on the watering can. Foliar feeding gives a quick boost to growth, but one should never rely on this form of feeding alone as it is not sufficient for the total needs of the plants. It should not often be necessary to apply foliar feeds, although they may be useful in very dry weather, and for correcting deficiencies of certain trace elements, although these are best corrected in the long run by adding plenty of garden compost or other organic matter to the soil.

From air, plant draws carbon dioxide (CO_2).

Sun's energy enables plant to manufacture sugars etc. from CO_2 and water.

Liquid fertilizers can also be absorbed through the leaves.

If the plant is removed the soil has lost some nitrogen etc. and has to replace this.

Right: intensive cropping and removal of plants from the soil for food eventually exhaust the soil of plant foods, which must be replaced by the addition of fertilizers and manures.

From soil plant takes food substances such as nitrogen, phosphorus and potash, as well as water.

A Guide to Fertilizers and Manures

Types of Fertilizer A basic division is into organic and inorganic fertilizers. The organic types are derived from natural sources (dead or waste plant or animal material) while the inorganic types are of purely chemical origin, and are obtained either through manufacturing processes (hence they are often called 'artificials') or by extraction from rocks or dried-up sea beds.

ORGANIC OR INORGANIC? Both types can be used to provide the various plant foods, but an increasing number of gardeners use only organic fertilizers for a number of reasons.

Generally speaking, organic fertilizers have a much longer-lasting effect, supplying plant foods over a far longer period than the inorganic types because they are broken down gradually by the soil bacteria and fungi. Inorganic fertilizers are easily washed, or 'leached', out of the soil by rain and not only are they then unavailable to the plant, but your money has been wasted and much of the leached-out fertilizer finds its way into streams, rivers and lakes where it causes serious pollution. Many gardeners believe that vegetables taste better grown without inorganic fertilizers, and there is some evidence to support this.

Inorganic fertilizers come from sources that are just as exhaustible as oil, so it is wise to minimize their use for this reason, too.

Organic fertilizers are generally just as easy to use as the inorganic types, as they are often specially processed for ease of application. They are usually more expensive than inorganic ones.

If you do use inorganic fertilizers, it is wise not to rely on them too much, restricting their use to boosts of food for growing plants, and using organic fertilizers as much as possible. You should never rely on fertilizers alone; it is essential to use bulky organic matter to add humus to the soil and improve its structure. If you do this regularly, you will find that plants require less extra feeding by fertilizers.

Fertilizers can also be divided into 'straight' and 'compound' types. A STRAIGHT FERTILIZER is obtained from a single source and supplies only one main type of plant food, though several others may also be supplied in smaller amounts, especially with straight organic fertilizers. A COMPOUND FERTILIZER is a mixture (generally man-made) of fertilizers which provide nitrogen, phosphates and potash in balanced amounts, the balance depending on the plants they are intended to feed.

Straight Organic Fertilizers DRIED BLOOD This is rich in nitrogen, in a form which is readily available to plants; it is one of the most quick-acting of all organic fertilizers. It can be applied in spring and summer as a top-dressing around growing plants at the rate of 30–90g per sq m (1–3oz per sq yd), but as it is expensive, most gardeners prefer to reserve it for greenhouse plants or pot-plants. One type is completely soluble in water and can be used as a liquid feed.

FISHMEAL This provides nitrogen, also phosphate and calcium. Potash is usually added as inorganic potassium chloride to modern fishmeal fertilizers, although it is possible to buy straight fishmeal. It may be dug into the soil at the rate of 90–120g per sq m (3–4oz per sq yd) before planting or sowing in the spring. Unless it is dug in promptly, it may be eaten by birds or go mouldy.

SEAWEED MEAL (dried seaweed) is an excellent all-round fertilizer containing mainly potash and nitrogen as well as a wide range of trace elements. Dig it in at 120g per sq m (4oz per sq yd) during spring and summer around growing plants, as it acts quite quickly. Some types have a general compound inorganic fertilizer added.

BONEMEAL This very popular fertilizer is an excellent source of phosphate, which is released steadily over a long period of time, and also supplies small amounts of nitrogen which are released quickly. It is most useful for adding in autumn to the planting sites of trees and shrubs (especially fruit), roses, herbaceous perennials and other permanent plants; it can also be applied around established plants in spring. Rake or hoe it into the soil lightly at the rate of 90–120g per sq m (3–4oz per sq yd) or more on poor soils. The finely divided sort, which used to be known as bone-flour, is quicker-acting than the coarse type, which releases its phosphate very slowly and is ideal for feeding fruit trees. Make certain you buy only sterilized (steamed) bonemeal, which is free from anthrax, or you may contract this serious disease.

MEAT AND BONE MEAL is a good, slow-acting general fertilizer, supplying mainly phosphate but also useful amounts of nitrogen (the proportions depend on the source). Fork in during autumn or winter at 120g per sq m (4oz per sq yd) before sowing or planting, or use as a tonic at double this rate.

HOOF AND HORN MEAL This is a mixture of finely ground animal hooves and horns which supplies nitrogen over a very long period; fine grades act more quickly than the coarser ones. Use in the same way as bonemeal at the rate of 120–180g per sq m (4–6oz per sq yd), but as it is more expensive, you may want to restrict it to greenhouse borders and pot plants.

WOOD ASH from garden bonfires or log fires provides a useful and free source of potash, but remember that smoking, open bonfires can be a health risk and are not allowed in some areas. Non-woody plant waste should be composted (see page 61), but cabbage stems, fruit-tree prunings and so on should be dried and burnt for the ashes. Young branches and twigs are much richer in potash than old wood. If you store wood ash, be sure to keep it somewhere dry; if it is exposed to rain, the potash will be washed out. Wood ash can be applied around any type of plant and may help to deter slugs, but is better given as a dressing at 120–240g per sq m (4–8oz per sq yd) in autumn or winter. Never give repeated heavy dressings, especially to chalky or heavy clay soils, as damage to the soil structure may result.

SOOT is a quick-acting source of nitrogen and useful amounts of trace elements. It should be stored under cover for three months before use, as fresh soot contains substances harmful to plants. Either rake it in after digging, at 120–180g per sq m (4–6oz per sq yd) or use as a top-dressing at the same rate, when its dark colour will absorb more of the sun's heat and thus warm the soil.

Straight Inorganic Fertilizers SULPHATE OF AMMONIA supplies nitrogen, though the speed of its release varies according to soil conditions. In cool, wet weather little nitrogen is available, but as the soil warms up soil bacteria work on the 'ammonia' part to liberate soluble nitrates. It can be used before sowing or planting, or around plants as a quick boost to growth, in spring or summer at the rate of 15–30g per sq m ($\frac{1}{2}$–1oz per sq yd), or as a liquid fertilizer, by dissolving two-thirds of a matchboxful in 4.5 litres (1gal) of water. It has an acidifying effect; this is an advantage on strongly alkaline chalky or limestone soils, but it may easily make other soils too acid if used often.

NITRATE OF SODA is similar to sulphate of ammonia, but is very quick-acting. Use it only as a growth-booster, if at all, at 15g per sq m ($\frac{1}{2}$oz per sq yd) in spring and summer at intervals of several weeks. Large or frequent dressings will destroy the crumb structure of many soils.

SUPERPHOSPHATE OF LIME supplies plants with phosphate (*not* with lime, too, despite the name). It can be raked in before sowing or planting or around growing plants, in combination with other fertilizers at the rate of 15–30g per sq m ($\frac{1}{2}$–1oz per sq yd). It is most suitable for seedbeds and root crops.

SULPHATE OF POTASH is a quick-acting supplier of potash. Again it is very often used with other fertilizers, but can also be used on its own in the spring and summer prior to sowing or planting or around growing plants. Apply at the rate of 30–60g per sq m (1–2oz per sq yd), or as a liquid fertilizer by dissolving 15g ($\frac{1}{2}$oz) in 4.5 litres (1gal) of water.

BASIC SLAG is a waste produce from blast furnaces and looks rather like soot. It provides phosphorus slowly over a long period of time when applied to the soil. It also contains some lime, so it can be used on acid soils low in phosphate, and can improve the texture of heavy clay and peat soils. Apply in autumn or winter before digging at the rate of 120–240g per sq m (4–8oz per sq yd), never at the same time as lime.

MAGNESIUM SULPHATE, also known as Epsom salts, should be used only for correcting magnesium deficiency in plants. It is very quick-acting and an improvement will be noticed within a matter of a few days. It is best used in liquid form, so dissolve 15g ($\frac{1}{2}$oz) in 4.5 litres (1gal) of water and apply around affected plants in spring or summer, or spray leaves with a solution of 7g ($\frac{1}{4}$oz) per 4.5 litres (1gal) of water.

SEQUESTERED IRON is used in liquid form to supply more iron for plants that lack it, especially for those growing in chalky soil where iron may be unavailable. Roses, hydrangeas, apples and many other trees and shrubs may suffer from a shortage of iron under these conditions. It should be used in the spring and summer, made up into a solution with water as directed by the makers, and watered around the plants showing symptoms of iron deficiency.

Compound Fertilizers When you apply a compound fertilizer you are providing the three main plant foods in one operation. As well as general-purpose compound fertilizers for all types of plants, there are specific compound types, such as those formulated for feeding lawns, roses, chrysanthemums or tomatoes; each of these groups of plants has different special needs.

Organic Compound Fertilizers BLOOD, FISH AND BONE COMPOUND releases its nitrogen, phosphorus and potash steadily over a long period of time. An excellent general compound fertilizer, it should be applied before sowing or planting or around established plants at the rate of 90–120g per sq m (3–4oz per sq yd).

Inorganic Compound Fertilizers NITRO-CHALK is a mixture of ammonium nitrate and chalk which supplies nitrogen and calcium. It is particularly useful on acid soils. Apply only in spring or summer before sowing or planting, or around growing plants, at the rate of 60g per sq m (2oz per sq yd).

GROWMORE is an extremely popular, well-balanced compound inorganic type. It can be used for all plants, applied in spring and summer before sowing and planting or around established plants at the rates recommended by the makers.

Liquid Fertilizers Proprietary compound fertilizers can often be bought in liquid form and these are generally organic in origin, such as liquid seaweed fertilizers. Liquid fertilizers are either applied to the soil or potting compost around growing plants in the spring and summer, or they may be intended for use as foliar feeds. Liquid fertilizers are very quickly absorbed by plants and should be considered as supplementary feeds during the main growing period; never rely on them alone.

Manures We now come to the bulky organic manures which are essential for supplying humus and improving the soil structure, as well as for their content of plant food, which however is variable and released slowly. They are generally dug into the soil in the autumn or winter or they can be used as a mulch in the spring or summer.

GARDEN COMPOST (see page 61) is a first-class soil conditioner and provides variable amounts of nitrogen, phosphate, potash and other plant foods, including trace elements.

LEAFMOULD is made by stacking fallen leaves in a compact heap which is best enclosed in wire netting to prevent wind blowing the leaves away. It is foolish to burn leaves and then buy peat. Do not use leaves of evergreens or any other tough leaves, or diseased fruit-tree leaves. The leaves will take about two years to rot down, though this will vary according to types of leaves used and weather conditions. Properly rotted leafmould should be dark and flaky and contain no whole leaves. Leafmould is an excellent soil conditioner for all soils, dug in at the rate of about 6.3kg per sq m (14lb per sq yd), and is excellent for mulching acid-loving plants such as rhododendrons and camellias.

FARMYARD MANURE may come from pigs, horses, cows or other animals, and usually contains their straw litter. It should not be used until well-rotted (after about six months in most cases) and provides the same foods as garden compost – again in widely varying amounts. Horse manure is the richest, followed by pig and then cow manure.

RABBIT, PIGEON AND POULTRY MANURES must also be rotted, but they are too concentrated to use as they are. They are very rich in plant foods and the dried manure, mixed with equal quantities of coarse sand and wood ash, can be used at about 240g per sq m (8oz per sq yd) lightly raked or hoed into the soil, as a stimulus to crop growth.

SEAWEED provides good amounts of the three main nutrients, especially potash, as well as other elements including trace elements, in addition to supplying plenty of humus. If you live near the sea, you can dig it fresh into the soil, and you can also mix it into the compost heap. Alternatively, dry it quickly in the sun and store under cover. Dig in fresh seaweed at about 4.5kg per sq m (10lb per sq yd) and dried seaweed at about 3.2kg per sq m (7lb per sq yd).

DRIED SEWAGE SLUDGE may be on sale by local authorities in some areas; it contains small amounts of nitrogen and sometimes phosphate and is a good soil conditioner, a useful lawn food, or a compost heap activator.

LAWN MOWINGS must first be rotted down before being dug into the soil or used as a mulch. Alternatively, mix them into the compost heap.

PEAT This is partly decomposed moss or sedge remains, sold in bales for garden use. Although it contains hardly any plant foods apart from small amounts of nitrogen, it can be dug in as a good soil conditioner, especially on lighter soils as it breaks down only very slowly and thus maintains its water-holding properties. Dig it straight from the bag at 2.2–4.5kg per sq m (5–10lb per sq yd); because it contains no nutrients, you should also apply blood, fish and bone compound or Growmore.

Plant Health

A visit to a garden centre or shop will reveal a vast array of chemicals for controlling plant pests and diseases, most of which are poisonous and long-lasting and can harm wildlife and the environment. Yet there is no need for the gardener to assemble such an armoury at home because many troubles can be avoided by various means; remember that prevention is better than cure.

Do Not Buy in Pests and Diseases
A lot of trouble can be avoided at the start by buying healthy plants. Before you make a purchase, inspect the plants really thoroughly to ensure they are free from pests and diseases. Once a pest or disease is introduced into a garden it is liable to remain and become established. For instance, avoid buying young plants of cabbages or other brassicas, and of wallflowers too, which you suspect have club root disease, because once this is introduced into your soil it is difficult to eradicate. When buying conifers, especially, be very wary of any that are starting to die from the base upwards as they could be suffering from one of the soil-borne root-rotting diseases; if these are introduced into your soil they are virtually impossible to control and could attack many other plants.

Whenever possible, try to buy plants or seeds which are known to be resistant to diseases. For instance, it is possible to buy varieties of annual asters (seeds or plants) which are resistant to the crippling wilt disease, and there are varieties of antirrhinum which are resistant to rust disease. There are also roses resistant to mildew and a parsnip variety resistant to canker.

With certain plants you should also try to buy varieties which are certified free from virus diseases; this is especially important with soft fruits such as strawberries and raspberries, top fruits such as apples and pears, and potatoes.

Grow Plants Well

Vigorous, strong-growing plants are less prone to most pests and diseases than weak ones making poor growth. And if strong-growing plants do happen to be attacked by diseases or insect pests they are better able to stand up to it and have a far greater chance of recovery.

So it really pays to maintain a fertile soil by manuring and applying fertilizers to ensure that your plants get all the nutrients they need. Also, you should keep plants well watered in dry weather. Foliar feeding (see page 26) may help a plant to quickly 'outgrow' an attack by a disease or pest. On the other hand, you must make sure that you give plant foods in the correct balance; for instance, plants given too much nitrogen develop soft, lush skins and foliage which are more easily eaten by pests.

You should also grow plants under the most suitable conditions in order to ensure strong, healthy growth. For instance, few plants like growing in deep shade, and if planted in such a situation will make thin weak growth which will be more prone to disease attack. Cabbages and other brassicas are more likely to develop clubroot when grown in acid soils, so lime may need to be added.

Avoid overcrowding plants: overcrowded plants will not grow strongly and will be more susceptible to fungus diseases. Sow or plant at the right distances apart, and thin at the right times. Many climbing and rambling roses are more prone to attack by the fungus disease rose mildew when grown against a wall, because this disease thrives in still, stale air, and such plants are better grown up an open trellis or over a pergola, to ensure good air circulation around them.

In the vegetable garden, it pays to carry out rotations of crops instead of growing the same types in exactly the same place year after year (see VEGETABLES, page 232), as this will help to prevent pests and diseases building up in the soil.

Similarly, if a tree or shrub dies and you have to grub it out, do not plant the same kind in that particular spot as the new plant could suffer from 'replant disease' and may even die. This applies especially to roses (see page 77). So plant the new tree some distance away from the original site, or if you wish to replant on the same site then choose a different kind of plant. For instance, if an apple tree dies, then you could plant in the same spot a plum or cherry. With roses, it is possible instead to replace the old soil with fresh and replant with roses.

Other Methods of Avoiding Troubles If possible, time sowing or planting to escape pests and diseases; e.g. turnips or radishes sown in June or later escape most attacks by flea beetles, and autumn and early spring sowings of broad beans are less likely to be attacked by blackfly aphids than later sowings, especially if the vulnerable soft new growth of the top 20cm (8in) of each broad bean stem is removed.

Growing onions from sets instead of from seed (see page 271) will greatly reduce the chance of onion fly attack.

Sowing 'companion plants' among vegetables and fruit may help to deter pests; strong-smelling herbs, such as parsley, fennel or coriander, may keep many insect pests at bay, as will sawdust or rags soaked in paraffin (see CARROTS, page 258).

Biological control methods are becoming more successful; it is possible to buy predators of red spider mites and whitefly for controlling these pests in greenhouses, from the source given at the end of the chapter.

Hygiene in the Garden You will have far less trouble from pests and diseases if you maintain hygienic conditions in the garden and greenhouse. For instance, never leave heaps of weeds or other garden rubbish or piles of pots lying around, as these will attract slugs, snails and woodlice and provide ideal hiding places for various other pests.

Weeds can attract a great variety of pests and therefore you should carry out regular weed control, even if the soil is not being cropped (see WEEDS AND THEIR CONTROL, below).

Regularly remove any dead and dying leaves from all plants, and especially from those under glass, as they can encourage a build-up of fungal diseases which could then attack healthy plant tissue. Also cut out completely any dead or dying shoots and branches from plants. Any plants which die should be dug up and burned immediately. It is safest not to incorporate any diseased or pest-ridden material into the compost heap, and no perennial weeds either, as the heap may not heat up thoroughly enough to kill them – burn them instead.

When pruning shrubs and trees it is very important to paint any cut surfaces over 4cm (1½in) in diameter with a bituminous tree paint to prevent diseases entering through the wounds.

Under glass, strict hygiene is particularly important as pests and diseases can build up rapidly, given favourable conditions. For instance, at least once a year, maybe in the autumn, the inside of the greenhouse should be thoroughly washed down with a solution of disinfectant such as Jeyes Fluid at the maker's recommended rate. This includes glass, walls, staging and paths. All pots and seed trays should be sterilized before use by being soaked in Jeyes Fluid solution and then allowed to dry off thoroughly. If you grow plants in soil beds in the greenhouse, such as tomatoes and late-flowering chrysanthemums, then the soil should be sterilized once a year after cropping, by soaking it with Jeyes Fluid solution as directed by the manufacturer.

The composts that you use for seed sowing and potting should be free from pests and diseases. This will certainly be the case if you buy them in bags from a garden centre, but if you mix your own then be sure to use sterilized loam in the mixes. Peat and sand, the other ingredients of composts, should already be free from harmful organisms and therefore do not need to be sterilized.

Under glass always maintain a healthy atmosphere by ventilating on all suitable occasions and providing heat if possible during cold damp weather. In a stale, damp atmosphere various fungal diseases such as botrytis or grey mould can build up. In the summer under glass you should try to encourage a humid (but not stale) atmosphere by damping down the paths and staging once or twice a day, as such conditions will help to control red spider mite, a serious pest under glass.

Dealing with Affected Plants

To minimize the use of chemicals in the garden, you should destroy any plants which are badly attacked by pests and diseases. This would apply more to plants that are grown only for a short time, such as tomatoes and potatoes suffering from potato blight, or broad beans and nasturtiums, for instance, suffering from a very heavy attack of blackfly. It would certainly apply to all plants suffering from viruses (see VIRUSES, below), as there is no cure for these.

Very often one can effectively control a pest or disease by cutting out the shoots or stems which are affected and burning them. Trees and shrubs which have cankered stems can have the entire stems or branches removed and the wounds painted with a bituminous tree paint.

Many pests, such as caterpillars, can be picked off the plants by hand and destroyed, again to minimize the use of chemicals.

Use the Least Harmful Chemicals

Despite maintaining hygienic conditions in the garden and greenhouse, destroying badly affected plant material, and hand picking pests, the problem may become so serious that some other form of control is necessary. If you have to use chemicals, do so only as a last resort and then only use those that do the least harm to wildlife and break down quickly so that they do not remain in the soil or become concentrated in the bodies of animals. A few pesticides are derived from natural plant sources, and these are the safest types to use; details are given below, under THE LEAST HARMFUL PESTICIDES.

Most modern synthetic pesticides, by contrast, are poisonous to a wide range of creatures besides those they are intended to kill, including beneficial insects. Because they are often very long-lasting, they can accumulate rapidly in the bodies of birds and other animals which eat the pests, and may kill them or make them infertile. Pests and diseases can build up resistance to many pesticides; obviously the more they are used, the more likely this is to happen. Finally, pesticides are expensive and a shelf full of chemicals will represent a considerable addition to your gardening budget. Even when you use the least harmful pesticides, there are some basic rules that you must follow to minimize danger.

Always follow the manufacturer's instructions concerning the period of time that must elapse before it is safe to eat sprayed fruit or vegetables. Never spray when it is windy, never allow any spray to drift onto neighbouring gardens, fields or water in ditches, ponds and so on. Do not make up any more spray than you need for a particular job, or you will have to dispose of the excess. Always wash your sprayer (never use a watering can used for watering plants), and your hands very thoroughly after spraying.

You must store any pesticides in tightly shut containers, clearly labelled 'poison' (preferably the original containers) well out of the reach of pets and children; *never* transfer them to containers such as lemonade or beer bottles – people have died as a result of this.

Encouraging Natural Predators On no account should you spray plants while their flowers are open, or you are very likely to kill pollinating insects such as bees. Always spray at or after sunset to avoid doing this. Also, do not spray any plants which have beneficial insects on them, such as ladybirds or hoverflies, as these insects are very efficient predators of pests and should be encouraged rather than destroyed. Ladybirds (adults and larvae) and hoverfly larvae eat large quantities of aphids. There are a number of excellent books that will help with identifying these insects; a particularly useful guide is the Ministry of Agriculture's Bulletin No 20, 'Beneficial Insects' published by HMSO,

Leatherjacket (Crane Fly larva)

Cutworm (Turnip Moth caterpillar)

Vine weevil and grubs (left)

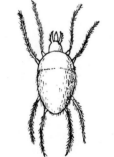

Red spider mite

P.O. Box 569, London, SE1. Birds, hedgehogs and toads are among the other animals that destroy huge quantities of insect and other pests, and they should be encouraged and protected.

The Way Pests and Diseases Attack Plants

Pests ROOT PESTS Some soil-dwelling pests attack the roots of plants and sometimes also the base of the stems, causing plants to wilt and maybe die. Common pests of this sort include wireworms, leatherjackets, cutworms, chafer grubs and vine-weevil grubs. All kinds of plants can be attacked, from herbaceous perennials and trees and shrubs, to lawn grasses and pot plants.

LEAF-EATING PESTS Other pests chew leaves, making holes in them or resulting in ragged edges; this can seriously weaken plants. Caterpillars of various kinds can, in a heavy attack, completely strip a plant of leaves if not controlled. Other leaf eaters include earwigs, capsid bugs, flea beetles (which produce a 'shot-hole' effect), slugs, snails, weevils and chafers.

SAP-SUCKERS Another range of pests sucks the sap of plants, generally from leaves, and this can have a very serious weakening effect on the plants. Aphids (greenfly and blackfly) are the main culprits, attacking a wide range of plants, and often their feeding habits result in severe distortion of leaves and young shoots. Other sap-suckers include leafhoppers, red spider mites and whitefly.

STEM PESTS Some pests attack the stems of plants; for instance, woolly aphids cause damage to the bark of fruit trees. Scale insects attach themselves firmly to bark and their feeding habits can result in damage to young shoots.

FLOWER PESTS Pests which damage flowers include earwigs, thrips, capsid bugs, and some birds which may peck out the flower buds on fruit trees.

FRUIT PESTS Fruits may be damaged by various pests which feed within them, such as codling moth and apple sawfly grubs in apples, and raspberry beetle grubs in raspberries, blackberries and loganberries.

The Least Harmful Pesticides

PYRETHRUM Sold by any garden shop and available as a dust or spray, this will destroy aphids and many other insect pests including caterpillars, as long as they have not grown too large. It is harmless to all warm-blooded animals, but kills some useful insects such as ladybirds and their larvae; however it breaks down within about 12 hours of application, so if sprayed in the evening it will be safe by next morning.

DERRIS Also very widely available, it is useful as a spray for killing caterpillars and other insects, and as a dust for the control of flea-beetles. Like pyrethrum, it is harmless to warm-blooded animals, but unlike pyrethrum it will kill fish, so take great care that none drifts or runs into ponds or streams. For the more resistant insect pests, mixtures of pyrethrum and derris, also readily obtainable, are more effective than either used alone.

NICOTINE This is much stronger than the above two, and will kill the tougher insect pests, such as weevils and large caterpillars, though it spares hoverfly larvae and both adult and larval ladybirds. You should be very careful when using a nicotine spray, as it is extremely poisonous to human beings and other warm-blooded animals; always wear rubber gloves when dealing with it and wash your hands thoroughly after use.

Nicotine breaks down within 48 hours and does not build up in the soil. Crops can be eaten after a week has elapsed.

It can be obtained from various suppliers, including Joseph Bentley Ltd, whose address is given at the end of this section, or you can make it easily as follows: collect 240g (8oz) of filter-tip cigarette ends or 120g (4oz) of ends from non-filter cigarettes, and boil them for 30 minutes in 4.5 litres (1gal) of water, in an old pan used for this purpose alone. When cool, strain the brown liquid through an old nylon stocking in a funnel and it will keep for up to four weeks in a stoppered bottle, clearly marked 'poison', kept in a dark place out of reach of children. Even better, prepare it only as you need it. This should be used diluted with four parts of water, or for a more effective action, mix it thoroughly with a solution of soft soap (from chemists, ironmongers or the address below) made by dissolving 30g (1oz) of soft soap in 4.5 litres (1gal) of water. This helps the nicotine penetrate the waxy coats of the pests.

Typical damage done inside an apple by the larva of the codling moth.

QUASSIA This is a particularly safe pesticide which will kill aphids as well as apple and gooseberry sawfly caterpillars and raspberry beetle grubs, but spares ladybirds, bees and many other predators (though not hoverfly larvae). Quassia chips are obtainable from good chemists or the same suppliers as nicotine, and will keep indefinitely. Simmer 30g (1oz) of these in 1.1 litres (2pt) of water for half an hour, topping up with water as necessary, mix in 30g (1oz) of soft soap and dilute the mixture when cool with another 3.4 litres (6pt) of water. As it tastes very bitter, allow two weeks before eating any crops sprayed with it.

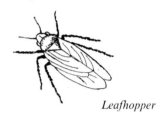

Leafhopper

Other safe aphid sprays can be made by cutting up 1.4kg (3lb) of rhubarb or elder leaves, boiling them for 30 minutes in 3.4 litres (6pt) of water and straining; when cool add the solution to a solution of 30g (1oz) of soft soap in 1.1 litres (2pt) of water. These are harmless to useful insects and other animals, as is a solution of 60g (2oz) soft soap alone in 4.5 litres (1gal) of hot water – allow to cool and use on aphids, whitefly and smaller caterpillars.

Aphid

Other Remedies for Pests SLUGS can be killed by using Fertosan slug destroyer, a herbal preparation that is watered onto the soil near the plants (but not onto their leaves). It is harmless to other creatures, unlike the modern metaldehyde or methiocarb slug pellets which can harm pets and kill slug-eating animals such as birds and hedgehogs. Slugs can also be killed by scattering a mixture of crushed potassium permanganate crystals (from chemists) and fine sand on the soil. Alternatively, trap them in saucers of diluted beer, brown sugar solution or milk, destroying your catch every morning.

Thrip

SOIL PESTS such as leatherjackets, chafer grubs and wireworms can be controlled with Jeyes Fluid as directed by the makers; this breaks down completely and quite quickly in the soil, unlike the very poisonous gamma HCH (BHC) and bromophos products which remain active for a long time and may also taint root crops. Unless you have a bad attack, you can keep many soil pests under control by digging or hoeing to expose them to birds or attracting them to traps of hollowed-out potatoes on skewers set just beneath the soil surface. Cabbage root flies and cutworms can be deterred by surrounding each seedling with a collar of tarred roofing felt or plastic at planting time.

Apple sawfly larva

HAND-PICKING is very effective for all larger, slow-moving pests such as caterpillars, scale insects and slugs – drop the pests into a strong salt solution if you dislike squashing them.

TAR-OIL WINTER WASHES are effective against the over-wintering eggs or pupae of many pests of fruit and ornamental trees and shrubs, although they will kill some insect predators too; it is best to use them only if you have had a bad attack.

GREASE BANDS fixed around the trunks in autumn are good, very safe methods of destroying trunk-climbing pests such as winter moths on apple and cherry trees.

EARTHWORMS are excellent soil improvers and should not be destroyed, but if you feel you have to control them in a fine lawn never use chlordane wormkillers which are very long-lasting and as well as harming wild-life, can be dangerous to humans, especially children, as the poison can penetrate the skin. Instead, use a solution of 30g (1oz) of potassium permanganate (cheap, from a chemists) in 4.5 litres (1gal) of water sprayed over each sq m (sq yd) of lawn; alternatively, buy a derris wormkiller, but do not use this if there is a risk of run-off into a pond or stream.

Diseases

ROOT DISEASES Various diseases can attack the roots of plants, such as clubroot of brassicas and wallflowers which causes the roots to swell and the plants to become stunted. Black root rot affects many plants, including geraniums and antirrhinums. Honey fungus attacks a wide range of trees and shrubs and results in their rapid death.

LEAF DISEASES Many diseases affect the leaves of plants and probably the most common is powdery mildew which appears as a white mealy layer on the foliage, often causing distortion. Rust (appearing as rust coloured spots) attacks many plants including roses. A wide range of hardy plants is affected by leaf spots of various types which cause dark-coloured spots to appear on the foliage – black spot of roses is the best known. Botrytis, or grey mould, affects many plants, both outdoors and under glass. It causes leaves and shoots to rot. There are various leaf-curling diseases; peach leaf curl is one of the most common.

STEM DISEASES Stems or branches of plants are also prone to various troubles; examples are bacterial canker of cherries, plums and other stone fruits which causes open wounds in the branches. There are various other cankers such as the one which attacks apples and pears. Coral spot (bright pink spots on stems and branches of trees and shrubs) generally only infects dead wood, but it sometimes attacks live shoots and ultimately causes their death. In seedlings, mainly under glass, there is a common fungal disease known as damping off, caused by wet, overcrowded conditions.

FRUIT DISEASES Fruits can be affected and spoiled by scab disease and also by botrytis and mildews.

VIRUS DISEASES Viruses are microscopic particles which infect many plants. They can be spread by insects, particularly aphids, on garden tools or on the hands. Symptoms include yellow spots or patches on leaves (mosaic viruses); distorted and crinkled foliage; brownish stripes on stems (streak viruses); and stunted growth. Many ornamental plants are liable to attack, and fruit is especially susceptible. There is no cure for viruses and affected plants should be dug up and burned. Try to prevent infection by buying healthy virus-free plants wherever possible and keeping aphids under control.

Controlling Diseases More Safely A wide range of modern chemicals is available, but these suffer from all the drawbacks of pesticides described above, and much safer controls are still available.

BURGUNDY MIXTURE is a good scab-killer for apple and pear trees, and will also control potato blight, leaf spot of tomatoes and various ornamental plants, various rusts, downy and powdery mildews, and brown rot of fruit. If you cannot buy it, make it up yourself by dissolving 90g (3oz) copper sulphate (from the chemists) in 4.5 litres (1gal) of hot water in a *plastic* bucket; leave this overnight, then add a solution of 120g (4oz) washing soda in 4.5 litres (1gal), mix the two solutions thoroughly, and spray. Wash any sprayed crops thoroughly before eating them.

BORDEAUX MIXTURE is a similar but weaker fungicide, which is more generally available from garden shops.

LIQUID COPPER FUNGICIDES are useful for killing canker, grey mould (botrytis) and many other fungal diseases.

BENOMYL and THIOPHANATE-METHYL are two modern systemic fungicides, both of which control a wide range of fungus diseases.

DOWNY MILDEWS can be controlled by spraying with a solution made by dissolving 450g (1lb) washing soda in 22.5 litres (5gal) of cold water, then stirring in 225g (8oz) of soft soap. A POWDERY MILDEW spray can be made by dissolving 15g ($\frac{1}{2}$oz) potassium permanganate in 13.5 litres (3gal) of water. Be sure to spray both sides of the leaves.

VIRUS DISEASES There is no cure, but remember that many suspected virus diseases turn out to be not true diseases at all, but deficiency disorders caused by lack of some essential nutrient – magnesium deficiency is quite common (see page 26).

Weeds and Their Control

What are Weeds? A common definition of weeds is that they are plants which are growing where the gardener does not want them. Generally speaking, weeds in British gardens are wild plants found growing naturally in the countryside and on waste ground. Those that appear in our gardens are those types that are most efficient at reproduction and the most adaptable. Many of them seed themselves very freely, especially the annual weeds, including groundsel, chickweed, hairy bitter cress and spurge.

The perennial weeds often have very deep root systems and are therefore difficult to control. Many of them propagate themselves by means of roots – it is quite possible that even pieces of root which have been left in the soil may produce new plants. Some of the most persistent perennial weeds include ground elder, bindweed, couch grass and mare's tail.

Manual Control of Weeds There are a number of ways of controlling weeds that avoid the use of chemicals. The most common practice is HAND-PULLING or HAND-FORKING of established weeds and this is suitable for the annual types. Perennial weeds, however, should be dug out completely, including their entire root systems, for the reason mentioned above, before sowing or planting.

Hand-pulling of annual weeds is sometimes too time consuming and it is quicker to HOE the soil regularly between plants to control weed seedlings. If you hoe just as weed seeds are germinating, then they will quickly shrivel up and die on the surface. Hoe as early as possible on a warm dry day when the surface of the soil is dry. Hoeing while the surface is wet is very difficult because the soil clings to the blade, and usually results in the weeds taking root again. You must hoe regularly

Ground elder

Bindweed (Convulvulus)

Couch grass

Mare's tail (Horsetail)

Groundsel

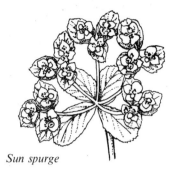

Sun spurge

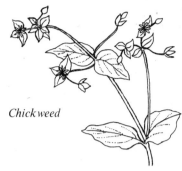

Chickweed

throughout the spring and summer to keep the soil free of weeds.

Another way of helping to control weeds is by MULCHING the soil between plants. The mulch can be a 5cm (2in) thick layer of farmyard manure, garden compost, lawn mowings (not treated with weedkillers), peat or other organic matter, applied from spring onwards. Never apply a mulch to dry soil. Any weeds that do germinate in the mulch are easily pulled out. In most cases, the organic matter will slowly supply nutrients to the plants (these will have to be added in the case of peat, see page 20). An alternative method is to mulch with six thicknesses of old newspapers weighted down with stones, after feeding and watering. When removed, the yellowed paper can be torn up and mixed into the compost heap. Mulching is particularly useful around plants such as currants, gooseberries, raspberries and roses which have shallow feeding roots which can be easily damaged by careless hoeing.

Small rotary cultivators are sometimes used between rows of crops for controlling germinating weed seeds. Never use them on land infested with perennial weeds, however, otherwise they will chop up the roots and make the problem even worse – get rid of every piece of perennial weed first.

Chemical Control of Weeds Most modern weedkillers (or herbicides) are potentially harmful to wildlife and the environment, being highly poisonous, and some take a long time to break down. All that was said above about modern pesticides applies equally to them; in addition it is sometimes difficult to restrict them to the weeds and avoid killing your crops or ornamental plants.

There are occasions when it may be difficult or impossible to hoe or hand weed, but again you should use the least harmful chemicals. The rules for applying pesticides given above apply equally to weedkillers; in addition, if using them on weeds near garden plants, use a dribble bar on the watering can or a hand sprayer, to avoid killing your plants. Be extra careful not to allow sprays to drift onto neighbouring gardens or other land.

Weedkillers are described as selective (destroying broad-leaved plants for example) or non-selective; none is truly selective however. AMMONIUM SULPHAMATE (sold as Amcide), although non-selective, is very safe, as it breaks down within several weeks to sulphate of ammonia, so although it should not be used among growing plants, you will be able to sow or plant a treated area within two months of applying it. As it works by 'choking' the weeds, use it when they are growing strongly in spring and summer. Be careful not to let it get on your skin, in your eyes, or into ponds or streams. A solution of 450g (1lb) of the white crystals in 4.5 litres (1gal) of cold water will be enough to treat 9.3sq m (100sq ft) and will kill couch grass, spear thistles, giant docks and other difficult perennial weeds as well as any annuals. It is obtainable from

Joseph Bentley Ltd (address at the end of this section) or from Battle, Hayward and Bower, Carrholm Road, Lincoln, Lancashire.
TAR-OIL WINTER WASHES are useful for removing weeds from gravel paths and are safer than the modern alternatives.

If you find it impossible to remove odd perennial weeds among cultivated plants, you could 'spot-treat' them using a hormone weedkiller such as 2-4-D with mecoprop applied on a small paintbrush directly to the weed, but this should be used only as a last resort.

Suppliers Supplies of safer pesticides and ammonium sulphamate can be obtained from Joseph Bentley Ltd, Barrow-on-Humber, South Humberside, DN19 7AQ and various other good horticultural suppliers.

Many of the remedies, including those for biological control, can be obtained from The Henry Doubleday Research Association, Convent Lane, Bocking, Braintree, Essex. This non-profit making body is the largest organized group of organic gardeners in Britain and carries out much valuable research into safe methods of controlling pests, diseases and weeds.

Propagation: How to increase your stock

Seeds

Growing from seed is one of the major methods of raising new plants and is very often a cheap one, particularly if you save your own. Even if you buy packets of seeds from a seedsman or garden centre you will be getting good value for money for they mostly each still cost only a matter of pence rather than pounds, and if they are sown carefully and the seedlings well cared for, they will provide you with a good quantity of new plants.

Sowing seeds outdoors and in seed trays in a greenhouse or indoors is fully discussed under BASIC TECHNIQUES on pages 58–60, so this section deals with collecting and storing seeds from plants in your own garden or greenhouse.

Saving Your Own Seed It is best to collect seeds only from true species of plants – those which are found in the wild and have been unaltered by man. The resultant seedlings will then be true to type – that is, will be identical to the parent plants. If you collect and sow seeds from highly bred plants – hybrids and cultivated varieties (cultivars) – such as hybrid tea roses or dahlias, then the resultant seedlings will be a very mixed batch and many will not have the same characteristics as the parent plants. Many of them will in fact be inferior to the original parent plant.

There are sure to be many plants in your garden or greenhouse from which you can collect seeds, such as trees, shrubs, conifers, climbers, herbaceous plants, alpines, hardy annuals, and greenhouse shrubs and perennials.

It is best to collect seeds when they are fully ripe but before they are shed by the plants. The main period for seed collecting is in the summer and autumn. Many plants produce seeds in dry pods and capsules and

Right: a garden in spring

Above: summer in the herbaceous border

Right: varied planting adds depth to a corner

Above: an alley of laburnums

Right: a cottage garden in summer

Left: wisteria, cheiranthus and silver tulips

Above: lacecap hydrangeas 'Bluewave'

an indication of ripening is a change in the colour of these, generally from green to brown or black. The pods and capsules usually split open to release the ripe seeds, so collect them just before this happens. Many plants produce their seeds in fleshy fruits and berries, such as those of holly and cotoneaster, and these generally turn from green to red or various other colours (depending on the plant) as the seeds within ripen. Conifers produce their seeds in cones and as the seeds ripen, the woody scales start to open and eventually the seeds fall out.

It is best to collect seeds on a warm dry day to ensure that the seed pods, capsules and so on are dry. Put them in paper bags and make sure you label each one correctly with the name of the plant and the date.

Seeds which are in dry pods and capsules should then be dried off for several weeks in a warm, sunny, dry, airy place, such as on a greenhouse bench or windowsill. Spread out the seed pods in a single layer on sheets of newspaper. Once thoroughly dry, the seeds should be separated from the pods, capsules or cones. You may find that many of the seed containers have split open and the seeds are lying on the newspaper ready to be gathered up. In other instances you will have to gently crush the pods and capsules to release the seeds. The best method is to rub them between your hands. You will now have a mixture of seeds and debris (known as chaff) and ideally the two should be separated. This is easily achieved by gently blowing the mixture – the lighter chaff will be blown away, leaving the seeds for you to collect up. There are special seed sieves on the market for separating seeds and chaff, but these are only recommended if you intend to clean large quantities of home-saved seeds.

Once the seeds have been separated, they should be put into paper envelopes and labelled. Then they should be stored in a cool room indoors (they must be kept dry and frost-free) until sowing time.

Most of the fleshy fruits and berries produced by trees and shrubs should be stored by a different method, known as stratification, and the idea of this is to soften the hard seed coats so that the seeds will germinate better when sown. For this method you will need a tin or a plastic pot for each subject. There must be drainage holes in the base. Place a 2.5cm (1in) layer of moist sand in the base, followed by a single layer of the fruits. Place a 2.5cm (1in) layer of sand over these, and then another single layer of fruits. Continue in this way until all the fruits are between layers of sand, and finish off with a layer of sand on top. Now place the tins or pots in a north-facing site out of doors so that the seeds are subjected to alternate freezing and thawing over the winter. By the following spring the seed coats should have become softened by this treatment and the mixture of seeds and sand can be sown.

Vegetative Methods
Cuttings An important method of increasing plants is by means of stem cuttings – shoots of plants which are encouraged to form roots so that they grow into new plants identical in every respect to their parents. Shrubs, conifers, soft fruits, perennials, alpines and many greenhouse plants can often be increased from various types of stem cutting.
SOFTWOOD CUTTINGS These are taken from soft, unripened side shoots of plants such as shrubs, perennials, alpines and greenhouse shrubs or greenhouse perennials. They are generally taken between April and the end of June. Cut side shoots from the plants and trim the base of each

Left: plants for city privacy

one immediately below a leaf joint (node) with a sharp knife to provide cuttings approximately 7.5cm (3in) long. Then cut off the lower leaves so that the lower third to half is leafless. Dip the base of each cutting in a hormone rooting powder formulated for softwoods to encourage rooting. Moisten the base first if it is dry.

The cuttings can be rooted in a mixture of equal parts peat and coarse sand in pots of a suitable size. Make the compost moderately firm and dibble in the cuttings up to their lower leaves. Use a wooden dibber or pencil to make the holes and lightly firm-in each cutting. Cuttings can be inserted around the edge of the pot and also in the centre, so that the leaves are only just touching. Water in with a fine-rosed can.

Softwood cuttings need heat to root successfully, an electrically heated propagating case being ideal. High humidity is also necessary, and this is also achieved in a propagating case. An amateur mist-propagation unit, although more expensive, is the ideal piece of equipment for rooting softwood cuttings. Failing these, one can root softwoods on a warm windowsill indoors. Slip the pot of cuttings into a polythene bag and secure the top with an elastic band – this will provide the desired humidity. The bag can be supported with a few split canes inserted in the pot. Ventilate the cuttings two or three times a week for an hour or so.

SEMI-RIPE CUTTINGS These are taken from shoots which are partially ripe or woody at the base but still soft at the tips. They are generally rooted at any time between July and late September. Shrubs, conifers, tender perennials and many greenhouse plants can be increased from semi-ripe material. They are also known as half-ripe cuttings and semi-hardwood cuttings.

The cuttings are made from side shoots and are prepared in the way described for softwood cuttings, except that a rooting powder specially formulated for semi-ripe cuttings should be used. Again, insert the cuttings in pots as described under softwood cuttings.

These cuttings do not necessarily need heat to root, although gentle bottom heat will speed up rooting. Many people root them in cold frames or on a greenhouse bench. A windowsill indoors would also be suitable.

The general method of rooting a softwood cutting is to remove the lower leaves of a side shoot, cut the stem just below a leaf joint, and insert in light compost up to the lower leaves. Several cuttings may be put round the edge of the same pot.

HARDWOOD CUTTINGS These are prepared from current year's shoots which are fully ripened or woody, and they can be rooted in a sheltered spot out of doors. Hardwoods are taken from October to December. Subjects easily raised from hardwoods include blackcurrants, red currants, gooseberries, willow, privet, Chinese honeysuckle, *Tamarix*, *Weigela*, and some roses and many other deciduous shrubs.

Use a pair of secateurs to prepare them, cutting just above a leaf joint (node) at the top and just below a node at the base. The average length should be about 20–30cm (8–12in). All the dormant buds are left intact, with the exception of red currants, gooseberries and roses; with these cut out all the buds except the top three or four. Dip the bases of prepared cuttings in a hormone rooting powder formulated for hardwoods.

The cuttings are then inserted in a slit trench (a V-shaped trench) made with a spade. Stand them upright in the trench, return the soil around them and firm well in. Cuttings should be inserted to about half their length – but with red currants and gooseberries some bud-free stem should show above soil level. Refirm after a frost if necessary, and by the following autumn the cuttings should be well rooted.

Grafting

Grafting involves joining together the parts of two separate plants to form a new plant, and is generally used to produce new trees, both ornamental and fruiting kinds. There are various reasons for grafting – mainly it is used to increase hybrid trees which would not come true to type from seeds. Many of these hybrids are also difficult to root from cuttings, and grafting provides the easier alternative. Many trees, particularly fruit trees such as apples and pears, do not grow well on their own roots, even if cuttings were successfully rooted, so that grafting is used to influence the growth rate. A piece of shoot of the variety to be propagated, known as the scion, is joined on to part of another plant which provides the root system only. The latter is known as the rootstock, and it is this which influences the ultimate vigour of the tree. In fruit-tree raising there are many different kinds of rootstock – some result in large vigorous trees suitable for orchards; some result in less vigorous trees, while others result in dwarf trees. The latter are necessary for trained forms of fruit trees such as cordons and espaliers.

The rootstock used for grafting is generally the common counterpart of the variety which is to be propagated; for example, varieties of birch are grafted onto common silver birch, *Betula pendula*; cherries onto the wild cherry, *Prunus avium*; and apples onto selected forms of wild apple rootstocks. Pears, however, are grafted onto the quince, *Cydonia oblonga*.

Rootstocks of some subjects can be raised from seed, like birch, ash and beech. Rootstocks for fruit trees are not generally raised by amateurs as it is a specialized process, so the gardener may have to beg some from a kindly nurseryman, or use rooted suckers produced by established trees in the garden.

Two-year-old rootstocks should be used for grafting and they should have been planted out for at least one growing season to become established.

The usual type of graft used to produce new trees is the WHIP AND TONGUE GRAFT, and this is made in February or March while the plants are dormant.

Firstly you will need to collect some previous year's shoots of the tree you wish to increase. With secateurs, these should be cut into four or five bud lengths, cutting just above a bud at the top and 2.5cm (1in) below a bud at the base. These are the scions which will produce all the top growth of the new tree. A 5cm (2in) long slanting cut is now made at the base of the scion from one side to the other, on the opposite side to the lowest bud. In the centre of this a short upward cut is made to form a tongue.

Now the rootstock is prepared, firstly by cutting it down to within 23–30cm (9–12in) of the ground. Next, a 5cm (2in) long slanting cut is made at the top of the rootstock from one side to another. In the centre of this a short downward cut is made to form a tongue.

The scion is now fitted to the rootstock by interlocking the tongues. To be successful, the cut surfaces of both scion and rootstock should match exactly. If they will not match all round, then move the scion to one side so that one edge is in contact with one edge of the rootstock cut. Now tie in the scion tightly with raffia and then seal the grafted part with a coat of bituminous tree paint. Put a dab of this on the top of the scion also. In about eight weeks the graft should have united, at which stage the tie can be carefully cut away.

Budding This is a form of grafting but instead of joining a scion on to the rootstock, one inserts a single growth bud. Budding is a good method of increasing hybrid roses, as well as some fruit trees and ornamental trees.

To obtain buds of the varieties to be increased, cut off strong current year's shoots, and discard the soft tips. A bud will be found in each leaf axil (where the leaf stalk joins the shoot). Remove the leaves but retain the leaf stalks (petioles).

Now prepare the rootstock by making a T-shaped cut as close to the soil as possible. First make a 3.8cm (1½in) vertical cut, followed by a short horizontal cut at the top. Prise up the bark on each side of the vertical cut to form two flaps.

Next you must remove a bud from one of the prepared shoots. Insert your pruning or budding knife below a bud, and draw it underneath so that it comes out above it. This should give you a shield-shaped piece of bark 3.8cm (1½in) long with a bud in the centre. There will be a thin sliver of wood behind the bud – this should be carefully flicked out with the tip of the knife blade or with your finger nail.

Holding the bud by the leaf stalk, slip it down underneath the bark of the rootstock and close the flaps of bark. Now tie in the bud with raffia, leaving the actual bud exposed; or use one of the proprietary rubber budding patches with a wire clip. The patch covers the bud and is held in place by a clip at the back of the rootstock. Within about six weeks the bud should have taken, in which case the ties should be removed. In February of the following year cut off the top of the rootstock just above the bud – this will stimulate the bud into growth.

Increasing large clumps of plants by division may be done by placing two garden forks back to back through the clump, then levering them apart.

Division

Division simply means splitting a plant into a number of smaller pieces. It is generally used for increasing herbaceous plants and other hardy perennials, including grasses and ferns. Many carpeting or mat-forming alpines can also be divided.

The best time for division is in the early spring – March or early April – or in the case of spring-flowering subjects, immediately after flowering.

Carefully lift the plants and tease away as much soil as possible. Many herbaceous plants make really large clumps which may be difficult to pull apart with the hands. In such cases, thrust two garden forks back to back through the centre of the clump and then prise them apart. This should give you two pieces, which can then be further divided by the same technique. The ideal size of divisions for replanting is about the size of your hand. It is best to replant divisions immediately to avoid the roots drying out. Remember that each division should consist of a good portion of roots plus some top growth or dormant buds.

Layering

This involves rooting a shoot or stem while it is still attached to the parent plant. It is an easy method of increasing many shrubs and trees, such as magnolias, rhododendrons, forsythias, camellias and so on. It is particularly useful for those which are difficult to increase from cuttings.

Layering can be done from April to August, using young stems, preferably those produced in the previous year. The ground where the shoots are to be pegged down should be forked over and ideally some peat and coarse sand incorporated.

Now the shoot for layering can be prepared. About 30cm (1ft) from its tip it should be wounded. Either give the shoot a sharp twist to partially break some of the tissues; or use a knife and make a 5cm (2in) long cut halfway through the shoot to form a tongue. Keep the tongue open with a small stone.

Using a galvanized wire peg the shape of a hairpin, peg down the shoot where it was wounded into a depression in the prepared soil. Cover with a layer of soil 10–15cm (4–6in) deep and firm. Now insert a short cane and tie in the shoot so that it is in an upright position.

Within 12 months (18 months for magnolias and rhododendrons) the shoot should be well rooted where it was pegged down. Carefully lift it, sever it from the parent plant and replant it in its permanent site.

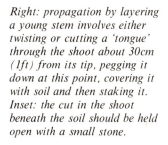

Right: propagation by layering a young stem involves either twisting or cutting a 'tongue' through the shoot about 30cm (1ft) from its tip, pegging it down at this point, covering it with soil and then staking it. Inset: the cut in the shoot beneath the soil should be held open with a small stone.

Air Layering In a way this is similar to layering mentioned above, except that the shoot is rooted above ground. It is useful for those trees and shrubs whose branches cannot be pulled down to ground level.

A shoot is prepared by cutting a tongue in it as described above. The tongue is kept open by packing it with moist sphagnum moss. Then the whole of the prepared part of the shoot is wrapped with moist moss.

Right: to air layer a branch, first cut a tongue in it and hold it open with damp sphagnum moss. Wrap polythene round the cut, tie the lower end as shown and pack more moss round the branch. Seal the top of the polythene tube and the long overlapping edge with tape to keep out rain.

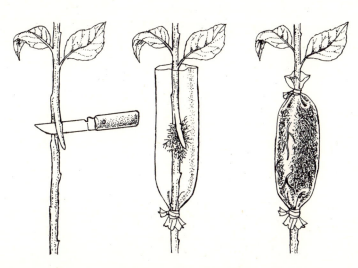

This is held in place with a bandage of clear polythene sheeting. The sleeve or bandage must be sealed to prevent rain entering: using waterproof tape, give a few twists around each end of the bandage and use a longer length of tape to seal the overlapping edge of the polythene.

Air layering is carried out in the period from April to August and the shoots may take 12 months to root. The time to remove the polythene and moss is when white roots can be seen through the polythene. The rooted shoot should be severed from the parent plant and planted out in the garden.

Basic Cultivation Techniques

Essential Garden Tools

Always buy the best tools that you can afford, to ensure that they last a good many years. These days many tools are made from stainless steel, and these are the best that money can buy; they are easy to use as soil does not stick to them, they do not rust, they are very strong and are easy to clean. If you cannot afford stainless steel tools, buy good-quality ones in ordinary steel.

Spade Choose a spade carefully – if it is too small it will take you too long to dig a piece of ground, and if it is too large and heavy, the work may soon tire you. The blade of a spade should preferably be a full-sized one: 29cm (11½in) long for deep digging. The usual width is 19cm (7½in). Women and children may find the smaller border spade easier to use, although it will not dig as deeply as a full-length one. Its blade size is generally 23cm (9in) long by 14cm (5½in) broad. A tread plate at the top of the blade makes digging easier on the boots and more comfortable. Spades may have Y-shaped or T-shaped handles – choose whichever you prefer. The shaft may be of ash-wood or of tubular steel coated with a thin layer of plastic, the latter being the lightest and also very strong.

Fork A four-pronged fork is the most useful, with 28cm (11in) long prongs. The usual width is about 16.5cm (6½in). A lighter border fork measures about 23cm by 14cm (9in by 5½in). As with spades, forks have either Y or T-shaped handles, and shafts in either ash or tubular steel. Flat-pronged forks are especially good for digging light sandy soils and for harvesting root crops, particularly potato tubers.

Rake For preparing a seed bed you will need a steel rake with 10 or 12 teeth. Choose one with a 1.5m (5ft) handle, either in ash or tubular steel. The latter will be lighter in weight. Rakes with cheap pressed steel heads will not last long.

Hoes There are various types of hoe on the market. The DUTCH HOE, with a stirrup-shaped blade almost in the same plane as the handle, is the most popular for cultivating the surface of the soil and controlling weed seedlings. It has one cutting edge and is pushed forward through the soil in short jerks.

The DRAW HOE is also used for weeding and cultivating and again has

Below, left to right: shears, dibber, trowel, hand fork, secateurs, digging spade and fork, border spade and fork, rake, draw hoe, two types of Dutch hoe, double-wheeled wheelbarrow.

one cutting blade. In this instance the hoe is used with a downward, chopping action, and then pulled towards you. It is particularly useful for hoeing heavy or very stony soils, or where there is a lot of weed growth. Another very important use of the draw hoe is in drawing out drills for sowing seed; pull the hoe with the blade on edge through the soil at the correct depth for the seed being sown. For broad drills, use the broader base of the blade.

The double-edged hoe (with two cutting edges) is used with a push-pull action and therefore very fast work is possible.

The usual length of hoe handles is 1.5m (5ft) and they may be made of ash or tubular steel. Choose a hoe with a 15cm (6in) wide blade.

Trowel and Hand Fork A hand trowel is essential for planting small plants. Choose one with a short handle and with a blade about 15cm (6in) in length. A small hand fork is useful for loosening the soil and digging out weeds between plants close together. It is also useful for lifting small plants. A hand fork generally has three prongs; choose one with a short handle.

Shears Short-handled shears are used for trimming hedges, lawn edges, dead blooms on various plants and so on. The blades are generally about 20–23cm (8–9in) long but lighter shears generally have shorter blades. Ensure that the ones you buy are made from Sheffield steel, hardened and with a machined cutting edge. Good shears will have a hardened-steel centre bolt with a self-locking nut to prevent the blades becoming loose during use.

Secateurs These are essential for pruning shrubs, trees and other plants. Buy good-quality steel as then the cutting edges will remain sharp. The parrot-bill types are better than the anvil types as they are less likely to crush or bruise the stems. They have two cutting blades, whereas the anvil types have one which cuts down onto a steel bar – the 'anvil'.

Dibber A dibber can be used when planting seedlings of plants such as brassicas, wallflowers and so on. It is pushed into the ground to make a planting hole, and is quicker than using a hand trowel. Stainless steel and plastic dibbers are available; if you buy a wooden one, choose one with a metal tip. The tip should be rounded, not pointed, or it may leave an air space beneath the seedling when it is planted.

Garden Line A garden line is necessary for marking out straight seed drills and rows for planting vegetables. Polythene or polypropylene lines are rot-proof, and for easy storage buy one with a reel of some kind for winding up the line after use.

Wheelbarrow This is essential in the average garden for moving rubbish, compost, manure, peat and so on. The most popular type is probably the galvanized-steel barrow, although more expensive kinds are available. There is the single-wheeled version or, perhaps more easily handled, the double-wheeled type. A really up-to-date rigid plastic barrow has a pneumatic ball-shaped wheel, and is light and easy to use.

Digging

There are many instances where digging is required. New gardens will need to be dug thoroughly before planting, laying lawns and so on; and vegetable plots and flower beds should be dug prior to sowing and planting.

What are the reasons for digging the soil? It enables essential organic matter such as garden compost and manures to be incorporated; it encourages better air circulation in the soil, so necessary for healthy growth; it helps to improve drainage of excess water by relieving compaction in the lower soil; it enables you to bury annual weed growth and other surface growth and to remove the roots of perennial weeds; and it exposes a larger surface area of soil to frost in the winter, so that the frost reduces the soil to smaller lumps, making it easier to prepare for sowing and planting in the spring.

There are various methods of digging, as discussed below, but, generally speaking, it is best to dig in the autumn so that the ground lies rough over winter, when frosts and wind will improve its structure. Avoid digging when the soil is wet and sticky or frozen. Dig in straight lines across the plot to ensure that all the soil is turned over and to produce a level surface. A garden line can be used to guarantee straight lines – follow the line, scoring a slit along the ground with a spade, and then remove the garden line while you dig. Always insert the spade or fork to its full depth – known as a single 'spit'.

Single Digging This is the most common type of digging, and involves turning over the soil to a single spade's depth, or spit. It is generally carried out annually on the vegetable plot and flower beds. If you have a wide plot, divide it into strips: work down the first strip, turn round and dig back up the next one, and so on until the whole site has been dug.

Begin by taking out a trench across one end of the strip and move the excavated soil close to the other end of the plot. The trench should be 25cm (10in) deep and 30cm (1ft) wide. Now, facing the trench and starting at one end, insert the spade about 15cm (6in) back from it, lever out a block of soil and throw it well forward into the trench, at the same time turning it over completely. Proceed along the trench in this way and when you get to the other end start taking out the next 15cm (6in) width, and so on. Fill in the final trench with the soil from the first. Organic matter, if added, should be placed along the bottom of each trench with a fork.

Half-Trenching (Bastard Trenching) This deeper digging is useful for soils where drainage is poor due to a hard pan of compacted lower subsoil. Again, divide the plot into strips. First make a trench 25cm (10in) deep and 60cm (2ft) wide and move the excavated soil to the other end of the plot. Then break up the bottom of this trench to the full depth of the spade or fork. If required, mix well-rotted manure or garden compost well into the subsoil with a fork. Next, mark out and excavate a second trench, throwing the soil forward into the first one and turning it over as you do so, so that you have another trench 60cm

To dig most efficiently, place one hand well down the shaft and, with the other gripping the handle, push the spade vertically into the soil with the foot to the full depth of the spade, that is, a spit.

(2ft) wide. Do this in several stages, as a 60cm (2ft) width is too large to move in one go. Dig or fork over the bottom, add organic matter and take out your next trench. Proceed in this way to the end of the plot and fill in the final trench with soil from the first.

Full Trenching or Double Digging This is the deepest sort of digging, recommended for improving badly drained heavy soils and for preparing a site for permanent crops, if you add manure or some other long-lasting organic source of humus and plant food at the same time. After dividing the plot, take out a trench 25cm (10in) deep and 90cm (3ft) wide, moving the topsoil to the end of the plot. Use the line to divide the trench in half, then dig out a further 25cm (10in) depth of soil from the front half; remove it to the end of the plot, but keep it separate from the first heap (because subsoil is less fertile than topsoil). Now break up the bottom of the first half of the trench to a depth of 25cm (10in) and fork in manure. Dig 25cm (10in) deep blocks of soil from the second half of the original trench and throw them forward onto the broken-up bottom of the first half. Break up the subsoil in the second half and incorporate manure in the same way as before. Next, mark out a strip 45cm (1½ft) wide directly behind the original wide one, and dig out 25cm (10in) of topsoil, then invert it onto the raised step of turned-over soil now lying in the front half of the original trench. Now dig out a second 25cm (10in) depth of soil from the second trench and throw it on top of the broken-up bottom of the rear half of the original trench. You can now break up the subsoil in the bottom of the 45cm (1½ft) trench. Carry on this way, removing a 45cm (1½ft) trench each time. When you get to the end of the plot, put the smaller heap of lower soil from the first trench into the base of the last trench, filling this in with the larger heap of topsoil from the first trench.

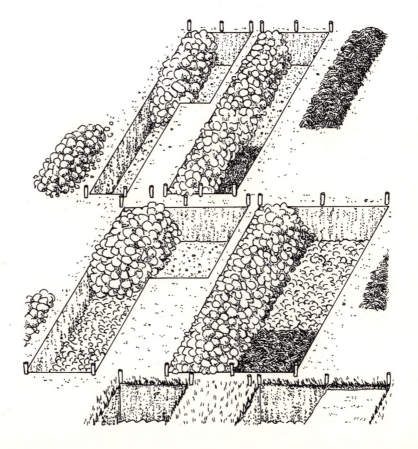

Right: single digging (above) involves digging to the depth of a spade (1 spit) in straight trenches 30cm (1ft) wide, piling the earth from one trench into the one previously dug. Half trenching (below) means working the soil two spits deep. Take out the first trench as in single digging but 60cm (2ft) wide. Break up the soil at the bottom of this trench to the full depth of the spade or fork, add manure, then excavate a second trench, throwing the soil from this into the first one.

Full trenching is useful for improving the soil in the garden of a new home, where the builders may have inverted the layers of topsoil and subsoil, so that the fertile topsoil is buried. Here, after removing any rubble, you will have to dig two spits deep as described above, but ensure that you reverse the order when you fill in the trenches, so that you end up with the darker, fertile topsoil on top and subsoil beneath. If the builders have removed all the topsoil, you will have to buy some: choose the best you can afford, and if possible a medium light loam.

Ridging This exposes a large surface area to the weather, and should be done in autumn on heavy clay soils so that the frost will have broken up the clods by spring. Divide the plot into 90cm (3ft) wide strips and deal with each in turn. Remove a 30cm (1ft) wide, 25cm (10in) deep trench across one end of the first strip. Now single dig down the length of the strip, but throw the soil from the left and right towards the centre, and the soil from the centre forwards. This forms the soil into a continuous ridge. Deal with each 90cm (3ft) strip in turn until the whole plot is a series of steep-sided ridges.

Sowing Seeds

Outdoor Seedbeds Whether sowing vegetables or flowers outdoors, you will need a well-prepared seedbed of fine soil. The site should ideally have been dug in the autumn ready for spring sowing, but if you have not done so, dig as soon as conditions allow to give the soil time to settle before sowing. Although the clods may have been partly broken down by frosts, the soil will still be in large lumps, so the first job is to break it down.

Seedbed preparation should be carried out only when the soil surface is just slightly moist – not wet and sticky. Take a fork and break down the soil so that there are no large lumps or clods, and make sure the surface is reasonably level.

You will need a rather firm surface for sowing, so the next stage is to systematically tread over the plot, using your heels, to firm the soil. Do this thoroughly, otherwise you will end up with 'soft spots' on the seedbed.

If you are adding fertilizer, do so at the recommended rate after firming. Spread it evenly all over the seedbed.

Now the final seedbed preparation can be undertaken – this is raking, using an iron rake. The object of raking is to reduce the surface soil to a fine crumbly state (tilth) so that it is suitable for small seeds. Raking also ensures a really level seedbed and allows you to remove stones and other surface debris to make seed sowing, and seed germination, easier. It also incorporates the fertilizer into the surface of the soil. Rake first in one direction and then again at right angles to the first raking.

Seeds are generally sown in straight rows, so you should stretch your garden line across the plot when preparing each row. The seeds are sown in a continuous shallow trench known as a drill. This is most conveniently made with the corner of a draw hoe blade (or the base of the blade for a very wide drill). Pull the hoe towards you alongside the garden line, walking backwards all the while.

The depth you should make the drill will depend on the size of the seeds – for instance very small seeds may be sown in 6–12mm ($\frac{1}{4}$–$\frac{1}{2}$in) deep drills, while large seeds like peas and beans will be sown up to 5cm (2in) deep.

Generally the right sowing depths are indicated on the seed packets,

Sowing seed outdoors.

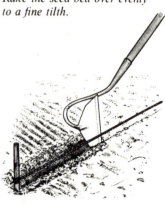

Rake the seed bed over evenly to a fine tilth.

Take out shallow drills by drawing a hoe alongside a taut line.

Sow thinly by allowing the seeds to run slowly out of your hand.

Using the back of the rake is an efficient way to draw soil back over the seeds after sowing.

but they have also been included in the A–Z descriptions of individual
vegetables (pages 232–285).

Sow seeds thinly in the drills to minimize subsequent thinning out of
seedlings, which is a wasteful process. Also, space out the seeds as
evenly as possible – seeds should not touch each other or be deposited
in thick patches. It is best to trickle the seeds from the palm of your
hand or from a small plastic seed-sower rather than from the packet, as
then you have better control over them.

Once each row has been sown you must cover the seeds shallowly
with soil. There are various methods of doing this – you can use a rake
to gently pull soil over them, or you can shuffle along the row (one foot
on each side of the drill) pushing soil into the drill. Whether or not you
firm the soil over the seeds is optional – if you wish to firm, then do so
very lightly by tamping down gently with the back of the rake. Keep
seeds moist at all times to ensure germination.

Seed Sowing Under Glass Plants raised from seed in a greenhouse or in
the house are sown in seed compost (see page 24), usually in standard-
size plastic or wooden seed-trays, although large seeds are often sown in
clay or plastic pots. These must be kept very clean; plastic trays and
pots are easier to sterilize. If you are using a John Innes seed compost
(see page 24) you must first cover the drainage holes in the base of the
pot or tray with a drainage layer consisting of pieces of broken clay pot
(crocks), small pebbles or other suitable material followed by a very
shallow layer of gravel or peat: this is to ensure that the hole does not
become blocked up with compost. Now, fill the tray with compost and
firm it all over gently with your fingers, paying particular attention to
the edges and corners. Level it off either with your fingers or with a
short length of wood. Finish off by firming the surface down gently
using an L-shaped piece of metal or a flat piece of wood with a handle
to keep a smooth level surface. The surface of the compost should be
12mm ($\frac{1}{2}$in) below the top of the tray.

Sow most seeds from the palm of your hand – hold your hand about
10cm (4in) above the tray and gently tap it with the other, so that the
seeds fall evenly over the compost. Sow half the quantity across the tray
and the other half from one end to the other to ensure even
distribution. Sow the seeds thinly to avoid overcrowding in the resultant
seedlings.

Large seeds, like those of cyclamen, can be hand spaced to ensure an
even sowing, while a pair of tweezers comes in useful for positioning
slightly smaller ones. Sow flattish seeds, such as those of cucumbers,
melons and marrows, on their edges. Very fine dust-like seeds, such as
those of begonia, can be mixed with a quantity of very fine dry silver
sand to bulk them up and make sowing easier. It is easy to see if you
are sowing evenly when using this technique.

Very fine seeds should not be covered with compost, but larger seeds
will need a covering, the correct depth being equal to about twice the
diameter of the seed. It is best to sift compost over the seeds, using a
small-mesh garden sieve. Make sure the layer is even all over. Using a
fine sprayer, water the compost in the trays or pots with clean water
until it is thoroughly moist. Never use a sprayer that has been used for
spraying chemicals such as weedkillers.

The seeds of most plants sown under glass need a soil temperature of
about 15–18°C (60–65°F) to germinate well, though some need more
heat while others do better at somewhat lower temperatures (e.g. most

vegetable seeds germinate best at a temperature of 13–16°C (55–60°F). The best place for germinating many greenhouse-sown seeds is in a propagator, of which there is a wide range available – from the simplest types, consisting of a seed tray topped by a plastic cover with two adjustable ventilators, which is placed on an electrically heated tray, to the most sophisticated thermostatically controlled ones large enough to take several trays and pots of seedlings or cuttings. It is also possible to use shelves above radiators or in airing cupboards or similar situations in the house for germinating seeds, but they must be away from strong sunlight and any draughts. Seeds of the more hardy plants can often be germinated in an unheated greenhouse or frame.

The compost must not be allowed to dry out, so some covering is necessary; also most plant seeds germinate better in dim light. A good method is to cover each container with a piece of brown paper topped with a sheet of glass or plastic. Check daily to see that the compost has not dried out (this is unlikely) and whether the seeds have germinated.

As soon as seedlings appear, remove the coverings to allow them plenty of light (though not strong direct sunlight) and air, so that they will grow sturdily and healthily. Not all the seed may germinate at once, but do not wait for all the seedlings to appear before taking the covers off. However, propagator covers can be left on until germination is complete; open the ventilators if conditions become excessively humid. If the seedlings are on a kitchen windowsill, turn the tray round regularly so that they do not grow over in one direction, and move them into a warm room at night; they will be killed by cold near the window.

Seedlings of the more tender plants are best left in the propagator until pricking-out (see section below), and then returned to the propagator until well established, but for most seedlings the temperature should be gradually reduced as soon as the oval first leaves, or seed-leaves, appear.

Potting

Pricking Out Also sometimes termed potting up, or potting off, this is the initial moving of young plants such as seedlings and rooted cuttings (see PROPAGATION, page 40) which have been raised in seed compost in trays into pots containing potting compost. Generally, seedlings are pricked off into small pots of 7.5–9cm (3–3½in) diameter, although it is sometimes more convenient to prick off into trays when seedlings are to be grown on in quantity, as with lettuces or annual bedding plants for example.

Either clay or plastic pots may be used, though plastic ones are easier to obtain, easier to sterilize, less breakable, and retain moisture and warmth better. Prepare the pots (or trays) as described in SEED SOWING UNDER GLASS above, putting in a drainage layer first if you use a loam-based John Innes compost, and filling with a potting compost (John Innes No 1 or an equivalent soilless type), which contains more plant food than a seed compost.

The failure rate is lowest if seedlings are pricked out as soon as they are large enough to handle, so that their delicate roots are damaged as little as possible and because they soon exhaust the limited food in a seed compost. Prick out your seedlings when two true leaves (small versions of the adult leaves) have appeared above the initial seed leaves.

It is worthwhile pricking out only healthy seedlings; weakly ones

Right: potting on. Turn the pot containing the plant upside down, holding the stem gently between the fingers. Tap the rim of the pot against a hard surface to remove the plant with its roots and compost in a single mass. Remove any drainage material from its base and place inside the new pot, having put crocks and a layer of compost in the pot first. Put more compost round the plant, firming it down with the thumbs until it reaches the level of the old compost.

stand little chance of recovery. Make sure that the potting compost is firm and moist before they go into it, and also moisten the seed compost they are growing in if necessary. It is a good idea to water the seedlings the day before you are going to move them. Now, using a miniature dibber or a pencil, make a little hole in the centre of the potting compost in each pot, deep enough to take the roots comfortably without being cramped. Next, *gently* lever up the compost beneath the seedlings in the tray to dislodge the roots. Now you are ready to move the seedlings into their holes in the pots. Always pick up a seedling by its leaves – *never* by its stem or roots, which are very fragile. With some seedlings, such as those of marrows, which have large leaves, you can pick up the seedling between your thumb and forefinger, but most are too delicate and you must use a pair of long, fine-tipped tweezers or a tool made by cutting a V-shaped notch in the end of a piece of wood. Still holding it by the leaves, put the seedling into its hole and push the surrounding compost in gently to cover the roots. You should now press the compost in carefully but firmly around the seedling with your fingers until the seed-leaves lie just above the surface of the compost.

Potting On This involves moving a plant from its present pot into a larger pot. Pot plants of all kinds often need regular potting on as they grow, to give them more room for root development.

Generally speaking potting on is carried out in the spring, but plants should be moved on before they become pot bound. This is when the pot becomes tightly packed with roots – the plant will then cease to grow, or make only very poor growth. Always move the plants into a pot one size larger.

Water the plant thoroughly beforehand, allowing the moisture to drain through. Have your fresh potting compost ready for use. If potting on into a clay pot, you should soak it thoroughly overnight; this is not necessary for plastic pots. Put a drainage layer in the base of the new pot unless you are using soilless compost, and then put in a shallow layer of compost. Turn the pot containing the plant upside-down, holding the stem gently between two fingers, and then tap the rim of the pot smartly on the edge of the potting bench, or other hard surface, when the plant complete with the compost surrounding its roots should come out as a single mass. Remove any old drainage material, and tease out the roots if they are tightly packed and tangled, but take care to avoid damaging them. Now place the plant on top of the compost layer in the centre of the new pot and gradually add fresh compost all round it, firming it down well with the thumbs and shaking now and then to remove air spaces. Continue adding compost until the pot is almost filled, leaving the usual space for watering, and the plant is at the same depth as it was in the old pot.

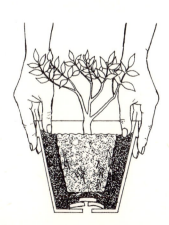

Finally, tap the pot sharply on the bench several times to settle the compost, firm once more and water thoroughly, keeping the plants out of direct sunlight for a few days until they start growing again.

RE-POTTING is necessary for mature plants grown in the same-sized container for years. The process is the same as for potting on except that some of the roots and the surrounding compost may need to be removed.

Making a Compost Heap

This is one of the most vital of all basic gardening tasks as, for a small initial outlay, you can quite easily convert kitchen and garden waste, which would otherwise burden the country's waste disposal system or be burned, into what is really an excellent substitute for animal manure.

Garden compost can be made from dead leaves, lawn mowings (as long as they have not been treated with weedkiller), non-woody prunings, leaves, stems and flowers of both ornamental plants and food crops (but none that suffered from pests or diseases), annual weeds (it is safer to exclude the more pernicious perennial weeds) and vegetable kitchen waste – tea leaves, orange peel, potato peelings, cabbage leaves and so on. Other materials you may be able to obtain free include straw, hay, sawdust and small amounts of animal manure such as rabbit or poultry manure for use as an activator (see below).

BASIC CONDITIONS FOR MAKING GOOD COMPOST The bacteria and other microorganisms that break down the waste into garden compost must have enough air, moisture and food (particularly nitrogen and phosphates) to do this work, and the heap must be insulated to retain the heat produced. Open heaps have to be very large if they are to heat up sufficiently, so it is advisable to make your compost in a container or 'bin'.

BUYING OR BUILDING A CONTAINER Proprietary compost bins are available in a wide range of different designs; good ones include the Huyker and the Rotocrop models. A cheaper and often better alternative is to make your own bin from lengths of old timber fixed together. Wood is a good heat insulator. Make the bin about 1–1.5m (3–5ft) square and roughly the same height, provide a removable door at the front so that you can shovel out the compost easily when it is ready, and fit a sloping roof on top to shed the rain, which can make the heap so wet that it becomes a sour and slimy mess. It is best to make a double bin (twice the length given above, divided in two by a wooden wall) so that as soon as one is full of material and being left to mature, you can start the next one.

Alternative home-made designs include those with walls made of corrugated iron or concrete breeze blocks anchored by wooden stakes, or a cylindrical bin of wire netting lined with waste timber or stout cardboard (such as boxes opened out).

MAKING THE HEAP Whatever the design of container, you should make the heap in the same way. First arrange a layer of old bricks or large stones at the base of the bin, after forking up the soil to allow the earthworms access to the heap. These bricks, with air spaces left between them, form an aeration layer and should be covered with thick woody prunings or tall, tough plant stems to prevent the air channels becoming blocked by compost.

Then heap on top of this the first 23cm (9in) deep layer of garden and kitchen waste; if necessary, moisten it first, and always mix in the kitchen waste as thoroughly as possible. Sprinkle the surface of this layer thickly with an activator; you can use a proprietary activator such as Fertosan, or Q.R., or animal manures, such as poultry, pigeon or rabbit manure; another very good activator is human urine diluted with three times its volume of water. The activator supplies the food needed by the bacteria, and because there should be sufficient food in the green vegetation in summer, an activator is not essential then.

Now add a further layer of well-mixed, moist, waste vegetable material, and sprinkle this layer with lime to prevent the heap becoming too acid (*never* add activator and lime to the same layer). Go on building up the layers in this way until the bin is full. Do not add a thick layer of any one material such as lawn mowings or leaves as this

There are many different types of container suitable for preparing compost. One of the simplest is a structure of stakes and wire netting (far right) with a layer of twiggy sticks at the base to keep the bottom of the heap aerated. A proprietary plastic bin container (right) has perforated sides to admit air. The compost material goes in the top and the side panels slide up to release finished compost. Ideally there should be two heaps, and a wooden double bin construction with slatted walls (below) is a good system.

would slow down or stop the composting process; each layer should be thoroughly mixed.

After adding each layer plus activator you can sprinkle a thin layer of soil onto the activator, and you should cover the heap with sacking or a piece of old carpet to retain the heat. If the heap dries out, water it, but do not let it become really wet.

It is usually a good idea to turn the heap so that the cooler outer portion is then inside so that it will rot thoroughly. If this is difficult, remove the outer 15cm (6in) before using the rest of the compost, and use it to start the next heap.

The compost is ready to use when it is dark brown, moist and crumbly, with no still recognizable half-decayed stalks or leaves. The whole process should take between three and four months for a heap started in spring and summer, but at least six months for one started in autumn or winter.

Use your garden compost either as a mulch at the rate of about one standard 9 litre (2gal) bucketful per sq m (sq yd), or dug in generally at the rate of about half a bucketful per sq m (sq yd), or more for poorer soils and particularly greedy plants, such as marrows or roses.

THE ORNAMENTAL GARDEN

Planning and Design

Vistas and Environments

It is possible to plan a garden with either of two very different aims. These aims are not necessarily incompatible, though either could be achieved without the other. The one most commonly recommended by those who write on the subject is to create a three-dimensional picture, or series of pictures, to be viewed from one or more points, the usual advice being to pay special attention to what will be seen from those rooms in the house that overlook the garden.

Many excellent gardens have been created in this way, but at least as many owe their charm to a quite different approach, not often discussed but frequently adopted instinctively. The aim is to create a congenial environment in which people can live, move and find enjoyment. It is closely akin to the designing and furnishing of rooms, and it is no accident that many gardens planned in this way are divided into several sections, each with its own character and purpose. Gardens of this kind do not have to be admired from certain viewpoints and may not have any vistas or focal points. Their purpose is to express a personality, create a mood or perform a function, often all three at the same time.

Division, if practicable, is useful because it enables the designer to contrast one kind of environment with another; to vary design, density of planting, colour and texture; and to meet several needs, such as a place in which to relax, another in which to grow crops and a third in which to enjoy plants.

So, before you allow your ideas to crystallize too firmly, consider carefully which kind of garden you really want or whether you would prefer to attempt the more difficult task of combining the two aims. This requires imagination in handling space and creating vistas. Some of these vistas may even continue outside the garden, being directed towards distant objects such as a fine tree or a church steeple, without destroying the sense of being in a private enclosure.

Making the Plan

Probably the worst way for most amateur garden designers to start is that which is most commonly regarded as essential, to draw a plan on paper. The trouble is that a plan of this kind only shows in outline what would appear if the garden could be viewed from above as from a balloon. Of course it is never seen in this way by those who use it, but from ground level or at most from the upper windows of a house, when it appears as a perspective view very different from that which appears on the plan.

Professional garden designers are trained to translate flat plans into three-dimensional views. Some amateur gardeners may be sufficiently gifted to do the same, but many are more likely to be misled by drawing a plan in the first place. It may come in very useful at a later stage when the design has to be transferred to the ground with the aid of stakes and string, but as an aid to designing initially, perspective sketches, however rough, are likely to be much more helpful. Another possibility is to make a model of the garden with pieces of cardboard cut out to represent trees, large shrubs, walls, screens, hedges and so on.

In a small garden it may be easier to dispense with desk work altogether and go straight to the plot armed with canes or sticks and a draw hoe, the former to be stuck in the ground to represent trees, shrubs or large plants that will play a key role or to mark the line of hedges and screens, the hoe to scratch on the ground the outline of paths, beds, lawns and other features. A length of hose can be useful, laid on the ground and moved about to try the effect of different curves until you hit upon the one you like most. When the whole thing is completed you can stand back and look at it from various angles using your imagination to clothe the sticks and canes with branches and leaves, fill the beds with foliage and flowers, carpet the lawns with grass and suitably pave the paths. You may not get it quite right at the first attempt but you are more likely to get close to it this way than indoors working on a sheet of paper.

Before starting to plan at all try to look at as many other gardens as possible. Those of your friends and neighbours may be useful if only, on occasion, as dreadful warnings of what not to do, but even large gardens and parks can have their useful lessons. It may be possible to scale them down to suit much smaller areas or to take small sections as models from which to build up something that would be appropriate. You may also note plant groupings that work well, and fine individual plants that could be used in key positions; maybe a lovely Japanese maple with finely divided leaves that could transform a patio or a beautifully coloured vine for use as a canopy to a pergola or arbour, or a happy association of climbing rose and clematis that would be just right as a drape for a wall or screen.

Sloping and Awkwardly Shaped Plots
Do not be afraid of oddly shaped plots, nor of sloping or contoured gardens. They may be a little more difficult to handle in the first place since it will not be easy to find other gardens that resemble them closely but, given time and thought, they can finish up by being a great deal more rewarding than gardens made on flat, rectangular plots. Indeed in these it may be necessary to make changes of level and of apparent shape to create variety and maintain interest, maybe by constructing raised beds or by masking straight boundaries with curving borders filled with dense banks of plants.

Try to work with the site as much as possible rather than making major alterations. This can save a great deal of labour and expense and is unlikely to land you with the problems that can occur when large changes in the character and levels of the site are attempted.

If you have to move a lot of soil to recontour the site, be sure to remove the dark, fertile, topsoil first (this layer varies from a shallow covering to 30cm (1ft) or more) and stack it safely out of the way while you reshape the lower subsoil. Then, when this task is done, return the topsoil and spread it evenly over the surface to its original depth. You should increase the depth of a shallow topsoil by regular addition of manure, garden compost, peat or other organic matter. Aim for a depth of at least 30cm (1ft).

Even in the most awkwardly shaped plots it is usually possible to mark out some areas which can be planned in a fairly conventional way, leaving the rest to be filled in with trees, shrubs or whatever seems most appropriate. However, before doing this, look carefully at the shape as a whole to see whether it suggests some treatment that will actually take advantage of its peculiarity. This is one instance where it may help to draw a plan on paper, marking the boundaries in ink but filling in details with an erasable pencil so that you can try out various schemes until you have discovered the right one.

Situation, Aspect and Soil

Situation and aspect will affect the choice of plants and so, to a lesser degree, will soil, though not so greatly as is sometimes supposed. Fortunately most plants are highly adaptable and, though they may prefer one kind of soil to another, will nevertheless grow well enough in most reasonably fertile soils that are neither very dry nor likely to remain waterlogged for long periods. The most fussy are likely to be the so-called lime-haters (see page 22).

Situation is important, mainly because it can affect both exposure to wind and temperature, two factors which can influence growth and even survival of plants. There are hillside and seaside gardens in which it is almost impossible to grow most plants until shelter has been provided, either with structures such as walls, fences or screens, or with belts of those evergreen trees and shrubs that are tolerant of such conditions.

Contrary to general opinion, winter temperatures in Britain (and it is these which determine what plants can and cannot be grown) follow not only a south to north distribution but also a west to east pattern. Many west coast gardens, even in the north of Scotland, suffer little frost because of the warming influence of the Gulf Stream Drift, whereas gardens in the east are often bitterly cold because of their proximity to Europe and consequent exposure to cold winds sweeping down from Scandinavia and Russia. (See also WEATHER, page 12.)

Before making a final choice of plants, look carefully around the locality and note what grows well there, and also talk to local gardeners and experts such as those in the nearest horticultural society or staff of the local park.

Aspect can be one of the most critical factors in determining which plants are most likely to succeed. Though most plants will survive in sun or shade, many prefer one to the other and grow poorly or even die if incorrectly sited. In the Northern Hemisphere, walls and fences facing in a southerly direction are likely to be sunny and warm, just the places for plants from warmer countries than our own, whereas those facing in a northerly direction will get little or no sunshine and so will be most suitable for plants that normally grow in woodlands and forests.

Trees in or near the garden will cast shade, so if you wish to grow plants beneath or to the north of them, you should choose those that will grow well with little or no sunshine. Rhododendrons, azaleas, camellias and hydrangeas are just a few of the many possible choices. If the right plants are chosen, there is no reason why shady spots should be dull places. Many foliage plants grow well in shade, including ferns, of which there are many fully hardy and highly ornamental kinds.

Meeting Personal Requirements

Of course every garden should be planned to cater for the requirements of those who are going to use it. This seems so obvious as to be scarcely worth saying, yet if you follow some of the plans published in books or magazines too slavishly you may well find yourself finishing up with a garden that does not really suit your needs. If you have children, they will need a place in which to play, which might suggest a sizeable lawn, but one sown with the coarser rye or meadow grasses rather than the fine fescues and bents which do not withstand rough usage so well. A sand pit could be just the thing for young children but, since they are unlikely to use it after a few years, it should be planned and sited for later conversion into a bed, rock garden or pool.

If you intend to do a lot of entertaining in your garden, you are likely to need a well-paved terrace or patio that can be used in comfort even when the grass is wet and thus easily damaged by heavy use and also unpleasant to walk or sit on. A barbecue can be built in as a feature, maybe with a pergola or arbour close at hand to make a pleasantly sheltered and private sitting-out place. A pool or water basin with a fountain would add the music and movement of water.

The best site for a vegetable garden is on a gentle south-facing slope, protected as much as possible from cold winds and not shaded by overhanging trees. This will ensure conditions which will help the vegetables to grow steadily and quickly and produce tender, full-flavoured crops. It is a good idea to site the vegetable and herb plots as near the kitchen door as possible. Make sure that wherever they are sited, they are served by a good path or paths.

You can grow bush fruit or cordon tree fruit as a screen to hide the vegetables from view; arrange them so that they cast as little shade as possible. See also VEGETABLES, pages 232–285.

A most important factor in siting a fruit plot is the necessity of avoiding frost, so beware of frost hollows (see WEATHER, page 12), give the trees and bushes enough space, and keep your fruit well clear of all places where cold air gathers. Fruit needs plenty of sunshine to ripen, so choose a south or south-west facing site if possible, and make use of house walls facing in this direction for growing fan-trained trees. See also FRUIT, pages 305–361.

You can fit fruit into a small garden by growing dwarf bush trees, cordons, espaliers or fans, while climbing vegetables also take up little horizontal space. Many fruit, vegetables and herbs are very ornamental, and can be grown among the flowers. Another way of saving space is to grow vegetables and fruit in tubs, large pots and other containers.

Alternatively, it is possible that you may require your garden to provide not only relaxation or food, but also a beautiful view to be enjoyed from the house as much as outdoors. If so, the planning should be directed partly to this end. In a small garden, it may be possible to place a mirror indoors to reflect the garden and possibly a second mirror at the far end of the garden to simulate a door leading to yet another garden.

Renovating Old Gardens
It is arguable whether it is an advantage or a drawback to start with a garden that has already been laid out. Much depends upon the quality of the original design and the way in which it has been maintained, but even when both are good, it may well be that the garden does not reflect the taste and requirements of its new owner. There is always some reluctance to sweep away what is already there, and so one may be persuaded to keep things that it would be better to destroy.

However, if the garden is established, it will certainly be wise to consider carefully how much of it you should retain. If the garden is also in poor condition, this may necessitate your waiting a whole spring and summer to clean things up and ascertain precisely what is there. During this period of reconnaissance, be careful to mark clearly everything that is to be scrapped as well as everything that you wish to retain. Make a note also of plants that are going to be useful, though not in the positions they already occupy. It does not matter too much if you cannot identify all the plants. Simply tie a label on each stating what it looks like, how high it grows and where you want to use it. Names are essential for communication but are unnecessary when you are actually planning or planting, provided you know the appearance of the plants you are handling.

The best period for transplanting most herbaceous plants, shrubs and trees, including fruit trees and shrubs, is between October and March. Herbaceous plants and evergreens are best transplanted at the beginning and end of this dormant period, while deciduous trees and shrubs, including bush, cane and tree fruit and roses, are moved most safely at a time well within these extremes, when they have shed their leaves. There are bound to be losses, especially with the larger plants, but it is possible to move plants from one part of a garden to another which would be almost impossible to move from nursery to garden. This is partly because there is so little change of soil or environment, but even more because the plants need only be out of the ground for minutes rather than hours or days, and can be lifted and moved with plenty of soil retained around their roots. For large shrubs, slip sacks or boards under them and use these to drag the plants to their new places.

Many old gardens can be greatly improved simply by thinning out the plants and pruning the trees and shrubs. If trees require drastic reduction in size, try to do it without spoiling their natural shape. It is usually better to remove whole branches than merely to shorten them, leaving stumps that may give the trees an ugly, pollarded appearance.

Form and Colour
Gardens can be made wholly with plants or very largely with artifacts such as walls, paths, terraces, steps, pools, statues and other ornaments or buildings but the best gardens usually result from a happy blending of the two. The structures will be there all the time, will not change with the seasons, and will give the garden form and character at all times, whereas the plants will be constantly changing in size and appearance, and the annual and bedding kinds will actually be renewed every year, or even two or three times a year. Many beautiful gardens are made by creating a firm design with the architectural components and then clothing this with a rich covering of plants.

Flowers provide much of the colour in gardens but foliage, with its immense variety of shapes, sizes and textures, and colours too, can be even more important in producing and maintaining the desired effects. Flowers may be compared with the paints used by an interior decorator and foliage with the fabrics and wall coverings. Just as it is usually desirable to restrict the range of colours used in a room, so in a garden it is usually best to limit the colours within one area.

The principles of using colour are just the same outdoors as in the home. One can plan for harmonies, that is to say for colours that are closely related to one another, or for contrasts made with colours of widely different hue or brilliance. Harmonies are usually easier to handle and less likely to go wildly astray, but strong contrasts can produce the most exciting effects when skilfully applied.

Much the same applies to form, particularly to the shapes of leaves and the branch patterns of trees and shrubs, except that with these it is usually the contrasts that are easiest to handle effectively. Evergreens contrasted with deciduous kinds, large leaves with small, finely divided or narrow leaves, or upright plants with those of spreading or prostrate habit are obvious possibilities.

Planting For Continuity

Not many plants flower continuously for a long time. Most have a comparatively short flowering season, three or four weeks at most, after which they turn their energies to seed production. Even modern roses, often described as perpetual flowering, actually bloom in two or three flushes, the major one in June or early July with more to follow in August or September but with plenty of gaps in between.

Many sub-tropical plants flower continuously for months on end or even the whole year round, and some of these are great favourites for use as bedding-out plants, being too tender to be left outdoors in winter but quite able to thrive and flower in summer. They include such favourites as zonal and ivy-leaved pelargoniums (bedding geraniums), begonias, marigolds, petunias, lobelias, heliotropes and scarlet salvias, all of which can be used for mass displays on their own or can be associated with other plants, herbaceous and woody, to prolong the display. Dahlias and fuchsias are useful in the same way, and many fuchsias are sufficiently hardy to be left outdoors all winter if their roots are protected with a good layer of peat. In the milder parts of the country and in sheltered town gardens dahlias will often survive in the same way, though it is more usual, and safer, to lift them in late autumn and store their tubers in peat in a dry, frost-proof place to be replanted the following spring (see DAHLIAS, page 221).

Another way to prolong colour in the garden is by planting for a succession of flowers. For example, spring-flowering bulbs can be planted with summer-flowering herbaceous plants. When the bulbs are in bloom, the herbaceous plants will be still dormant or only just starting to grow. By the time the latter are ready to flower, the bulbs will have conveniently died down out of the way. Daffodils are particularly good for this kind of two-tier planting as they survive well even when there is a good deal of competition for root space. Crocuses are excellent in the front line and so are grape hyacinths (muscari), scillas and chionodoxas. Tulips are a little more difficult as they do not really enjoy competition and are best lifted and replanted annually.

Summer-flowering lilies associate well with spring-flowering shrubs, such as azaleas and the smaller rhododendrons. Here the sequence is reversed, the lilies being dormant or only just starting to grow when the shrubs are in bloom but later sprouting up through them to get the benefit of the sunlight on their leaves, while retaining shade and coolness around their roots, which is just what they need. Of course the height of shrubs and lilies must be carefully matched so that the lilies will be able to overtop the shrubs rather than being smothered by them.

Then there are autumn bulbs such as colchicums, *Crocus speciosus* and autumn-flowering sternbergias, which do not start growing until September and have completely died down by the following May or June. Another useful winter plant, this time for foliage, is *Arum italicum* with shiny, dark green, white-veined leaves which appear in autumn, remain all winter and die down in the spring. (See also BULBS, page 203.)

Climbers and scramblers can be added to this mixture to prolong the display still further. The less vigorous varieties of clematis look lovely creeping over beds of heather, particularly those varieties with yellow or copper coloured leaves. Clematis can also be allowed to climb into evergreens such as the neater forms of cypress and juniper or into climbing roses. Sweet Peas also combine well with roses and can very usefully fill in the gaps between their flowering. (See CLIMBING and TRAILING PLANTS, page 226.)

Yet when all is said and done, flower colour tends to be brief and ever-changing, and so must not be relied on too heavily unless you are either prepared to change the flowering plants frequently (the bedding-out system) or to treat certain areas of the garden as purely seasonal, to be visited when in bloom and more or less ignored for the rest of the year. Nowadays, few garden owners have the means to do the former or the space to do the latter. Small gardens usually need good architectural features combined with good foliage and branch patterns to keep them interesting and attractive at all times.

Special Plants
However, there is another side to garden design besides its overall appearance. It should be a place in which to grow much-loved plants, even if they make little contribution to the mass display. It is delightful to go into the garden in December and be able to pick Christmas Roses (*Helleborus niger*) or to walk in it in January and find it full of the sweet perfume of Witch Hazel (*Hamamelis*) and Wintersweet (*Chimonanthus*). Even in summer a single rare bloom can give as much pleasure as a whole border filled with colour.

Plant lovers often look down on garden designers, just as the latter find the gardens of collectors disorganized and uninspiring. Yet there is room for both elements, even in a tiny garden. Special plants can be given special places where they will thrive and be sought out in season without ever being expected to play any part in the master plan.

Formality and Informality
Gardens are sometimes classified as being either formal or informal, terms which might be interpreted on a garden plan as being regular or irregular, geometric or freehand. Formal gardens often follow an axially matched pattern with a central path or lawn and identical features on each side. By contrast, informal gardens are pictorial rather than patterned, scarcely ever repeat the same idea, and are more likely to be composed in flowing curves than in straight lines, circles, ovals or other geometric shapes.

It is often said that formality suits the area near a house and that the further one gets away from it the more informal the garden design can become. This is a formula that can work well, but it should not be regarded as a rule which must never be broken. A formal design is, in general, easier to handle than an informal one, since it requires less imagination and usually does not depend so strongly on being visualized as a three-dimensional entity before it is created. Curving lines can be beautiful if they contribute to some well composed scheme, but it is easy to allow them to become meaningless and irritating.

Before deciding whether formality or informality suits your requirements best, or whether a combination of the two is most desirable, look at examples of each kind in other gardens. Note that in many gardens an underlying formality in design is often masked by great informality in planting, producing the kind of luxuriant riot of plants which we tend to associate with cottage gardens. This can produce the most delightful results, but requires a great deal of care in the selection, association and subsequent management of plants, some of which must be kept in check so that they do not grow out of scale.

There are even occasions when an element of formality can be introduced to the least formal parts of the garden; a lovely urn, for example, standing on a pedestal in a patch of long grass with scattered bulbs and overhanging trees.

Maintenance

When planning a garden, it is never wise to lose sight for long of what it will cost in labour and money to maintain. Some plants require a lot of care, some very little. Trees and shrubs are the least labour-demanding of plants, unless they are planted in such confined places that they require frequent pruning to keep them within bounds. Many fast-growing herbaceous perennials must be lifted, divided and replanted every second or third year but others, such as peonies, hostas and hellebores, can be left undisturbed for a long time with advantage to the plants themselves as well as to their owners. (See also HERBACEOUS PERENNIALS, pages 132–149.)

Hardy annuals have to be sown every year and may need to be thinned if they come up too thickly. Half-hardy annuals must be raised in a greenhouse or other protected place, transplanted in similar conditions and then hardened off for planting outdoors when there is no longer danger of frost; four processes that can take up quite a lot of time, unless you are prepared to purchase plants at the right planting-out season. Much the same applies to half-hardy bedding plants; these may also need to be overwintered under glass, which can be quite costly. (See also ANNUALS, BIENNIALS and HALF-HARDY ANNUALS, pages 210–215.)

Ground cover plants – those that make a low, dense and more or less permanent carpet over the soil – can save you a great deal of weeding provided that you weed the ground thoroughly before planting them out. If you do not make a proper job of this preliminary weeding, strong-growing weeds, such as couch grass, bindweed, docks, thistles and nettles, may appear, and it can become almost impossible to remove them, without ruining the ground-cover plants.

Open Spaces

Open spaces are as important to a design as well-planted borders. British gardeners usually want a lawn somewhere in the garden and it is true that our damp, temperate climate is well suited to grass, and there is no substitute for a good lawn. (See LAWNS, pages 150–165.) Yet lawns, particularly in tiny gardens, may not always be the best way of providing open space. Grass soon wears out if much walked on, and can look unattractive if not maintained in good condition. Gravel and/or paving may be more satisfactory; it can look better, cost less to maintain and be much drier to walk on.

Paving can contribute to the pattern, texture and colour of the garden. Many materials are available; examples are natural and artificial paving slabs, bricks, gravel, cobbles and concrete. Some of these can be laid in patterns, and most can be associated to emphasize the pattern or vary the texture. The loose grittiness of gravel can be contrasted with the smooth solidity of paving slabs, or inserts of cobbles can be used to give greater variety to either paved or concreted areas and, incidentally, to deter people from walking where they are not wanted, since large, rounded cobbles are uncomfortable underfoot. Concrete itself can be given a variety of finishes according to the aggregate used in its preparation and the treatment given to it as it is drying, e.g. raking, brushing or scoring with the point of a mason's trowel. Concrete can also be coloured, the colourant being added to the mix so that the colour cannot wear out. (See also CONSTRUCTION IN THE GARDEN, pages 364–380.)

It is also possible to carpet open spaces with plants other than grass; with chamomile or clover, for example, or the cultivated varieties of Wild Thyme, *Thymus serpyllum* ($= T. drucei$). Another possibility is to cover the surface with chippings or gravel and plant small alpines in it; choose those kinds described as liking scree. The maintenance problem may be greater than that of grass, but the effect can be delightful, and this is yet another way of increasing the variety of plants in a small garden.

Water and Rock Gardens

Yet another possibility is to make open spaces with water. After a water garden is planted, weeds are sure to appear and must be raked out or otherwise removed. The plants themselves will grow too large in time and will then have to be lifted, divided and replanted just like herbaceous plants in borders. Even so, water gardens can be less exacting in time and labour than gardens made on soil, and water has the added merits of introducing a new and entirely different texture to the garden as well as acting as a mirror to the sky and surrounding objects. Water can be used for movement and sound, splashing, tumbling, bubbling and playing in streams, cascades, waterfalls and fountains of all kinds. Modern techniques have made it easy to include water features, with polythene and butyl rubber sheets or preformed glass fibre to line the pools and make watercourses and cascades, and submersible pumps to recirculate the water. Here again the features may be formal or informal to suit the surroundings, the water confined to regularly shaped rills, canals or basins or in irregularly shaped pools, streams and cascades. Water gardening is described in more detail in the chapter on WATER GARDENS, starting on page 191.

Rock gardens are another possibility, though they are often introduced in situations in which they are not really appropriate. They should appear reasonably natural, as if they really belonged to the site. (See ROCK GARDENS, pages 186–191.)

Ornaments and Furnishings

Ornaments and furnishings can be an important part of any garden, even the most informal ones, but they need to be chosen with discrimination to suit the setting. Good statues and ornaments can be very expensive but some reasonable plastic or fibreglass reproductions are also available. Another possibility is to use natural objects such as large pieces of driftwood or rocks selected for their interesting shape.

Topiary, that is, evergreen shrubs trained and clipped to artificial shapes, can form an excellent substitute for statues and other ornaments. Yew and box are the two best shrubs to use and can be purchased in either green or golden leaved varieties. Shapes can be as simple or as fantastic as you wish; balls, columns, cones, spirals, broody hens, peacocks or running dogs. For simple shapes, clipping alone will be sufficient, but for some of the more complex forms it may be necessary first to construct a framework of wire or canes over which stems can be trained to give a rough outline of the shape required.

Some evergreen shrubs are so naturally neat in their growth that they produce a similar effect to that of topiary specimens with little or no clipping. These include Irish Yew (*Taxus baccata* 'Fastigiata') and Irish Juniper (*Juniperus communis* 'Stricta'), *Juniperus virgininia* 'Skyrocket', *Thuja occidentalis* 'Rheingold' and a dwarf form of White or Canadian Spruce (*Picea glauca* 'Albertiana Conica') as well as numerous varieties of Lawson cypress (*Chamaecyparis lawsoniana*).

Privacy and Enclosure

Climbers can be useful for clothing walls or fences, and also in the open, ascending pillars or tripods or trained over arches, pergolas and arbours. They are often a vital ingredient in garden making, especially in those gardens planned as outdoor rooms, where they help to complete the feeling of enclosure.

Do not forget that climbers ascend by various means. Some, such as ivies, ampelopsis, *Parthenocissus* (Virginia Creeper) and climbing hydrangeas, are self-clinging; others such as clematis and vines hold on by tendrils which require slender supports such as wires, trellis or twigs; yet others, such as wisterias and honeysuckles, twine around their support. There are also shrubs such as pyracanthas, chaenomeles, ceanothus and *Cotoneaster horizontalis*, which are not really climbers at all but can be readily trained and pruned to grow against walls and fences. (see also CLIMBING AND TRAILING PLANTS, pages 226–229.)

Many otherwise excellent gardens fail through lack of elevation and enclosure. They lack trees or other fairly tall objects to give them a fully three-dimensional effect and a comfortable sense of protection. 'Too much sky in that garden', visitors may complain, and most people will know exactly what they mean. Sky is an essential part of almost every garden yet, like everything else, it needs to be in due proportion and there are only occasional situations where it should become dominant. However, do not shade any areas where you wish to grow sun-loving plants.

When to Buy Plants

Plants that have been grown in containers at nurseries or garden centres can be planted out in the garden at any time of the year when the soil is in reasonable condition – neither very wet, nor very dry, and never when it is frozen. The secret of success, particularly with out-of-season planting, is to keep roots and soil as nearly as possible intact so that there is little check to growth.

If you buy plants that have been dug up from nursery beds, the planting season is restricted to those periods when they will suffer least check. For deciduous trees and shrubs, including roses, the best period is from early November until late March, but you should not attempt to plant if the soil is frozen or waterlogged. Evergreens usually transplant best in March, April and October.

Herbaceous plants are best moved in March, April, September and October. Spring and early-summer-flowering bulbs are mostly planted in September and October, bulbs flowering from July to September are mainly planted from March to early May, and autumn-flowering bulbs are planted in July and August.

Where to Buy Plants

Many popular plants can be obtained from garden centres and at these most of them will be container-grown. For a wider selection, it will be necessary to buy from nurseries which grow their own plants. The following firms are representative but there are many others supplying plants of equally good quality.

General Nurseries

Bees Ltd, Sealand, Chester
By Pass Nurseries, Ipswich Road, Colchester
A. Goatcher and Son, Washington, Storrington, Sussex
Hillier Nurseries (Winchester) Ltd, Ampfield, Romsey, Hants.
Notcutts Nurseries Ltd, Woodbridge, Suffolk
Pennell and Sons Ltd, Princess Street, Lincoln
R.V. Roger Ltd, Whitby Road, Pickering, Yorkshire
L.R. Russell Ltd, Richmond Nurseries, Windlesham, Surrey
Scotts' Nurseries (Merriott) Ltd, Merriott, Somerset
John Waterer Son and Crisp, Twyford, Reading, Berks.

Rose Nurseries

Cants of Colchester, Stanway, Colchester
James Cocker and Sons, Whitemyres Lane, Lang Stracht, Aberdeen
C. Gregory and Son Ltd, Toton Lane, Stapleford, Nottingham
R. Harkness and Co Ltd, The Rose Gardens, Hitchin, Herts.
John Mattock Ltd, The Rose Nurseries, Nuneham Courtenay, Oxford

Herbaceous Perennials

Bressingham Gardens, Diss, Norfolk
Thos. Carlile (Loddon Nurseries) Ltd, Twyford, nr. Reading, Berks.
Treasures of Tenbury Ltd, Tenbury Wells, Worcs.

Scarce Plants

Beth Chatto, White Barn House, Elmstead Market, Colchester
Hillier Nurseries (see GENERAL NURSERIES)
The Orpington Nurseries Ltd, Rocky Lane, Gatton Park, Reigate, Surrey
G. Reuthe Ltd, Jackass Lane, Keston, Kent
South Down Nurseries, Redruth, Cornwall

Rock Plants

W.E.Th. Ingerwersen Ltd, Gravetye, East Grinstead, Sussex
Jack Drake, Inshriach Alpine Plant Nursery, Aviemore, Inverness-shire
Robinsons Hardy Plants, Crockenhill, Swanley, Kent

Bulbs

Walter Blom and Son Ltd, Leavesden, Watford, Herts.
Broadleigh Gardens, Barr House, Bishops Hall, Taunton, Somerset
De Jager & Sons Ltd, Marden, Kent
Spalding Bulb Co Ltd, Queens Road, Spalding, Lincs.
Van Tubergen, Willowbank Wharf, Ranelagh Gardens, London SW6

Roses

There is a bewildering range of different types of rose and a vast number of varieties. These include miniatures that grow only 15cm (6in) high, suited to the smallest of gardens, as well as bush roses of various sizes, climbing roses, short and tall, and the vigorous tall-growing ramblers, which, with support from a tree, may attain heights of up to 12m (40ft).

The flowers also vary from the exquisite simplicity of the single-flowered types, through the more complex though no less beautiful semi-double or double flowers in some of the species roses and especially in the old roses, to the perfect symmetry of the spiralled hybrid tea varieties and the large clusters of the floribundas. The range of flower colour is enormous, from the most delicate pale pinks on the one hand to the most brilliant oranges or the deepest crimsons on the other, and many varieties have been bred with bi-coloured flowers. A truly blue rose, however, has yet to be produced.

Many of the old fashioned shrub and species roses extend this range of form and colour yet further. The elegantly arched branches of many of these bear attractive red fruit, called 'hips', in autumn, and some provide a further bonus in the form of strikingly coloured foliage, ranging from crimson-purple in some species to russet-brown in others. This contrasts beautifully with the green leaves of other roses.

A Classification of Roses

First of all, roses may be classified according to the shape and growing habit of the entire plant, into a number of major groups. Instead of being grown on their own roots, all hybrid roses are usually propagated in the nursery by budding the cultivated variety (the 'scion') onto a 'rootstock' (or 'stock'), which is a wild rose or one of its close relatives.

Classification According to Growing Habit

BUSHES AND DWARF BUSHES These are the roses most commonly planted in formal beds and mixed borders. They are not always very bush-like, as they have widely-spaced branches and relatively sparse foliage.

STANDARDS These are produced in the nursery by budding a bush or dwarf bush variety onto a rootstock with a tall stem, up to 60cm (2ft) high in a half standard, 1m (3½ft) high in a full standard, and even taller in a weeping standard. In modern half standards and full standards, the budding variety is usually a hybrid tea or floribunda (see below), although species or shrub roses (see below) may be used instead. A weeping standard has a 1.5m (5ft) tall stem onto which has been budded a drooping rambler rose.

CLIMBERS Often confused with ramblers, some of these have arisen as mutations or 'sports' of certain bush roses, while others have been bred from species roses (see below). Some of the latter are as vigorous in their growth as the ramblers, but there are many excellent varieties such as those derived as sports from the hybrid teas or floribundas (see below) and the Kordesii hybrids that are less rampant and can be grown in a smaller garden. These have the same types of flowers as their parents; the flowers are larger than those of the climbers derived from species roses, and they may be borne singly or in small clusters. These sports, however, have the disadvantage of producing only a few main flushes of flowers in summer, and of requiring care in pruning if they are not to revert to their original form (see under PRUNING, page 92). The Kordesii hybrids have ousted the sports in popularity, being just as compact, but flowering over a much longer period – almost six months in many cases.

Climbers derived from species roses have smaller flowers that usually appear in one main flush during June and July, though sometimes with smaller flushes in autumn.

RAMBLERS These are vigorous growers derived from a few species roses; they have more flexible stems than climbers, bear clusters of smaller flowers and generally bloom prolifically over a short period. Like climbers, ramblers can be trained up pergolas, arches and trelliswork, or into trees and large shrubs; they can also be allowed to sprawl across the ground instead of being treated vertically, when they may be used to cover unsightly objects such as tree stumps or manhole covers; peg them down to control their rampant growth.

MINIATURES These are sometimes known as fairy roses. Most bushes are between 15cm (6in) and 36cm (15in) high; the flowers and thorns are miniature as well as the overall size of the plant. Delightful little plants with flowers that are dainty replicas of the hybrid tea and floribunda blooms, they are ideal for the smallest gardens. They produce their flowers in small clusters in June and July and are usually repeat-flowering after cutting. Their stems are much-branched and almost thornless. They are available as small standards and climbers as well as in the usual miniature bush form.

Classification According to Origin The following classification is based on the origin and type of flowers of the roses:

HYBRID TEAS These, along with the next group, are the most common type in modern gardens. Often called simply HT's, they bear beautifully-shaped, double flowers singly or in small groups; these are larger than those of the floribundas and usually produced over a long period. Many hybrid teas are too vigorous for a very small garden, although excellent low-growing varieties are available. They can be grown as bushes, dwarf bushes, half standards or full standards.

FLORIBUNDAS These are distinguished from the hybrid teas by bearing their flowers in large, dense clusters or trusses, with many blooms opening simultaneously in each truss. The flowers are generally of a less perfect form than those of the hybrid teas; they may be single, semi-double or fully double. Compared with the hybrid teas, few varieties have scented flowers.

Floribundas are vigorous in growth, and more productive of blooms than the hybrid teas. They are also more recurrent-flowering than the latter.

HYBRID TEA-FLORIBUNDAS These have been produced by crossing the two types to give roses combining their best characteristics. They are sometimes known as Grandifloras, and bear perfectly formed hybrid-tea-type flowers in large clusters.

SPECIES ROSES These are the true, wild species of roses, referred to by their Latin names (e.g. *Rosa gallica*), and varieties bred from them. Many are originally natives of Asia, though some are found in the wild in Europe. They are the ancestors of modern roses and although many are large shrubs or ramblers, others are smaller and suitable for the average garden. They are easily grown, often thriving even on poor soils, need little pruning and are often resistant to pests and diseases.

Many of them bear masses of beautiful flowers (usually single in the true species, but often semi-double or double in cultivated varieties), usually for a short season, although there are notable exceptions, such as *R. rugosa*. Many species roses bear striking red hips in autumn. They usually form large bushes.

OLD SHRUB ROSES This is a very large and varied assortment of old-fashioned roses. They are hybrids or sports of species roses, and like the latter, they should be grown more frequently, as they are very beautiful. Although their flowering season is usually shorter than that of modern shrub roses, they make up for this by having richly scented, subtly-coloured flowers. Some have single flowers, others semi-double or double, while some have 'quartered' blooms, with tightly packed, flattened inner petals arranged in four quarters. Most grow into large bushes. This group includes the Albas, Bourbons, Damasks, Gallicas, Hybrid Musks, Hybrid Perpetuals, Hybrid Rugosas, Hybrid Sweetbriars (Penzance Briars), Moss Roses, Polyantha Pompons (or Dwarf Polyanthas) and Scotch Roses.

MODERN SHRUBS These are hybrids, mainly between the species roses and old roses, and make graceful, tall bushes suitable for hedging, for growing as specimen plants or together with other shrubs at the back of a mixed border; some varieties have elegantly arching branches. Modern shrubs have the advantages of only needing light pruning and usually produce their single, semi-double or double flowers throughout the summer. Some varieties have flowers resembling those of the old roses, while others have flowers like those of the floribundas or hybrid teas.

Buying Roses

Roses can be bought from specialist rose-growers as well as from garden centres and garden shops, and they are also offered for sale on market stalls and in the gardening departments of large stores. To avoid disappointment, it is generally safer to buy from a reputable nursery, garden centre or shop supplying strong, pest and disease-free stock; bargains can sometimes be found, but they need to be examined by an expert eye to make sure that they are really bargains and not inferior plants. You should make sure that the plants have at least two or three strong, sound stems and plenty of roots.

First of all, after reading through this chapter, look at some rose growers' catalogues and, even more important, look at roses growing in gardens and parks. When you have decided what types of roses will suit your garden, you can start narrowing down the choice to particular varieties.

Avoid the temptation of speeding up the process by relying solely on the pictures in the catalogues, as however well they may be printed, the colours are not always true to life. Try to see the varieties you have chosen actually growing under garden conditions, by visiting friends' gardens, public parks and gardens, demonstration plots at rose nurseries, or the display grounds of the National Rose Society at St Albans, if you are a member (see address on page 87).

Container-Grown Roses are generally rather more expensive than bare-root roses dug up from the nursery bed, and the choice of varieties is more restricted. However, they can be planted at any time of the year (unlike bare-root roses), even when the plants are in flower, and are particularly useful for quick results, as when replacing roses in a neglected bed.

Modern Roses: Hybrid Teas and Floribundas for general garden display.

'Alec's Red'
0.9m (3ft). This hybrid tea produces its heavily-scented cherry-red flowers freely in summer and autumn, with some flowers in between. A sturdy grower with shiny foliage.

'Alexander'
Can attain 1.5m (5ft). A hybrid tea with brilliant vermilion flowers which withstand rain well. Rather tall for small gardens. Flowers freely for a long period and in autumn makes a good hedge.

'Arthur Bell'
0.9m (3ft). A fairly tall upright floribunda which produces its shapely flowers freely over a long season. The golden-yellow flowers pale to cream but retain their charm and fragrance.

'Blessings'
0.9m (3ft). An attractive floribunda which flowers freely over a long season. The soft coral-pink flowers are fragrant, lovely for cutting or garden decoration. Vigorous, bushy.

'Cheshire Life'
Usually under 0.6m (2ft). A very prolific variety flowering freely over a long period. The blooms are brilliant vermilion-orange and withstand wet weather.

'City of Leeds'
0.9m (3ft). A fine floribunda which continues to produce its rich salmon-pink flowers right through the summer. A first-class vigorous garden rose.

'Dame of Sark'
1.1m (3½ft). A very healthy, easy to grow floribunda. Good for beds or hedges, producing its rich orange flowers, which are marked with paler orange, most freely.

'Dearest'
0.8m (2½ft). An attractive bedding floribunda, but its fragrant soft salmon-pink flowers are easily ruined by rain, so it is not suitable for wet districts.

'Diorama'
0.9m (3ft). A fine hybrid tea, very free-flowering, particularly in autumn; the large, fragrant apricot-yellow flowers stand up well to rain. Outstanding in this colour group.

'Elizabeth of Glamis'
0.9m (3ft). A beautiful floribunda for warm, sheltered gardens with sweetly scented apricot-flushed salmon-pink flowers. Do not plant in cold heavy soil or exposed sites.

'Escapade'
0.9m (3ft). A vigorous, bushy floribunda which produces freely its musk-scented, almost single, light rose-magenta flowers. A charmer for those who appreciate the unusual colour; nearly always in flower and lovely for cutting. Disease-resistant.

'Evelyn Fison'
0.8m (2½ft). Vigorous and bushy in growth, this floribunda is seldom out of flower. The vivid red flowers, which are marked with shades of scarlet, stand up well to wet weather and make an effective bright display.

'Eye Paint'
1.1m (3½ft) or more if lightly pruned. A beautiful single-flowered floribunda, which can be grown as a hedge. The scarlet flowers have a creamy-white eye which enhances the golden yellow stamens. Vigorous in growth.

'Glenfiddich'
0.8m (2½ft). A lovely floribunda, particularly when grown in cooler gardens of the north. Flowers are well-formed, amber with yellow tints freely produced. An upright grower and most attractive as a cut flower.

'Grandpa Dickson'
0.9m (3ft). A vigorous upright-growing hybrid tea with cool lemon-yellow flowers, classically shaped, and ideal for exhibition. Has densely-thorned stems. Planted under 0.6m apart, is good for decoration in the garden and resists rain. Also resistant to disease.

'Iceberg'
1.2m (4ft), a favourite floribunda, seen in all parts of the country as a bed or hedge or as individual plants. The pure white flowers are lovely for cutting, but this rose sometimes suffers from mildew in autumn. Also susceptible to black spot.

'Just Joey'
0.8m (2½ft), a very free-flowering hybrid tea which has rapidly gained popularity because of its unusually attractive, large, fragrant, coppery-orange and fawn flowers, which have frilled edges. Good for cutting. Leaves are red at first, then dark green.

'Kerryman'
0.9m (3ft), a floribunda with large flowers of unusual pink shades, which deepen in colour at the edges of the petals. Flowers most profusely over a long season.

'Korresia'
0.8m (2½ft). A golden-yellow floribunda with perfectly shaped fragrant flowers freely

produced on a bushy plant. Seems destined to become popular.

'Lilli Marlene'
0.8m (2½ft). A compact-growing floribunda with the ideal habit of growth for garden decoration. The scarlet-red, semi-double flowers are freely produced in neat trusses throughout the season. Has abundant, bronze-tinted foliage. Susceptible to mildew.

'Litakor'
0.9m (3ft). A light copper-gold flowered hybrid tea of perfect form which is ideal for garden decoration, or for cutting, as new flowers appear quickly after removal of blooms (known as 'repeat flowering').

'Living Fire'
0.9m (3ft). A bright orange-flame flowered floribunda which is usually particularly good in autumn. Grows well and looks effective in the garden.

'Margaret Merril'
0.9m (3ft). A floribunda with flowers of the most delicate shade of satin-pink and exquisite form. Has an unforgettable perfume and is well worth trying as a cut flower.

'Matangi'
0.9m (3ft). A floribunda of spectacular appearance. The orange-vermilion flowers have silver shadings and underside (or 'reverse') and are freely produced, particularly in autumn.

'Memento'
0.8m (2½ft). A slightly fragrant floribunda with flat salmon-vermilion flowers which are produced freely on a bushy plant over a long period and are resistant to bad weather. A new variety, introduced in 1978.

'Mischief'
0.8m (2½ft). A hybrid tea which is exceedingly valuable as a garden rose. The shapely sweet-scented coral-salmon flowers are freely produced over a long season, are weather resistant, and also good for cutting. A first class variety.

'Molly McGredy'
0.9m (3ft). A free-flowering vigorous floribunda, giving a great crop of shapely cherry-red flowers with a silvery reverse over a long period.

'Moon Maiden'
0.8m (2½ft). A slightly scented floribunda which produces creamy yellow flowers in abundance over a long season, and is particularly good in autumn. Blends nicely with other varieties and also useful for cutting.

'Mullard Jubilee'
0.8m (2½ft). A robust hybrid tea, freely producing clusters of large, scented, rose-pink flowers. Somewhat later in flowering than many varieties, but very impressive in the garden.

'National Trust'
0.8m (2½ft). A hybrid tea with finely shaped crimson-scarlet flowers on a neat compact shrub. Very free-flowering right into autumn.

'News'
0.8m (2½ft). A recent floribunda which has extended the colour range of this type of rose. The beetroot-red buds open to flat purple flowers which are produced freely over a long season. Most effective in the garden when planted with the creamy 'Moon Maiden' or grey foliage plants.

'Paddy McGredy'
0.6m (2ft). A compact floribunda which produces a tremendous crop of hybrid-tea-shaped blooms. These are carmine pink with a salmon flush, and are abundant in summer; there is a gap until autumn, when it flowers less freely. Susceptible to mildew.

'Pascali'
1.1m (3½ft). The best white hybrid tea rose at the present time. Stands wet weather and is an ideal rose for cutting, the flowers being pure white, beautifully shaped with firm slim stems, and lasting well.

'Peace'
1.2m (4ft). A famous hybrid tea which grows into a large bush requiring at least 0.8m (2½ft) between the plants. The large flowers are yellow, edged with pink, and are produced freely in summer and autumn. Resists wet weather well.

'Pernille Poulsen'
0.8m (2½ft). A fragrant pink floribunda which flowers early and most freely; most attractive for garden display.

'Picasso'
0.8m (2½ft). A unique floribunda, known as the 'Hand Painted Rose', because of its unusual cherry-red flowers, flecked with silvery-white. Remarkably free flowering, and particularly so in autumn. Not very resistant to bad weather.

'Piccadilly'
0.8m (2½ft). A first class bedding hybrid tea rose freely producing scarlet and yellow flowers, which are weather resistant. Flowers reappear quickly after cutting. This is the most popular bicolour at present. Has produced

several sports, of which 'Super Sun' and 'Harry Wheatcroft' are quite distinct.

'Pink Favourite'

0.8m (2½ft). A vigorous hybrid tea which produces fine, shapely, bright rose-pink flowers, which when disbudded reach exhibition standard. A fine variety for bedding and noted for its handsome foliage. A sport, 'Honey Favourite', is identical in habit, but has pale pink flowers. Almost immune to diseases.

'Pink Parfait'

0.8m (2½ft). A floribunda, whose slightly fragrant light salmon-pink flowers, suffused with creamy-yellow, are produced lavishly over a long season and are weather-resistant. Excellent for cutting and garden decoration.

'Precious Platinum'

1.2m (4ft). A vigorous hybrid tea which should be allowed 0.8m (2½ft) between plants to do it justice. The fragrant crimson blooms are well formed and produced most freely. A spectacular bedder, though susceptible to mildew in some areas.

'Queen Elizabeth'

1.5m (5ft). An exceptionally vigorous floribunda which requires 0.9m (3ft) between plants. It is a most popular variety, with clear pink flowers, which are produced freely and are good for cutting. Has long stems with few thorns. Makes a fine hedge and useful also amongst mixed shrubs. Resists wet weather well, but has little scent.

'Red Devil'

1.1m (3½ft). A fragrant hybrid tea, popular with exhibitors because of its enormous light crimson-scarlet blooms. These require protection in wet weather. Not suitable as a garden variety in wet districts.

'Roaming'

1.1m (3½ft). A scentless hybrid tea of strong, vigorous growth which produces its reddish-pink flowers very freely on a healthy plant, especially in autumn.

'Rob Roy'

1.1m (3½ft). A floribunda whose large trusses of slightly fragrant, brilliant crimson flowers are most freely produced and are outstanding for colour. Useful for cutting or as an informal hedge.

'Rose Gaujard'

1.1m (3½ft). An outstanding hybrid tea for the garden, it has rose-red flowers with carmine veins and silvery reverses. A particularly good variety for the beginner, being easy to grow, disease-resistant, good for garden display

(especially in autumn) and also producing some blooms of exhibition standard.

'Silver Jubilee'

0.9m (3ft). A vigorous hybrid tea noted for its healthy growth. The slightly fragrant flowers are an attractive combination of coppery salmon-pink and peach-pink shading. Freely produced over a long season, they are of exhibition standard if disbudded early. Exceptionally fine flowers have been produced under glass.

'Southampton'

1.2m (4ft). A fragrant, vigorous floribunda which produces orange-apricot flowers, flushed with red, freely over a long period. Outstandingly healthy, good for a hedge or a large bed and for cutting.

'Sunblest'

0.9m (3ft). A good hybrid tea which grows well and produces its golden-yellow flowers freely on nice straight stems. Good for cutting, holding its colour well.

'Sunsilk'

0.9m (3ft). Produces its fragrant, lemon-yellow, hybrid-tea-shaped flowers so freely that it is often classified as a floribunda. An outstanding performer in autumn, but may be susceptible to black spot.

'Sutters Gold'

0.9m (3ft). This hybrid tea exudes its fragrance freely but takes time to become established. Well worth waiting for, the pale orange-yellow flowers are flushed red and produced most freely; an excellent bedding rose and outstanding for cutting.

'Troika'

0.9m (3ft). A fine orange-bronze flowered hybrid tea. The fragrant blooms are beautifully shaped and freely produced. A vigorous healthy plant which makes a fine bedding rose and is good for cutting.

'Typhoon'

0.9m (3ft). A hybrid tea of good bedding habit with fragrant, salmon-pink, orange-shaded flowers, enhanced by dark foliage.

'Wendy Cussons'

0.9m (3ft). A fine hybrid tea, with large cerise-scarlet flowers which have a strong fragrance. Vigorous in growth, very fine as a standard; one of the most reliable varieties for garden purposes, which may produce some flowers suitable for exhibition.

'Whisky Mac'

0.9m (3ft). A hybrid tea which responds well to

good cultivation. The bronze buds open into elegant golden-amber flowers with tangerine inner petals; these are fragrant, freely produced and ideal for cutting. Requires watching in autumn for mildew.

'Yvonne Rabier'

45cm (1½ft). Not a floribunda but a veteran polyantha-pompom (see page 79) introduced before World War I. The rosette-shaped, medium-sized flowers are freely produced at all seasons in small trusses. White with a hint of sulphur yellow, they are very sweetly scented, and should be hard pruned to keep the plants low and compact.

Compact Floribunda Roses

These are suitable for small gardens and should be planted about 0.5m (1½ft) apart for the purpose of garden display. None grow more than about 0.8m (2½ft) tall.

'City of Belfast'

A free bushy grower with bright, vermilion-scarlet flowers freely produced.

'Esther Ofarim'

An attractive orange with a yellow base. Responds to good cultivation. Does well as a cut flower when grown under glass.

'Golden Slippers'

This has flowers that are orange-flame inside and pale gold outside. Although most attractive, it seems to have been overlooked despite the fact that it is vigorous, and free-flowering.

'Kim'

Very bushy grower with canary-yellow flowers flushed red, particularly in autumn; an attractive cushion plant.

'Little Stephen'

A delightful little rose producing small pink flowers of hybrid tea form in clusters and singly.

'Marlena'

A profuse producer of its double crimson-scarlet flowers, especially good in autumn; a good ground cover variety.

'Meteor'

The bright orange-scarlet double flowers are freely produced; ideal for massing in a small bed.

'Mrs Walter Burns'

A very healthy little rose, whose warm rose-pink flowers have an appealing old-world appearance. An attractive newcomer.

'Snowline'

A compact white-flowered variety with a long season of flower.

'Stargazer'

A most attractive single-flowered variety. The orange-red, yellow-eyed flowers change to carmine and are freely produced on a fine compact plant. Small, matt-green leaves.

'Tip Top'

Has delicately fragrant warm pink flowers with salmon-pink shading borne freely in large clusters. Now seems to be becoming better known and more widely planted.

'Topsi'

Is very free-flowering; its semi-double glowing scarlet flowers are most effective for small beds. Vulnerable to black spot.

'Warrior'

0.8m (2½ft). A vigorous newcomer of considerable promise, with fully double flowers, which are scarlet-red and freely produced.

Summer-Flowering Shrub Roses giving one main display.

'Canary Bird'

Height and spread up to 2.1m (7ft) in good soil. This is a species rose, a hybrid from *Rosa xanthina*. Should be planted 1.5m (5ft) apart, so that you can appreciate the beauty of the arching branches with delicate leaves, swayed down with masses of scented, single, canary-yellow flowers. One of the earliest roses to flower, generally beginning in May.

'Celestial' (Céleste')

Height 1.5m (5ft), spreading to 1.2m (4ft). A delightful shrub belonging to the group of old roses called Albas. A great favourite amongst lovers of the old roses because of its combination of grey-green foliage and large delicate blush-pink flowers. Sweetly scented and beautifully shaped, a charming rose, which benefits greatly from the removal of old and weak growths after flowering.

'Complicata'

Up to 2.4m (8ft) high, and spreading as wide as this, if supported by a tree or pillar. One of the Gallica group of old roses, its origin is unknown but it is one of the finest single-flowered roses, worthy of a place in any garden of sufficient size, growing well on light soils. The freely produced, clear pink flowers have a white centre, like a much more dramatic version of the dog rose.

'Constance Spry'

Height and spread up to 2.4m (8ft). A modern shrub of great vigour, most effective if supported by a pillar or wall. The large cupped fragrant glowing pink blooms are freely borne in arching sprays in early summer.

'Fritz Nobis'

Height and spread 1.5m (5ft). A modern shrub of medium vigour, producing a great number of semi-double pale salmon-pink flowers in June and July. A beautiful rose.

'Frühlingsgold'

Will grow up to 2.1m (7ft) high and the same spread. A vigorous modern shrub which should not be planted closer than 1.8m (6ft) apart to do it justice. A wonderful sight in May and early June when its branches are festooned with the large, open, semi-double creamy-yellow flowers, which are sweetly fragrant. Grows well on light soils and most others. Known also as 'Spring Gold'.

'Frühlingsmorgen'

Height and spread up to 1.8m (6ft). Fairly vigorous, this modern shrub has very beautiful single rose-pink flowers with yellow centres. A free-flowering, early summer beauty with a few late blooms in September.

'Golden Chersonese'

Height and spread may be as much as 1.8m (6ft). An upright-growing modern shrub with small dense leaves and dark stems. The single flowers are fragrant, intense yellow, and produced freely along the branches in May. Plant 1.5m (5ft) apart.

'Marguerite Hilling'

Height and spread 1.8m (6ft) or more. A sport from 'Nevada', which it resembles in all respects except flower colour, which is light pink with deeper shades.

'Nevada'

Height and spread 1.8m (6ft) and upwards on good soil. A modern shrub unsurpassed as a specimen. A magnificent sight at its best, the arching stems festooned with the very large semi-double creamy white flowers all along their full length, almost obscuring the leaves and reaching the ground if isolated. Some flowers appear later but do not bear comparison with the June display.

Recurrent-flowering Shrub Roses

These varieties, mostly modern shrub roses, can be grown as specimen shrubs or in the mixed shrub border where they will look most effective, particularly as they flower repeatedly, an advantage not possessed by many shrubs.

'Angelina'

An attractive shrub which, when established and treated well, may attain height and spread of 1.5m (5ft). A dainty plant, quite suitable for modestly sized gardens, with delightful light pink, semi-double flowers which have prominent stamens. May require watching for black spot in some areas. Flowers over a long season.

'Ballerina'

Height and spread 1.2m (4ft). This musk-type shrub is quite suitable for a bed, or may be planted in a mixed border where it will fit in well. The delicate pink, single flowers have white centres, and are produced abundantly in large trusses. They have a slight musky fragrance. Makes a very decorative standard, which looks well in autumn.

'Buff Beauty'

Height and spread 1.8m (6ft). Grown in good soil in a bed or against a wall, this is one of the best of the Pemberton Musk Roses, with spreading arching branches. The very fragrant, deep apricot-yellow, double flowers are produced in abundance in summer and again in late autumn. One of the most beautiful shrub roses.

'Chinatown'

Height up to 1.5m (5ft), spread 0.9m (3ft). A vigorous, somewhat stiffly growing floribunda shrub which makes a fine hedge or a good background to other roses. The large, double, fragrant flowers are deep yellow, sometimes with a pink edge, and are recurrently produced.

'Fountain'

Height and spread 1.2m (4ft). A very free-flowering shrub of medium size with big, bright crimson double flowers over a long season.

'Frank Naylor'

Height and spread 1.2m–1.5m (4–5ft). A distinctive shrub, especially in the spring when its small leaves are maroon in colour. The single flowers of deep crimson-maroon have attractive golden centres. May require protection from black spot in worst-affected areas.

'Fred Loads'

Height 1.8–2.1m (6–7ft) spread 1.2–1.5m (4–5ft). A vigorous upright shrub with scented, single or semi-double light vermilion flowers in large clusters of the floribunda type. May be classified either as a modern shrub or floribunda. Popular for its bright colour, freedom of flowering, and as a background plant. It is also popular amongst exhibitors of floribunda roses.

'Golden Wings'

Can attain a height and width of 1.8m (6ft) if lightly pruned, but somewhat less if hard pruned in spring. A most delightful modern shrub for those who like large single flowers. These are light primrose-yellow with a large central mass of buff-yellow stamens and are produced continuously over a long period. Produces abundant hips in a good autumn. Cut out older branches in winter and reduce others by a third, more in small gardens.

'Joseph's Coat'

May grow to a height of 1.8m (6ft) and spread of 1.2m (4ft) if lightly pruned, but can be kept down to about 1.2m (4ft) if pruned severely in spring; if this is done, it could be grown in a large bed. A versatile modern shrub variety, it may also be trained as a climber. The semi-double flowers are bright yellow flushed with orange and red, very freely produced, and put up a particularly bright display in autumn.

'Magenta'

Height and spread 1.2m (4ft). A floribunda-type shrub with a somewhat sprawling habit caused by the weight of flowers it produces so freely. These have very full, beautiful lilac-pink to soft deep mauve petals, which are sometimes quartered, and are delightfully perfumed.

'Marjorie Fair'

Height and spread 1.2m (4ft). A very free-flowering hybrid musk shrub bred from 'Ballerina', and best described as a reddish carmine flowered form of that variety. A much stronger colour.

'Penelope'

Height and spread 1.5m (5ft). A vigorous Pemberton Musk which is one of our most valuable shrub roses for the garden. Recurrent flowering, usually providing a fine display in early autumn. The semi-double flowers are pale salmon-pink, tinged with apricot, and are strongly scented. Makes a good informal hedge and if not dead-headed produces unusual coral-pink hips in late autumn.

'The Fairy'

Height and spread 0.9m (3ft). This polyantha pom-pom is a vigorous grower of spreading habit producing its soft pink double flowers in masses from July onwards. Ideal for bedding or in a mixed border, and fine for standards. Resistant to bad weather.

'Yesterday'

0.9m (3ft). A dainty floribunda-type shrub with semi-double, small, flat-spreading, fragrant flowers, pale pink with red-lilac shades, which can be used effectively for beds or in mixed borders. Flowers freely over a long period.

Species Roses

Rosa davidii

Height up to 2.7m (9ft). A vigorous shrub with single pink flowers in loose clusters. It produces bunches of bright orange-red, flask-shaped hips in autumn.

Rosa rugosa **'Frau Dagmar Hastrup'**

Height 0.9m (3ft). A compact shrub belonging to the rugosa group, which is suitable for small gardens. The single delicate pink flowers are produced recurrently and followed by large, globular, tomato-like hips in clusters. Can be grown as a hedge, when it should be clipped in winter to keep it even.

R. × highdownensis

Height and spread 3m (10ft) or more on fertile soil. A seedling of *R. moyesii*; the single deep pink flowers have white centres. The beautiful flask-shaped hips are glossy orange-red and as fine as any in this group.

R. holodonta

Grows up to 2.7m (9ft). Is very similar to *R. moyesii* but not quite so vigorous; indeed, it is considered by some botanists as a variety of *R. moyesii* under the name *rosea*. The deep rose-pink single flowers are succeeded by a profusion of orange-red flask-shaped hips, unsurpassed in beauty by any other species.

R. moyesii

Height 3m (10ft). This very popular shrub has single deep blood-red flowers in June followed by glossy, orange-red, flask-shaped hips. These are set off beautifully by the dark green foliage, and persist from late August to October.

R. moyesii **'Geranium'**

Grows up to 2.1m (7ft). A better choice for smaller gardens, being somewhat dwarfer than its parent. The bright geranium-red single flowers are followed by an abundant crop of hips which are even larger than those of the parent, making a glorious sight in autumn.

R. rubrifolia

Height 2.1m (7ft). This is a handsome shrub, its attractive purplish grey stems and blue-grey foliage looking most decorative in the garden, especially with a grey stone background. It is much used for cutting. The somewhat inconspicuous clusters of small pink flowers are followed by a heavy crop of mahogany-red hips during September and October.

R. rugosa 'Scabrosa'
Height 1.5m (5ft) or more, spreading to 1.2m
(4ft). A fine *rugosa* variety with large single
mauve-red flowers, strongly fragrant and
continuously produced over a long season. Can
be grown as a specimen plant, or makes a very
fine hedge if planted 1.2m (4ft) apart and
pruned to keep it neat. Very fine round orange-
red hips appear in early autumn.

'Scharlachglut' ('Scarlet Fire')
Height up to 2.4m (8ft) in fertile soil. A very
vigorous shrub with large, single crimson-
scarlet flowers borne very freely in June. A
crop of large pear-shaped hips in heavy clusters
follows, becoming orange-scarlet and most
decorative during early winter. A very fine
shrub which may be trained against a wall.

R. sweginzowii
Height 2.1m (7ft) and upwards on fertile soil.
The bright single rose-pink flowers are
followed by very striking flagon-shaped scarlet
hips which colour in August. An erect shrub.

Climbers and Ramblers
A selection suitable for walls or fences.

'Bantry Bay'
Height 3m (10ft). A vigorous climber which
produces its pleasing semi-double light pink
flowers freely throughout the summer. These
have striking yellow stamens.

'Compassion'
Height 3m (10ft). a fragrant climber which
repeats quickly. The double hybrid-tea-type
flowers are salmon-pink with a hint of orange.

'Crimson Shower'
Height 2.4m (8ft) or more. A rambler which
produces small rosette-type flowers freely in
July and August – later than most roses in this
group. True to its name in flower colour. Ideal
for a weeping standard. Prune away the
flowering growths when they are finished in
late August and allow the young basal growths
to replace them. Useful for pillars or arches.

'Golden Showers'
Height 1.8–3m (6–10ft). A very free-flowering
climber, the blooms recurring over a long
season. The dainty buds open into deep golden
yellow double blooms which change to cream
and are pleasantly fragrant.

'Handel'
Height 3m (10ft) or more. A fine climber,
unexcelled for beauty and abundance or
flowers, and length of flowering period. The
buds when half open are classical in shape,

opening up into double flowers that are cream,
flushed and heavily edged with deep pink: an
attractively dainty combination. Can also be
grown as a shrub. Susceptible to mildew.

'New Dawn'
Height 2.4m (8ft). A repeat-flowering rambler
of bushy form which can be grown on pillars,
fences, walls or as a shrub. The sweetly
fragrant double flowers are pale silvery pink,
most effective around midsummer.

'Parkdirektor Riggers'
Height 3.7m (12ft) or more. A vigorous
climber which has proved very reliable and
popular, being a repeat-flowering variety,
producing semi-double deep crimson blooms
well into autumn. Better on tall pillars or
fences than on walls, where it may be sensitive
to black spot or mildew.

'Pink Perpetue'
Height up to 3m (10ft). A continuous repeat-
flowering climber which is exceptionally prolific
in autumn. The medium-sized, slightly fragrant
double flowers are bright rose-pink and
produced in large clusters. Can be grown as a
shrub or hedge by some attention to pruning.

'Sander's White Rambler'
Height 3m (10ft) or more. A vigorous rambler,
very suitable for fences, pillars or arches and in
particular weeping standards. The flowers,
which are produced most freely in large
clusters in June and July, are clear white with a
yellow eye, and very fragrant, but do not
repeat. Prune out old growths after flowering.

'Schoolgirl'
Height 3m (10ft). A vigorous repeat-flowering
climber, popular because of its lovely scented
apricot-orange hybrid-tea-shaped blooms; a
beautiful colour. Apt to become leggy if not
pruned and trained. Disease-resistant.

'Veilchenblau'
Height 3.7m (12ft). This rambler is included
here although it is not recurrent because of its
beautiful scented and distinctively coloured
flowers; these are purplish-violet with white
centres, fading to lilac grey. Thornless, or
nearly so, it is a typical rambler in growth and
ideal for a shady wall.

'Zéphirine Drouhin'
Height up to 3m (10ft) when trained to a
support. This climber may also be grown as a
shrub or hedge with suitable pruning. This is a
famous example of one of the old Bourbon
roses and it is also known as the Thornless
Rose because of its unarmed stems. The

medium sized semi-double flowers are cerise carmine-pink in colour and strongly scented. A most recurrent flowering variety, still very popular although now in its second century. Susceptible to mildew and also to black spot.

Miniature Roses Miniature roses often look at their best grown in an area of their own, or in a raised bed. Mixed with other roses or plants they not only look out of place but can easily become overwhelmed and disappear from view. Groups of three or five plants each of several different varieties can make a delightful display. They are ideal for modern small gardens, or grown in window boxes or troughs of sufficient depth – about 25cm (10in). An average planting distance of 30cm (12in) to 37.5cm (15in) should be sufficient.

'Angela Rippon'
Dainty double salmon flowers.
'Baby Darling'
Orange to orange-pink flowers.
'Baby Masquerade'
Flowers are yellow splashed pink and red; nearly always in bloom, taller than most miniatures. Especially good grown as a hedge.
'Coralin'
Attractive, deep orange-red flowers, which, like the leaves, are rather large.
'Darling Flame'
Flowers are bright orange-vermilion, shaded gold; glossy foliage, very neat growth.
'Dresden Doll'
A miniature moss rose, with lovely china pink buds, well covered with scented mossy glands; these open into shell-pink flowers with yellow stamens, flowering all summer.
'Easter Morn'
Small, shapely ivory-white flowers, produced very freely.
'Fashion Flame'
Flowers somewhat larger, of brilliant coral pink.
'Fire Princess'
Fiery scarlet-vermilion flowers.
'Golden Angel'
Larger flowers, golden yellow.
'Gold Pin'
Golden yellow, fragrant flowers; bushy.
'Green Diamond'
A most unusual flower, opens pale pink, changing to soft green pom-poms.
'Judy Fischer'
Delicate pink flowers with undertones of yellow.

'Lavender Lace'
Flowers are fine lavender; free-flowering.
'Little Flirt'
Double flowers are orange-red with yellow reverse.
'Magic Carousel'
Carmine and ivory flowers in clusters; a repeat-flowering variety.
'Perla de Alcanada'
Deep crimson flowers on a bushy plant.
'Pour Toi'
Flowers white, with cream at base of petals.
'Rise 'n Shine'
A new buttercup-yellow flowered variety.
'Rosina'
A popular variety with bright yellow, classically shaped flowers produced continuously; a good miniature.
'Stacey Sue'
True miniature-type pale pink flowers.
'Starina'
Has shapely, very colourful scarlet and gold flowers.
'Stars 'n Stripes'
A newcomer; flowers uniquely striped with red and white, freely produced on a sturdy plant.
'Yellow Doll'
Fragrant, yellow to cream flowers, freely produced on a bushy plant. One of the best yellow miniatures.

Miniature Climbing Roses
'Climbing Jackie'
Flowers are a soft yellow, becoming cream; produced freely in spring, with some recurrent bloom. Climbs up to 1.5m (5ft) high.
'Lozomi'
0.9m (3ft). Can be trained upwards or allowed to spray out naturally. A distinct plant producing masses of single, very pale pink flowers over a long period, but does not repeat.
'Pink Cameo'
0.9m (3ft). A small-leaved, upright plant which produces its small, double, rose-pink flowers continuously throughout the summer.
'Pompon de Paris'
1.8m (6ft) or more. Small double, pompon-like red-pink flowers produced freely in early summer.

You can obtain full details of membership of the National Rose Society from: The Secretary, The National Rose Society, Chiswell Green Lane, St Albans, Herts.

Soil and Site for Roses

Soil Roses are tough plants and can be grown well in many different types of soil, if it has been properly prepared, though they do have several dislikes. First, they grow badly on poorly-drained soil liable to waterlogging. Second, most roses grow poorly on chalk soils, especially if these have only a thin layer of topsoil overlying the chalk. Chalky soils are also strongly alkaline, which roses dislike. Third, they dislike very acid peaty soils. The ideal soil is a fertile, well-drained, slightly acid medium to heavy loam.

Site Roses do best in an open position, and, apart from climbers, they should not be planted near a wall. They should not be hemmed in by shrubs, nor should they be overcrowded, as they need a free circulation of air or growth will be poor and they will be far more susceptible to diseases. The site must also be as sunny as possible.

Preparing the Site If you are lucky enough to garden on a well-drained medium to heavy loam, little preparation will be necessary apart from digging and weeding the site and enriching it with organic matter. Heavy clay soils are likely to be poor-draining and prone to waterlogging in winter and drying out in summer. They are greatly improved by digging in large quantities of organic matter, and also by adding lime or gypsum (see page 23). However, you must avoid overliming, as roses prefer a slightly acid soil; do not add lime unless the soil structure needs improving or if the soil is very acid, as with many gardens in cities or industrial areas suffering from air pollution. Light, freely-draining sandy soils should also have liberal amounts of organic matter added, in this case to help them retain more moisture and to replace nutrients leached away.

Thin, chalky soils present more of a problem; again the best course is to add as much organic matter as possible or, if the topsoil is very thin, to buy in quantities of good quality heavier topsoil. Very acid peaty soils will have to be improved by laying drains, liming and feeding.

Prepare the soil at least a month in advance of planting, if possible, and preferably more, to give it a chance to settle. It is best to carry out double digging (as described on page 57), so that the topsoil will be aerated and the hard subsoil layer broken up, improving drainage; it will also ensure that the plant food in the manure or other organic matter that you incorporate will be available to the rose roots at as great a depth as possible, which will encourage a good strong root system. As you dig, remove any weeds, taking particular care to eradicate every piece of the deep-rooting perennial weeds.

Incorporate well-rotted farmyard manure in the lower layers, covering it with at least 5cm (2in) of fine soil, as it will harm the rose roots if in direct contact with them. If you cannot obtain farmyard manure, use garden compost.

Renovating Neglected Rose Beds Soils in which roses have been growing continuously for about seven years or more may be suffering from what is known as 'rose sickness' or 'specific replant disease'. If you remove the old roses and replant with new ones, whatever the variety, the new plants may become severely stunted and will never recover completely, though the original plants may have been flourishing. The exact cause of this trouble is not known, but there is a method of avoiding it. Remove the soil to a depth of at least 38cm (15in) and replace it with topsoil in which roses have not been grown. The old soil can be moved to any site where plants other than roses are to be grown.

Planting Roses

When to Plant Roses BARE-ROOT ROSES can be planted at any time between October and March, while they are dormant, as long as the soil is not waterlogged or frozen. In nearly all cases, however, best results come from autumn planting, between late October and the middle of November, as the soil should still be warm enough then to produce good root growth before winter. This will help to reduce the risk of the plant being lifted by frost and make sure that it is well established by the next growing season. On sites that are low-lying or on very heavy clay soil, which run the risk of waterlogging, delay planting until March. CONTAINER-GROWN ROSES can be planted at any time of the year.

Preparing Roses for Planting When you receive your roses, first remove any paper or other coverings and check each plant for broken or damaged roots, removing these with a clean, sharp pair of secateurs, and also shorten any unduly long roots. Do not remove any of the thin, fibrous roots. Next check the shoots and cut out any that are broken or damaged, and also any extra long ones, to lessen the chance of wind damage. This trimming may have been done for you already in the nursery. If the roots are very dry or the stems shrivelled, immerse the roots in a bucket of cold water for 24 hours. Cut off any leaves, fruits or flower buds that may still be present.

If the soil is frozen or very wet so that you cannot plant them immediately, you must store your roses in a cool but frost-free shed or other place, removing wrappings, and covering the roots with a thick layer of clean straw, peat or bracken over which you should place thick sacking, until conditions are suitable for planting.

If the soil is in suitable condition, but you have not quite finished preparing the planting site, you can heel the roses into a shallow trench, making sure that the roots are completely covered with soil; as long as there is no severe frost, they can remain there safely for a few weeks.

Container-grown roses need no root trimming; trim shoots if necessary, keep the root-ball moist, and protect from frost if planting is delayed.

Just before planting, you should prepare a planting mixture, consisting of moist peat, finely-sieved soil, sterilized bone-meal and hoof and horn meal, in the proportion of two handfuls of bone meal and one of hoof and horn to each standard 9 litre (2gal) bucketful of a two-thirds peat and one-third soil mixture.

Planting Distances These vary according to the vigour of the particular variety and the effect desired, but some general rules are useful. Miniatures can be planted as close as 25–30cm (10in–1ft) apart. Most modern hybrid tea and floribunda bushes can be spaced about 45cm (1½ft) apart, but more vigorous varieties will need at least 60cm (2ft) and very vigorous ones at least 75cm (2½ft). Species roses, old roses and modern shrubs should be set between 1.5m (5ft) and 3m (10ft) apart, depending on their vigour. Standards need a spacing of at least 1.4m (4ft). Weeping standards need at least 1.8m (6ft) between plants. If you grow more than one climber, space the plants at least 2.1m (7ft) apart, increasing this to 3m (10ft) for ramblers. If planting roses in mixed borders, add about 45cm (1½ft) to each of the above distances. No roses except miniatures should be planted closer than 30cm (1ft) from the edge of a bed or border.

Planting Procedure When planting on a windy day, take care not to let the fine fibrous roots dry out; cover the roots with sacking. The following account applies to bare-root roses; planting from containers is dealt with at the end of this section.

PLANTING BUSH VARIETIES This applies to all types of roses grown as bushes. If the plant has roots that radiate in all directions, dig out a hole deep enough and wide enough to hold the roots comfortably when they are spread out naturally, without being bunched together. Then put two trowelfuls of your prepared planting mixture into the bottom of the hole and heap it up to form a mound about 5cm (2in) high at the centre. Next, place the plant with its crown on this mound, spread out the roots fanwise, and then sprinkle more planting mixture over the roots until they are covered. You must hold the rose firmly by one of its stems during the whole process; it is easier to get someone else to help.

As you add the planting mixture, shake the plant gently up and down to remove any air pockets which will prevent the roots making good contact with the soil. Then add the original soil taken from the hole, until the hole is half filled, firming it down thoroughly by gentle treading, working inwards towards the main stem and taking great care not to damage the roots. Firm planting is essential, but do not tread too heavily. Then add more of the excavated soil until the hole is full and tread in as before. Level up with a little more soil, leaving this loose. It is most important that the crown or 'bud union', where the stem of the cultivated variety was budded onto the rootstock, is covered by 2.5cm (1in) of soil. This bud union can be recognized as a noticeable bulge.

PLANTING STANDARD ROSES All standard roses must be staked or they will be damaged by wind. Use strong, sound wooden stakes at least 3.8cm (1½in) square and treat the bottom half with a horticultural wood preservative such as Green Cuprinol, which will not harm the plants. Before planting, drive each stake at least 30cm (1ft) into the soil next to the planting position, on the side from which the prevailing wind blows.

After planting firmly, you must tie the stem to its stake in three places: just above the soil, just below the top of the stake and midway between. Use a proprietary expandable rose-tie or a strip of strong rubber. Wrap the rubber twice around the stem, then twice around the stake, tying and nailing it to the latter.

PLANTING CLIMBERS AND RAMBLERS These are planted as described for bush roses. Do not plant climbers too near a wall as the soil there is likely to be very dry; plant about 45cm (1½ft) away from the wall and train the shoots back to the wall.

Climbers and ramblers will need their stems tying to the support after planting; use soft fillis string. Against a wall, use trelliswork as a support, attached to blocks of wood screwed firmly into wall plugs; this method allows for the best air circulation. If you are unable to provide a wall or trellis, you can grow many climbers and ramblers as pillars. Train climbers round and round the support, whereas ramblers are better fastened to the post in a vertical position, and should have their lateral branches pinched back as they form.

PLANTING CONTAINER-GROWN ROSES Unless the soil in which they are growing is thoroughly moist, give the containers a good soaking in a bucket of water. Dig a hole just a little deeper than the container and wide enough to leave a 5cm (2in) space all round it. Cut away the bottom and sides of the container, keeping the ball of soil around the roots intact. Gently place the rose centrally in the bottom of the hole and fill in the gap around the root ball with planting mixture, then firm in, ensuring that the bud union is at the correct depth below the surface.

General Cultivation Throughout the Year

Looking after your roses will not prove a problem if you carry out the basic tasks outlined below. Pruning is dealt with later.

Spring and Summer CHECKING FOR FIRMNESS At the end of winter and during early spring, make sure that all your roses are still standing firm; some may have become loosened by frosts or gales, and will need refirming. Replace any broken stakes, trelliswork, ties etc.

MULCHING This is an important task that should be done in late spring, when the soil is still moist but has begun to warm up. It will retain moisture (so never apply a mulch to dry soil), keep the soil temperature steady, suppress weeds, lessen the chance of attacks of some fungus diseases and add valuable humus to condition the soil. Also, if you mulch with well-rotted farmyard manure or garden compost, this will supply the roses with considerable amounts of slowly released plant foods. If you use peat as a mulch, make sure it is moist. Peat, and also shredded bark, make the beds look neat and attractive, but contain hardly any plant foods, so you should add a fertilizer such as fish meal at about 70g per sq m (2oz per sq yd) or the soil may be robbed of nitrogen. Well-rotted leafmould can also be used as a mulch, as can lawn mowings, provided they have not been treated with a weedkiller.

Spread your mulch about 5cm (2in) deep. Leave a narrow gap around the base of each plant to avoid the risk of damage from the heating up of the mulch as it decomposes.

FEEDING Provided that you incorporated plenty of manure or garden compost into the soil at planting time, the roses should not need further feeding in their first growing season, but they will need it in subsequent years. You can feed from late spring onwards, the most important time being during summer when most roses are in bloom and preparing to flower again. Organic fertilizers such as those based on fishmeal and seaweed manure are quick acting and supply good amounts of the main plant foods. The liquid types can be watered onto the soil after being diluted at the manufacturer's recommended rate, while the dry forms should usually be applied at the rate of about 135g per sq m (4oz per sq yd). Remove the mulch before applying any food, replacing it afterwards. If you use inorganic fertilizers, do not overfeed with nitrogenous fertilizers as this will result in soft, disease-prone stems; use a fertilizer specially formulated for roses instead. Do not feed later than the end of July.

WATERING Newly planted roses, especially those planted in early spring, may suffer badly from lack of moisture, particularly in dry areas or during cold, drying winds, and these should be thoroughly watered. Because they have strong rooting systems, established roses should need little watering except in very dry weather.

Roses grown in sandy or chalky soils, and climbers against walls, will need more water than other types. Give bushes and standards at least 4.5 litres (1gal) of water per plant and climbers up to 13.5 litres (3gal).

WEED CONTROL Hand-weed regularly to remove any weeds not smothered by the mulch, but if you hoe, do so only very shallowly or you will damage the delicate fibrous feeding roots of the roses.

DISBUDDING Many hybrid teas usually produce more than one flower bud at the end of each shoot – two or more side buds and one terminal bud at the very tip. If you want large, exhibition-quality blooms, you should remove the side buds by rubbing them out with thumb and finger as soon as they are recognizable, thus allowing the stronger terminal bud to grow to its maximum size. This process is known as disbudding and will obviously result in fewer though larger blooms. Buds appearing lower down the stem may be left alone. Do not practise disbudding with any other types of rose.

CUTTING FLOWERS Take care not to weaken your roses by taking off too much of the stem with the flower; never remove more than one-third of the flower stem and always cut just above a plump, outward-facing bud (see under PRUNING below). The cut stems should bear no leaves if the bush is not growing vigorously; remove only a few blooms without any leaves from roses in their first season.

DEAD-HEADING To ensure repeat flowering, it is essential to remove spent blooms as soon as they fade. Cut the flower stems as described in the paragraph above. Take off hardly any stem when removing faded flowers from first-year roses. Do not dead-head roses grown for their hips.

OTHER TASKS Keep an eye open for pests and diseases, remove any suckers (see under TROUBLES below) and adjust ties if too tight.

Autumn and Winter FEEDING Sterilized bone meal or meat and bone meal are good organic fertilizers to use; because they are slow acting, they should be applied in autumn each year, raked gently into the bed at the rate of about 135g per sq m (4oz per sq yd). Roses appreciate potash, which helps to strengthen stems and ripen flowers. Seaweed meal contains potash, and this can be augmented by gently raking in wood ash collected from a bonfire and stored under cover. Do not use wood ash too often, particularly on clay soils, as it can make them sticky and unworkable, or on chalky soils, as it may make them more alkaline. An alternative is to rake in sulphate of potash in spring at the rate of 35g per sq m (1oz per sq yd).

Gently rake the mulch into the soil in October; it will improve the soil structure and add plant nutrients.

PREVENTING WIND DAMAGE Cut back extra tall stems of bushes by half in November (read the PRUNING section first) to reduce the risk of strong winds dislodging the plants.

Pruning

A look at any neglected rose bed will make it evident that roses benefit from pruning. Although often puzzling to the novice, pruning is straightforward once you have understood the following basic points.

Unlike those of many other trees and shrubs, which continue to grow until mature, the shoots of roses die when they reach a certain size, to be replaced by new shoots. The dying shoots sap the young shoots of nutrients and may also harbour disease if many are left on the plant, so they must be cut back each year. Also, if roses are not pruned, new growth tends to come from the top, leaving the plants with bare, dead wood below and lots of top-heavy, crowded, soft disease-prone growth above, which results in poor-quality flowers.

Pruning encourages new growth to grow from the base, and is essential to keep the plants open, especially at the centre, so that light and air can reach all parts, discouraging disease and allowing the young growth to ripen properly before winter sets in.

The Best Time for Pruning Roses can be divided into two main groups: those that flower on the new shoots produced during the current season, which are best pruned in late winter and early spring (all types except true ramblers and weeping standards) and those that bloom on last year's wood, which must be pruned immediately after flowering, in

Right: three common faults in rose pruning are shown here (the correct cut is shown bottom right): top left, the cut is too close to the bud which may therefore be damaged; top right, the cut slopes towards the bud, allowing water to drain on to it; bottom left, the cut is too far away from the bud and the shoot will die back.

autumn (true ramblers and weeping standards).

In exceptionally warm areas where severe frost is seldom experienced and the garden is well sheltered, pruning of all roses except ramblers and weeping standards can be done at any convenient time during winter or early spring. In most areas, however, it is unwise to prune too early or frost damage may result; wait instead until the bushes are just starting into new growth. This is between late February and mid-March in most southern and extreme western gardens, though it is more likely to be in late March in the Midlands and the north, and as late as early April in northern Scotland and on high ground in England and Wales.

Pruning too late, on the other hand, results in the plants being weakened; once the buds have really started growing, sap will be flowing strongly and pruning will cause the cut shoots to bleed, losing nutrients and water and being open to attack by pests and disease. Pruning cuts made at the right time will heal quickly.

Roses to be planted in early spring should be pruned before planting.

Pruning Tools The most common pruning tool is a pair of secateurs; it is vital to use them properly and keep them sharp or you will crush the stem, causing damage and allowing pests and diseases to enter. Experienced rose-growers often prefer a pruning knife, and in skilled hands this is the more effective tool. If you can learn to use one properly, do so. As with secateurs, keep it constantly sharp.

If faced with a neglected rose with thick stems, you may need to use a pair of long-handled pruners designed for such heavier tasks. Narrow-bladed or curved pruning saws are invaluable for removing thicker stems in congested, hard-to-reach places.

If you have to remove diseased wood, it is wise to dip the pruning tool in an antiseptic solution afterwards to help prevent spreading the disease to other plants. A strong pair of gloves is essential when dealing with all but a few thornless varieties.

Making the Correct Cut If you examine a growing rose shoot, you will see that it bears buds arranged so that they alternately point in opposite directions, towards the inside or the outside of the plant. Whatever the type of rose, all pruning cuts should be made just above an outward-pointing bud, so that the new shoots grow outwards and the centre remains open and free from crossing branches. In the case of a horizontal stem of a rambler or climber allowed to sprawl over the ground before climbing, the outward-pointing bud is in fact upward-pointing, but the principle is exactly the same.

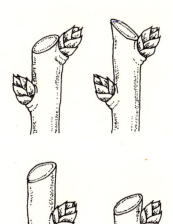

Each pruning cut must slope downwards away from the bud, so that it will shed water; if moisture collected on the bud it would be likely to become diseased and rot. Common faults in pruning are shown in the diagram on this page – study it carefully. All cuts over 1.5cm ($\frac{1}{2}$in) in diameter should be treated with a proprietary wound-healing paint.

Pruning Routine Whenever you prune a rose, always follow the same basic routine:
1. Cut out completely all dead and diseased or damaged wood.
2. Remove any suckers, but *not* by cutting (see TROUBLES, below).
3. Cut out completely all branches growing inwards that cross and rub against each other.
4. Cut out completely any very thin, straggly stems and any that are unripe (if the thorns bend or tear off easily, the stem is unripe). If allowed to remain, such stems will be of little use but will use up nourishment needed by the more robust ones.

5. Only healthy, ripe stems should now remain. Prune these as described below, depending on the particular type of rose.

Degrees of Pruning It is a good idea to remember the old saying 'Growth follows the knife'. Thus whenever you remove a branch, a number of previously dormant buds will be stimulated into growth and you will end up with more branches and a bigger bush. The more vigorous the variety, the more dormant buds will burst into life. Accordingly, very vigorous roses such as the hybrid tea 'Peace' should be pruned only lightly, whereas weak-growing varieties should be pruned more severely. There are three different degrees of pruning:

HARD PRUNING involves cutting a shoot back to only two or three buds from the base, leaving a short stubby piece of stem about 10cm (4in) high. Although favoured by many exhibitors for producing a few superb blooms on hybrid teas, such extremely hard pruning is not recommended for established roses grown for garden display; but it is necessary for newly planted roses to encourage them into strong growth, and sometimes also for weak-growing or neglected roses.

MODERATE PRUNING involves cutting stems back to about half of their length, although the weaker stems should be cut back slightly more. This is the type of pruning that you should practise on established hybrid tea bushes and on hybrid tea and floribunda standards, and, in a modified form, on floribunda bushes, as described below.

LIGHT PRUNING involves cutting back stems to about two-thirds of their length – sometimes called 'tipping'. This is recommended only for vigorous hybrid teas or for roses growing in poor soils or a very polluted atmosphere, or it will result in tall bushes with weak, spindly stems and poor flowers.

How to Prune Different Types of Roses In the following account, 'newly planted' refers to roses in their first season, i.e. those planted the previous autumn or winter or due to be planted in early spring. 'Established' refers to those in all subsequent years.

HYBRID TEA BUSHES Newly planted bushes should be hard pruned to stimulate growth of new shoots from the base; some varieties produce new growths naturally and, if well ripened, these should be allowed to replace the older growth which should be removed to make room. Established bushes should be moderately pruned, although light pruning is recommended in a few cases (see under LIGHT PRUNING above).

FLORIBUNDA BUSHES Newly planted bushes should be pruned hard, though not quite as hard as for hybrid teas. Established bushes should basically be moderately pruned, but some older stems should be hard pruned, while the new shoots that have arisen from close to the base the previous year should be only lightly pruned; the idea is to end up with stems of varying lengths, ensure a long period of continuous flowering.

HYBRID TEA AND FLORIBUNDA STANDARDS Newly planted standards require hard pruning, but not so hard as for newly planted bushes: cut back to about five or six buds from the base. Established standards should be moderately pruned; cut the main branches so that they are approximately equal in length.

WEEPING STANDARDS Newly planted trees should be hard pruned. Established trees need similar treatment to ramblers. In autumn, remove all branches that have flowered and any new season's growth that is overcrowded or reaching the ground. This leaves vigorous new shoots that will flower next year.

RAMBLERS Newly planted ramblers should have their stems cut down to

Right: both hybrid tea and floribunda bushes in their first spring (top) should be pruned as indicated by the lines marked on the stems. Hybrid tea roses in their second and subsequent years (centre) should first have all dead, diseased, weak and inward-growing shoots cut out, then be pruned as indicated by the lines marked on the stems. To prune floribundas in their second and subsequent years (below), hard prune the older stems and lightly prune the newer growth.

about 60–90cm (2–3ft) after planting, though this is likely to have been done in the nursery. Established plants need to have their old shoots pruned in autumn after they have ceased flowering. The new shoots, which will produce next year's flowers, are then tied onto the support.

In one group of varieties, including 'Dorothy Perkins' and 'Sander's White Rambler', nearly all the new shoots arise from the base and the task is simply one of cutting out all the old shoots at the base and tying in the new ones. In the other group, which includes 'New Dawn', 'Emily Gray' and 'American Pillar', new shoots are produced mainly from higher up on the old wood. For each old stem, choose a strong, healthy new shoot as a 'leading shoot' and cut the old wood back to the point where this leading shoot emerges. Tie in the leading shoots ready for flowering next year and cut out all the shorter lateral shoots which they bear to two or three buds from their point of origin. Cut out completely any old wood which bears no new shoots, to prevent overcrowding. Ramblers in this group may become bare at the base; if this happens, cut one or two stems down to a bud about 30cm (1ft) above the base. If too few new growths are produced to allow the above treatment, retain the best of the old shoots and cut back all the laterals to two or three buds.

CLIMBERS Newly planted climbers should not be pruned at all, apart from removing dead tips or diseased stems, because many of them are climbing sports of hybrid teas or floribundas, and may revert to the bush form if cut in their first year. Established climbers need little pruning apart from that done to maintain health, prevent overcrowding and keep the plant within bounds. Reduce small laterals to about 7.5cm (3in) in spring.

MODERN SHRUBS, OLD SHRUBS AND SPECIES ROSES Newly planted roses should not be pruned at all. Established plants need very little pruning apart from removal of dead, diseased or overcrowded wood and cutting to control size and shape. If they become bare at the base, cut down one or two of the older shoots to a bud about 23cm (9in) from the base, every spring for three years.

MINIATURES Newly planted miniatures need pruning as for hybrid teas. Established plants should have all strong growths cut back to five or six buds and weak ones to one bud above the base. Remove completely any extra-vigorous shoots which upset the plant's symmetry.

Hygiene After Pruning Never leave prunings lying about, as they will harbour pests and diseases; always burn them or remove them from the garden as soon as possible.

Troubles

Removing suckers Suckers are shoots that originate from the base of the plant, usually from beneath the soil in a bush rose, sometimes at a fair distance from the plant. They grow from the rootstock and not from the budded variety (the scion). If allowed to remain, they will sap the plant's strength and may so weaken it that they will take over completely: this is known as 'reversion'. They are typically paler green than the normal scion shoots and the leaflets are usually smaller, differently shaped and sometimes more numerous. If in doubt over identification, remove soil carefully and trace the suspected sucker to its point of origin; if it comes from the rootstock (i.e. below the bulge of the bud union), your suspicions are confirmed.

To remove a sucker, do *not* cut it out, as this will encourage dormant buds on the rootstock to develop, sending up more suckers. As soon as the sucker is large enough to handle, wrench it out cleanly to destroy the budding system. Hold the base of the plant firmly in place with one foot or you may dislodge the roots.

Pests Aphids should be kept under control as they carry virus diseases, for which there is no cure. Encourage natural predators and if your area suffers from aphids badly, prevent the population building up by spraying after sunset with pyrethrum or nicotine and quassia; see page 35. Do this early in spring, making sure that all parts of the plant are drenched. A tar-oil winter wash applied in winter will destroy aphid eggs as well as many of the various caterpillars that may attack buds and leaves; do this only if you had a bad attack of these pests the previous summer. Caterpillars and other pests such as leaf-hoppers and chafer beetles can be hand-picked or shaken off and then destroyed, if in small numbers. A derris or nicotine spray (see page 35) will destroy large infestations of these pests, as well as capsids, thrips and others. The pink, spongy, moss-like 'robin's pincushions' that may appear on the leaves are caused by gall wasps; they do no great harm and can be left there. Cut off the affected leaf if you dislike its appearance.

Diseases The three most serious rose diseases are mildew, black spot and rust, all caused by fungi.

POWDERY MILDEW is the most widespread, appearing as a white, powdery mould on leaves, buds and young stems, usually in summer or early autumn. Some varieties are more susceptible than others, particularly if the plants are kept very dry at their roots, as often happens with climbers planted too near a wall. Fungus diseases are also more likely when air circulation around the plants is poor.

Remove and burn any infected parts and spray with Nimrod-T systemic fungicide (see also PLANT HEALTH, page 31).

BLACK SPOT is most prevalent in the south-west of Britain, especially in regions where the air is particularly unpolluted (conversely, it is rare in cities and industrial areas). The black spots appear like splashes of ink with a fringe around the edge, and spread rapidly, causing the leaves to fall. It is encouraged by potash deficiency and by warm, wet summers.

Remove and burn all infected leaves and spray with Burgundy mixture, or with Nimrod-T fungicide or benomyl if the disease persists. Further attacks of black spot, and of rust too, can often be prevented by remembering to remove and burn all dead leaves in autumn (the disease spores are spread from these onto the new season's growth in spring, partly by splashing raindrops), to burn all prunings promptly, and to apply a mulch to prevent infection from the soil.

RUST is not common except in the south-west, but often kills the plant when it does strike. Moist, warm weather encourages the disease, and some varieties are more susceptible. Rust appears as rounded, orange swellings on the undersides of leaves and on stems; these swellings turn black at the end of summer. Prevent as described above under black spot; remove and burn infected parts, if rust appears, and spray if necessary with Burgundy mixture, colloidal copper, or with Zineb or Plantvax as a last resort.

It is far better to adopt a policy of spraying as little as possible, and then with the safest pesticides only, as described above and on pages 35–7. Best of all is to encourage natural predators and to reduce the chance of a build-up of pests and diseases by keeping your roses well-fed and growing strongly, and by good garden hygiene.

Right: 'Blessings', a floribunda

Above: 'Alec's Red', a very fragrant hybrid tea

Right: pink and red climbing roses

Above: Helleborus niger, the Christmas rose

Right: 'Southampton', a vigorous floridunda

Left: delphiniums, lupins, lilies, aquilegias

Above: early-flowering irises

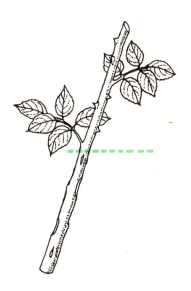

Above: a rose cutting prepared for rooting, with all except two leaf shoots removed. It should be inserted into soil to just below the lower leaf axil, as indicated by the dotted line.

Propagation

The easiest way for the amateur to increase his stock of roses is by growing from HARDWOOD CUTTINGS. Plants rooted from cuttings have the advantage that suckers are not a problem, as all shoots will be of the cultivated variety and need not be removed. However, some less vigorous hybrids will not grow successfully on their own roots.

The root systems of rooted cuttings are less extensive and the plants may suffer more from drought or frost than do budded roses. Nevertheless, rooted cuttings are often very successful with many of the more vigorous floribunda bushes, some of the most vigorous hybrid teas, vigorous climbers and most ramblers, and with vigorous shrub roses and species roses. Miniature roses should always be propagated from cuttings, as they generally retain their dwarf character better.

The general principles of rooting hardwood cuttings are described on page 50. Take cuttings of roses in late September or October. Select young but well-ripened non-flowering lateral shoots (which have been produced the same year), about the thickness of a pencil and about 23cm (9in) long, or 7.5cm (3in) long for miniatures, cutting just below the lowest bud and just above an upper bud with the usual slanting cut. Remove all leaves except the top two or three. Dip the moistened base of each cutting into hormone rooting powder and place it in the bottom of a V-shaped trench 18cm (7in) deep and lined with coarse sand, then fill in with soil, tread down firmly and water the foliage thoroughly and the soil too if it is at all dry. Choose a sheltered site for your trench and allow about 10cm (4in) between cuttings and 30cm (1ft) between trenches. Take a good number of cuttings, as some are likely to fail. Leave the cuttings until next autumn, when they should be transplanted into their permanent quarters.

BUDDING is the method used by commercial growers to propagate most roses. It is a form of grafting (see page 51) in which a single bud, or eye, of the cultivated variety (the scion) is grafted onto the rootstock, rather than a short length of scion shoot. Refer to one of the many good books on growing roses for fuller details of this process.

Shrubs, Trees and Hedges

Unlike many other spare-time pursuits, gardening offers a choice of different approaches, suited to individual tastes and abilities. Nowadays, with so many competing attractions for weekend gardeners, ways of cutting down on routine garden jobs are most welcome.

In recent years, there has been a trend towards the wider use of trees and shrubs as a way of lessening the workload. Annuals need frequent attention during their growing season, perennials require periodic lifting and dividing, and some bulbs, corms, rhizomes and tubers must also be lifted, stored and replanted annually, whereas most trees and shrubs, once established, demand little attention, apart from pruning.

A careful choice of subjects in these two categories can provide colour in the garden the whole year round. It is not for their flowers alone that trees and shrubs score so highly but also for the beauty of their fruits and foliage and the value of their architectural form.

Left: Michaelmas daisies

Trees

The selection of trees suitable for a garden of small to average dimensions must be made with great care. You do not want your plot to be overshadowed by giant elms, oaks or beeches, so planting of the larger, more vigorous types of tree should be avoided in any garden of less than 2,000sq m (half an acre) in extent. The choice of suitable material for plots of more modest dimensions is wide. It ranges from ornamental cherries, crab-apples, thorns, laburnums and the like, down to slow-growing dwarfs like the Japanese maples and pygmy willows which could be accommodated in a large pot.

Another important factor to bear in mind is the ultimate height and spread of the subjects chosen. In this connection, the descriptive lists appearing below, which include approximate height and spread in average conditions, eight to ten years after planting, will help, as also will the excellent descriptive catalogues of many nurserymen.

Success with trees lies, to a large extent, in the correct initial preparation of their planting holes. Although some trees are now obtainable in containers for planting at any time of year, it is still preferable, in most cases, to plant specimens that were raised in the open ground during their dormant season, from about the middle of October to the end of March, provided that weather conditions are favourable. For evergreens, this period can be extended to mid-September at one end and the middle or end of May at the other.

It pays to order as early as possible from the nursery and to obtain a firm delivery date so that the planting holes can be ready when the trees arrive. If planting conditions are unsuitable when delivery is made – either because the soil is waterlogged by heavy rain or rock hard owing to severe frost – the wrappings should be removed and the trees heeled into a trench to protect their roots and prevent them from drying out.

Planting holes must be deep and wide enough to accommodate the roots without bunching or overcrowding. For the majority, holes 75cm (2½ft) wide and deep should be sufficient. The soil in the bottom of the hole should be broken up with a fork. It is often better to plant in sifted garden soil, enriched with well-rotted garden compost, peat or leafmould and a scattering of bonemeal. The use of animal manure when planting is not advisable but if it is used it must be completely rotted down and care must be taken to see that it does not come into contact with the roots by covering it with several inches of soil.

It is important to choose a stout enough stake for support. Too often one sees the tree supporting the stake instead of the opposite. Stakes should act as crutches for young trees for their first three or four years.

Shrubs

Similar procedures apply to the planting of shrubs, except that they will not require staking in any but the most exposed and windswept areas. Many shrubs make useful individual specimens but they are usually planted in borders devoted entirely to shrubs or in mixed borders.

The site for a shrub border, which for the garden of average size should not be less than 3m (10ft) wide, is best prepared several weeks in advance of planting. Double digging, which involves breaking up the subsoil with a fork and the incorporation of plenty of humus-rich materials such as garden compost, leafmould, peat or well-rotted manure, will make certain that the soil is in a condition that will get the shrubs off to a good start (see also BASIC TECHNIQUES, page 54).

Above: it is important that the planting hole for a tree be dug deep and wide enough for the roots to spread out, and that the stake be attached before the hole is filled in (top). A stick laid across the rim of the planting hole (bottom) will enable you to ensure that the tree is planted at the right depth, up to the level of the soil mark on the trunk.

Aftercare of Trees and Shrubs

The first two seasons after planting are a time of great importance for establishing vigorous, healthy specimens. Newly planted trees or shrubs should be watered liberally during any dry spells. In this connection, it is better to give a thorough soaking at weekly intervals – up to 9 litres (2gal) per plant – than sporadic sprinklings that merely wet the surface of the soil. Moisture can also be retained over long periods by the use of mulches, using partly rotted leaves, lawn-mowings, peat, leafmould or garden compost, and making sure that the mulch is removed from around the base of the plants before watering and replaced afterwards.

Regular mulching of this kind will ensure that the soil in the border is always rich in humus. During the first few seasons after planting, rotted manure can be used as a surface mulch. An application of a general fertilizer at the rate of 70–100g per sq m (2–3oz per sq yd) during spring will take care of any other nutritional requirements.

During the first few years, the space surrounding trees and shrubs should be kept free from weeds and grasses. Mulching will, to a certain extent, help to keep down the weeds, but you should also hoe regularly during the growing season. Any weeds that appear in places inaccessible to the hoe should be removed by hand. Forking over the soil in the vicinity of trees and shrubs is a practice to be avoided if possible. It tends to disturb or damage surface roots.

As a last resort, weeds could also be kept down by the use of a paraquat-based weedkiller, which destroys most weeds without damage to trees or shrubs, since it is neutralized on contact with the soil.

Severe frost conditions sometimes lift newly planted trees and shrubs partly out of the ground. After spells of hard weather, it is advisable to go round and inspect them, firming back any that have been disturbed.

Container-Grown Plants

Although container-grown trees and shrubs can be planted out at almost any time of year, it is better not to transplant them during very dry spells. They should preferably be left in their containers and watered regularly until conditions are more favourable.

Pruning

Irreparable damage can be done to trees or shrubs by careless use of the secateurs or pruning saw. A knowledge of the habits and characteristics of the plants involved is very important before you start to prune them. Some shrubs require drastic annual pruning; others, less vigorous in character, are best left well alone. For example, the Butterfly Bush, *Buddleia davidii*, should be cut back hard each spring almost to the point at which the previous year's growth started. Camellias and Rhododendrons, on the other hand, require little or no attention.

It is difficult to lay down any hard and fast rules for pruning. In general, however, you should prune, firstly, to remove dead and diseased stems and branches and to achieve a well-balanced shape; secondly, to increase the number of flowers produced or to form larger or better blooms; and finally, to restrict the growth of too-rampant subjects.

Usually, shrubs that flower on the previous year's growth should be pruned as soon as the blooms have faded, whereas those that flower on the current year's growth are normally cut back in spring. Examples in the former category are flowering currants, Winter Jasmine, deutzias

Above: a Butterfly Bush in full flower before pruning (top), and the same bush (bottom) after hard pruning.

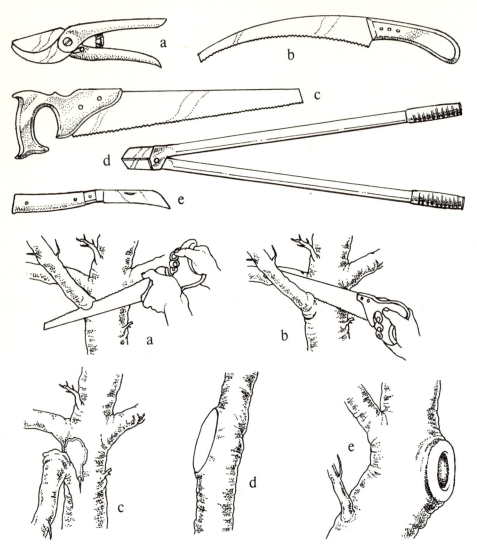

Left: pruning tools include (a) secateurs, (b) a Grecian saw, (c) a pruning saw, (d) long-handled secateurs, and (e) a pruning knife. A good knife and a pair of secateurs are essential equipment for all gardeners.

Left: to prune a large branch, first (a) make an undercut with a saw, then (b) cut off the branch as close to the trunk as possible. Failure to make an undercut (c) will result in the branch tearing the bark of the main trunk. Make the cut surface elliptical (d) and coat with preservative paint. Healing starts from the edges, producing a raised edge (e) which eventually meets in the centre.

and philadelphus; most buddleias, santolinas and tamarisks, on the other hand, need hard pruning in spring. Others that need this latter treatment each year are partly tender shrubs such as fuchsias, whose old growths are susceptible to frost damage. Similar treatment, although for a different reason, is given to the red and yellow-stemmed dogwoods and willows with coloured stems, the new growths of which have strikingly-coloured bark.

Other methods of pruning include the spurring back of side growths to five or six leaves in July and August to encourage the formation of flower buds for the following season. These shoots are shortened again to two or three dormant buds during the following winter. This is a good way of dealing with wisterias and pyracanthas.

Propagation

Many kinds of trees and shrubs can be grown from seed. With the exception of a very few, however, such as brooms, lavenders and sun roses, which often come into flower two seasons after sowing, this is apt to be very much a long-term project. With most shrubs, faster results are obtained from cuttings or layers.

The former can be of several kinds. Those taken from young shoots of the current year's growth are known as 'soft' cuttings, more mature ones are called 'semi-ripe'. Those taken from ripened stems are 'hardwood' cuttings.

Soft cuttings root quickly but are not easily kept alive without special equipment such as propagators and mist sprays. For the amateur, hardwood cuttings offer the easiest method of increase. Many useful garden shrubs and trees, including willows, poplars, escallonias, forsythias, Winter Jasmine, Garryas, cornus, privets, loniceras, lavenders, rosemary and heathers, readily strike from cuttings of this kind. They should be taken with a heel of old wood and inserted in a shallow trench with a layer of sharp sand at its base, preferably in a shaded and north-facing border.

Rhododendrons and many other shrubs with low, sweeping branches can be propagated by means of layering. For further details of propagation methods, see under PROPAGATION, pages 40–54.

Pests and Diseases

The majority of garden shrubs in general cultivation are not unduly susceptible to pests and diseases, apart from such commonplace ones as aphids, slugs and snails, and so on, and various kinds of mildew. Much depends on maintaining healthy soil conditions and correct feeding during the first few seasons.

Among the more serious diseases affecting trees and shrubs are honey fungus (*Armillaria*), canker, various kinds of leaf spot, rusts, mildew and silver leaf disease. Fortunately, these are comparatively rare.

Honey fungus is a killer; affected shrubs or trees may die suddenly for no apparent reason. Its presence is indicated by dark brown string-like threads growing into the roots and by the appearance of light brown toadstools at or near the bases of the plants. Any trees or shrubs thus affected should be dug out and burnt, roots and all. Soil in the immediate area should be removed and replaced with clean soil (preferably sterilized) from another part of the garden before replanting.

Canker, often accompanied by gummy exudations, attacks ornamental cherries, crab-apples, peaches and plums, causing affected branches to 'die back'; starting at their tips, the young shoots die back, and this may be followed by the death of older wood. Any such dead branches should be cut right back to sound wood. Spraying with a copper fungicide in early autumn helps to keep the disease in check.

There are many different kinds of leaf spot. Bordeaux mixture, captan and other copper or sulphur sprays and dusts which are sold under a variety of proprietary brand names are useful in combating these. Attacks vary according to season and situation and, unless extremely severe, are unlikely to have any permanent effect on the plants.

Bad attacks of rusts and mildews can also be combated with sulphur sprays or other fungicides.

AN ALPHABETICAL LIST OF SHRUBS

The figures in metres and centimetres with equivalents in feet and inches indicate the approximate height and spread attained after eight to ten years' growth in average conditions; details after each description give flowering period, whether suitable for sun or shade, and soil preferences.

Artemisia   90 × 90cm (3 × 3ft)
Evergreen shrubs of moderate size, with silver-grey or grey-green aromatic foliage. The best-known species is *A. abrotanum*, popularly known as 'Old Man' or 'Lad's Love', with finely cut feathery foliage.
Foliage plant   Sun   Any soil
Azalea – see under *Rhododendron*

Above: top, light pruning; bottom, heavier pruning.

Berberis (Barberry)   Various heights and spreads – see below
This large group of shrubs provides many useful garden all-rounders
noteworthy for the beauty of their flowers, fruits and foliage. It includes
forms for every kind of situation, ranging from dwarfs no more than
30cm (1ft) tall, suitable for the rock garden, to vigorous, tall-growing
kinds up to 3m (10ft) in height. The deciduous species are grown
primarily for the beauty of their autumn and winter fruits and the
brilliance of their autumn foliage. Evergreen barberries are notable for
their abundance of colourful blossom and glossy dark green foliage.

B. aggregata, which grows to 1.5m × 90cm (5 × 3ft), is a handsome
deciduous shrub of dense habit with yellow flowers followed by large
numbers of coral-red berries, and striking autumn leaf colour.
Early summer   Sun or light shade   Any soil

B. thunbergii is a small dome-shaped deciduous shrub and ranks
among the finest *Berberis* for colour of berries and autumn foliage. The
purple-leaved forms are especially striking. These include *B. t.
atropurpurea*, 1.8 × 1.5m (6 × 5ft), with leaves of a rich crimson purple,
and its dwarf form 'Nana', 45 × 45cm (1½ × 1½ft). 'Rose Glow',
90 × 90cm (3 × 3ft) is a curious variety whose young purple foliage is
splashed with silvery pink.
Spring   Sun or part shade   Any soil, but preferably lime-free

B. wilsonae, growing to 90cm × 1.2m (3 × 4ft), is a medium-sized
deciduous shrub of prostrate habit useful as ground cover. The yellow
flowers are followed by an abundance of translucent coral berries. In
autumn the soft green foliage flushes to purple to provide an effective
complement to the coloured berries.
Summer   Sun or part shade   Any soil

B. darwinii, 2.5 × 1.5m (8 × 5ft), is an evergreen species which makes a
fine specimen shrub with small, dark green, shield-shaped leaves and
masses of orange-yellow blossom followed by deep purple fruits.
Spring   Sun or part shade   Any soil

B. × stenophylla, 2.5 × 3m (8 × 10ft), is an evergreen hybrid barberry
with several good named varieties. The small dark green leaves are
borne on long arching stems. 'Coccinea' is more compact than the type
with crimson-budded flowers opening to orange. 'Corallina' has coral-
pink buds; 'Pink Pearl' is an interesting form with purple foliage
streaked with pink and cream.
Spring   Sun or part shade   Any soil

Buddleia davidii (Butterfly Bush)   3 × 2m (10 × 6½ft)
Vigorous and fast-growing deciduous shrubs, useful as gap-fillers and
for rapid results in new gardens. They are renowned for attracting
butterflies when in bloom in late summer. Buddleias need cutting back
hard each spring, almost to the point where the previous year's growth
commenced. The Butterfly Bushes are valuable for their late summer
display, bearing long spikes of vanilla-scented bloom from late July to
the end of August. Good named varieties include 'Black Knight', deep
violet; 'Ile de France', deep purple; 'Royal Red', wine-red and 'Peace'
with attractive creamy-white blossom.
Late summer   Sun   Any soil

Calluna vulgaris   Heathers: see also *Daboeica* and *Erica*   60 × 60cm
(2 × 2ft)
This is the Heather or Ling of our moors and downlands. The many
outstanding named varieties make a colourful and long-lasting display
on dry banks and in the rock or heath garden. Once the plants are

established, the dense evergreen foliage provides an extremely effective ground cover. In association with the Winter Heather, *Erica carnea*, callunas will furnish the garden with colour the whole year through. The callunas will not tolerate lime and do best in an acid peaty soil. Clipping in spring prevents the plants from becoming too straggly.

The following are some of the best named varieties: 'H.E. Beale', double pink; 'J.H. Hamilton', bright pink dwarf form; 'Alba Plena', a fine double white and 'Ruth Sparkes', a more compact double white. Other kinds, including 'Orange Queen' and 'Tricolor' are grown primarily for the beauty of their coloured foliage.
Late summer   Sun   Well-drained lime-free soil

Camellia 4.5×1.5m (15×5ft)
Camellias are among the choicest of evergreen flowering shrubs. They are completely hardy in themselves but the opening flower buds can be damaged if a rapid thaw occurs after night frosts in spring. The plants, therefore, should be sited either in light overhead shade or in a north- or west-facing situation where the sun will not reach them until late morning. Although more tolerant of lime than rhododendrons and azaleas, they do best in a neutral or acid soil that is rich in humus.

There are many fine varieties of *C. japonica*, among the best of which are 'Adolphe Audusson', with scarlet flowers; 'Lady Clare', having peach pink blooms, and 'Contessa Lavinia Maggii', with pink striped white blossom, all with double flowers. If space restricts planting to only one or two specimens, the best choice is offered by the *williamsii* hybrids, which have an exceptionally long flowering season, from February to April. The widely-grown 'Donation' is an outstanding semi-double pink and 'J.C. Williams' a fine single pink.
Early spring   Sun or part shade   Lime-free peaty soil

Caryopteris (Blue Spiraea) 1.2m $\times 90$cm (4×3ft)
These deciduous shrubs are useful for their late flowering season. Their compact habit makes them suitable for the small garden. The grey-green aromatic foliage provides an attractive background for the bright blue flowers that appear in August and September. *C. $\times$ clandonensis* and its varieties 'Arthur Simmonds' and 'Heavenly Blue' are the best forms.
Early autumn   Sun   Any soil

Ceanothus (Californian Lilac)   up to 3×2m ($10 \times 6\frac{1}{2}$ft)
A large group of deciduous and evergreen shrubs, noteworthy for the beauty of their masses of brilliant blue flower spikes. In the open garden they need a sheltered position in full sun; in colder districts they are best grown against a south- or west-facing wall. Ceanothuses will not thrive on shallow chalk soils.

The deciduous kinds should be lightly pruned in spring; evergreen species need only light pruning after flowering to keep them trim and tidy. The latter, with dark green, glossy foliage that remains decorative throughout the year, include such fine hybrids as 'Autumnal Blue' and 'Burkwoodii', which flower in late summer and autumn, also 'Cascade' and 'Delight', which bloom in late spring or early summer.

Two of the best deciduous forms are 'Gloire de Versailles', free-flowering, with large panicles of powder-blue flowers, and 'Topaz', a deeper indigo, both blooming in summer.
Various seasons (see above)   Sun   Well-drained loam

Ceratostigma (Hardy Plumbago) 90×75cm ($3 \times 2\frac{1}{2}$ft)
Small deciduous shrublets for the front of the border. *C. willmottianum* bears cobalt-blue flower spikes from July to October. The crimson-red

autumn foliage is a decorative autumn bonus. Plants should be cut back to ground level each spring.

Summer/autumn   Sun   Any well-drained soil

Chimonanthus (Wintersweet)   2 × 1.8m (6½ × 6ft)

This group of shrubs is usually represented in the garden by *C. praecox*, a deciduous winter flowering shrub with waxy yellow flowers, blotched with purple at their centres, borne on bare stems and intensely fragrant.

  Wintersweet takes five years to come into flower and is not a suitable shrub for the colder parts of Britain.

Winter   Sun   Any soil, including chalk

Choisya (Mexican Orange Blossom)   1.5 × 2m (5 × 6½ft)

C. ternata is a handsome evergreen shrub of moderate size with dark green glossy trifoliate leaves, aromatic when crushed. The small white flowers, borne in clusters, are sweetly scented and appear from late spring to early summer with a repeat flowering in autumn. They are particularly useful in seaside districts.

Late spring and autumn   Sun or shade   Any soil, including chalk

Cistus (Rock Rose or Sun Rose)   90 × 90cm (3 × 3ft)

Sun-loving evergreens of medium height and spread that make useful subjects for dry banks or in large rock gardens. They are not fully hardy in the colder parts of Britain, but are extremely tolerant of wind and thrive in milder coastal areas. The flowers resemble those of the wild rose, and are white or pink in most varieties, blotched with crimson at their centres. There are numerous named hybrids and cultivars of which *C. × corbariensis*, with crimson-tinted buds opening to white, is one of the hardiest. Two other worthwhile forms are 'Sunset', which makes a compact rounded bush of sage-green foliage decked with deep pink flowers at midsummer, and 'Warley Rose' with darker leaves and flowers of a similar colour.

June/July   Sun   Any well-drained soil

Cornus (Dogwood)   Various heights and spreads – see below

A versatile race of deciduous shrubs, grown variously for their beauty of foliage, coloured stems and blossom. They vary greatly in dimensions. *C. canadensis*, for example, is a small creeping shrublet, not more than 10–15cm (4–6in) in height, with showy white bracts surrounding inconspicuous flowers, followed by scarlet berries.

  The two species grown for their winter bark colouring are *C. alba sibirica* and *C. stolonifera* 'Flaviramea' with scarlet and butter-yellow stems respectively. 'Westonbirt' is the finest red-stemmed dogwood, with far more conspicuous bark colouring than that of the type. Both kinds should be cut back hard each spring as shoots of the current season are the most brightly coloured. Both these species have an ultimate height and spread of around 1.5 × 1.5m (5 × 5ft).

  C. kousa and *C. mas* are much taller, being almost tree-like in appearance, with dimensions of up to 4.5 × 4m (15 × 13ft). In June, the stems and branches of the former species are thickly clustered with white flower bracts that are followed by strawberry-like fruits. The bare twigs of *C. mas* are massed with small yellow flowers in winter. These are followed by scarlet edible fruits known as 'cornelian cherries'. *C. mas* also displays striking autumn leaf colour.

Various seasons: see above   Sun or part shade   Any soil

Cotinus (Smoke Bush)   2 × 1.8m (6½ × 6ft)

The Smoke or Wig Bush is one of the most colourful of the larger deciduous summer-flowering shrubs, with vivid red autumn foliage and

curious pinkish flowers that turn grey in late summer to give this shrub its popular names. The best named forms are 'Royal Purple', with leaves of a deep wine red, and 'Flame', with autumn leaves of brilliant orange.
July/October   Sun   Acid or neutral soil

Cotoneaster   Various heights and spreads – see below
An extensive group of deciduous and evergreen shrubs of varying dimensions and characters. The genus contains some of the most popular and useful subjects for the shrub garden. Cotoneasters are mainly noteworthy for the decorative effect of their leaves and berries; the flowers, usually white or faintly tinged with pink, are fairly inconspicuous.

Prostrate species such as *C. adpressus*, which is deciduous, and the evergreen *C. dammeri* make useful ground cover on banks or in the rock garden.

'Cornubia', 4.5 × 2.5m (15 × 8ft), is a partly evergreen hybrid, with glossy dark green leaves and large bunches of scarlet berries, and 'John Waterer', 5 × 4m (16 × 13ft), is of similar character. 'Hybridus Pendulus' is an evergreen hybrid with pendent branches. These can be restricted to a single stem to make an attractive small weeping tree.

C. horizontalis, 1.2 × 3m (4 × 10ft), the Herringbone Cotoneaster, and *C. salicifolia* 'Autumn Fire', 60 × 75cm (2 × 2½ft) are both prostrate forms of spreading habit, with brilliant scarlet berries. They are useful for covering banks or clothing the lower parts of a wall. They will thrive on any aspect. The Herringbone Cotoneaster, so called because of the way its branches are arranged, has fiery autumn foliage to complement its display of berries.
Autumn leaf and/or berries   Sun or shade   Any soil

Cytisus (Broom) – see also *Genista* and *Spartium*   Various sizes
Brooms are a useful group of shrubs for planting in a new garden for quick results. Most are vigorous but short-lived, providing a good display of bloom the first or second season after planting. With the exception of the semi-prostrate dwarf brooms such as *C.* × *beanii*, with deep yellow flowers, and *C.* × *kewensis*, which has paler yellow flowers, the garden forms average 1.5 × 1m (5 × 3ft). Attractive hybrids of our native yellow broom include 'Golden Cascade', yellow; 'Wings', deep red; 'Sunset', yellow, pink and purple and 'Zeelandia', pink and red.

C. battandieri, 3 × 2.5m (10 × 8ft), the Pineapple Broom, named for its distinctive scent, has dense clusters of yellow flowers. This is a larger and longer-lived species with silvered silky three-lobed leaves. It likes a sheltered position and makes an interesting wall shrub.
Early summer   Sun   Neutral or slightly acid soil

Daboecia cantabrica (St. Dabeoc's Heath)   60 × 90cm (2 × 3ft)
This attractive heath has larger bell-shaped flowers than the ericas and an exceptionally long flowering period – from midsummer to early winter. There are many good varieties, including 'Alba', white; 'Atropurpurea', deep purple; and the unusual 'Bicolor' which bears white, purple and purple and white striped blooms on the same plant.
July/October   Sun   Acid or neutral soil

Daphne   Various heights and spreads – see below
Compact deciduous and evergreen shrubs, all with exceptionally fragrant flowers in winter or early spring. *D. cneorum*, the Garland Flower, 30 × 60cm (1 × 2ft), is a dwarf semi-prostrate evergreen that bears clusters of scented pink flowers in late spring; *D. burkwoodii*, another evergreen kind, is dense and bushy with pink-tinged flowers. It

makes good ground cover. *D. odora* produces its purple-budded white flowers in March and April. This species is rather tender; the variety 'Aureomarginata', with gold-edged evergreen foliage, is hardier.

Flowering in January on bare stems, *D. mezereum*, 120×60cm (4×2ft) has very fragrant purple flowers followed by poisonous scarlet berries. There is a white form 'Alba' and another, 'Grandiflora', with larger flowers.

Winter or early spring   Sun or part shade   Moist well-drained soil

Deutzia

Easily grown deciduous shrubs with a lavish display of blossom around midsummer. They are fairly compact in habit, reaching 1.2×1.2m (4×4ft). 'Mont Rose' and 'Grandiflora' are two of the best kinds, both with large white blooms suffused with pink. All old twiggy growths on deutzias should be cut out after flowering.

June/July   Sun   Any well-drained soil

Elaeagnus

Vigorous shrubs grown for the decorative quality of their evergreen foliage, useful as windbreaks and good in maritime districts. *E. pungens* 'Variegata', 2×1.5m (6$\frac{1}{2}$×5ft), is the most widely grown form. It has striking gold-splashed foliage. *E. ebbingei*, 3×2.5m (10×8ft), grows faster than the former and has small scented ivory flowers in autumn. The large oval leaves of this species are jade-green, with silver undersides.

Foliage plants   Sun   Any soil except chalk

Erica   Heathers: see also *Calluna* and *Daboecia*

An extensive group of small to medium-sized evergreen shrubs flowering at various seasons, thus making it possible to have heathers in bloom at almost any time of the year. Ericas make good ground cover and, once established, will smother any but the most persistent weeds. With the exception of *E. carnea* and its varieties, the ericas are lime-haters and do best in acid peaty soils. They can be grown in partial shade but are seen at their best in full sun. Those kinds grown for their coloured foliage do not colour well in shade. Ericas can be lightly pruned after the flowers have faded. This will prevent them from becoming straggly.

E. carnea, 30×90cm (1×3ft), is the Winter-flowering Heath that provides a wealth of colour in the garden from November to March. There are many named varieties with different coloured flowers, among the best of which are 'Winter Beauty', clear rose-pink; 'Eileen Porter', carmine-red; 'Vivelli', deep wine-red; and the prostrate, fast-spreading 'Springwood White'. 'Aurea' is a form with pink flowers that is grown primarily for the beauty of its golden foliage.

E. × darleyensis, which also blooms in winter, is slightly taller than *E. carnea*. 'Arthur Johnson' is the most outstanding form, with long dense spikes of magenta flowers.

E. arborea alpina, 1.5×2m (5×6$\frac{1}{2}$ft), is the hardiest of the so-called 'tree' heaths, with dark green foliage and masses of scented white flowers in May.

Other erica species that flower between June and October are our native Bell Heather, *E. cinerea*, 20×30cm (8in×1ft) and the Cornish Heath, *E. tetralix*, of similar dimensions.

Various – see above   Sun or light shade   Light, acid soil

Escallonia – see HEDGES, page 126.

Euonymus   Various heights and spreads – see below.

An extensive group of deciduous and evergreen trees and shrubs that includes our native Spindle, *E. europaeus*. Their flowers are relatively insignificant, and they are grown mainly for the decorative effect of their fruits and/or foliage.

E. fortunei is a trailing evergreen species that can also be used as a clinging wall shrub. 'Silver Queen', with leaves edged with creamy-white, and 'Variegatus', which has grey-green and white leaves with a tinge of pink, are two of the best varieties.

E. alatus, 1.5 × 1.2m (5 × 4ft), is a slow-growing deciduous shrub of medium height and spread with autumn foliage of a striking crimson pink. In winter, an added attraction is provided by the winged stems with their curious corky bark.

Foliage plants   Sun or part shade   Any soil

Fatsia japonica   3 × 4.5m (10 × 15ft)

Handsome evergreen shrub of great architectural value, useful for focal planting. The palmate (hand-shaped) leaves are dark green and glossy, measuring more than 30cm (1ft) across. Large clusters of creamy-white flowers appear during late autumn.

October/November   Part shade   Any well-drained soil

Forsythia (Golden Bells)   Various – see below

These deciduous flowering shrubs are widely grown on walls and fences and in the open garden. Their golden-yellow flowers, thickly festooning the bare stems, make the forsythias among the showiest of early spring shrubs. 'Beatrix Farrand' and 'Lynwood', 2 × 1.5m (6½ × 5ft), are two of the best named forms. *F. suspensa*, 3 × 2m (10 × 6½ft), which is loose and rambling in habit, is best grown as a wall shrub.

February/March   Sun   Any soil

Fuchsia – see also HEDGES, page 126.

Although often thought of solely as greenhouse or pot plants, many fuchsias are completely hardy in the milder districts of the British Isles. Others, although cut back to ground level by frost, make strong new growths each following spring.

Fuchsias give good value in the garden, flowering profusely from early July to late autumn. Among the hardiest are 'Alice Hofman', scarlet and white; 'Mrs. Popple', crimson; 'Mme. Cornelissen', red and white, all about 60 × 45cm (2 × 1½ft), and the dwarf 'Tom Thumb', 30 × 30cm (1 × 1ft). *F. magellanica* 'Versicolor' is an outstanding variety. Its leaves are variegated with copper and pink; the flowers are crimson and purple.

July/October   Sun or part shade   Any moist soil

Garrya elliptica   3 × 1.8m (10 × 6ft)

Decorative evergreen shrubs with dark green leaves and conspicuous jade-green catkins in winter. They are useful for seaside planting or in colder districts will do well on a north wall. The male forms should be planted as they bear the longer catkins, up to 30cm (1ft) in length.

January/February   Sun or shade   Any well-drained soil

Genista (Broom) – see also *Cytisus* and *Spartium*

A useful group of deciduous shrubs, flowering later than *Cytisus* and including several dwarfs suitable for the rock garden. The Mount Etna Broom, *G. aetnensis*, 3.5 × 1.8m (12 × 6ft) is one of the larger species, bearing masses of yellow sweet-pea-like flowers in August. *G. hispanica*, the Spanish Gorse, is a prostrate shrub 60cm (2ft) tall, and makes good ground cover. It is smothered in golden blossom in May and June. *G. lydia*, only 40cm (15in) tall, has spikes of pale yellow flowers in June.

Various (see above)   Sun   Neutral or acid soil

Hamamelis (Witch Hazel)   2 × 1.5m (6½ × 5ft)
Deciduous shrubs with hazel-like foliage bearing a profusion of spidery, yellow, scented flowers on their bare stems during winter. *H. mollis*, the best-known species, has several varieties with more showy flowers than those of the type. These include 'Brevipetala', with orange flowers; 'Goldcrest', yellow, with petals blotched with red at their base; and 'Pallida', sulphur-yellow.
December/March   Sun   Any soil

Hebe   Various heights and spreads – see below
Evergreen flowering shrubs with interesting foliage, especially useful for seaside districts. Not all kinds are hardy in colder parts of the British Isles. Height and spread vary, ranging from dwarfs such as *H. pinguifolia* 'Pagei', 30cm (1ft) in height, with glaucous (blue-grey) foliage and white flowers, to 'Midsummer Beauty', 1m × 75cm (3 × 2½ft), with reddish leaves and long spikes of purple flowers throughout summer. 'Autumn Glory' is a useful later-flowering variety with spikes of deep violet-purple. 'Alicia Amherst', 30 × 30cm (1 × 1ft), has deep blue flowers in late summer. There are also several forms, such as *H. × andersonii* 'Variegata', with cream-variegated foliage that provides a delightful complement to the lavender flowers.
July/October   Sun   Any well-drained soil

Hibiscus (Tree Hollyhock)   2 × 1.5m (6½ × 5ft)
The so-called 'Tree Hollyhock', *H. syriacus*, is a fairly large deciduous shrub with a profusion of mallow-like single or double flowers from July to October. It is very late in coming into leaf, sometimes not before the beginning of June. It needs fairly drastic pruning and the side shoots should be cut back to two or three dormant buds in February.

Good named varieties include 'Blue Bird', having violet-blue flowers with maroon centres; 'Hamabo', pink with crimson centres; and 'Woodbridge', a large-flowered pink form with darker centres. All of these are singles; 'Duc de Brabant', deep rose-purple, is a good double.
August/October   Sun   Any well-drained soil

Hydrangea   Various sizes (see below)
This large family contains some of the most widely grown flowering shrubs, with a season that lasts from midsummer to late autumn. There are various species and hybrids of differing habits and character. Those most widely grown are the hortensias and lacecaps, both of which belong to the *macrophylla* group. These are seaside shrubs *par excellence* but they will also do well in sheltered gardens in mild inland districts. Old flowering shoots should be cut back hard as soon as the blooms have faded, except in colder districts, where it pays to leave pruning until spring in order to give protection from frost to the dormant buds.

Hortensias average 1.5 × 1.5m (5 × 5ft), but grow taller in the shade. Worthwhile varieties include 'Altona', deep pink; 'Ayesha', white with unusual lilac-type flowers; 'Générale Vicomtesse de Vibraye', rose-pink; 'Madame E. Mouillière', white with a pink eye; and 'Parsifal', with large deep pink blooms.

The two best-known lacecap hydrangeas are 'Bluewave' and 'Whitewave' with pink and white blooms respectively. They grow about the same size as the hortensias. The pink colouring of some varieties will be a rich blue in acid soils or in slightly alkaline soils treated with a blueing compound such as alum (aluminium sulphate).

Another deservedly popular species is *H. paniculata*, whose flowers are more pointed than those of the hortensias and lacecaps. These are

cream in colour, gradually turning to a pale carmine-pink as they mature, and lasting for a very long time. 'Grandiflora' is the best form, with much larger flowers. Hard cutting-back in spring improves the size and quality of the blooms. It grows to 1.2m (4ft) or more.
July/October   Prefer some shade   Any moist soil except chalk

Hypericum (St. John's Wort)   up to 1.2m × 75cm (4 × 2½ft)
A very large family of decorative shrubs of moderate size producing yellow rose-like blooms over a long period. There are some good named hybrids, including 'Hidcote', with bright yellow saucer-shaped flowers from July to October, and 'Rowallane', a semi-evergreen with large golden cup-shaped blooms up to 8cm (3in) across. The latter is not completely hardy in colder districts.

   H. calycinum, the Rose of Sharon, spreads rapidly and makes a first-rate ground cover plant. It bears masses of yellow flowers in late summer and is semi-evergreen.
Late summer to autumn   Sun or part shade   Any soil

Jasminum nudiflorum (Winter Jasmine)   2 × 2m (6½ × 6½ft)
The Winter Jasmine is one of our most popular winter-flowering shrubs. It is usually grown on walls or fences where it produces its masses of bright yellow blooms on the bare stems during any mild spell from November to February. Straggly growths should be cut right back as soon as the flowers have faded.
November/February   Sun or part shade   Any soil

Kerria japonica (Jew's Mallow)   1.5m × 90cm (5 × 3ft)
This is a useful deciduous shrub that thrives in any soil or situation. Although the double-flowered 'Pleniflora', with orange-yellow tassel-like flowers, is the kind most often seen, the single species, whose smaller cupped blooms mass the bare stems in spring, has a charm of its own. An added attraction of both is their conspicuous green stems in winter.
Early spring   Sun or shade   Any soil

Lavandula (Lavender)   Up to 90cm × 1.2m (3 × 4ft)
The most widely grown of grey-leaved aromatic plants, the lavenders make small shrubs up to 90cm (3ft) tall. Old English Lavender, L. spica, is the most fragrant, with long spikes of lavender-blue flowers. 'Hidcote' and 'Munstead' are two of its more compact varieties, with deeper violet flowers than those of the type. 'Twickel Purple' makes a rounded bush with long-stemmed, lavender-blue flower spikes. Lavenders have a tendency to legginess; this can be prevented by light pruning in spring.
July/August   Sun   Any well-drained soil

Lavatera (Mallow)   1.5 × 1.2m (5 × 4ft)
Deciduous shrubs with saucer-shaped flowers and palmate leaves that are especially useful in seaside districts. L. maritima has grey-green downy foliage and stems with purple-centred flowers of pale lilac.
July/October   Sun and shelter   Any soil

Mahonia   1.5 × 1m (5 × 3ft)
Handsome evergreen shrubs with holly-like leaves and yellow flowers in late winter or early spring, followed by clusters of purple, grape-like berries. M. aquifolium, the Oregon Grape, is one of the best evergreen shrubs for dense shade. It can also be grown in full sun, when its leaves will often colour strikingly in winter.

   M. japonica makes a lovely specimen shrub, with long racemes of Lily-of-the-Valley-scented flowers from December to April!. 'Charity', a hybrid of M. japonica and M. lomariifolia has erect, yellow flower spikes.
Winter   Sun or shade   Any well-drained soil

Olearia (Daisy Bush)   Up to 2 × 1.5m (6½ × 5ft)
Evergreen shrubs of Australasian origin that are ideal for maritime
districts and exposed situations, but not completely hardy in colder
parts of Britain.

O. macrodonta, the New Zealand Holly, has greyish-green holly-like
leaves up to 9cm (3½in) long, with a lavish display of white blossom in
June.

O. × haastii, a dense rounded bush, has smaller, oval leaves, and is
massed with white daisy-like flowers in August.
Various (see above)   Sun   Any well-drained soil

Osmanthus delavayi   1.5 × 1.8m (5 × 6ft)
An attractive small-leaved evergreen with dark green foliage and masses
of tiny tubular flowers in spring, which are exceptionally fragrant.
April   Sun and shelter   Medium loam

Paeonia suffruticosa (Tree Peony)   2 × 1.5m (6½ × 5ft)
The so-called 'tree' peonies are among the aristocrats of flowering
shrubs, with handsome cut foliage and giant peony-like flowers 15cm
(6in) or more in diameter in late spring. Because of their tolerance of
lime, they make good alternatives to azaleas on alkaline soils.

There are many excellent varieties, including 'Duchess of Kent', with
bright rose-pink flowers; 'Lord Selborne', salmon-pink; 'Mrs. William
Kelway', pure white and 'Superb', a rich cherry-red. Crosses with *P.
lutea* have produced some fine yellows such as the sulphur-yellow
'Chromatella' and the golden-yellow 'Souvenir de Maxime Cornu'.
May/June   Sun   Any well-drained soil

Pernettya   75 × 90cm (2½ × 3ft)
Attractive berry-bearing evergreen shrubs of moderate size, requiring a
soil that is lime-free. They form dense clumps of wiry stems with small
dark green leaves and bear heath-like white flowers in late spring. These
are followed by marble-sized berries ranging in colour from white to
deep purple. Pernettyas should be planted in groups of three or more to
ensure cross-fertilization. 'Snow White' has pure white berries, those of
'Mother of Pearl' are pale pink, while those of 'Crimsoniana' and
'Signal' are crimson and deep red respectively.
May/June   Autumn berries   Sun or part shade   Acid peaty soil

Perovskia atriplicifolia (Russian Sage)   90 × 45cm (3 × 1½ft)
Grey-leaved aromatic shrublets with tall spires of lavender-blue flowers
in late summer. 'Blue Spire' has deeply cut foliage and larger flower
spikes than those of the type. The stems should be cut back almost to
ground level each spring.
August/September   Sun   Any well-drained soil, including chalk

Philadelphus (Mock Orange)   Various sizes (see below)
This is a useful group of deciduous shrubs that includes species and
varieties to suit gardens of all sizes. In most forms, the 'orange blossom'
flowers that appear in July are rich in fragrance. Varieties worth
growing include 'Belle Etoile', 1.5 × 1.5m (5 × 5ft), an established
favourite with large ivory flowers blotched with mauve at their centres;
'Silver Showers', 1.5m × 90cm (5 × 3ft), with pure white flowers; and
'Virginal', with masses of pure white, scented, double blooms.
More compact in habit and ideal for the smaller garden are *P.
microphyllus*, 90 × 90cm (3 × 3ft), with small but very fragrant white
flowers, and 'Manteau d'Hermine', 90 × 75cm (3 × 2½ft), another
favourite with dainty double white flowers.
July   Sun or part shade   Any soil including chalk

Phlomis fruticosa (Jerusalem Sage)   1.2m × 90cm (4 × 3ft)
Compact grey-green shrublets with whorls of yellow flowers
complemented by the thickly felted leaves.
Midsummer   Sun   Any well-drained soil

Phormium tenax (New Zealand Flax)   3 × 2m (10 × 6½ft)
Magnificent shrubs of Australasian origin, hardy in any but the coldest
parts of the British Isles. Sword-like evergreen leaves set off the striking
bronzy-red flower spikes which grow as much as 3m (10ft) tall.
Phormiums are useful for focal planting or for creating an exotic sub-
tropical effect. The variety 'Purpureum' has purplish-bronze foliage,
while 'Variegatum' has cream and green striped leaves.
July   Sun   Any good soil

Pieris   2 × 1.5m (6½ × 5ft)
Dense and compact evergreen shrubs that produce their pitcher-shaped
flowers in spring. A feature of some species is the brilliant red or coral-
pink of their young foliage. 'Firecrest' and 'Forest Flame' both have
vivid red young growths and pendent clusters of ivory flowers.
April/May   Part shade and shelter   Neutral or acid soil

Potentilla fruticosa   Up to 1.2m × 90cm (4 × 3ft)
Hardy deciduous shrubs of small and compact character. They are
noteworthy for their long flowering season, lasting from early summer
to autumn. The flowers, which are white, yellow or orange, resemble
miniature wild roses. Among the best of the named forms are
'Buttercup', 'Farrer's White' and 'Tangerine', whose names are sufficient
description of their flower colour. 'Katherine Dykes', with primrose
yellow flowers, is a more vigorous form than most.
June/October   Sun or part shade   Any soil

Pyracantha (Firethorn)   3 × 3m (10 × 10ft)
Evergreen shrubs grown for the decorative quality of their scarlet,
orange or yellow berries. They are often used as wall shrubs (see
CLIMBING AND TRAILING PLANTS, page 226). The leaves are small and
toothed and the stems armed with sharp spines up to 5cm (2in) long.
Clusters of hawthorn-like blossom appear around midsummer.
Pyracanthas do well in towns.
   P. coccinea 'Lalandei', with large orange fruits, is the most widely-
grown form. Others, equally worthwhile, are *P. atalantioides*, with
scarlet berries, and its attractive yellow-berried variety 'Buttercup'.
June/July   Sun or shade   Any soil

Rhododendron (including Azaleas)   Various sizes – see below
Rhododendrons and Azaleas probably represent the most popular and
widely-grown group of garden shrubs. This group includes species and
varieties of greatly differing sizes and character, most of which are
relatively slow-growing, evergreen and free-flowering. They are all lime-
haters that will thrive only in acid, well-drained peaty soils.
   Gardeners on alkaline soils can grow some of the smaller kinds in a
lime-free peat compost in tubs or raised beds. Rhododendrons do not
need regular pruning but flower production will benefit by the removal
of blooms as soon as they have faded.
   In general, the plants prefer partial shade, although the popular hardy
hybrids do well in full sun, provided that the soil is moist and well-
drained. These hybrids, which are the kinds most widely grown in
modern gardens, range in size from dwarf and prostrate forms to others
as large as small trees, so that there is a choice for even the smallest of
plots. The varieties listed will attain heights between 1.5 and 3m (5–10ft).

Small to medium size

'Bluebird'	Violet-blue flowers in small trusses
'Blue Tit'	Violet flowers, white at the throat
'Carmen'	Bell-shaped, deep crimson flowers
'Elizabeth'	Clusters of dark red, trumpet-shaped flowers
'Praecox'	Valuable for its early-flowering habit; the lilac-pink flowers appear in March
'Yellow Hammer'	Small, tubular, creamy-yellow flowers

Larger hybrids

'Betty Wormald'	Huge pink flowers in large trusses
'Britannia'	Bell-shaped scarlet flowers
'Cynthia'	Deep rose with conical flower heads
'Lavender Girl'	Lilac-mauve flowers opening to pale lavender
'Mother of Pearl'	Large blush-pink blooms freely borne
'Mrs. G.W. Leak'	Bright pink flowers with brownish 'eye'
'Pink Pearl'	Large pink blooms; vigorous and free flowering. The most widely planted of all rhododendrons
'White Swan'	White flowers suffused with pink

Evergreen Azaleas

These are comparatively dwarf in character, up to 1.2 × 1.8m (4 × 6ft), with a slow growth rate. The flowers are so profusely borne that the leaves are scarcely visible when the display is at its peak. The flower colour is given for a range of varieties listed below. The evergreen azaleas will thrive in full sun or part shade.

'Addy Wery'	Scarlet
'Blaauw's Pink'	Salmon-pink
'Hatsugiri'	Vivid magenta
'Hinodegiri'	Crimson-scarlet
'Hinomayo'	Clear pink
'Palestrina'	White with greenish throat
'Polar Bear'	White

Deciduous Azaleas (Ghent, mollis and Exbury hybrids)

These are larger, with bigger flowers, than the evergreen kinds and equally noteworthy for the brilliance of their display. The leaves of the mollis hybrids turn a fiery scarlet in autumn. In the following list, the flower colour is given for each form.

'Bouquet de Flore' (Ghent)	Salmon-rose
'Comte de Gomer' (mollis)	Rose-pink, spotted orange
'Daybreak' (Exbury)	Orange, suffused red
'Homebush' (Ghent)	Rounded heads of semi-double pink flowers
'Spek's Brilliant' (mollis)	Orange-scarlet
'Strawberry Ice' (Exbury)	Flesh pink and gold

Since the choice of species and varieties is very wide, these lists can only be a purely representative selection.

Mainly May/June   Sun or light shade   Acid peaty soil

Ribes sanguineum (Flowering Currant)   1.5 × 1.5m (5 × 5ft)

Popular deciduous shrubs of medium size with pendent clusters of pink or crimson flowers in spring. The bushes should be pruned as soon as the flowers fade. The two most popular varieties are 'King Edward VII', with deep crimson flowers, and 'Pulborough Scarlet', with crimson-red blooms.

April   Sun or part shade   Any soil

Santolina (Cotton Lavender)   60 × 30cm (2 × 1ft)
Aromatic evergreen sub-shrubs with grey-green foliage and yellow
button-shaped flowers in summer, grown primarily for the attraction of
their finely-cut silvery leaves. Cutting back hard each spring will keep
the plants from becoming leggy. *S. chamaecyparissus* and *S. neopolitana*
are the two most widely-grown species.
July   Sun   Any well-drained soil

Senecio laxifolius   60 × 90cm (2 × 3ft)
Evergreen spreading shrubs of medium size, with silver-grey leaves,
which turn green at maturity, and loose clusters of sulphur-yellow
flowers in summer. These shrubs should be cut back hard in spring to
prevent them from straggling. The senecios are good for planting in
coastal gardens and those in very exposed situations, as they are
extremely wind-resistant.
July   Sun   Any well-drained soil

Skimmia japonica   90 × 90cm (3 × 3ft)
Slow-growing evergreen shrubs with very fragrant but relatively
inconspicuous white flowers, followed by brilliant scarlet berries if both
male and female forms are planted. A combination of the vigorous
'Foremanii' (female) with the male form 'Fragrans' should result in a
lavish display of globular red berries. Skimmias are useful shrubs for
gardens in maritime and industrial districts.
April/May   Sun or shade   Any soil

Spartium junceum (Spanish Broom)   1.5m × 90cm (5 × 3ft)
Vigorous shrub with bright green stems and scale-like leaves, bearing
large yellow pea-like flowers over a long period in summer and early
autumn. It makes a good plant for seaside districts. Spartiums should be
pruned in March, taking care not to cut back into old wood. Keep
pruning to a minimum if botrytis (grey mould) is prevalent.
June/September   Sun   Any well-drained soil

Spiraea   Up to 1.5m × 90cm (5 × 3ft)
A large group of deciduous flowering shrubs, varying considerably in
habit and appearance. *S. × arguta*, the Bridal Wreath, and
S. × vanhouttei both bloom in spring. The former masses its stems with
small clusters of white flowers in May; *S. × vanhouttei*, similar in
character, blooms a few weeks later. *S. × bumalda* 'Anthony Waterer', a
popular summer-flowering spiraea, bears flat heads of bright crimson
flowers from July to September and has variegated pink and cream
young leaves on some shoots.
Various – see above   Sun   Any soil

Symphoricarpos (Snowberry)   90 × 90cm (3 × 3ft)
Deciduous shrubs of suckering habit that bear tiny pink and white bell-
shaped flowers that are followed by conspicuous marble-sized berries
ranging in colour from pure white to pinkish-purple. 'Magic Berry', with
rose-pink berries; 'Mother of Pearl', with pearly-white berries; and
'Constance', with large pure white berries, are all good hybrid forms. The
berries last well into winter.
Autumn and winter berries   Sun or shade   Any soil

Syringa vulgaris (Lilac)   Up to 3.5 × 2m (12 × 6½ft)
Deciduous shrubs of medium to large size. The numerous named
varieties are widely grown for the beauty and fragrance of their flowers
in late spring. The faded flower heads of lilacs should be removed
promptly and annual dressings of compost or well-rotted manure given
to encourage flower production.

A good selection, with a range of flower colours, would include the
following: 'Ambassadeur', lilac with white eyes; 'Marechal Foch',
carmine-rose; 'Maud Notcutt', pure white; and 'Souvenir de Louis
Späth', wine-red, which are all singles, and double lilacs such as 'Belle
de Nancy', lilac-pink; 'Charles Joly', deep purple; 'Katherine Havemeyer',
lavender-purple; and 'Madame Lemoine', white.
May/early June   Sun   Any soil including chalk

Tamarix pentandra (Tamarisk)   1.5m × 90cm (5 × 3ft)
Good seaside shrubs extremely resistant to wind and exposure. The
greyish feathery foliage makes a perfect foil for the plumes of tiny rose-
pink flowers. This is one of the showiest of late-flowering shrubs. A
tendency to legginess can be prevented by cutting back fairly hard in
spring. 'Rubra' is a variety with deeper flower colour than that of the
type.
July/September   Sun   Any soil except chalk

Viburnum   Up to 2 × 2m (6½ × 6½ft)
An extensive group of evergreen and deciduous shrubs flowering at
different times of the year, some with exceptionally fragrant flowers,
others with decorative autumn berries or foliage.

V. × *bodnantense* 'Dawn' is an outstanding winter-flowering hybrid,
producing spikes of sweetly-scented pinkish-white flowers which open
during any mild spells from October to March. Others grown for their
flowers and fragrance are *V.* × *burkwoodii*, with flat heads of creamy-
white blossom, and *V. carlesii*, with pink-budded flowers opening to
white.

V. opulus is the popular Guelder Rose with scented white flowers and
dark green, maple-like foliage, which colours well in autumn. The
variety 'Sterile', popularly known as the Snowball Bush, has large,
globular flower heads, each bloom being greenish in bud and opening to
pure white. 'Xanthocarpum' bears beautiful rich yellow berries in
autumn.

V. plicatum tomentosum bears flat heads of lacecap flowers, followed
by shiny red berries. 'Lanarth' is the best form.

V. tinus (Laurustinus) is the most widely grown of the evergreen
viburnums. It is a vigorous shrub with dark green glossy leaves and
pink-budded white flowers in flat clusters that start to open in late
winter.
Various – see above   Sun   Any well-drained soil

Vinca (Periwinkle)   25 × 50cm (10 × 20in)
Prostrate evergreen shrubs that make useful ground cover. *V. major*,
with larger leaves and flowers, is faster-growing than *V. minor*. The
trumpet flowers of the former species are bright blue and there are
varieties with variegated green and white foliage. *V. minor* has varieties
with purple or white flowers in addition to those of the type, and one
with variegated green and yellow leaves.
April/June   Sun or shade   Any soil

Weigela   1.5 × 1.8m (5 × 6ft)
Deciduous flowering shrubs of moderate dimensions that bear a
profusion of tubular, foxglove-shaped flowers in early summer. *W.
florida* 'Variegata' is a popular variety whose cream-edged foliage makes
a perfect foil for the pale pink flowers. There are many other fine
varieties and hybrids including 'Abel Carriere', with large rose-carmine
flowers; 'Eva Rathke', with crimson-red flowers; 'Le Printemps', with
peach-pink blooms; and 'Mont Blanc', with white flowers.

The flowering shoots should be cut back as soon as they finish blooming.
May/June   Sun or part shade   Any good soil
Yucca (Adam's Needle)   Various sizes (see below)
Evergreen shrubs of exotic appearance with sword-like leaves and tall
spikes of ivory-coloured bell-shaped flowers, which do not appear until
the plant is several years old. *Y. gloriosa* has grey-green leaves tipped
with sharp spines. It grows on a single stem, and may reach 1.8m (6ft)
high and spread almost as wide. *Y. filamentosa* is a more compact,
stemless species which produces clumps of broadsword-shaped leaves
edged with curling white threads. It grows to about 75cm (2½ft) high
and 90cm (3ft) broad.
June/July   Sun   Any well-drained soil

AN ALPHABETICAL LIST OF ORNAMENTAL TREES
Acer (Maple)   Japanese maples up to 4.5m (15ft)
Although the larger maples are unsuitable trees for the small garden,
there are many kinds that make good lawn specimens, as well as the
delightful Japanese maples, some of which are dwarf enough for the
rock garden.

    A. palmatum is the Japanese Maple from which many outstanding
garden cultivars have been raised. Most of these are not much larger
than a big bush or small tree at maturity and will take as long as ten or
twenty years to reach such dimensions. All have lobed leaves, finely-cut
and lacy in the 'Dissectum' group, seven-lobed in the 'Septemlobum'
(or 'Heptalobum') group.

    The Japanese maples need moist, rich soil conditions and a position
sheltered from cold winds. There are numerous good named forms,
including the relatively vigorous 'Atropurpureum', with bronzy-crimson
foliage; 'Corallinum', whose young stems are coral pink and whose
leaves open shrimp-pink and turn green as they mature; and 'Aureum',
with young foliage of a bright gold colour.

    Some of the most striking members of the 'Dissectum' group are
'Dissectum' itself, both in the green and purple-leaved forms; 'Dissectum
Palmatifidium' with exceptionally lacy foliage; and 'Dissectum
Variegatum', whose leaves are bronzy-red, variegated with cream or pink.

    'Osakazuki' is the finest variety in the Septemlobum group, with green
leaves that are a blaze of scarlet in autumn. 'Septemlobum Elegans
Purpureum' with deep bronze-red leaves and 'Senkaki' ('Sangokaku'),
the Coral Bark Maple, with golden-yellow foliage and coral-pink stems
are two other kinds well worth growing.
Flowers inconspicuous   Sun and shelter   Moist well-drained soil
Ailanthus (Tree of Heaven)   Up to 18m (60ft)
Deciduous, fast-growing trees with very large, divided ash-like leaves.
They make a rapid impact in the garden as specimen trees. Good for
towns and industrial areas, as they tolerate atmospheric pollution.
Flowers inconspicuous   Sheltered situation   Rich soil
Alnus (Alder)   Up to 9m (30ft)
Although the Common Alder, *A. glutinosa*, and the Grey Alder, *A.
incana*, are not suitable for the average-sized garden, there are several
forms of these trees that are worth planting on the boundaries or in the
shrub border since they are compact and shrub-like in habit. 'Laciniata'
is an attractive variety of the common alder with finely-cut lacy foliage.
'Aurea', a form of *A. incana*, has striking golden foliage. Alders bear
abundant purplish-brown catkins in spring and brown cones in autumn.

Catkins, March/April   Damp situation   Any soil except·chalk

Amelanchier canadensis (= *A. laevis villosa*) (Snowy Mespilus)   Up to 6m (20ft)

A fine tree of moderate size that is noteworthy for its profusion of white star-shaped flowers in spring and brilliant red or gold autumn leaf colour. It has woolly, sharply-toothed leaves.

April   Open situation   Well-drained soil, preferably lime-free

Arbutus (Strawberry Tree)   Up to 6m (20ft)

Extremely attractive small evergreen trees that stand up to the fiercest gales and are ideal for maritime districts, although young trees should be protected from frost in winter with straw or bracken until they are established. Strawberry Trees have reddish trunks with handsome dark green glossy foliage and bear white pitcher-shaped flowers and inedible but decorative strawberry-like fruits. *A. unedo* is the hardiest species, with orange-red fruits. The flowers often appear at the same time as the previous year's fruit. The form 'Rubra' has flowers tinged with pink.

August/September   Open situation   Any soil

Betula (Birch)   Up to 9m (30ft)

There are several forms of our native Silver Birch, *Betula pendula*, that make attractive specimen trees for the garden. The common Silver Birch is semi-weeping in habit but does not compare in beauty of form with Young's Weeping Birch, *B. pendula* 'Youngii'. This makes an elegant weeping tree that seldom reaches a height of more than 6m (20ft). Birches bear 5cm (2in) long pale yellow male catkins (the flowers) and much smaller, insignificant female catkins in spring.

Catkins, April/May   Any situation   Any soil

Catalpa (Indian Bean Tree)   Up to 10.5m (35ft)

Catalpa bignonioides is a handsome and exotic-looking tree with a rounded head, grown primarily for the decorative quality of its large heart-shaped leaves. The white foxglove-like flowers, marked with yellow and purple, are very striking but do not start to appear until the tree reaches maturity. The long green fruit pods, ripening to reddish brown in winter, have given the tree its common name; they are not edible. 'Aurea' is a form with yellow leaves. The Indian Bean is not suitable for exposed situations as the large, soft-textured leaves, which do not appear until June, are susceptible to frost and wind damage.

July/August   Sheltered situation   Any well-drained soil

Cercis siliquastrum (Judas Tree)   Up to 5m (16ft)

A small compact tree, useful in the smaller garden, with round leaves and masses of rosy-purple pea-type flowers on the bare branches in spring.

May   Full sun   Well-drained soil

Crataegus (Thorn)   Up to 7m (23ft)

Some of the best all-rounders for the small garden are found in this group of trees and shrubs, including the colourful 'May' or Common Hawthorn, *C. monogyna*, which is abundant in hedges throughout Britain. As well as the ordinary white-flowered kind there are pink-leaved and weeping forms. The best garden kinds, however, are varieties of the wild Midland Hawthorn, *C. oxyacantha* (= *C. laevigata*). These include 'Paul's Scarlet' (or 'Coccinea Plena'), which bears scarlet double flowers, and 'Rosea Flore Pleno', with attractive deep pink double flowers.

May/June   Open situation   Any soil

Eucalyptus   Up to 18m (60ft)

Although the majority of the eucalypts are not sufficiently hardy to survive a really severe British winter, there is one species that has proved itself to be almost completely hardy. This is the Tasmanian form of *E. gunnii* which came through the exceptionally severe winter of 1962/3 unscathed. *E. gunnii* is a handsome, fast-growing tree with silvery bark and 'evergrey' foliage which, in the young tree, is disc-like in appearance. As the trees mature, the leaves become sickle-shaped and bluish-green. The flowers, which are borne in clusters, are creamy-white. Late summer   Sunny situation, sheltered from cold winds   Any soil except chalk

Laburnum   Up to 9m (30ft)
One of the most popular of the smaller ornamental trees, with long, pendulous racemes of yellow blossom in early summer. The light green trifoliate leaves are also attractive. 'Vossii' is the most outstanding cultivar, with racemes of flowers 30cm (1ft) or more in length.
June   Sun   Any soil

Malus (Flowering crab-apple)   Up to 6m (20ft)
The ornamental crab-apples, together with the Japanese cherries, are generally the first choice of gardeners with plots of small to medium size. Some are noteworthy for their blossom, others for their colourful fruits, many of which make first-rate crab-apple jelly. There is a great number of species and varieties, and those listed below are a few examples only of those worthy of a place in your garden. The first five varieties are grown for their blossom.

M. atrosanguinea is a small tree, which is smothered in rosy-red blossom in mid-May.

M. floribunda is similar to the former species but bears clouds of frothy white blossom in late April and May and is of a semi-weeping habit.

M. 'Lemoinei' (flowering April–May) and 'Profusion' (flowering mid-May) are two of the best purplish-crimson-flowered varieties, the brilliant flowers of the latter being particularly striking.

M. sargentii is a small bushy species with glossy leaves and white flowers borne in early to mid-May.

Among the best of the ornamental fruiting crabs are 'Golden Hornet', a small, erect tree which bears prolific crops of oval golden-yellow fruits that remain on the branches until well after Christmas, and 'Wintergold', another small form which bears large clusters of smaller rounded fruits, which last until late February.

The red or yellow-fruited Siberian crabs are equally decorative, while two of the best crab-apples for making jelly and wine are 'John Downie' and 'Dartmouth Crab'. Both of these have rosy-cheeked apples like miniature pippins.

Prunus (Flowering cherries, plums, peaches and others)   Up to 8m (26ft)
This extensive group of trees and shrubs includes the Japanese cherries; there are kinds suitable for even the smallest garden. It also contains other fine ornamental trees such as the purple-leaved plums, *P. blireiana* and *P. cerasifera* (the Cherry Plum), both of which make attractive small lawn specimens or trees for boundary planting.

The flowering almonds and peaches are also members of the *Prunus* group. The almonds, among the first trees to come into flower in late winter or early spring are forms of *P. dulcis* (= *P. amygdalus*). The variety 'Roseoplena', with pink double flowers, is the best one to plant.

The best forms of *P. persica* (the Common Peach) for decorative effect are 'Klara Meyer', with double pink blossom; 'Russell's Red', a crimson double; and 'Alboplena', double white.

Of the superb Japanese cherries, a good representative selection would include 'Fugenzo' with coppery-red young leaves and large double pale pink flowers; 'Hokusai' with bronzy-coloured young leaves and semi-double pale pink blossom; 'Tai Haku', considered by many to be the finest white-flowered cherry; and 'Kanzan', the most widely planted of all the ornamental cherries, with double purplish-pink flowers.

Weeping cherries make very effective lawn specimens and 'Cheal's Weeping' ('Kiku-Shidare Sakura') is unrivalled in this category. For a restricted area, the flagpole cherry, *P. serrulata erecta*, usually known as 'Amonogawa', is ideal. Its slender column, up to 6m (20ft) in height, does not exceed 2m (6ft) in diameter. In late spring it is a pillar of pale pink blossom and its leaves colour brilliantly in autumn.

Early to late spring   Sun   Any soil

Pyrus salicifolia (Willow-Leaved Pear)   4.5m (15ft)

This is one of the loveliest ornamental trees for the small garden. The cultivar 'Pendula' has slender weeping branches densely clothed with silvery willow-like foliage. The creamy-white flowers are comparatively insignificant and are followed by minute green 'pears'. It is a useful subject for very dry soils.

April   Sun   Any soil

Robinia pseudoacacia (False Acacia)   6m (20ft)

Most of the False Acacias (or Locust Trees) are too large for the average garden, but the variety 'Frisia' is an exception. This is a delightful ornamental tree of medium height and spread, with brilliant golden-yellow pinnate foliage. The pendent sweet-pea-type white flower clusters appear around midsummer. Robinias are robust, drought-resistant trees which can tolerate atmospheric pollution. Their brittle branches should be protected from strong winds.

June   Sun   Any well-drained soil

Salix (Willow)   4.5m (15ft)

Although the better-known forms of weeping willow grow too big for most gardens, there is one that makes an excellent lawn or poolside specimen for the smaller garden. This is the American Weeping Willow, *S. purpurea pendula*. The leaves are felted with silver-grey and it bears attractive catkins in spring. The greyish-purple bark is an added bonus in winter.

Early spring   Sun or part shade   Moist loamy soil

Sorbus   Up to 9m (30ft)

This group of trees includes the native Rowan or Mountain Ash, *S. aucuparia* and the Common Whitebeam *S. aria*. Both species have produced varieties and cultivars suitable for the small garden.

S. aucuparia itself bears creamy scented flowers which are followed by clusters of orange-red fruits that ripen in August. Two similar species, the Chinese Scarlet Rowan, *S. discolor* (= *S.* 'Embley') and *S. sargentiana* have foliage that colours to a fiery scarlet in autumn.

The best of the whitebeams is *S. aria* 'Decaisneana' with much larger greyish-white leaves than those of the type, up to 15cm (6in) long. These make a perfect background for the large crimson fruits in late summer.

May/early June   Sun or part shade   Any well-drained soil

HEDGES

Hedges act as a frame for the garden picture, enhancing the beauty of what they enclose. Their most important functions, however, are to afford protection and privacy.

Various factors, including soil, situation, cost and the amount of time involved in clipping will decide the choice of hedging subjects. It is a wide choice, since a hedge can be either formal or informal, evergreen or deciduous, flowering or coniferous.

Boundary hedges are of primary importance, but low-growing interior hedges can effectively act as dividers between different parts of the garden. Dwarf shrubs such as Rosemary, Lavender and *Santolina* (Cotton Lavender) are good for this purpose.

Preparation of the planting site for a hedge should be carried out with as much care as for individual specimen shrubs. The width of a bed for a boundary hedge should not be less than 60cm (2ft); for small internal hedges 30cm (1ft) will usually suffice.

Hedge plants, which are generally planted much closer together than individual shrubs, need to be fed properly. The site should be double-dug with plenty of well-rotted manure or garden compost incorporated into the lower spit. Planting distances vary according to subject and, together with the approximate price of 100 plants from the average nursery, are given in the list of shrubs below; although prices inevitably change, these figures give a very good idea of the relative cost of each kind.

Evergreens and conifers will benefit from staking during the first two seasons after planting. Conifers make excellent hedging material. The fastest growing of these is the hybrid *Cupressocyparis × leylandii* (Leyland Cypress) which increases in height and spread by more than 60cm (2ft) annually. At the opposite end of the scale are Yew and Box, the aristocrats of evergreen hedging plants, with a very slow growth rate. This, however, makes them ideal for a formal garden.

Flowering hedges are attractive and colourful, but they cannot usually be cut back hard without spoiling the display of bloom. For informal hedges, however, they are ideal.

Many of the plants listed in the shrub section make first-rate hedging material, among them barberries (see under *Berberis*) and cotoneasters.

Pruning

Two hedging plants that need constant clipping are the Common Privet, *Ligustrum ovalifolium*, and the Shrubby Honeysuckle, *Lonicera nitida*. The former is a voracious feeder that will rob any neighbouring plants of nourishment. The Honeysuckle responds well to hard clipping but quickly becomes leggy with neglect.

Most other hedges need one, or at the most two, cuts each year. August and September are the best months for this operation (with the second pruning, if given at all, in spring), but with flowering hedges, the time and types of flowering will have to be taken into consideration.

The leading shoots of hedging plants should normally be allowed to reach the required height for the hedge before being topped. Side shoots can be cut back as they develop. The right shape for a hedge is broad at the base, tapering slightly towards a rounded or ridged top – not a flat one. This helps to minimize damage after heavy snowfalls, and also produces a denser hedge.

In most cases, frequent pruning in the first year or two is necessary to produce a dense, well-shaped hedge; fast-growing species, such as Lawson's and Leyland Cypresses, Honeysuckle or Privet will benefit from harder and more frequent pruning than slow-growing ones, such as Box, Yew or Holly.

Thin hedges can be thickened by pushing some of the autumn prunings (in effect, half-ripe cuttings) into the soil; a number of these should have rooted by next spring.

AN ALPHABETICAL LIST OF HEDGING PLANTS

The figures quoted after each subject represent planting distances and approximate cost per 100 plants.

DECIDUOUS HEDGES

Beech (*Fagus sylvatica*)

Beech is actually a tree but it is deservedly popular as a hedging plant because it clips well and, when grown as a hedge, retains its dead leaves during winter. The russet beauty of the latter is rivalled only by the pale green, lacy foliage of the young leaves in spring.

Beech thrives in almost any soil except heavy wet clays.
30cm (1ft)   £20–£30

Cotoneaster simonsii

A semi-evergreen, upright in habit, with small oval leaves and a lavish display of bright orange berries in autumn and early winter. It makes a hedge of moderate height, up to 1.2m (4ft), that needs minimal clipping.
30cm (1ft)   £50

Hawthorn (*Crataegus monogyna*)

Hedges of Hawthorn (also known as Quickthorn or May) are uninteresting in appearance when the leaves fall but among the most economical hedging plants where long stretches are needed. Also, they have pretty white, strongly scented flowers and glossy dark green leaves, and produce attractive fruit (the 'haws') in autumn. Their spiny stems make an impenetrable hedge and the twigs are dense enough to act as a winter windbreak. Will make a hedge up to 2.5m (8ft) tall.
25cm (10in)   £8–£12

Hornbeam (*Carpinus betulus*)

Deciduous trees of similar character to Beech, but more suited to heavy wet soils. The leaves are rather smaller than those of the Beech, but like the latter, they change colour in autumn, to a golden hue.
30cm (1ft)   £15–£25

Myrobalan or Cherry Plum (*Prunus cerasifera*)

Myrobalan is a fast-growing small tree that will quickly make a dense hedge with pale green foliage and white blossom in spring. A rampant grower, it needs cutting back hard each year once the desired size has been reached. The purple-leaved form 'Pissardii Nigra' (or 'Atropurpurea') is showier and also slower-growing than the former. Both will make a good hedge up to 3m (10ft) tall.
40cm (1¼ft)   £15–£10

Prunus × cistena

This is another member of the *Prunus* family that is becoming increasingly popular as a hedging plant. It is less vigorous than the Myrobalan and is best topped at around 1.2m (4ft). The foliage is a rich red that contrasts well with the white flowers in spring and makes a blaze of colour throughout summer and autumn.
45cm (1½ft)   £50

EVERGREEN HEDGES

Berberis (Barberries)

Several of the Barberries make first-class hedges. *B. stenophylla* will produce its masses of orange-yellow bloom more freely if pruning is delayed until after mid-July. It is a shrub of rapid growth; up to 30cm

(1ft) annually. *B. darwinii* is similar in character but less rampant. Either of these will make a dense hedge up to 2.4m (8ft) in height.
45cm (1½ft)   £60

Box (*Buxus sempervivens*)

Next to Yew, Box is the hedging shrub most commonly seen in the gardens of our stately homes. It is slow-growing, dense and a vivid deep green in colour, needing little clipping. It is not suitable for hedges more than 90–120cm (3–4ft) tall. With Yew, it is ideal for topiary work. The variety 'Handsworthensis' is best for hedging.
40–45cm (1¼–1½ft)   £75–£100

Holly (*Ilex*)

Although Holly is relatively slow-growing for the first few years after planting, its rate of growth is greatly accelerated once the plants are established. Most species and varieties have prickly leaves and make dense impenetrable hedges, up to 3m (10ft) or more in height. If the 'Gentle' Holly, 'J.C. van Tol' (= 'Polycarpa') is planted, however, it will make a hedge practically free from prickles.
45cm (1½ft)   £150

Honeysuckle (*Lonicera*)

The Shrubby Honeysuckle, *L. nitida*, makes a dense small-leaved hedge that is almost comparable in appearance with Yew if it is clipped four or five times annually during the growing season. It should, however be restricted to a height of about 1.2m (4ft). Above this height it tends to get leggy and bare at the base. *L. yunnanensis*, a close relative of the former, is more upright in habit and has small scented flowers in spring followed by inconspicuous black berries.
40cm (1¼ft)   £20–£25

Laurel (*Prunus laurocerasus*)

The Common Laurel is a large-leaved evergreen of medium growth rate that is unsuitable for low-growing hedges. The optimum height for a laurel hedge is between 1.5 and 3m (5 and 10ft). The variety 'Rotundifolia' is the best for hedging.
60cm (2ft)   £40–£65

Lawson's Cypress (*Chamaecyparis lawsoniana*)

This is a popular hedging conifer, more widely grown before the arrival of the much more vigorous Leyland Cypress (see below). The foliage stands up well to clipping. Lawson's Cypress makes a dense hedge up to 3m (10ft) tall. 'Green Hedger', with greener foliage and a more rapid growth rate than the type, is the form most often recommended.
90cm (3ft)   £90–£150

Leyland Cypress (× *Cupressocyparis leylandii*)

This remarkably quick-growing conifer is very popular for hedging, being especially well suited to rapid screening of unsightly views or to establish a wind-break as quickly as possible. Because it grows so quickly, it will need frequent cutting if it is not to grow straggly. 'Haggerston Grey', 'Leighton Green' and 'Naylor's Blue' are good varieties. Often known as 'leylandii'.
90–105cm (3–3½ft)   £90–£120

Privet (*Ligustrum ovalifolium*)

Although Privet has a bad reputation as a soil robber, there can be few other shrubs that will produce a dense evergreen hedge in so short a time. However, like the Shrubby Honeysuckle, it needs constant clipping during the growing season. The golden form 'Aureo-marginatum' is much less rampant. It is more costly but its brilliant foliage makes it a

good choice where a hedge of not more than 1.5m (5ft) is required.
30–45cm (1–1½ft) £15–£20 ordinary £40–£50 golden

Thuja plicata (Western Red Cedar or Arborvitae)

Although, like Lawson's Cypress, somewhat eclipsed by 'leylandii' since its introduction as the fastest hedging plant, *Thuja* (or *Thuya*) makes a handsome dark green hedge that stands up well to clipping. It is comparatively rapid in growth and remains dense and well-clothed with foliage up to 5m (16ft). It makes a good choice for wet soils, since it thrives in moist conditions, but it is not suitable for chalk.
60–75cm (2–2½ft) £75–£100

Yew (*Taxus baccata*)

As already mentioned, Yew, although very slow-growing, is one of the finest and longest-lived of hedging subjects and is one that has been used with outstanding effect in our gardens since Tudor times. Yew can be stopped at any height up to about 3m (10ft). Only very light annual trimming is needed. With Box, it is the best hedge for topiary work.
60cm (2ft) £100–£150

INFORMAL HEDGES

The shrubs listed below will make informal hedges with a loose, open type of growth. It is advisable, wherever practicable, to trim such hedges with secateurs rather than with shears.

The best time for this operation is in early spring, before the new growth starts, except in the case of flowering hedges, which should be pruned as soon as the flowers have faded.

Choisya ternata (Mexican Orange Blossom)

This shrub makes a dense evergreen hedge that does equally well in sun or partial shade. The richly perfumed ivory flowers appear in early summer and stage a repeat performance on a less lavish scale later in the year. *C. ternata* will make a hedge up to 1.5m (5ft) tall.
90cm (3ft) £50–£60

Elaeagnus

Several of the *Elaeagnus* species make good evergreen hedges and one of the fastest-growing is *E. ebbingei* with handsome olive-green leaves attractively silvered on their reverse. The tiny creamy-white flowers, which appear in the axils of the leaves in autumn, are inconspicuous, but intensely fragrant. *E. pungens* 'Variegata' is slower-growing, but its gold-splashed foliage makes a more striking display than that of the former. Both will eventually make a dense hedge up to 1.5m (5ft) tall.
90cm (3ft) £50–£75

Escallonia

Escallonias are among the best of the flowering evergreens for hedging with a rapid rate of growth and a colourful display. They stand up well to clipping and can be cut back hard as soon as the flowers have faded. 'Crimson Spire' and 'Ingramii' are two of the best forms for hedging. *E. macrodonta* is not completely hardy but makes an outstanding choice in milder coastal districts. The dark green glossy leaves are larger than those of other escallonias and the flowers are a rich crimson. All the escallonias will make dense hedges up to 2.5m (8ft) tall.
60cm (2ft) £50–£60

Euonymus japonicus

A non-flowering evergreen, with dark green glossy foliage, *E. japonicus* is especially useful as a hedging plant in exposed situations at the seaside. It is impervious to salt spray and the fiercest gales. There are gold and silver-variegated forms that are particularly eye-catching.

90cm (3ft)   £60–£75

Fuchsia

For milder districts and especially those near the sea, the vigorous *F. magellanica riccartonii* makes a colourful hedge massed with small scarlet and violet flowers from July to October. It is deciduous and needs only light annual pruning, making a dense hedge up to 1.8m (6ft) tall that will do equally well in sun or partial shade.

60cm (2ft)   £50

Griselinia littoralis

This is another evergreen that is specially recommended for exposed situations and seaside districts. *Griselinia* makes a dense hedge up to 1.5m (5ft) in height. Its oval leathery leaves, pale green in colour, are very attractive. It is not a suitable subject for cold inland districts.

90cm (3ft)   £60–£75

Laurustinus (*Viburnum tinus*)

Laurustinus makes a good choice where an evergreen flowering hedge is required for a partly shaded situation. Although rather a slow starter, Laurustinus will make a useful windbreak in about five years, up to 1.8m (6ft) high. The flat heads of white flowers, pink in bud, are borne continuously throughout winter.

90cm (3ft)   £75–£100

Olearia

The Daisy Bush, *O. × haastii* and the New Zealand Holly, *O. macrodonta*, are both evergreen shrubs of Australasian origin, hardy in most parts of the British Isles. They have greyish-green foliage, holly-like in the case of *O. macrodonta*, smaller and oval in *O. × haastii*. Both bear a great profusion of white daisy-like flowers in summer. The olearias make excellent hedges for exposed situations, and clip well up to 1.5m (5ft) or more.

90cm (3ft)   £50–£75

Pyracantha

Most of the Pyracanthas (see also SHRUBS AND TREES, page 105) make dense spiny hedges up to 3m (10ft) in height that stand up well to clipping. The attractive glossy foliage is enlivened by the hawthorn-like blossom in summer and the colourful winter berries. *P. atalantioides* and its cultivar 'Orange Glow' are two of the best hedging kinds.

90cm (3ft)   £50–£75

Rhododendron ponticum

Given the necessary acid soil, the common purple rhododendron, which has naturalized itself in many parts of Britain, would be a first-rate choice for a hedge that needs a minimum of attention. Although slow-growing at first, *R. ponticum* in time forms a dense impenetrable screen, massed with purple flowers in late spring. It does equally well in sunny or partly shaded situations.

1–1.2m (3–4ft)   £75–£100

ROSE HEDGES – see ROSES, page 77.

DWARF SHRUBS FOR INTERIOR HEDGES

Miniature hedges of dwarf shrubs make neat divisions between various sections of the garden. They are useful for making gardens within gardens, or for segregating groups of similar plants, such as herbs, roses or those with silver and grey foliage. Dwarf shrubs can also be used as dividers between the ornamental garden and the fruit or vegetable plot, or they can act as a frame for pools or patios. There are miniature versions of many popular shrubs as well as small and compact ones.

Lavandula (Lavender)

Lavender has always been one of the most popular subjects for dwarf hedges. There is a choice of several different kinds, most of them cultivars of the Old English Lavender, *L. spica*. These include the type plant, which will reach a height of 90cm (3ft) with dense spikes of spicily fragrant blooms on long stems. 'Hidcote' and 'Munstead' are more compact; not more than 25cm (10in) tall. The former has deep violet flower spikes, while those of the latter are lavender-blue.

Lavender hedges should be lightly clipped yearly, care being taken not to cut back into the previous season's wood.

30–40cm (1–1¼ft)   £25–£30

Rosmarinus (Rosemary)

Like Lavender, Rosemary is an aromatic herb that is often used for interior hedges. It should be lightly pruned each spring to prevent legginess. The pale blue flowers appear in late spring. The best form for hedging is 'Miss Jessop' ('Jessop's Upright'), of dense and erect habit, with less tendency to straggle than the common kind and growing up to 90cm (3ft) in height.

Rosemary is somewhat tender and will need a sheltered situation in colder districts. It is particularly suited to seaside gardens.

45cm (1½ft)   £25–£30

Herbaceous Perennials

Definition and Characteristics

Any plant that does not produce persistent woody stems is botanically described as 'herbaceous', a term that by common usage is mainly associated with perennial plants which die down in the autumn, persist in a semi-dormant or dormant state throughout the winter, and re-emerge the following spring. The majority of herbaceous perennials that are readily available are hardy throughout the British Isles, and can occupy a key position in both large and small gardens. They harmonize well with trees, shrubs and roses, many make an attractive ground cover to carpet the soil and deter weeds, and when brought together in a border provide a most economical means of creating a garden of colour and interest.

Herbaceous Borders and Island Beds

The traditional method of growing herbaceous perennials in large single or double borders, separated by a wide grass path, and made one-sided by being surrounded with a tall evergreen hedge, is now a rarity to be seen in relatively few gardens, mainly those associated with stately homes or maintained by public authorities. Elsewhere, as gardens have decreased in size, and labour is now scarce and expensive, beds flanking a wall or hedge have become much smaller and the concept of 'island beds' has increasingly been applied. In these, plants of low or medium height are brought together in beds sited in the open. There is no enclosing hedge, wall or fence to shade the plants or protect them from wind and consequently they grow to maturity with sturdy stems that are mostly self-supporting, thus largely doing away with one of the most laborious tasks associated with the old herbaceous border, that of staking. Island beds can be viewed from all sides, a great advantage.

Planning Island beds may not be easy to fit into an existing formal garden, but structural changes to existing features may make it possible and, in the end, worth the effort. The shape and size of each bed should preferably be decided at an early stage in the design of the garden. Length is not critical, but very wide beds can pose problems of access to the plants at the centre.

Before attempting to plant, a picture of the bed or border should be drawn on graph paper to scale, marking in the positions of the different plants. It is a good idea to supplement this plan with a perspective sketch or even a rough cardboard model. Although it is not usually wise to design the entire garden as a flat plan, it is important to draw up accurate plans of individual areas, such as herbaceous borders. The time taken by such preliminary planning will be well repaid by good results (see PLANNING AND DESIGN, pages 66–76).

Choosing the Right Plants For most gardeners, deciding what to plant is likely to be a compromise between variety among the different kinds to be grown and a display of mass colour. Planting single specimens of most kinds offers little in the way of display so, whenever possible, even in fairly small beds of roughly 8sq m (10sq yd), it is best to plant in groups of three, increasing the number to 10 or more for large borders of over 83sq m (100sq yd).

When deciding the height of the tallest plants, a useful guide is that it should not be greater than half the width of the bed or border.

Figures given for height in books and catalogues should always be regarded as approximate, since the plant size varies so much with soil fertility, water availability and growing position. It is important not to overlook the fact that the space between different groups should be more than that between plants in the same group. Plants with similar rates of growth should be grouped together. Some plants spread many times faster than others and if these are placed in adjoining groups the slower spreading are bound to suffer.

It is usually best to restrict low-growing plants to the front of the bed, backing them with plants of increasing height, but with a large bed a flat effect can be avoided by bringing occasional taller plants, including those with tall flower spikes, to the front. This also means that late-flowering plants can be used to fill in the spaces left as plants such as *Dicentra spectabilis* that flower early in the season die down.

When planning and planting, flower colour usually receives most attention, but foliage is another factor of equal, if not greater, importance. Some plants are grown solely for their leaves, for example, ferns and ornamental grasses; others have leaves that complement their own flowers as well as the blooms of other plants nearby that appear at different times of the year. Consideration has to be given to the texture of foliage, its period of duration and colour at all times of the year; these often vary with the season. There is a remarkable diversity of form available from which to choose; in colour, every shade of green as well as glaucous-blue, grey, purple-bronze and near black; there are also plants with variegated leaves, with white, cream, red or brown.

The suggested plans for an island bed and a rectangular border given below indicate how it is possible with plants to compose a picture that will change with the seasons, but never lack interesting flowers, foliage or both. Possible plant associations are almost limitless and can be tailored to personal requirements. The plans do not have dimensions, but it may be helpful to note that if for the island bed only one plant of each kind were to be put in, a site of 5sq m (6sq yd) in area would be required, measuring, for example, 3m × 1.7m (10ft × 5½ft). For the rectangular border an area of 4sq m (4¾sq yd) would be needed, for example 4m × 1m (13ft × 3¼ft).

Plant Names

In the lists of plants that follow, the common or English names are given. Unfortunately, not all plants have a common name, and even when one exists it cannot be used for several members of the same family. To add to the confusion some plants have more than one common name and these can vary from one part of the country to another, and between countries. To overcome these difficulties, botanical names are used to ensure national and international recognition. Difficult though these may be to pronounce and memorize at first, they are the best way of getting to know plants, especially as they are used by the nursery trade in catalogues, and by botanical gardens when labelling. The first name is that of the genus, or group, to which the plant belongs; the second its species, and the third the variety.

Site and Soil

Most herbaceous perennials grow best in an open sunny position away from the shade of trees, but there are plants adapted to grow in conditions of all kinds. The following lists of plants (which include those for grasses and ferns) give details of the best soil and site for each.

The soil should be fertile and free of perennial weeds. Few plants will flourish if the soil is full of water in the winter when the plants need it least and parched in summer when water requirement is greatest. Drains may have to be laid to remove excess water (page 18), but this should be done only as a last resort on very waterlogged sites; deep cultivation will improve drainage and aeration of the soil, and encourage roots to go down in search of moisture. Adding organic matter, such as farmyard manure, garden compost, peat or forest bark, will increase soil fertility and improve the drainage of heavy clay soils and the water-holding capacity of light soils. Lime should only be applied if the soil is acid; growth of most plants is best when the soil is slightly acid, pH 6.5–7.

Planting

The best time to plant herbaceous perennials is in the autumn, whenever the soil is moist enough to enable the roots to become established quickly, but not so wet that it sticks together in unmanageable clods. If the plants arrive from the nursery dry, they should be soaked in water before planting, and subsequently thoroughly watered if the weather remains dry. Plants arriving in winter when the soil is frozen or too wet for planting are best taken out of their packages and covered with moist soil, peat or sand in a cool well-drained spot until planting is possible. Spring planting should be successful as long as the plants do not suffer from drought.

Before starting to plant, mark out the groups and individual planting positions on the bed with sticks. When the soil is workable with a trowel or spade dig a hole deep enough to enable the crown buds to be covered by about 2–5cm (1–2in) of soil. The hole must be wide enough for the roots to be spread out comfortably in all directions. Next, fill the hole in stages with fine soil, each layer being firmed as the work proceeds. Take great care not to damage the crown buds. Label each group clearly, and when growth starts, protect the plants from pests.

General Care

Staking Plants in windy situations, and those with top-heavy flowers, such as the Oriental Poppy, may require some support. The best kind of stakes are twiggy branches or pea sticks which should be inserted around the clumps of plants when the shoots are 15–20cm (6–8in) tall. They should be pushed well into the soil, preferably when it is moist to ease the task, and must be tall enough to support the plant when full-grown, but not so tall as to protrude over the top of it when in flower. Although at first you might find the stakes unsightly, the plants soon grow through them and hide them.

Feeding and Top-Dressing The best way to feed herbaceous perennial plants is by incorporating organic manures into the soil during cultivation, *before* planting. The roots will then go down in search of nutrients and moisture and produce sturdy, wind-resisting shoots. Sandy, quick-draining soils which lack organic matter may need extra feeding with a liquid organic fertilizer (such as seaweed fertilizer), meat-and-bonemeal or a balanced inorganic fertilizer, all of which will act as a quick tonic; for slower feeding, use bonemeal or apply a mulch.

Mulching Plants on all soils appreciate a surface mulch of organic matter, such as well-rotted manure, garden compost, leafmould or peat, applied in the late spring, which will help to conserve moisture, smother weeds and provide nutrients in a slowly available form.

If you use peat it should be thoroughly moistened, and if the mulch is to provide food, bonemeal or a general fertilizer should be added at a rate according to the maker's instructions.

If you are applying a mulch on dry soil, always water the soil first.

Watering Plants growing in deeply worked soil, well supplied with organic matter, will not normally need to be watered over-much once they are established. Leafy plants and those growing in sandy, chalky or gravelly soils will respond to water in times of drought, and especially in early summer when in full growth and preparing to flower. You must apply enough water to ensure that it penetrates right down to the roots of your plants; it is generally best to give water as a fine spray. It is not beneficial to the plants to give a mere surface watering. If the soil lacks nutrients a liquid fertilizer can be mixed with the water as directed by the manufacturer. For soil known to dry out in summer, the need for watering can most easily be reduced by selecting when planning the bed those plants naturally adapted to dry conditions. See the DESCRIPTIVE LIST OF HERBACEOUS PERENNIALS, on pages 138 to 149.

Weeding Assuming that the soil is free of perennial weeds before planting, your task is to control annual weeds and prevent seedling perennial weeds from becoming established. Shallow hoeing or hand-weeding when the soil is dry and crumbly will control annual and biennial weeds, and perennial weed seedlings. See WEED CONTROL, pages 38–40.

Autumn Clearance

As the plants die down, the dead tops should be cut off at ground level and put on the compost heap (or burnt if diseased). Plants yet to bloom, such as the Christmas Rose (*Helleborus niger*) and the Algerian Iris (*I. unguicularis*), should be given as much light as possible. As the weather deteriorates cloche protection can be given, not because the plants are tender, but to protect the blooms from wind and mud.

Vigorous plants which have become too large and are tending to die out at the centre should be lifted at this time, divided and replanted into soil enriched with an organic fertilizer. (See pages 40–54.)

Many gardeners fork over the beds in the autumn or early winter, burying the rubbish and summer mulch, but they are not aware of the damage this can do to the roots of the plants. Forking improves the appearance of the beds and may expose some soil pests to birds, but it also brings weed seeds to the surface which will grow as soon as spring arrives. Mulching the soil surface with organic matter will make the beds look neat without the disadvantages and hard labour of forking.

Winter Protection

Winter protection for most perennials is unnecessary, but plants introduced to Britain from countries with warmer or dryer winters

---

SUGGESTED PLANTING SCHEMES

These contain easily grown herbaceous perennials selected for a colourful, long-lasting effect.

Island Bed Planting Scheme
1. *Hosta fortunei* 'Aurea'
2. *Heuchera sanguinea* 'Bressingham Hybrids'
3. *Anaphalis triplinervis*
4. *Coreopsis verticillata*
5. *Sedum spectabile* 'Autumn Joy'
6. *Geum × borisii*
7. *Veronica gentianoides* 'Variegata'
8. *Pulmonaria saccharata*
9. *Dicentra formosa* 'Bountiful'
10. *Euphorbia myrsinites*
11. *Achillea* 'Moonshine'
12. *Armeria maritima* 'Vindictive'
13. *Helleborus orientalis*
14. *Anthemis cupaniana*
15. Aster × *frikartii*
16. *Aconitum napellus* 'Bressingham Spire'
17. *Helenium autumnale* 'Coppelia'
18. *Geranium* 'Johnson's Blue'
19. *Solidago* 'Goldenmosa'
20. *Papaver orientale* 'Mrs Perry'
21. *Anemone × hybrida* 'September Charm'
22. *Monarda didyma* 'Cambridge Scarlet'
23. *Phormium tenax* 'Purpureum'
24. *Verbascum* 'Pink Domino'
25. *Miscanthus sinensis* 'Variegatus' (ornamental grass)

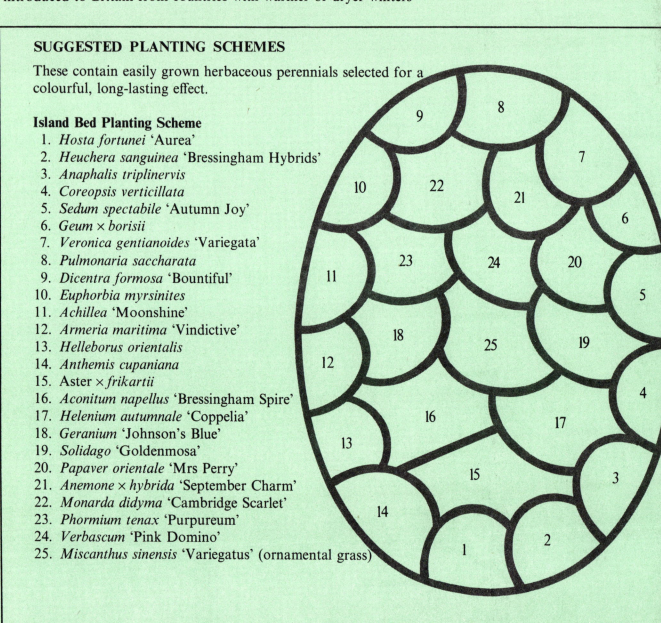

which are not fully hardy here, such as African Lilies (*Agapanthus*), kniphofias and the Globe Artichoke (*Cynara scolymus* 'Glauca'), need protection, which can be given by covering the crowns with 30cm (12in) of straw or bracken until March. As the plants mature, their resistance to cold increases, especially on well-drained soil.

Some herbaceous perennials bear basal leaves or small shoots right through the winter. Others are completely deciduous and remain leafless until new growth starts in the spring.

Spring Treatment

Before annual weed seedlings get a chance to emerge, give the bed a thorough but shallow hoeing and hoe or hand weed any weeds that appear subsequently. Tender new shoots are very susceptible to slugs, so it is wise to set up slug traps or use the herbal slug killer Fertosan; do not use metaldehyde or methiocarb slug baits or liquids, as these can be very harmful to wildlife and to pets (see page 34).

Formal Border Planting Scheme

Front row
1. *Alchemilla mollis*
2. *Doronicum plantagineum* 'Miss Mason'
3. *Anthemis cupaniana*
4. *Aquilegia vulgaris* 'McKana Hybrids'
5. *Artemisia schmitdiana* 'Nana'
6. *Aster amellus* 'Violet Queen'
7. *Pulmonaria angustifolia*
8. *Bergenia cordifolia* 'Purpurea'

Middle row
9. *Campanula glomerata* 'Superba'
10. *Dicentra spectabilis*
11. *Digitalis × mertonensis*
12. *Hosta sieboldiana* 'Elegans'

13. *Erigeron speciosus* 'Rotes Meer'
14. *Euphorbia polychroma*
15. *Gaillardia* 'Mandarin'
16. *Hemerocallis* 'Golden Chimes'
17. *Phlox paniculata* 'Harlequin'

Back row
18. *Kniphofia* 'Atlanta'
19. *Rudbeckia fulgida* 'Deamii'
20. *Salvia haematodes* 'Indigo'
21. *Phormium* 'Yellow Wave'
22. *Acanthus spinosus*
23. *Papaver orientale* 'Mrs Perry'
24. *Euphorbia wulfenii*
25. *Miscanthus sinensis* 'Zebrinus' (ornamental grass)

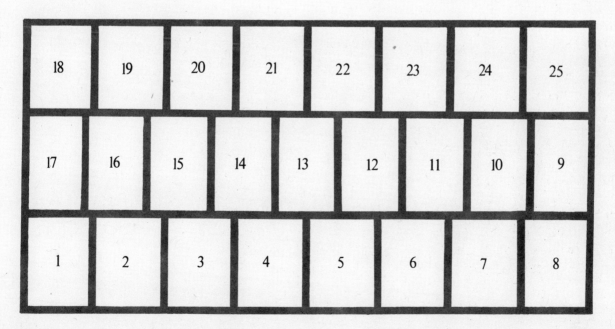

A–Z LIST OF HERBACEOUS PERENNIALS

Below is a selection of the best plants for the
small or average size garden, together with
some of the cultivated varieties currently
available. There are so many plants from
which to choose that some favourites may have
been omitted. The common name (if any) is
followed by details of the most suitable site
and soil for the plant genus; this is followed by
a description of each species.

Symbols

C   Suitable for cutting

SH   Good seed-heads or fruit for flower
      arrangement

D   Plant density; the number indicates how
      many plants are needed per square metre

PH   Plant height: the figure quoted represents
      the average height reached by mature
      plants, and this may vary according to
      soil, site and climate.

Flowering periods are also indicated, e.g.
'June–August'.

Acanthus

Bear's Breeches. Ordinary soil, sun or light
shade. C, SH.

mollis latifolius

Leaves arching, undulating, PH to 60cm (2ft).
Flowers foxglove-like, lilac-rose in spikes.
110cm (3ft 8in), D3, July–September.

spinosus

Leaves dark green, divided, with spiny points,
to 60cm (2ft). Flowers in spikes of mauve-
purple. PH 1.2m (4ft), D3–4, July–September.

Achillea

Yarrow. Fertile soil in sun. C, SH.

filipendulina 'Coronation Gold'

Leaves mid-green. Flowers in flat heads,
yellow. PH 90cm (3ft), D4, June–September.

millefolium 'Cerise Queen'

Leaves deep green. Flowers cherry-red in loose
flat heads. PH 75cm (2½ft), D4, June–August.

'Moonshine'

Leaves silver, filigree. Flowers pale yellow.
PH 60cm (2ft), D4–5, June–August.

ptarmica 'The Pearl'

Sneezewort. Leaves narrow, mid-green. Flowers
double, daisy-like, in clusters of 5–10cm
(2–4in), PH 75cm (2½ft), D3, June–August.

Aconitum

Monkshood. Fertile moist soil in sun or partial
shade. (N.B. All parts of the plant are
poisonous.) C.

napellus 'Bicolor'

Leaves dark green on branching spikes.
Flowers hooded, blue-and-white. PH 1m (3½ft),
D5, July–August.

'Bressingham Spire'

Leaves dark green, divided. Flowers violet-blue
in spikes. PH 90cm (3ft), D5–7, July–August.

septentrionale 'Ivorine'

Leaves dark green; flowers white. PH 90cm (3ft),
D4–5, May–July.

Agapanthus

Love Flower or African Lily. Winter
protection advisable in cold districts.

campanulatus

Leaves strap-shaded, mid-green, sometimes
evergreen. Flowers funnel-shaped 2.5–7.5cm
(1–3in) long in terminal clusters, blue. PH 75cm
(2½ft), D4, July–August, C, SH.

'Headbourne Hybrids'

Flowers from pale China-blue to deep violet-
blue. PH 75–90cm (2½–3ft), D4, July–August,
C, SH.

Alchemilla

Lady's Mantle. Ordinary soil, sun or shade. C,
SH.

mollis

Leaves light green, hairy, lobed, on which water
droplets sit. Flowers tiny green-yellow, in
branched heads. PH 45cm (1½ft), D4–5,
June–August.

Anaphalis

Everlasting Flower or Pearl Everlasting.
Ordinary soil, sun or shade, C, SH.

triplinervis

Leaves grey and woolly, forming mats; flowers
white in clusters. PH 30–38cm (12–15in), D4–5,
July–September.

yedoensis

Grows to 75cm (2½ft).

'Summer Snow'

A recent introduction growing to 25cm (10in),
D3, July–September.

Anchusa

azurea (= *A. italica*) 'Little John'

Leaves mid-green, coarse, hairy. Flowers
salver-shaped, bright blue. PH 45cm (1½ft), D5,
June–August.

'Opal'
Flowers Cambridge-blue. PH 90–120cm (3–4ft),
D4, June–July.

Anemone
Windflower. Fertile soil in sun or light shade. C.
× *hybrida* (=*japonica*) 'Bressingham Glow'
Leaves mid-green, 3–5 lobed. Flowers semi-
double, cup-shaped, rosy-red, 7.5cm (3in)
wide. PH 45cm (1½ft), D5–7, August–October.
'White Queen'
Flowers large and white. PH 90–120cm (3–4ft),
D5, August–October.
'September Charm'
Flowers soft pink, 10cm (4in) across. PH 45cm
(1½ft), D3, August–October.

Anthemis
Chamomile. Ordinary soil in sun. C.
cupaniana
Leaves grey, aromatic, finely cut, carpeting.
Flowers large, daisy-like, white. PH 30cm (1ft),
D5, May–August.
nobilis
The Common Chamomile, also known as
Chamaemelum nobile. Leaves finely cut,
aromatic, mid-green, carpeting. Single white
daisy-like flowers. PH 15–23cm (6–9in), D5,
June–August. For a small lawn choose the
non-flowering variety 'Treneague'.
sancti-johannis 'Mrs. E.C. Buxton'
Leaves grey-green, hairy. Flowers lemon-
yellow, 5–7cm (2–2½in) across. PH 75cm (2½ft),
D4–5, June–August.

Aquilegia
Columbine or Granny's Bonnet. Ordinary soil
in sun or partial shade. C.
vulgaris 'McKana Hybrids'
Leaves pale green. Flowers bonnet-shaped with
long spurs in cream, yellow, pink, red, crimson
and blue, 7.5cm (3in) long. PH 75cm (2½ft), D5,
June–August. Many other good varieties and
hybrids available.

Armeria
Thrift or Sea Pink. Ordinary soil in sun.
maritima 'Vindictive'
Grass-like, dark green leaves in tufts. Flowers
in tight heads, rose-red. PH 30cm (1ft), D3,
June–July.

Artemisia
Wormwood. Ordinary soil in sun. C.

absinthium 'Lambrook Silver'
Leaves silver-grey, deeply divided. Flowers
yellowish. PH 90cm (3ft), D4, July–August.
maritima Nutans
Leaves evergreen, silver-grey. Flowers
insignificant. PH 60cm (2ft), D5.
schmidtiana 'Nana'
Leaves silver-grey. Flowers dull yellow,
enclosed in woolly silvery bracts; like tiny
balls. PH 7.5cm (3in), D5, August–September.

Aruncus
Goat's Beard. Deep moist soil in partial shade. C.
sylvester (=*Spiraea aruncus*)
Leaves, made up of several leaflets, pale green.
Flowers cream-white in plumes 20–25cm
(8–10in) long. PH 1.5m (5ft), D3, June–July.
'Kneiffii' is only 60–90cm (2–3ft) tall.

Asclepias
Milkweed. Moist soil in sun. C.
incarnata
N. American swamp milkweed. Leaves narrow,
mid-green; flowers flesh pink. PH 1.2m (4ft),
D4, July–August.
tuberosa
Leaves oblong, mid-green. Flowers orange in
broad heads. PH 45cm (1½ft), D6, July–August.

Aster
Michaelmas Daisy. Fertile soil in full sun. C.
amellus
Leaves grey-green. Flowers 6cm (2½in) across
with yellow or orange centres contrasting with
outer petals. Many varieties such as 'King
George', violet-blue, PH 60cm (2ft), D5,
August–October; 'Sonia', pink, and 'Violet
Queen', both PH 45cm (1½ft), D5, August–
October.
× *frikartii*
Leaves mid-green, flowers lavender-blue with
orange centres. 90cm (3ft), D5, July–October.
novae-angliae
Leaves narrow, dull green. Good varieties
include: 'Elma Potschke', carmine-rose, PH 1m
(3½ft), D4–5, September–October and
'Harrington's Pink', PH 1.2m (4ft), D4,
September–October.
novi-belgii
Leaves deep-green, pointed. Some of the best
varieties include: 'Ada Ballard', mauve-blue,
PH 90cm (3ft), D5, August–October; 'Blandie',
white, semi-double, PH 1.2m (4ft), D4, August–
October; 'Chequers', violet-purple, PH 60cm

(2ft), D5, August–October: 'Marie Ballard', light blue, double, PH 90cm (3ft), D5, September–October; and 'Winston S. Churchill', Ruby-red, double, PH 75cm (2½ft), D5, September–October. Dwarf varieties: 'Jenny', violet-purple, double, PH, 45cm (1½ft), D5, September–October; 'Lady in Blue', semi-double, PH 25cm (10in), D5, August–October; 'Little Pink Beauty', pink, semi-double, PH 40cm (16in), D5, September–October, and 'Snowsprite', semi-double, white, PH 30cm (1ft), D4, September–October.

Astilbe
Moist soil essential, tolerates light shade. C.
× *arendsii*
Leaves mid to dark green, deeply divided. Flowers plume-like. Many varieties including: 'Bressingham Beauty', pink flowers, PH 60–75 cm (2–2½ft), D4, July–August; 'Deutschland', white, PH 60cm (2ft), D5, June–July, and 'Fanal', red, PH 45cm (1½ft), D5, June–August.
chinensis pumila
Flowers lilac-rose, in short spikes. PH 30cm (1ft), D5, July–September.
taquetii 'Superba'
Flowers rose-lilac on imposing spikes. PH 1.2m (4ft), D4, July–August.

Astrantia
Masterwort. Moist soil in sun or light shade. C, SH.
carniolica 'Rosea'
Leaves mid-green, much divided. Flowers purple-red, star-like. PH 75cm (2½ft), D5, July–September; 'Margery Fish', whitish flowers. PH 80cm (2¾ft), D4, June–October.

Bergenia
Ordinary soil, sun or relatively deep shade. C.
'Ballawley'
Sometimes called 'Delbees'. Leaves round, mid-green, glossy. Flowers rose-red in small spikes. PH 30cm (1ft), D3, April–May.
cordifolia
'Purpurea' leaves tinged purple, flowers pink-purple. PH 30cm (1ft), D3–4, March–April; 'Silberlicht', flowers white suffused pink. PH 30cm (1ft), D3–4, April–May; 'Sunningdale' flowers deep pink, leaves richly burnished in winter. PH 45cm (1½ft), D3, April–May.

Brunnera
Ordinary soil, sun or shade. C.

macrophylla
Leaves heart-shaped, mid-green. Flowers blue, resemble Forget-Me-Nots. PH 40cm (16in), D4, April–June. The form *B.m.* 'Variegata', with cream and green leaves, is especially attractive.

Campanula
Bellflower. Fertile soil in the sun. C.
carpatica
Leaves rounded, with toothed edges, mid-green; clump forming, carpeting. Flowers light blue in 'Blue Moonlight' and white in 'Bressingham White'. PH both 20–30cm (10–12in), D5–6, June–August.
glomerata 'Superba'
Leaves as *C. carpatica*. Flowers in dense heads, violet blue. PH 75cm (2½ft), D4–5, June–July.
lactiflora 'Pouffe'
Mounded plants, with rounded light green leaves. Flowers pale lavender-blue. PH 25cm (10in), D4–5, June–September.
poscharskyana
Quick-spreading ground cover plant. Mid-green, rounded, toothed leaves. Lavender-blue star-like flowers, 2.5cm (1in) across, in long sprays. PH 25cm (10in), D4, June–November.

Catananche
caerulea
Cupid's Dart. Ordinary soil in sun. C. Leaves narrow, grey-green. Blue-purple cornflower-like blooms. PH 60cm (2ft), D5, June–September. 'Perry's White' has white flowers, 'Major' has larger lavender-blue flowers.

Centaurea
Perennial Cornflower. Ordinary soil in sun. C.
dealbata
'John Coutts'
Leaves deeply cut, grey-green. Flowers large, up to 7.5cm (3in), and pink with pale yellow centres. PH 60cm (2ft), D4, June–August.
montana
'Violetta', flowers deep blue. PH 60cm (2ft), D3–4, May–June. 'Rosea' has pink flowers, 'Alba' white ones.

Chrysanthemum
Fertile soil in sun. C.
maximum
'Wirral Supreme'
Shasta Daisy. Leaves dark green. Flowers daisy-like, semi-double, white with golden centre. PH 90cm (3ft), D5, July–September.

Cimicifuga
Bugbane. Moist soil in partial shade. C.
americana (= *C. cordifolia*)
Leaves dark green, rather fern-like. Flowers small, cream-white on slender spikes. PH 1.2m (4ft), D4, August–October.

Coreopsis
Fertile soil in sun. C.
verticillata
Leaves dark green, finely divided. Flowers somewhat daisy-like, 4cm (1½in) across, yellow. PH 60cm (2ft), D5, July–September.

Crocosmia
Fertile well-drained soil in sun, but tolerates semi-shade. Needs plenty of water in summer. C.
masonorum
Leaves slender, iris-like, light green. Flowers bright orange on arching stems. PH 60cm (2ft), D7–9, July–September. Striking new hybrids include: 'Emberglow', 'Lucifer', 'Blaze' and 'Spitfire'.

Cynoglossum
Hound's Tongue. Ordinary, well-drained soil, sun or light shade. C.
nervosum
Leaves narrow, grey-green. Flowers tubular, intensely blue. PH 45cm (2½ft), D4–5, June–August.

Delphinium
Perennial Larkspurs. Deep fertile soil in sun, preferably in sheltered position.
'Belladonna hybrids'
'Blue Bees', light blue flowers, and 'Peace', deep blue, both good for the smaller garden. PH 1.2m (4ft), D4, June–August. 'Pink Sensation', PH 90cm (3ft).
'Pacific hybrids'
Reliable varieties include: 'Black Knight', dark blue flowers; 'Blue Jay', mid-blue with a white eye; 'Astolat', pink, and 'Galahad', white, all PH 1.2–1.5m (4–5ft), D4–5, June–August.

Dianthus
Border pinks and carnations. Fertile, alkaline soil in sun. C. Leaves evergreen, narrow, grey-green. Garden Pinks consist of Old-Fashioned Pinks and Modern Pinks.
Old-Fashioned Pinks
Some good varieties include 'Excelsior', double pink flowers; 'Mrs Sinkins', double white, both PH 25cm (10in), D4–5, May–July.

Modern Pinks
'Doris', double pale salmon pink; 'Show Portrait', crimson; both PH 25–30cm (10–12in), D3, June–September.
plumarius
The original Garden or Scotch Pink, one of the Species Pinks. Flowers fringed, fragrant, rose, purple, white or variegated. PH 30cm (1ft), D4–5, June–July.

Dicentra
Dutchman's Breeches. Fertile soil in sun or semi-shade, protected from strong winds and frost. C.
formosa 'Bountiful'
Leaves fern-like, glaucous. Flowers in arching sprays, tubular, deep pink. PH 30cm (1ft), D4, April–June; maybe also smaller display in autumn.
spectabilis
Bleeding Heart. Leaves delicate, light green. Flowers rose-red, heart-shaped. PH 45–75cm (1½–2½ft), D4, May–June.

Dictamnus
Burning Bush or Dittany. Fertile, alkaline soil in sun. C.
albus (= *D. fraxinella*)
Leaves dark green, glossy, compound. Flowers in spikes, fragrant, white; aromatic oil released from the flower-heads, the vapour from which can sometimes be ignited by a match held just next to a mature flower. PH 75cm (2½ft), D4–5, July–September. 'Purpurea' has pale pink flowers striped with red.

Dierama
Wand Flower or Angel's Fishing Rod. Fertile soil in sun. C.
pendulum
Leaves grass-like, mid-green semi-evergreen. Flowers bell-shaped, pendulous on wiry, arching stems. PH 75cm (2½ft), D4–5, July–September.

Digitalis
Foxglove. Moist soil in semi-shade. C.
grandiflora (= *D. ambigua*)
Leaves mid-green, hairy. Flowers in one-sided spikes, yellow netted with brown. PH 60–90cm (2–3ft), D5, June–August.
× *mertonensis*
Flowers bold, dark pink. PH 75cm (2½ft), D5, June–August.

purpurea
Common Foxglove, which is a perennial under ideal conditions, but often grown as a biennial. Oblong rich green leaves in a rosette. Flower spikes of spotted flowers up to 90cm (3ft) high. Good strains are 'Excelsior', PH up to 1.5m (5ft) high, with white, cream, yellow, rose-pink or purple flowers all round the spikes; 'Foxy', similar colours, but with several side shoots surrounding a leading flower spike and much shorter, PH 75cm (2½ft); and 'Shirley', with white, pink, red or purple flowers, PH 2.1m (7ft). D3–4, June–July.

Doronicum
Leopard's Bane. Fertile soil in sun or partial shade. C.
plantagineum
Leaves bright green, heart-shaped. Flowers daisy-like, yellow. 'Miss Mason' has bright yellow flowers, 6cm (2½in) across, PH 45cm (1½ft), D5, April–June. 'Harpur Crewe' has larger, golden-yellow flowers, up to 7.5cm (3in) across, PH 60cm (2ft), April–May.

Echinacea
Purple Cone Flower. Fertile, moisture-retaining soil in sun. C.
purpurea
Leaves mid-green, rough. Flowers daisy-like, 10cm (4in) across. 'Robert Bloom' is one of the newer 'Bressingham Hybrids' with freely-produced rose-purple flowers. PH 1m (3½ft), D5, July–September.

Echinops
Globe Thistle. Fertile soil in sun. C, SH.
ritro
Leaves grey-green, without spines. Steel-blue flowers in globular heads, up to 5cm (2in) across, which do not fade when dried. PH 1m (3½ft), D4, June–September.

Epimedium
Barrenwort or Bishop's Hat. Fertile soil in semi-shade. Leaves evergreen, lop-sided, heart-shaped, mid-green, in many forms tinged with red when young and beautifully veined, turning bronze, yellow and red in autumn. C.
grandiflorum = (*E. macranthum*)
'Rose Queen'
Mid-green leaves. Flowers delicate, saucer-shaped, deep pink on thin wiry stems. PH 30cm (1ft), D5, April–June.

Eremurus
Giant Asphodel or Foxtail Lily. Deep fertile soil in sun, with wind protection.
elwesii
'Highdown Pink, White and Yellow'. Leaves strap-shaped, light green. Flowers in majestic spikes. PH 1.8–2.7m (6–9ft), D1–2, May–June.

Erigeron
Fleabane. Fertile well-drained soil in sun. C.
speciosus
Leaves mid-green. Flowers daisy-like, lavender-blue, PH 45cm (1½ft). 'Charity', pink flowers, PH 60cm (2ft); 'Darkest of All', violet-blue with golden centre, PH 60cm (2ft); 'Rotes Meer', near red, semi-double, PH 50cm (20in); 'Schwarzes Meer', lavender-violet, PH 60cm (2ft). All D5, June–August.

Eryngium
Sea Holly. Fertile soil in sun. C, SH.
bourgatii
Leaves glaucous, deeply cut. Flower-heads silver-blue, teasel-like. PH 45cm (1½ft), D6, June–August.
× *oliverianum*
Leaves round, blue-green, deeply cut. Flower-heads deep blue. PH 90cm (3ft), D5, June–August.
variifolium
Evergreen glossy dark green leaves marbled with white. Flowers round, blue. PH 60cm (2ft), D5, July–September.

Eupatorium
Hemp Agrimony. Moist soil in sun or semi-shade. C, SH.
purpureum
Leaves mid-green, slender, pointed. Flowers small, rose-purple, in heads. PH 1.5m (5ft), D3–4, August–September.

Euphorbia
Spurges. Ordinary soil in sun. C.
cyparissias
Cypress Spurge. Leaves narrow, pale green. Flower-heads yellow-green. PH 25cm (10in), D4, April–June.
griffithii 'Fireglow'
Leaves narrow, pale green. Flame-orange bracts surround insignificant flowers in heads. PH 75cm (2½ft), D4–5, May–June.
myrsinites
Leaves rounded, blue-grey, on trailing stems.

Sulphur-yellow bracts surround heads of
flowers. PH 15cm (6in), D4–5, March–May.
polychroma (=*epithymoides*)
Leaves rounded, bright green. Bracts sulphur-
yellow. PH 45cm (1½ft), D4–5, April–May.
wulfenii (=*veneta*)
Leaves evergreen, glaucous, narrow. Yellow-
green bracts on tall flower-heads, 23cm (9in)
long. PH 1.2m (4ft), D4, May–July.

Filipendula (=*Spïraea*)
Moist soil in sun or semi-shade. C.
camtschatica
Leaves mid-green, five-lobed. Flowers small,
white and fragrant, borne in 15–20cm (6–8in)
wide heads. 'Rosea' has deep pink flowers. PH
1.2–1.8m (4–6ft), D3–4, July–August.
palmata (=*digitata*)
Leaves dark green and five lobed. Flowers
cerise pink, 15cm (6in) wide heads. PH 75cm
(2½ft), D5, June–August. Dwarf form 'Nana'
PH 25cm (10in).
ulmaria 'Aurea'
Meadow Sweet. Needs partial shade. Pinnate
leaves, gold when young, turning green later.
Flower-heads creamy white, 15cm (6in) across.
PH 45cm (1½ft), D5, June–August.

Gaillardia
Blanket Flower. Fertile soil in sun. C.
aristata (=*grandiflora*)
Leaves narrow, grey-green. Flowers daisy-like,
yellow with red centres. PH 60cm (2ft), D5,
June–October. 'Ipswich Beauty' has orange
flowers with brown-red centres; 'Mandarin' has
flame orange and red flowers; 'Burgundy' has
dark wine-red flowers, and 'Goblin', a dwarf
cultivar growing only to 23cm (9in) high, has
smaller bright yellow flowers with deep red
centres.

Gentiana
Moist soil in semi-shade. C.
asclepiadea
Willow Gentian. 'Knightshayes' is a fine
variety. Leaves mid-green, willow-like on
arching stems. Flowers rich deep blue, trumpet-
shaped. PH 60cm (2ft), D5, July–September.
lutea
Yellow Gentian or Gentian Root. Leaves
rounded, mid-green. Flowers star-like, yellow
in whorls up stem. PH 90cm–1.5m (3–5ft), D4,
July–August.

Geranium
Cranesbill. Vigorous plants, many of which are
tolerant of soil and situation. C.
endressii
'Wargrave Pink'. Leaves five-lobed, deeply cut,
mid-green. Flowers pink, saucer-shaped. PH
45cm (1½ft), D4, June–September.
'Johnson's Blue'
This hybrid has dark green, lobed leaves.
Flowers light blue. PH 38cm (15in), D5,
May–August.

Geum
Avens or Herb Benedict. Fertile soil in sun. C.
× *borisii*
Leaves pinnate, mid-green. Flowers orange-
scarlet, bowl shaped. PH 30cm (1ft), D5,
May–September.
chiloense
Good varieties include 'Lady Stratheden',
double yellow flowers; 'Mrs Bradshaw', semi-
double, red. Both PH 60cm (2ft), D5,
June–September.

Gypsophila
Baby's Breath. Fertile, alkaline soil in sun. C.
paniculata
'Bristol Fairy' leaves slender, grey-green.
Flowers small, round in sprays, white. PH
90cm (3ft), D3, June–September; 'Rosy Veil',
shell-pink, double. PH 25cm (10in), D4,
June–September.

Helenium
Sneezewort. Fertile soil in sun. C.
autumnale
Mid-green narrow leaves. Flowers daisy-like.
'Bressingham Gold' has gold-crimson flowers.
PH 90cm (3ft), D5, July–August; 'Coppelia',
copper orange, PH 90cm (3ft), D5,
July–August; 'Golden Youth', yellow with a
darker yellow centre, PH 75cm (2½ft), D4–6,
June–July; 'Moerheim Beauty', rich crimson
with a dark centre, PH 90cm (3ft), D5,
July–September.

Helianthus
Perennial Sunflower. Fertile well-drained soil in
sun. Staking essential. C.
decapetalus
'Loddon Gold', leaves mid-green, rough, ovate
with toothed edges. Flowers yellow, double,
10cm (4in) across. PH 1.5m (5ft), D4, July–
September.

Heliopsis
Orange Sunflower. Fertile soil in sun. C.
scabra
'Golden Plume', leaves rough, mid-green. Flowers daisy-like, double, rich yellow. PH 1.2m (4ft), D4–5, July–September.

Helleborus
Hellebores. Moist, rich, well-drained soil, in semi-shade. C.
argutifolius (=*corsicus*)
Leaves evergreen, three-lobed, mid-green, spiny. Flowers cup-shaped, yellow-green, PH 60cm (2ft), D4–5, March–May.
foetidus
Stinking Hellebore. Leaves evergreen, narrow, deeply cut, dark green. Flowers in clusters, yellow-green. PH 45cm (1½ft), D5, February–May.
niger
Christmas Rose. 'Altifolius' is an improved form. Leaves evergreen, leathery, deeply cut. Flowers white, saucer-shaped. PH 30cm (1ft), D5, December–March.
orientalis
Lenten Rose. Leaves evergreen in mild areas, broad, dark green. Flowers saucer-shaped, usually cream speckled inside with crimson, but often flowers are crimson, purple, pink or white. PH 45cm (1½ft), D5, February–April.

Hemerocallis
Day Lily. Fertile soil in sun or light shade. Has clumps of strap-shaped, arching, mid-green leaves. Flowers lily-like and trumpet-shaped, borne over long period, though each bloom will last for only one day. Many garden hybrids available: 'Black Magic', with deep ruby-purple flowers, yellow throat. PH 90cm (3ft), D4, June–August. 'Giant Moon', pale yellow. PH 75cm (2½ft), D4, June–August. 'Golden Chimes', deep yellow. PH 45cm (1½ft), D5, July–August. 'Morocco Red', maroon-red with yellow throat. PH 60cm (2ft), D4, June–August. 'Pink Damask', warm pink with yellow throat. PH 75cm (2½ft), D4, June–August. 'Zora', orange. PH 45cm (1½ft), D5, May–July.

Heuchera
Alum Root or Coral Flower. Light, well-drained soil in sun or semi-shade. C.
sanguinea
Leaves evergreen, heart-shaped. Flowers in

arching sprays. 'Bressingham Hybrids' is a mixed strain with red, pink, white and near yellow flowers. PH 60cm (2ft), D4–5, June–July.

Hosta (=*Funkia*)
Plantain Lily. Ordinary, moist soil in sun or preferably semi-shade, especially for the variegated kinds. C.
decorata (= 'Thomas Hogg')
Leaves long, stalked, ovate, ribbed or boldly veined, margined cream. Flowers tubular on thin arching stems, purple. PH 45cm (1½ft), D4–5, June–July.
fortunei 'Aurea'
Leaves gold edged with green in spring, light green in summer. Flowers lilac. PH 60cm (2ft), D4, June–July.
plantaginea 'Grandiflora'
Leaves large, glossy, yellow-green. Flowers white, scented. PH 60cm (2ft), D4, August–September.
sieboldiana (=*glauca*) 'Elegans'
Leaves large, broad, glaucous. Flowers pale lilac. PH 90cm (3ft), D3, July–August.

Iris
Fertile, well-drained soil in a sunny position for most kinds. C.
germanica and hybrids
German Iris or London Flag (Bearded Flags). Leaves sword-shaped. Flowers sweetly scented and borne at the end of long stems. In *I. germanica* they are dark and pale purple with a white beard. Many hybrid varieties also available, some of the best being: 'Berkeley Gold', with deep golden-yellow flowers; 'Black Swan', with very dark, blue-black flowers; 'Gudrun', large white flowers; 'Jane Phillips', intense pale blue; 'Paradise Pink', bright flamingo pink; 'Quechee', garnet red; 'Staten Island', gold and maroon; and 'Wabash', white and violet. PH 90cm–1.2m (3–4ft), D5, May–June.
foetidissima
Gladwyn or Gladdon Iris. Shade tolerant with evergreen, dark green leaves. These give off a strong, rank smell when bruised. Bears beautiful seed pods bursting with scarlet seeds in autumn. PH 60cm (2ft), D5. Flowers insignificant pale purple, in June.
pallida
Glaucous leaves; variety 'Variegata' has cream, stripes. Flowers violet-blue. PH 60cm (3ft), D5,

June–August.
pumila hybrids
One of the Dwarf Bearded Irises. Available in several varieties. PH 10–20cm (4–8in), D7, April–May.
sibirica hybrids
Available in several varieties for moist soil or water-side. PH 90cm (3ft), D4, June–August.
unguicularis (=*stylosa*)
Algerian Iris, winter flowering, best at the foot of a warm wall. PH 30cm (1ft), D5, November–March.

Kniphofia (= *Tritoma*) hybrids
Torch Lily or Red Hot Poker. Fertile soil in sun or semi-shade. C. Leaves evergreen, long and thin, mid-green or deep green. Flowers tubular and arranged in bottlebrush-like spikes at the ends of long stems. Many varieties available including: 'Atlanta', yellow and red, PH 90cm (3ft), D3, June–July; 'Bee's Sunset', flame orange, PH 90cm (3ft), D3, June–July; 'Jenny Bloom', salmon-pink, PH 90cm (3ft), D3, June–July; 'Little Maid'; cream-yellow, PH, 60cm (2ft), D4, September–October; 'Maid of Orleans', ivory cream, PH 75cm (2½ft), D3, July–September; 'Samuel's Sensation', bright scarlet, 1.5m (5ft), D3, July–September; 'Royal Standard', red and yellow, PH 1m (3½ft), D3, June–August.

Lamium
Dead Nettle. Tolerant of soil and site.
maculatum
'Chequers', leaves mid-green, heart-shaped with a silver stripe. Flowers hooded, tubular, pink. PH 30cm (1ft), D3, April–June. 'Beacon Silver', Leaves evergreen, silver. Flowers pink. PH 10cm (4in), D4, April–June.

Ligularia (= *Senecio*)
Moist soil, sun or semi-shade. C.
clivorum (=*dentata*) 'Desdemona'
Leaves rounded, purple. Flowers orange, strong stems. PH 1.2m (4ft), D3–4, July–September.

Limonium (= *Statice*)
Sea Lavender or Statice. Also known as Everlasting Flower.
Ordinary soil in sun. C, SH.
latifolium
Leaves tough, downy, mid-green in a rosette. Bright flowers in open clusters in white, yellow, pink, lavender and dark blue. 'Violetta' has

deep violet-blue flowers. PH 60cm (2ft), D4, July–September.

Linaria
Toadflax. Ordinary soil, in sun.
purpurea
Narrow, mid-green leaves. Small snapdragon-like flowers in slender spikes. 'Canon J. Went' is a good variety, with pink flowers. PH up to 1.2m (4ft), D4, July–September.

Lupinus
Lupin. Ordinary well-drained soil in sun. Has long, handsome spikes of flowers of both one and two colours. It is best treated as a short-lived perennial, propagating new plants from seed or cuttings (pure strains) every three years or so. C.
polyphyllus hybrids
Russell hybrids include many named varieties (pure strains) with flowers ranging from blue, mauve, pink and white to orange and yellow, and 'Russell Strain Mixed' producing a full range of shades from one sowing. PH 90 cm (3ft), D3–4, May–July. 'Dwarf Lulu', a selection of the best hybrids with flowers of Russell hybrid colours, including bicolours. PH 60cm (2ft), D4, May–July.

Lychnis
Campion or Catchfly. Ordinary soil, sunny positions. C.
coronaria (=*Agrostemma coronaria*)
Rose Campion. Woolly silvery leaves. Flowers 4cm (1½in) across, bright pink. PH 45cm (1¼ft), D5–6, July–September.
flos-jovis
Stems and thick leaves silvery or grey. Flowers 1.3cm (½in) across, red or purple, in loose clusters. PH 60cm (2ft), D5–6, June–August.

Lysimachia
Moist soil, but will tolerate quite dry soil. Sun or partial shade. Can be very invasive.
nummularia
Creeping Jenny or Moneywort. Vigorous, trailing, with rounded, mid-green leaves. Flowers, bright yellow, cup-shaped; an excellent ground cover plant. 'Aurea' has yellowish leaves. D4, June–August.
punctata
Yellow Loosestrife. Mid-green leaves and tall spikes of yellow cup-shaped flowers. PH 90cm (3ft), D4, June–August.

Lythrum

Purple Loosestrife. Moist soil in sun or semi-shade. C.

salicaria

Leaves mid-green. Small flowers closely packed in long spikes. PH 75cm (2½ft) or more, D5, June–September. 'Robert' has light rose-pink flowers, 'The Beacon' deep carmine-red flowers and those of 'Dropmore' are rosy-purple.

Monarda

Sweet Bergamot or Horsemint, also known as Bee Balm or Oswego Tea. Fertile soil in sun.C.

didyma

Leaves mid-green, aromatic. Flowers hooded, tubular in whorls. PH 90cm (3ft), D4, June–September. 'Cambridge Scarlet' has bright scarlet flowers, 'Blue Stocking', violet-purple and 'Snow Maiden', white.

Nepeta

Catmint or Catnip. Ordinary, well-drained soil, preferably light, in sun or semi-shade. C.

×fassenii

Leaves aromatic, ovate, grey-green. Flowers small, tubular, hooded, violet-blue. PH 38cm (1¼ft), D5, May–September.

Oenothera

Evening Primrose. Fertile, well-drained soil in sun or semi-shade. C.

missouriensis

Leaves mid-green on prostrate stems. Flowers cup-shaped, up to 7.5cm (3in) across, yellow, opening in the evening and living for several days. PH 25cm (10in), D5, June–August.

Paeonia

Peony. Deep fertile soil in sun. C.

lactiflora (=*albiflora*)

Leaves dark green, deeply cut, tough. The often fragrant flowers, borne at the ends of strong stems, are 10–18cm (4–7in) across. Some of the best varieties include: 'Edulis Superba', pink, scented; 'Felix Crousse', carmine red; 'President Roosevelt', deep red; 'Duchesse de Nemours', white; and 'Sarah Bernhardt', pale pink, scented. All these have double flowers. Single-flowered varieties, which have prominent yellow stamens at the centre of the flower, include 'Augustus John', deep cherry-pink; 'Globe of Light', pale rose pink; and 'Whitley's Major' ('The Bride'), white. PH 75–90cm (2–2½ft) tall, D3, June–July.

Papaver

Deep fertile soil in sun.

orientale

Oriental Poppy. Leaves coarse, hairy, mid-green. Flowers top-heavy, borne at the ends of long stems that usually need support. Some of the best varieties include: 'Fireball', orange, double, PH 25–30cm (10–12in), D5, May–July; 'Goliath', crimson; 'Mrs Perry', pink; and 'Perry's White', all single-flowered and PH between 75–90cm (2½–3ft), D4, May–July.

Phlox

Fertile soil in sun or semi-shade. C.

douglasii

Forms a dense carpet of prostrate, awl-shaped mid-green leaves, covered with pale lavender flowers in late spring. PH 7.5cm (3in), D5, May–June.

paniculata (=decussata)

Leaves mid-green on stiff stems. Flowers in dense terminal clusters, fragrant. Many varieties – some of the best include: 'Fairy's Petticoat', pale mauve with dark mauve centre; 'Gaiety', orange-red; 'Harlequin', variegated leaves, bright purple flowers; 'Mount Fujiyama', white; 'Pinafore Pink', 'Prince of Orange' and 'Starfire', brilliant deep red; all PH 75–90cm (2½–3ft), D4–5, July–October.

Phormium

New Zealand Flax. Fertile, moist soil in sun with wind protection.

tenax and *cookianum* hybrids

Grown for its ornamental leaves. The flowers are dull red and appear from July–September. Varieties available include: 'Purpureum' in which the sword-like leaves are purple; PH to 2m (6ft), D1. 'Dazzler' has arched, fan-like leaves, reddish-brown overlaid with carmine; PH 60–90cm (2–3ft), D2–3. 'Yellow Wave', leaves golden-yellow margined green; PH 60–90cm (2–3ft), D1–2. 'Thumbelina', purple leaves; PH 30cm (1ft), D1–2.

Physalis

Cape Gooseberry or Chinese Lantern. Ordinary soil in sun. SH.

franchettii

Leaves mid-green, flowers white, followed by orange fruit enclosed in papery orange bladders that dry well for winter decoration. PH 75cm (2½ft), D4, fruits September–October.

Polemonium
Ordinary soil, sun or partial shade.
caeruleum
Jacob's Ladder. Neat tufts of arching mid-green leaves divided into leaflets and small five-petalled blue or white flowers. PH 60cm (2ft), D4, April–July.

Polygonatum
Solomon's Seal or David's Harp. Any soil, as long as roots are protected from sunlight. Good for growing in shade; thrives in quite deep shade. Drought-tolerant.
×*hybridum*
Arching stems with mid-green, oblong leaves clasped around them. Ivory-white tubular flowers borne along stem in clusters of 2–5. PH 90cm (3ft), D5, May–June.

Polygonum
Knotweed. Ordinary soil, sun or semi-shade. C.
affine
Narrow, dark-green leaves, which remain brown and papery on the plant throughout the winter. Flowers in spikes. 'Darjeeling Red' has pink flowers. PH 25cm (10in), D3–4, May–August.
bistorta 'Superba'
Snakeweed or Bistort. Leaves rounded, light green. Flowers clear pink. PH 90cm (3ft), D3–4, May–August.

Potentilla
Cinquefoil. Fertile soil in sun. C.
atrosanguinea hybrids
Leaves strawberry-like, grey or green. Flowers in open sprays. 'Gibson's Scarlet', bright red, single, semi-prostrate plant; 'Yellow Queen', semi-double yellow flowers and silver foliage. PH 30cm (1ft), D5, June–August.

Primula
Border primulas are described here. Moist, fertile soil. Sun or partial shade.
denticulata
Drumstick Primrose. Broad, pale green leaves form a compact rosette. Numerous small purple, pink or white flowers borne in dense round heads on short, thick stalks. Varieties include 'Superba', with lilac-blue flowers; 'Ruby', rose-purple, and 'Alba', white. PH 45cm (1½ft), D5, March–May.
bulleyana
Dark green oblong leaves. Tiered spikes of

light orange flowers. PH 60cm (2ft), D5, June–July.
florindae
Giant Cowslip. Mid-green, toothed leaves. Fragrant heads of pale yellow cowslip flowers borne on graceful, drooping stalks. PH 90cm (3ft), D4, June–August.

Pulmonaria
Lungwort. Moist soil in semi-shade. C.
angustifolia (=*azurea*)
Leaves mid-green. Flowers tubular, cowslip-like, gentian-blue. PH 23cm (9in), D5, April–May.
saccharata
Bethlehem Sage. Leaves bright green marbled with white. Flowers open pink, mature to sky blue. 'Pink Dawn' has bright rose-pink flowers. PH 25cm (10in), D5, March–April.

Rodgersia
Moist soil in semi-shade, needs a sheltered site. C.
pinnata 'Superba'
Leaves chestnut-like, mid-green turning bronze-purple. Pink, starry flowers borne in sprays on strong branching stems. PH 90cm (3ft), D3–4, July.

Rudbeckia
Cone Flower or Black-eyed Susan. Fertile soil in sun. C.
fulgida (=*speciosa*, =*newmanii*)
Leaves mid-green. Large flowers, dark purplish-brown cone-like centre. PH 90cm (3ft), D5, July–October. 'Deamii' has yellow petals and flowers up to 10cm (4in) across; 'Goldquelle', large double yellow; 'Goldsturm', yellow, larger flowers, and 'Speciosa', orange flowers.

Salvia
Sage. Fertile soil in sun. C.
haematodes
Basal rosette of grey-green. Flowers lavender on branching spikes. 'Indigo' has blue flowers. PH 90cm (3ft), D5, June–September.

Scabiosa
Scabious or Pincushion Flower. Alkaline soil in sun. C.
caucasica
Leaves narrow, mid-green. Large bluish flowers, borne on long, stiff almost leafless stems. PH 75cm (2½ft), D5, June–September.

'Clive Greaves' has lavender-blue flowers; 'Miss Willmott', white.

graminifolia
Silvery-grey foliage, light mauve flowers (soft pink in variety 'Pincushion'). PH 30cm (1ft), D5, June–September.

Sedum

Stonecrops or Ice Plants. Ordinary soil in full sun; drought resistant.

spectabile
Leaves thick, pale glaucous. Flowers in large, flat heads, attract butterflies. 'Autumn Joy' has pinkish-red flowers; 'Meteor', deep carmine-red. PH 45–60cm (1½–2ft), D4, August–October.

spurium
Leaves dark green on prostrate stems. Flowers in small heads. 'Green Mantle' has pink flowers; 'Album', white. PH 10cm (4in), D4, July–August.

Solidago

Golden Rod. Ordinary soil in sun or light shade. C.

hybrids (*S. hybrida* or *S. arendsii*)
Many hybrids including: 'Golden Thumb', leaves mid-green. Flowers mimosa-like, yellow. PH 25cm (10in), D5, August–September. 'Cloth of Gold' with yellow-green foliage. PH 45cm (1½ft), D4, August–September; 'Goldenmosa', yellow-green foliage. PH 75cm (2½ft), D5, August–September.

Stachys

Lamb's Tongue or Sow's Ear. Ordinary soil in sun or semi-shade. C.

lanata
Leaves covered with silvery hairs, so that they appear woolly. Flowers small and purple, borne in spikes on strong stems. 'Sheila MacQueen' is an improved form. 'Silver Carpet' is a non-flowering form useful for ground cover.

Thalictrum

Meadow Rue. Fertile soil in sun or semi-shade.

flavum 'Glaucum'
Grey-green leaves, compact heads of fluffy yellow flowers. PH 1.5m (5ft), D5, July–August.

minus (=*adiantifolium*)
Grown for its finely-divided leaves, grey-green and like those of the Maidenhair Fern in shape.

Greenish-purple flowers almost insignificant. PH 90cm (3ft), D5, June–July.

Trollius

Globe Flower. Moist soil, in sun or partial shade. Water well in dry weather; never let roots dry out. C.

× *hybridus* (=*europaeus*)
Rich green leaves made up of deeply cleft, toothed lobes. Globe-shaped flowers like large, closed-up buttercups. Good varieties include 'Canary Bird', with pale yellow flowers; 'Goldquelle', golden yellow, and 'Salamander', fiery orange. PH 75cm (2½ft), D4, May–June.

Verbascum

Mullein. Ordinary soil in sun. C, SH.

hybrids (=*V. hybridum*)
Low-growing hybrids include: 'Golden Bush', leaves grey-green; flowers yellow. PH 60cm (2ft), and 'Pink Domino', deep rose-pink. PH 1m (3½ft), both D5, June–August.

Veronica

Speedwell. Ordinary soil in sun or semi-shade. C.

gentianoides
Leaves mid-green, forming a basal rosette. Flowers pale blue in dainty spikes. 'Variegata' has leaves marked with white. PH 60cm (2ft), D5, May–June.

incana
Leaves silver-grey, toothed. Small, blue flowers in spikes. PH 30cm (1ft), D5, June–August.

Viola

Violets and Pansies. Fertile, moist but well-drained soil, in sun or partial shade. They can easily become overpowered in a herbaceous border or island bed, but are good for edging paths. There are many species and varieties.

labradorica 'Purpurea'
Rounded mid-green leaves, suffused with purple. Mauve flowers. PH 12.5cm (5in), D5, April–May.

odorata
Sweet Violet. Heart-shaped, dark green leaves. Flowers purple or white. PH 15cm (6in), D5, February–April (and sometimes in autumn). Pansies are best grown as biennials, and are described under this heading on page 210.

Zantedeschia

Arum Lily or Calla Lily. Rich, moist or wet soil. Needs protection in winter. C.

aethiopica
'Crowborough' is usually a hardier variety than others. Leaves triangular, dark green, on long stems. The flowers are borne on a prominent yellow fleshy spike (the 'spadix') surrounded by a large white modified leaf (the 'spathe') and are carried at the ends of long stems. The spathe is up to 23cm (9in) across. PH 90cm (3ft), D5–6, June–September.

ORNAMENTAL GRASSES
All these are valuable for flower arrangers and can be dried for winter decoration, cut before the flower heads are fully mature.

Avena
Ordinary soil in sun.
candida (*Helietotrichon sempervivens*)
Leaves evergreen, very slim, arching, grey-blue. Buff-coloured flower-spikes. PH 30–45cm (1–1½ft), D3–4.

Carex
Sedge. Moist soil in sun.
morrowii
'Variegata' has slender, arching evergreen leaves margined with white. Green flowers in large branched clusters. PH 40cm (15in), D5, March–May.

Cortaderia
Pampas Grass. Ordinary soil in sun, but protected from wind.
selloana (= *argentea*)
'Pumila' is a more compact form suited to the smaller garden. Leaves long, slender, arching, evergreen. Flowers on tall stems in silky, silvery white plumes. PH 1.8m (6ft), D1, September–October.

Festuca
Grey Fescue Grass. Ordinary soil in sun.
glauca (= *ovina* 'Glauca')
Dainty tufts of bristle-like, blue-grey leaves. PH 15–23cm (6–9in), D5.

Hakonechloa
Moist soil in sun.
macra
'Aureola' has green-gold leaves with pink and cream markings. PH 25cm (10in), D5.

Luzula sylvatica 'Marginata'
Wood Rush. This form is suitable for a relatively dry soil in shade. PH 30cm (1ft), D5.

Millium
Bowles' Golden Form of Wood Millet. Moist soil in semi-shade.
effusum 'Aureum'
A graceful grass for a shady border. PH 60–90cm (2–3ft), D3–4, June–August.

Miscanthus
Ordinary soil in sun.
sinensis
'Variegatus' has pale green and yellow leaves. 'Zebrinus' has reddish-green leaves banded with yellow. PH for both 1.2m (4ft), D4.

Stipa
Feather Grass. Ordinary soil in sun.
pennata (= *Lasiogrostis splendens*)
Graceful mid-green foliage in clumps. Flowers in splendid silvery-buff plumes. PH 90cm–1.2m (3–4ft), D4, June–August.

HARDY FERNS
Grow all these in cool, moist soil in shade or in a north-facing bed.

Adiantum pedatum
Maidenhair Fern. Dainty, gracefully drooping, light green fronds. PH to 45cm (1½ft), D5, C.

Athyrium filix-femina
Lady Fern. Lacy, fresh green fronds. 'Plumosum' has golden-green fronds. Both PH up to 90cm (3ft), D5, C.

Dryopteris filix-mas
Male Fern. Deep green fronds unroll. PH 90cm (3ft), D1, C.

Matteuccia struthiopteris (= *Onoclea germanica*)
Ostrich Feather Fern or Shuttlecock Fern. The fronds open in spring to form a shuttlecock shape; the tall sterile outer fronds are golden-green and the shorter inner fronds are fertile and dark brown. PH up to 1.5m (5ft), D3, C.

Osmunda regalis
Royal Fern. Elegant fresh green fronds, turning to a beautiful russet colour in autumn. Does well beside water. PH 1.5m (5ft), D1, C.

Lawns

A perfect lawn of top-class bowling green quality would require so much maintenance that for most gardeners the effort could not be justified. However, a good lawn requires only a moderate amount of attention if it has been well made. First and foremost, you must decide what purpose you want your lawn to serve, and where it is to be situated, so that you know whether to use seed or turf, and if seed, which mixture to sow.

Seed or turf?

Firstly, it must be said that turf, if you can get it, is best for any garden with really poor soil (such as many town gardens) in areas where it would be prohibitively expensive or impossible to obtain good replacement soil. A lawn can be made from turf in a short time, whereas a seeded one may take a good deal longer. However, it is difficult in many areas to obtain suitable turf. You should beware of cheap offers of turf containing coarse grasses and weeds. It is best to use good-quality turf from the same type of soil as your own.

On the other hand, it is usually possible to buy a grass-seed mixture to suit your soil. A local garden shop should be a reliable source, because it is very likely to sell seed that suits the district. By using seed, you can use different grasses for different parts of the garden – under trees, on moist patches, and so on. This would be very difficult to do with turf. Preparing the site for your intended lawn will take about the same time for both a seeded lawn and a turfed one. On balance, then, making a lawn from seed is in most cases the better proposition.

Grass-seed mixtures

Standard lawn-seed mixtures are available, some containing ryegrass and others ryegrass-free. If you want to make a rough lawn to fill in a bare corner of the garden, or for heavy use by children or dogs, then save your money and sow a ryegrass mixture. If you want a reasonably good lawn, then choose a ryegrass-free mixture, which will cost a little more. If you want a really fine lawn, choose a mixture of bents and fescues.

The grasses of any good lawn must contribute dwarfness, fineness, vigour, resistance to and quick recovery from wear, resistance to drought and disease, and ability to withstand regular mowing. No single species has all these characteristics, so mixtures are made up of bents, fescues and other grasses in varying proportions.

Fescues (*Festuca*) are tough, drought-resistant, fine-leaved grasses which grow well in poor soil.

Bents (*Agrostis*) are also fine, but are even more resistant to adverse conditions than the fescues.

Meadow Grasses (*Poa*) are coarser grasses, more suitable for pastures than for fine lawns, although they do help to make good recreation lawns. When mixed with the finer grasses, they protect these during their rather slower development period.

Perennial Ryegrasses (varieties of *Lolium perenne*), already mentioned above, give a serviceable if coarse lawn on all but very acid soils.

Crested Dog's Tail (*Cynosurus cristatus*) is a hard-wearing, drought-resistant, cold-tolerant grass. It is not suitable for fine lawns, but is good for a tough lawn on a chalky or light soil.

Timothy Grass (*Phleum pratense*) Aberystwyth improved strain S50, is coarse, quick growing and ideal for wet places and heavy, moist soil.

Some typical grass seed mixtures

	Kg	lb		Kg	lb
1. For a fine lawn:			**4. For a lawn in a damp, shady place:**		
Chewing's Fescue	1.36	3			
Browntop Bent	1.36	3	Creeping Bent	0.91	2
Creeping Red Fescue	1.82	4	Ryegrass (S23)	2.27	5
	4.54	10	Rough-stalked		
			Meadow Grass	1.36	3
				4.54	10
2. For a hard-wearing lawn on moist soil:			**5. For a lawn in a dry, shady place:**		
Chewing's Fescue	2.74	6			
Browntop Bent	0.45	1	Browntop Bent	1.36	3
Creeping Red Fescue	0.45	1	Fine-leaved Fescue	0.91	2
Crested Dog's Tail	0.45	1	Sheep's Fescue	1.82	4
Timothy Grass (S50)	0.45	1	Creeping Red Fescue	0.45	1
	4.54	10		4.54	10
3. For a hard-wearing lawn on a dry soil:			**6. For a lawn in a town garden:**		
Chewing's Fescue	1.81	4	Ryegrass (S23)	1.82	4
Browntop Bent	0.91	2	Rough-stalked		
Creeping Red Fescue	0.91	2	Meadow Grass	1.36	3
Crested Dog's Tail	0.91	2	Annual Meadow Grass	1.36	3
	4.54	10		4.54	10

Preparation of the site for a lawn

Generally speaking, sound preparation is at least half the battle; remember that your lawn will be there for many years to come and it is worth taking trouble to ensure that it is as good as you can make it, bearing in mind its purpose. The best time to prepare the soil depends on whether you propose to use turf or sow seed. For turf, it is best to do the work in autumn, while preparation for a seeded lawn is best done in autumn or spring. For autumn sowing and for turfing, you should prepare the site in summer and allow the soil to settle for at least six weeks. For spring sowing, you should do your initial digging in late autumn and leave the soil rough for the frost to break up the clods.

On a new plot, where the topsoil is buried under subsoil and brick dust, full trenching is essential after removing debris. For established sites, half-trenching will do: the lower layer, of subsoil, is broken up and manure or garden compost is forked into it. If the ground is clean and drainage is good, you can merely turn over the top spit of soil, incorporating organic matter as you do so. (See BASIC CULTIVATION TECHNIQUES.)

If you have a heavy clay soil, make it more porous by incorporating sand as well as manure or other humus-forming organic matter; for a light, sandy soil, dig in extra organic matter to make it retain more moisture. (See SOIL AND COMPOSTS.) You should aim for a minimum soil depth of 15–22.5cm (6–9in) after allowing one-fifth extra for settling.

Hand-digging versus power-digging You may be tempted to use a cultivator if you are preparing a large site. If the area is very large, it may be the only way you will get the work done, but it is far better to dig by hand. Hand-digging makes it much easier to pick out coarse grasses and perennial weeds. A cultivator is likely to cut them up and spread the pieces about so that your weed problem will be greatly increased.

Drainage You cannot create a good lawn on waterlogged soil. If your drainage is bad, you must improve the situation by the method described on page 18.

Levelling A lawn should have a reasonably level surface, without any humps or hollows. This does not mean that it must be absolutely horizontal, unless you want a top-quality bowling green, but if there is a slight slope in any direction it must have a running level, i.e. run smoothly. If the change in gradient is small, it can sometimes be corrected simply by adding topsoil. In such cases, it is possible to level the slope by eye. Where a major alteration is necessary, remove the topsoil and set it aside, then level the subsoil by the following method:

Equipment needed Wooden pegs, 45cm (18in) × 2.5cm (1in) × 2.5cm (1in), the number of pegs depending on the size of the lawn. You will need a peg for each 2.1m (7ft) of lawn. Paint the top 20cm (8in) of each peg white to make it more visible. Also, draw a line around each one in indelible pencil, at a distance from the top equal to the depth of topsoil.

A straight-edge: a wooden board 2.1m (7ft) × 10cm (4in) × 2.5cm (1in).

A spirit level, securely strapped to the centre of the narrow face of the straight-edge.

Mallet, spade, fork, rake and wheelbarrow.

Procedure Drive a peg into the ground to the depth of the pencil line, close to a side boundary, so that its top represents the general level required. Knock in a second peg about 2.1m (7ft) away along the line across the site. Bridge the gap between them by placing the straight-edge, with the spirit level attached, across their tops. Then drive in the second peg until the bubble of the spirit level is central or a little to one side or the other, according to the direction of the running level. Repeat this at a third peg on the line and so on until the whole distance is completed. From the first peg, mark the beginning of a second line by levelling a peg, positioned 2.1m (7ft) away and at right angles to the original cross line. Then insert pegs to traverse the second line. Repeat this until the whole lawn surface is covered with a network of pegs 2.1m (7ft) apart, the tops of which mark the required level.

Rake the subsoil to bring its whole surface level with the pencil mark on each peg. Then cover the subsoil with successive layers of topsoil to a maximum depth of 7.5cm (3in) so that, when they are firmed and settled, they reach the tops of the pegs throughout the area.

Settling and weeding After the soil has been dug over and broken up, allow it at least six weeks to settle, during which period you can weed out any invading coarse grasses. If this is during the growing season, the plot may be treated with a selective weed killer, which will kill the perennial weeds. Alternatively, to avoid the use of chemical controls, remove these by hand, being sure to pick out every fragment of stem and root. All the annual weeds that appear after the lawn is made will eventually be killed by mowing. After a week or so, you can make your seed bed.

Preparation of the bed Before sowing your seed, you must create a fine tilth, free from stones; for a turfed lawn, it is not necessary to be quite so particular. You should then rake a lawn fertilizer into the seedbed

Below: a simple method of levelling. Drive in the first peg so that its top represents the level required (top and centre), then drive in the second peg, bridging the two pegs with a spirit level attached to a straight-edge (bottom) to check that they are at same level. Repeat the process until the required area is covered with pegs.

Bottom: a close-up of the spirit level attached to the straight-edge, placed over the pegs which are adjusted until they are at the correct level.

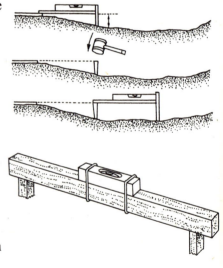

Right: the almond (Prunus)

Above: the shrub Vibernum in winter   *Right: carnation 'Arthur Sim' for greenhouses*

Above: dogwood and winter-flowering heaths

Right: Acer palmatum, the Japanese Maple

Left: Pieris forrestii, an evergreen   *Above: begonia and cineraria planted out*

soil in amounts recommended by the manufacturer, together with peat if the soil is dry and sandy. The fine tilth is achieved by cross-raking, followed by treading on a dry day to firm the soil, and then a final cross-raking. All stones and other debris should be removed by this process. The resulting fine tilth should be about 10cm (4in) deep.

Making a lawn from seed
Sowing seed should be done on a windless day, when the soil is not wet enough to cling to your boots. The time of year for sowing is not absolutely critical, although the best time is August or September, when the soil is still warm and likely to stay moist. April is the next best sowing time. If sowing in summer, make sure the soil is moist. Recommended sowing rates are 50gm per sq m (1½oz per sq yd) for fine lawns, and 67gm per sq m (2oz per sq yd) for other lawns. It is a good idea to obtain seed treated with bird repellent, which does not harm the birds but prevents them from eating it.

Before you buy your seed, you must calculate the area of your lawn to find out how much you need. This is easily done for a square or rectangular lawn, by multiplying the length by the breadth. The best method for an irregularly shaped lawn is to treat the area as if it was one or more rectangles.

Sowing can be done more evenly with a mechanical distributor, but this is not essential. When hand sowing, it is much easier if you bulk up the seed with an equal or greater amount of silver sand, and divide your seed/sand mixture into two halves. Then, walking steadily across the bed, cover it as evenly as you can with the first half. Next, sow the second half, this time walking at right angles to your first sowing. This will give reasonably good coverage, but for best results, divide the seedbed into squares by means of parallel strings, about 1m (3ft) apart, and laths placed across them at the same distance apart. After sowing, lightly rake the seed in, first one way and then at right angles, so that it is just covered by soil. If your seed is not treated with bird-repellent, protect it with silver foil bird-scarers or netting.

The first rolling When it is about 3.75cm (1½in) high, the new grass should be *lightly* rolled, but do not roll if it is at all wet. A roller mower, preferably a hand one, with its cutting blades tilted upward so that the grass is not damaged, is heavy enough for the job.

The first cutting On a dry day, when the grass is dry and about 7.5cm (3in) tall, it can be cut, preferably using shears. If you have to use a mower, use a hand mower, with the blades set high and without the grass box. With subsequent mowings, gradually reduce the grass height to 1.3cm (½in) and keep the grass at this height for the rest of the first year.

Weeds and coarse grasses It is important to dig out any coarse grasses as they appear, using a trowel or hand fork, otherwise they will take over. They are not destroyed by selective weedkillers. It is not advisable to treat young grass with selective weedkillers, except those mentioned under WEEDS on page 39.

The edges of a seeded lawn Many gardeners want their lawns to have clean, sharp edges. To ensure these, you should make the seedbed 15cm (6in) wider all round than the intended final size of the lawn. When the seed is rooted and the soil consolidated, you can cut a good lasting edge with an edging iron. If your soil is very light, the edge may need the support of a flexible plastic or aluminium strip, which is sold in lengths.

Left: rock plants in a raised bed

Making a lawn from turf

When to lay turf The traditional, and best, time to lay turf is between September and early February, when it is not frosty, although it may be done at other times. It is, however, most important not to select a time when drought is likely to follow; this could kill the turf. Lay the turves as soon as possible after delivery. If they must be stored, unroll them and lay them out flat, and do not stack them.

The size of each turf is usually 90cm (3ft) × 30cm (1ft) × 3.2cm ($1\frac{1}{4}$in), but they are occasionally 30cm (1ft) square. They must be of uniform thickness, or they will produce an uneven lawn.

Marking the boundaries If a lawn is square or rectangular, it is easy to mark the edge with a line. For one with a curved edge, it is best to mark it out by looping string around stakes about 5cm (2in) beyond the intended edge, so that this can eventually be cut sharply.

Laying the turf When the soil surface is dry, lay a row of turves, tightly abutting one another along one side. Then lay a second row, the joints of which are staggered with those of the first row, just like in a brick wall. Continue laying rows like this until you reach the opposite side. Tap each turf down lightly with the head of a rake, but do not compress it. Work forward, and stand on a plank so that the turves already laid are not damaged by your heels. Next, fill up the joints by brushing into them a top dressing of equal parts of fine topsoil, coarse sand and damp peat, sprinkled on with a trowel. Brush away any excess so that the grass is not smothered.

Finally, firm in the turves by light rolling or by walking along a plank placed over them.

You must keep your new lawn well watered, especially if you laid it in spring, when a dry spell may follow. When the grass starts to grow, mow it carefully.

Dealing with sunken edges Often the outer turves sink after they have been laid. To remedy this, dig out a channel 15cm (6in) wide, and the same depth as the turf, around the outside of the lawn bed and fill it with turves cut in half lengthways. Firm them in lightly. Now lay the outside turves on top of the half-turves. When they have become consolidated, you can cut sharp edges.

Care and maintenance of the lawn

Tools With the right tools, caring for a lawn can be a pleasure. Essential ones are shears, a spring tine rake, a fork, an edging iron, a broom and a mower.

SHEARS Short-handled shears are essential, being used for cutting the grass in its early stages and, on an established lawn, for trimming inaccessible patches or long stems missed by the mower. A long-handled version obviates the need for bending. Battery-operated shears can be operated with one hand, and are supplied with a mains battery charger.

EDGE TRIMMERS Long-handled edging shears are made with sideways-facing blades for trimming grass at the lawn edge. One type of mechanical trimmer has a rotating star-shaped cutter mounted on a non-slip rubber roller which overhangs the edge. As you push it along, the cutter trims the edge. Re-chargeable battery trimmers are also available. Edging irons have a half-moon shaped metal blade mounted on a long shaft, and are pushed into the turf to slice off a clean edge.

SCARIFYING TOOL The important job of scarifying involves stirring up the lawn surface and removing dead matted grass or weeds which would

Right: tools for lawn maintenance include (a) an edging iron, (b) long-handled shears, and (c) a spring-tine rake for scarifying the lawn surface and collecting leaves.

Right: a lawn aerator.

choke the grass. This can be done with a spring-tine rake.

LEAF SWEEPERS A spring-tine rake can be used to collect leaves. For larger lawns, hand-pushed leaf sweepers are available. They have bristle brushes mounted on a roller, to lift leaves, dead grass and so on into a fabric bag fixed at the back. Power-driven sweepers collect the leaves by vacuum.

AERATORS Regular aeration is essential for the health of the lawn. It reduces compaction, assists the draining of any surface water that might encourage fungus diseases, keeps down moss and enables fertilizer to reach the grass roots. It can be done by inserting the prongs of a garden fork deeply into the lawn at intervals of 15cm (6in), but is more efficiently done with a special tool, of which there are three kinds: solid-tine aerators for light soils, hollow-tine tools, which remove plugs of soil and relieve compaction in heavy soils, and slitters, which divide the grass roots and encourage their growth, so that the sward is thickened.

SPREADERS Seed or fertilizer is placed in a hopper mounted on wheels and distributed evenly and accurately as this is wheeled steadily over the lawn.

SPRINKLERS Watering is best done by an oscillating sprinkler on a hose.

ROLLERS Rolling should be done as little as possible; it is only necessary once or twice in early spring to consolidate turf loosened by frost. Hire or borrow a lightweight lawn roller, no heavier than 100kg (2cwt); a heavy one will do a great deal of damage. Never try to correct bumps with a roller.

Mowers There are two main types of mower: cylinder and rotor. The former are either side-wheeled or roller models.

Cylinder mowers SIDE-WHEEL TYPES These have a cutting cylinder with a grass box in front and a small roller behind. They cannot cut along the edge of a lawn, but are good for cutting rough and overgrown grass and the long stalks raised by scarifying, because these are not flattened as they would be by a mower with a heavy roller.

ROLLER TYPES On a hand-driven type, the cylinder is between the rear, heavy roller and a small roller and the grass box in front. It is more expensive than the side-wheel type, but will cut along the edges. An electrically driven type may be powered direct from the mains or by batteries. The mains type needs less maintenance than a petrol-driven mower, is quieter when running and should present no starting problems. Its greatest disadvantage is the inconvenience of the cable, especially in a large garden. Also, mains-operated mowers, both cylinder and rotary, are poor performers on rough ground.

A battery model is not difficult to use. Re-charging, particularly with a built-in charger, and refilling of batteries are not arduous tasks if carried out regularly. The life of a battery is about four years. For most models, about 670sq m (800sq yd) of lawn can be cut between chargings.

A petrol-driven roller mower needs more maintenance, is often more difficult to start and is more expensive than an electric one. However, it has more power and greater mobility, and is suitable for rough ground.

Rotary mowers These have a whirling horizontal blade, and deal better with long grass than the cylinder type, but do not cut so finely or leave a striped lawn. They are easy to handle and do not need resharpening.

The petrol-engined type has a recoil starter, operated by pulling a cord. Some models have a grass box or a flexible collecting bag, although with long grass it is easier to allow the mowings to fall to the ground, or the collector will fill too quickly. If the collector is not used,

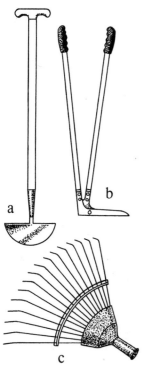

you should ensure that the ground is free from stones beforehand as otherwise there is the danger of those hit by the blade flying up and injuring someone; you must also rake up the mowings afterwards.

There are a few mains-operated rotary mowers, but no battery-operated ones. HOVER MOWERS are rotary mowers which literally hover above the grass on a 6mm (¼in) cushion of air. Easy to handle, they are especially efficient on steep banks. The cuttings have to be collected. They are best for rough work and cannot give a close finish.

With all rotary mowers, and particularly with hover mowers, it is very important to wear stout boots when using them and take great care not to let your feet get too near the fast-whirling blade.

Tasks See the GARDENING CALENDAR, pages 381–391, for further information on lawn maintenance throughout the year.

REPAIRING EDGES Damaged lawn edges should be repaired in autumn. Do this by cutting out the damaged turf, replacing it with the broken edge on the inside, and firming it in. Fill in gaps at the joints with sifted soil mixed with grass seed to produce a continuous growth.

REMOVING HUMPS AND HOLLOWS Get rid of these by making an H-shaped cut with a spade or edging iron over the hill or hollow, then folding back the two flaps of turf to expose bare soil. Remove or add soil accordingly, until the surface is flat, then replace the flaps and firm down.

Lawn Troubles

FUSARIUM PATCH DISEASE

Although this fungus can appear at any time, it is most likely in a mild September or October. Brown patches appear in the lawn; these spread and eventually join up. During wet weather and after snow, white or pinkish threadlike growths develop. Again, lack of aeration and drainage is often the cause, as with so many lawn problems, so deal with this if necessary. Also, avoid feeding late in summer. For a bad infestation, apply a good proprietary lawn fungicide (such as benomyl systemic fungicide). If this fails, dig out the offending patch and re-sow or re-turf.

CORTICUM DISEASE

This fungus, also known as Red Thread, particularly infests fine grasses, and is most common on sandy soils. In a wet autumn, yellow patches tinged with pinkish-brown appear; minute coral-red needles cling to the grass blades. Growth of this fungus indicates that the lawn needs nitrogen. The remedy is as for Fusarium Patch.

LEATHERJACKETS These are the brownish-grey, tough-skinned larvae of crane-flies, or daddy-long-legs, and they live beneath the soil. They damage turf by eating the roots and lower stems. Their presence is often revealed by the dying grass above them; sometimes large tufts of grass become loose and can be pulled out easily. A timely warning is often given by large numbers of starlings or other birds feeding on them on the lawn. An effective treatment is to wet the lawn and cover the damaged areas with black polythene sheeting or old sacking overnight. The next morning the leatherjackets will have risen to the surface, and you can remove and destroy them or leave them for the birds to eat.

COCKCHAFERS The larvae of these insects eat grass roots. They are commonest in sandy soil. Deal with them as for leatherjackets.

MOLES These may make their characteristic 'hills' in your lawn. Unfortunately, they are difficult to control. There are certain proprietaries that aim at their destruction and traps can be set to catch them, but these methods are not very satisfactory. Normally they are

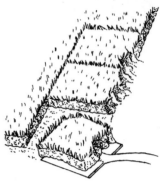

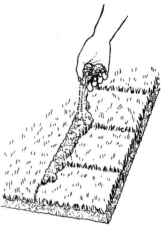

Above: repairing the broken edges of a lawn may be done by reversing the turves (cut with an edging iron) so that damaged edges are on the inside (top). The damaged area is then filled with fine soil containing grass seed (bottom).

Below: to remove small lumps and hollows from an established lawn, an H-shaped cut can be made and the turf rolled back so that either excess soil can be removed or more added.

found only in turf where earthworms are plentiful, so controlling the earthworm population might prove to be the answer. Planting Caper Spurge (*Euphorbia lathyrus*) around the lawn may drive the moles away.

PEARLWORT is a particularly troublesome weed. It can be confused with fine grasses and, if then left alone, will spread rapidly. It can be eliminated by 'spotting' the patches with a selective weedkiller containing MCPA or a mixture of 2,4-D and mecoprop at double strength.

FAIRY RINGS These stubborn fungi usually occur in summer, appearing as rings of lush, bright green grass with dead grass inside them. Small toadstools emerge from time to time. To eliminate the fungus, remove the turf from the affected area, break up the soil and apply a formalin solution: 3.41 litres (6pt) of 40 percent formaldehyde and 284ml ($\frac{1}{2}$pt) of wetting agent in 45.5 litres (10gal) of water. Then cover the area with moist sacking or cloth for 10 days, after which you should fork the soil well, then allow it to stand for a further 14 days. Finally, add fresh soil, up to the level of the surrounding turf, and re-seed the affected area.

Greenhouses, Frames and Cloches

Owing to the extremely changeable and often destructive nature of our weather, most outdoor gardeners experience disappointment at some time or other. Frequently this can be simply avoided by giving cloche or frame protection, but a greenhouse provides much greater scope. Even an unheated greenhouse enormously extends the range of plants that can be grown.

It is misleading to pretend that a small greenhouse kept well heated for sub-tropical and tropical ornamental plants will not prove to be a luxury – it must be regarded as a delightful but quite expensive hobby. However, a greenhouse that is unheated, or maintained just frost-free, or even one kept at a minimum temperature of about 7°C (45°F), can be a very profitable proposition indeed. The cost of the structure can soon be recovered in the value of the produce.

Nowadays cloche, frame, and greenhouse gardening is often reserved for producing a supply of delicious fresh vegetables and fruit the whole year round. This will help greatly to reduce your food bill, especially when out-of-season winter salads are grown, which are usually very expensive to buy in the shops. Cloches can be used for protecting flowers for cutting and hardy pot plants, as well as for the less tender food crops. Frames and greenhouses can provide a supply of beautiful bedding and border plants for the garden, and attractive pot-grown plants for the house; all these make splendid gifts, too. Many of these are costly to buy as plants but can be easily raised from seed.

Greenhouse gardening is specially suited to the not-so-young, the handicapped and the infirm. The protection from the weather, particularly in winter, will be welcomed by such gardeners.

There are very many specialist fields for the greenhouse enthusiast to explore. Certain plants lend themselves to specialized cultivation. Examples are chrysanthemums, carnations, foliage plants, tomatoes, cucumbers, orchids, various fruits, alpine plants, and ferns. Some gardeners like to have a greenhouse devoted to just a few of these or even to one particular group only, so that conditions can be arranged to grow them to perfection. The plants may be exhibited at shows, sold for profit, or raised purely to give pleasure and a sense of achievement.

Choosing a Greenhouse

Greenhouse Design Nowadays there is a great number of different greenhouse designs to choose from, and this can confuse the beginner. Generally speaking, for greatest versatility, the conventional 'BARN' shape, having vertical sides and covering a rectangular or square area of ground, will be found best for a free-standing greenhouse. It allows for the maximum use of the space available. The same applies to a vertical-sided LEAN-TO greenhouse. SLOPING SIDES were introduced to improve light transmission in winter, the sun's rays then having less thickness of glass to pass through. However, where the home gardener is concerned, it is doubtful whether this advantage can be fully exploited and is worth while. It is true that sloping sides will also give extra stability to a greenhouse structure, especially where there are high winds, and in this situation, such a design may be helpful. However, it is now possible to get metal or timber-framed houses which are of very robust construction even though they have vertical sides.

Small CIRCULAR GLASSHOUSES can look attractive and may make an interesting feature for the garden or patio, but are best used for decorative plants and as display houses. DOMED GREENHOUSES have also been introduced. Here again they make eye-catching display houses or conservatories, but are not really the best choice for general purpose growing. A very recent design, of a shape to trap the most sunlight, is the HIGH SOUTH-WALL greenhouse. This has one sloping side which must face south, and a roof which is inclined to meet a much lower sloped north side. It can be fitted with glass or with rigid plastic.

For the widest range of applications, a greenhouse glazed to ground level, or almost so, is to be recommended. This is known as a GLASS-TO-GROUND GREENHOUSE. However, for some purposes a low base wall, made from timber or brick or concrete, may be preferred. This type of greenhouse is called a PLANT HOUSE. Both types may be fitted with wide wooden or metal shelving, known as STAGING, on which pot plants, seed-trays and so on can be arranged. The space under the staging in a plant house will not receive so much light, but may be useful for shade-loving plants. A house with a base wall is likely to retain artificial warmth better, but it must be remembered that it will also cut out some sunlight, a source of free natural warmth.

Below: there are many different designs of greenhouse including, left to right, a barn type with low wooden walls; a glass-to-ground greenhouse; a glass-to-ground lean-to; a circular glasshouse; a lean-to model with low wooden walls; and a high south-wall type.

Lean-to greenhouses serve as excellent conservatories or sun rooms, or as home extensions when they can be entered from the dwelling house. A design that deserves more attention is the combined shed/greenhouse. This may have the greenhouse in the form of a lean-to against the shed, or it may be a continuation at one end of the shed. The greenhouse should preferably be entered from the shed. The shed section helps to reduce heat loss from the greenhouse and it makes a very useful place for potting, sowing, and other jobs.

Glass or Plastic? Plastics are now extensively employed in greenhouse construction. It must be realized that they are not substitutes for glass and are unsuitable for a permanent greenhouse expected to last many years. The plastics are softer than glass and do not weather so well, some being very short-lived. Polythene, for example, may need replacing every few years. For horticultural use a special grade of polythene should be used, called UVI or UV Inhibited (the letters 'UV' standing for 'ultra-violet').

Despite their limited lives, plastic houses have special applications and are particularly useful as extra houses where space in a glass house may be short and they can take over the growing of the more hardy plants, and for growing fruit and vegetables. In the latter case a plastic house is often light enough to be rotated with a crop on a vegetable plot.

The Greenhouse Framework When choosing material for the framework of a greenhouse, ALUMINIUM ALLOY is worth giving first consideration. If you find the appearance of metallic aluminium unattractive, frames can now be obtained with special weather-resistant white or green plastic coatings.

The advantages of aluminium are that it is lightweight, and thus easily transportable should it be required to move the greenhouse at any time; it is very strong, so that only narrow glazing bars are necessary, allowing as much light as possible to enter; and it will not warp, rot, or become attacked by fungi or wood-damaging insects. Moreover, an aluminium house usually needs no maintenance whatsoever.

All TIMBER frames will require either painting or treatment with a restorative or preservative at intervals of a few years, if they are to remain in good condition and not rot or warp. If timber is chosen, it is wise to select one of the more weather-resistant types, such as western red cedar or teak. The latter is more expensive and many people prefer the mellow look of cedar, which has proved very popular. Cheaper woods will need proper treatment and painting.

GALVANIZED STEEL is another strong material for the framework, but like cheaper wood, it should preferably be painted. Once the zinc

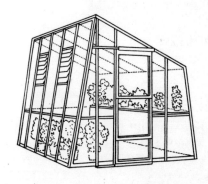

coating is scratched or damaged, it is liable to rust.

For some specialist crops or plants, there are special designs. For alpines there is a house provided with high staging to bring the plants nearer to eye-level, and extra ventilation. For carnations extra ventilation is also necessary, but the house should have very low staging or none at all. A lean-to facing south is good for fruit which can be trained against the rear wall. A plant house with a good heat-retaining base wall is sometimes preferred for warmth-loving plants.

Some useful general features to look for when buying a greenhouse are as follows:

Extendibility, in case you want more room later.

The possibility of fixing dividing partitions in case you want more than one temperature level or other different conditions for different plants.

The largest size you can afford and accommodate, since a large greenhouse is easier to manage than a small one and more convenient to work in.

A door wide enough to admit a wheelbarrow comfortably, and, if possible, a sliding one which can be used for extra ventilation.

Guttering, which helps to prevent waterlogging of the ground in winter. A good roof slope to lead condensation to one side and prevent light obstruction and dripping water (condensation is especially common with plastic houses).

Good facilities for ventilation in all cases, with as many ventilators as possible; this is particularly important with plastic houses.

Ease of erection. Some modern designs are especially simple to put up.

Siting and Erecting the Greenhouse

It is quite common to see a greenhouse sited in a remote, out-of-the-way part of the garden. It is a much better idea to put it as near your house as is convenient. This allows water and electricity services (and perhaps also natural gas for heating) to be connected easily and cheaply. Such a greenhouse is likely to get more frequent visits and more attention even when the weather is disagreeable.

Nevertheless, an open site receiving all the sunlight possible should always be selected, if this is feasible. If it is not, there are plants that can be grown very well in more shady greenhouses, but the plant selection will be very restricted. Remember it is simple to shade, but not so easy to provide artificial light to make up for inadequate daylight or sunshine (and artificial light costs money). The maximum sunlight in winter also means lower fuel bills if the house is heated.

Do not put a greenhouse near large trees, especially evergreens. They cast shade, exude gums that dirty the glass, shed leaves and possibly branches which may break the glass, and their roots may upset the foundations. Some trees also harbour pests and diseases that can affect greenhouse plants, and roosting birds may foul the glass.

Small ornamental trees at a reasonable distance will do no harm, and neither will nearby hedges, walls, fences, and the like, which may be useful windbreaks if sited on the side of prevailing wind. They should not cast shade, however. Avoid wet ground (or see that it is drained) and hollows or the foot of a hill, as frost will accumulate there.

Most modern prefabricated greenhouses can be erected single-handed in a matter of hours. Take special care if the house is plastic to see that the maker's instructions for anchoring are strictly obeyed; plastic houses have been known to blow away in a gale.

The manufacturers or suppliers should also give recommendations for laying the foundations. Rarely is anything elaborate necessary. A simple foundation for solid brick or wooden walls can usually be made by digging out a shallow trench a few inches deep (down to the hard subsoil layer), and filling with a very liquid concrete mix sufficiently fluid to find its own level. However, always check final levels with a spirit level.

Any painting or wood treatment should be completed before glazing. The glazing should be done during dry weather and the glass, when delivered, stored in the dry. It is particularly important to have dry conditions for glazing when using putty or mastic. When a timber frame is used, be very careful in your choice of preservative. Creosote must *never* be used, since it will give off fumes harmful or lethal to plants over a long period. It will also stain and sometimes weaken plastic.

If possible, position a greenhouse east–west, with the door preferably facing west. This ensures maximum entry of sunlight in winter when the sun is low in the sky, and in summer it is often necessary to shade only the south-facing roof and part of the side.

Guttering is an advantage, to keep the ground from becoming waterlogged, but the water should either be led into a soakaway or collected in a butt for use on the garden. Rainwater collected in this way is not suitable for greenhouse plants, as it is too contaminated.

Equipping the Greenhouse

In the average small amateur greenhouse on a permanent site, it is best not to grow plants in the ground soil. This does not apply to movable plastic houses, which can be rotated with crops if the soil becomes 'sick'. Nowadays there are many excellent special seed and potting composts free from pests and disease and weed seeds. These can be used in pots or other containers, or in grow-bags (plastic bags filled with compost) for the larger plants such as tomatoes, cucumbers, chrysanthemums, and so on. A soil floor can therefore in most cases be firmed and levelled, and strewn with clean shingle to give a neat appearance. This type of floor will hold moisture to maintain humidity in summer when it is 'damped down' (see page 174), without allowing puddles to form. To keep this type of floor clean and free from weeds and algae, it should be treated with a total weedkiller such as sodium chlorate and a proprietary algicide when necessary.

Greenhouses can be erected on concrete or asphalt, and for conservatories, display houses, or greenhouses used as garden rooms, a firm impervious floor is desirable. To give a decorative effect, modern vinyl floor coverings are useful and very resistant to ill treatment.

Staging and Shelving For short pot-plants, bedding plants, propagation and the like, STAGING is usually desirable to keep much of the work at waist height, and in a glass-to-ground house there should be enough light under the staging to make it useful for growing too. Nowadays PORTABLE STAGING that can be moved around, or even dismantled when not required, is becoming popular; this is usually made of aluminium.

Staging bought with a greenhouse usually has to be fixed to the sides. Sometimes it is convenient to have staging along only one side of a greenhouse, keeping the south side free for tall plants, such as tomatoes. In a house 3m (10ft) wide or wider, it is usually possible to have a run of staging down the centre and a path around it, as well as some staging along the sides.

During summer, the top of the staging should be covered with some moisture-retaining material to maintain humidity. Polythene sheeting covered with moist grit, modern plastic capillary matting, or a water-holding material such as Hortag can be used for this. For winter this should be removed or allowed to dry out, to keep down the humidity when conditions are cool. NARROW SHELVING is often useful when space is in demand in spring, and sometimes this can also be removed for winter to admit maximum light. TWO-TIER STAGING is available for glass-to-ground houses and TWO-LEVEL SHELVING is now also designed for suspending from the roof bars of aluminium houses.

Pots and Other Containers For general growing, PLASTIC POTS are now widely used, since they are easily cleaned and retain moisture longer than clay pots. However, a few CLAY POTS will be useful for plants that prefer a dryish, well aerated compost. For alpine plants, bulbs, and dwarf-growing plants, trailers and the like, also for plants with small root systems, HALF-POTS, which are half the depth of normal flowerpots, are very useful. GROW-BAGS are large plastic bags filled with a suitable compost and set on their sides. Holes through which to set the plants are then cut in the sides. Proprietary grow-bags are available, or you can fill your own plastic bags with home-made potting compost. For RING CULTURE, special rings made from bitumenized card or fibre are sold. They are usually about 25cm (10in) in diameter.

Other Useful Greenhouse Equipment Unless the facilities of a potting shed are available, a small home-made POTTING BENCH of a portable nature will be found very helpful. It can consist of a three-sided tray made to fit a section of staging and is best constructed from aluminium sheet or timber covered with a plastic such as formica. On this potting, sowing, and small-batch compost mixing can be done.

BLINDS for shading are best attached to the exterior of the roof and rested on rails a few inches from the glass for maximum cooling effect. Interior blinds are available, but they are far less efficient. (See also SHADING, page 174.)

PARTITIONS with communicating doors are worth consideration, so that compartments of different environmental conditions and temperature can be maintained for particular groups of plants. For example, a home greenhouse of good size could have two partitions, giving three sections: an unheated compartment at the door end, a warm compartment in the middle, and a cool compartment at the far end. Some makers of greenhouses supply these dividing partitions as extras, but for temporary divisions polythene sheeting can be used.

A small PROPAGATOR is an invaluable piece of equipment; some are heated by paraffin, and others by electricity. The latter is more convenient since very accurate temperature control is possible. You can make your own large propagator, using a lightweight aluminium frame on the staging heated by electric soil warming cables, which can be bought from a good garden shop or centre. The propagator will be required for seed germination and starting off bulbs and other storage organs, as well as for rooting cuttings of various kinds.

A MAXIMUM AND MINIMUM THERMOMETER is an essential piece of equipment, since it is vital to keep a check on the highest and lowest temperatures reached during your absence. A HYGROMETER may be helpful to give an indication of the humidity of the air, and beginners may find a MOISTURE METER helpful in watering. A moisture meter has a probe which is inserted into the compost before giving water to a plant.

Above: the usual greenhouse staging is open-slatted. However, many plants need humidity, and to provide this the staging can be covered with sheeting or matting which is in turn covered with moist grit.

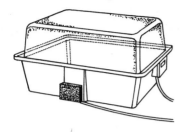

Above: a seed propagator may either be bought (top) or home-made (bottom) using electric soil-warming cables through a bed of sand. Seed boxes are placed on the sand, and pots pressed into the sand and surrounded by peat. A peat and sand mixture may be put on top of the sand bed and used for rooting cuttings.

It will indicate 'dry', 'moist' or 'wet' and hence gives a guide to how much water, if any, to give. A FERTILIZER INDICATOR is now also available which gives audible clicks when the probes are inserted in the compost. The slower the rate of clicks the less of a particular nutrient there is present. Another new introduction is a GREENHOUSE LIGHT-METER which helps to assess the right lighting conditions for plants.

Water can be supplied to the greenhouse via plastic alkathene tubing which will not burst if the water freezes in winter. Natural gas should be installed by an expert and according to the Gas Board specifications. Electricity must similarly be installed by a professional. Special fittings are designed for the damp conditions of the greenhouse and should always be used. Domestic electrical fittings and equipment are *not* suitable and would be extremely dangerous. If in doubt, consult your local Electricity Board.

Heating Your Greenhouse

It is important to remember that glass has special properties that enable structures made from it to trap solar heat. A well sited greenhouse will cost less to heat than one partly in shade, and it is particularly desirable for a greenhouse to be in an open position if it is not artificially heated.

For most plants grown in the average home greenhouse a minimum winter temperature of about 1.7°C (35°F) is perfectly adequate. If a temperature of about 4.4–7.2°C (40–45°F) can be maintained as a minimum, a vast range of plants from the world over can be overwintered. Temperatures above this level become rather expensive to maintain, even in a small greenhouse. However, small sub-tropical and tropical plants can be grown economically inside the greenhouse, in frames heated by soil warming cables. In this case, a winter minimum of from 12.8°C (55°F) to about 18.3°C (65°F) will be necessary.

Many beginners tend to aim at temperatures which are far too high, and quite unnecessary, indeed often undesirable, for ordinary plants. Many of the relatively hardy vegetables grown for winter cropping need only protection from the harsh weather, and those varieties suitable for forcing need only modest artificial warmth. Most of the popular decorative pot plants such as cinerarias, calceolarias, fuchsias, pelargoniums, primulas and the like, are happy if kept merely frost free.

When buying or installing heating equipment, it is most important that it should be capable of giving out enough heat to maintain the minimum temperature required during the coldest periods. If given the greenhouse size, area of glass, walls, floor, etc., and the minimum temperature needed inside and the lowest temperature expected outside, makers of equipment will advise what rating the heater should have.

Different Types of Heater. The old fashioned wick-type PARAFFIN OIL HEATER is still convenient and popular. It is most wise to have one of these heaters at hand with a stock of paraffin, whatever form of main heating you have, to bring into use during emergencies, such as power breakdowns, strikes, or periods of exceptionally cold weather when the main heating may not be able to cope. Wick heaters should be properly designed for the greenhouse and preferably have heat-distributing tubes. A small amount of ventilation must be constantly allowed while the heater is in use. This is to admit air (containing oxygen) for proper combustion of the paraffin, and to allow the products of combustion to disperse. To avoid fumes the heater must be kept clean, the wicks trimmed, and only best quality domestic paraffin used. Be careful when buying a paraffin heater to see that it has a high enough BTU output.

Next in order of popularity, and especially efficient, clean and convenient is ELECTRIC HEATING. However, it has an unjustified reputation of being expensive. Taking into account that electricity needs no attention whatsoever, and that the greenhouse atmosphere is kept pure and free from waste products of combustion, ensuring extremely healthy plants and excellent growing conditions, it can compare favourably with other fuels.

For the home greenhouse an ELECTRIC FAN HEATER is ideal, but it should be of a type in which the fan and heat output are controlled together by a thermostat – not with a fan running all the time – for greatest economy. The intermittent air circulation gives very healthy conditions for the plants and there is minimal need for ventilation in winter, resulting in little waste of electricity. If a greenhouse is lined with polythene for heat insulation (see below), a continuously running fan can be used since much less warmth will be lost. ELECTRIC CONVECTOR HEATERS also give good air circulation. For smaller houses, ELECTRIC HEATING TUBES are useful and are usually rated at about 60 watts per 30cm (1ft) run. It is best not to put them too near the greenhouse sides; if possible, they should be set alongside a central pathway.

HOT WATER PIPES are not used so much nowadays, but are still useful where higher temperatures are needed. They then give greater efficiency than if employed merely for keeping out frost. They can be heated by fuel oil, paraffin, natural gas, or solid fuels. The last mentioned is relatively cheap compared with others, but hot-water-pipe heating equipment is among the most expensive to install.

NATURAL GAS is not poisonous to plants and is now being used in small heaters without flues. These are much the same as paraffin wick heaters where the atmosphere of the greenhouse is concerned, water vapour and carbon dioxide being the products of combustion. Constant ventilation is again essential. It has also been found that some natural gas heaters do evolve oxides of nitrogen under certain conditions when thermostatically controlled. This gas is toxic to plants and can cause some damage. Because of the water vapour evolved, both paraffin and natural gas tend to make the air very humid.

Greenhouse Insulation

To conserve greenhouse warmth, be sure that the house is reasonably airtight and that doors and vents do not admit draughts. To reduce heat losses during winter by about 40 per cent, line the house inside with clear thin polythene sheet leaving a gap of about 1.3–2.5cm ($\frac{1}{2}$–1in) between the glass and the polythene. It is this air gap that forms the heat insulation. Cellular polythene has lately been introduced. This is a very efficient heat insulator but reduces light entry.

It is best to remove the polythene lining as soon as the weather becomes warmer, or you will have problems with condensation.

General Greenhouse Cultivation
Growing in Pots, Seed-Trays and Other Containers For successful results under glass when growing plants in pots, seed-trays and other containers, care must be taken over the type of growing medium used.

For seed sowing and for potting, special composts should be employed. The first and best known are the John Innes composts. These are still excellent but should be bought from suppliers who are members

Right: ways of growing greenhouse tomatoes include the grow-bag method (above) and ring culture (below), where the plants are grown in rings made of card or fibre filled with compost and placed over a layer of moist peat.

of the John Innes Association to ensure reliable formulation and correct manufacture. There are now many other proprietary seed and potting composts, mostly based on peat. For economy, some balanced fertilizers, such as Phostrogen, can be added to a peat/grit mix according to the maker's specifications. This is helpful when a large quantity of compost is needed for troughs, frames, tubs, and ring culture, or when many pot plants are grown, and also to fill seed trays for bedding plants. Both seed and potting composts should be stored in *closed* bags or in bins closed with tight-fitting lids when not being used.

For seed sowing, the plastic seed trays generally available should be used for greenhouse subjects and preferably also for the sowing and pricking-out of bedding plants. Many greenhouse pot plants can also be grown in seed trays in the early stages to reduce the need for potting. When potting, always keep the pot size to the minimum necessary for the plant. As a plant grows, it is best to 'pot on' through several sizes of pot as the need arises. This ensures that the plant always has reasonably fresh compost around the newly forming roots.

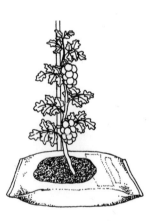

PEAT POTS are very useful, especially for plants with delicate roots which react badly to being transplanted, as the plants do not need to be removed from the pots. For example, sweet corn seedlings raised in peat pots in a greenhouse can be planted outdoors complete with the pots, which rot down in the soil.

For certain crops such as tomatoes, cucumbers, climbing French beans, and chrysanthemums, RING CULTURE can be used. With this technique the plants are grown in cylinders of bitumenized card or fibre, usually about 25cm (10in) in diameter, and filled with moist compost before being stood on a base of water-retaining aggregate. At one time ballast (a mixture of coarse sand and small stones) was popularly used for the base. However, it is more convenient to use a layer of peat about 10–15cm (4–6in) thick. This should be spread on polythene sheeting slit at intervals to allow excess water to drain away.

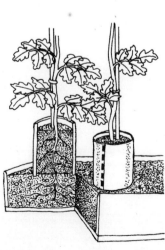

When growing by ring culture, the base aggregate is kept constantly moist either manually or by some automatic method. The compost in the rings will consequently remain moist by capillary absorption and should not need to be watered. However, liquid feeds are given via the compost, because it is in this that most of the fine roots form which are adapted to absorb nutrients. Those that take up water form lower down in the aggregate.

Growing Directly in the Greenhouse Soil When plants are grown directly in the greenhouse soil, it should be prepared in much the same way as an outdoor site. However, farmyard or other animal manures should not be used. These are liable to introduce pests and diseases, which under cover multiply rapidly. Proprietary dried sterilized products made from animal manures are all right, and so is well-fermented garden compost that has reached a temperature high enough to destroy pests, diseases, and weed seeds.

Growing Round The Year For the cold greenhouse the hardy spring-flowering bulbs and corms are started in autumn, and so are the 'prepared' types for flowering in a heated greenhouse. From about February onwards, the many summer and autumn-flowering bulbs and other storage organs are started into growth. Seed sowing of both bedding and greenhouse plants also begins at about this time. Nearly all tender shrubs should be pruned after flowering if there is any doubt about when this should be done. For winter and early spring-flowering pot plants for the frost-free greenhouse, another important sowing period is from about June to August.

General Routine Management

CONTROL OF TEMPERATURE is usually the first consideration in greenhouse management. It must be kept within the limits suitable for the well-being of the plants. Excessively high temperatures are just as much to be avoided as very low ones, and in all cases wide fluctuations can be very damaging. Generally, plants prefer to be cool when the weather is dull and at night. Active growth cannot take place without light and it is then that warmth can be utilized as a source of energy to aid the chemical reactions that take place in plant growth.

It is during good light conditions too, that water and plant nutrients can be taken up and used by plants. The rule, then, is to be moderate in WATERING AND FEEDING during winter when plants are growing slowly. Dormant plants may not need water at all and should certainly not be fed, and the colder the conditions the more restraint is needed. In summer, however, actively growing plants demand generous treatment and their roots should be kept constantly moist. This means neither waterlogged nor bone dry. Both LIQUID AND FOLIAR FEEDS can be applied, preferably in moderate concentrations but often.

Another general rule is to keep down the HUMIDITY of the air in winter when conditions are cool, and to do all that is possible to maintain a nicely moist air when it is hot in summer. Damp conditions in winter promote the growth and spread of various moulds and mildews. In summer a damp atmosphere reduces the rate at which plants lose moisture from their foliage, and hence the need for watering. In summer the greenhouse should be frequently damped down when it is very warm. This means splashing water about the floor and keeping the staging moist. It is usual to have some sort of moisture-retaining material on the staging (see page 169). Since water absorbs heat as it evaporates, damping down also helps keep the house cool.

VENTILATION is important too in keeping down temperature, and to give some air circulation which deters fungoid diseases. The ventilators of the greenhouse should be used with regard to the prevailing wind direction and to ensure that air is freely admitted – but not a gale-force wind. Too great an airflow will hasten drying out.

Sometimes in summer if the weather is poor, and particularly in autumn, it may be necessary to close the ventilators early in the afternoon to retain what warmth has been trapped from the sun. This is especially necessary when the more tender plants are grown.

Proper SHADING in summer is absolutely vital. Many beginners neglect this task and may lose a house full of plants in a few hours. An unshaded house, especially if its owner has forgotten to open the vents, can reach temperatures exceeding 48°C (120°F), which will upset even tropical plants and will soon shrivel temperate ones. For years green shading has been used, but in recent years this has been shown to be completely the wrong colour; white is the best choice.

An excellent new type of shading material is Coolglass electrostatic paint. This can be applied to the glass by means of a spray or on a soft brush. It has the curious property of resisting rain, but it can be wiped off with ease when dry (by means of a duster tied around a broom). It is white and reflects back heat rays, though allowing rays useful to plant growth to pass through it.

Blinds can be used instead, but if they are allowed to touch the glass on the outside, heat absorbed from the sun can be transferred directly to the glass and the cooling effect will be lost. Badly fitted blinds may make the house hotter – as also can green shading. Shading may need attention quite early in the year if early-flowering decorative pot plants are grown. Even from February onwards, strong sunshine can make temperatures shoot up.

Hygiene is also an important consideration in the greenhouse.
The basic principles of watering described above are generally well known. However, it is not so often realized how important it is to always use *clean* water for greenhouse irrigation. It is not unusual for gardeners to use water collected from roofs and gutters in the mistaken belief that rainwater must be good for the plants. In fact such water usually is a veritable 'soup' of pest and disease organisms, weed seeds, slime-moulds and algae. It is pointless to use clean sterilized seed and potting composts if you ruin their benefits by applying contaminated water. If lime-free water is needed for lime-hating plants like primulas, azaleas, and plants that naturally grow in acid woodland soils or peaty areas, collect clean rainwater in clean bowls or other vessels and store it in a clean container provided with a tightly fitting lid.

Strict cleanliness is always vital in the greenhouse. Dead or decaying plant material and sickly plants must be promptly removed and burnt. A daily check must be made for pests or diseases, paying special attention to underneath leaves where the signs often first appear.

Automation in the Greenhouse

All greenhouse gardeners will find some forms of automation helpful, but it is especially valuable to those who have to be away from home all day. AUTOMATIC WATERING is usually given first consideration and there are many systems now available. It is an advantage to have a mains supply of water in the greenhouse, although some systems can use water from a storage tank which is filled with a garden hose when necessary.

One method of CAPILLARY WATERING uses a layer of grit or sand kept moist by means of wicks dipped into a tank of water, which is kept topped up by a ball valve. Plants in plastic pots are then pressed into the grit or sand so that the compost in which they grow makes good contact via the drainage holes in the pots. Water will then pass from the sand into the compost automatically as required by the plants' roots. In recent years, this system has been greatly improved by replacing the sand or grit layer with a special type of porous plastic fibre matting. This can be spread over a layer of polythene on the greenhouse staging or floor. It is lightweight and can be washed and put away in autumn, and it can be cut with scissors to fit any size or shape of staging.

The flow of water can be very accurately controlled by ELECTRICAL SENSORS which operate an electromagnetic water valve. The best of these is photoelectric and will supply water according to the intensity of the sunshine falling on it. It can be worked from a low-voltage transformer so that there is no need for mains electricity to be connected to the greenhouse if this is inconvenient. Other sensors work by evaporation of moisture from a porous block or from a special surface between electrical contacts. These too control a magnetic water valve. Where there is mains pressure, these systems can also operate misting jets for overhead watering or automatic damping-down.

VENTILATION can be very effectively controlled by temperature. A non-electrical device, which works by the expansion and contraction of a special compound in a piston, is very convenient. However, one such device has to be fitted to each vent. Thermostatic electric fans are also highly efficient, but are best operated in conjunction with some form of automatic watering or damping down in summer, otherwise the greenhouse may dry out very rapidly.

EXTERIOR BLINDS can be controlled by photoelectric cells, but these are rather expensive to install and have to be custom made. PEST CONTROL using vaporizing chemicals has also been semi-automated, but pests may become immune to the pesticides and it is possible to inhale the harmful vapours.

Most forms of HEATING equipment are thermostatically controlled, even if only to some extent. They include solid-fuel hot water systems. Wick-type oil heaters have also been thermostatically controlled, but so far not very efficiently, and there is risk of fumes. Electrical heating can be extremely accurately controlled thermostatically.

Cloches and Frames

Cloches The name is derived from the French word for 'bell', owing to their original shape – still sometimes used. No vegetable garden is complete without a few cloches, but they are now usually in the form of 'tent', 'barn' or 'tunnel' shapes. Cloches are used to give protection against excesses of wind, wet and cold, and also often against animal pests. Glass cloches will trap a considerable amount of the sun's heat and help you to produce much earlier crops and enable the growing of more tender plants outdoors. However, since a great deal of warmth is rarely required or desirable, plastic cloches have become very popular owing to their light weight, portability, easy storage and unbreakability. Tunnels of polythene supported on semicircles of wire are very useful for covering rows of crops in the vegetable garden.

The cloche can often be useful, too, in the herbaceous border to protect the more tender perennials, or those that are liable to rot during a wet winter. Tent or barn cloches can be turned on their side to give wind protection to delicate young plants.

The vegetable-garden soil for a cloche site should be well prepared: remove all weeds and make it friable and moisture-retaining, so that it will not be necessary to remove cloches for watering. Water will penetrate through the soil after draining from their roofs, and keep the roots of the plants moist. Before winter and early spring sowings, the cloches should be placed in position a few weeks beforehand to allow the soil to warm up and to become merely moist rather than to remain wet after rainfall.

Left: a barn cloche provides excellent protection for all kinds of crop, and is easy to move. Far left: polythene tunnel cloches are useful for rows of strawberries, spring-planted lettuce, and early plantings of peas and runner beans. The polythene sides may be raised to allow watering and air circulation.

Frames A frame can be considered as a miniature greenhouse and used as such, taking over much of the work usually done in a greenhouse proper. It can certainly be used to grow most plants which do not grow very tall, and consequently can save much valuable space. In addition it can be used for raising bedding plants, for seed-sowing and other propagation, and the storage of dormant plants. Frames can be economically warmed with electric soil-warming cables, which widens their scope even further. They then also become ideal for growing winter salads and for forcing. Heated frames can also be used in a greenhouse as a propagator or for accommodating small tropical plants.

There are many frame designs, but modern ones tend to be lightweight and easily portable, usually being made from aluminium and glass. Plastic frames are also available, but these need firm anchoring to make them windproof and are not so warm. For most greenhouse work, the frames are best sited on the north side of the greenhouse and adjacent to it. Too much sunlight is often a disadvantage for frame

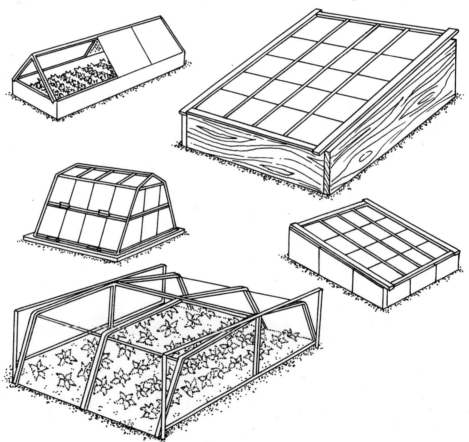

Right: five different types of garden frame, which may be made of aluminium, plastic, wood or bricks.

growing, unless the frame is to be used for winter crops, but a portable frame can be moved about according to the season's requirements.

The top of the frame is called the 'light'. This is either hinged or can be slid to one side and removed entirely. It should have a good slope to allow condensation and rain to run off. The sides may be transparent, or constructed of concrete blocks, bricks, sheet metal or timber. It is also possible to place lights over a pit dug in the ground. Frames with metal sides should have the sides lagged with expanded polystyrene sheet or cellular plastic in winter to keep them warmer. Where a large area of frame space is needed to take over much greenhouse work, roller frames are very convenient. These have sides of concrete blocks and lights that can be slid aside on nylon rollers at the touch of a finger.

POPULAR GREENHOUSE ORNAMENTALS

Name	Description	Flowering time	Height	Sow/plant	Minimum temperature	Cultivation
Abutilon hybrids	Maple-like foliage, bell-shaped flowers various colours. Perennial. Flowers first year	June–Oct	60–90cm (2–3ft)	Sow March 21°C (70°F)	Frost free	Easy. Shade in summer but not in winter. Can be cut back early spring to keep neat
Abutilon megapotamicum	Climber with lantern-shape flowers, red and yellow. Patio in mild areas. Perennial	May–Oct	1.8–2.4m (6–8ft)	Plant spring	Frost free	Slight shade, airy greenhouse, keep moist. Needs support but can be grown as shrubby pot plant if growth restricted
Agapanthus	Neat grassy foliage. Large umbels of blue or white flowers. Perennial. Good for patio pots	July–Aug	60–75cm (2–2½ft)	Plant spring	Frost free	Hardy in mild places. Slight shade. Tubs or large pots. Keep moist in summer
Aphelandra squarrosa	Perennial evergreen. Cream veined foliage. Unusual yellow flowers	June–Nov	60–75cm (2–2½ft)	Plant any time	10°C (50°F)	Slight shade. Moist atmosphere. Water well in summer but sparingly in winter
Asclepias curassavica	Perennial shrub with clusters of red-orange flowers first year. Summer patio plant	June–Sept	60–120cm (2–4ft)	Sow March 21°C (70°F)	Frost free	May die back in winter in cold conditions but new growth appears in spring. Slight shade. Water well in summer
Asparagus species	Several grown for evergreen feathery foliage. Some bushy, others trailing. Patio in summer	Flowers insignificant, some have showy berries	30–90cm (1–3ft)	Sow March 21°C (70°F)	Frost free	Very slight to slight shade. Moist in summer. Trailers are good for hanging baskets
Beloperone guttata	Evergreen shrub with unusual shrimp-like pinkish flowers	Almost the year round	45–60cm (1½–2 ft)	Plant any time	7°C (45°F)	Good light brings out best colouring, but will grow in slight shade. Good house plant
Bougainvillea glabra	Climber or wall shrub with brightly coloured bracts. Suitable for patio in pots for summer	June–Sept	90cm–2.4m (3–8ft)	Plant spring	7–10°C (45–50°F)	Can be kept short and shrubby by vigorous pruning in February, otherwise train on supports or along wires
Browallia speciosa	Perennial pot plant with violet-blue flowers in abundance	Summer onwards. Winter in warmth	45–60cm (1½–2ft)	Sow early spring 21°C (70°F)	10°C (50°F)	Slight shade in summer, full light in winter. Best if young plants are frequently raised from seed
Calceolaria (herbaceous)	Very popular biennial pot plants with masses of showy pouch-like flowers. Patio, after risk of frost only	December to spring depending on sowing time and variety	15–45cm (6in–1½ft) (dwarf and tall types)	Sow May–July 18°C (64°F)	Frost free	Keep moist and shaded in summer. Watch for aphids. Keep cool and shaded during flowering. Discard plants after flowering is over.
Campanula (various species)	Biennials and perennials with blue or white bell-shaped flowers. Patios in summer	May–Sept	Varies with species, some erect some trail	Sow or plant spring. *C. isophylla* cannot be sown	5°C (41°F)	Most prefer slight shade. 25cm (10in) pots for biennial *C. pyramidalis*. Baskets for *C. isophylla* and *C. fragilis*

POPULAR GREENHOUSE ORNAMENTALS

Name	Description	Flowering time	Height	Sow/plant	Minimum temperature	Cultivation
Capsicum annuum	Annual pot plant with orange to red bright berries.	June–Nov	15–30cm (6in–1ft)	Sow spring 18–21°C (64–70°F)	5°C (41°F)	Easy plant. Several varieties with different shaped berries. 12.5cm (5in) pots. Discard when no longer decorative
Carnations	Perpetual flowering types grown in greenhouse. Perennial	Almost year round	45cm–1m (1½–3½ft), short and taller varieties	Plant Dec–March, April–July, Sept–Nov	5°C (41°F)	Buy plants from specialist grower. Usually full instructions supplied. Airy conditions. Good light
Cineraria	Very popular biennials. Pot plants with richly coloured daisy flowers in profusion	Dec–spring according to sowing time and variety	30–60cm (1–2ft)	Sow May–July 18°C (64°F)	Frost free	Keep cool and shaded in summer. Watch for aphids. Keep moist and cool and shaded when in flower. 12.5–17.5cm (5–7in) pots
Citrus (various species)	Orange, lemon, grapefruit and others. Evergreen. Scented flowers waxy white. Patio in summer	April–June or longer	Varies, up to about 1.5m (5ft)	Plant any time. Best not grown from seed	5°C (41°F)	*C. mitis* is dwarf. Best bought as pot plants from specialist. Slight shade and lime-free compost. Give iron feed occasionally
Clivia miniata	Perennial with bold strap-like leaves and umbels of large orange showy flowers	March–May	45cm (1½ft)	Sow spring 21°C (70°F) or pot any time when not in bloom	Frost free or 5°C (41°F)	Takes over 3–4 years to flower from seed. Water well in summer, little in winter. Slight shade. 25cm (10in) pots
Cobea scandens	Perennial climber usually grown as annual, with purple bell flowers. Good patio climber	June–Oct	1.8m (6ft)	Sow spring 18°C (64°F)	5°C (41°F)	Good light. Need support of canes or trellis. Quick growing. A white flowered form is sometimes available
Coleus	Very popular colourful foliage plant grown as annual	Flowers usually removed	30–60cm (1–2ft) or taller	Sow March 21°C (70°F)	10°C (50°F)	Good light brings out best colours. Keep moist. 12.5cm (5in) pots. Dwarf type 'Sabre' can be specially recommended
Cuphea ignea	Perennial grown as annual. Neat pot plant with many small tubular scarlet 'flowers'	Nearly all the year	30cm (1ft)	Sow March 21°C (70°F)	5°C (41°F)	Easy but prone to red spider attack. Slight shade or bright conditions. 12.5cm (5in) pots
Eccremocarpus scaber	Perennial climber grown as annual. Orange to yellow showy flowers. Good patio climber	June–Oct	90cm–1.8m (3–6ft)	Sow Feb–March 21°C (70°F)	Frost free or 5°C (41°F)	Good light to partial shade. Ultimately 20–25cm (8–10in) pots needed. Give support of canes or trellis. Hardy in very mild areas.
Exacum affine	Neat annual for pots with scented purple flowers	July–Sept	15–30cm (6in–1ft)	Sow Feb–March 21°C (70°F)	10°C (50°F)	Transfer several seedlings to each 12.5cm (5in) pot. Slight shade. Choose varieties noted for scent and compact habit

POPULAR GREENHOUSE ORNAMENTALS

Name	Description	Flowering time	Height	Sow/plant	Minimum temperature	Cultivation
Francoa ramosa	Perennial with long stems of white to pink flowers	May–July	45–75cm (1½–2½ft)	May–June 21°C (70°F)	7°C (45°F)	Slight shade. Grow on in frames in summer. Final 12.5cm (5in) pots. Repot yearly
Fuchsia	Very popular pot plants. Can be trained in various ways. Good patio plants	May–Nov	Varies with type and training	Best potted early spring	Frost free to 10°C (50°F) for trained specimens	Slight shade in summer and cool and moist airy conditions. Buy from specialist and note varieties suited to different forms of training
Gerbera	Perennial with large beautiful daisy flowers in subtle colours. Ideal cut flower	July–March	45cm (1½ft)	Sow spring 21°C (70°F), plant spring–summer	7°C (45°F) for winter flowers	Slight shade in summer, but good light in winter. 12.5–17.5cm (5–7in) pots. Pull flower stems for vases – do not cut
Grevillea robusta	Handsome foliage plant with ferny foliage. Good summer patio plant	Evergreen in warmth	Usually up to 1.8m (6ft), but a tree naturally	Sow March 21°C (70°F)	7°C (45°F)	Slight shade. Will survive frost free but loses foliage which grows again in spring. Keep moist. Acid compost
Gynura sarmentosa	Perennial foliage plant with purple-red velvety leaves, small orange flowers	Jan–March	45–60cm (1½–2ft)	Plant any time but preferably spring	10°C (50°F)	Slight shade in summer and high humidity. 5in pots. Keep foliage dry if possible. Repot April–May
Heliotropium peruvianum	Best grown as annual pot plant. Sweetly scented violet flower heads	June–Oct	30–60cm (1–2ft)	Sow March 21°C (70°F)	7°C (45°F)	Slight shade, airy but humid. Keep moist. Stop seedling to obtain bushy plants. May need cane for support
Hibiscus	Shrub usually grown as annual in the variety 'Southern Belle'. Enormous plate-sized flowers, white to rose	Summer–autumn	60cm–1.2m (2–4ft)	Sow Feb 21°C (70°F)	10°C (50°F)	Good light. 8 to 10in pots, the smaller for more dwarf forms. Stout cane for support. Keep moist and well fed
Hoya carnosa	Evergreen climber with scented pinkish flowers	July–Oct	90cm–1.8m (3–6ft) or more	Plant spring	Survives frost free or 7°C (45°F)	Slight shade. Humid in summer. Little water in winter. Best effect when trained up into roof so that flowers hang
Hydrangea	Popular shrubs with pink to blue flower heads	April–Sept	45–90cm (1½–3ft)	Plant spring	Frost free	Under glass plants are usually grown from cuttings and gently forced for early bloom. Lime-free compost
Impatiens	Popular perennial pot plants often best as annuals. White to salmon coloured flowers	Almost year round	15–45cm (6in–1½ft)	Sow March 21°C (70°F)	10°C (50°F)	Good light to slight shade. Keep moist. 5in pots. Compact F_1 hybrid varieties are best. Some can be bedded out for summer

POPULAR GREENHOUSE ORNAMENTALS

Name	Description	Flowering time	Height	Sow/plant	Minimum temperature	Cultivation
Ipomoea	Annual climber with large blue, pink or red flowers. Good patio plant	July–Sept	1.8m (6ft)	Sow March 21°C (70°F)	10°C (50°F)	Grows poorly if too cool. Good light to slight shade. Keep moist. 5in pots or several seedlings in larger pots or small tubs
Iresine herbstii	Perennial foliage plant with rich purple-red leaves	—	45cm (1½ft)	Plant spring	13°C (55°F)	12.5cm (5in) pots. Water well in summer. Keep slightly moist in winter. Good light
Jacaranda mimosaefolia	Handsome foliage plant with fine ferny leaves. Good for patios	—	Reaches several feet (tree)	Sow March 21°C (70°F)	10°C (50°F)	Will survive frost free but loses foliage – grows again in spring. 7in pots to small tubs
Jasminum polyanthum	Vigorous climber with scented white flowers	Nov–April	90cm–1.8m (3–6ft)	Plant March	7°C (45°F)	Can be grown in small pots as young plants. Canes or trellis for mature plants. Slight shade. Keep moist
Lapageria rosea	Evergreen climber with showy waxy tubular flowers, rose, pink, white. Patios in mild areas only	July–Oct	To 1.8m (6ft)	Plant spring	Frost free	Shade. Good for north facing lean-to. Grow on wall trellis. Keep moist. 10in pots to small tubs
Lobelia tenuior	Large flowered form of border types good for patio in summer	May–Oct	15cm (6in) with spreading habit	Sow spring 21°C (70°F)	10°C (50°F)	Grow several seedlings to each half pot or hanging basket. Does not like chill. Slight shade
Maranta	Several species of beautiful foliage plants. Oval leaves	Small flowers of no consequence	15–30cm (6in–1ft)	Plant spring	10°C (50°F)	Will survive almost frost free but then deteriorates severely. Grows again in spring. Shade. Moist. Humid
Mimosa pudica	Strange touch-sensitive plant. Leaves fold up with dramatic effect	Small flowers in summer	15–60cm (6in–2ft)	Sow March 21°C (70°F)	10°C (50°F)	Usually grown as annual. Young plants most sensitive. 12.5cm (5in) pots Slight shade. Keep moist
Nerium oleander	Handsome evergreen shrub with single or double flowers freely produced. Rose, pink, white. Good patio plant	June–Oct	60cm–1.2m (2–4ft)	Sow spring (3 years to flower), pot spring	Frost free to 7°C (45°F)	Can be stood out in summer but keep nicely moist. Water sparingly in winter. Can be cut back to keep neat shape
Nierembergia caerulea	Low shrub with purple *Campanula*-like flowers	June–Sept	15–30cm (6in–1ft)	Spring 18°C (64°F)	5°C (41°F)	Put several seedlings in each 12.5cm (5in) half pot. Use twiggy sticks for support. Good light. Little water in winter

POPULAR GREENHOUSE ORNAMENTALS

Name	Description	Flowering time	Height	Sow/plant	Minimum temperature	Cultivation
Passiflora	Several species with exotic flowers, vigorous climbers	June–Oct	Up to 1.8m (6ft) or more	Spring 21°C (70°F)	Frost free to 10°C (50°F)	*P. caerulea* is hardy but rampant under glass. A fine species is *P. quadrangularis* (tender). Good light. Trellis for support. Humid
Pelargonium	Popular 'geranium' and 'ivy' types, and regal or show types. Good patio plants	Some nearly year round in warm greenhouse	15–60cm (6in–2ft) according to type	Sow F_1 hybrid 'geranium' seed in Feb 21°C (70°F), pot in spring	Frost free to 10°C (50°F)	New F_1 hybrid seed can be highly recommended. Good light. Keep on dry side in winter. Do not be afraid to cut back straggly plants
Peperomia	Attractive foliage plants. Several species. Some trailers. Catkin-like 'flowers'	Varies with species	15–45cm (6in–1½ft) according to species	Pot in spring	5–10°C (41–50°F)	Most like shade, moisture and good humidity. *P. sandersii* is more difficult, needing good warmth
Pilea cadierei	Pretty foliage plant with silver marked leaves	—	15–30cm (6in–1ft)	Pot in spring	7–10°C (45–50°F)	Use 12.5cm (5in) pots. Slight shade. Water with Epsom Salt solution occasionally to avert magnesium deficiency
Primula	Several species with pretty flowers. Also Polyanthus. Good for patios	Dec–April	15–45cm (6in–1½ft)	Sow Jan–May	Frost free to 5°C (41°F)	Up to 12.5cm (5in) pots. *P. obconica* perennial. Cool, moist, slight shade. Some species cause a skin rash on allergic people
Saintpaulia	Well known house plant. Blue, white and pink	Almost year round	To 15cm (6in)	Sow Jan–Feb 21°C (70°F)	13°C (55°F)	Good for warmed cases or frames in the greenhouse. Moist, humid, shade, but not excessive
Strelitzia reginae	Famous Bird of Paradise flower. Strange bloom like bird's head. Showy	Often twice yearly when established	90cm (3ft)	Sow spring 26°C (79°F)	Frost free to 7°C (45°F)	Much easier and more hardy than generally realized. Takes several years to flower from seed. Slight shade. Little water in winter
Streptocarpus	Perennial pot plants with lovely trumpet flowers. Various colours	May–Oct	30cm (1ft)	Sow Feb 21°C (70°F)	7°C (45°F)	Plants, such as John Innes hybrids, can be bought from specialists. Slow from seed. Warmth, shade, humidity
Thunbergia alata	Annual climber or trailer with striking black-centred orange flowers in profusion	May–Sept	To 90cm (3ft) or more	Sow spring 21°C (70°F)	5°C (41°F)	Discard seedlings with eyeless or pale flowers. Watch for red spider. Good for hanging baskets, also train up canes

POPULAR GREENHOUSE CROPS

Name	Particulars	Minimum temperature	Cropping time	Suitable varieties, sowing/planting time, cultivation hints
Asparagus	Forced shoots	16–18°C (60–65F)	Winter	Most varieties. Take crowns from outdoor bed in November. Plant in boxes under staging. Keep dark with black polythene. Cut shoots when 15–20cm (6–8in) long
Aubergine	All varieties; also called Egg-plant	10°C (50°F)	Summer to autumn	Money Maker, Long Purple. Sow Feb 18°C (65°F). Pot on to 18–20cm (7–8in) pots. Sow later in unheated greenhouse. Good light. Keep moist. Allow 3–4 fruits per plant
Beetroot	Round varieties	10°C (50°F)	Spring	Boltardy, Globe, Early Bunch. Sow Feb–March 10°C (50°F) or slightly higher. Good light. Useful catch crop when fitted in with others. Also for frames
Cabbage	Early varieties	Frost free	May onwards	Hispi, May Star (F_1 hybrids). Sow Jan–March 7°C (45°F) in seed trays, then prick out into small pots, subsequently planting outdoors. Cloche initially
Cape Gooseberry	Fruits size of large cherries. Golden, sweet	16°C (60°F) or higher	Summer– autumn	Golden Berry. Sow March onwards 18°C (65°F). Pot on to 25cm (10in) pots. Grow like tomato but do not stop or deshoot. Good light.
Carrot	Early salad types	7–10°C (45–50°F)	April–May	Amsterdam Forcing, Early Nantes, Parisian Rondo. Sow Jan onwards 10°C (50°F). Good light and ventilation. Useful catch crop
Cauliflower	Early varieties	7–10°C (45–50°F)	May–June	Varieties listed in catalogues for sowing under glass Sept–Oct, or Jan–Feb. Good light and ventilation. Sow at about 10°C (50°F). Move to ground soil or 25cm (10in) pots or troughs
Celery	Self-blanching early varieties	5°C (41°F) in greenhouse	August	Golden Self-blanching. Sow early in year 10°C (50°F) and transfer plants to cloches or frames in April about 15cm (6in) apart. Remove protection about May. Plants are self-blanching provided planting is close
Chicory	Salad 'chicons' and newly introduced varieties resembling cos lettuce	10°C (50°F) for roots. Frost free for others	Winter– spring	For forcing: Witloof, Red Verona. Cos type: Sugar Loaf, Crystal Head. Lift roots from outdoors in autumn. Plant in boxes under staging and cover with black polythene. Cut when chicons are 15cm (6in) long. Sow from October–March in cold greenhouse. Cos types: no blanching
Chinese Gooseberry	Elongated fruit about golf ball size. Delicious grape flavour. Wall shrub	Frost free but hardy	Autumn	The plant is *Actinidia Chinensis*. Plant against lean-to wall and train along. For best fruiting a male plant should be planted near. This can be outside the greenhouse. Good light and ventilation. Prune in Feb. Cut back young plants to encourage spreading shoots
Climbing French Bean	Green and purple podded types. Stringless	13°C (55°F)	April–May	Earliest of All, Purple Podded, Violet Podded, Romano, Coco. Sow Feb 18°C (65°F). Transfer to small pots then grow on like tomato 38cm (15in) apart. Stop laterals and secondary lateral shoots at third joint. Pick young for best flavour. Good light, warmth and humidity. Good pre-tomato crop

POPULAR GREENHOUSE CROPS

Name	Particulars	Minimum temperature	Cropping time	Suitable varieties, sowing/planting time, cultivation hints
Cucumber	House and frame varieties	18°C (64°F) or higher	Usually early summer to autumn in home greenhouse	Telegraph, Butchers, Sigmadew, Conqueror. New all female types: Femspot, Rocket (F_1 hybrids). Sow and grow as for tomato, but train along wires 15–20cm (6–8in) apart (usually 5 wires) stretched end to end of greenhouse. Stop laterals two leaves on from where fruit forms. Remove male flowers from non all-female vars. Slight shade. Keep moist, humid, not waterlogged
Dwarf French Bean	Green and white podded varieties. Stringless	10°C (50°F)	April–June	The Prince, Masterpiece, Kinghorn (white). Sow Feb–March 16°C (60°F). Put 3–4 plants in each 20cm (8in) pot. Use canes or wires and twine for support
Fig	Several varieties	Frost free	2–3 crops per year	Brown Turkey is most popular: grow similar to outdoors, but best trained on wall of lean-to. Plants in pots can be stood out in summer
Grape	Green, purple and golden varieties	Frost free, rising to 21°C (70°F) when flowers set	Summer	Black Hamburgh, Royal Muscadine (both good for limited pot culture), Foster's Seedling (green), Primavis Frontignan (golden), both for unheated house. Plant Jan. There are many specialist books on vine culture which should be consulted for full details; also growers' catalogues
Herbs	Various	Frost free	Spring and almost year round	Most types and varieties. Lift mint roots from garden in November. Plant in pots or boxes to yield leaves in spring. Sow parsley in July and give glass protection from Oct onwards. Most other herbs can be pot grown
Leek	Outdoor varieties	Frost free	Winter	Most varieties can be sown under glass Feb–March and subsequently planted out with cloche protection for early cropping
Lettuce	Mostly cabbage types. Few cos types	Frost free or warmer	Winter–spring	Kweik (sow Aug for Dec cropping), Kloek (Oct for March), Sea Queen (Aug to Feb for Dec to April), Emerald (as for Sea Queen), May Queen (Oct to March for March to June), Little Gem (cos type), sow Feb onwards, Winter Density (cos), sow autumn. Good light and ventilation. Watch for grey mould fungus
Melon	Casabar and Cantaloupe	10°C (50°F) or warmer	Summer to Autumn	Unheated house: Sweetheart, No Name, Dutch Net, Burpee Hybrid. Heated house: Superlative, Hero of Lockinge, Emerald Gem. Germinate and grow as for tomato in early stage. Train along wires as for cucumber. Pollinate female flowers. Keep about 3–4 fruits per plant. Good light
Mushroom	'Cultivated' varieties	10°C (50°F)	At least 3 crops per year	Mushroom spawn is sold by specialists. There are now also ready-planted containers supplied with full instructions. A good under-staging crop. Light is not essential and neither is blacking out
Mustard and cress	White and curled varieties	13°C (55°F)	year round	Curled Cress, White Mustard. Sow cress 3–4 days before mustard. The so-called 'mustard' is usually rape seed. Warmth. Good light. Good frame crop

POPULAR GREENHOUSE CROPS

Name	Particulars	Minimum temperature	Cropping time	Suitable varieties, sowing/planting time, cultivation hints
Peach, Nectarine, Apricot	Early unblemished fruit	Frost free	Summer–autumn	Peach: Hale's Early, Duke of York. Nectarine: Lord Napier, Early Rivers. Apricot: Moorpark. Best trained against wall of sunny lean-to. Plant and grow much as outdoors, but pollinate flowers under glass with fluffed cotton wool on a stick. Good humidity, but do not spray blossom or fruit
Potato	First early varieties	Frost free	Late Dec onwards	Sprout seed potatoes in autumn then transfer to compost in boxes or pots (about one per 25cm (10in) pot) 7.5cm (3in) deep. Slightly warmed frames are better
Radish	Summer radish varieties	Frost free or warmer	Almost year round	Saxerre (round), Red Forcing (round), French Breakfast (elongated white/red). Sow Jan onwards 10°C (50°F) or warmer for early development. Good catch crop
Rhubarb	Forced early	7°C (45°F) or warmer	December onwards	Lift crowns in November and leave until well frosted on ground surface. Transfer to boxes of peat in greenhouse and keep completely dark. Forced roots cannot be replanted after cropping
Seakale	Swiss chard (forced shoots)	Frost free or warmer	Winter	Lift mature roots in autumn and plant the crowns in soil under the staging. Black out with black polythene and keep moist
Strawberry	Unblemished large fruits, early crops	Frost free	April–May	Buy plants from specialist grower. Grandee is good cold house variety. Suppliers often give growing instructions. Under glass hand pollinate flowers as described for peaches, etc. Bright conditions and airy
Sweet Pepper (Capsicum)	Pimiento, green and red fruits	10°C (50°F)	Summer–autumn	Ace, Canapé and other F_1 hybrids. Sow as for tomatoes and grow similarly in early stages. 20cm (8in) pots adequate with stout cane support. Good light. Keep moist. Remove some young fruits if overcrowded
Tomato	Red, yellow, large and small vars. Fancy shapes	10°C (50°F)	Summer–autumn	Alicante (excellent generally), Kingley Cross (small G.H.), Big Boy (large fleshy fruit, fine flavour), Yellow Perfection (yellow exquisite flavour), San Marzano (elongated Italian type), Gardener's Delight (small, tangy for garnishing), Supercross F_1 (good disease resistance). Sow February onwards according to G.H. temp. 18°C (65°F) for germination. Keep in small pots first. Transfer to 25cm (10in) pots, troughs or ring culture. Train clockwise around strings. Deshoot shoots forming between leaf and main stem. Good light. Even watering, temperature and feeding. Slight shade when fruiting
Turnip	Early forced	Frost free	Spring	Snowball, White Milan. Sow early Feb 10°C (50°F). Thin to 10cm (4in) apart. A little extra warmth (warming cables) gives quicker development and better flavour. A good frame and catch crop

Rock Gardens

Rock plants are ideal for today's small gardens, for a rock garden can be fitted into the smallest back yard, and there is scope for as many as 50 carefully chosen rock plants to be grown in an area no larger than a billiard table. Even without a garden, rock plants can be enjoyed in old sinks, windowboxes, or pots on balconies belonging to flats and maisonettes. What is more, they can be of interest all year round, especially if those with handsome foliage, such as sempervivums and silver-encrusted saxifrages, are included.

Nowadays the cost of rock and the high price of carting it, as well as the time involved in having to hand-weed such creations, have helped influence a change in fashions. Less bulk of rock tends to be used, limiting it to bold bluffs from which flow gentle slopes of soil mixture covered with stone chippings.

Raised beds and artificial stone sinks have become popular, for these are constructed to lift the little plants to table height, where their intricate beauties can be enjoyed closer to eye-level. Cultivation is easier too, making bending unnecessary – a boon if you are elderly or crippled.

What Are Rock Plants?

It has been said, unfairly, that an alpine plant is a rock plant for which a nurseryman can charge extra. For practical purposes the terms 'rock plant' and 'alpine' are synonymous. At one time an alpine was strictly a plant that grows wild in the Alps. But a rock plant or alpine need not be a native of any mountain region. Appropriate-looking, neat, small hardy perennials or shrublets are just as likely to come from lowland areas, such as *Morisia hypogea* from sunny Mediterranean shores.

Siting A Rock Garden

Deciding to use rock plants because 'nothing else will grow there' spells disaster. Sprawling clumps of arabis, aubrietia and yellow alyssum tolerate all sorts of conditions. But to grow choicer, more exciting rock plants means choosing a place in the sun, open and airy without being draughty. If possible, avoid sites hemmed in by shrubs and trees as their falling autumn leaves will smother the plants. If you live on the shady side of the street, there is no need to do without rock plants, provided that your selection of plants is limited to shade-tolerant kinds including ramondas, haberleas, certain primulas and ferns.

Choosing the Right Type of Rock

Rock provides a traditional setting, and in some areas, such as the Cotswolds, parts of Devon and Yorkshire, it is literally on your doorstep. To choose rock from another locality would look odd. When buying the best, the choice lies between limestone, which is unsuitable for the few plants that hate lime, or sandstone. Natural weathered or water-worn pieces, such as grey Westmorland limestone, are costlier than angular quarried pieces. These rocks, particularly Cotswold and Dorset limestones, bear faint markings called 'strata' created by sand or shell grit laid down millions of years ago in layers, and eventually hardened into stone. To copy nature, all pieces of rock must be laid so their strata run in the same direction, preferably slightly sloping or horizontally.

It is a disadvantage to have larger pieces than one person can handle; a strong sack for hauling pieces of rock and a crowbar for levering them up are helpful. Gardeners unable to lift heavy weights find a light, pumice-like rock called tufa very handy. Finger-size holes can be bored into it very easily and some rock plants, such as silver-encrusted saxifrages, haberleas and drabas, can be planted in these, ramming the roots securely with soil compost.

Construction
A sloping site is ideal. On flat ground excavate shallow paths and valleys and throw up the soil into shaped heaps. A rise of 30–45cm (1–1½ft) to every 1.5m (5ft) of ground gives a nicely proportioned result.

Rock plants cannot tolerate waterlogging. On heavy clay and other soils liable to hold stagnant water, a 7.5cm (3in) layer of broken bricks and stones should be spread approximately 38cm (15in) below the surface. The soil is then put back over this, mixing it with other materials to improve its texture, and taking out weeds. Sandy soils, gravels and clays can be mixed with ½–⅓ (by bulk) their amount of leafmould or peat. Clays need a similar proportion of coarse sand (never builders') or weathered ashes mixing in. Add about four handfuls of fortified hop manure to every bucket of soil, a half bucket of hop manure to every barrowload. On no account use farmyard manure.

Rocks Placing The largest rocks occupying the most prominent places, called keystones, should be put in first, anchoring each by partly burying it. Smaller pieces are then used, building outwards from these keystones. Pieces laid next to one another should be of similar thickness, colour and character, with strata markings running parallel. Rocks laid sloping slightly inwards, into the soil, allow water to trickle towards the plants, which also means that less soil will be washed away. Use a rammer, such as a dibber, to firm soil around the rocks.

A terraced effect can look attractive, each terrace with 'walls' 15–30cm

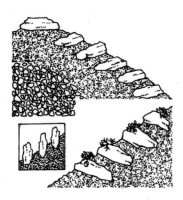

Below: rocks should be placed in the mound of soil built up over a layer of broken bricks or stones to ensure adequate drainage. Inset: the wrong way to lay rocks. Below right: rocks laid correctly, sloping slightly backwards.

Right: terraced rockwork has the retaining rocks placed to give a stepped effect.

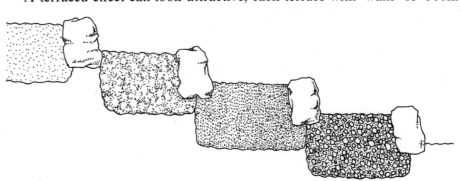

(6–12in) high. Harsh surfaces of newly broken rock soon develop moss and look as old as the hills, if painted with dilute liquid manure or milk.

Screes
Many choice rock plants, especially the tight cushions of douglasias, drabas and silver saxifrages, grow well in imitation screes. A natural scree is a mound of shattered rock fragments, broken from solid rock by weathering, which has accumulated on a mountain slope. It is extremely free-draining and low in soil content. A good garden scree mixture consists of 50 per cent stone chippings and small pieces of rock ranging from walnut to fist size, 20 per cent peat or sieved leafmould,

20 per cent sieved loam, and 10 per cent coarse sand. The natural temptation is to make a scree too rich.

Screes can be arranged either by piling up the scree mixture to create slopes, or holes can be excavated 30–38cm (12–15in) deep and filled with a 13–15cm (5–6in) depth of drainage material – pieces of brick, stones, or gravel, topped by 23–25cm (9–10in) of the scree mixture. The surface is then covered with a layer of stone chippings.

Alpine Lawns

A flat area, especially where a rock garden merges into other features, often harmonizes pleasantly when treated as an alpine lawn. A lawn which is never mown, is not even composed of grasses, and where stones are an advantage sounds unlikely. But these are characteristics of alpine lawns, inspired by alpine meadows in the Swiss Alps.

They are easier to make than conventional rock gardens. Soil is prepared in a similar way and flattish-topped stones are partly buried at intervals to take the heaviest tread, giving a boulder-strewn moorland appearance. This is a convincing way of using smooth, roundish stones.

A three-tier system is the most effective. The basic planting consists of low carpeting plants such as *Acaena microphylla, Antennaria dioica, Cotula squalida, Dryas octopetala*, alpine phloxes and mossy saxifrages. These carpeters form the lowest tier, with dwarf bulbs such as tiny narcissi, tulips, scillas and crocuses growing up through them. These constitute the second tier. The third consists of a very few carefully chosen taller plants which lend height. Suitable dwarf conifers are the Noah's Ark Juniper, *Juniperus communis compressa*, and *Picea albertiana conica*. Other appropriate tall plants include *Linum arboreum, Pulsatilla vulgaris, Sedum populifolium* and *Penstemon scouleri*.

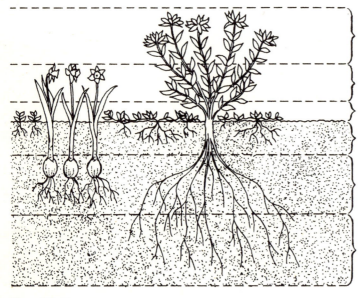

Occasional taller rock plants and dwarf shrubs (Layer Three)

Dwarf flowering bulbs (Layer Two)

Low, spreading ground cover plants (Layer One)

Shallow roots of low, ground cover plants (Layer One)

Roots area for dwarf bulbs (Layer Two)

Roots of taller rock plants and dwarf shrubs (Layer Three)

Left: a cross-section of an alpine lawn showing the different layers of roots in a three-tier planting.

Dry Walls

Wherever ground has to be cut away or built up, leaving an unstable, almost vertical bank, a rock-built dry wall will not only prevent soil from slipping down, but will provide homes for flowers. A free-standing dry stone rampart, visible from both sides, may be constructed too, consisting of two parallel back-to-back walls with a 15–23cm (6–9in) soil-filled cavity between them. These walls are called 'dry' because cement is not used. For details of their construction see pages 374–5.

Raised Beds

Raised beds are extremely popular and may be made any convenient shape, though usually rectangular or square. Their walls, about 60cm (2ft) high, may be constructed of rock in similar fashion to dry walls. Artificial stone blocks are often used, but old wooden railway sleepers are most favoured. One sleeper laid edgeways gives a height of 25cm (10in). Beware of making the beds so wide that the plants in the middle are out of reach; between 90cm and 1.2m (3–4ft) is best.

Rubble should be used to fill the bottom third of the space inside the sleepers or blocks, to provide sufficient drainage, topped up by a soil mixture chosen to suit particular plants. A general-purpose mixture consists of equal parts soil, peat and sand. A scree mixture, or a peaty mixture for lime haters, are other possibilities. The entire 'table top' can be landscaped with rocks and have trailing plants such as phloxes cascading over the sides.

Peat Beds

Where the local soil contains sufficient lime to kill lime-hating rock plants, such as most Asiatic gentians and miniature rhododendrons, these plants may be nurtured in special beds. They can be constructed in a similar manner to raised beds. The sides are best built up of thoroughly moistened peat blocks sold for the purpose, which may also be built into terraces on banks. Fill up the hollow centre with a mixture of peat and leafmould, plus about a quarter of lime-free soil or sand.

Sinks or Troughs

Old stone sinks have become very fashionable as homes for the tiniest rock plants and convincing, cheaper versions can be made by covering glazed sinks with hypertufa cement. There is a tendency to overdo drainage when preparing these sinks. John Innes potting compost No 1 mixed with a few stone chippings makes a good growing medium.

Planting

Provided the soil is neither waterlogged nor frozen, theoretically any rock plant grown in a pot can be planted out at any time. In practice, however, it is dangerous to move hairy and silver-leaved plants in winter when their foliage becomes clogged with moisture. Slightly tender species such as crassulas and any which die down to their roots for the winter are also safer planted between May and July. These include several campanulas, dwarf delphiniums, geraniums, oxalis, and primulas.

Plants lifted from open ground are best moved in spring soon after growth recommences. A trowel is the most practical tool to use. Firm planting is half the secret of green fingers. Never move a dry plant; water it the night beforehand.

General Cultivation

Weeds and Hygiene Provided roots of persistent weeds such as dandelions and creeping thistles are thoroughly removed when the rock garden is made and annual weeds, like groundsel and shepherd's purse, are kept cleared so they cannot seed, weeds need not be a major problem. The worst weeds are tiny annual grasses, and small, white flowered bitter cress. Avoid all chemical weedkillers. An old dinner fork is most useful. Dead leaves and stems must be picked from plants to prevent them rotting and spoiling the crowns.

Feeding Giving rock plants manures and fertilizers is like giving a baby a pork chop. Hop manure is the safest pick-me-up, pricked in with a handfork during spring, when a topdressing of fresh compost is also helpful. Screes need 'topping-up' with more chippings once a year, preferably in autumn, tucking chippings under cushion plants to keep their necks dry.

Watering Although rock plants insist on thorough drainage, most enjoy plenty of water during spring and early summer, coinciding with melting snows in the mountains. On very hot days, they benefit from regular hosing, with a very fine mistlike spray directed over them.

Winter Protection During autumn and winter, alpines in their natural habitat are normally tucked away dry and safe under snow. Silvery, hairy and woolly foliage kinds such as androsaces, drabas and helichrysums should be protected in the garden by glass propped over them. Remember to label those kinds which disappear below ground for winter *before* they do so. These include dwarf delphiniums, codonopsis, dodecatheons, oxalis and some primulas.

Pests Fortunately, rock plants suffer from few pests. Pyrethrum is a safe insecticide to use against caterpillars, aphids, etc. Slugs can be controlled by means of slug traps (see page 36) or you can try herbal slug-killers. Look out for ants nesting in cushion plants and use an antkiller. When plants wilt unexpectedly, suspect bugs eating their roots, especially vine weevil grubs in pots. Dig up affected plants and search out the culprits, and water neighbouring plants with lindane solution.

Propagation

One of the great pleasures in growing rock plants is raising your own cheaply, principally from seeds, cuttings, root cuttings and division.

Seeds Many rock plants can be raised from seeds sown in pans or pots, using John Innes seed compost, with plenty of drainage crocks in the bottom. Easy kinds include alpine poppies, *Papaver alpinum*, *Erinus alpinus*, tiny aquilegias such as blue *bertolinii*, purply-red *Dianthus deltoides*, small primulas such as pink *frondosa*, and *Pulsatilla vulgaris*. Fluffy seeds, like pulsatilla, are best covered with coarse sand or stone chippings. Others simply need 'sugaring over' with silver sand through a fine sieve. Seeds are sown in winter and the pots stood outdoors to be frozen, which will help them germinate in the spring.

Cuttings Some plants do not 'come true' from seed. For instance, red-flowered sun roses or helianthemums might produce yellows, pinks or oranges from seed, whereas plants from cuttings are identical to their parents. Cuttings can be taken from most alpines except bulbs. Sideshoots from 1.3–7.5cm ($\frac{1}{2}$–3in) long make good cuttings, trimmed cleanly with a sharp knife just below a stem joint. They are firmed into holes made with a pencil into sandy compost in pots, which are watered and stood in a greenhouse or frame, out of direct sunshine. June is a good month to take cuttings.

Root Cuttings For these, you should remove pieces of root, usually no thicker than a pencil lead, and 1–2cm ($\frac{1}{2}$–1in) long. They are buried, vertically and the right way up, in holes in sandy compost in a pot so that their tops are just below the surface. This is done in February or March, keeping the pots in a frame. Suitable plants include dodecatheons, pulsatillas, morisia, erodiums and *Primula denticulata*.

Division Digging up and splitting up clumps of rock plants into smaller pieces, each with roots attached, is the easiest means of increasing them.

Though possible at almost any time, spring, after flowering, and early autumn generally prove best. Kinds increased by division include sisyrinchiums, geraniums, armerias, campanulas and sedums. Some rock plants produce offsets – rosettes of leaves with their own roots which can be removed from the parent plants. Sempervivums, androsaces and saxifrages are examples.

After-Care Seedlings with two pairs of true leaves are pricked out, either singly into 5cm (2in) pots or 2.5cm (1in) apart in pans, again using seed compost, or a scree mixture for difficult kinds. Cuttings are treated similarly when well rooted.

Water Gardens

Water can be used with good effect both formally and informally, and introduces a unique range of plants for growing on and in it, as well as many that luxuriate in boggy conditions.

Water has considerable benefit for wildlife; birds in particular will benefit from being able to drink and bathe in it at all times of the year. A pool or fountain sited in view of the main living-room windows will give endless pleasure. Properly planted and stocked with fish, the water should not need to be changed but will remain permanently clean, fresh and free from infestation by mosquitoes or other pests.

Aquatic plants, especially waterlilies, prefer still water and an open, sunny position well away from trees and falling leaves that foul the water. Trees such as the weeping willow, though intimately associated with water, should not be planted without careful consideration. An average weeping willow will reach about 7m (25ft) in height and have a spread of over 9m (30ft), and its ramifying roots are a potential threat to drains, greenhouse foundations and other garden features.

Types of Pool

In gardens where there is a boggy patch it is possible, with earth-moving equipment, to excavate a pool about 1m (3ft) deep at the centre with a gentle slope at the margin. It can be lined with puddled clay or with one of the pool liners described below.

For the very small garden, tubs are an excellent means of growing water plants, as shown in the diagram (page 192). There are plastic pools and those of fibre-glass bonded with resins available in a variety of shapes and sizes; shaped on a mould, these have a rigid structure and are ready to install.

Sheet Liners Larger pools can be lined with sheeting made of PVC (also available reinforced with a network of terylene fibres) or of BUTYL RUBBER, which has an almost indefinite period of use, being very resistant to both mechanical damage and ultraviolet rays. The liner should be laid on a bed of sand, sawdust or fine soil free from sharp stones, once the hole has been dug to the required shape: 38cm (15in) deep for a small pool and 45–60cm ($1\frac{1}{2}$–2ft) deep for a larger one.

Shelves, on which plants can be stood in suitable containers, are introduced at intervals round the margin at a depth of about 23cm (9in). The walls of the pool should have a 20° slope, i.e. 7cm (3in) horizontally for every 23cm (9in) in depth. To calculate the size of a

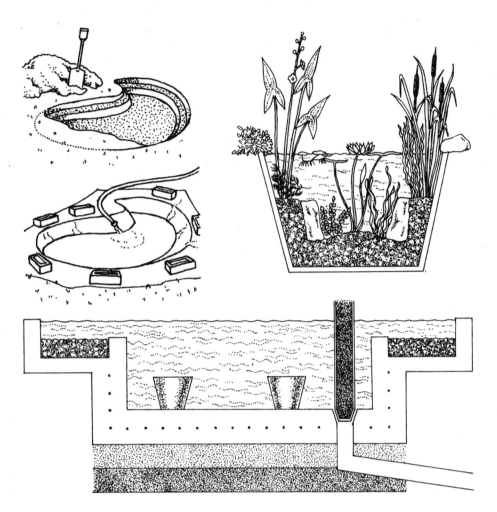

Far left: after excavating the site for a plastic-lined pool (above), put down a layer of sand, sawdust, or fine soil. The sheeting is held in place temporarily by bricks (below), while water is gently run in from a hose.

Left: a water garden in a tub is a good way of growing water plants even in a small garden.

Left: a cross-section of a concrete pool, showing the outlet pipe and marginal troughs for shallow water plants.

liner, regardless of the shape, size or position of the marginal shelves, add to the length of the hole twice its maximum depth, and repeat the same calculation for the width. For example:

A hole 300cm (10ft) long and 110cm (7ft) wide with a depth of 45cm (18in) will require a liner 390cm (13ft) long and 300cm (10ft) wide. When laying a liner it should first be stretched over the hole and loosely held in place with a few smooth, rounded stones. Water is then introduced and its weight presses the liner down until it is moulded into shape. Any surplus material at the edges can then be removed, leaving enough to allow the edge to be secured and disguised by stones, soil and edging plants.

Concrete Linings A firm foundation is essential for concrete pools or the lining may easily become cracked. Clay subsoils need to be covered with a layer of ash and light sandy soils topped with a 10cm (4in) layer of hardcore. The method of construction usually adopted is shown in the diagram on this page.

Use fresh Portland cement, mixing thoroughly one part by bulk with two of coarse sand and three of clean aggregate in sizes ranging from 50mm ($\frac{3}{16}$in) to 2cm ($\frac{3}{4}$in). For large pools, heavy gauge netting is needed as reinforcement, and wooden shuttering will be required to support the walls until the concrete sets. The base and side walls should be 12–15cm (5–6in) thick which, allowing 13cm (5in) for soil, enables you to fill the pool with water to a depth of 38cm (15in). The walls of the marginal troughs need be no more than 10cm (4in) thick, and

Right: winter buttercup (Eranthis)

Above: colourful annuals and bedding plants

Right: an exhibition chrysanthemum

Above: Fritillaria meleagris (snakeshead)   *Right: collerette dahlia with pink collar*

Left: *water garden at Malahide Castle*

Above: *spring-flowering Anemone apennina*

should be deep enough to contain 7.5cm (3in) of soil and the same depth of water.

Maturing Concrete pools constructed, filled and left to stand for the winter can be planted the following spring. Alternatively, a proprietary compound can be applied to seal the pores and neutralize or lock in the harmful alkalines that would otherwise leach out of the new concrete.

Planting

The best effect is produced if only about one-third of the water surface is obscured with plants. Planting before filling the pool simplifies the task. Plant firmly and just about cover the crowns using fertile soil, and then anchor with stones. Let in just enough water to cover the crowns and subsequently add water in small quantities as the plants grow. For direct planting into filled pools, or into natural lakes, the plants should be put into plastic planting crates or suitable substitutes and lowered into the water to a depth that should be increased in stages as growth proceeds. Only soil of low fertility needs additional fertilizer, given either as bone meal when mixing the compost or in sachets specially formulated for aquatic plants.

Fish

No pool is aesthetically or biologically complete without fish. A number of different kinds are suitable for a small pool; choose them from a reputable dealer. To allow room for future growth, healthy breeding pairs should be introduced at the rate of 5cm (2in) of fish per 930sq cm (1sq ft) of surface area. The fish should not be introduced until the plants are well established, i.e. at least three weeks after planting.

Keeping the Water Clean

After planting, algae will rapidly appear and spread, turning the water green or rusty-red but, as the aquatic plants grow, shading the water and lowering the level of nutrients, a point of balance will be reached and the water will clear. If algae are particularly troublesome a harmless proprietary chemical is available for their control.

To neutralize any impurities in the water it is essential to have enough submerged oxygenating plants to absorb surplus carbon dioxide and replace it with oxygen. A small pool requires more oxygenating plants than a large one where there is a greater surface area for air exchange. About 24 will be needed in a pool 2.4 × 1.8m (8 × 6ft) in area.

Pool Maintenance

At the first signs of pest attack spray forcibly with water under pressure; dislodged and in the water, pests are an easy prey for fish. Pools must be kept free of weeds, and of decomposing leaves, especially in the autumn. In cold weather toxic gases can accumulate under the ice, but by keeping an area of the surface ice-free, possibly with an electrical pool heater, you will remove this risk. After about three years the most vigorous plants will have to be divided and replanted.

Hardy Waterlilies (*Nymphaea*)

Choice of Varieties The size of pool and the depth of water must be taken into account when deciding which varieties to grow. Waterlilies, especially those with yellow flowers, resent root disturbance and may not move easily: they may take some time to become established and at

Left: crocus 'Cream Beauty'

first produce flowers not true to colour. A visit in the summer to a nursery specializing in aquatic plants is advisable so that a personal selection can be made.

Flowering and Foliage Plants for Pools

These will grow in shallow water up to 15cm (6in) deep and in moist soil above the water level

Acorus calamus 'Variegatus'	Variegated sweet flag	Leaves iris-like, aromatic, striped cream	Green flowers on conical spadix	Division
Calla palustris	Bog or water arum	Creeping rootstock with dark, heart-shaped leaves	White spadix, June–July, 30cm (1ft). Red berries	Division
Caltha palustris and its forms 'Alba', white, and 'Plena', double	Marsh marigold	Bold tufts of round, dark green, shiny leaves	Large buttercup-like flowers. March–May 23–38cm (9–15in)	Division or seed
Cyperus longus	Sweet galingale	Tufts of grassy foliage	Dark brown umbels 60cm–1.2m (2–4ft)	Division or seed
Glyceria maxima (or *aquatica*) 'Variegata'	Variegated reed, sweet or meadow grass	Broad grass-like leaves striped white and yellow 45–60cm (1–1½ft)	Greenish spikelets	Division
Hypericum elodes	Marsh St John's wort	Creeping stems with woolly leaves	Flowers yellow, August, 15cm (6in)	Division

Prefers boggy soil or standing water only a few cm deep

Iris laevigata		Narrowly sword-like leaves, deciduous to 45cm (1½ft)	Flowers violet-blue, 10–15cm (4–6in), June	Division or seed
Juncus effusus 'Spiralis'	Corkscrew rush	Stems spirally twisted, evergreen, 45cm (1½ft)	Flowers insignificant brown clusters, June	Division
Lysichitum americanum	Yellow skunk cabbage	Leaves with silvery sheen, 1m (3½ft)	Flowers yellow, arum-like, March, 30cm (1ft)	Division or seed
Mentha aquatica	Water mint	Leaves fragrant, ovate, hairy	Flowers lilac in whorls. Aug–Sept 30–90cm (1–3ft)	Division, cuttings or seed
Menyanthes trifoliata	Bog bean	Creeping stems with trifoliate, glossy leaves	Flowers in clusters, white, May–July 30cm (1ft)	Division
Mimulus ringens	Lavender water musk	Leaves dark, narrow, 75cm (2½ft)	Flowers lavender to violet blue, 2cm (¾in) Aug–Sept	Division or cuttings
Myosotis scorpioides (*palustris*)	Water forget-me-not	Leaves evergreen, spoon-shaped, 23cm (9in)	Flowers dainty blue, April–July	Cuttings or seed
Pontederia cordata	Pickerel weed	Leaves ovate, glossy on stiff stems	Flowers purple-blue, terminal spikes, 45–75cm (1½–2½ft)	Division or cuttings
Ranunculus lingua 'Grandiflorus'	Great spearwort	Leaves ovate, blue-green, on erect stems 60–75cm (2–2½ft)	Flowers yellow, 5cm (2in) in loose sprays	Division
Sagittaria latifolia	Duck potato	Leaves ovate, light green on 60cm (2ft) stems	Flowers white, three-petalled, 2cm (¾in), July–Aug	Detach and replant tubers in spring
Scirpus (*Schoenoplectus*) *tabernaemontani*	Zebra rush 'Zebrinus'	Soft stems banded green and white, 90cm (3ft)	Insignificant brown flowers	Division
Typha minima	Dwarf reedmace	Leaves pale green, grass-like, 45–75cm (1½–2½ft)	Flower-heads brown, 3cm (1¼in), June–July	Division

Bulbs

Cultivation of most bulbous plants is simplicity itself. Each bulb
contains not just the potential of the flower to come but the flower
itself. It takes relatively little care and even less knowledge to bring that
flower to perfection. But if bulbous plants are to be a part of the garden
scene year after year, without having to be replaced each season, it is
wise to understand how these plants work.

What is a Bulb? A 'bulb' is, in general terms, an underground food
storage organ from which roots, leaves and flowers spring forth, and the
layman's use of this word embraces several different forms of
subterranean parts, derived from different parts of the plant. These may
be true bulbs, corms or tubers.

A BULB consists of fleshy leaf-bases or modified leaves wrapped tightly
around each other with a vestigial flower inside. A CORM consists of a
thickened stem base, at the top of which is a bud, from which new shoots
and roots will arise. A TUBER is a thickened root or underground stem.
The connection between them is that they are all attempts by the plant
species which have evolved them to survive in difficult climatic conditions,
and knowing this can help us to cultivate them more successfully.

Requirements of Bulbs Most bulbs come from areas with a more or less
extreme climate, having a short period of rain and a baking summer:
the 'Mediterranean climate' of mild moist winters followed by hot dry
summers, which occurs not only in the Mediterranean region, but also
in California, South Africa, parts of Australia and much of what used
to be called Asia Minor, always produces quantities of bulbous plants.
Here are the origins of the typical growth pattern: root development in
early autumn (lift an established daffodil in August and the new roots
will already be starting), shoot-tips above ground around Christmas,
flowering in early spring, followed by rapid seed production and a quick
return to the protection of the soil.

All this helps to explain the cultivation methods we should adopt for
bulbous plants. It shows the need for planting as early as possible and
why those end-of-season offers, however apparently attractive, are
usually a mistake. It indicates, too, something of soil and weather
requirements – too much moisture in winter, a problem particularly with
heavy soils, may do harm. Summer heat can seldom be too great, and a
thorough ripening of the bulb is essential for good flowering the
following year. So too is that generally disregarded period between
flowering and the dying off of the leaves. During this time, the green
leaves are busily building up the subterranean food store and actually
laying down the foundations for the next flower: aggressively tidy
gardeners who itch to cut down the leaves before they have finished
their job are diminishing future pleasures for a very temporary
satisfaction. All these plants are naturally perennials and attention to
their inbuilt needs ensures that they can go from strength to strength.

Many gardeners naturally associate spring with *the* season of bulbs –
the first crocuses to open and the lengthening daffodil stems are some of
the most heartening signs that winter really is being left behind.
However, it cannot be over-emphasized that there are bulbs for all
seasons, indeed for every month of the year, which can be grown
without greenhouse protection.

Bulbs for Winter and Early Spring Flowering

January is the most difficult month; although February can be just as cold, by then the days are beginning noticeably to lengthen and this is one of the greatest spurs to plant growth. Nonetheless, the first month of the year is represented by the CROCUSES. *Crocus imperati*, an attractive little species from Italy, has purple-streaked buff outer petals and bright purple inner ones, and *C. laevigatus fontenayi*, which has similar flowers, can even be open on Christmas day. The genus *Crocus* is a huge one, with wild species ranging from Spain, through the Mediterranean countries and the Alps into Asia Minor and Iran. Because they come from areas having light soil, they need good drainage at their roots.

Crocuses are small plants with thin leaves unsuitable for naturalizing in rough grass. However, because the foliage is not obtrusive and disappears by early summer, they are one of the few groups of bulbs that can be planted in rough-cut lawns. Best for this are the robust Dutch varieties and the more delicate and earlier *C. tomasinianus* which can be increased freely from seed.

Crocuses are a fine example of plants to grow in as large a quantity as can be afforded; it is almost impossible to have too many. The smaller kinds are suitable for rock gardens or raised beds or for planting in drifts in front of shrubs, and so long as they are left alone, they will increase in beauty and in numbers from year to year. 'Left alone', however, means not only by people. Birds and mice can be a maddening problem, the former shredding the flowers and the latter eating the corms underground. Depredations by sparrows are particularly unpredictable, but where the habit occurs, the larger yellow crocuses are the most likely to be attacked and it is best not to grow them. Mice or voles are more likely to be a serious problem in rural areas; dust the corms with a proprietary animal repellent. Small-mesh wire netting, laid 5cm (2in) above the corms and 1cm ($\frac{1}{2}$in) beneath the soil surface should protect any especially prized stock.

Many SNOWDROPS, on the other hand, are originally natives of moist woodlands. Our common (and perhaps truly native) February-flowering snowdrop is *Galanthus nivalis*, from which has been developed a number of varieties, ranging from the old 'cottage-garden' double forms to unusual (and expensive) varieties such as the oddly eared *G.n.* 'Poculiformis'. People always expect these snowdrops to be the first flowers of the year: as described above, crocuses gain this distinction, though other species of snowdrop from south-east Europe extend the season in both directions. *G. corcyrensis* from Corfu and the Grecian *G. reginae-olgae* push up their flowers through the fallen leaves of autumn, to be followed by *G. graecus* and *G. byzantinus* in January. One of the finest and easiest of the exotic snowdrops is *G. elwesii* which flowers with our native snowdrop in February and early March. It has broad grey-green leaves and fine large flowers on stalks up to 20cm (8in) high.

Most snowdrops are bought in autumn as dry bulbs but they all establish themselves better if it is possible to obtain and separate the growing plants as soon as they have finished flowering in early spring. This is the best time to increase your own stock; while it will gradually happen naturally (provided that soil and site are suitable), the process will be greatly speeded up if you lift the clumps every three years and divide carefully, separating each bulb with its roots and leaves intact.

Less common than the snowdrops, but no less delightful, are the

SNOWFLAKES. *Leucojum vernum* has flowers like chubby, bell-shaped snowdrops; they appear in February and March. Its surprisingly large daffodil-like bulbs again like woodland conditions: moist soil and some shade, though they appreciate sun as long as the soil does not dry out. The so-called Summer Snowflake, *L. aestivum*, in fact flowers in April and May. It is a taller plant, growing as high as 60cm (2ft), and enjoying moist semi-shade: its delicate green-tipped white flowers are held in heads of half-dozen or so. This is a very easy plant to cultivate, and it is a pity it is not grown more often.

A difficulty similar to that with snowdrops is establishing dry tubers of the WINTER ACONITE, *Eranthis hyemalis*, whose golden flowers are borne from February onwards on naked stems, each flower being surrounded by a ruff of pale green bracts. A few specialist nurseries now offer growing plants in the spring. These are more expensive than tubers but losses are far less likely. Again, winter aconites are naturally plants of leafy soil in woodland: in gardens, therefore, clumps left undisturbed under shrubs are most likely to succeed and increase.

Flowering with the snowdrops are the first of the IRISES. These early rock-garden or front-of-the-border types are very different from the splendid great 'flags', such as the Bearded Irises described under HERBACEOUS PERENNIALS on page 132. They may not perform well year after year when treated as perennials although bulbs can be bought every year and the plants treated as annuals. Nevertheless, while the stored flowers will give of their best when the time comes, it seems a pity for the plant not to be encouraged to go on producing them from year to year.

In spite of this, however, it is generally true that one of the earliest of the bulbous irises, *I. danfordiae*, a 10cm (4in) tall yellow-flowered species from the Taurus Mountains of eastern Turkey, must be planted annually. After flowering once, the bulbs often break up and, although sending up leaves in subsequent years, often fail to flower again.

Fortunately others are less temperamental. Also flowering in February or even earlier is *I. histrioides*; it grows to about the same height as *I. danfordiae*, and has surprisingly large flowers of rich clear blue that appear before the leaves. This is a much more reliably perennial plant that *I. danfordiae*, as is the group of lovely varieties derived from *Iris reticulata*. The species itself grows up to 23cm (9in) high, and bears deep mauve flowers with gold on the falls (the three outer petals). Several forms are now available, such as 'J. S. Dijt' (reddish-purple), 'Cantab' (clear pale blue) and 'Harmony' (sky-blue with bright yellow on the falls). Most catalogues also offer a mixture of varieties which are lovely for massing with low shrubs and other bulbs.

Later bulbous irises for borders include the so-called Dutch, Spanish and English types. All are planted in autumn and begin to send up leaves almost at once, though they do not flower until late May, continuing to do so throughout June. Dutch and Spanish Irises are frequently grown as cut flowers in frames or in a cold greenhouse, but can be grown just as well outdoors without protection in well drained soil. English Irises are more robust and in rather heavier soil make fine, truly perennial plants, as long as they are protected from attack by slugs. They associate particularly well with the early flowering dwarf gladioli mentioned below.

In small clumps in the rock garden or in great swathes under shrubs in a light soil, few spring sights are more rewarding than those provided by CHIONODOXAS (commonly known as Glory of the Snows) and SCILLAS, close relatives of the native English Bluebell. These both bear flowers that are, in most species, a clear, very bright, sky-blue colour, though in chionodoxa this is modified by a white eye. The best species to grow are *Scilla sibirica* and *Chionodoxa luciliae*. There are also white and rather dingy pink forms of these bulbs.

Like a rather large, single-flowered chionodoxa is *Ipheion uniflorum* (sometimes listed as *Brodiaea*, *Triteleia* or *Milla uniflora*). This is one of the most unduly neglected of bulbs – perhaps only needing a popular name to make it catch on – despite the fact that it is inexpensive and easy to grow. From low clumps of leaves which appear before Christmas, the starry, violet-scented Dresden-china-blue flowers appear over a long season from March to May. *Ipheion* thrives whether in half-shade or sun in a well-drained soil. There are varieties with paler blue and white flowers.

Shades of blue are repeated with most of the GRAPE HYACINTHS (*Muscari*). These all bear spikes of small bell-shaped flowers but some have the disadvantage of having rather coarse leaves. They need a long growing season; the leaves begin to appear in September but the flowers do not follow until March or April. Nonetheless, they make a fine, bright display when in flower, and are easily grown plants which increase freely. *M. botryoides* has a worthwhile white-flowered variety, 'Album', while *M. comosum* and *M. moschatum* bear unusual tufts of sterile florets at the top of their flower spikes in May.

Spring-flowering anemones which, unlike the summer and autumn-flowering types, are grown from root tubers, require a rich, moist but well-drained soil. They include the small, early-flowering *Anemone blanda*, available in white, pink, mauve or pale blue forms. The taller, mid-season *A. coronaria* hybrids, commonly known as Poppy Anemones, have single flowers in the De Caen varieties and double or semi-double ones in the St Brigid varieties; these are available with red, white or blue flowers, which are marked with white in some forms. *A.* × *fulgens* bears its scarlet flowers with their white centres as late as May. The last two anemones generally deteriorate quite quickly, and should be replaced with new stock after about three years.

Plants which are less easy to grow inevitably, and unfairly, have a fascination which the common sorts lack. Two related genera come into this category – though not all are difficult – and also into the category of mid-spring flowering bulbs. These are the FRITILLARIES (*Fritillaria*) and DOG'S-TOOTH VIOLETS (*Erythronium*). Of the former, perhaps none is more charming than our own Snake's-Head, *Fritillaria meleagris*, with its nodding chequered purplish bells. Now a rare plant in the wild in Britain, being found in a few moist meadows, it is cheap to buy and easy to establish in similar situations such as an old orchard. More unusual are the 30cm (12in) high *F. acmopetala* and *F. pyrenaica* with brownish-green flowers. Even odder is *F. camtschaticus* from Alaska with near-black flowers, while *F. persica* has fine spikes of grape-bloomed purple bells. Quite different in appearance is the old cottage-garden Crown Imperial (*F. imperialis*), which in its orange, red and yellow forms is the most stately of spring bulbs, growing up to 1.2m (4ft) high under the right conditions. It needs limy well-drained soil in half-shade when it will readily put up its strange flower heads. Each head is composed of a ring of pendulous tulip-shaped flowers surmounted by a tuft of spiky leaves, standing proudly at the top of the stout bare stem which rises from whorls of narrow leaves lower down. Crown Imperials are very much a part of the flower paintings by the Dutch old masters.

Erythroniums like damp positions in semi-shade and a leafy soil: it is important that the tubers do not dry out before planting. The popular name of Dog's-Tooth Violet refers to the little pointed tubers of the European *Erythronium dens-canis*; this produces lovely spotted leaves and starry, nodding flowers of a clear pink. More robust – up to 30cm (1ft) high – are two varieties of Californian species. Both *E. revolutum* 'White Beauty' and *E. tuolumnense* 'Pagoda' (golden yellow) resemble small Turk's-Cap Lilies. These two flower in May.

While there are yet more small spring-flowering bulbs which can be discovered in specialist catalogues or in botanic and other gardens, the main display is generally bound to devolve upon the three great genera of *Narcissus* (daffodils and their relatives), *Tulipa* (tulips) and *Hyacinthus* (hyacinths) and their innumerable hybrid progeny. Both the wild species and the cultivated varieties have their place in every garden. As the first narcissi precede the earliest tulips by a short head – or a couple of weeks – we will begin by discussing these.

The earliest DAFFODILS are the small wild species which are often found growing, like crocuses in the Alps, through the melting snows of the high Spanish Sierras. Some are the so-called 'hoop-petticoats', almost all trumpet and no petal – *N. bulbocodium* and its tribe. 'Conspicuus' is the easiest and most robust of the cultivated varieties, but none is more than 15cm (6in) in height. They are therefore plants for sunny pockets in the rock garden which provide as much direct sunlight as possible and some frost and wind protection for flowers that are so precocious as to be out in late January or February.

Often as early as the first hoop-petticoats is the dwarfest typical daffodil, *N. asturiensis* (= *N. minimus*), also from Spain. This little gem is a perfect miniature only 7.5cm (3in) high; it needs and deserves a sheltered spot and protection against slugs.

March brings into flower a number of exciting little species varying considerably in form. Most odd is *N. cyclamineus*, with its long deep yellow trumpet and equally long petals swept back in exactly the same plane. This naturalizes readily in damp spots as, for instance, in a whole meadow at the Savill Gardens, Windsor Great Park. *N. triandrus albus* and *N.t. concolor* (Angel's Tears) and *N. canaliculatus* are examples of multiple flowered-heads; all are delicate little plants.

In recent years many fine hybrids have been raised by crossing taller species with dwarf ones, thus combining the grace of the wild plant with a rather, more robust habit. 'February Gold', 'Tète-à-Tète' and 'Peeping Tom' have *N. cyclamineus* as a parent and are excellent for naturalizing in grass, while 'Rippling Waters' is a robust, and easier, Angel's Tears hybrid. Gardeners interested in growing these hybrids and those who have a small garden but still wish to grow a range of daffodils should write to the specialist bulb growers, from whose catalogues they will get an idea of the large selection available, which increases all the time. As usual, the older hybrids are the least expensive.

Many other gardeners, however, expect their daffodils to be bigger, but no less various in colour and shape. The range for this type is now extremely extensive and for convenience, the hybrids are listed in the catalogues according to flower type by divisions, *1a* for example containing forms that have the big yellow trumpets of the 'typical' daffodil. Here the old 'King Alfred' is a prime example. Length of trumpet, colour of petals and trumpet (the same or contrasting colour) and even double flowers give an endless range of variations and everyone will have their own favourites. In the garden, care should be taken not to try to outshine the colour catalogues but to group similar, complementary colours and to consider the other March and April-flowering plants in the same part of the garden, in order to build up attractive colour schemes.

In borders, narcissi are best planted 12.5cm (5in) deep, as early as possible, in groups of between 10 and 20. They are also ideal for naturalizing in grass, when the bulbs should be planted a little deeper still. As they will have plenty of competition from the grass or other plants in such situations, it is false economy to buy old forced bulbs in quantity for this job. Colour combination should again be considered: a gradual blending effect of related shades can be achieved with about a hundred bulbs of, say, five varieties; a group of a variety with white flowers (such as 'Polar Ice') leading on to a cream-flowered one (such as 'Mount Hood'), then on to a soft yellow (such as 'Carlton') and so on. This is much more effective than either a random mixture or bold contrasts. Bulbs for naturalizing should be scattered in groups and planted where they fall to obtain a random, 'natural' effect. As always with bulbs, it cannot be over-emphasized that it is of vital importance not to remove the leaves after flowering but to let them die down at their own speed; this is to allow the foliage to feed the bulbs so that they will produce next year's flowers. An application of a foliar feed after flowering is an aid to this end, although it will add to your budget.

Discussion of TULIPS is bound to follow a similar pattern in that their season opens with the dwarf species and their hybrids and continues with the large garden varieties in all their diversity of colour and form. Tulips are not, generally, plants for naturalizing in grass (though on light warm soil this can be tried) nor are they so permanent as daffodils. Their shorter growing season – November is not too late to plant them – also makes them much better for spring bedding schemes.

The season begins with the Water-Lily Tulip *T. kaufmanniana*, which opens its flat white flowers, which are flushed with yellow and red on the outside, during the first sunny days of March or even at the end of February. This is followed by *T. greigii*, with orange-red flowers, notable for its lovely marbled leaves, and the much taller *T. fosteriana*, with huge scarlet flowers up to 23cm (9in) across. All now have many brilliant named varieties. Much more restrained for rock gardens are little gems such as the cream-yellow *T. batalinii*, the pink and white Lady Tulip (*T. clusiana*) and the many-headed yellow and white *T. tarda*. These are all plants that enjoy full sun and limy soil and, given these conditions, may go on flowering from year to year.

Big bedding tulips, for use from April through to late May, are available in every colour to complement whatever plants you choose for your spring bedding scheme – whether they are multicoloured polyanthuses, orange wallflowers or blue forget-me-nots. Again, you should look at the catalogues, remembering the scale and position of the area to be planted and in exposed spots avoiding those such as the gorgeous but heavy-headed peony-flowered doubles. Mendel, Darwin and Cottage Tulips have conventional bowl-shaped blossoms, whilst the Lily-Flowered varieties have delicately pointed petals and those of the Parrots are fringed and flamed. If they are to be grown in beds needed for summer annuals to follow at once, they should be lifted carefully and heeled in elsewhere to die down naturally. If then put out into the shrub border, a few will flower the following year, although most will take longer to build up their reserves again.

Although hyacinths are more usually grown indoors or in the greenhouse, it is also possible to grow them outdoors. When buying hyacinth bulbs for this purpose, do not choose those that have been specially prepared for forcing into early flowering in pots indoors, though you can plant old forced hyacinths outdoors in March or April after they have flowered, when they stand a good chance of recovering and flowering again year after year, if they are not disturbed.

Dutch hyacinths (*Hyacinthus orientalis* hybrids) are available in a wide range of colours, from pure white, through yellows, oranges, reds and pinks to blues and purples. The smaller Roman Hyacinths (*H. orientalis albus*) are available in white, pink and blue-flowered varieties, but these are best grown indoors.

Bulbs for Summer and Autumn Display
The ALLIUMS or ornamental onions offer great diversity of form between May and August, from the early dwarf *A. karataviense*, with broad grey-blue leaves and large round heads of pale pink flowers in May and June, and the mid-season *A. albopilosum*, 60cm (2ft) high, and bearing even larger globes of rosy-purple flowers from late June to the late-blooming *A. beesianum*, which bears its nodding, tubular blue flowers at the end of 23cm (9in) stems in July and August. All are easy to grow in light, well drained soil. *A. beesianum* is grown from a leek-like stem as it does not form a round bulb.

The ARUM family contains a number of attractive species, including the Monks-Cowls (*Arisaema*). These, together with members of the allied genus *Arisarum* are always worth a search through the specialist catalogues. South Africa is the original home of many of our summer and autumn bulbs, with the GLADIOLI taking pride of place. The big hybrids are magnificent just as the first, lower, flowers open, but these look shabby by the time the buds further up the stem have opened. For this reason, large gladioli are really best grown as a row in the kitchen garden and used for cut flowers. For general use, the smaller and more delicate Butterfly and Primulinus hybrids are to be recommended. They make good groups with shrubs and herbaceous plants and are especially useful planted among flag irises where they will give another later show on the same patch of ground. Gladioli corms usually have to be lifted in late autumn and gradually dried off for winter storage, but in sheltered areas many survive if left outside.

Whereas gladioli prefer a warm dry soil, LILIES need one that is deep, leafy and damp – though not waterlogged. Few plants are more lovely than lilies, and there are nearly 100 species and many hybrid strains to choose from. Lily bulbs are made up of leafy scales without a surrounding protective coat, so they dry out easily; also many of their roots are perennial. Because of this, they should be out of the ground for as short a time as possible and bought bulbs should be firm and plump. Those which produce roots from up the stem as well as from the base, such as *L. henryi* and *L. regale*, need the top of the bulb planted 10cm (4in) below soil surface while those without these stem roots are planted much more shallowly – the Madonna Lily (*L. candidum*), indeed, must have its tip just above the soil and is planted when dormant in August. All other lilies are best put in during October, or as soon as they are available.

Among the easiest and best are the Turk's-Cap (*Lilium martagon*), *L. regale* and, although not likely to last many years, the remarkable Golden-Rayed Lily (*L. auratum*) from Japan, which has great scented flowers, 20cm (8in) or more across, on stems up to 2.1m (7ft) high. Brilliant colours are provided by the Mid-Century, Harlequin and Bellingham hybrids.

In September and October two other bulbs of South African origin are predominant. These are the Belladonna Lily (*Amaryllis belladonna*) and *Nerine bowdenii*. Neither are true lilies, belonging to a related family, the *Amaryllidaceae*. Both send forth from leafless bulbs fine spikes of clear pink flowers – those of *Amaryllis* being bigger and heavier and marked with cream on the throat. They need a warm site against a wall, because not only do they flower late, but having done so, the leaves then appear and remain green over winter until the following May or June. The large bulbs should be protected with peat in badly frosted regions. Both these plants make splendid cut-flowers and are worth every effort. Like most bulbs, they need well-drained soil. When given the right conditions, they increase readily: unless flowering appears to decline, old clumps should be left undisturbed.

Related to *Amaryllis*, *Nerine* and the true lilies are the COLCHICUMS. These are sometimes erroneously called autumn crocuses (true crocuses are members of the iris family), and this causes confusion because *Crocus zonatus* (= *C. kotschyanus*) and a few other true crocuses flower in autumn, too. Colchicums have large, goblet-shaped flowers, usually in shades of pink, again emerging from the leafless bulbs (not corms as with true crocuses). *Colchicum speciosum*, with mauve flowers, and its double hybrid 'Waterlily' are two of the best. Other hybrids are available with flowers of different shades of mauve or purple, and there is a fine white form, 'Album'. All are good in shrub borders or naturalized in grass, where the huge flat green leaves do not look out of scale when fully developed in spring. All these autumn-flowerers are planted when dormant in mid-summer.

This season, as already mentioned, brings on plants such as crocuses and snowdrops which we always consider to belong to spring. It is also the main season for planting bulbs and so the cycle begins again; it is always moving forward and always giving pleasure.

Annuals, Biennials, and Half-hardy Annuals

For colourful displays in spring and summer there is nothing to beat hardy annuals, biennials and half-hardy annuals. They are easy to raise from seed and their cultivation generally presents no problems.

Most kinds are very adaptable and will thrive in any ordinary soil – the main requirement is good drainage. Some plants do have their particular fads – for instance, nemophilas (hardy annuals), *Digitalis* (foxgloves), primulas and violas (biennials), and begonias and impatiens (half-hardy annuals) prefer moist soil conditions. It is safe to say that all of these plants can be grown in full sun, and in fact the majority need an open sunny situation. Some which like partial shade include *Digitalis*, primulas and violas (biennials) and begonias (half-hardy annuals).

Annuals are sown, produce flowers and seeds, and then die all in the same year.

Biennials are sown one year, they flower in the spring or summer of the next year and then they die. Gardeners do, however, treat some perennial plants as biennials, such as *Bellis*, hollyhocks and polyanthus, discarding them after the first flower display.

Hardy Annuals

Uses Very often hardy annuals are grown in their own special bed or border to provide a riot of colour from May to September. One should aim for a reasonably large or bold group of each variety grown, at least 1×1m ($3\frac{1}{2} \times 3\frac{1}{2}$ft) and each group should be informal in outline. It is a good idea to plan an annual border on paper before sowing it, so that you can place each group for maximum effect.

Many annuals are excellent for cutting, and these could be grown in a utility area such as a vegetable plot. Dwarf annuals like nemophila are ideal for sowing in a rock garden or in window boxes.

Sowing Hardy annuals are generally sown in spring, where they are to remain for the rest of their lives, but some (see the chart on page 213) can also be sown in August or September for earlier flowering the following year. Prepare the seed bed as described in the chapter on TECHNIQUES (page 54). Then, if you are sowing a complete border or bed, mark the outline of each group with a trickle of sand. The seeds should then be sown in drills 15cm (6in) apart, within each group.

Thinning and Cultivation When the seedlings are large enough to handle, they should be thinned out to stand about 15cm (6in) apart in the rows.

Some of the taller annuals will need the support of twiggy hazel sticks or similar supports. These should be pushed in around the seedlings so that the plants grow up through them. Keep the young plants weeded and watered throughout the season.

Biennials

Uses The spring-flowering kinds, such as *Bellis*, wallflowers, *Myosotis* and polyanthus, are generally used in bedding displays, often in combination with bulbs, such as tulips and hyacinths.

The other kinds, both spring and summer-flowering, make excellent plants for a mixed border and should be mass planted for a good effect. Some, like Sweet Williams, make good cut flowers.

Sowing The seed is sown out of doors in nursery beds and details of seed-bed preparation and sowing will be found in the chapter on TECHNIQUES (page 54). The time to sow is May or June for most kinds.

Some kinds are best sown in seed trays in a cold frame: polyanthus, primroses, violas and pansies come into this category.

Transplanting and Aftercare Once the seedlings are large enough to handle easily, they should be transplanted to nursery beds where they can grow on. Set them out in rows about 30cm (12in) apart with 15cm (6in) between the plants in the rows. In October or November the young plants should be lifted from the nursery beds and planted in their flowering positions. Final planting distances are given in the chart on page 214.

Polyanthus sown in trays in August should be pricked out into trays and kept in a frame over winter, and planted into nursery rows in the spring.

Half-hardy Annuals

Uses Half-hardy annuals are generally mass planted in beds to give colour from late May or early June until the autumn. All are tender and will be killed by the first autumn frosts, and so new plants are raised each year. Some are true annuals (dying after flowering in their first year) but some are perennials – capable of living for a number of years. However, even the perennial kinds are generally treated as annuals and scrapped in the autumn.

There are countless combinations of plants that one could use for summer bedding displays, such as orange pelargoniums with purple petunias; mauve ageratums with pink or red begonias; and yellow or orange marigolds with blue or purple heliotrope. It is best to jot down ideas on paper as you see pleasing schemes in public parks and other people's gardens.

Many half-hardy annuals are suitable for window boxes and tubs – such as begonias, impatiens, lobelias, pelargoniums, petunias, salvias, marigolds and verbenas. Some are used in hanging baskets, especially trailing lobelias and petunias.

Sowing and Pricking Out Seeds are sown in trays in the spring (see sowing times in the chart on page 214) and are germinated at a temperature of 18–21°C (65–70°F). Details of sowing in trays will be found in the chapter on TECHNIQUES (page 54). An electrically heated propagator is useful for germinating seeds.

When the seedlings are large enough to handle, they must be pricked out or transplanted into further seed trays to give them room to grow. Generally speaking, you should aim to prick out 24 seedlings into a standard-size tray in six rows each of four plants.

Use John Innes No 1 potting compost for pricking out, or an equivalent soilless type. You will need a miniature dibber for pricking out – a pencil will be ideal. Carefully lift a few seedlings with the fingers and gently separate them out. Mark out the rows on the surface of the compost and then start to plant. Make a hole for each seedling with the dibber, dangle the roots in it and lightly firm in with dibber or fingers. The seedlings should be inserted up to the seed leaves or lower leaves (correctly cotyledons). Always handle the seedlings by the seed leaves, never by the stems. After completing a tray, water the seedlings with a fine-rosed can and place the tray on the greenhouse staging or in a heated frame. Give adequate light, keep moist and above all keep free from frost. Many subjects need a minimum temperature of 10°C (50°F) and some, such as salvias, like it warmer – up to 16°C (60°F).

Hardening Off and Planting Out Two or three weeks before planting outdoors, the young plants should be transferred to a cold frame to harden off, or gradually become acclimatized to outdoor conditions. This means giving them increasing amounts of ventilation during the daytime but closing the frame at night. By planting time the plants will be receiving full ventilation, at night as well as by day.

Do not plant out until all danger of frost is over – which is generally the end of May in the south and the first week of June in the north.

Hardy Annuals Botanical Name	Common Name	Colour	Height	Flowering Time	Sowing Time	Soil Preferred
Alyssum maritimum	Sweet Alyssum	white, purple	10–15cm (4–6in)	September	April–May or August–September	Any
Calendula	Pot Marigold	yellow, orange	45–60cm (18–24in)	June–September	March–May or August–September	Light
Centaurea cyanus	Cornflower	Blue, lavender, pink, red, crimson, white	30–90cm (12–36in)	July–August	March–May or August–September	Light
Chrysanthemum carinatum	Tricolor Chrysanthemum	yellow, red, orange, white	60 90cm (24 36in)	June–August	March–May	Wide range
Clarkia elegans		pink, red, mauve, purple, white	45–60cm (18–24in)	June–August	March–May or September	Light, well drained
Delphinium ajacis	Larkspur	pink, red, purple, lavender, white	60–90cm (24–36in)	June–August	March–May or September	Light
Eschscholzia californica	Californian Poppy	orange, yellow, red, crimson, pink, white	30cm (12in)	June–September	March–May or August–September	Light
Godetia		pink, mauve, red, white	20–60cm (8–24in)	June–August	March–April or September	Light
Iberis umbellata	Annual Candytuft	pink, purple, white	20–40cm (8–16in)	June–September	March–May or September	Wide range
Lavatera trimestris	Annual Mallow	pink	90–120cm (36–48in)	June–September	March–May	Wide range
Layia elegans	Tidy Tips	yellow and white	30–40cm (12–16in)	June–August	March–May	Dry
Limnanthes douglasii		yellow and white	20–30cm (8–12in)	May–July	March–May or September	Any, including moist
Linaria maroccana	Annual Toadflax	all colours	20–30cm (8–12in)	June–September	March–May or September	Light
Malcolmia maritima	Virginian Stock	red, lavender, white	20cm (8in)	June–August	March–May or September	Light
Nemophila	Baby Blue Eyes	blue	15cm (6in)	June–August	March–May or September	Cool and moist
Nigella	Love-in-a-mist	blue, purple, white	40–45cm (16–18in)	June–September	March–May or September	Any
Papaver rhoeas	Shirley Poppy	pink, red, crimson, white	75cm (30in)	June–September	March–May or September	Any, including poor and dry
Phacelia campanularia		blue	20cm (8in)	June–August	March–May	Light, well drained
Reseda odorata	Mignonette	red and green	30cm (12in)	June–August	March–May	Chalky or limy
Tropaeolum majus	Nasturtium	orange, yellow, red, crimson, pink	20–30cm (8–12in) also climbing	July–September	April–May	Any, especially poor types

Hardy Biennials

Botanical Name	Common Name	Colour	Height	Flowering Time	Final Planting Distances	Soil Preferred
Althaea rosea	Hollyhock	pink, mauve, red, crimson, yellow, white	150 240cm (60–96in)	July–August	60–90cm (24–36in)	Well drained
Bellis perennis 'Monstrosa'	Double Daisy	red, pink, white	15cm (6in)	March–May	15cm (6in)	Any
Campanula medium	Canterbury Bell	blue, lavender, pink, white	45–60cm (18–24in)	June–July	45–60cm (18–24in)	Well drained
Cheiranthus allionii	Siberian Wallflower	orange, yellow	40cm (16in)	March–June	30cm (12in)	Any, including chalky or limy
Cheiranthus cheiri	Wallflower	yellow, white, orange, red, crimson, purple, pink	30–45cm (12–18in)	March–May	30cm (12in)	As above
Dianthus barbatus	Sweet William	red, pink, crimson, white	15–45cm (6–18in)	June–July	30–45cm (12–18in)	Any, especially chalky or limy
Digitalis purpurea	Foxglove	pink, purple, red, white	90–150cm (36–60in)	June–July	60cm (24in)	Moist
Erysimum	Alpine Wallflower	yellow	15–20cm (6–8in)	March–May	30cm (12in)	Well drained
Lunaria annua	Honesty	purple, white	60cm (24in)	May–June	30cm (12in)	Any, including chalky
Matthiola incana	Brompton Stock	pink, red, crimson, lavender, white	45–60cm (18–24in)	March–May	30cm (12in)	Well drained, light
Matthiola incana	East Lothian Stock	pink, red, crimson, lavender, purple, white	30–45cm (12–18in)	April–September	30cm (12in)	Well drained, light
Myosotis	Forget-me-not	blue, pink	15–40cm (6–16in)	March–June	15cm (6in)	Any, especially moist
Papaver nudicaule	Iceland Poppy	orange, yellow, red, pink, white	60–75cm (24–30in)	May–July	30–45cm (12–18in)	Well drained, light
Primula elatior	Polyanthus	all colours	30–40cm (12–16in)	March–June	30cm (12in)	Moist and cool
Primula vulgaris	Coloured Primroses	all colours	15cm (6in)	January–May	30cm (12in)	Moist and cool
Viola species	Pansies and Bedding Violas	yellow, orange, mauve, lavender, blue, purple, white	15–20cm (6–8in)	March–October	15–30cm (6–12in)	Moist

Half-Hardy Annuals

Ageratum	Floss Flower	blue, mauve, purple, white	15–20cm (6–8in)	June–August	February–March	15cm (6in)	Any
Antirrhinum	Snapdragon	yellow, orange, pink, red, white	15–90cm (6–36in)	June–September	January–March	30–45cm (12–18in)	Any
Begonia semperflorens	Fibrous-rooted Begonia	pink, red, crimson, white	15–30cm (6–12in)	June–October	January–February	15cm (6in)	Moist

Botanical Name	Common Name	Colour	Height	Flowering Time	Sowing Time	Final Planting Distance	Soil Preferred
Callistephus	China Aster	blue, lavender, purple, red, crimson, pink, white	30–75cm (12–30in)	July–September	March–April	30–45cm (12–18in)	Any well drained soil
Cosmos bipinnatus	Cosmea	pink, crimson, white	45–60cm (18–24in)	July–September	February–March	45–60cm (18–24in)	Light
Gazania		yellow, pink, red, orange	10–30cm (4–12in)	June–September	February–March	30cm (12in)	Well drained, dry
Heliotropium	Heliotrope	blue, purple	45–60cm (18–24in)	June–September	February–March	30–45cm (12–18in)	Any
Impatiens holstii and *I. sultanii*	Busy Lizzie	pink, red, purple, white	15–40cm (6–16in)	May–October	March–April	30cm (12in)	Moist
Lobelia erinus and *L. tenuior*	Bedding and Trailing Lobelia	blue, pink, purple, crimson, white	15–20cm (6–8in) and trailing	May–September	January–March	15cm (6in)	Any
Mesembryanthemum criniflorum	Livingstone Daisy	pink, red, orange	prostrate	June–September	February–March	15cm (6in)	Well drained, dry
Nemesia		many colours	20–30cm (8–12in)	June–September	February–April	15cm (6in)	Cool, moist
Nicotiana	Flowering Tobacco	red, pink, green, white	30–75cm (12–30in)	June–September	February–April	45cm (18in)	Deep and rich
Pelargonium zonale (F_1 hybrids)	Zonal Pelargonium or 'Geranium'	pink, red, crimson, orange, white	45–60cm (18–24in)	June–October	December–January	30–45cm (12–18in)	Well drained
Petunia		many colours	30–45cm (12–18in)	June–September	February–March	30cm (12in)	Light and rich
Phlox drummondii	Annual Phlox	pink, red, crimson, purple, white	15–45cm (6–18in)	June–August	February–April	15cm (6in)	Moist and fertile
Salvia splendens	Scarlet Sage	red, pink, purple	15–60cm (6–24in)	June–September	January–February	30cm (12in)	Any well drained soil
Tagetes erecta	African Marigold	yellow, orange, cream	20–60cm (8–24in)	July–September	February–March	30cm (12in)	Light, well drained, even poor and sandy
Tagetes patula	French Marigold	yellow, orange, crimson	15–30cm (6–12in)	July–September	February–March	15–30cm (6–12in)	As above
Verbena hybrids	Vervain	pink, red, crimson, blue, mauve	15–30cm (6–12in)	July–September	January–March	30–45cm (12–18in)	Rich and well drained
Zinnia		pink, red, purple, yellow, orange	15–90cm (6–36in)	July–September	March–April	30cm (12in)	Rich and well drained

Chrysanthemums and Dahlias

CHRYSANTHEMUMS

Technical Terms

A chrysanthemum bloom is made up of a large number of small flowers or FLORETS. The florets are of two kinds – the coloured portion of the bloom is made up of RAY FLORETS (often incorrectly called 'petals'), while the cushion in the centre of the bloom is composed of DISK FLORETS, the sole producers of pollen.

A STOOL is the root of an old plant with a portion of the old stem and its surrounding young shoots.

A SUCKER is a rooted shoot growing from the old root.

A CUTTING is an unrooted leaf growth taken either from the old root or from the old stem.

STOPPING is the act of removing the tip of a growth.

BREAKING is when the plant branches or sends out side growth.

A LEAF AXIL is the space between the stalk of a leaf and the stem to which it is attached.

SECURING THE BUD is the act of removing all leaf axil shoots and unwanted buds, leaving only the bud which is to develop into a flower.

THE BREAK BUD is the flower bud which, if the plant is left to grow naturally, finally appears at the end of the solitary main stem before it branches or breaks.

THE FIRST CROWN BUD is the first bud which appears at the end of a lateral growth from the main stem of the plant.

SECOND CROWN BUD. If the tips of the lateral growths from the main stem are removed, further side growths will develop in the leaf axils of these laterals. These further side growths then grow on until a bud is produced at the end of each of them, and this is termed a second crown bud.

Flower Types

A list of recommended varieties of chrysanthemum is given on page 225. First, there are those held in particularly high esteem by the connoisseur, with their immaculate INCURVED blooms. In contrast, there are the gracefully REFLEXED blooms in which each floret evenly overlaps the next. Then there are those with SPIKY florets which do not form a smooth surface. INCURVING blooms (or INTERMEDIATES) have florets arranged in a loosely incurving formation so that they do not close over on the top, thus revealing the deeper colour of the inner sides of the florets to produce a bi-coloured effect. SINGLES are daisy-shaped flowers having a central disk and approximately five rows of ray florets. ANEMONES are similar, but here the predominant feature is the central cushion which is deep and dome-shaped. SPRAYS can be grouped into four categories: Anemones, Pompons, Reflexed and Singles. The plants are allowed to develop their blooms without any disbudding, thus providing an attractive spray of small flowers. Finally, there is the giant Japanese type known as LARGE EXHIBITION, with football-sized blooms.

Below: how a chrysanthemum grows.

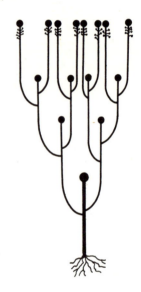

Right: some types of chrysanthemum flower. From top to bottom: reflexed, reflexed decorative, pompon, exhibition incurved, single, incurving.

General Cultivation

To grow chrysanthemum plants successfully and to obtain high quality blooms, new plants should be raised each year by obtaining leafy vegetative cuttings from plants grown to maturity the previous year.

In the first season of growing chrysanthemums, young rooted cuttings should be purchased from a reputable chrysanthemum specialist; thereafter the plants should be treated as advised later.

It is most important to carry out stock selection by retaining for propagation purposes the plants that have produced the best blooms the previous season. Stools of Early-Flowering types can be left in the open garden until early November (when the temperature is occasionally below 4°C (40°F) to provide a period of 'vernalization': this process subjects the stools to winter conditions and encourages the production of vegetative cuttings.

The main stems should first be cut down to 15cm (6in), all leaves removed and all green growth cut off at ground level. Lift the stools carefully with a fork; it is advisable also to wash off the soil using a little Jeyes Fluid in the water to remove any pests.

Plant the stools in clean boxes or trays to a level no deeper than the original soil mark using John Innes No 1 compost or a mixture of equal parts loam, peat and grit. Water the stools in well to settle the compost. Make sure the stools are labelled correctly. They should then be placed somewhere dry such as a cold frame where they can have plenty of light and air but be kept free from frost. Probably no more water will be needed until the boxes go into the greenhouse in January. Keep an eye on them so that you can deal with any diseases such as mildew or botrytis which may appear and could ruin the flowers. Dusts of flowers of sulphur (or captan sprays) will cope with attacks of these troubles.

With the higher temperature in the greenhouse, young growth will emerge from the base of the stools to provide cutting material for the coming season.

In the meantime, start preparing the site where the plants are to be grown. Remove all dead leaves and large weeds and burn all such material to avoid spreading disease. If the ground is heavy, December and January is the time to dig it, incorporating well-rotted manure into the top spit, and leaving it rough for the frosts to weather.

Propagation

In early February you can start propagating new plants for the coming season. The rooting compost can be John Innes Potting Compost No 1 or a mixture of equal parts by volume of peat, loam and coarse grit, or one of the many soilless composts now on the market. Depending upon the number of cuttings to be rooted, you have the choice of inserting three round the edge of a 9cm (3½in) pot, or 18 in a standard-sized seed tray 36cm (14in) × 21cm (8in) × 5cm (2in) deep, in which case the compost should be firmed with a board and a layer of sharp sand sprinkled on the surface. Space the cuttings in the tray 5cm (2in) apart each way.

Water the stools well the day before to plump up the cuttings. snap off the cutting between finger and thumb, about 5cm (2in) in length, just below a leaf joint. Dip the bottom 1.3cm (½in) of stem into a hormone rooting powder and make a hole 1.3cm (½in) deep in the compost using a dibber about the diameter of a standard pencil. Place the cutting in the hole and press the compost up to the stem. Some of the sand sprinkled on the surface of the compost will fall to the bottom of the hole and the drainage thus created will help to prevent decay. Water the trays or pots well.

The time taken for rooting will depend upon the conditions provided. In a rooting box with a bottom heat of about 15°C (60°F) and an air temperature above of approximately 4°C (40°F), they should root in 14 days. On an open bench with a general temperature of 10°C (50°F) they will take a week or so longer. Cuttings can be rooted without heat when the risk of frost is over, but they take longer to root this way and the delay will affect the timing of blooms. Propagation can continue throughout February until early March.

Growing On

As soon as the cuttings are rooted, they should be removed to a cooler part of the greenhouse. Slow and steady growth is required to produce a short sturdy plant with a big root system, and the best place to produce this type of growth is in a cold frame. Place the frame on top of a 15cm (6in) bed of weathered clinker or ashes. Then make up a bed of compost 10cm (4in) deep using John Innes Potting Compost No 2. The rooted cuttings can be set out 10cm (4in) apart into the bed, or alternatively they can be moved on into larger boxes at least 10cm (4in) deep, which are then placed in the frame.

The move into the cold frame should take place during March. From then on, give the plants as much light and air as possible. Leave the frame lights off whenever the weather permits and, when they are on, keep them raised a little at all times unless there is a risk of frost. During the early spring, frosts usually occur at night and under such conditions cover the frame lights with sacks or old carpets. Water should be given sparingly, just enough to keep the plants going.

While the plants are in the frames, the ground where the early-flowering chrysanthemums are to be grown must be finally prepared for planting. Dig it over roughly in December or January, or even as late as March if it is very light ground. Then on a dry day in April, when the ground is fit to walk on, rake it over thoroughly to obtain a fine tilth, the object being to create a crumb structure similar to the compost in which the young plants have been growing. Incorporate a balanced fertilizer into the top 10cm (4in) of soil at the rate of 170g per sq m (5oz per sq yd). Allow two to three weeks for the beds to settle before planting out.

Stopping and Timing

Stopping is the removal of the growing point of a plant to encourage lateral growths to develop from the leaf axils. Gardeners keen on exhibiting their chrysanthemums are always anxious to learn the 'correct stopping dates' for particular varieties in order to obtain blooms of the highest quality on the date of the show for which they are required (such meticulous timing is not necessary if the plants are not to be exhibited). However, there is no such thing as a 'correct stopping date' that can be acted upon regardless of growing conditions. The date of chrysanthemum flowering, whatever the natural habit of the variety, is influenced by several factors, the most important being the date of rooting the cuttings, the date of stopping the plants, the date of securing the buds, the altitude at which the plants are grown, the aspect of the site, the seasonal conditions and the absence or abundance of sunshine.

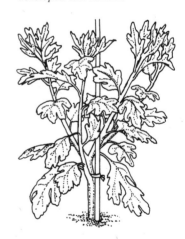

Below: a chrysanthemum plant after stopping, with four evenly developed side-shoots.

For Early-Flowering Chrysanthemums the time required from rooting to stopping is approximately 12 weeks, while for Late-Flowering Chrysanthemums it is about 14 weeks. Many chrysanthemum varieties will break naturally and produce blooms fully developed in time for September and November shows. Late-Flowering varieties must be stopped to encourage earlier breaks and to give sufficient time for the lateral growths to develop and form flower buds which will mature in time for show purposes.

To sum up with regard to the stopping and timing of chrysanthemums, the varieties can be divided into three groups: firstly, varieties which are naturally early in their particular season; these require late rooting and should be allowed to break naturally; secondly, varieties which naturally bloom at the period required; thirdly, varieties which are naturally late and must be rooted early and stopped at a recommended date to accelerate the flowering.

Most specialist nurserymen give stopping dates in their catalogues.

Planting Out Early-Flowering Chrysanthemums
From the 1st to the 14th May is an approximate date for planting. Do not be in a hurry – you should not plant out when the ground is very wet or when frost threatens. It is better to wait a few days.

When planting, the more space you can give a plant the better. A spacing of 45cm (1½ft) between plants and 60cm (2ft) between rows is ideal. However, if you cannot afford to give so much space, give as much as you can.

Planting is quite simple. Take out a hole just large enough to accommodate the soil ball of the plant. Set it in about 1.3cm (½in) lower than it was in the previous container and return the soil around the stem, pressing it in firmly to make a slight saucer-shaped depression that will take up water. Provide each plant with a cane 1.2m long and 1.3cm thick (4ft × ½in) and when tying the plant, leave a space between the stem and the cane of approximately 1.3cm (½in) for expansion.

Hoeing in the early part of the season will prevent the soil from cracking, retain moisture and keep down the weeds. As the season progresses the plant roots become nearer to the surface and hoeing could be dangerous, so that any weeds must be removed by hand.

A good method of moisture conservation at this stage is mulching, which creates a barrier to stop the sun's rays drying out the soil.

Feeding
To what extent this is necessary will depend upon the type of soil and the thoroughness with which it was prepared, and the purpose for which the plants are being grown. On reasonably heavy soil, a bed dug in the autumn, with manure incorporated, which was subsequently given a dressing of fertilizer at planting time will carry a good crop of flowers for garden display and probably produce good show blooms without further feeding. A light soil, however, will benefit from some supplementary feeding. As a general guide, a nitrogenous feed should be given about a week after planting, using synthetic urea at the manufacturer's recommended rate. Towards the end of June give a dry feed of a balanced general chrysanthemum fertilizer well watered in. Then a month later give another dry feed, say of an early-flowering chrysanthemum fertilizer or of the general chrysanthemum fertilizer, again well watered in. This treatment should produce good blooms.

Flowering Laterals

These arise from the stopping of plants or as a result of their breaking naturally. When growing for garden display and cut-flower purposes, remove all except six evenly matched laterals. If you are growing for exhibition, you should retain only the three strongest laterals in order to produce larger blooms.

As the laterals lengthen, they will produce further side growths from the leaf axils. When these are about 1.3cm (½in) in length, they should be carefully removed, leaving the main lateral, the tip of which will produce a flowering bud.

Late-Flowering Chrysanthemums

The cultivation routine for Late-Flowering Chrysanthemums to flower in pots in the greenhouse from October to Christmas is very similar to that given for the Early-Flowering types. However, after the cuttings have been rooted they should be moved on into progressively larger pots, starting with pots of 7.5cm (3in) diameter, then on to 12.5cm (5in) pots, the final pot being one of 20cm (8in) or 23cm (9in) diameter. Each move should be made when the roots have filled the pot.

For the 7.5cm (3in) pots use John Innes Potting Compost No 1; for the 12.5cm (5in) ones, John Innes Potting Compost No 2; and for the final pots, John Innes Potting Compost No 3. The move into the final pot is the most important, the plant remaining there for several months.

With these soil-based composts proceed as follows: place some crocks at the bottom of the pot to provide adequate drainage, followed by a layer of peat about 2.5cm (1in) deep, then partly fill with compost and firm gently with a rammer. Place the plant in the centre of the pot and fill in around the plant with compost. Do not fill the pot; allow 5cm (2in) for future top-dressing. Next, ram down the compost firmly using a potting stick. Stand the pots close together to give the plants a certain amount of shade. Withhold water for 10–14 days to encourage the roots to grow into the new compost. An overhead spray in the evenings should prevent undue flagging.

Late-Flowering Chrysanthemums can also be grown satisfactorily in one of the proprietary soilless composts – with these there is no need to place crocks at the bottom of the pot. Do not allow these composts to dry out completely, or it will prove difficult to re-moisten them.

Standing-Out Ground for Late-Flowering Plants This should be a level site in full sun if possible. The aim should be to give each plant as much room as you can spare. The pots should stand in rows, preferably on an ash base, and each one should stand on a slate or tile to prevent worms from entering the compost through the drainage holes.

Strong posts should be driven into the ground at the end of each row with wires stretched between them. The canes should be fastened to the wires to prevent the plants from being blown over.

Watering procedure is similar to that recommended for the Earlies. Give an overhead spray on warm evenings and water the plants only when necessary, and then give a good soaking. With the restrictions of a pot, watering should be more frequent than with the Earlies and because of the more frequent watering a certain amount of the food in the compost will be leached out of the pot.

About six weeks after their final potting, you should feed the plants. A level teaspoonful of a balanced chrysanthemum fertilizer should be applied to the pot every 10–14 days until the buds show colour.

Right: some types of dahlia flower. From top to bottom: single-flowered, anemone-flowered, collerette, paeony-flowered.

Top-Dressing Late Chrysanthemums in Pots Towards the end of July, roots will appear on the surface of the compost. It is now the time to apply a top dressing of the final potting compost about 1.3cm (½in) thick. Further top dressings will be required approximately every three weeks thereafter.

As with the Earlies you must decide how many blooms you wish to grow and restrict the laterals accordingly.

Housing Late-Flowering Chrysanthemums Wash down the glass and framework of the greenhouse and fumigate to destroy any pests in readiness to house the plants. As soon as the buds show colour and before frost arrives, remove all dead or infected leaves and any weed seedlings, wash the outsides of the pots, move them into the greenhouse and spray the leaves with pyrethrum (or pirimicarb) if there are aphids.

Doors and ventilators should be left fully open for as long as possible to enable the plants to become acclimatized to the change of environment. Make sure the house is well ventilated. High temperatures are not necessary – you need only enough heat to keep the air moving and to maintain a temperature of 10°C (50°F). A fan heater is most suitable as it will give both warmth and air movement.

DAHLIAS

Types of Dahlias

The main groups of dahlias are the BORDER DAHLIAS and the BEDDING DAHLIAS, and there is further division into types, based on different flower size and structure.

Border Dahlias

SINGLE-FLOWERED

Height: 45–75cm (1½–2½ft). Planting distance: 45–60cm (1½–2ft). Diameter of bloom: 10cm (4in). Each flower has a single row of broad, flat, usually overlapping florets, surrounding a central disc.

ANEMONE-FLOWERED

Height: 60cm–1m (2–3½ft). Planting distance: 60cm (2ft). Diameter of bloom: 10cm (4in). These have double flowers with broad and flattened outer florets surrounding densely-packed central florets, often of contrasting colour.

COLLERETTE

Height: 75cm–1m (2½–3½ft). Planting distance: 60–75cm (2–2½ft). Diameter of bloom: up to 10cm (4in). Flowers have an outer ring of flat ray florets, sometimes overlapping, and an inner ring of smaller florets surrounding the central disc.

PAEONY-FLOWERED

Height: 90cm (3ft). Planting distance: 60cm (2ft). Diameter of bloom: up to 10cm (4in). These have semi-double flowers, with two or more rings of flat, broad ray florets and a central disc.

DECORATIVE

There are five groups, classified by bloom size. Their double flowers are composed of broad, normally slightly twisted, bluntly pointed, flat ray florets.

Giant. Height: 1.2–1.5m (4–5ft). Planting distance: 1.2m (4ft). Diameter of bloom: more than 25cm (10in).

Large. Height: 1–1.2m (3½–4ft). Planting distance: 1.2m (4ft). Diameter of bloom: 20–25cm (8–10in).

Medium. Height: 1–1.2m (3½–4ft). Planting distance: 90cm (3ft).

Diameter of bloom: 15–20cm (6–8in).

Small. Height: 1–1.2m (3½–4ft). Planting distance: 75cm (2½ft). Diameter of bloom: 10–15cm (4–6in).

Miniature. Height: 90cm–1.2m (3–4ft). Planting distance: 75cm (2½ft). Diameter of bloom: up to 10cm (4in).

BALL

There are two types of ball dahlias, once again divided according to the size of their blooms. Both are fully double and ball-shaped, occasionally flattened at the top. Their ray florets, which have blunt or rounded tips, are arranged spirally. Their sides are rolled inwards for more than half their length.

Ball. Height: 90cm–1.2m (3–4ft). Planting distance: 75cm (2½ft). Diameter of bloom: 10–15cm (4–6in).

Miniature ball. Height: 90cm–1.2m (3–4ft). Planting distance: 75cm (2½ft). Diameter of bloom: up to 10cm (4in).

POMPON

Height: 90cm–1.2m (3–4ft). Planting distance: 75cm (2½ft). Diameter of bloom: up to 10cm (4in). The flowers are fully double and similar to those of ball dahlias, but appreciably smaller and more spherical. Their blunt or rounded florets are rolled inwards along their whole length.

CACTUS AND SEMI-CACTUS

Again, both these groups are classified according to their bloom size. The fully double flowers have pointed ray florets. With cactus dahlias these are rolled outwards or quilled for more than half their length, whereas with the semi-cactus type, they are broader and quilled for half their length or less.

Giant. Height: 1.2–1.5m (4–5ft). Planting distance: 1.2m (4ft). Diameter of bloom: more than 25cm (10in).

Large. Height: 1.2–1.5m (4–5ft). Planting distance: 1.2m (4ft). Diameter of bloom: 20–25cm (8–10in).

Medium. Height: 1–1.35m (3½–4½ft). Planting distance: 90cm (3ft). Diameter of bloom: 15–20cm (6–8in).

Small. Height: 1–1.2m (3½–4ft). Planting distance: 75cm (2½ft). Diameter of blooms: 10–15cm (4–6in).

Miniature. Height: 90cm–1.2m (3–4ft). Planting distance: 75cm (2½ft). Diameter of bloom: up to 10cm (4in).

Bedding Dahlias Bedding dahlias may belong to any of the above classes, but they must not exceed 60cm (2ft) in height. There are comparatively few named varieties.

Buying Dahlias

Dahlias are offered for sale by specialist nurserymen, garden centres and similar suppliers either as rooted cuttings or as tubers, which are the roots which have formed at the base of a plant grown the previous season.

Cultivation

Site Dahlias prefer an open sunny position, but they will tolerate partial shade, providing there are no nearby trees.

Soil and its Preparation Any good soil is suitable, providing it is well-drained and enriched with compost, farmyard manure or peat.

As dahlias are shallow rooted, it is normally only necessary to single-dig the bed.

A month before planting, break up the soil to a fine tilth and rake

Above, top to bottom: decorative, ball, pompon and cactus dahlias.

bonemeal, at a rate of 120g per sq m (4oz per sq yd) into the top 5cm (2in).

Planting Tubers This applies both to pot tubers that you buy from the nursery and to your own ground tubers, which you dug up the previous year and stored through the winter (see under LIFTING AND STORING TUBERS below). Tubers may be planted either before or after they have sprouted.

UNSPROUTED TUBERS These should be placed in a hole, 15cm (6in) deep, in late April, or early May in colder gardens, and covered with fine soil. The crown should be 7.5cm (3in) below the surface of the soil.

SPROUTED TUBERS The dormant tubers should be started into growth in pots or boxes of moist soil or peat, with their crowns uncovered in mid February. Keep them in a fairly warm place and keep the soil or peat damp without wetting their crowns. When the shoots are well developed, harden them off and plant out in late May or early June.

Planting Rooted Cuttings These, whether purchased already potted or taken from sprouted tubers and raised in pots (see under PROPAGATION below), should be planted in late May (early June in colder areas). Plant each cutting in a hole large enough to take the root ball comfortably. Water the pots one hour before planting and water the plants in after planting.

Staking Border dahlias, but not bedding dahlias, should be staked, using 2.5cm (1in) square stakes or bamboo canes for shorter varieties, about 30cm (1ft) shorter than the ultimate height of the plant. Insert the stakes firmly into the planting hole to a depth of 30cm (1ft) before planting. When the dahlias reach 23cm (9in) high, the main stems should be loosely tied in; go on doing this as the plants grow.

Watering All dahlias should be watered freely during hot spells.

Weeding The soil should be kept free of weeds by shallow hoeing for three or four weeks after planting, but this must then cease, to avoid damaging their shallow roots.

Mulching Mulch the soil when it is thoroughly moist from rain (or after a thorough watering) with a 7.5cm (3in) layer of garden compost, well-rotted manure or peat. This will help control the weeds and keep the soil moist.

Pinching Back (Stopping) When five pairs of leaves have developed, the growing tips of all types of dahlias should be pinched out to encourage bushiness.

Dead-heading To encourage continuous flowering, all dead blooms should be removed.

Feeding Dahlias benefit from feeding, starting in late June with a high nitrogen content fertilizer, which encourages the growth of foliage and stems, applied every ten days until the buds show colour. Then it should be replaced by a high potash feed, which strengthens the shoots, improves flower colour and encourages tuber development.

Side Shooting and Disbudding Stopping (see PINCHING BACK above) applies to all types of dahlias. Side shooting and disbudding are essential for border dahlias required to produce quality blooms for cutting or showing.

SIDE SHOOTING All unwanted laterals are removed.

DISBUDDING All side buds are removed from a stem, leaving the central terminal bud to develop.

Lifting and Storing Tubers
Except in the mildest districts, tubers must be lifted and stored during

the winter. A week after frost has blackened the foliage, cut down the plants to 15cm (6in) from the ground. Then dig up the tubers by making a cut, with a spade, one spit deep, around the plant, 30cm (1ft) from its centre. Holding the stem, gently lift the tubers on the spade blade, taking care not to damage the base of the stems from which new shoots will develop. Any very damaged tubers should be discarded.

Label each tuber clearly, with the name of the variety and the date. Tie the label to the base of the stem. Stand the tubers upside down for a week under cover, so that any water drains from the hollow stalks.

Next, trim off the thin stringy roots from the ends of the tubers, and cut the stems down to 5cm (2in). Also cut away any damaged parts of the tubers and dust the wounds with flowers of sulphur.

Place the tubers in damp peat in shallow boxes, leaving their crowns exposed, and store in a cool, frostproof place.

During the winter, inspect the tubers frequently, discarding any diseased ones and plumping up any that have shrivelled by soaking them in water overnight, drying them and returning them to store. Any damage found must be cut away and the wound dressed with flowers of sulphur.

Propagation

Border Dahlias Border dahlias are propagated vegetatively, because seeds do not breed to type. This is done either by division or by rooting cuttings.

BY DIVISION This method requires no heat. With division, flowering is several weeks earlier than with plants raised from cuttings.

The dormant tubers are first started into growth as described under PLANTING above.

When the 'eyes', or buds, have begun to swell, usually after two or three weeks, make a cut down the centre of the stem between the buds, right through the tuber. You can often make further divisions, but each piece must include a portion of the stem attached to a piece of the crown bearing an eye and at least one portion of a swollen tuber. It is advisable to dust each cut part with flowers of sulphur.

Either plant the divisions outdoors in early May or grow them on in seed boxes under glass and put the plants out in late May after hardening them off.

FROM CUTTINGS Undamaged tubers are made to sprout in the manner described under PLANTING. When the shoots are 7.5cm (3in) long, cut them off with a sharp knife at a point 6mm ($\frac{1}{4}$in) from the crown; this allows further shoots to grow.

Then remove the lower pair of leaves, moisten the base of the cutting and dip it in hormone rooting compound. Insert four cuttings round the edge of a 7.5cm (3in) pot containing cutting compost.

Water the pots thoroughly and put them into a propagator at 15–18°C (59–64°F), shielding them from direct sunlight.

When growth starts, pot on each cutting into a 7.5cm (3in) pot containing potting compost, and place the pots in a frost-proof frame. After hardening off, plant the new plants out in late May or early June.

Bedding Dahlias Although these can be propagated by division and from cuttings, they are often treated as annuals and grown from seed.

Sow the seeds under glass during February or March in trays or pans of sowing compost and germinate at 16°C (61°F).

When they are large enough to handle, prick off the seedlings into

SOME RECOMMENDED VARIETIES OF CHRYSANTHEMUM

Early Flowering (Garden Display)

	Type	Colour	Height	Stopping Date	Flowering Period
'Julie Ann'	Incurving	Light Pink	1m (3½ft)	End May	Mid-August/September
'Autumn Days'	Incurving	Orange Bronze	1.2m (4ft)	End May	Mid-August/September
'Nuflair'	Reflexed	Bright Red	1m (3½ft)	End May	Mid-August/September
'Allbright'	Reflexed	Rich Yellow	1m (3½ft)	Mid May	Mid-August/September
'Early Bird'	Spiky	Light Purple	1m (3½ft)	Mid May	Mid-August/September
'Cornish'	Incurving	Cream	1m (3½ft)	Mid May	Mid-August/September

Early Flowering (Sprays)

	Type	Colour	Height	Stopping Date	Flowering Period
'Lucida'		Yellow	90cm (3ft)	End May	Mid-August/September
'Anna Marie'		White	90cm (3ft)	End May	Mid-August/September
'Pennine Dancer'		Pink	90cm (3ft)	End May	Mid-August/September

Early Flowering (Exhibition)

	Type	Colour	Height	Stopping Date	Flowering Period
'Ginger Nut'	Incurving	Light Bronze	1m (3½ft)	Mid May	September
'Yellow Ginger Nut'	Incurving	Yellow	1m (3½ft)	Mid May	September
'Peter Rowe'	Incurved	Yellow	1m (3½ft)	Mid May	September
'Sam Oldham'	Reflexed	Red	1.2m (4ft)	Mid May	September
'Bruera'	Reflexed	White	1.2m (4ft)	End May	September
'Timmy Gray'	Reflexed	Purple	1m (3½ft)	7 May	September
'Kingston Imperial'	Reflexed	Pink	1.2m (4ft)	Mid May	September
'Grace Riley'	Reflexed	Bronze	1.2m (4ft)	Mid May	September

Hardy Koreans

	Type	Colour	Height	Stopping Date	Flowering Period
'Doris'	Single	Light Bronze	60cm (2ft)	1 June	August/September/October
'Wendy'	Single	Cream	60cm (2ft)	1 June	August/September/October
'Honey'	Single	Dark Yellow	60cm (2ft)	1 June	August/September/October

Late Flowering

	Type	Colour	Height	Stopping Date	Flowering Period
'Gigantic'	Large Exhibition	Pink	1.4m (4½ft)	25 May	November
'Connie Mayhew'	Medium Exhibition	Yellow	1.4m (4½ft)	{ 30 March 10 May	November
'Minstrel Boy'	Exhibition Incurved	Light Bronze	1.2m (4ft)	15 June	November
'Chesswood Beauty'	Single	Red	1.5m (5ft)	{ 14 April 20 June	November

A SELECTION OF DAHLIAS

Variety or Strain	Type	Colour	Height cm	ft	Flowering time (until frosted)	Remarks
'Alva's Doris'	Cactus (Small)	Deep blood red	105	3½	From early August	
'Bishop of Llandaff'	Paeony	Scarlet	75	2½	From early August	Dark foliage
'Blue Perfection'	Pompon	'Near blue'	105	3½	From early August	
'Colour Spectacle'	Semi-Cactus (Large)	Red and white	120	4	From late August	
'Coltness Gem'	Single (Bedding)	Scarlet	45	1½	From July	
'Comet'	Anemone-Flowered	Maroon	105	3½	From early August	
'David Howard'	Decorative (Miniature)	Orange bronze	105	3½	From early August	
'Deepest Yellow'	Ball	Yellow	90	3	From August	
'Drakenberg'	Cactus (Large)	Purple	150	5	From late August	
'Dr John Grainger'	Ball (Miniature)	Golden orange	105	3½	From early August	
'Frau Louis Mayer'	Cactus (Small)	Lemon yellow	60	2	From August	Good for bedding
'Gerrie Hoek'	Decorative (Medium)	Pink	105	3½	From mid August	
'Glory of Heemstede'	Decorative (Small)	Yellow	120	4	From early August	
'Happy Mood'	Semi-Cactus (Miniature)	Yellow	105	3½	From early August	
'Hit Parade'	Semi-Cactus (Small)	Scarlet	135	4½	From early August	
'La Cierva'	Collerette	Purple and White	105	3½	From early August	
'Lavender Perfection'	Decorative (Large)	Lavender pink	120	4	From late August	
'Libretto'	Collerette	Red, white and carmine	105	3½	From early August	
'Little William'	Pompon	Red and White	105	3½	From early August	
'Magnificat'	Ball	Rosy orange	90	3	From August	
'Majuba'	Decorative (Large)	Deep red	120	4	From early Sept	
'Morning Kiss'	Semi-Cactus (Medium)	Pink and white	120	4	From mid August	
'Orfeo'	Cactus (Medium)	Deep purple	120	4	From mid August	
'Polar Sight'	Cactus (Giant)	White	120	4	From early Sept	
'Princess Marie Jose'	Single	Pink	45	1½	From early August	
'Respectable'	Semi-Cactus (Giant)	Yellow	120	4	From early Sept	
'Rigoletto' Strain	Bedding (Double)	White, bronze, orange, coral, pink, red	38	1¼	From July	

boxes, and later transplant them into 7.5cm (3in) pots of potting
compost. In about April, harden them off in a cold frame and then
plant them out in their flowering quarters in late May, or later.

Climbing and Trailing Plants

Walls and fences provide opportunities – sometimes overlooked by
gardeners – to increase the numbers and variety of plants grown. This
is particularly important where the garden is small and space is at a
premium.

Climbing plants and wall shrubs occupy very little ground area in
relation to their height so that more can be grown in a given space.
Sheltered south and west-facing walls also allow partially tender subjects
to be grown that would not survive a severe winter in the open garden.

Unsupported, many of these plants can be used to trail over difficult
beds and banks, old tree stumps and other similar objects. The more
rampant kinds, such as ivies and some of the honeysuckles, will act as a
ground cover, smothering weeds with a dense carpet of foliage.

Before starting to plant against walls, it must be remembered that the
soil at their base will, in all probability, be poor and certainly
exceptionally dry. Also, the soil next to the walls of new houses is likely
to contain large quantities of mortar and builders' rubble, which is
unsuitable for most shrubs and could mean death to lime-haters.

The best procedure, therefore, is to take out the soil to a depth and
width of 45cm (1½ft) at the base of the wall, replacing it with good soil
from another part of the garden, enriched with peat, leafmould or well-
rotted compost. Alternatively, if this seems too formidable a task, the
planting holes alone can be prepared in this manner.

Wall shrubs and climbers should be planted at a minimum distance of
30cm (1ft) from the wall in order to minimize the effects of soil dryness.

Most types of wall plant fall into one of three categories – clingers,
twiners or wall shrubs. Obviously, those in the first category are the
most trouble-free since they are completely self-supporting. Virginia
creepers and some of the ornamental vines support themselves by small
sucker pads that attach them to the wall surface; others, such as the
ivies, by roots on their stems that cling to the wall.

Clinging plants support themselves by twining stems, leaf stalks or
tendrils. Wisteria, clematis and various vines are examples of these.
Clingers will need the support of wires, trellis or a host plant through
which they can scramble.

Most wall shrubs that do not fall into the above-mentioned classes
will need training and tying in to some kind of support. In many cases,
this will be necessary only until a basic framework of erect and lateral
branches has been formed. Various kinds of support can be used,
including wooden or plastic trellis, wire netting, lengths of galvanized
wire stretched between vine eyes or the special wall nails with lead heads
that are sold for the purpose.

In other parts of the garden, plants can be trained on pergolas and fences, or used to camouflage sheds, outbuildings and other unsightly objects. In the borders, posts or tripods will provide support for roses and clematis, while old fruit trees, past their prime, make excellent 'hosts' for the more vigorous types of climber.

A Selection of Climbers and Wall Shrubs
Actinidia
There are two worthwhile garden species of this Asiatic shrub, both hardy and vigorous deciduous twiners. *A. chinensis*, the Chinese Gooseberry, is noteworthy for its magnificent heart-shaped leaves, up to 20cm (8in) long. The stems are covered in crimson hairs and in favourable seasons and districts, the plants will bear the succulent gooseberry-like fruits that are responsible for its popular name. *A. kolomikta*, the Kolomikta Vine, is somewhat less rampant and is grown for the unusual effect of its harlequin foliage, transversely banded with green, pink and white.
Aspect: S or W
Aristolochia (Dutchman's Pipe)
Only one species of these twining plants is suitable for outdoor cultivation in the British Isles. This is *A. sipho*, also known as *A. durior* and as Dutchman's Pipe, from the curious appearance of its saxophone-shaped yellow flowers. Given a suitable host plant, it will reach a height of 9m (30ft). The heart-shaped leaves grow up to 30cm (1ft) in length.
Aspect: Any
Clematis
Often called, and justly so, the 'queen of climbers', clematis comes in many forms varying greatly in character, shape of blooms and flowering season. Clematis thrive on any aspect provided that the plants have a cool moist root run. Most of the species, such as *C. montana*, *C. orientalis*, *C. tangutica* and *C. viticella*, are easy to establish, but the cultivation of the large-flowered hybrids is bedevilled by the killer disease known as clematis wilt for which, at the present time, no certain cause or cure has been discovered.

This, however, should not deter anyone from planting such outstandingly beautiful named forms as 'Nelly Moser', whose large cyclamen-pink blooms are barred with carmine; 'Hagley Hybrid', shell-pink with brown anthers; 'Lasurstern', a large lavender-blue clematis with white stamens; and 'Marie Boisselot' (or 'Mme. Lecoultre'), the finest white clematis.

Others well deserving of a place are 'Gipsy Queen', violet-purple with velvety sepals; the old favourite, the purple-flowered 'Jackmanii'; 'Barbara Dibley', violet barred with carmine; and 'Vyvian Pennell', violet-blue and one of the finest doubles.
Aspect: Any
Clianthus
The 'Lobster Claw' or 'Parrot's Bill', *Clianthus puniceus*, is a partly tender deciduous wall shrub with exotic scarlet blooms that give the plant its popular names. The ferny foliage makes a perfect setting for these scarlet claw-like flowers.

This shrub needs a sheltered south wall and some kind of protection from frost in winter in any but the most favoured districts of Britain.
Aspect: S
Hedera (Ivies)
The numbers of species and varieties of ivy are very large, *Hedera helix*,

the native Common Ivy, alone having more than twenty varieties. One of these, 'Buttercup' (known also as 'Golden Cloud' or 'Russell's Gold'), is the finest golden ivy. 'Glacier' has silver-grey foliage edged with white and 'Gold Heart' (or 'Jubilee') is a showy cultivar whose emerald-green leaves are conspicuously splashed with gold at their centres.

'Tricolor' and 'Chicago' are smaller and less vigorous than the above-mentioned forms. 'Tricolor' is a dainty small-leaved ivy with white-edged grey-green leaves that become tinged with pink in winter. 'Chicago' has small dark green leaves edged with bronzy-red.

The Persian Ivy, *H. colchica*, is a vigorous and handsome species, noteworthy for the size of its leaves which, in some forms, are as much as 20cm (8in) long. The cultivars 'Dentata' and 'Dentata Variegata' have even larger leaves than the type. In the latter, they are broadly margined with gold.

Aspect: Any

Hydrangea

The Climbing Hydrangea, *H. petiolaris*, makes a good all-rounder for a north wall. In addition to the lavish display of creamy-white flowers in June, there is a colourful bonus of golden foliage in autumn followed by the rich cinnamon brown of its bare stems and branches in winter.

Aspect: Any

Jasmine (*Jasminum*)

There are two species of jasmine that are useful plants for walls or fences. The Winter Jasmine, *J. nudiflorum*, opens its bright yellow trumpet flowers during any mild spells in late autumn and winter.

The Summer Jasmine, *J. officinale*, is a vigorous clinging plant, with white, intensely fragrant flowers.

Aspect: Winter Jasmine: Any   Summer Jasmine: S or W

Lonicera (Honeysuckle)

The honeysuckles are hardy and vigorous twining plants that will thrive in almost any soil or situation. Their somewhat untidy habit of growth makes them more suitable for clothing outbuildings or pergolas than for the walls of the house.

Most kinds, including our native Woodbine, *L. periclymenum*, flower from June to October and are noteworthy for the rich fragrance of their flowers. Among the exceptions are 'Dropmore Scarlet' which compensates for its lack of scent by the showiness of its scarlet flowers.

The two most widely-grown cultivars of the Woodbine are 'Belgica', the so-called Early Dutch Honeysuckle, with its clusters of reddish-purple tubular flowers, and the Late Dutch Honeysuckle, 'Serotina', with flowers of a richer shade of purple.

The Japanese Honeysuckles are exceptionally vigorous and will reach heights of up to 9m (30ft) given suitable support. 'Aureoreticulata' is grown mainly for the beauty of its bright green foliage which is conspicuously netted with gold. 'Halliana', which also makes dense ground cover when grown unsupported, has masses of small yellow flowers whose fragrance is rich and penetrating. Both these honeysuckles are evergreen.

Aspect: Any

Parthenocissus (Virginia Creeper)

The Virginia Creepers, formerly known as *Ampelopsis* and *Vitis*, are a group of rampant climbers that support themselves by tendrils or sucker pads. They include the popular *P. tricuspidata* 'Veitchii', which clothes walls in sheets of scarlet and orange in autumn. The true Virginia Creeper is *P. quinquefolia*, which is looser and more open in habit. Its five-lobed leaves, however, colour just as brilliantly as those of 'Veitchii'.

Where wall space is restricted, a more suitable choice would be the somewhat less vigorous *P. henryana*, an attractive species whose greenish-purple leaves are veined with pink and silver and change colour to a vivid scarlet in autumn.
Aspect: Any

Polygonum baldschuanicum (Russian Vine)
This exceptionally rampant twiner, sometimes known as the 'mile-a-minute' vine, should be introduced into gardens with caution. Once established, it almost lives up to its popular name and spreads rapidly in every direction by underground suckers. It can produce stems as much as 12m (40ft) long in a single season. There is, however, no better quick camouflage for unsightly sheds or outbuildings or as a shrub for scrambling through tall trees, where the beauty of its pink-tinged feathery blossom can be seen to best advantage.
Aspect: Any

Solanum crispum (Climbing Potato)
This climbing species of the potato family is an interesting subject for a sunny south or west wall. It is evergreen or semi-evergreen, exceptionally vigorous, and flowers over a very long period from the first season after planting.

The flowers are very similar in form to those of the potato, but slaty-blue in colour with a prominent yellow 'beak' of stamens at their centre. 'Glasnevin' is the best form. *S. crispum* is useful for chalk soils.
Aspect: S or W

Vitis vinifera
This group of vines, which includes the cultivated grapes, also contains some vigorous ornamental twiners that support themselves by means of tendrils. They bear bunches of small grapes that ripen outdoors in good summers. Among the most decorative are the Parsley Vine, with lacy, finely-cut foliage and the Teinturier Grape, *V. vinifera* 'Purpurea', with leaves of a deep greenish-purple that turn to a deeper crimson in autumn.

'Brant' is a hybrid dual-purpose vine, one of the best outdoor-fruiting varieties of grape. It bears bunches of small black grapes and is also noteworthy for the striking colouring of its purple foliage.

The most spectacular of all the ornamental vines, however, is undoubtedly *V. coignetiae*, the so-called 'Giant Vine'. This is a vigorous non-fruiting species with heart-shaped leaves up to 30cm (1ft) across. It will quickly climb to the top of a tall tree. Its autumn display of brilliant scarlet and orange leaf colour is magnificent.
Aspect: S or W

Wisteria
This deciduous twining climber is one of the showiest for clothing a south or west wall or a pergola. *W. sinensis* is the species most widely grown and the type plant bears long racemes of scented lilac-mauve pea flowers in June. There is also a white form, *alba*.

The most spectacular of all, however, is the cultivar 'Macrobotrys', sometimes listed as *W. multijuga*. This has flower trusses as much as an incredible 1m (3ft) long.
Aspect: S or W

THE KITCHEN GARDEN

Vegetable Growing

If you already grow your own vegetables, you will know that there is nothing to beat the flavour of home-grown crops. If you are a newcomer to vegetable growing, you will soon discover that there are flavours to enjoy which you could not even imagine when you were buying all your vegetables from shops or supermarkets. You will also be able to eat unusual vegetables, which are no more difficult to grow than carrots or lettuce.

Soil and Soil Preparation

In the matter of soil, do not despair if your garden seems to consist of nothing but clay, which clings like glue in wet weather and bakes like concrete when it dries out, or if it is full of hard core left behind by builders. Gardening will present more problems in such circumstances, but with careful soil preparation and cultivation you can grow virtually any crop in virtually any soil, even though not always to perfection.

If you are tackling a new garden, the best time to start is autumn, whether it is a bleak, rubble-covered patch or a wilderness covered with weeds. If you start work in spring or summer, do not attempt to establish order in the vegetable garden and produce crops the same year. This is a good time for planning what crops to grow and where to grow them (see CROP ROTATION, INTERCROPPING and CATCH CROPPING, pages 233–234).

Then, in autumn break up the soil on your intended vegetable patch, using a fork, spade or even a pick-axe if necessary. Do not try to work the soil down to a fine tilth as you go. All you have to do is to turn over every bit of the patch, making sure by deep digging and thorough searching that all of the tenacious perennial weeds are completely uprooted; this means removing every *piece* of root that you can find. Cart away any stones, brickbats, slabs of broken concrete and other rubble. Then leave the roughly-dug soil for winter frosts to break it up.

Towards the end of winter, there should be short spells of fine, dry weather (usually with cold winds, but working will soon warm you up). This is the best time to go over your roughly-dug patch, collecting any plant debris for a garden bonfire and then shaking out each forkful of soil. You will find that the clods have been broken up by frost action and that extricating any remaining weed roots from the soil is easy. When all the rubbish is removed, you will discover that raking over the soil will soon reduce it to a fine tilth. That is all you need to do. Indeed, with a heavy clay soil, it is best not to attempt to dig it again in spring.

If you are lucky enough to be starting your garden on an old grassfield, dig with a spade, turning over each spit and burying the turf root-side uppermost. Leave the patch in this rough state and rake over the surface in spring, but do not dig again then.

In your first year, on a new plot, you should not need to apply organic manures. Healthy soil which has not previously borne a vegetable crop should have enough nutrients for at least one year.

In later years, when the fertility of the soil needs replenishing, dig in manure in autumn, leave the surface rough and rake it down in spring. On no account attempt to dig again in spring, or you will only bring to the surface the manure you buried in autumn.

Rotation of crops means that you grow each crop on a different plot each year. If you grew cabbages, for example, in the same part of the garden year after year, two things would happen – firstly, the supply of nutrients in the soil needed by cabbages would soon become exhausted and, secondly, there would be a build-up of those pests and diseases that attack cabbages. This is why crop rotation is so important.

When planning a rotation, a little botanical knowledge is necessary. It is, for instance, essential to know that cabbages, cauliflower, kale, kohl rabi, Brussels sprouts, turnips, swedes and radishes are all members of the Brassica clan. They extract the same nutrients from the soil and are subject to the same pests and diseases. Similarly, carrots and celery belong to a separate family, and onions and leeks to another.

A simple rotation is based on the division of plants into three groups:
a Brassicas
b Root-crops (excluding Brassica roots)
c Miscellaneous crops, such as beans, peas and lettuce

Put into practice, this means that the bed which produces Brassicas one year will grow root crops in the second, followed by peas, beans, lettuce, or some other crop in the third, and then, in the fourth year, it will be used to grow Brassicas again.

Although there are other cropping plans, this one gives a good rotation, because peas and beans, along with other legumes, have the valuable ability to 'fix' nitrogen gas from the air, that is, to convert it into nitrogen compounds that can be taken up by plants (it is the microscopic bacteria in the root swellings, or 'nodules', of the plants, and not the plants themselves, that effect this transformation). After harvesting, dig in the roots (and also, if possible, the green 'haulms' or stems) of the peas and beans and you will have increased the nitrogen

Using the Vegetable Plot
Crop Rotation

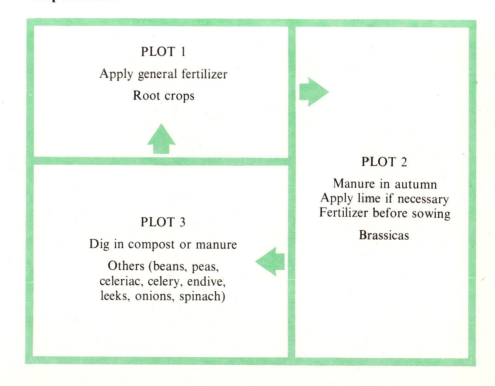

Right: the principle of crop rotation, in which each group of vegetables is moved to a different site every year.

PLOT 1
Apply general fertilizer
Root crops

PLOT 2
Manure in autumn
Apply lime if necessary
Fertilizer before sowing

Brassicas

PLOT 3
Dig in compost or manure

Others (beans, peas, celeriac, celery, endive, leeks, onions, spinach)

content of the soil, which is just what the Brassicas need.

It is as well to be fairly strict about crop rotation. For instance, when digging out a crop of potatoes you are almost sure to miss one or two of the smaller ones, and these tubers will sprout the following spring. The temptation is to leave them to grow and produce an early crop (which they are capable of doing), but digging them up and destroying them is a wiser course, because any tubers that are left will not only upset your rotation but are likely to have been host to pests and diseases through the winter.

Intercropping

Intercropping is the growing of a quick-maturing crop between the rows of a slower-growing one, so as to economize on space. For example, you can fit in a crop of lettuces between rows of slower-growing parsnips. The lettuces will be harvested before the parsnip plants need the space.

Intercropping may seem to contradict the concept of crop rotation, but need not do so if you are careful in your choice of crops. You should also take care not to let your intercropping plants be shaded by the main crop, or to compete with it for moisture.

Other quick-growing crops which can be used for intercropping are radishes, beetroot, carrots and spinach, but be cautious in your use of radishes, remembering that they are Brassicas. Chinese cabbage, another Brassica, is useful for intercropping in the second half of the year, for it takes up little room, grows quickly, and can withstand partial shade.

Catch Cropping

Catch cropping means fitting an extra, quick-growing crop into the rotation; it is another way of getting the maximum out of the available space. For example, if you harvest your early potatoes in June, you can easily fit in a crop of lettuce, spinach, radishes, carrots or turnips on the same plot before winter. Broad beans and early crops of peas, carrots and lettuce are among other vegetables which are harvested in time for another crop to be grown on the same patch in the same year.

Successional Sowing

It is very important, particularly in a small garden, to avoid producing a glut of crops. Instead of sowing large amounts of a particular vegetable,

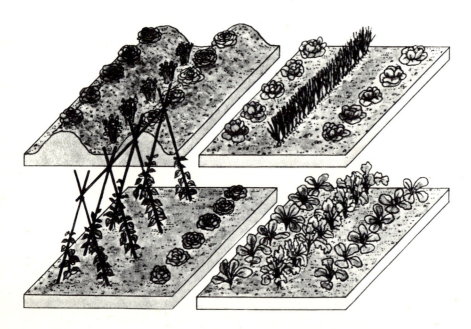

Left: catch cropping may be done with different combinations of vegetables, such as (top) lettuce and celery, and spring onions and winter cabbage, or (bottom) lettuce and runner beans, and turnips and autumn cauliflower.

it is better to sow small quantities of seed at, say, three-weekly intervals throughout the growing season. This 'successional sowing' is particularly suited to quick-growing crops such as lettuce, radishes, turnips, carrots, beetroot and spinach.

Green Manuring

Some gardeners broadcast mustard seed all over the plot as soon as the early crops are removed, digging it in as green manure when it is about 30cm (1ft) high, *before* any flowers appear. As an alternative to mustard, use annual lupins, rape, winter spinach or winter tares (vetch), or proprietary mixtures of green manure crops. (See also under MUSTARD in the A–Z list of vegetables.)

When dug in, a green manure crop will provide small amounts of plant foods, but its main value is that it will increase the humus content of your soil, which improves the soil structure and absorbs plant foods that might otherwise be washed out of the soil.

Unless the green manure crop consists of peas, beans, clover, tares or other legumes, it is very important to add a nitrogenous fertilizer (such as granular ammonium sulphate) at the rate of 60g per sq m (2oz per sq yd) before digging it in, because the soil bacteria that are responsible for the early stages of breaking down the green manure need nitrogen to do this work. If you do not provide nitrogen, these bacteria will rob the soil of any nitrogen it contains, so that it will become 'nitrogen-starved', and cannot produce good crops.

Nursery Beds

It would not be a good idea to use every vacant patch for catch cropping or green manuring. You should reserve some plots vacated by early crops, particularly potatoes, as nursery beds into which you transplant seedlings of cabbage, cauliflower, kale, broccoli, leeks and other crops which are to survive the winter and come to maturity in the following spring.

Raising Vegetables from Seed

Apart from the preparation of the soil during autumn and winter, the basic tasks in growing vegetables from seed are sowing, thinning or transplanting, and harvesting. However, if you did nothing but these basic tasks, your crop would probably be a poor one. To achieve the best results you need to undertake certain important subsidiary operations.

Thwarting the British Climate Only three months of the year can be relied upon to be frost-free (and not always those in many parts of the country). Our growing season is uncomfortably short, though our high latitudes provide some compensation by giving us long hours of daylight around midsummer. In general, however, you will find it necessary to use every possible ruse to thwart the hazards of the British climate.

The best method with those plants which are too tender (at least at the seedling stage) to withstand frost, is to grow them under glass. With some crops unheated glass, such as cloches, cold frames or a cold greenhouse, will be sufficient. Others require moderate heat. If you have no glass, it is as well to buy plants rather than seed.

Fortunately, many crops can endure moderate frosts, while others grow so quickly that they may be sown after all danger of spring frosts is past and still produce a crop before the autumn frosts begin. You should make yourself familiar with the needs and potentialities of each crop before planning your vegetable plot.

A Good Start in Life Generally speaking, vegetables are most vulnerable at the seedling stage. Birds are among the commonest causers of damage. When the sun radiates more heat in spring, and the soil begins to warm up, sparrows love to dust-bathe along the rows of newly sprouting seeds. Birds may also eat many of the seedlings, too. Some protection must be given, and one of the most effective measures is to cover the rows with netting of 19mm ($\frac{3}{4}$in) mesh. Alternatively, you can create an entanglement of black cotton. Make an irregular mesh of it about 2.5cm (1in) from the ground, stretching the cotton tight between pegs or sticks. The birds cannot see it and so when, alighting on the plot, they find the cotton touching their legs or wings, they fly away in panic. Make sure you use *cotton* and not nylon thread, as the latter does not break easily and will entangle the birds, injuring or killing them.

Mice also attack some young seedlings, such as beans and peas, at an early stage, and may also eat the seed beneath the soil. Sow pea or bean seed treated with mouse repellent, or soak them in paraffin.

Watch out for damage by slugs, snails and insect pests such as flea beetles and take appropriate action by hand-picking, setting slug-traps or dusting with derris (see page 38).

Even seeds sown in boxes under glass are not immune to trouble; they are particularly susceptible to fungal diseases, especially those known collectively as 'damping off'. However, damping off may usually be prevented by proper attention to details, such as avoiding over-watering or sowing the seed too thickly. As a precaution, it is often wise to water the compost or the seedlings with Cheshunt Compound, which will prevent damping off. This is available at any good garden shop.

Pelleted seed This is available for the more popular varieties of a number of different vegetables. Pelleted seeds have a coating of a clay-like material which greatly increases their size, making it easy to pick them up and sow them individually at precise distances apart. This avoids the necessity for thinning and gives each seedling plenty of room.

F$_1$ Hybrid seed When looking through seed catalogues, you will notice the term 'F$_1$' or 'F$_1$ Hybrid' after certain varieties of vegetable. Seedsmen produce F$_1$ hybrids by crossing two different, specially selected parent plants. Plants grown from F$_1$ hybrid seed are of exceptionally good quality, vigour and uniformity. Because seed has to be produced afresh each year and it is a complicated job involving hand-pollination, F$_1$ seed is more expensive than ordinary seed, but is worth the extra cost.

Growing the Plants to Maturity

Firstly, in spring and summer, there is vigorous competition for sunlight, air and the nutrients in the soil. Native weeds have an advantage over your crops, particularly the more tender ones. Much of your time in summer will be spent in dealing with weeds. Controlling weeds will also help to reduce the chance of pests and diseases.

Secondly, competition from other plants of the same crop can be quite as disastrous as that from weeds. This is why close-growing seedlings must be thinned out or transplanted; either eat the thinnings or put them on the compost heap, provided that they are not suffering from pests or diseases.

As a general rule, root vegetables are thinned rather than transplanted, but there are exceptions, details of which are given in the A–Z account of growing each crop (below).

Thirdly, you must keep an eye open for attack by any pests or diseases.

Finally, remember that plants can absorb nutrients only in solution. The soil may be rich in all the essential plant foods, but if it is bone dry the plants cannot use any of them. Frequent and copious watering is therefore essential in hot, dry weather.

Harvesting

The commonest fault in harvesting is allowing the vegetables to become too old. Peas and beans should be picked before the pods have hardened; beetroot should be pulled when they are no larger than cricket-balls (or smaller for summer use); marrows cut when they are still growing fast. Harvest at the most succulent stage and use immediately. This applies equally to vegetables intended for deep-freezing. Root vegetables for storing, on the other hand, should usually be allowed to mature.

After harvesting, clear away the remains of each crop as soon as possible. Burn any woody stalks too hard to decay readily and also any plants affected by pests or diseases. Put the rest on the compost heap.

Blanching

Amateur gardeners sometimes shy away from the unknown when confronted with the demand for blanching. There is no need to do so. The technique is simple. All you have to do is exclude light from the growing plant. Full instructions for doing this are given for relevant crops in the growing guide (below).

A–Z VEGETABLE GROWING GUIDE

ARTICHOKE, GLOBE (*Cynara scolymus*)

Perennial, but not completely frost-hardy in the British climate. Grown for its edible flower-buds. You can also blanch the leaf shoots to produce a secondary crop, which can be cooked in the same way as celery or seakale beet.

Varieties Gardeners usually have to take what is available. Green Globe (or Green Ball), Purple Globe, Vert de Laon and Grande Beurre are the commonest of the limited number of varieties.

Soil and Site This crop needs a good, fertile soil, well drained but not so porous that it dries out too quickly. As the plants will remain in position for three or four years, the soil should be well supplied with organic manure in advance.

When choosing a site, bear in mind that the mature plant is a large, bushy one, requiring a space 90–120cm (3–4ft) in diameter which it will occupy for several years, and probably attaining a height of 120–150cm (4–5ft). Allow ample space, on a site where it will not shade other crops. The Globe Artichoke prefers sunshine to shade.

Sowing and Planting Globe artichokes are generally propagated from rooted suckers, or 'offsets', which occur as side growths on mature plants. Split these off in November and allow them to take root in pots of John Innes potting compost No. 1. Keep the potted plants in a frost-free greenhouse or frame during winter, and plant them out in their permanent site in spring. Alternatively, remove the offsets in April, making sure they each have a good amount of root growth, and plant them out as for the pot-grown plants. To economize on space, if that is necessary, plant three plants in a clump, about 45cm (18in) apart, and then allow a space of 90–120cm (3–4ft) to the next clump.

Alternatively, the plants can be grown from seed. Sow in March in a heated greenhouse at a temperature of 12–16°C (55–60°F). Prick out the seedlings into 7.5cm (3in) pots and in May start to harden them off under cloches. Plant out at 15–22.5cm (6–9in) spacing in a nursery bed in late spring, and move to permanent positions the following spring.

Alternatively, sow outdoors in late May, after the last frost, and thin to 15cm (6in) apart. Choose the best plants and discard the weaker ones during summer.

Cultivation Keep well watered. A sprinkling of nitrogenous fertilizer may be applied in spring. Mulch with garden compost, well-rotted farmyard manure or other organic matter in summer. It is a good idea to support tall-growing varieties with stakes.

On no account allow the plants to flower in their first year; pinch out any flower buds. When the plants are mature and in full bearing, restrict the number of main terminal buds or 'king heads' to five or six.

Harvesting Cut the king heads when they are about 10cm (4in) across, snipping off the stem about 15cm (6in) below the base of the bud. Smaller lateral heads will then develop, thus extending the cropping season. Once the flower has expanded, the head is inedible. If there are more heads ready for harvesting than you can use, you should still harvest them all. If the stems are pressed into wet sand the buds, or 'chokes', will last for a week or more.

Producing Blanched Stems After the harvest of buds, if these cease to appear in late summer, cut down the foliage. The plant will then produce new shoots in autumn. When these are 45–60cm (1½–2ft) tall, tie them together and blanch as for celery (using brown paper, black polythene, or drainpipes). Blanching takes five or six weeks, and the blanched stems should be cooked like celery. It is probably as well to reserve this treatment for plants which have come to the end of their bud-bearing life and would otherwise be discarded.

Aftercare Globe artichokes are not completely hardy. In autumn their foliage will wither and should be cut down. In exposed sites, earth up the crowns and cover them with bracken, forest bark or some similar material, but not too deeply or they will rot. Remove the covering in early spring.

During winter, fork in well-rotted manure or garden compost around the plants. Globe artichokes are gross feeders.

Although the Globe artichoke is a perennial, it will produce a worthwhile crop for three or four years only. Discard it after the fourth harvest, having taken steps to ensure a continued supply of plants from rooted suckers.

Problems The crop is usually trouble free, apart from the ubiquitous garden pests such as slugs, snails and earwigs. In some years the buds may be affected by black aphids and these should be picked off or washed off before cooking; a spray will not reach them.

The flower buds may be attacked by a disease known as petal blight in wet, cool summers, particularly in gardens where chrysanthemums, dahlias, anemones or cornflowers are grown. The bud becomes covered with small brown spots and may start to rot. Spray with Zineb.

Root rot will sometimes kill off artichoke plants in winter, particularly in wet, cold soils. It is a sign that the garden drainage needs attention.

ARTICHOKE, JERUSALEM (*Helianthus tuberosus*)
Perennial, but usually grown as an annual, the tubers being planted like potatoes to produce a crop for winter use. Completely frost-hardy.
Varieties Only a few varieties are available, the two principle ones being Purple and White. The White is the better-flavoured. If you find them difficult to obtain from a nursery, use tubers from a greengrocer.
Soil and Site Not a fastidious crop, Jerusalem artichokes will grow in almost any soil that is not waterlogged or excessively acid. They can be left in the same plot for years, though usually do best when replanted annually. Very acid soils should be treated with lime, and an application of potash a few days before planting will be productive: for this you can use fishmeal at the rate of 100g per sq m (3oz per sq yd), or a heavier application of wood ash.

These are tall plants closely related to the Sunflower, and will grow to a height of 2.4m (8ft) or more. Choose a site, therefore, on the north side of the garden, where they will not shade other crops but will make a useful windbreak.
Planting Plant like potatoes, in late February or early March, choosing medium-small tubers. Plant in holes 15cm (6in) deep in rows about 1m (3ft) apart, with 45–60cm (1½–2ft) between plants in the rows.
Cultivation Very little attention is needed, except to give some support to the tall stalks at the height of summer on an exposed site if they start to sprawl. A few stakes linked by string on each side of the stems should be adequate. Alternatively, the tops may be snipped off at a height of 1.5–1.8m (5–6ft), to prevent them from becoming too unwieldy. Weeding is seldom necessary, as the luxuriant foliage smothers most weeds. Some gardeners earth up their artichokes, as with potatoes, to encourage the production of more tubers.
Harvesting In late autumn, when the foliage dies, cut off the stalks about 30cm (1ft) above ground. Lift tubers as required for use throughout autumn and winter. They can be lifted and stored in peat or sand, but retain their flavour better if left in the soil and are not harmed by frost.

Unless you intend to allow the plants to grow on the same site in the following year, finish lifting the crop by the end of winter. It is most important to try and remove every single tuber; even a tiny tuber left in the soil may grow into a troublesome weed the following year. Save some good tubers for replanting next year.
Uses The tubers may be cooked as potatoes; they can be boiled, mashed, baked or fried or made into soup. The slightly smoky flavour is not to everyone's liking. They may also be diced raw and used as a salad.
Problems The crop is usually trouble-free. Tubers left in the ground throughout the winter are sometimes attacked by slugs or grubs. Control these as described on page 36.

Occasionally the stems or tubers are attacked by sclerotinia rot, caused by clearly visible growths of a white, fluffy fungus. The disease is particularly liable to attack stored roots. Burn affected plants or tubers.

ASPARAGUS (*Asparagus officinalis*)
Hardy perennial. Grown for its young shoots, regarded as a delicacy.
Soil and Site Asparagus prefers a light, sandy soil, although this should be enriched with well-rotted farmyard manure or garden compost. In a garden blessed with such soil there is no need to construct the raised beds on which asparagus is often grown; they are required only when it

is necessary to raise the plants above a heavy, waterlogged soil.

Take considerable care with the making of a permanent bed, remembering that, once the plants are established, they will remain there for a long time – perhaps 20 years. Choose a sunny, sheltered site.

Varieties Most readily available are: Connover's Colossal (seeds or crowns), Purple Argenteuil (seeds), Martha Washington (seeds), Limburgia (F_1 seed), Brocks Imperial (F_1 seed) and Sutton's Perfection (crowns).

Sowing and Planting One of the deterrents to asparagus growing is the gap of three years between sowing the seed and harvesting the first crop. Most gardeners shorten this waiting period by purchasing one- or two-year-old crowns. Plant in late March or early April.

The crowns have long, spidery, spreading roots, which will grow much longer. Prepare the bed by digging out a trench about 30cm (1ft) deep, then, using some of the excavated topsoil, form a central ridge in the trench, with its top about 10cm (4in) below the surrounding soil level. Lay the crowns on this ridge, with the roots draped over the sides. Cover with fine sifted topsoil to a depth of about 10cm (4in), and press this down firmly. Plant in single rows, allowing 30–45cm (1–1½ft) between each plant and the same distance between rows. Water generously until the plants are well established.

To grow from seed, soak it in water for several hours to hasten germination, then sow in April in drills 3cm (½in) deep, in rows 45cm (1½ft) apart. Thin, in two stages, to a spacing of about 30cm (1ft) between plants in the rows. Cut down the foliage almost to ground level when it starts to turn yellow in autumn and apply a mulch of garden compost. Transplant into the permanent bed in spring.

Cultivation Repeat the autumn trimming and mulching annually; asparagus particularly appreciates seaweed manure. Feed with potash in the form of wood ashes at the rate of 120g per sq m (4oz per sq yd) during late winter.

Keep the bed free from weeds at all times as asparagus is especially vulnerable to competition, but never hoe deeper than 5cm (2in), or you will damage the shallow roots. Keep the plants well watered in summer.

New asparagus beds may be intercropped with lettuce, radishes and other quick-growing crops, but not after they are three years old.

When the plants are two years old, you should be able to tell which are male and which female (females produce green 'berries', which ripen to red, in autumn); get rid of any female plants as they are only half as productive as the males.

Harvesting Resist the temptation to cut any shoots for the first two seasons after planting, or future crops will suffer greatly. Cut the young shoots when they are 10cm (4in) high, severing them about 10cm (4in) below soil level. Use a sharp knife, ideally a serrated one. The harvest season lasts only about six weeks, from late April to the middle of June. During that period cut every shoot, *except* in the first harvesting year, when only two or three shoots should be taken from the three-year-old plants. The thin, straggly ones can be used for soup. After the end of June, allow the foliage to grow freely; do not cut it for flower arranging, or you will weaken the plants.

Forcing Asparagus can be forced in heated greenhouses for winter use. Choose only crowns at least four years old, lifting them in autumn, after the foliage has died down, and plant in boxes or in beds under greenhouse staging. Plant close together and cover with 5–10cm (2–4in) of sifted soil. Keep them well watered and at a temperature of 16–18 C (60–65°F). Shoots should be ready for cutting after about three weeks.

After forcing, the crowns may be replanted outdoors but they will probably take two years or so to recover.

Problems

Asparagus Beetle The larvae (greyish, hump-backed grubs) attack the shoots and foliage from early summer onwards. Good garden hygiene, including cleaning all beds thoroughly in autumn, is the best precaution. To combat an attack, dust with derris or pyrethrum powder.

Asparagus Fly The larvae, which are tiny white grubs, tunnel in the stems of young shoots and cause them to become distorted and dwarfed. Cut out and burn any affected shoots or stems.

Asparagus Rust This disease sometimes appears in wet summers, producing rust-coloured spots on shoots. Practice good garden hygiene, and cut off and burn affected shoots.

Violet Root Rot A soil-borne fungus disease which attacks a number of other garden crops, including carrots, parsnips, potatoes and beetroots. The foliage turns yellow. On examination, the roots are seen to be entangled in a web of violet-coloured strands. There is no cure. Dig up and burn infected plants. After a bad infestation, do not grow asparagus or other susceptible vegetables on the site for two years.

BEAN, BROAD (*Vicia faba*)

Hardy annual. Grown for the beans, which are gathered when green, shelled from the pods and cooked.

Varieties There are two main groups – those sown in late autumn, of which the commonest is Aquadulce; and those sown in February and March, of which a wide choice is available, including Masterpiece Green Longpod, Meteor, Imperial White Windsor and Green Windsor. There is also a dwarf variety, The Sutton, suitable for growing under cloches.

Soil and Site Broad beans like a rich soil but one which has been prepared for a previous crop and is not freshly manured. They do well in heavy soils, but soil acidity should be corrected by liming.

Choose a reasonably sunny position; a shady site will produce tall, straggly stalks and few beans. The plants will eventually form a dense hedge, so make sure they will not shade other crops.

Sowing An autumn sowing of a suitable variety may be made in November, or up to the end of the first week of December. Do not sow earlier, or the stems will grow too tall and be damaged by frost. The maincrop is sown in February and March, and additional later sowings may be made in April for a succession of crops.

Sow about 5cm (2in) deep in double rows 60–75cm (2–2½ft) apart. Put the seeds in one row opposite the gaps in the other. Allow 15–23cm (6–9in) between plants. Alternatively, sow two or three rows close together, when the plants will help support each other.

Some gardeners draw out a shallow trench and drop the beans into it. Others put in each bean separately with a dibber or a trowel. It is useful to have a plot for raising spare plants in a corner of the garden. Sow surplus seed there and transplant into any gaps that occur in the rows. Alternatively, in a cold area, beans for an early crop may be sown in pots in a cold frame or greenhouse in late January or February and planted out in March or April. Allow only one plant per pot.

Cultivation Broad beans need little attention after sowing. Hoe regularly to keep down weeds, and water well during a drought. As the plants are shallow-rooted they may need to be supported, particularly in windy areas. Stake at intervals round the row, with connecting strands of twine.

The later crops, and sometimes the earlier ones too, are almost certain to be attacked by the Black Dolphin Aphis, better known as the blackfly. This can be controlled by spraying or dusting with derris, but you can greatly reduce the likelihood of an attack by pinching out the tops of the plants, where the aphids congregate, as soon as all the flowers have opened. This will also encourage the formation of pods.

Harvesting Pick the beans when the pods have filled but before they become too hard. Each row should yield several pickings, the pods lowest on the stalks being ready first. The harvesting period is from June to August. The beans can also be picked at an earlier stage, when the pods are tender, and can be cooked whole.

After Harvest It is possible to take a second, though less prolific, crop if desired. When the first crop is finished, cut off the stalks 2.5cm (1in) or so above the ground. The plants will then send up new stems, which in due course will bear flowers and pods.

When you pull up the plants, be sure to add them to the compost heap; the roots in particular are very rich in nitrogen. Alternatively, you can leave the roots in the ground for a following crop that will benefit from the extra nitrogen, such as spinach, lettuce or other leaf vegetables.

Problems The chief pest is blackfly (see above, under CULTIVATION). The seed is often attacked in the ground by mice; soak it well in paraffin. Protect the young plants from birds with netting.

BEAN, FRENCH OR DWARF (*Phaseolus vulgaris*)

Half-hardy annual. Grown chiefly for the green bean pods, but haricot varieties are grown for dried beans which are allowed to ripen and are shelled before use.

Varieties There are three main types of French bean – dwarf, climbing and haricot.

Of the dwarf types, which are those most frequently grown, there are many varieties, including The Prince, Canadian Wonder, Masterpiece, Sprite, Tendergreen and Kinghorn Waxpod (cream-coloured waxlike pods). Blue Lake (with bluish or purple pods) and Purple-Podded Climbing are climbing varieties. Round-podded varieties, such as Kinghorn Waxpod and Tendergreen, are more inclined to produce poorly-shaped pods than are the flat-podded varieties.

Soil and Site These beans will grow in almost any soil or situation. They prefer, however, a sunny, sheltered plot, with a fairly light soil manured for a previous crop.

Sowing Do not sow outdoors until all danger of frost is past, or sow earlier with cloche protection. French beans may be started indoors, but they do not transplant well. Use pots (one plant per pot) rather than trays, and disturb the roots as little as possible when transplanting Peat pots are ideal in this respect.

Outdoors, seeds may be scattered thinly in a flat drill 7.5–10cm (3–4in) wide and about 5cm (2in) deep. To economise on space, sow in double rows, about 30cm (1ft) apart, with a space of 60–90cm (2–3ft) to the next pair of rows. The bean plants in the rows should be about 15cm (6in) apart; thin if necessary.

Cultivation Hoe regularly; this serves the dual purpose of checking the weeds and preventing a hard crust forming on the soil, which will prevent water reaching the roots. Beans like plenty of water, and also benefit from occasional applications of liquid manure, but take care not to splash this on the leaves. A mulch of clean, dry straw will help to conserve moisture and keep the beans clean.

The climbing varieties need stout support from canes or stakes, as with runner beans. The dwarf and haricot varieties do not, but it can be an advantage, especially on an exposed site, to support them with short twiggy sticks. Bean pods which trail on the ground may be eaten by slugs.

Harvesting With dwarf and climbing beans the pods will be ready for picking 8 to 12 weeks from sowing time. Once you start harvesting, you should continue to pick pods every two to four days. The pods mature with surprising rapidity, but as long as you keep picking them the plant will continue to produce more. When ready for picking, a pod should snap easily. If it does not, it is too old and fibrous, but pick it off anyway or its presence will only inhibit the growth of new pods.

Gather the pods carefully. Expert gardeners snip them off with thumbnail and fingers. If you cannot master this technique, use scissors instead. Do not pull them off, or you may pull up the whole plant.

Haricot beans are allowed to ripen thoroughly. Harvest in autumn, when the pods are brown, paper-like and beginning to split. Shell the beans, allow them to dry on trays placed in a light, airy place, and store in glass jars or other damp-proof containers.

Problems There should be very few. Take precautions against slugs, as outlined above. Occasionally blackfly can be a problem; spray or dust with derris and remove and burn infected tops as soon as enough pods have formed. Fungus diseases, such as botrytis (grey mould) and root rot, can be a nuisance in a wet summer or on cold, badly drained soils. Destroy any affected plants or parts of plants.

BEAN, RUNNER (*Phaseolus multiflorus*)
Half-hardy perennial, but always grown as an annual.
Varieties Numerous; among the best known are Enorma, Prizewinner, Streamline, Scarlet Emperor, Kelvedon Marvel, Fry (white-flowered) and Sunset (with salmon-pink flowers).
Soil and Site This is a crop which likes a well-manured plot. Ideally, dig a trench two spits deep and half fill it with well-rotted farmyard manure, then cover with soil. Up to about 90g per sq m (3oz per sq yd) of a balanced compound fertilizer may be incorporated with the soil at the same time, but choose a fertilizer rich in phosphates and potash rather than nitrogen, which promotes lush growth of foliage at the expense of crops. Apply lime if the soil is acid.
Sowing In the soil over the trench, either draw a drill about 10cm (4in) wide and 5cm (2in) deep, in which the beans are placed in a double row, 10–15cm (4–6in) apart, or, alternatively, plant them in the same pattern with a dibber, inserting each bean to a depth of about 5cm (2in). It is a good idea to insert the bean poles before or at the time of planting, to avoid disturbance to the roots of the growing crop later (for details see CULTIVATION, below).

Sow after the normal date of the last frost. Alternatively, sow under cloches a few weeks earlier, placing the cloches in position two or three weeks before sowing to help the soil to warm up. Many gardeners achieve an early start by sowing in boxes or pots in a greenhouse or frame and transplanting the young plants after the danger from frost is past. It is, in any case, a good idea to have a reserve of plants available in pots or boxes or on an odd plot, to fill in any gaps.

The normal procedure is to sow or plant in rows, 90–120cm (3–4ft) apart, but an alternative is to sow in a circle, with the poles arranged wigwam fashion. Another method is to sow three or four beans in the pattern of a cross around a single pole.

Choose a sunny site, but remember that the plants will grow 1.8–2.1m (6–7ft) high and form a dense hedge, shading any crops on the lee side.

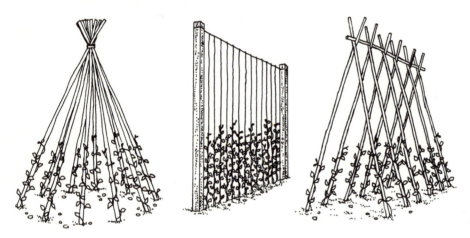

Left: there are various ways of growing and training runner beans, including (left to right) round a 'wigwam' of strings or canes, up a row of strings supported by poles at each end, or as a double row up sloping canes or strings attached to a crossbar.

Cultivation The most important task with runner beans is to get them properly staked; a row of runner beans is very heavy and also vulnerable to strong winds. The traditional method is to use locally cut poles of hazel or chestnut, or stout bamboo canes, but large mesh nylon netting, supported by poles, is more popular nowadays. When the beans are planted in rows, insert the poles in either side of the row, driving them 45cm (1½ft) into the ground, and slanting them slightly inwards so that they cross 1.35–1.5m (4½–5ft) above the ground. Lay a crossbar immediately above the point of intersection and tie the poles together firmly. The climbing stems may also be supported by lengths of twine supported by a crossbar.

For the wigwam support, tie the poles together at about the same level. Strings, trellises, poles or nets may be used to support beans grown against a wall.

The beans will wind naturally around the supports, but if any stray, lend them a hand and, if really necessary, tie them in. When the stems reach the top of the supports it is as well to snip off the tips.

Weed conscientiously in the early stages; later the plants themselves will smother most competition. Beans like to be kept thoroughly moist though not, of course, waterlogged. When watering during spells of dry weather, give enough water to saturate the soil. A mulch of straw, lawn mowings, peat or other material will help to conserve moisture.

Harvesting The beans should be picked green and fresh when they have just attained their full size (or earlier) and before they harden. As they develop very quickly once they have formed, the plants should be examined every other day after picking starts, which is usually in August, 10 to 14 weeks after sowing. Do not allow any pods to ripen on the plant if you wish for a succession of succulent beans for the kitchen. The plants should keep bearing till they succumb to frost.

When clearing the ground at the end of the season, leave the bean roots in the soil; they are a valuable source of nitrogen.

Problems This is a relatively trouble-free crop, most gardeners encountering problems only with slugs (in the early stages) and blackfly.

The latter may be plentiful enough to cause damage and should then be dusted or sprayed with derris; preventative measures are the same as for French and Broad Beans.

BEETROOT (*Beta vulgaris*)

Half-hardy biennial, grown as an annual. Grown for its roots. For leaf beets, see under that heading.

Varieties Two main types; globe and long-rooted. Of the globe varieties Boltardy, Sutton's Globe and Detroit are among the best known. There is also an orange-skinned, yellow-fleshed variety, Burpees Golden, and a white one, Snow White. The commonest long-rooted variety is Cheltenham Greentop.

Soil and Site Beetroots will grow in almost any soil but prefer a light, sandy loam enriched by previous manuring. The crop does particularly well after potatoes, beans or other crops which have been heavily manured. If the soil lacks manure, you can dig it in the previous autumn. It does best on a sunny site. Lime an acid soil.

Sowing Delay sowing until mid May or later, according to the district, as beetroot seedlings are susceptible to frost. Earlier crops can be brought on under cloches. Sow 2.5cm (1in) deep in drills 30–45cm (1–1½ft) apart. Do not transplant, but thin the seedlings in two stages until they stand 10–13cm (4–5in) apart. Successive sowings can be made until early July.

Cultivation Keep the crop free from weeds, by hoeing or mulching, and keep it well watered.

Harvesting Many gardeners do not carry out their second thinning until the largest roots are the size of a table-tennis ball. These are then pulled to allow the others to develop. Small beetroot are the best, although the roots can be allowed to grow to tennis-ball size for winter storage.

After pulling, wash or rub off the soil; do not attempt to clean them with a knife, for the beets will 'bleed' if their skin is broken. Twist off the leaves; do not cut them.

Storing Beetroot for winter use may be left in the ground until required. Cover them with straw or other suitable material in frosty weather. Alternatively, lift in late autumn and store in a box of peat or sand in a cool but frost-proof shed, or in an outdoor clamp (see under POTATO).

Problems Failure to produce beetroot of good quality can be due to leaving the roots to become too large and fibrous; growing in recently manured soil, which will cause the roots to fork or split; or inadequate watering.

Beetroot are also occasionally prone to trouble through mineral deficiencies of the soil. The most likely is crown rot, or heart rot, caused by a deficiency of the trace element, boron. This is most common on light sandy soils in dry weather, or on highly alkaline soils. The leaves die back and the roots may start to rot from inside. The condition can be corrected by adding a little boracic powder, but adequate applications of well-rotted manure, garden compost or seaweed fertilizer in autumn are the best preventative.

Pests which attack beetroot include the Mangold Fly, whose leaf-mining larva produces pale brown blotches in the leaves; pick off and burn infected leaves and encourage plants to grow quickly, to recover from attack. Another pest is the Beet Carrion Beetle, the grubs of which attack leaves of young plants in spring; spray or dust with derris.

The mud-coloured caterpillars of the Swift Moth may eat into the roots; hoe to expose the pests so that the birds will eat them, and keep weeds to a minimum. As a last resort in a severe attack, spray with trichlorphon.

Diseases include scab, usually associated with excessively alkaline soils, Violet Root Rot (see under ASPARAGUS) and Crown Gall, caused by bacteria which abound in badly drained soils and usually enter through a wound. Dig up and burn infected roots.

BORECOLE – see **Kale**

BROCCOLI, SPROUTING (*Brassica oleracea botrytis cymosa*)
Hardy or half-hardy perennial, grown as an annual, biennial or perennial. There are four types of sprouting broccoli: purple, white, green (or Calabrese) and perennial.
Varieties *Purple sprouting:* Early Purple Sprouting, for harvesting from late February (or late January in warm gardens or very mild years) to April, and Late Purple Sprouting, for use from April to May. *White Sprouting:* Early White Sprouting, for use from March to April and Late White Sprouting, for harvesting from April to May. *Calabrese:* A range of varieties is available, maturing from August to November, including Green Comet (F_1) and Express Corona (F_1), both ready from August, followed by Green Duke (F_1) and the late season Autumn Spear. *Perennial:* There is only one variety available, Nine Star Perennial, which will produce a number of creamy white heads each year for four or five years.
Soil and Site As for CABBAGE.
Sowing As for Winter Cauliflower (see CAULIFLOWER), except for Calabrese, which should be sown where it is to mature and then thinned, instead of being transplanted.
Transplanting As for CAULIFLOWER, except for spacing: purple and white sprouting and perennial types should be planted to stand 60–75cm (2–2½ft) each way, and Calabrese with 37cm (15in) between plants and 60cm (2ft) between rows.
Cultivation As for CAULIFLOWER, except that it is not wise to apply nitrogenous fertilizers, although you can mulch with organic matter. By mid-July, stake or earth up stems of purple, white and perennial sprouting broccoli so that they can withstand winds.
Harvesting *Purple and White Varieties:* harvest the stronger central shoots first, and the plant will go on producing smaller side shoots. Snap off the shoots when they are about 10–15cm (4–6in) long, leaving 5cm (2in) of stalk to develop another crop of shoots.
Calabrese: harvest the main central head first, which will encourage the plant to form smaller side-heads.
Perennial type: harvest in the same way as for white and purple varieties, but make sure you remove all heads, even if you do not use them, before they go to seed, and mulch after harvesting.
Problems See under CABBAGE.

BRUSSELS SPROUTS (*Brassica oleracea gemmifera*)
Hardy biennial, usually grown as an annual, primarily for its tight buds, or sprouts; the leafy tops are also delicious when cooked.
Varieties A large range of varieties is available, providing a succession of crops from late summer to the following spring. In the past, gardeners preferred to grow tall plants with large sprouts, but now the

emphasis is more often on smaller sprouts of uniform size, suitable for deep freezing. Varieties include Bedford-Fillbasket, various Roodnerf varieties, Bedford-Winter Harvest, Peer Gynt and Citadel. Rubine is a variety with reddish-purple leaves, stems and sprouts.

Soil and Site These are as for CABBAGE. Avoid a site that is exposed to the wind, bearing in mind that Brussels sprouts are tall plants and that most varieties will be there throughout the winter.

Sowing Brussels sprouts need a long growing season, so you should start them off as early as possible. This means sowing under glass, especially for autumn crops. In the south, it is sometimes possible to sow in September, protecting the plants with cloches during hard weather, for transplanting in spring. Later crops may be sown outdoors in March or early April. Sow 1.3cm ($\frac{1}{2}$in) deep in a well-prepared seed-bed.

Transplanting Allow plenty of room. Transplant, when the plants are 10–15cm (4–6in) high, into rows 60–90cm (2–3ft) apart, with the same distance between the plants in the rows. Plant firmly and fairly deeply, up to the first true leaf.

Cultivation As for CABBAGE, but do not give too much nitrogen.

Harvesting Pick the sprouts as they mature, working from the bottom upwards. It will be possible to make a succession of pickings. Towards the end, cut off the leafy tops, which can be cooked as cabbage. As harvesting proceeds, remove any leaves which turn yellow and put them on the compost heap.

Problems See CABBAGE.

CABBAGE (*Brassica oleracea capitata*)
Hardy biennial, grown as an annual for its tight-hearted crown of leaves.

Varieties There are a great number of varieties. The main groups are:

Round-headed spring-sown cabbages – such as golden Acre, Primo (F$_1$), Christmas Drumhead and Autumn Monarch. White cabbages include Holland Late Winter and Minicole (F$_1$).

Pointed-headed spring-sown cabbages – such as Greyhound, Winnigstadt and Hispi (F$_1$). Hispi can be sown all year round. Both types of spring-sown cabbages are harvested in late summer, autumn or winter.

Autumn-sown cabbages (for harvesting in the following spring and early summer) – such as Wheeler's Imperial, Harbinger and Offenham. These are usually called 'spring cabbages'.

Savoys (*Brassica oleracea bullata major*) are very hardy, spring-sown cabbages with crinkly leaves – varieties include Winter King, Best of All and Ormskirk. (Note: January King is midway between a winter cabbage and a savoy.)

Red Cabbage – sown in spring, harvested in autumn, and often grown for pickling. There are several varieties, all extremely hardy, including Ruby Ball (F$_1$) and Blood Red.

Chinese Cabbage – a quick-growing Brassica, resembling a cos lettuce, for use in late summer. See below, under CABBAGE, CHINESE.

Soil and Site Cabbages are well suited to the British climate and will flourish on almost any soil or site. They are gross feeders and thrive on heavily manured land. Cabbages grown for their hearts do best in open situations; those for spring greens will thrive in partial shade.

Sowing Cabbage may be sown at almost any season, according to variety, but be careful to match the variety to the season. Spring-sown varieties may be sown outdoors in March and April, or they may be started in boxes in greenhouses in January or under cloches in

February. Savoys and red cabbage may be sown outdoors in spring. Autumn-sown cabbages (which are usually and confusingly known as 'spring cabbages' because some mature in the following spring) are sown in early August, earlier in cold gardens.

For outdoor sowing in a seed-bed, sow seeds 1.3cm (½in) deep in rows 15cm (6in) apart. Under glass, sow thinly in boxes and prick out as soon as the plants are large enough to handle.

Transplanting and Thinning Most cabbage crops are best transplanted. Transplant cabbage plants grown outdoors in spring into their permanent sites in June. Those started in July–August may be transplanted in September, but a reserve should be left in the rows throughout the winter, for filling in gaps in spring.

Transplant cabbages when they have four or five leaves. If dry, water both soil and plants thoroughly the day before transplanting. Use a dibber or a trowel to make a planting hole bigger than the root-ball, and drop the seedling in until the lowest leaf is almost touching the soil. Firm in with the feet or by pushing the dibber into the ground at a slight angle alongside the plants to press soil against roots and stem.

Allow 30–50cm (12–20in) between plants in the rows, according to size of variety, and 60cm (2ft) between rows.

It is not necessary, however, to transplant autumn-sown cabbages intended for harvesting as spring greens before they develop hearts. Thin these to 7.5–10cm (3–4in) apart.

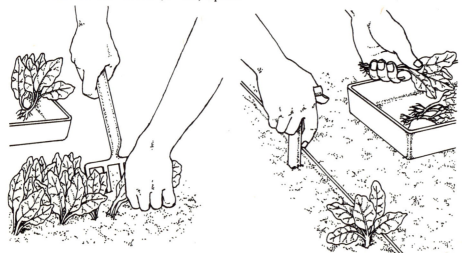

Far left: when transplanting cabbages, loosen the soil with a fork before lifting the plants, taking care not to damage the roots. Left: make the planting hole bigger than the ball and drop the plant in until the lowest leaves almost touch the soil. Firm in well.

Cultivation Cabbages require little attention after transplanting, apart from regular hoeing to control weeds and watering, especially in dry weather. Liquid feeding or monthly applications of dried blood, hoed in, can be beneficial during the growth period (but not in autumn).

Harvesting Cut as required. By proper selection of varieties it is possible to have cabbages available throughout the year. It is possible to store mature cabbages with hard hearts by placing them on racks in a frost-proof shed for up to a month or so in winter, but usually this is not necessary, for savoys and the hardier varieties of cabbage can withstand almost any degree of frost.

Problems Cabbages are liable to attack by a number of pests and diseases. Young seedlings at the two-leaf stage are very vulnerable to flea-beetles, which eat circular holes in the tiny leaves and can quickly devastate a crop. They can be killed by dusting the leaves with derris powder; regular hoeing helps prevent attacks because it disturbs the beetles, discouraging them from laying eggs.

Facing page: above left, the salad onion 'White Lisbon'; above right, early leeks 'Lyon – Prizetaker'; below, carrots 'St Valery'

This page: above, Globe artichokes
'Round French Green'; left, early
lettuces and peas under cloches; below
left, Japanese F1 hybrid onions for
autumn sowing; below, 'Hurst Green

Cabbages are prone to attack by many common garden pests, notably slugs and caterpillars and especially the caterpillars of the cabbage white butterflies and the cabbage moth. In some years these pests reach epidemic proportions. Remove the caterpillars and spray with derris.

Cabbage whiteflies, which look like tiny white moths, sometimes occur in immense numbers, rising in clouds from the leaves when disturbed. They are unfortunately not killed off by winter. Spray with bioresmethrin if you have a bad attack and burn infested leaves.

Cabbage-root fly maggots may attack the roots. Control as described in PLANT HEALTH, page 31.

Club root is a fungus disease of brassicas which generally appears when a proper rotation has not been followed. Once it has occurred, give the plot on which the plants grew a rest from brassicas for five years. It is often associated with badly-drained or very acid soils.

CABBAGE, CHINESE (*Brassica chinensis*)

Half-hardy biennial, grown as an annual. Chinese Cabbage looks rather like a cross between a cabbage and a giant cos lettuce. Most varieties have crunchy white hearts, blanched by the outer leaves.

Varieties Several are now available to the home-grower. These include Sampan (F_1), Nagoka 50 Days (F_1), Pe Tsai, and Round-leaved Santo. All except the last-named form hearts.

Soil and Site The ideal soil is a rich one that retains moisture well and is not markedly acid. If possible, choose a plot that was well-manured at the beginning of the season. If necessary, add lime before sowing. Chinese Cabbage prefers a semi-shaded position and is a good crop for intercropping, also for catch-cropping. When choosing a site, bear in mind that Chinese Cabbage reacts badly to transplanting and so should remain in the same place from sowing until harvesting time.

Cultivation The main problems with Chinese Cabbage are that it tends to 'bolt' (run to seed) in hot dry weather and it will not withstand frost. If the weather is warm and wet, little attention should be necessary, apart from weeding and the occasional watering, but in dry weather, take care to supply plenty of water so that growth is rapid and without check. Mulching with garden compost or lawn mowings will help prevent water loss. Do not give fertilizer as this will encourage bolting.

Sowing and Thinning This is a very quick-growing vegetable ready in about 10 weeks after sowing, so several small successional sowings are advisable. You should start sowing from about mid-June and finish in mid-August. Sow thinly in drills 1.5cm ($\frac{1}{2}$in) deep and about 30cm (1ft) apart and thin the seedlings to about 30cm (1ft) apart. If it is dry at sowing time, water the soil well before sowing and cover seeds with dry soil to act as a moisture-retaining mulch. It is a good idea to tie the heads with soft garden string or raffia to blanch the hearts.

Harvesting and Use Cut them whole as you would a hearting cabbage and use them as soon as possible. Remove the heads as soon as they are ready, or they will bolt. The crisp hearts are delicious cut up and served raw in a salad, or the heart and the outer leaves can be cooked as greens, having the advantage that they have none of the typically strong smell of cabbages, or by the Chinese 'stir-fry' method.

Problems Apart from the danger of bolting dealt with above, there should be few problems with this crop. There should be little trouble with pests and no diseases; if flea beatles attack the seedlings badly (small holes in the leaves) dust with derris.

Facing page: above, kohl rabi 'Early White Vienna'; far left, runner bean 'Enorma'; centre right, first early peas 'Kelvedon Wonder'; below right, potato plants in ridges

Chinese Mustard or Pak Choi (*Brassica pekinensis*) is a closely related vegetable with mild-flavoured green leaves that do not form a heart, somewhat hardier than Chinese Cabbage.

CARROT (*Daucus carota*)
Hardy biennial, grown as an annual for its roots.
Varieties *For forcing* – Amsterdam Forcing, Early Nantes, Konfrix. *Stump-rooted* – Chantenay Red-Cored, Nantes-Champion, Scarlet Horn, Parisian Rondo (round). *Intermediate and Long-rooted* – James' Scarlet Intermediate, Pioneer (F_1), St Valery, Autumn King – Vita Longa.
Soil and Site As with other root crops, freshly manured soil should be avoided, or split and forked roots will result. A sandy loam is best but the soil should not be too light and porous. Choose an open, sunny site.

Work the soil down to a fine tilth. While doing so, you can rake in a granular compound fertilizer low in nitrogen at a rate of 60–120g per sq m (2–4oz per sq yd).
Sowing Sow the seed in shallow drills about 0.6cm ($\frac{1}{4}$in) deep and cover gently with soil. The space between rows should be 15–23cm (6–9in).

As carrot seed is very small and should not be sown too thickly it is a good idea to mix it with sand, sawdust or radish seed (the latter will be ready for harvesting before the carrots and will not compete with them). Alternatively, use pelleted seed. Sow the carrots where they are intended to grow; this is not a crop for transplanting, but for thinning.

Sow a succession of crops throughout spring and summer, the first outdoor sowing (of stump-rooted varieties) being made in early March. For the earliest crop use cloches if available, placing them in position to warm the soil a few weeks before sowing. Outdoor sowing can continue until mid-July.

Under glass, seeds of a forcing variety can be sown from October to March and, if heat is provided, will give you very early crops.

For extra large carrots, use a crowbar to bore holes 45cm ($1\frac{1}{2}$ft) deep and fill them with fine, rich compost. Sow three or four seeds per hole and thin out the weaker seedlings, leaving one strong plant.
Thinning and Cultivation The vital task of thinning should begin when the foliage is 2.5cm (1in) high; thin to a final distance of 5cm (2in) between plants for early crops and 10–15cm (4–6in) apart for maincrops. Thin in the evening, when carrot flies are not likely to be about, and take care not to break or bruise the foliage, as the smell will attract the pests. For the same reason, burn all leaves of thinnings immediately, or bury them in the middle of the compost heap, and keep the soil moist and firm by watering if necessary, as this will also discourage carrot flies from laying their eggs. Keep the hoe going, as carrots compete poorly against weeds. Water well during dry spells.
Harvesting The thinnings should be used as an early harvest. Thin progressively, for a succession of roots. The maincrop can stay in the ground until mid-October, when it should be lifted and stored, or the roots are likely to suffer slug and insect damage.
Storing Clean the carrots as you lift them and cut the foliage about 1.3cm ($\frac{1}{2}$in) above the crown. Store in an outdoor clamp, covered with soil (see under POTATO), or in boxes of peat or dry sand kept in a cool, dry, frost-proof place.
Problems The worst enemy of the carrot is the carrot fly, whose pale yellow maggots eat into the roots, making them unusable. The main above-ground symptom is reddened, wilting foliage. Sowing early, and

then making no further sowings until the end of June, will often avoid attacks completely. Sow seeds as thinly as possible to reduce the need for thinning (see also above, under THINNING). Rows of parsley or onions sown between those of carrots may deter carrot fly, as will a rag soaked in paraffin pulled between the rows now and then (the fly is attracted mainly by the smell of the carrots).

Wireworms, slugs and eelworms can also be troublesome, and aphids sometimes attack in dry weather. Wireworms and slugs are controlled chiefly by good cultivation and garden hygiene; eelworms are a symptom of over-cropping with one crop, the remedy being to give the plot a long rest from carrots. Hand-pick aphids or spray with a derris-pyrethrum mixture; if the attack is really bad, use bioresmethrin.

Fungus diseases may attack the stored roots if dampness seeps in.

CAULIFLOWER (*Brassica oleracea botrytis cauliflora*)
Half-hardy or hardy biennial, generally grown as an annual, for its clusters of thickened flower-buds.

Although there is little difference in taste between them, there are really two different sorts of cauliflower. Winter cauliflowers, or heading broccoli, are hardier than the summer or autumn cauliflowers and can withstand a moderate British winter to produce fine heads, or 'curds', the following spring. This is because they were originally developed from the hardy sprouting broccoli and not from the tender cauliflower. For this reason, we have divided the list of varieties into these two main groups (although seedsmen have now produced crosses between them).

Varieties *Summer or Autumn Cauliflowers* A series of varieties is available, providing a succession of crops maturing from early June to late autumn. Snow King (F_1), Snowball, Alpha Polaris and Mechelse Delta are example of the earliest varieties; Dominant and All the Year Round are for general summer use; Autumn Giant-Autumn Protecting, Flora Blanca and White Heart are for cutting in autumn. There is also a group of Australian varieties of dwarf growth, such as Brisbane, Barrier Reef and South Pacific, which produce pure white heads from September to November.

Winter Cauliflower Here again, a succession of crops is available, extending the harvesting season from January to early June. The varieties maturing from January to March should, however, be grown only in southern or coastal districts, as they are not entirely winter-hardy; these include Angers No. 2 – Snow White, English Winter – Leamington and Angers No. 1 – Superb Early White. Those for heading in April include the Walcheren series, Armado April and English Winter – Reading Giant; those for May and early June use include English Winter – Late Queen, most of the Armado series, English Winter – Progress and Angers No. 5 – Summer Snow.

Soil and Site As for CABBAGE, but take care to avoid frost pockets.

Sowing Seeds of the earliest varieties are usually sown under glass: some in the previous autumn and some, with heat, from January to March of the cropping year. Seeds of late summer and autumn varieties and of all winter cauliflowers are sown outdoors in April to May, thinly in drills 1.3cm ($\frac{1}{2}$in) deep and about 23cm (9in) apart. Thin the seedlings to about 10cm (4in) apart.

Transplanting Do this in suitable weather when the seedlings have four or five true leaves. Space according to variety: for early varieties, allow 45cm ($1\frac{1}{2}$ft) between plants and about 60cm (2ft) between rows, for later

varieties, 60cm (2ft) between plants and 6–90cm (2–3ft) between rows.
Cultivation Water generously, never allowing the soil to dry out, and
keep well weeded. Feed with nitrogenous fertilizer, such as dried blood
at 60g per sq m (2oz per sq yd) or nitro-chalk at 30g per sq m (1oz per
sq yd) and water this in well; alternatively, mulch with garden compost
or well-rotted manure – this will also help to control weed growth.
Harvesting Cut when the curd is fully exposed. If too many heads
mature at once, you can prevent them from discolouring and becoming
unpalatable for up to a week by breaking the mid-ribs of a few leaves
and bending the leaves over the curds; or by lifting the root half out of
the soil and heeling the plant over, so that the curd faces north; or by
tying the leaves over the curd with raffia or string (this can also be used
to protect winter cauliflowers from frost).
Problems See under CABBAGE.

CELERIAC (*Apium graveolens rapaceum*)

Celeriac may be regarded as a type of celery grown for its 'root'
(actually a swollen stem) instead of its stalks (it is botanically a sub-
species of celery). Follow the instructions for growing self-blanching
varieties of CELERY.

Celeriac is, however, hardier than most varieties of celery and will
stand moderately hard frost. Except in very severe winters it may be left
in the ground till required for use; the 'roots' should be earthed up as
far as the base of the stem, to protect against frost and prevent them
from becoming bitter-tasting. Alternatively, it can be lifted in November
and stored in layers in boxes of dry sand, peat or sifted soil, kept in a
dry, frost-proof shed. When storing, retain the innermost leaves on each
root but remove the others.

In the later stages of growth, the leaves of celeriac can be used to
provide a secondary crop. Blanch them by drawing earth up around
them, or wrapping them in cardboard or black polythene.

Most catalogues offer only a few varieties of Celeriac. Globus, Marble
Ball and Dolci are among them.

CELERY (*Apium graveolens*)

Hardy biennial, grown as an annual. Grown for its leaf stalks, which
can be used as either a salad or a cooked vegetable.
Varieties There are many varieties, which can be divided into four main
groups, namely White, Red or Pink, Self-blanching and Green. In the
first category are Giant White, Solid White and White Ice, and in the
second, Giant Red, Giant Pink, Superb Pink and Standard Bearer Red.
The self-blanching varieties include Golden Self-blanching and Lathom
Self-blanching. The Green varieties are relatively recent introductions
from America, and include American Green, Utah and Greensleeves;
they are eaten green and do not need blanching.

An alternative division of celery varieties is into summer and winter
types. The summer varieties, which are mostly white or green, must be
harvested before the first frosts. Sizes range from giant to dwarf varieties.
Soil and Site Celery needs a good, deep, reasonably rich and well-
drained soil. Self-blanching celery may be grown on the flat. It is
sufficient to dig in ample well-rotted manure or garden compost one spit
deep in late winter. For other varieties the ground is usually trenched.
Dig a trench two spits deep in late autumn, and fork as much well-
rotted manure as possible into the bottom; a layer 15–20cm (6–8in) deep

is not too much, as celery is a gross feeder. Cover this lightly with soil but leave the trench open, heaping up the soil on either side. The width of the trench should be about 45cm (1½ft), with a space of about 90cm (3ft) between trenches.

Choose a sunny but sheltered site. Do not grow on a site occupied by carrots in the previous year.

Sowing In Britain celery is normally sown in seed compost in boxes and transplanted. Celery seed is very small, so sow not more than about 6mm (¼in) deep. Water it in gently and cover the compost with paper or hessian to retain the moisture. Keep the boxes in a frost-free place, such as a greenhouse or under a cloche. Outdoors, or in unheated soil, the seed may take as long as five weeks to germinate. There is therefore a great advantage to starting it in a heated greenhouse; if you do not have one, it may be sensible not to bother about raising plants from seed, but to buy them at the transplanting stage from garden shops. Not many plants are needed; a dozen or two will be ample for an average family.

In heated greenhouses, seed is usually sown about mid-March, in order to have plants ready for transplanting towards the end of May or in early June. Alternatively, seed may be sown in an outdoor seed-bed in April. Protecting with cloches helps; these should be placed in position a fortnight or so before sowing, but even so the plants will be ready for transplanting later than those brought on in heat.

Transplanting Transplant all but the self-blanching varieties into the prepared trenches in double rows when they are about 7.5cm (3in) tall. Allow about 20–23cm (8–9in) between plants in both directions for a double row.

Self-blanching and green varieties are best transplanted in a block rather than in rows, allowing a space of about 23cm (9in) each way between plants. Transplant with care, keeping a ball of soil around the roots of each plant.

Cultivation At all times keep the plants well watered. Self-blanching varieties need little further attention, apart from weeding, but the other varieties have to be earthed up. Begin this operation when the plants are 30–38cm (12–15in) high. One method is to tie the stems together just below the leaves and then to draw soil around them in stages, taking great care not to allow it to get between the stems and into the heart. Alternatively, bind cardboard or plastic collars around the stalks; then earth up. An even simpler device is to slip a length of drainpipe over the growing plant, which will grow up through it. Blanching, whatever method is used, will take seven or eight weeks.

Pick off and burn leaves showing celery fly damage during the growth period. Remove any side suckers that appear on the plants.

Harvesting Self-blanching varieties are generally ready for lifting from early August. The trench varieties will follow in autumn and can be harvested right on into winter. Lift the plants with a spade or fork, as they will be firmly rooted.

If plants are still in the ground when frosts become hard, provide some protection in the form of a straw or bracken covering.

Problems There are plenty. Lack of quality in the crop is generally due to inadequate watering or to faulty earthing up, or as a result of attempting to transplant too early, when the soil was cold.

Pests are numerous. One of the commonest is the Celery Fly, whose tiny maggots are leaf-borers, producing pale brown blisters on the leaves and causing them to shrivel and die. Spraying with derris is a

Above: young celery plants should be transplanted into a trench about 20–23cm (8–9in) apart.

precaution, and you should cut off and burn any affected leaves as soon as you see them.

The larvae of the Carrot Fly will attack the roots of young celery plants as well as carrots (both plants being members of the family *Umbelliferae*), which is the reason why these two crops should never be grown in succession in the rotation. See under CARROT.

Slugs are an ever-present menace and are particularly troublesome to mature plants. Control as described on page 36.

Among diseases, Celery Leaf Spot is probably the one most frequently encountered. The leaves are stippled with small brown spots of fungus, each with a black centre. Buy seed that has been given preventive treatment. If an attack occurs, spray with Bordeaux mixture.

Celery Heart Rot occurs chiefly in late crops which have been too long in the ground, exposed to attacks by slugs and other pests and harassed by frost. Lift before that stage is reached. Switch to a distant site the following year.

There are also several virus diseases, sometimes the result of planting in eelworm-infested soil. Some are transmitted by eelworms while others are carried by insects that have been feeding on marrows, cucumbers and other plants of the family *Cucurbitaceae*. Keep celery well away from these in the garden.

CHICORY (*Cichorium intybus*)

Hardy perennial grown as an annual. Grown primarily for its leaves which, forced and blanched, are used as a winter salad.

Varieties The best-known variety is the Witloof or Brussels, listed in most catalogues. Alpha and Normato are newer varieties of similar type; Red Verona has crimson-red foliage and is smaller and less compact. Sugar Loaf Chicory is so different as to be regarded as a distinct crop. It resembles a Cos lettuce and is used similarly for an autumn and early winter salad.

Soil and Site Chicory is a deep-rooted plant and prefers soil well-manured for a previous crop. Dig the site deeply. A sunny site is preferable but the plants will succeed in partial shade.

Sowing Sow 1.3cm ($\frac{1}{2}$in) deep in drills 30–45cm (1–1$\frac{1}{2}$ft) apart in late April or early May. With Sugar Loaf Chicory, delay sowing till June or July.

Thinning Although chicory can be transplanted, thinning is more usual. Thin to a spacing of about 23cm (9in) at the three-leaf stage, 25–30cm (10–12in) with Sugar Loaf Chicory.

Cultivation There is little to do in summer, apart from keeping weeds under control. Cut off any flower-stems that appear.

Harvesting Lift maincrop chicory from November onwards. The roots can be stored for forcing later, or they can be left in the ground till needed for forcing. They are unlikely to be damaged by frost. Dig them up carefully, to avoid damage, as they may be as much as 30–45cm (1–1$\frac{1}{2}$ft) long. If well grown they should have a diameter of 5cm (2in) or more at the top, tapering like a parsnip. Trim off the remains of the foliage just above the crown. For storing, place in layers in boxes of moist sand and keep in a frost-proof place, or stack them outdoors in a deep trench and cover with soil and straw.

Force in batches of six to eight roots at a time throughout the winter. Cut the roots back to a length of about 20cm (8in) and pack them upright about 5–7.5cm (2–3in) apart in containers (boxes, barrels, large pots, or even black polythene bags), filled with damp sand, light soil, peat, or a mixture of any of these. The crowns should, ideally, be 2.5–5cm (1–2in) below the surface. It is important to cover the containers so that light is completely excluded. Store where the temperature is unlikely to fall below 10°C (50°F).

The young, blanched shoots, known as 'chicons', will be 12.5–15cm (5–6in) tall and ready for cutting at any time from four weeks after planting. Lift each root gently and cut off the chicon with a sharp knife just above the crown. If the root is then carefully replaced it will later produce a second, though smaller, chicon. Afterwards, discard the root.

Do not attempt to force or blanch Sugar Loaf Chicory but use it as lettuce, cutting as required throughout autumn and early winter. Even after the outer leaves are damaged by frost, the heart remains sound for a long time, but it is a good idea to cloche the plants in October.

The young green leaves of most varieties of chicory may also be used as green salad during summer and early autumn, but do not weaken the root growth by stripping off all the foliage.

Problems There should be few problems. The larvae of the Swift Moth (large, mud-coloured caterpillars) may attack the roots in some years.

CHINESE CABBAGE – see **Cabbage, Chinese**

COURGETTE – see **Marrow**

CRESS (*Lepidum sativum*)
Hardy annual grown for salads.
Varieties For Cress which is to be harvested at the seedling stage, varieties are not normally named. Land Cress, or American Cress, is grown for its leaves which are used for salads throughout the winter; it may be regarded as a garden variety of the familiar Watercress, which can be cropped in summer.
Soil For seedling cress, grow in shallow boxes of fine soil or on flannel or some similar material. Land Cress requires a rich soil. Well-rotted manure or compost can be added just before sowing. Land Cress will grow in a sunny site or partial shade.
Sowing For cress sown in seed-boxes, the seed should be sprinkled on the surface and pressed in. If it is to be grown with mustard, sow the cress three or four days earlier than the mustard, as it takes longer to germinate.

Land Cress should be sown 6mm ($\frac{1}{4}$in) deep in drills about 30–38cm (12–15in) apart. Sow a succession of crops at intervals of four to six weeks throughout spring, summer and autumn.
Cultivation Cress for harvesting at the seedling stage should be kept at a temperature of not less than 10°C (50°F). It is frequently grown indoors in winter, being started off in dark cupboards until the seed has germinated. Alternatively, the boxes can be covered with black polythene or brown paper. Keep well-watered at all times.

Land Cress germinates slowly and needs frequent attention to keep weeds under control, especially in the early stages. Water generously. A mulch will help to conserve moisture. Thin to 20cm (8in) spacing when the plants can be handled. They may also be transplanted.

Land Cress seed sown in summer or autumn will continue producing leaves during the winter, if protected by cloches (which should be covered with sacking in very cold weather).

Harvesting Seedling cress is ready for cutting 7–11 days after sowing. Cut it with scissors and discard the roots.

Once it has survived the seedling stage, Land Cress grows quickly, forming rosettes of leaves 15–20cm (6–8in) across. They may be ready for cutting at any time from eight weeks after sowing. Cut sparingly at first, snipping off the outer leaves with scissors. Later, as the outer leaves grow old and hard, use the inner ones.

Continue to keep well watered and pinch out any flower stems.

Problems Virtually none, except for slugs and snails (see page 36).

CUCUMBER (*Cucumis sativus*)

Tender annual, grown for its fruit which is used in salads.

Varieties There are two main types, namely, frame or greenhouse cucumbers and ridge or outdoor cucumbers. Of the former, Butcher's Disease-resisting, Femspot (F_1) and Conqueror are good varieties, while among ridge varieties, Burpless and Baton Vert (F_1) can be tried. Gherkins, such as Venlo Pickling, are small varieties of ridge cucumber, grown for pickling. Many varieties are F_1 hybrids, of which it is useless to save the seed. Apple-shaped cucumbers are a novelty variety (Crystal Apple) with round, pale green fruits, and a white outdoor variety, Long White, is also available.

Soil For ridge varieties, as for MARROW. For greenhouse varieties, prepare a hotbed of loamy soil on a foundation of fresh, strawy manure and cover with another layer of manure, this time well-rotted, and finally with another layer of fine, sifted soil.

Sowing For ridge varieties, as for MARROW. For greenhouse varieties, sow seed in seed compost in 7.5cm (3in) pots in a heated greenhouse, at a minimum temperature of 18°C (64°F), in February or early March.

Transplanting For ridge varieties, see MARROW. For greenhouse varieties transfer from 7.5cm (3in) pots to 12.5cm (5in) pots containing John Innes potting compost No. 2 when plants have three true leaves and white roots show on outside of rootball. Maintain the temperature and keep the atmosphere humid. When the roots fill the 12.5cm (5in) pots, pinch out the growing point of each plant and pot on to 23cm (9in) pots containing John Innes potting compost No 3.

When the plants have eight or nine leaves and are 45cm ($1\frac{1}{2}$ft) high, transplant them into the permanent hotbed, setting them 60cm (2ft) apart, after saturating the bed with water. Raise the temperature to 21°C (70°F) and maintain high humidity.

Cultivation For greenhouse varieties, train each plant to horizontal wires fastened at 15cm (6in) intervals to the greenhouse framework. Allow the leading tip to reach the fifth wire, then pinch it out. Stop the lateral stem at the second leaf.

Female flowers have a miniature cucumber at their base; male flowers do not. Remove all male flowers as they open and leave only two female flowers per lateral stem. Some modern varieties produce only female flowers. You should also remove all tendrils. Note: You must *not* remove male flowers of ridge varieties, as the female flowers must be fertilized before fruits will develop. Greenhouse cucumbers produce fruit without fertilization; if the fruit are fertilized they will be bitter and swollen at one end.

Keep the cucumbers well watered and maintain the high humidity, but also provide adequate ventilation. As the sun grows stronger, shade the greenhouse. Supply liquid fertilizer, rich in *organic* nitrogen, about once every 10–14 days.

For cucumbers grown in frames, employ the same basic principles, training the plants to fill the space available, which will mean fewer female flowers per plant than in greenhouse cucumbers. Ventilate with caution.

Harvesting Cut every cucumber while still young.

Problems For ridge varieties, as for MARROWS. Trouble with greenhouse varieties is often due to faults in the environment, such as incorrect temperature, ventilation or humidity level. Drying up and falling of the immature fruits is usually due to inadequate water supplies, or to badly-drained soil. Greenhouse cucumbers are subject to the usual greenhouse pests, notably Red Spider Mite.

CUSTARD MARROW – see **Marrow.**

ENDIVE (*Cichorium endivia*)
Half-hardy annual, whose leaves are grown for salads.

Varieties There are two main groups, the Curled, which is grown for late summer and autumn use, and the Lettuce-leaved, which is a winter crop. In the first group, Moss Curled and Exquisite Curled are probably the best known varieties; Broad-leaved Batavian is the most commonly grown Lettuce-leaved variety.

Soil and Site Endive requires a fairly rich, well-drained soil. The autumn varieties do best in partial shade; the winter ones in a sunny position.

Sowing Sow a succession of curled endive at intervals from early June to late July. Sow seeds 1.3cm ($\frac{1}{2}$in) deep in drills 30–45cm (1–1$\frac{1}{2}$ft) apart. Winter varieties may be sown from July until September, especially if grown in frames or under cloches.

Thinning Thin to 30–38cm (12–15in) spacing. Do not transplant.

Cultivation Hoe and water as necessary: keep the soil moist.

Harvesting Endive leaves are bitter and must be blanched. When each plant is fully grown, which will be 12 to 16 weeks after sowing, cover it with a flower pot (with the drainage hole blocked up to exclude all light), box or some other container, or lift the endive and replant it in a box or pot, to be kept in a dark cellar or cupboard. Alternatively, gather the leaves together and tie them to exclude light from the heart; this method is generally used with winter varieties. Blanching will take one to two weeks in summer, three to four weeks in winter.

Problems Like lettuce, summer crops of endive are very liable to bolt; hence the advice to grow in partial shade and sow late. By regularly watering, you should avoid any check to growth. When blanching, examine the plants frequently as, if left after they have been blanched, they may soon dissolve in a fungal rot.

KALE (or Borecole) (*Brassica oleracea acephala;* also *Brassica napus*)
Hardy biennial, grown as an annual. Grown for its leaves, which are cooked. There are also some perennial varieties.

Varieties The type most often grown is the Curled, of which there are several varieties, one or two of which are dwarf. Hungry-Gap Kale is a dwarf type grown for fresh shoots in spring. Among the less common varieties are Cottager's Kale, which has purple leaves, and Russian Kale, which has silver-grey foliage. Thousand-headed Kale is a perennial.

Soil and Site Like other brassicas, kale thrives in a rich loamy soil, although it is not fastidious. Avoid freshly manured plots if possible,

and correct any soil acidity by liming. A sunny site is preferable, but should be sheltered from strong winds, for most varieties grow tall.
Sowing Sow 1.3cm ($\frac{1}{2}$in) deep in rows 15cm (6in) apart for varieties which can be transplanted (see below), 45–60cm ($1\frac{1}{2}$–2ft) apart for those which are not. Sow maincrop varieties between April and June. The Rape Kales, which are those derived from *Brassica napus*, and which include Hungry-Gap and Russian Kale, are sown in July. Propagation of perennial varieties can also be by cuttings.
Transplanting and Thinning Transplant plants sown between April and June when they have four to five true leaves, at a spacing of about 60cm (2ft) in rows 45–60cm ($1\frac{1}{2}$–2ft) apart. Those remaining in the seed-bed can be thinned, to the same spacing, but results from such plants are generally inferior to those from the transplanted ones. Thin the July-sown crops to a 30cm (1ft) spacing. Do not transplant these varieties.
Cultivation Keep well hoed and watered. If growing on an exposed site, earth up the plants in autumn, to give extra support to the stems.
Harvesting Kale is a hardy stand-by, for use when other green crops are becoming scarce. Frost improves its flavour. Probably the first cutting will not be made until late winter, and with Hungry-Gap not until spring. With most varieties cut the crown leaves first. The woody stems will subsequently produce a profusion of side-shoots, which can be picked as required, until the plants start to produce flowers in May.

When the plants are discarded, burn the stems, as they are too hard, and fibrous to rot down in a reasonable time on the compost heap.
Problems Kale is subject to all the ailments and pests common to Brassicas. See also under CABBAGE.

KOHLRABI (*Brassica oleracea gongyloides*)
Half-hardy biennial grown as an annual for its swollen stem, which resembles a bulbous root. After the skin has been removed, this can be boiled or fried and eaten hot, or grated and used in salads. The leaves can also be cooked like cabbage.
Varieties There are two main varieties – Purple and White, sometimes listed as Purple Vienna and White Vienna.
Soil and Site Kohlrabi is not a fastidious crop. It will grow in almost any type of soil, but do not grow it in freshly manured ground. It also dislikes an acid soil, so correct any acidity with lime. When planning the rotation, remember that Kohlrabi is a brassica and therefore should not be grown immediately after cabbage, Brussels sprouts, broccoli or other brassica crops. It prefers a sunny site, but will grow in partial shade.
Sowing Sow about 1.3cm ($\frac{1}{2}$in) deep in drills 38–45cm (15–18in) apart. Make the first sowing outdoors in early or mid-May, unless protected by cloches, when it can be earlier. Thereafter make successive sowings until about mid July.

Alternatively, the seed may be sown in trays and the seedlings transplanted. This does not always ensure an earlier crop, for transplanting imposes quite a severe check on the plants.
Transplanting and Thinning Thin to a spacing of 10–15cm (4–6in) between plants. Later, as the plants become large enough to harvest, continue thinning to a final spacing of 20–25cm (8–10in).

If transplanting, move the plants when they are large enough to handle and plant to a spacing of about 25cm (10in) between plants.

Keep the plants well watered, especially when thinning and transplanting and keep the hoe busy, both to suppress weeds and to loosen the soil. Do not earth up the plants; the bulbous stem should lie entirely above the surface of the soil.

Harvesting Do not delay too long; start to harvest the globes when they are about 5cm (2in) in diameter. If allowed to grow larger than about 7.5cm (3in) in diameter, they will become hard and lose their flavour.

Kohlrabi should be used when freshly harvested, although the globes will keep for a few weeks stored in layers in boxes of dry peat. They are also suitable for deep freezing; pull them when young and tender and blanch them whole.

Problems Kohlrabi are beset by the normal Brassica troubles (see under CABBAGE). However, once the plants are well established and growing satisfactorily there should be few problems. Poor crops are usually a result of inadequate watering, especially in the early stages.

LEAF BEETS: Spinach Beet and **Seakale Beet,** or **Swiss Chard** (*Beta vulgaris cicla*)

Hardy or half-hardy biennials, grown for their leaves and broad leaf mid-ribs.

Varieties Of the two main types, Spinach Beet has broad succulent green leaves which, apart from their colour, resemble those of ordinary beetroot. Seakale Beet (Swiss Chard) has similar, though often larger, more crinkly leaves with broad white mid-ribs and leaf-stalks. Rhubarb Beet is a very ornamental variety of Seakale Beet with red mid-ribs and stems and purplish-red leaves.

Soil and Site Leaf beets will thrive in most soils. They benefit from large quantities of well-rotted manure, to promote luxuriant leaf growth, and will succeed in a sunny site or in partial shade.

Sowing Sow 2.5cm (1in) deep in drills 38–45cm (15–18in) apart. April or early May sowings will provide a summer and autumn crop. Sowings in July and August will supply a harvest in winter and spring.

Cultivation Thin to 20cm (8in) between plants; do not transplant. Keep well watered; this is a leaf crop and needs to be kept growing strongly without a check. A mulch is better than the hoe for weed control, as it helps to conserve moisture.

Harvesting Pick the leaves as they become large enough, starting with the outer ones. Do not use a knife; pluck them, breaking off each stem as near the rootstock as possible. Take a few leaves at a time from each plant; never strip any plant of all its leaves. Cut off any flower stems.

The spring-sown crop will yield a succession of pickings throughout the summer. Do not discard the plants at this stage but allow to remain in the soil through the winter. You can then take a further harvest of leaves in the following spring, until the plant sends up strong flower-stems. Top dress with a nitrogenous fertilizer as the leaves start to grow.

Problems This vegetable is virtually trouble free, apart from the ravages of slugs. Unsatisfactory crops are generally due to either insufficient watering or inadequate thinning.

LEEK (*Allium ampeloprasum porrum*)

Hardy biennial grown as an annual for its succulent stem.

Varieties Early varieties include Lyon, Early Market and Lyon – Prizetaker. Mid-season varieties are Musselburgh, Giant Winter – Highland Giant and Autumn Mammoth – Walton Mammoth. For late season there are Giant Winter – Royal Favourite, Winter Crop and Catalina.

Soil and Site Use ground heavily manured with well-rotted manure or compost in the previous autumn or else manured for a previous crop. Leeks thrive in a deep, rich soil, though they will grow in most gardens that are reasonably well drained.

Leeks are one of the crops which are transplanted, thus requiring both a seed bed of fine soil and a permanent site. For the latter many gardeners prefer to grow their leeks in trenches. These should be about 30cm (1ft) deep and must be prepared well in advance. If dug two spits deep, manure or compost can be incorporated in the bottom spit.

Leeks will succeed in either sunlight or partial shade.

Sowing For early leeks, sow seed in trays under glass from January onwards. For main crops, sow outdoors from mid-March onwards. Sow thinly in drills about 7mm (¼in) deep and 10cm (4in) apart.

Transplanting It is advisable always to transplant leeks, after an initial thinning to 10cm (4in) apart, though those left in the seed-bed can be thinned again to a 15cm (6in) spacing. They will, however, be shallow-rooted and so should be earthed up.

The aim is to grow leeks with long, stout, blanched stems. Transplant when they are about 20cm (8in) tall. When transplanting, make a hole 15cm (6in) deep with a dibber, insert the leek and water it in. The water will wash the soil in around the roots, and this is sufficient; do not press down the soil firmly. When transplanting into a trench, follow the same technique and do not fill in the trench immediately. Trim off the ends of the leaves at transplanting time, to promote vigorous growth and to prevent them from trailing in the soil and rotting.

Cultivation As the leeks grow, draw in the soil around them, a small amount at a time. This, of course, is easier in trenches, for surplus loose soil is ready to hand. Some gardeners tie collars of cardboard or black plastic around the stems to blanch the stems and also to keep them clean. As the stems grow longer and fatter the collars may be replaced by lengths of drainpipe. Good stout leeks, though not perhaps of exhibition standard, may, however, be grown without collars.

Keep the plants well watered and weeded throughout the growth period. They may be fed, about once a fortnight, with liquid manure.

Harvesting Early leeks should be harvested in autumn. The later

Below left: leek plants being dropped into 15cm (6in) deep holes and watered in. Below right: soil drawn up around the plants helps to blanch the stems.

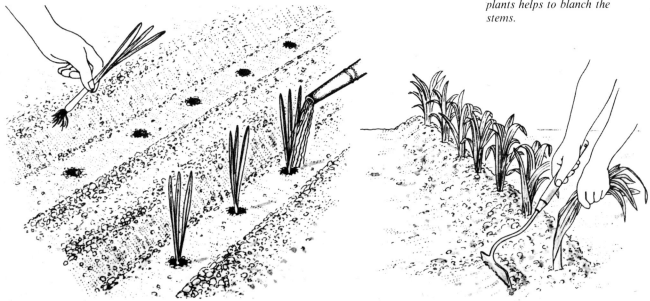

varieties are completely frost hardy and may be left in the ground till
needed. They make considerable growth in late autumn and will start to
grow again in spring, so do not be in a hurry to dig them until they are
needed. They will probably not send up flower stems till early May.

Lift them carefully, using a spade to lever out the roots, which will be
deep and well anchored.

Problems This crop is usually trouble-free. Occasionally it is attacked by
Onion Fly maggots. See under ONION.

Occasionally, too, Leek Moth caterpillars can be troublesome. These
are leaf-mining caterpillars, whose tunnels cause white streaks to appear
in the leaves and sap their strength. Control by using nicotine spray.

Several rots and rusts may attack the plants, though they are not
usually troublesome. Plants grown in good, well-drained soil in a proper
rotation are seldom affected. Leek rust disfigures the leaves with
brownish, powdery spots. It may indicate an imbalance of plant
nutrients, with an excess of nitrogen. A bad infestation can be
controlled with a zineb spray. White rot produces as symptoms
yellowing leaves and white, fluffy, fungus growth at the base of the
plant. There is no satisfactory control for this; destroy affected plants.

LETTUCE (*Lactuca sativa*)
Half-hardy and hardy annuals.
Varieties There are two main types, cabbage and cos, and one less
frequently grown, loose-leaf.

Of cabbage lettuce there are numerous varieties. Those for forcing
under glass in winter and early spring include Unrivalled, May King,
Dandie and Kloek. Maincrop varieties for spring and summer sowing in
open ground include All the Year Round, Appia, Tom Thumb (a dwarf
variety) and Buttercrunch, all of which are soft, round lettuces known
as butterheads. Crisp-hearted varieties, also for summer sowing, include
Webb's Wonderful and Windermere. Cos lettuces, which are tall and
cylindrical and have crisp, sweet leaves, include Lobjoit's Green, Winter
Density and Little Gem, the last two being dwarf varieties. Of the loose-
leaved or non-hearting varieties Salad Bowl is one of the best. Several
cabbage varieties, such as Valdor and Arctic King, are very hardy and
were bred for autumn sowing outdoors.

The crisp-hearted and cos varieties take longer to mature but
withstand drought better than most of the butterhead varieties.
Soil and Site A sunny site is desirable. Lettuces will grow in almost
any soil but succeed best in fertile, well-drained ground, preferably
not freshly manured. Correct any acidity by liming. Lettuces can often
be grown as a catchcrop between rows of slower growing vegetables
such as celery.
Sowing Sow 1.3cm ($\frac{1}{2}$in) deep in rows 38–45cm (15–18in) apart.
Germination takes 4–12 days. Early crops may be brought on under
glass and transplanted, or they may be sown under cloches.
Thinning or Transplanting Early and late crops may be transplanted.
With maincrops, however, the check imposed by transplanting in warm,
sunny weather often causes the plants to bolt. With summer crops, thin
when the plants are large enough to handle. For most varieties, thin to
25–35cm (10–14in), or transplant to the same spacing. Cos varieties
need less space, and dwarf varieties, such as Tom Thumb, even less.
Cultivation The main preoccupation with lettuce is to avoid any check
to growth. Therefore keep the soil well watered at all times, but do not

drown the plants. Mulching with well-rotted manure, garden compost or other organic matter will feed the plants, retain moisture and help suppress weeds. Control weeds also by hoeing and hand weeding.

Harvesting In spring, start by using the fresh young thinnings for salads. Maincrops come to maturity 42–80 days from sowing. Autumn-sown crops of the correct varieties will withstand a normal winter and produce succulent hearts the following spring. They may be protected by cloches. Cut leaves from a lettuce with a sharp knife or pull them up and cut off the roots if you wish to store them for a few days.

Problems The chief cause of failure is premature bolting. There will often be a few plants which throw up a flowerhead early, but wholesale bolting should not occur if enough water was given and if transplanting was done with care. Inadequate thinning always produces poor crops.

Chief pests are slugs, millipedes and sometimes cutworms. Under wet conditions the plants are occasionally attacked by grey mould (botrytis). Remove and burn diseased plants.

MARROW (including **Custard Marrows, Squashes, Courgettes** and **Pumpkins**) (*Cucurbita pepo ovifera*; also *C. maxima* and *C. moschata*) Tender annuals, grown for their fruits (which are used as vegetables).

Varieties Of the common marrow there are two main types – Trailing and Bush. The varieties within these types are usually named according to colour, e.g. Improved Green Trailing or White Bush.

Courgettes, or Zucchini, are immature marrows. They are usually dark green, but there is a golden type called burpee's Golden Zucchini.

Custard Marrows resemble in shape the popular idea of a 'flying saucer' with scalloped edges.

Pumpkins are massive spherical cucurbits, mostly orange-buff in colour. Although perfectly edible, and indeed, if properly prepared, delicious, they are often grown for decoration and competition.

Soil and Site All types of marrow do best in the richest possible soil, though they can be grown in any normally fertile garden. They will flourish on a well-rotted heap of farmyard-manure; trenches or pits may be dug instead, and filled with manure or garden compost. Provided they are kept well watered, they like a sunny site.

Sowing Marrows are often raised in seed-boxes under heated glass and transplanted, to give them a flying start. They can, however, be sown in seed-beds outdoors when all danger of frost is past. Sow the seeds individually about 2.5cm (1in) deep and 7.5–10cm (3–4in) apart.

Transplanting Transplant when frosts are no longer a danger. Handle the plants carefully, keeping a ball of soil around each root. Allow a space 1.2m (4ft) in diameter for bush types and 1.8m (6ft) across for trailing types. Pumpkins need even more – about 2.1m (7ft).

Cultivation Your most important task is to keep the plants generously watered, so that they never experience a check. Keep the site weeded, especially in the early stages; later the spreading leaves will smother weeds.

Harvesting Cut as fast as the fruits develop (except if grown for size). Young tender fruit are much to be preferred to mature, hard-skinned ones. Courgettes in particular should be cut when no more than about 10cm (4in) long.

If the last fruits are allowed to grow to full size and to ripen they may be stored in a dry, frost-proof place for several months.

Problems The chief problem is getting the timing for transplanting just right in spring. If too early, the plants are checked by cold weather; if too late, valuable growing time is lost. Learn from experience.

The plants are unlikely to be attacked by any pests (although black aphids can occasionally be troublesome). Several fungus diseases, particularly grey mould (botrytis), may cause the fruit to rot, especially towards the end of a wet summer. Remove and destroy affected fruits.

MUSTARD (*Sinapis alba*)

Hardy annual. Grown for two purposes: for green salad at the seedling stage and for green manuring.

Varieties Usually only one is listed – White Mustard.

Soil and Site Mustard for salad is grown in very fine soil in seed trays or other containers, or on pads of flannel or similar material. Mustard for green manuring will grow in any soil.

Sowing For both purposes, sow broadcast. For salad mustard, sprinkle seed on the surface of the soil or material and press it in firmly. Salad mustard is usually sown with cress. It germinates rather more quickly than cress and should be sown three to four days later if the crops are to be harvested together.

Mustard seed for green manuring should be raked into the soil.

Cultivation For salad mustard, the seed-trays should be kept at a temperature of not less than 10°C (50°F). They can be covered with black polythene or brown paper or kept in a dark cupboard until the seed has germinated. Keep them well watered with tepid water.

Harvesting Mustard seedlings should be ready for cutting from four to seven days after sowing. Cut them at the two-leaf stage.

Mustard for green manuring should be allowed to grow to a height of 15–30cm (6–12in) and then dug in before it flowers. It should reach this stage in about five or six weeks from sowing. Tread or cut it down first, after sprinkling it with a nitrogenous fertilizer at 60g per sq m (2oz per sq yd) so that the soil is not robbed of nitrogen (see page 235).

Problems None should arise with salad mustard. Flea-beetles may attack mustard sown outdoors and could destroy the crop at the seedling stage. Combat with derris only if really necessary.

Remember that mustard is a brassica and that its use as a green manure can upset the rotation, giving an opportunity for typical brassica diseases, such as club-root, to develop.

NEW ZEALAND SPINACH – see **Spinach**

ONION (*Allium cepa*)

Hardy biennial grown as an annual for its bulbs, which are used as a vegetable; includes spring onions grown for green salad. There are a few perennial onions.

Varieties Spring-sown onion varieties include Bedfordshire Champion, Rijnsburger, Hygro and White Lisbon (this last is usually grown for salad onions). Hardy varieties for autumn sowing include Solidity, Ailsa Craig and Giant Zittau. In recent years Japanese varieties, which are sown in August to provide bulb onions in June and early July, have become popular; these include Express Yellow (F_1) and Senshyu. Onion sets are small onions which have been lifted in autumn and heat-treated so that they can be replanted in spring without fear of them bolting in the summer. The bulbs produced are often larger than from spring-sown seed. Sturon and Stuttgart Giant are good varieties.

The Welsh Onion (*Allium fistulosum*) is a perennial grown for its green leaves. It does not produce a bulb.

Soil and site Onions like a rich though light soil but not one recently manured. Any organic manuring should have been done in the previous autumn. Correct any acidity by liming. Work down to a fine tilth before sowing and make into a firm seed-bed.

Sowing Sow maincrop onions 1.3cm ($\frac{1}{2}$in) deep in drills 30–45cm (1–1$\frac{1}{2}$ft) apart between the end of February and the end of April. Salad onions may be sown at intervals throughout spring and summer for a succession of crops.

For an early crop, sow in seed-trays in a cool greenhouse and transplant, or protect early sowings with cloches.

For autumn sowing, sow in early September, but sow Japanese varieties about mid-August. Sow rather more thickly than with spring-sown onions, to allow for losses.

Transplanting and Thinning Transplant onion plants from trays 10–12.5cm (4–5in) apart in rows 30–45cm (1–1$\frac{1}{2}$ft) apart. Autumn-sown onions may be either thinned (to the same spacing) or transplanted. Spring-sown onions may also be transplanted but are usually thinned, the thinnings being used as salad onions. Do not transplant the Japanese varieties.

When transplanting, allow a hole deep enough for the roots to be well buried in the soil but ensure that the base of the bulb is no more than about 1.3cm ($\frac{1}{2}$in) below the surface. Plant firmly.

Plant onion sets in March and April in rows 30–45cm (1–1$\frac{1}{2}$ft) apart. Allow 10–15cm (4–6in) between plants. Plant with the tips of the sets just above the soil surface. Avoid planting in cold soil; this may mean waiting until April.

Cultivation Onions, with their thin upright leaves, do not compete well against weeds. In addition to keeping the hoe busy between the rows, hand-weeding will probably be necessary. When hoeing, do not disturb the soil too close to the plants. Keep the patch watered in dry weather, until the bulbs start to ripen. Feed occasionally with liquid fertilizer.

Harvesting Japanese varieties will be ready for harvesting in June and July. They are for immediate use and will not keep. Autumn-sown onions and onion sets should be ready in July or August, the maincrop about a month later.

Try to harvest during a spell of dry weather. When the leaves have turned yellow and shrivelled, the onions are ripe. Ease the roots out of the soil with a fork. In sunny weather they may be left to dry on the ground, on a dry sack, or on a frame of wire-netting; in rainy weather, dry them off indoors in a greenhouse or shed.

Storing When dry, onions are ideally stored by tying them in ropes and hanging in a frost-proof shed, a cellar or even a kitchen. Alternatively, place them in a single layer on trays.

Problems A problem likely to be encountered with onion sets is that they may rise out of the soil. Examine the rows frequently and replace any that have moved out of rank. Birds are inclined to pull up the young plants, too, and scatter them, so protect the seedlings with nets.

The most prevalent insect pest is the Onion Fly, the larvae of which tunnel into the bulb and stem of the young plant. As the flies are about in May, early sowing is helpful, and autumn-sown onions are less likely to be attacked than spring-sown ones. Trichlorphon watered into the soil in May and June is a fairly effective treatment for a serious attack.

Eelworm infestation, which causes deformity in the plants, results from failure to follow a proper crop rotation. Several fungal diseases, notably neck rot and soft rot, may attack onions in store. Examine the bulbs from time to time and burn any infected ones.

PARSNIP (*Pastinaca sativa*)

Hardy biennial grown as an annual for its roots.

Varieties Varieties are grouped according to the length of their roots. Long-rooted are perhaps the most popular type; examples are Improved Hollow Crown and Tender and True. Medium-rooted varieties include White Gem and Offenham. Short-rooted varieties are less common; the best known is Avonresister.

Soil and Site It is important that the soil is not freshly manured with organic manure, or forked and misshapen roots will result. A stony soil will produce the same result. Otherwise soil type is not really important, provided there is a good depth of soil. Choose a sunny position.

Sowing Parsnips are slow to germinate and grow and so should be given as long a growing period as possible. Sow as soon as the soil is in fit condition at the end of winter or in early spring 2–2.5cm ($\frac{3}{4}$–1in) deep in drills about 45cm ($1\frac{1}{2}$ft) apart. As germination at this season can take as long as a month it is helpful to sow quick-germinating seeds, such as radish or lettuce, with the parsnip seed, to mark the position of the row.

For extra long parsnips, dig a hole 1m (3ft) deep, or make it with a crowbar, and fill with compost. Sow three seeds in each hole, removing the two weakest seedlings later.

Thinning Thin the plants to 15–23cm (6–9in) apart when they are large enough to handle; do not transplant.

Cultivation In the early stages it will be necessary to hoe frequently; later in summer the foliage will smother most weeds. Parsnips like a moist soil; if watering is necessary do it thoroughly. Make a shallow depression around each root and pour in sufficient water to saturate the soil and penetrate to the tip of the root. Remove any catchcrops sown with the parsnips before they start to compete. Weed carefully, taking care not to damage the roots with the hoe.

Harvesting Parsnips, being thoroughly hardy, may be left in the ground until required for use. Mark the rows as the tops will die right down. The flavour of parsnips is commonly considered to be improved by frost. If the plot is needed, however, they can be lifted and stored in layers of dry sand or peat, in a dry, dark place. Cut off leaves close to the crown before storing.

When lifting long-rooted parsnips dig a deep hole at one side of the root and lift it out sideways, to avoid damage.

Problems Parsnips are fairly trouble-free. Canker is the most prevalent disease. Its symptoms are orange-brown discolourations and patches of decay on the shoulder of the root. These will eventually extend down the root and destroy it. There are no easy remedies, though Avonresister and Tender and True are resistant varieties.

When Celery Fly are present in the garden some may transfer their attention from the celery to the parsnips. The tiny maggots burrow in the leaves, producing brown blisters and can severely check the growth of young plants. Remove by hand-picking and hang paraffin-soaked rags near the parsnips to discourage the flies from egg-laying. Spray with nicotine or malathion after removing affected leaves.

Wireworms, which tunnel into the roots, are occasionally

troublesome, though usually only on soil freshly reclaimed from grassland.

PEA (*Pisum sativum*)
Hardy annual, grown for its immature seeds.

Varieties There is a very large range of varieties, developed to mature in succession throughout the summer. Among the earliest varieties are Pioneer, Kelvedon Wonder, Gradus and Little Marvel. Second-earlies include Hurst Green Shaft, Onward and Fek. Onward is also used as a maincrop, as are Lord Chancellor, Victory Freezer, Senator and Achievement. All of these are wrinkle-seeded. Round-seeded varieties, of which Pilot and Meteor are examples, are hardier and may be sown in late autumn for maturing in early summer, although there is always a risk of damage by frost or excessive rain in winter.

In addition, there are several special varieties, such as Petit Pois and Sugar Pea, as well as the Asparagus Pea, which is not botanically a pea at all but a kind of Lotus.

Soil and Site Peas like a rich, well-cultivated soil but not one which has been freshly-manured, for that would promote leaf growth at the expense of pods. Correct any acidity with lime. Choose an open site, although not one exposed to strong winds. Orientate the rows in a north–south direction, so that all the plants get their share of sunlight. Note the height to which each variety is likely to grow, and do not plant the tall ones where they will shade another sun-loving crop.

Sowing Make a succession of sowings from early spring onwards (and from late autumn through the winter in favourable districts or if grown under cloches). The early crops (except the autumn-sown ones) take 11–12 weeks to produce a crop; the second earlies, 12–13 weeks; and the maincrop varieties, 13–14 weeks. The last summer sowing should be made in early June and should be of one of the early, quick-growing varieties; Kelvedon Wonder is a good choice.

With a hoe draw out a flat drill 10–15cm (4–6in) wide and 5cm (2in) deep and sow in a double staggered row with about 5–7.5cm (2–3in) between each seed (more thickly with autumn and early crops, to allow for wastage). As protection against mice, try to obtain seed dressed with a repellent chemical. If this is not available, soak the seed in paraffin. Allow 60–120cm (2–4ft) between rows, according to variety.

Peas are not normally transplanted or thinned, but it is possible to bring on early peas in pots (one per pot) under glass and transplant, disturbing the roots as little as possible. Peat pots are best for this.

Cultivation All except the dwarf varieties need staking. The traditional method is to use twiggy hazel-sticks, but these are often difficult to obtain and plastic netting is a modern alternative. Anchor the netting firmly at either end of the row. Note the height to which each variety grows when selecting seed and plan accordingly. Weed regularly, but be careful not to damage the roots when hoeing.

Keep the crop well watered to avoid a check in growth. Mulches of organic matter will help retain moisture and deter weeds.

Harvesting Pick the pods when they are young, green and fresh. They will harden and lose their flavour if left for even a day or two after the critical stage. Two, sometimes three, pickings can be expected from each row of peas.

After that, remove the haulm quickly and put it on the compost heap if not diseased. Leave the roots in the soil; they are rich in nitrogen and will improve the fertility for the next crop.

Problems As already indicated, mice can play havoc with the seed as soon as it is sown. Sparrows and other birds are very prone to attack the seedlings, which will probably need to be protected by netting.

The white maggots often found in the later crops of peas are the larvae of the Pea Moth. Partial control is effected by spraying with fenitrothion when the peas are in flower, but in districts where the maggots are a perennial problem it is much better to concentrate on the early crops, which are seldom attacked. Several other insect pests, notably thrips, may attack maincrop varieties; treat with derris.

Of the various fungal diseases which may attack peas powdery mildew is the commonest. It appears as white powdery patches on leaves and pods. The plants may be sprayed with benomyl, but it is better to concentrate on adequate watering which will help the plants to develop their own defences. Burn any badly affected plants.

POTATO (*Solanum tuberosum*)

Half-hardy perennial grown as an annual for its tuberous roots.

Varieties There is a large number of varieties, though many are difficult to obtain. Among the popular *First-early* varieties, which produce crops from June onwards, are Home Guard, Arran Pilot, Duke of York and Sutton's Foremost. *Second-earlies* include Vanessa, Craig's Royal and Maris Peer. Of *maincrop* varieties, Majestic and King Edward VII were long supreme, but Desirée, a pink potato, has now become a firm favourite, and new varieties such as Pentland Crown are popular, while Golden Wonder has high quality and flavour.

Soil and Site Potatoes will grow in almost any soil. They prefer slight acidity to an excess of lime and do not object to a heavy clay soil. Prepare the soil the previous autumn by digging in plenty of well-rotted manure or compost, and leave it rough for the frost to break down.

Planting Potatoes are propagated by planting medium-small tubers, or 'sets' (also confusingly called 'seed potatoes'). Make sure you order these in good time. Do not buy sets that are not certified as disease-free. Most gardeners buy sets every year, but you can grow from tubers of your own crop every other year. To give the sets an early start, set them out singly in trays in a light, cool but frost-proof shed in mid to late winter, to sprout. This is most important with early varieties; it is of less importance with the maincrop.

Plant them 10–12.5cm (4–5in) deep. For early and second-early varieties plant 30cm (12in) apart and allow 50–60cm (20–24in) between rows. For maincrops, plant 40cm (16in) apart with 75cm (30in) between rows. Some gardeners draw out a V shaped trench with a hoe and plant the tubers in the bottom: others put them in with a trowel.

Date of planting varies with the district and variety; it can be as early as February in the extreme south-west for earlies and as late as late April or May in the north-east for maincrops. The earliest crops are brought on in a cool greenhouse or under cloches.

Cultivation The fresh young shoots are very susceptible to frost. Protect them with ample layers of straw on nights when frost is forecast. Protection may also be given by drawing soil up around the shoots. This will be a preliminary operation to earthing up, which is done when the foliage is about 15cm (6in) high.

Many gardeners earth up their plants by instalments, raising the height of the ridges as the foliage grows. The purpose is to encourage the growth of lateral roots, on which the potatoes form, and also to protect the tubers from light, which causes their skins to turn green.

When drought intervenes in the middle of the growth period, water by flooding the trenches between the ridges, if possible. A mulch of straw helps to retain moisture, suppresses weeds, and is also an aid to growth. Weed regularly but do not hoe too near the plants.

Harvesting Dig early potatoes as soon as they are large enough to eat. Do not wait for them to attain full size; they will be appreciated for their freshness. It is possible to draw back the soil from the sides of the earliest roots, harvest a few potatoes and replace the soil so that more tubers are formed.

Maincrop potatoes should be dug when fully mature, from September onwards. If possible, dig on a dry day and allow the tubers to dry for a few hours before storing them. Be careful to collect all the tubers, even the smallest; otherwise any left in the ground will grow and may harbour pests and diseases. Cut off the haulms when they start to die.

Storing Stored potatoes need to be kept cool but frost-free. Ideally, store them in trays covered with black polythene or some other cover to exclude light, or on a floor thickly covered with dry straw, with barriers to exclude draughts; cover the heap thickly with straw. If, in default of any better method, the potatoes have to be stored in sacks, use hessian sacks, not paper ones. Outdoor clamps are another possibility, but are only worthwhile if fair quantities of potatoes have to be stored. Dig a shallow trench; line it thickly with straw; heap up the potatoes; and cover with first a 15cm (6in) layer of straw and then a 15cm (6in) layer of soil. Insert at the apex of the heap several twists of straw, to provide ventilation. Do not open the clamp in frosty weather.

Problems Potatoes are affected by numerous pests and diseases. The most prevalent disease is undoubtedly Potato Blight, which occurs most years from July onwards. Symptoms are dark brown patches on the leaves. Spray plants with Bordeaux mixture; this will not eradicate the disease, but will hold it at bay while the tubers mature. Cut off the haulm before the disease spreads down the stem and into the roots. Do not store any affected tubers.

Potato Root Eelworm is a serious pest which occurs in soil overcropped with potatoes. The remedy is to rest that plot from potatoes (and tomatoes, which are closely related to them) for at least five years.

Scab is a blemish which often occurs on the surface of the tubers, especially in soils with an excess of lime. It is only skin-deep and does no harm, apart from making the potato unsightly. Wart disease, however, which is characterized by ugly warts near the eyes of the tubers, is serious and is legally notifiable to the Ministry of Agriculture, as is any occurrence of the Colorado Potato Beetle, which is mercifully extremely rare in this country. Potatoes are subject to various virus diseases carried by aphids. For this reason it is advisable to use fresh sets for planting, raised in countries such as Scotland, N. Ireland and the Isle of Man, which are relatively aphid-free.

Slugs may be a nuisance beneath the surface. A well-drained soil is not likely to be heavily infested with underground slugs and growing second earlies instead of maincrops will help, as they are dug up before the slugs cause much damage.

PUMPKIN – see **Marrow.**

Below: a cross-section of a potato clamp, showing the potatoes stored inside a thick layer of straw and a thick layer of soil, with the ventilation hole at the top filled with straw.

RADISH (*Raphanus sativus*)

Hardy biennial, grown as an annual. Grown for its roots, which are used in salads; winter radishes may also be cooked like turnips.

Varieties Scarlet Globe, Saxa, and Cherry Belle and Inca are among the round varieties of summer radish, while the French Breakfast varieties are typical of the cylindrical summer type. There are also a few long-rooted summer varieties, of which Long White Icicle is probably the most frequently grown. Among the large winter radishes are Black Spanish (round and long varieties) and China Rose (oval-shaped).

Soil and Site Radishes require a very fine, fertile soil, though it should not have been manured recently. In spring choose an open, sunny site, while for summer crops partial shade is best, as plants grown in full sunlight tend to bolt quickly.

Sowing Sow thinly 7mm ($\frac{1}{4}$in) deep in drills 15cm (6in) apart, covering lightly with fine soil. Radishes are often used as a catch crop or for intercropping; for example, between rows of lettuce or onions or on the ridges of celery trenches. The seed is frequently mixed with that of slow-germinating seeds, such as parsnip, to mark the drills, the radishes being ready to harvest before the parsnips are big enough to compete. Sow all except winter varieties from March to August, making small successional sowings.

For winter varieties, delay sowing until after the beginning of July at the earliest and not later than the end of August.

Thinning Thin at an early stage, to a spacing of 5cm (2in) between plants, or up to 15cm (6in) for late crops and winter radishes.

Cultivation Keep the crop well watered, as a check in growth will cause the plants to bolt.

With spring and summer crops, weeding will probably be unnecessary, as the radishes will be ready for pulling before the weeds become a problem. With winter radishes, keep the rows well hoed. With radishes grown under cloches in late winter, cover the cloches with sacking in frosty weather.

Harvesting Summer varieties are usually ready for pulling three to six weeks after sowing. Harvest them while the roots are young and crisp; if left they will become fibrous and hot-tasting.

Winter radishes, which may weigh 0.5kg (1lb) or more each, can be treated like other hardy root vegetables. They can be left in the ground until required for use, or they can be lifted and stored in layers in boxes containing damp sand. They will not deteriorate quickly as summer varieties do. When used in salads, winter radishes should be peeled.

Problems Like other brassicas, radishes are very vulnerable to flea-beetles in the seedling stage (see CABBAGE).

Failures through the plants bolting and sending up flower stalks rather than forming succulent roots are frequent, and are generally due to thinning too little and too late, or to inadequate moisture. Club-root disease may occur where rotation has not been followed (see CABBAGE).

RHUBARB (*Rheum rhaponticum*)

Hardy perennial grown for its stems, which are cooked as a fruit.

Varieties Victoria and Hawke's Champagne are good sound varieties. Timperley Early is an early one, popular for forcing.

Soil and Site Rhubarb is a perennial and resents interference, so prepare a good, rich permanent bed, with plenty of well-rotted manure or garden compost dug in.

Choose a sunny but sheltered site, away from trees, shrubs or hedges. Avoid making the bed in a frost-pocket, for rhubarb produces its crop quite early in the season and is susceptible to frost. Weed thoroughly, removing all traces of the roots of perennial weeds.

Sowing or Planting While most gardeners start a new bed by transplanting roots, or 'crowns', it is also possible to grow rhubarb from seed. Sow in April 2.5cm (1in) deep in rows 15cm (6in) apart. Thin to 15–20cm (6–8in) apart during summer and transplant to the permanent bed in the following autumn or winter. Plants grown from seed require several years to become thoroughly established and should be cropped sparingly while young and not at all in the first year. Crowns are planted in late autumn or early spring about 90cm (3ft) apart each way. Dig an ample hole and plant the crowns so that the topmost bud is just above the surface of the soil. Press the soil firmly around them.

It is a good idea to lift the plants and make a new bed every five to eight years, but many thriving rhubarb beds are much older. When lifting and splitting crowns for a new bed, discard the older central part and use the newer outer parts, ensuring that each crown is showing at least two pink buds.

Cultivation Each autumn cover the bed with a generous layer of well-rotted farmyard manure or garden compost. An application of a balanced compound fertilizer at 90–120g per sq m (3–4oz per sq yd) may be made in early spring, and a further dressing of a nitrogenous fertilizer, at the same rate, during the growing season will also be helpful. Cut off any flower stems as soon as they appear; on no account allow them to develop. Water during summer droughts.

Harvesting Do not pull from newly-planted beds for the first two years and after that only lightly for another year or two. Then pull as required, taking three or four stems per plant at a time. Pull, with a twisting motion, as far down the stem as possible; do not cut. The harvesting season is normally from late April to the end of June inclusive. *Never* eat rhubarb leaves; they are very poisonous.

Forcing It is possible to have early crops of rhubarb in late winter, when most fruits are scarce. To force a crop from roots growing in an established bed, cover selected crowns with an open-ended box or barrel, filling it loosely with straw. Alternatively, keep the straw in position by boards or other means. This can be done at any time from December onwards.

Another method is to lift crowns at the same season, and pack them into boxes filled with light loam in a heated greenhouse or under a bench where the temperature does not fall below 10°C (50°F). Exclude all light.

Crowns that have been forced in outdoor beds should be left uncropped in the following year. Crowns that have been forced indoors are best discarded.

Problems There should be few problems. Occasionally the crowns may be attacked by a bacterial rot. Dig up affected plants and destroy them.

SALSIFY (*Tragopogon porrifolius*)
Hardy biennial, grown as an annual, chiefly for its roots but also for its young foliage in spring.
Varieties Seed merchants usually offer only one variety – Mammoth Sandwich Island.
Soil and Site This plant has a long, tapering root and therefore needs a

deep soil, as free as possible from stones. The best sort is a light sandy loam which has been enriched with well-rotted manure or other organic matter for a previous crop. If this is not possible, you can add manure in the autumn prior to sowing, but no later, or it will encourage the roots to fork. Salsify likes a reasonably sunny site.

Sowing Sow in drills about 1.5–2.5cm ($\frac{1}{2}$–1in) deep and 38cm (15in) apart in April. For large, straight roots, make holes 60–90cm (2–3ft) deep with a crowbar and fill with compost. Sow two or three seeds in each hole, removing the weakest plants later to leave one per hole.

Cultivation Keep the site well weeded because salsify, having tall, flat, narrow grass-like leaves, does not compete well against weeds. However, do not use the hoe too close to the roots, as they are easily damaged. A mulch is beneficial, as it helps to keep the roots moist as well as being a check to weeds. Water regularly in dry weather.

Harvesting The roots can be left in the ground until required for use, for they are not harmed by the frosts experienced in a normal British winter. If you want to clear the ground, they can be lifted, stored in damp sand and kept in a cool, dry airy shed, but there is really no need to do so unless the ground is required for some other purpose, and there is a danger of damaging the roots, which will then lose their flavour in storage. When lifting, twist off the leaves – do not cut them – and do not trim or break the roots as they 'bleed' very easily. Salsify roots can either be grated and eaten raw in salads, or cooked.

Leave some roots in the ground, for the tender young shoots to be used as green vegetables in spring. Cut the shoots when they are about 15cm (6in) high and cook them as you would asparagus. Alternatively, they can be blanched by drawing soil over the crowns of the plants to a depth of about 15cm (6in) after cutting down any leaves in December so that about 2.5cm (1in) of stem remains above soil level. Keep the soil fairly dry by covering with pots. Cut the blanched shoots, or 'chards', at just above crown level when the tips appear above the surface. You cannot use the roots left to produce chards as these would be too tough.

Problems There are very few with this crop. Shallow, stony or freshly manured soil will result in forked and ugly-shaped roots.

SCORZONERA (*Scorzonera hispanica*)

Hardy perennial, grown as an annual (or sometimes as a biennial) for its blackish roots which have white flesh. It is sometimes known as black salsify. The leaves are similar to those of salsify, but broader.

Varieties The variety marketed by most seedsmen is Russian Giant.

Cultivation See under SALSIFY.

SEAKALE BEET – see Leaf Beet

SHALLOTS (*Allium cepa* Aggregatum)

A hardy biennial, grown for its small onion-like bulbs used for cooking or pickling.

Varieties Giant Red (Dutch Red), Giant Longkeeping Yellow (Dutch Yellow) and Native de Niort.

Soil and Site Select a site manured for a previous crop and worked down to a fine tilth. A light, loamy soil is best, though shallots will succeed in heavier soils provided they are not waterlogged. Shallots, like onions, need plenty of sunshine.

Planting Shallot bulbs are planted like onion sets and not grown from seeds. Plant in February or March, about 15–20cm (6–8in) apart in rows 38cm (15in) apart. Loosen the soil and insert each bulb so that just the tip protrudes.

Cultivation Keep the rows well weeded, but take care not to damage or disturb the bulbs. Water sparingly in dry weather.

Harvesting When the shallots are growing well they will begin to produce sideshoots which, if left, will form a small cluster of new bulbs around the parent one. Some of these shoots may be removed and used in spring salads. Towards midsummer, the foliage will turn yellow and die down, and the bulbs will ripen. When they are fully ripe, lift them carefully, using a fork, and lay them out to dry thoroughly before storing. Burn any diseased bulbs.

Shallots may be stored all winter, either by hanging them in nets in a dry shed or placing them in trays. Examine for disease symptoms from time to time; do not store diseased bulbs as they will infect the others.

Problems Birds frequently attack newly planted shallots, pulling them out of the ground. Protect by cloches, netting or entanglements of black cotton. Cut off any dead, withered leaves before planting, to lessen the chances of birds being attracted by them.

Always buy a certified virus-free strain from a reputable dealer, otherwise you may have problems with virus diseases. The only pest you are likely to face is the Onion Fly (see ONIONS).

SPINACH (*Spinacea oleracea*) and **New Zealand Spinach** (*Tetragonia expansa*)

True spinach is a hardy annual, while New Zealand spinach, a completely unrelated plant increasingly grown as a spinach substitute, is half-hardy. Both are grown for their succulent, tasty leaves. Spinach beet is another spinach substitute (see LEAF BEET).

Varieties There are two main groups: summer and winter spinach. The summer varieties include Long-Standing Round, Greenmarket and Viking; the winter, Broad-Leaved Prickly and Sigmaleaf. Only one variety of New Zealand spinach is available.

Soil and Site The richer the soil, the better for spinach – dig in as much as 10kg per sq m (22lb per sq yd) of well-rotted manure or garden compost. The soil should retain moisture well. New Zealand spinach, on the contrary, prefers a sunny site and a fairly light soil, which should be alkaline rather than acid; it does well on chalk and limestone soils.

Sowing Sow 1.5cm ($\frac{1}{2}$in) deep in drills 30–38cm (12–15in) apart. Make a succession of sowings of summer spinach from February to August. Winter spinach should be sown in August and September. New Zealand spinach, being a trailing plant, requires much more space. Allow 90cm (3ft) between rows and 45–60cm ($1\frac{1}{2}$–2ft) between plants. As New Zealand spinach is half-hardy, it is usually better started off in pots in a greenhouse or frame and transplanted when all danger of frost is past; outdoors, do not sow it before May. New Zealand spinach seed should be soaked overnight before sowing, as it has a very hard casing.

Transplanting or Thinning Transplanting is worthwhile only with the greenhouse-raised New Zealand spinach. These should be set 90cm (3ft) apart, and the plants grown wholly outdoors should be thinned to the same distance, as New Zealand spinach spreads quickly over a wide area. Thin the seedlings of summer spinach first when they are 5cm (2in) high to stand 15cm (6in) apart, and then when the leaves of adjacent plants touch, to a final spacing of 30cm (1ft) apart. Winter spinach plants are smaller, so they can be finally thinned to 23cm (9in) apart.

Cultivation Hoe shallowly, both to remove weeds and provide a mulch of loose soil to conserve moisture. Never let the soil around summer spinach dry out in hot weather, or the plants are likely to bolt (see PROBLEMS). Summer spinach must have a steady supply of water throughout its growing season; bolting may also result from sudden overwatering after a prolonged drought. New Zealand spinach will not bolt during drought, but it must be watered regularly for good crops. Winter spinach should be protected from frost and mud with layers of clean, dry straw or bracken, or under cloches.

Harvesting Do not pick many leaves off any one plant, or you will kill it; this applies to all types of spinach. Start picking the leaves as soon as they are large enough, and continue to harvest them until the plant sends up a flower head. This happens quite quickly with summer spinach; hence the need for a succession of sowings. New Zealand spinach, which should be ready from about 35–40 days after sowing, will continue to produce leaves for the rest of the summer, until destroyed by frost. If the leading shoots are pinched out the plant will be encouraged to spread.

Problems New Zealand spinach is normally trouble-free. Summer varieties of spinach are often attacked by slugs and are also vulnerable to mildews and other fungal diseases, but the crop is seldom in the soil long enough to warrant remedial treatment. Disappointing results with summer spinach tend to result from late and inadequate thinning and insufficient watering, when the plants invariably bolt.

SPINACH BEET – see **Leaf Beet**

SPROUTING BROCCOLI – see **Broccoli, Sprouting**

SQUASH – see **Marrow**

SWEDE (*Brassica napus napobrassica*)
Hardy biennial, grown as an annual for its large, swollen, yellow-fleshed roots, which have a milder, sweeter flavour than turnips.

Varieties There are two main types, Purple Top and Bronze Top. Of the Purple Top varieties, Western Perfection, Laurentian and Marian are examples. The most easily available Bronze Top is Mancunian.

Soil and Site As for TURNIP.

Sowing Sow seed 1.3cm ($\frac{1}{2}$in) deep in rows 45cm ($1\frac{1}{2}$ft) apart. In the South, do not sow before the end of May to avoid mildew, to which swedes are very susceptible. In the North, this hazard is much less likely and sowing can be made early in May. Thereafter make successional sowings until August, the last sowing to provide greens for the following spring. However, if you wish to store the crop for winter use, make only one sowing, in June.

Thinning and Cultivation As for TURNIP.

Harvesting Swedes are in general hardier than turnips and can often be left safely in the ground throughout the winter; their flavour is usually improved by a touch of frost. Any that are left at the end of winter will provide green foliage for use as a vegetable in spring. Alternatively, the roots may be lifted in autumn and stored in frost-proof clamps (see under POTATO). Swedes may be left to grow much larger than turnips without their quality deteriorating; indeed, roots weighing several pounds can be perfectly sound and remarkably tender.

Problems As for TURNIP except that mildew is more prevalent and more serious (see above under SOWING). Spraying with dinocap or benomyl can help if a severe attack develops; a safer chemical control is to spray with a solution of 15g ($\frac{1}{2}$oz) of potassium permanganate in 13.6 litres (3gal) of cold water.

SWEET CORN (*Zea mays*)

Half-hardy annual, grown for its cobs or 'ears', containing tightly-packed rows of seeds or kernels.

Varieties Most of those listed are F_1 hybrids, and for these you must buy fresh seed each year rather than taking it from your plants. Varieties commonly grown include John Innes Hybrid (F_1), Early Xtra Sweet (F_1), Earliking (F_1), Kelvedon Glory (F_1) (and several others of the Kelvedon series), Golden Bantam and Sugar King (F_1). Some F_1 hybrids must not be grown anywhere near other sweet corn varieties, or cross-pollination may occur and the resulting cobs will taste unpleasant.

Soil and Site A sandy loam is best. Ensure that the soil is well drained. Ideally, it should have been well-manured for a previous crop. If this is not possible, dig in garden compost; on a light, quick-draining soil, do this in late winter, but if it is heavy clay soil, do so as early as possible in winter.

Choose a sunny site, but bear in mind that, as sweet corn is a tall, shallow-rooted plant, it is best sheltered from strong winds. Make sure that it does not shade neighbouring crops – different varieties grow to heights of 1.2–2.4m (4–8ft).

Sowing You can sow outdoors in milder areas from early or mid-May onwards. Sow as early as possible in drills 2.5cm (1in) deep and 60–90cm (2–3ft) apart, but bear in mind that sweet corn is susceptible to frost. Protection by cloches is helpful; these should be placed in position two or three weeks before sowing, to warm up the soil.

Many gardeners start their seedlings under glass in April and transplant when danger of frost is past. This method has the additional advantage of providing protection against bird damage until the plants are past the vulnerable stage. On the other hand, sweet corn dislikes having its roots disturbed, so it is best to sow in peat pots, which can be planted direct into the garden plot. Use 7.5cm (3in) diameter peat pots, sowing three seeds per pot. Press them in about 1.8cm ($\frac{3}{4}$in) deep and when the seedlings are large enough to handle, thin to leave the strongest on its own.

Sweet corn can be grown in rows 60–90cm (2–3ft) apart, with about 35cm (14in) between each plant, or in blocks with the plants about 45cm (18in) apart each way. The latter is the better method as the mature plants help to shelter each other against the wind, and pollination is made easier. If you decide to plant only a single row, orientate the row so that the prevailing wind blows *along* it rather than *across* it. This is because the female flowers, which produce the cobs, are fertilized by pollen blown by the wind from the male flowers.

Thinning From outdoor sowings, thin the seedlings to the advised spacing when they are 20–25cm (8–10in) high. Take great care not to disturb their roots. Protect them by cloches from frost.

Cultivation If you use a hoe to weed, go carefully, as sweet corn has shallow, spreading roots which are easily damaged. It is better to weed by hand. Weeding should only be an important task during the early stages; when the plants grow taller they can compete well with weeds.

Keep the plants well watered during dry spells, though do not water too lavishly. Watering with liquid fertilizer is helpful while the cobs are forming and growing. A mulch of clean dry straw will conserve moisture. The plants may also be earthed up in the same way as potatoes; this seems to encourage more vigorous root growth.

Pollination can usually be left to look after itself, but if there is little or no wind when the male flowers (the spikes or tassels at the top of the plant) are ready to shed their pollen, give the plants a gentle shaking.

Harvesting Harvest the cobs when they are full and plump and when the silken tassel at the tip turns dark brown. The generally advised test is to dig a thumb-nail into one of the kernels, when a milky liquid should spurt out. If no liquid appears, the cob is too old; if the liquid is watery, leave the cob a little longer. Before long, experience should make this test unnecessary.

To pick a cob, grasp it firmly and split it from the stalk by a downward movement. The cobs nearer the base of the stalk will be ready first. When they have been removed the plant will switch its resources to ripening the smaller ones higher up the stem.

All vegetables are best used when fresh, and this is particularly true with sweet corn. As soon as the cobs are picked, the sugars they contain start to turn into starches. Keep them for 24 hours and they are no longer *sweet* corn. If left to become too ripe on the stem they also lose much of their sweetness. On no account remove the husks from the kernel until you are ready to put the cobs into the saucepan.

Problems Sweet corn has very few enemies in Britain. It may be attacked by Frit-fly maggots, which bore into the tips of the young plant. Spray or dust with gamma HCH (BCH) soon after transplanting or when the plants are about 15–20cm (6–8in) high. In a very wet summer, the plants may suffer from various fungus diseases, but fortunately this does not often happen. If a serious attack develops, destroy the plants and try again next year – on a different site.

SWISS CHARD – see **Leaf Beet**

TOMATO (*Lycopersicon esculentum*)
Tender or half-hardy annual. Grown for its fruit.
Varieties You must select a variety bred for the purpose you have in mind. Those for use in a heated greenhouse include Eurocross BB, Seville Cross, Extase and Amberley Cross, all of which are F_1 hybrids. For the unheated greenhouse, suitable varieties include Moneymaker, Isabelle (F_1), Potentate–Best of All, and Ailsa Craig. Quick-growing varieties suitable for outdoor cultivation include Alicante, Moneymaker and Harbinger. Bush tomatoes have a spreading bush growth and do not need pruning or staking; varieties include Sigmabush (F_1), The Amateur and the dwarf variety Tiny Tim. Most tomatoes are bright red, but there are some yellow varieties such as Golden Sunrise and Yellow Perfection; also a number of novelty varieties, such as Sugarplum (the name deriving from the size and shape of the fruit) and Tigerella, whose red skins are striped with yellow.
Soil and Site Whether for outdoor or indoor cultivation, seed should be sown under glass for transplanting. Sow in John Innes seed compost.

For greenhouse crops, transplant into John Innes potting compost No. 3 or into a specially prepared mixture consisting of 3 parts sterilized loam, 1 part coarse sand and 1 part dry, well-rotted manure (parts by volume). Alternatively, use one of the proprietary growing bags. It is essential to use fresh compost each year.

For outdoor cultivation prepare during autumn and winter a rich soil incorporating generous quantities of well-rotted manure or garden compost. Select a sunny, sheltered site, ideally by a south-facing wall.

Sowing and Pricking Sow the seeds about 0.5cm ($\frac{1}{4}$in) deep and 2.5cm (1in) apart, in seed-boxes or seed-trays, and prick off when they are large enough to handle into 7.5cm (3in) pots of potting compost or into peat pots. Alternatively, sow two or three seeds per 7.5cm (3in) pot and thin to leave the strongest seedling. Cover the seed only very lightly with compost or place a sheet of glass and brown paper on top of the seed-tray, removing this after germination. The seeds require a temperature of at least 16°C (60°F) to germinate.

Transplanting Transplant carefully, allowing 38–60cm (15–24in) between each plant, whether outdoors or indoors. Rows should be 60cm (2ft) or 120cm (4ft) apart, giving bush tomatoes the wider spacing. Transplant when the young plants are 15–17.5cm (6–7in) high. With outdoor crops, cover the plants with cloches, plastic tunnels or inverted pots at night for the first week or so.

Cultivation Tomatoes, except for bush varieties, need supporting. Train to single stakes; tie the stems loosely to the supports with soft fillis string as the plants grow. In a greenhouse, an alternative method is to twine the stems gently around soft fillis string tied vertically between two horizontal wires at the top and bottom of the greenhouse.

Pinch out any side-shoots that appear, and ensure that the plants are always well-supplied with water. Feeding with a proprietary tomato fertilizer when the fruit is growing gives higher yields.

Indoor tomatoes may need some assistance with fertilization, by spraying the plants lightly with a fine mist of water when the flowers are wide open or by shaking them gently, or even by pollinating individual flowers by means of a camelhair brush. This is not necessary with outdoor tomatoes.

When six or seven trusses of fruit have formed on indoor tomatoes, snip out the growing tip of the plant just above a leaf. With outdoor tomatoes do so in August, regardless of how many trusses have formed. Remove all yellowing leaves, and in the later stages cut off any other leaves that are shading the fruit and hindering ventilation and circulation of air around the plants, but remember that the leaves are the food factories of the plant and it is unwise to remove many.

Do not prune or stop bush tomatoes.

Above: tomato side-shoots must be removed when small. Snap them off cleanly between thumb and forefinger.

Harvesting Pick fruit as it ripens. When the first frosts come, pick any outdoor tomatoes that have not yet turned completely red, wrap them in tissue paper or wax paper, and place them in a drawer in a warm room to ripen. Use green fruit for chutney.

Problems With outdoor tomatoes, most problems may be avoided by using fresh soil each year and keeping the plants adequately supplied with water. Tomatoes may be affected by Potato Blight; spray the leaves with Bordeaux mixture at the end of July and each fortnight thereafter if there is potato blight about or if the summer is wet and cool.

Indoor tomatoes are subject to most of the usual greenhouse pests and diseases, including moulds, rots, red spider mites and glasshouse whitefly, and also to eelworm damage. Certain varieties have some resistance to fungus diseases.

TURNIP (*Brassica rapa*)

Hardy or half-hardy biennial, grown as an annual primarily for its roots, but also for its green leaves, which can be used as a vegetable.

Varieties Globe varieties, in which the root is ball-shaped, are the most popular. There are also long-rooted and flat-rooted varieties. It is important to grow varieties suited to the season. Some are developed to grow quickly in spring and summer, but are not frost-hardy. Others may grow more slowly, but can stand moderate frosts and may be stored for winter use.

Among the early varieties are Early Snowball – Early White Stone, Milan White and Purple Top White Globe. Maincrop varieties include Green Globe, Golden Ball and Manchester Market.

Soil and Site Turnips are one of the less fastidious crops, but avoid using freshly manured soil. Correct acid soils by applications of lime, though this should be done at least two months before sowing. Choose an open, sunny site.

Sowing Sow 1.5cm ($\frac{1}{2}$in) deep in drills 30cm (1ft) apart. Sow for a succession of crops, beginning with early varieties in mid-March and continuing until late July. Turnips are a very useful catchcrop, for sowing on a plot vacated in summer by other crops. A further sowing may be made in September to provide greens in late autumn and again in spring. This late sowing need not be in rows; the seed may be scattered at random.

Cultivation Thin to a spacing of 15–23cm (6–9in) for early varieties; 30cm (1ft) for maincrops; do not transplant. Turnips must grow without any check, or they will quickly develop a hard skin and a woody interior, so keep them well watered in times of drought. Hoe frequently, not only to control weeds, but also to keep the soil loose and hence conserve moisture.

Harvesting With early crops, pull while the turnips are young – no larger than a tennis ball and preferably smaller. Leave the maincrop in the ground until required. While some varieties will be untouched by a moderate frost, it is advisable to have most of the crop lifted and stored by the end of November. Turnips are usually stored in an outdoor clamp (see POTATOES) or in layers in boxes filled with dry peat or sand.

Problems Probably the worst hazard is the Turnip Flea Beetle which eats small circular holes in the leaves of the seedlings, especially at the two-leaf stage. These beetles often occur in large numbers and can clear a young crop within a few days. Dust with derris.

Club root is a fungal disease which is generally associated with overcropping of brassicas. To prevent this, follow a strict rotation and use lime to correct any soil acidity, but do not overdo it.

Powdery mildew causes powdery whiteish patches to appear on the leaves, usually in time of drought. Prevention is better than cure; keep the crop well watered.

ZUCCHINI – See **Marrow**

Herbs

Where shelter from cold winds can be provided, herbs should flourish, because their cultural requirements are so few. They will not grow beneath overhanging trees and need moderately fertile soil, reasonable drainage and good light, but apart from this, they are the most accommodating plants in the garden.

For general kitchen use as fresh herbs, few plants are required, so they can be grown among other plants in either the vegetable or flower garden. Where they are grown in the kitchen garden they are to hand when vegetables are harvested (for example, the mint is there when the peas are being picked), and generally they will take up less space where they can be grown in rows. A corner near to the kitchen door is not necessarily the most suitable for the herbs themselves, although it is frequently suggested as a convenient spot. It does have the advantages of quick and easy access to the plants, however.

If herbs are grown with the intention of harvesting and drying them for storage, then far more need to be cultivated. Usually eight times as much fresh material needs to be gathered when it is to be dried, because the plants will forfeit about seven-eighths of their weight and bulk in the drying process.

Preparation of the Site

Initial preparation of a site is always rewarded. Perennial weeds should be removed, the soil surface generally forked over and levelled, and where the soil is very dry a little garden compost, well-rotted manure or other moisture-retentive organic matter added. Really heavy sticky clays are perhaps the most unsuitable for herbs, but much can be done to ameliorate the environment for the plants, by the addition of fine gravel, sand or peat to lighten the soil (see also SOIL AND COMPOSTS, page 17).

Annuals

Those herbs which are annuals, or grown as such, are raised from seed, sown in spring as soon as the soil has warmed up and a good tilth can be obtained by raking. Annuals include cumin, coriander, borage, dill, summer savory and chervil. When seed is saved, it is best to sow that of chervil as soon as it is ripe in the late summer, to provide good fresh leaves in the spring.

Usually, cumin and coriander are sown in drills, both to facilitate thinning the seedlings and hoeing to keep weeds down in the early summer, because the seedlings are very delicate and easily smothered by the weeds. By contrast, the seed of other herbs, such as borage, may be scattered, or 'broadcast', as the seedlings, if thinned, will be sufficiently robust to smother annual weeds that may trespass on their territory.

Biennials

Angelica is an example of a biennial herb, taking two years to complete its life cycle. Once introduced into the garden a fresh crop of seedlings will appear each autumn, and the best can be used to maintain the crop. Caraway is a biennial too, and for both these plants flowering should be discouraged, by removing the flowering shoots when young. This will stimulate the growth of foliage and allay the early death of the plant.

Although parsley is a biennial, the plant can be made to go on producing fresh leaves for three or four years by cutting away the flowering stems as soon as they are seen to be forming. As for annuals, the seedlings of biennials should be thinned out, removing the weaker and overcrowded ones; also, the ground must be kept free of weeds.

Angelica will dominate the plot on which it is grown so put it towards the centre of the bed, or at the back if the herbs are grown in a one-sided border. Parsley provides an attractive edging to paths in the vegetable garden, or even to rose beds, and it should be sown in drills about 15cm (6in) away from the edge and parallel to it.

Perennials

A stock of perennial herbs, such as winter savory, sorrel, sweet Cicely, thyme and marjoram, can be raised from seeds sown in spring, as for annuals and biennials. But many perennials, such as sage, bay and rosemary, are of shrubby growth, or have a good clump-forming habit like chives and lemon balm, or spread quickly in the way that mint does. These plants respond best to vegetative propagation, that is, either from cuttings or by being divided.

Cuttings of sage, rosemary, marjoram, thyme, and winter savory should be made in spring or early summer, and inserted in a porous cutting compost. They can then be planted out into their permanent positions in the autumn or the following spring.

Dividing root clumps is the simplest method of increasing stock and is best done in spring or autumn. It is successful for sweet cicely, round-leaved sorrel, winter savory, mints, lovage and pot marjoram, whereas plants of alecost and tarragon profit best by being divided about every third year in spring.

Growing Herbs in Containers

The undemanding nature of many culinary herbs make them ideal plants to cultivate in somewhat unlikely places. In towns, provided the atmosphere is not polluted, they thrive perfectly happily in troughs, window boxes or in pots placed on balconies. By nipping off shoots judiciously, as they are required in the kitchen, small plants can be contained within bounds for two or three years.

In pots, troughs or hanging baskets, the simplest way of starting off your herbs is to plant rooted cuttings. Another method is to plunge small pots containing rooted cuttings to rim level in the soil of a window-box or other large container. Mint roots need to be contained within a plastic bag to prevent them from insinuating themselves throughout the entire volume of compost. With either method, the herb plant can be replaced by another with a minimum of disturbance to the remaining arrangement, should it fail, or outgrow its attractiveness.

Two golden rules for successful cultivation of pot-grown plants are to ensure that the compost is kept evenly moist and never allowed to dry out between soakings, and that adequate drainage material in the form of broken pieces of clay pot (crocks) or gravel is provided at the base of the container. Lack of drainage and overwatering both lead to sourness of compost with the subsequent failure of plants.

For window boxes, balconies and patios where plants are to be grown in containers of some sort, thyme, marjoram, borage, tarragon, parsley, mint, chives and dill are easy herbs to grow. Dill or borage seed may be sown directly into the compost. For larger-growing plants such as sage and rosemary, rooted cuttings should give better results.

Probably the most popular container-grown herb is bay, and while it can be propagated from cuttings taken at the end of the summer, or from branches layered in July, it is often difficult to raise without some heat. For this reason, it is more usual to buy small bay trees in tubs. The little bushes can be kept trim by clipping; the leaves removed in this way can then be dried off for use in the kitchen.

Herbs in Raised Beds

An increasingly popular way in which to cultivate herbs is in a raised bed. Several plants that tend to sprawl or flop about such as sage, thyme and marjoram are seen to greater advantage when grown in this way. Provided a sense of proportion is achieved all herbs may be grown in raised beds if the situation is suitable and the compost not too rich and adequately drained. Watering is essential during dry weather. Mint, as always, must be introduced with discretion and its roots contained.

Growing Herbs Indoors

An almost foolproof way of cultivating herbs indoors is to grow rooted cuttings in pots. Several small pots can be introduced into a larger container, jardinière or window-sill trough, packed around with peat and pebbles spread over the surface. Provided that there is sufficient light, and watering is not neglected, the plants will thrive. Annuals are not really suitable but parsley, grown from seed in a specially designed container, which has a number of holes in its sides, makes a decorative feature in the kitchen once the plants are flourishing.

AN A–Z OF CULINARY HERBS

Alecost or costmary (*Tanecetum balsamita*)   60–90cm (2–3ft)
The flowers of alecost resemble small yellow buttons and bloom in August above greyish-green leaves which are strongly aromatic. It flourishes in a light to medium soil, revelling in the sun. When it is grown in a herb border, together with other herbs, staking is not usually necessary, as all the plants support each other. Growth needs to be cut back to ground level in the autumn, and this is a good time to divide the plant to increase the stock. Spring division is preferable in the colder districts or, alternatively, the plant may be propagated from spring-sown seed. Young leaves make a refreshing addition to salad if chopped and sprinkled with sugar for an hour before being served.

Angelica (*Angelica archangelica*)   1.3–1.8m (4½–6ft)
A striking plant for the back of the herb border, or for incorporating in a herbaceous border, angelica is truly a biennial, and if it is prevented from flowering it will behave as a perennial. A moist soil with some shade encourages softer growth, which is preferable if the leaf stalks are to be harvested in May and early June for crystallizing to use in cakes and confectionery. A second crop may often be taken in August.

The stems are ribbed and hollow, and stand erect without staking. It is essential to allow the plant sufficient room. The cream-coloured flowers are carried in rounded heads, and can be left to form seed. In autumn, self-sown seedlings ensure a continuation of the stock and may be transplanted when small. Seed is best sown once it is ripe, because if it is kept until the following spring it may no longer be viable.

Bay (*Laurus nobilis*)   90cm–3m (3–10ft)
A small evergreen tree, popularly grown in tubs, but perfectly suitable for a sheltered situation in an outdoor herb garden in all but the very coldest districts, bay, or sweet bay, as it is sometimes called, has attractive, shiny green leaves. When properly dried, they can be stored for considerable periods without losing their aroma, and are then used to flavour potted meats, pâtés, casseroles and other dishes. The bush requires no staking and lends itself to clipping. If left to grow freely, it

Facing page: above, 'Cobham Bush Green' marrow; below, 'Early Snowball', a globe variety of turnip

This page: top, rosemary; above, thyme   *Facing page: crops on a vegetable patch*

Facing page: above left, chicory seedlings; above right, salad onion seedlings; below left, lettuce; below right, radishes. All these crops may be grown in pots

This page: right, 'Golden Queen' tomatoes, which may be grown under glass or outdoors; below right, 'Tanja', a greenhouse tomato; below left, harvested heads of celery 'Lathom's Self-blanching'

This page: above, raspberry 'Malling Delight'; below left, 'Black Hamburgh, the finest greenhouse grape; below, 'Careless', an easily grown and very reliable gooseberry

Facing page: above, frame-grown 'Charantais' melons; below, 'Cambridge Vigour', an early-ripening strawberry

*Left to right, top row: chervil,
caraway, rosemary, bay.
Bottom row: angelica,
coriander, common thyme.*

Below: mint.

produces cream-yellow flowers in May followed by purplish berries in
favourable seasons. Difficult to propagate from summer cuttings, unless
heat can be provided, bay can be increased instead from layers pegged
down in late July and August, and severed the following spring. Cold
wind is the main enemy of young plants and sometimes of the young
growth of established plants, and protection against this should be
provided for a season or two for newly-planted specimens.

Borage (*Borago officinalis*)   45–90cm (1½–3ft)
If borage can be planted where it will catch the light, or a beam of the
evening sun, there is no more decorative plant for the herb garden. Its
pink buds, deep blue flowers and silver-haired stem make it instantly
recognizable. Borage is an annual, but is sometimes grown as a biennial,
when the seeds are sown in summer and the small rosettes allowed to
overwinter. The resultant plants are superbly handsome. Early spring-
sown seed, in boxes, pots or frames, produces lovely plants to flower in
late June. Alternatively, seed sown later in a dry warm soil will provide
blooms in August. The rough foliage can be infused to make a pleasant
drink, while the stems, peeled, are an excellent substitute for cucumber.

Caraway (*Carum carvi*)   45–60cm (1½–2ft)
Caraway is an umbelliferous plant, like chervil and dill. It resembles many
of its relatives, so that it is often not identified very easily when it is first
seen. A biennial, its white flowers appear in May. The seed, which is the
part harvested, ripens in June and July. Choose a light soil in a well-

drained position and sow the seed in early summer where it is to grow. Thinning is necessary to leave sufficient room for the plants to develop. The roots may be lifted and used as a vegetable, like carrots, in the second autumn, but it is for the ripened seed as a flavouring in cake and bread making and in other cooking that the plant is chiefly grown.

Chervil (*Anthriscus cerefolium*)   30–40cm (1–1½ft)

The seed leaves of chervil are strap-shaped but soon the characteristic feathery foliage develops, which is used to provide one of the ingredients of *fines herbes*. An annual plant, sometimes behaving as a biennial, chervil prefers a fairly rich soil but will thrive in most soils other than a heavy clay. Successive sowings may be made throughout the summer months because the plants have a tendency to bolt. Seed sown as soon as it is ripe is the most successful. The white flowers bloom from May to July from a spring sowing, and the leaves should be harvested just before the plant comes into full flower. The leaves are used to add pungency to game soups, pâtés and other dishes.

Chives (*Allium schoenoprasum*)   15–45cm (6in–1½ft)

A bulbous perennial, chives make a first-rate edging to beds in the herb or kitchen garden. Propagation may be from spring-sown seed, but it is more usual to divide clumps in spring or after flowering, and most market plant stalls have a stock of chives. A dry sandy or chalky soil suits them well, but should be enriched with some moisture-retentive material to produce rich leaf growth. Once established, the clumps can be left to maintain themselves, provided that the flowers are removed and some leaves clipped off for use from time to time. When allowed to bloom, the flowers appear as attractive rounded heads of a beautiful rose-pink colour during the summer, and can be put into salads.

Coriander (*Coriandrum sativum*)   20–60cm (8in–2ft)

A truly accommodating plant, happy in most soils, coriander is an umbellifer grown mainly for its round seeds which are an ingredient of curry powder and can also be used in sausages. Germination is rather slow, so seed is usually sown in drills once the soil has warmed up in early May, and the plants subsequently thinned to 23cm (9in) apart. The flowers are white or pinkish white, appearing in July and August. The whole plant, particularly the stem, assumes an unpleasant aroma once the seeds have set. As soon as the seed ripens and is ready for harvesting, the aroma becomes pleasant. Leaves may be gathered for drying prior to flowering time, and used to flavour soups and curries.

Cumin (*Cuminum cyminum*)   30–60cm (1–2ft)

Bearing a strong resemblance to fennel in its foliage, but not reaching the same height as the latter, cumin is an annual with umbels of white or pink flowers in high summer. It appreciates a well-drained soil and an open, sunny situation. Seed should be sown in drills in late April or early May. After germination, the seedlings should be thinned to about 15cm (6in) apart, when they will sprawl about because the stems are weak. The part harvested is the seed, which is pungent and is used in Indian and Mexican dishes as a flavouring.

Dill (*Anethum graveolens*)   45–75cm (1½–2½ft)

Dill is a pretty plant, bearing yellow umbelliferous flowers in July and August followed by seed which is harvested when ripe. An annual, it is raised from seed sown in drills in March and April, or even earlier, as soon as a seedbed can be made, as it is perfectly hardy. The seedlings should be thinned to 30cm (1ft) apart two or three weeks later. Almost any soil and situation is suitable, provided a good seed bed, with a fine tilth, can be made. The foliage is fine and feathery, and is used to garnish potatoes and for sauces to accompany fish dishes. Leaves should preferably be taken from the plant before flowering time. They do not dry well and lose their flavour quickly, so it is better to use them fresh. The seed is used to flavour pickled cucumbers and sauerkraut.

Fennel (*Foeniculum vulgare*)   60–90cm (2–3ft)
The delicate, thread-like foliage of fennel makes a very decorative addition to the herb border, and it is particularly attractive in the bronze-leaved or 'black' form. A remarkably upright-growing perennial plant, it appreciates a soil enriched with compost and a warm sunny situation. Sow the seed in spring, thinning the seedlings to 45–50cm (18–20in) apart. Provided that the plants are discouraged from flowering, they will last for several years. If the stems of some plants are cut right back in summer there will be a further crop of fresh green leaves. These have a pleasant aniseed flavour and can be chopped finely and added to fish dishes, poultry, salads and cooked vegetables. The 'seed' (actually the fruit) may be harvested from plants which have been left to flower, and is used in omelettes, cottage cheese, and biscuits.

Lemon Balm (*Melissa officinalis*)   60–90cm (2–3ft)
A good plant for semi-shade on a light dryish soil, or in full sun where the soil is richer, lemon balm is a perennial with rather nettle-like leaves. Their pleasant lemon scent remains after the leaves have been harvested, and is perhaps the strongest scent of this kind among the aromatic herbs. The leaves may be used fresh at any time of the year with restraint, to impart flavour to stuffings for meat or poultry, or infused to make a refreshing drink. Leaves for drying should be harvested in July prior to flowering. The plant appreciates a sheltered situation, and is attractive especially in the variegated leaf form. Balm can be propagated from spring-sown seed, but the more usual method is by division of plants in either spring or autumn.

Lovage (*Levisticum officinale*)   90cm–1.5m (3–5ft)
The handsome clear green foliage of lovage ensures it a place in the herb border for its wholesome appearance alone. It is a fine, upstanding plant, smelling of yeast. It does best on a deep, moist soil, but will thrive on all but heavy clays provided good compost or other moisture-retentive material is incorporated into the ground. It will not be as luxuriant of growth on drier soils. The top growth dies right down in winter and old stems should be removed at ground level in the autumn. Both leaves and young stalks, with their yeasty taste and aroma, are a good addition to meat and vegetable soups and stews, especially as a substitute for celery, although lovage must be used with restraint. The stems are hollow and can be candied like those of angelica. The crushed seed is sometimes sprinkled on bread and biscuits for a spicy flavour.

Propagation is best achieved by dividing the strong roots in spring and setting out the pieces at least 60–90cm (2–3ft) apart because the resultant plants are strong growing perennials. They can also be propagated from seed. Sow seed in summer as soon as it is ripe, otherwise germination tends to be patchy. The seedlings can be transplanted to about 60cm (2ft) apart early the following spring.

Scotch lovage or Scotch parsley, *Ligusticum scoticum*, 15–90cm (6in–3ft), is a wild plant of coarser growth with bright green leaves. In the past it was much used as a pot herb and called shumis.

Black lovage, *Smyrnum olusatrum*, is also known as Alexanders. It grows up to 90cm (3ft). The leaves may be chopped and put in salads.

Marjoram, Pot (*Origanum onites*)   Up to 60cm (2ft)
Although inferior in flavour, pot marjoram is most frequently grown
because the sweet or knotted marjoram *O. marjorana* is not truly hardy
everywhere. Given a warm situation and a light soil, pot marjoram is a
useful plant both for its attractive appearance and in the kitchen. The
leaves dry or freeze well and can be used to flavour stews, meats and
stuffings to accompany roast meats and game. They can also be used
fresh.

Propagation is by seed, though germination is slow, or by cuttings
taken from established plants in early summer.

Marjoram, Sweet or Knotted (*Origanum marjorana*)   20–25cm (8–10in)
This has a much milder and more pleasant flavour than pot marjoram.
It prefers a slightly richer soil and is usually grown as an annual
because it is doubtfully hardy as a perennial. The wild marjoram
Origanum vulgare is also cultivated, thriving best on its native chalk or
gravelly soils. Propagation of both these species is by seed, which may
be slow to germinate as with pot marjoram. As the seeds are very small,
they are best mixed with sand or dry soil to ensure even distribution.

Flowers of all the marjorams are purple, appearing from July to
September. The foliage of sweet and wild marjoram is used in the
kitchen in the same way as that of pot marjoram, except that sweet
marjoram can be used in greater quantity, because of its milder flavour.
Marjorams make effective garden plants forming dense mats of foliage
when they become well established. There is a pleasing form of *O.
vulgare* called golden marjoram. It has a particularly attractive effect in
spring before the flower stalks rise, when the golden foliage has a
flowerlike quality.

Mints (*Mentha* species)   30–100cm (1–3½ft)
There is a profusion of form and a reputation for variable
characteristics among the mints but it is generally considered that about
six species are commonly grown in herb gardens. All are perennial.

Spearmint, *Mentha × spicata* (sometimes called *M. viridis*) is readily
distinguished by the absence of leaf stalks and rarely exceeds 60cm (2ft).
The flowers are lilac-pink and are borne in a terminal spike during July
and August. The leaves often take on a purplish bronze sheen.
Commonly known as garden mint, like most other mints it varies in
flavour according to the soil on which it is grown. This is the mint used
to make mint sauce.

Peppermint, *Mentha × piperita citrata* (often called *M. citrata*), which
grows up to 30cm (1ft) high, provides many of the variations on the
theme of mints, for in its abundant guises it is the bergamot mint, Eau
de Cologne mint, orange mint and pineapple mint. Its true quality is as
a medicinal plant from which oil of peppermint is extracted and it is
invaluable as an ingredient of *pot pourri*. It has the reputation of
enhancing the perfume of any plant grown in association with it. There
are other decorative mints which deserve a place in the herb garden, all
of which have edible leaves. These include apple mint, *M. rotundifolia
variegata* (or more properly *M. suaveolens*), and ginger mint, *M. gentilis*,
which is good in salads and is also known as Scotch mint.

Pennyroyal, *Mentha pulegium*, is a little different from other mints,
and is easily distinguished by its smaller leaves and robust habit. It is
the prostrate form of this plant that is used to make mint lawns and
paths, which require mowing only a couple of times a year.

Local conditions often decide which is the best mint to grow in a garden and the round-leaved mints *M. rotundifolia*, which include those known as apple mint, woolly mint, fox-tail mint and the well known garden form 'Bowles's Variety' or 'Bowles's Mint' (a hybrid between *M. spicata* and *M. suaveolens*), should not be scorned for culinary use. The leaves need to be washed more carefully, but the hairiness disappears when they are chopped. 'Bowles's Mint' has a rich flavour.

Leaves of all the mints can be harvested at any time, but are best in quality and highest in essential oils just before the plant flowers in summer. This is the best time to harvest them in order to dry them for winter use. (The hairy mints wilt very quickly and are therefore not nearly so easy to handle for drying.)

All these mints prefer a moist rich soil, free from overhanging trees, although some shade is preferable to a completely open situation. Nevertheless, the mints are singularly undemanding and will propagate themselves very readily by creeping about across the soil surface with their insinuating runners. A piece broken off will quickly establish itself elsewhere. It is best to confine mint roots by growing the plants in an old bucket, oil drum or other suitable container plunged into the soil to rim level, or by lining the area to a depth of 30cm (1ft) with black plastic sheeting.

Parsley (*Petroselinum crispum*)   15–20cm (6–8in)
The vernacular name 'parsley' is a tag for a range of wild plants, and the garden parsley itself has in the past been variously called percil, persele, perseley and other names. This parsley is a biennial, grown for its crisply curled leaves of intense bright green. This is the form grown in Britain and America, but in other countries it is almost unknown, and the plain-leaved kind, also known as French parsley, is preferred. Seed of the latter is obtainable in Britain, and the plain-leaved type is preferred for continental cookery; you should need only a pinch of seed because this parsley provides numerous self-sown seedlings.

A permanent supply of curled parsley may be obtained by sowing seed in spring and again in late summer, although there are strains such as Sutton's Claudia which are claimed to allow continuous cutting from a single sowing. By preventing the plants from flowering, a supply of fresh, good-flavoured leaves can be ensured for a longer period.

Parsley seed is notoriously slow to germinate, sometimes taking as much as seven or even eight weeks before the seed leaves appear.

Generally speaking, the warmer the soil or compost at sowing time, the more quickly the seed will germinate. Wait until the soil has warmed up in late spring, warm it up by means of cloches, or water the drill with boiling water before sowing for quicker results.

Seed is best sown in drills, which need not be in the kitchen garden, but can be drawn parallel to the edge of a path or lawn in the decorative garden, making use of the plants as a decorative edging.

The plant lends itself to cultivation in a window box or in a container for growing indoors, when a supply of fresh green leaves is always close at hand. Recommended varieties are Moss Curled and Green Velvet. Parsley is best used fresh as a garnish; although the leaves can be frozen or dried, their effectiveness as an attractive addition to a dish is lost completely because they do not remain crisp. Parsley is also used in sauces and soups, and as an ingredient of *bouquet garni* and *fines herbes*.

Another kind of parsley is Hamburg or turnip-rooted parsley, *Petroselinum crispum* 'Tuberosum'. This makes a much larger plant, growing to 60cm (2ft), and it is much easier to germinate. The leaves

Left to right: fennel, marjoram, parsley, chives and sage, all of which may be grown in pots.

can be used in just the same way as the plain-leaved parsley and moreover, the roots, shaped like parsnips, are a good winter vegetable, tasting like a cross between celeriac and parsnip.

Purslane (*Portulaca oleracea*)   10–15cm (4–6in)

Given a sunny situation and warm dry soil, this half-hardy annual will provide deliciously fleshy leaves as a salad in summer and the stems may be used as well. It is possible also to cook the leaves as in French cooking in the soup *Bonne Femme*, and you could also try them pickled.

Sow the seed in shallow drills in May and thin the seedlings out to 10–12cm (4–5in) apart. Start picking the leaves as soon as they are ready, to encourage the growth of fresh leaves. The golden-leaved variety Golden Purslane, *P.o. sativa*, is a somewhat hardier form which should be grown in exactly the same way.

Rosemary (*Rosmarinus officinalis*)   90cm–1.5m (3–5ft)

An evergreen shrub, rosemary is a really valuable plant in the herb garden. Put it towards the back of the border where its floppy habit will not detract from the overall appearance. Its pale blue flowers bloom in spring and early summer, but in sheltered localities often appear as early as the end of February. It is a satisfactory hedge plant which tolerates clipping, and the summer clippings of the non-flowering shoots provide good cuttings from which to propagate. Rooted cuttings may be put into their permanent positions the following spring.

Leaves or small sprigs may be nipped off the bushes at any time of the year and used fresh as a garnish for fatty meats, or sparingly in soups, stews and other dishes. Flowers and leaves are useful as an ingredient of *pot pourri*. Several good varieties are available.

An attractive variety for seaside gardens and those of other favoured localities is *Rosmarinus lavandulaceus* (sometimes catalogued as *R.o. prostratus*). It is a good carpeting plant, very useful in raised beds.

Sage (*Salvia officinalis*)   45–60cm (1½–2ft)

Sage is a highly aromatic, low-growing, evergreen shrub. The grey-green leaves are strongly pungent and have a wrinkled texture. It is really at home on dry chalky soils, but provided the drainage is good, it should succeed anywhere. It is important, when selecting a sage bush intended for culinary use, to find one suited to the particular soil. This may well need a little trial and error, but you will be rewarded by a crop of leaves devoid of bitterness.

In general, the narrow-leaved forms are more pungent than the broad-leaved forms, possibly because the latter rarely flower. Sages with different-coloured leaves are equally useful for culinary flavouring, although the same patience is needed to find an acceptable plant as with the green-leaved forms. Purple sage, *S. officinalis* 'Purpurascens', with its soft plum-purple new shoots, is a delight in any garden and the variety 'Tricolor', in which the grey foliage is variegated with carmine and cream earning it the tag of painted sage, provides a splash of colour.

The bushes should be layered every three or four years, or they will become leggy and untidy; simply peg down lower branches and allow them to take root, when they can be severed from the parent and replanted. Propagation may also be by cuttings taken in summer. Seed is sometimes available, but is usually of the narrow-leaved sorts.

Savory, Summer (*Satureia hortensis*)   15–30cm (6–12in)

There are two distinct forms of savory. This one is an annual, usually sown in April once the soil has warmed up. Few plants are needed, as it is robust and the flavour of the leaves is such that it is usually used only sparingly.

Seed can be sown outdoors in April in a sandy seedbed in an open position, and the seedlings thinned to 15cm (6in) apart once they are big enough to handle. Pale pink flowers appear in July, but it is advisable to harvest the leaves just before the plant flowers.

Savory, Winter (*Satureia montana*)   30cm (1ft)

Winter savory is a small, hummock-forming evergreen, curiously overlooked in the garden though by no means as neglected as the annual summer savory *S. hortensis* (see above).

Winter savory is a perennial which grows best in well drained, rather alkaline soil in full sunshine. It is especially suitable for the tops of banks or walls. The pale pink flowers appear in August and September, after which the little bushes ought to be clipped to encourage the bushy habit and keep them from straggling. The foliage is best used fresh, picking only a few leaves at a time; dried leaves are very tough and brittle. Their flavour is similar to that of summer savory, and they should be used in the same way (see above). Propagation is from spring cuttings, or the plants may be lifted and the roots divided in spring.

Sorrel (*Rumex acetosa* and *R. scutatus*)   60–75cm (2–2½ft)

Common or garden sorrel (*Rumex acetosa*) is a broad-leaved plant, occasionally called broad-leaved sorrel. It is a cultivated form of the wild sorrel (also *R. acetosa*), but has a more refined flavour. It has large, pale green, slightly fleshy leaves. Unfortunately, some confusion arises between *R. acetosa* and *R. scutatus*, as both are at times called French sorrel.

Given good soil and a sunny situation, garden sorrel can be grown from spring-sown seed, and will provide good leaves the first summer if the seedlings are kept growing strongly.

Thinning to 20cm (8in) apart is essential; then the seedlings can be transplanted in June into holes made with a dibber and filled with garden compost. This may seem an unnecessary operation for a plant which grows so prolifically in the wild, but the object is to produce good fleshy green leaves which are not too bitter in flavour.

Rumex scutatus, on the other hand, has smaller, grey-green, shield-shaped leaves which, unlike those of garden sorrel, are borne on trailing stems. Like garden sorrel, it likes a good soil in an open spot. There is no need to transplant the seedlings in the same way as for *R. acetosa*, but they should be thinned to the same spacing. The leaves usually have a more refined flavour than those of garden sorrel.

The fresh leaves of both these plants can be used in salads, sandwiches and sorrel soup, or wrapped around a joint of meat to make it more tender. They have an interesting but sharp taste, so use them sparingly. The acid content of the leaves precludes the use of iron cooking pots, or any utensil or chopping instrument other than one of stainless steel.

Sweet Cicely (*Myrrhis odorata*)   90cm–1.2m (3–4ft)

One or two plants of this tall-growing umbelliferous herb are more than enough in the kitchen garden, but its white flowers, and spreading, lacy, almost downy foliage would earn it a place in the ornamental garden. Beyond requiring good drainage, it is quite undemanding as regards soil and position, and seems to flourish equally well in both sun and slight shade. A perennial, it is easily propagated from seed, but can also be increased by division in autumn. If the flower shoots are removed as they appear through the summer, the leaves can be used from February, or even earlier, until October or November. If the seed is to be harvested then the plants should be allowed to flower and the mature seed gathered when ripe.

Both leaves and seed are used in moderation for cooking sharp-tasting fruit, imparting a sweet aniseed-like flavour. Formerly, the roots were used as a vegetable, or candied and served as a sweetmeat.

Tarragon, French (*Artemisia dracunculus*)   60–90cm (2–3ft)

The refined growth and flavour of French, or true, tarragon merit it a place in the herb border. Its dark green leaves are long and narrow and form a bushy perennial which, if it does flower, will produce nondescript, small, grey-green blooms.

Plant young plants in a well drained spot in sun or partial shade, ensuring that some moisture-retentive organic matter is incorporated in the border at planting time. Crowns may need to be protected in winter by a mulch of leafmould or peat, or they may even be moved to a frame where a supply of shoots will continue to be produced throughout the winter months. Tarragon does not set seed, so propagation is from division of the brittle white rhizomes early in the spring. Alternatively, shoots pulled away from the plant with a heel will make successful summer cuttings. Harvest leaves or shoots before the plants reach summer maturity, for making tarragon vinegar or in cooking. They can be used fresh, and can also be dried or frozen. The leaves are excellent for flavouring chicken and egg dishes in particular.

Russian tarragon (*A. dracunculoides*, or more correctly, *A. dracunuculus inodora*), is hardier and taller, attaining perhaps 1.5m (5ft), and is altogether less stocky than French tarragon. It is inferior in flavour to French tarragon, what little it has being rather bitter.

Thyme (*Thymus* species) 5–30cm (2–12in)

Of the many cultivated thymes, three species earn a certain place in the herb border for their distinctive flavour. Perennials, with wiry stems and tiny evergreen leaves, they are creeping plants that are excellent for the front of the border, edging paths, tucking in between paving stones or growing in troughs and containers. Sharp drainage is essential if they are to spread and form good ground cover.

Lemon thyme, *Thymus × citriodorus*, and its cultivar 'Silver Queen' with cream-marked silver leaves and 'Aureus' (with golden leaves) are small and need sheltered sunny spots.

Garden thyme, *T. vulgaris*, forms good hummocks and bears clusters of small lilac flowers in midsummer. The foliage is dark green, but in the cultivars 'Aureus' and 'Variegatus' it is yellowish and dense, and variegated green and white and very fragrant respectively. There is also *T. v.* 'Silver Posie' quite similar to 'Silver Queen' but with pinkish stems and somewhat hardier. Most of these cultivars of *T. vulgaris* generally form smaller hummocks than the type plant.

Another culinary thyme, not seen so frequently today, is the caraway thyme, *T. herba-barona*, the leaves of which were once used for rubbing over a baron of beef to impart their individual flavour. It is a small plant, whose stems arch close to the ground and root as they make contact with the soil, so that a loose mat is soon formed.

Small shoots of all the thymes can be picked off the plants throughout the summer, though preferably not during the flowering period, and used fresh, or dried for future use. Thyme is one of the ingredients of *bouquet garni*, and may also be used with sage in stuffings for meat.

Propagation is by seed, sown in spring, or from cuttings taken early in the summer. Plants may also be divided in spring, or layered at the same time. The tip-rooting habit of caraway thyme means that a ready supply of new little plants can usually be found. All plants should be thinned to 30cm (12in) apart each way.

Fruit Growing

Fresh fruit provides a valuable low-calorie contribution to your diet, containing a number of mineral salts and a certain amount of vitamin C – a high amount in the case of blackcurrants and strawberries.

The chief value of fresh fruit, however, is that it brings an enjoyable variety to your meals and the value of growing it in your own garden is that the fruit will be fresher, and therefore richer in vitamin C and much tastier, because it does not have to be harvested slightly unripe to allow for the rigours and time-lapse of distribution from grower to greengrocer. Furthermore, home growing can save the pocket and cater for personal preferences seldom satisfied by shop produce.

Fruit in the garden can also be very decorative. Well-tended trees are a feature in their own right, the beauty of tree fruits in blossom is proverbial and the ripening fruit always delight the eye.

Although a few fruits may well be grown for their ornamental effect in addition to their crop potential, it is sound policy to group most fruit together in one plot. Exceptions, for which a place should be found in the vegetable plot, are melons, an annual crop, and strawberries, which need fresh soil every three or four years if they are not to become weak and diseased, and so must be worked into your crop rotation scheme.

Grouping the same kinds of fruit together makes manuring, spraying, pruning and picking easier and also reduces the cost of protection against birds. In many suburban or rural areas birds are such a problem that the only way to succeed with fruit is to cage in the entire fruit plot.

Protection against birds should be considered in advance by all intending fruit-growers. Trees against walls are fairly easily covered with netting while the fruit is ripening, or in winter when the buds are under attack. Where the crop is small, fruits can be protected individually by slipping muslin or ventilated polythene bags or even old nylon stockings over them but this is a tedious process. A well-constructed permanent fruit cage is the best solution to the problem.

Strawberries should be protected by netting on a low semi-temporary support structure. Other soft fruits can be given a degree of protection from birds with black cotton but not, repeat not, nylon thread which does not break and may inflict horrible wounds on the birds or even kill them. An even better alternative is to shroud the fruit in strands of fine rayon web which are sold for this purpose.

The next consideration is your soil. Nearly all fruits prefer a slightly acid soil, while blueberries and cranberries need a very acid soil. Most fruits will tolerate neutral conditions but few will thrive in alkaline soils.

Good drainage, too, is essential for all fruits. The soil should be well dug at least one spit deep, the subsoil being thoroughly broken up with fork or spade. This will improve surface drainage and allow you to eliminate perennial weed roots. Such deep digging will never be possible again once the trees or soft fruits are planted. (See also BASIC TECHNIQUES, page 54.)

Digging will also give you an opportunity to mix well-rotted manure or garden compost into the subsoil to improve the moisture-holding capacity of light, gravelly soils and to break down heavy clay ones. (No manure or fertilizer should ever come in direct contact with the roots.)

Generally speaking, a reasonably good average garden soil which has been cultivated for a number of years will need no special treatment, other than digging, to prepare it for tree fruits. The soft fruits, particularly strawberries, require rather richer conditions, and the soil must hold moisture well in summer.

When planting, it is most important that the soil should be in a friable condition, not too wet and not too dry: it must break down easily into fine particles which will make close contact with the roots.

Should the soil be too wet, so that it is sticky and clammy, or the surface entirely frozen over, or if for any other reason planting has to be deferred when the plants arrive, the parcel should be opened and stored somewhere out of the wind and protected from pests.

As soon as conditions permit, the trees, bushes or canes should be temporarily heeled-in outdoors. This procedure consists of taking out a shallow trench with one side sloping at about 45°. The trees or bushes are laid in this, against the slope, the roots covered with soil and firmed in with the heel. The stems should be covered only up to the soil mark.

Below: heeling in, the way to protect plants when the weather makes the soil unsuitable for planting.

Before planting any trees or bushes, check to see that they have not dried out. If in doubt, soak the roots in a bucket of water for an hour.

Also inspect for damage and cut back all wounded roots to sound tissue, making cuts sloping on the underside of the root.

All tree fruits need staking at first, and apples on dwarfing root-stocks will need support all their life. Cordons, fans and espaliers will have to be secured to canes fastened to horizontal wires. For trees buy pressure-treated stakes if you can. Never plant alongside a freshly creosoted stake; use a copper-based preservative (such as Green Cuprinol) which will not harm the plant. Stake *before* covering the roots, not after.

Also have ready in advance the necessary materials for tying: soft string for fastening cordons, espaliers and fans to canes and either stout cord or patent plastic ties for the tree fruit. If you use cord, you must first bind the tree trunk with a strip of sacking or rubber to prevent chafing. Next, make several circles of cord around tree and stake, leaving a space of 2.5cm (1in) or so between them, the cord then being lapped several times across this space before being knotted, thus forming a buffer.

The patent plastic ties incorporate a buffer and have the great advantage of being subsequently adjustable.

Examine all fastenings a few weeks after planting, when the soil has had time to settle, to ensure that the tree is not being suspended by its tie. After this make an annual inspection in April to check that growth has not made ties too tight, and replace or adjust them as necessary.

The reader about to plant any tree fruit is advised to read the section below on planting apples. The general procedure applies to all fruit trees.

Pruning requirements are dealt with under the individual fruits. You need a sharp pair of secateurs: use them decisively to make a clean cut, always just beyond a bud and sloping very slightly to just behind it.

Tree fruits are not usually grown on their own roots and therefore have to be budded or grafted onto a rootstock. The propagation of tree fruits is a specialist's business and should be attempted only by the professional or the experienced amateur. Accordingly, this subject is not covered here. In any case, the necessary rootstocks are very difficult to obtain in small quantities.

Soft fruits are a quite different proposition, being grown on their own roots; their propagation is relatively simple and is described below under the accounts of individual fruits.

A Model Fruit Garden

The plan for a model fruit garden shown on page 309 is only a suggestion. Thousands of variations are possible and every gardener has to plan according to his or her own particular circumstances and needs.

A number of important factors have been taken into consideration. First, it is assumed that this is a suburban or rural garden where, very commonly, birds are a problem and will on occasion attack all ripening fruit, including apples. The fruit plot, therefore, is entirely caged in with netting. The roof can be removed when snow threatens. The fruit cages generally advertized are usually only 1.8m (6ft) high, occasionally as high as 2m (6½ft). The latter would be well worthwhile but even here, height would limit what can be grown. Vigorous varieties of raspberry need a top support wire at 1.8m (6ft) high and canes will grow above that. Pyramid plums need a height of at least 3m (10ft) and any vigorous bush apple will reach 3.6m (12ft).

Below: types of trained fruit trees include (top to bottom) the espalier, the double cordon, the single cordon, and the fan.

The dimensions of this plot are really governed by what is being grown, but its shape is almost square, the most economical shape to enclose with netting.

The fan-trained plums are to be supported by a free-standing system of horizontal wires. As two plums are grown, either self-fertile or suitable cross-pollinating varieties may be selected.

The different fruits in this plot are so grouped that the potash-lovers – the apples, raspberries, gooseberries, and red and white currants – are together, while those with above-average nitrogen requirements – the pears, plums and blackcurrants – are in another group.

Possible average yields from the fruit garden shown are:
Plums 14kg (30lb), pears 38kg (84lb), blackcurrants 19kg (42lb), gooseberries 12kg (27lb), red currants 10kg (22lb), white currants $2\frac{1}{4}$kg (5lb), raspberries 14kg (30lb) and apples 33kg (72lb).

SOFT FRUIT

BLACKBERRIES (*Rubus fruticosus* and others)
Blackberries are worth growing in the garden because the fruits will be of higher quality and easier to pick than those from the hedgerows. Thornless varieties are now available which make the care and harvesting of this fruit much more pleasant than formerly. Blackberries are an undemanding fruit as to soil and site, they are hardy, and they flower late, escaping frost, but they do need wires for their support.
Site and Soil Although the earliest crops and best results will be achieved in full sun, blackberries will tolerate partial shade.

Sound drainage is essential, but dry conditions in summer will result in tiny, hard berries, so improve the moisture-holding properties of a sandy or gravelly soil by digging in plenty of well-rotted strawy manure or garden compost. Where neither is available, peat or bark fibre may be used, but then extra nourishment should be provided by adding a good general garden fertilizer according to the maker's directions.
Planting Autumn planting is generally preferable, but on a very heavy soil wait until early spring. Spread the roots out and do not plant too deeply. Allow a lateral spacing of at least 3.0m (10ft), with 2.1m (7ft) between rows. The variety Merton Thornless is less vigorous and can be spaced only 1.8m (6ft) apart, but Himalaya Giant grows very strongly and is better at a spacing of 4.5m (15ft) to 6.0m (20ft).
Pruning and Training Immediately after planting, cut all the shoots down to within 23cm (9in) of the soil. During the summer new shoots will appear and these will bear fruit the following summer.

Each year cut out the old canes immediately after harvesting and train in the new canes of the current year's growth. To prevent disease infection via dripping rain, keep the new shoots always tied in above the old canes, or quite separate by training all new canes to one side one year and all the next year's new canes to the other side.

There are several ways of training the canes to the supporting wires, which should be at heights of 90cm (3ft), 1.2m (4ft), 1.5m (5ft) and 1.8m (6ft) above the ground (see the diagram overleaf). Where space is extremely limited, the weaving method may be adopted but this is much more troublesome to establish.
Cultivation Keep down weeds during the growing season either by very shallow hoeing or by hand-weeding.

Conserve moisture by applying in spring a mulch up to 5cm (2in)

Right: a plan of a model fruit garden.

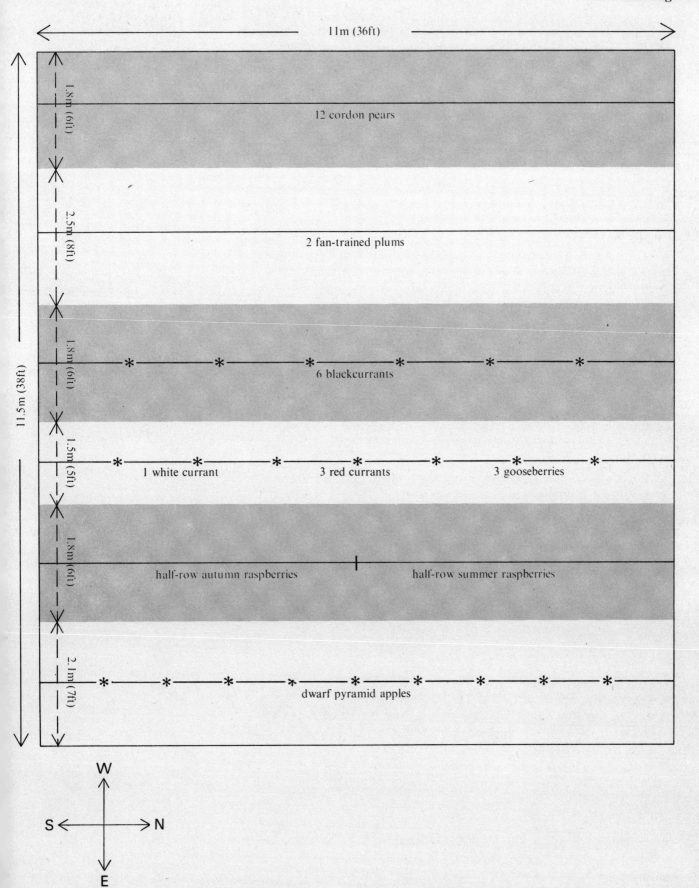

11m (36ft)

11.5m (38ft)

1.8m (6ft)

12 cordon pears

2.5m (8ft)

2 fan-trained plums

1.8m (6ft)

6 blackcurrants

1.5m (5ft)

1 white currant   3 red currants   3 gooseberries

1.8m (6ft)

half-row autumn raspberries   half-row summer raspberries

2.1m (7ft)

dwarf pyramid apples

W

S ← → N

E

deep of well-rotted manure or garden compost. Water well in dry weather. Gently mix the mulch into the top soil in late autumn.

No further manuring is necessary on good soil, but where farmyard manure or garden compost is unavailable, use peat or bark fibre after applying 70g per sq m (2oz per sq yd) of sulphate of ammonia and 27g per sq m ($\frac{3}{4}$oz per sq yd) sulphate of potash in early spring, scattering these over the surface of the bed and lightly raking them in.

Harvesting Because fruit is produced only on the previous year's wood, you will not have a crop the first year. In subsequent years, harvest as soon as the berries are ripe and black; pick them regularly as over-ripe fruit will encourage pests and diseases.

Troubles Few troubles bother the blackberry. Cane spot disease can usually be prevented from becoming serious by keeping young canes away from the old (see above). Virus disease may stunt growth and reduce cropping, and as there is no cure, affected plants should be dug up and burned. Replace with new plantings on a fresh site.

The raspberry beetle sometimes attacks blackberries. Spray with pyrethrum 10 days after the first blossom opens, and again 10 days later, as a preventative if this pest is a problem in your area. If you do not notice an attack until later, spray from when the first fruits begin to turn pink. Do not spray until just before sunset, to spare bees and other beneficial insects.

Propagation New plants are easily produced by bending over a new cane in summer, as soon as it is long enough, and burying about 15cm (6in) of the tip. Refirm the soil and keep the tip buried by tying the cane down with a string to a peg in the ground. Sever the new plants from the parent when new above-ground growth appears, and transplant them to their permanent site a year later.

BLACKCURRANTS (*Ribes nigrum*)

These fruits are famed for their high vitamin C content and from late June into August they provide fresh fruit for cooking. The surplus may be made into jam and juice for the winter, or preserved by bottling or freezing.

Site and Soil Although they will give their earliest and best crops in a sunny position, blackcurrants will tolerate partial shade and are

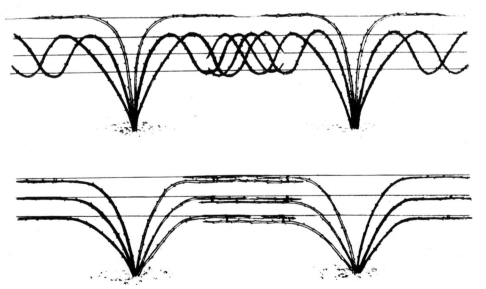

Left: train blackberries to keep fruiting and young canes apart. Cut out the old wood after fruiting, and either weave in young replacement canes (top) or use the one-way system (bottom), training young wood of adjacent bushes to left and right.

Top right: immediately after planting blackcurrants, cut back all shoots to a bud less than 2.5cm (1in) above soil level. Centre right: in winter, prune established plants by removing one third of the old wood.

Below right: neglected bushes will respond to removal of all old wood, and any broken, diseased or overcrowded branches.

therefore useful for planting in a border on the north side of a wall or the house. Avoid situations exposed to frosts and strong winds.

Blackcurrants are greedy feeders and so do best in a rich soil. On a light, rather poor soil they will succeed, however, if they are fed liberally.

Light land which dries out rapidly can cause problems and it is best to improve the moisture-retaining property of the soil before planting by digging in generous amounts of well-rotted farmyard manure or garden compost or, failing these, peat or bark fibre with artificial fertilizer.

Planting The planting season extends from October until March. Buy from reputable growers who have their stock certified as disease-free by the Ministry of Agriculture. Allow 1.8m (6ft) between bushes, each way. Plant firmly, setting the bushes slightly deeper than they were in the nursery: you can see the nursery soil mark on the stems.

Immediately after planting cut every shoot down to a bud less than 2.5cm (1in) above soil level.

Pruning Blackcurrants are grown as shrubby bushes with a number of shoots springing from ground level, never on a 'leg' as is usual with gooseberry or redcurrant bushes. The young, one-year-old shoots of a blackcurrant, identified by their lighter colour, crop most heavily, while the older shoots bear less and less well as they age. The technique of good management, therefore, is to encourage as high a proportion of young wood as possible while keeping as much old wood as may still be profitable without inhibiting the production of more young growth. You must therefore adjust your pruning year by year according to growth.

To leave the shoots at full length after planting would severely weaken your chances of success for several seasons. In the first summer, new shoots will grow from near or below ground level and if these are all sturdy, no further pruning is called for in autumn or winter. Cut down any weak shoots, however, to less than 5cm (2in) from the ground.

In the second summer you should be able to harvest your first crop, and thereafter it pays to prune as soon as picking is completed. At this first annual pruning of the young bush it will probably be sufficient to cut out about one quarter of the shoots to near the soil.

If in subsequent years you cut out between a third and a quarter of all shoots, you will maintain an approximate balance between old and young wood, and no bush will contain wood older than four years.

Where growth is exceedingly vigorous you can improve the next year's crop by pruning less severely; where growth is weakly, you will encourage stronger young growth in future by pruning more drastically.

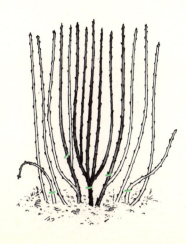

Cultivation Early in the spring following planting spread a 5cm (2in) mulch of well-rotted farmyard or stable manure, or garden compost, over the soil around and between the bushes. This will conserve moisture and discourage weeds, but be ready to water liberally in dry spells. Deal with weeds by hand pulling. Much damage is done to the shallow roots of blackcurrant bushes by cultivating the soil too deeply close around them. Light hoeing is permissible, but not forking.

Feeding As previously mentioned, blackcurrants need a good deal of feeding, especially on light sandy or gravelly soil. The best possible feed is a mulch of well-rotted manure or garden compost applied every year in late winter or early spring. 2.8kg per sq m (5lb per sq yd) – approximately equivalent to one average garden wheelbarrow load per 4.8sq m or 6sq yd – should be adequate. Pig manure and poultry litter may also be used but only up to 1kg per sq m (2lb per sq yd).

In addition to these bulky organic foods, you can give an annual spring dressing of 35g per sq m (1oz per sq yd) of sulphate of ammonia and a third as much of sulphate of potash. Every third year, you can give 35g per sq m (1oz per sq yd) of superphosphate. Where the soil is very acid, use nitro-chalk instead of sulphate of ammonia. If you want to use organic fertilizers instead, apply 70g per sq m (2oz per sq yd) each of sterilized bone meal and hoof-and-horn meal.

Harvesting When the berries have turned completely black, pick by removing the little bunches entire. If you strip the berries off the stalk, or 'strig', they are liable to be damaged. Those destined for preserving should be ripe but still firm. Currants for immediate use may be left on the bush as long as possible. All the currants on a bush tend to ripen at the same time, so growing several varieties will lengthen the picking season.

Troubles DISEASES Reversion is the most serious disease as it can reduce cropping to zero and there is no cure. It prevents fruiting, but not flowering, and the blossoms on an infected bush look pinker just before they open than those on a healthy one. This is because the healthy flower buds have more hairs.

Another symptom, and a more difficult one to distinguish, is to be seen in June when the leaves on an infected bush will be observed to be simpler in outline, with fewer lobes than those on a healthy bush. It looks as if the leaves have reverted to the simpler pattern of some distant wild ancestor. A healthy leaf has from five to eight sub-veins on either side of the central vein of the top lobe, while in a reverted leaf there will be only four or less.

Dig up reverted bushes and burn. Replant new, certified bushes on a fresh site. This disease is caused by a virus spread by gall mites (see below).

Leaf spot is a fungus disease which causes dark brown spots on the leaves in the early summer. These may grow and join together until the whole leaf surface is covered. Leaves may then fall prematurely in July and the berries will shrivel. Collect and burn any fallen spotted leaves.

To control a serious attack of leaf spot, spray with benomyl when the blossom buds look like miniature bunches of grapes and repeat three times at fortnightly intervals. If symptoms are still visible at picking time, spray with benomyl after picking, and repeat fortnightly.

Alternatively, use thiophanate-methyl, spraying when the first flowers open and again repeating at fortnightly intervals two or three times.
PESTS Gall mites, causing the condition popularly known as 'big bud', are serious because they not only destroy the fruiting buds but also transmit Reversion Disease. Suspect this trouble if some buds start to swell abnormally in winter, look promising by spring but never open.

Hand-picking big buds in early March will help to contain this pest but if you are faced with a bad attack, spray with malathion or a potassium permanganate solution when the first flowers open.

Aphids may infest the leaves, causing stickiness and stunting growth. Spray with pyrethrum or derris (or with malathion or dimethoate) before the blossom opens and in winter with a 5 per cent tar-oil wash.

Propagation Provided your blackcurrants are absolutely healthy, you can increase your stock easily by rooting cuttings.

Early in October cut pieces of the current year's well-ripened wood. Cut off unripened wood at the tip, cutting just above a bud, and trim off at the base, just below a bud, to leave a piece about 23cm (9in) long.

Plant the cuttings about 15cm (6in) deep and the same distance apart in a shallow slit-trench which has had a little washed river sand sprinkled in it. Return the soil to the little trench and tread firm. Inspect occasionally and refirm if frost has loosened the cuttings.

By November just over a year later, the cuttings should have rooted well and may be transplanted to their permanent quarters, after which you should cut down all growths to within 2.5cm (1in) of soil level.

BLUEBERRIES (*Vaccinium corymbosum*)

The American Highbush blueberry is related to our native bilberries (also known as blaeberries or whortleberries) but bears larger fruits with a distinct waxy 'bloom' on their surface, which are sweet and of better flavour. They are excellent in pies and flans and can be made into jam or frozen. Although blueberries are partly self-fertile, success is more likely to follow the planting of at least two varieties to ensure cross-pollination.

Soil and Site Blueberries need a very acid soil, such as that suitable for rhododendrons and azaleas. While it needs to be reasonably well drained, it must never be allowed to dry out. A very thin sandy soil can be improved by digging in peat. Never try to grow blueberries in an alkaline soil. Although full sun is preferable, blueberries will tolerate partial shade. See that they are sheltered from cold winds.

Planting The planting season extends from November to March. Add no manure but work a little peat around the roots and set the plants a little deeper than they were in the nursery, and 1.8m (6ft) apart each way.

Cultivation Mulch with well-rotted manure, garden compost or peat in early spring and water liberally whenever necessary.

On a relatively poor soil, you can give an annual March dressing of 35g per sq m (1oz per sq yd) sulphate of ammonia and half as much sulphate of potash.

Harvesting The berries ripen between mid-July and the end of September and several pickings may be necessary to clear each bush. Pick them when they are firm and very deep blue.

Pruning Little pruning is necessary, and none during the first three years. Then, early in winter tip the leaders to promote bushy growth and occasionally cut out old branches entirely to stimulate new shoots from the base.

Troubles Few troubles may be expected but netting against birds is essential and should be in place long before the berries ripen.

Propagation You can increase your stock by layering branch tips in spring or semi-hardwood cuttings from mid-July until early August. Layered tips should be ready for severing and replanting after one or two years; the cuttings should be rooted in a cold frame, potted singly and then grown in a nursery bed until ready to plant out permanently after two or three years.

GOOSEBERRIES (*Ribes grossularia*)

The gooseberry is a useful garden fruit because of its long cropping season. The earliest varieties may provide small immature berries for the first pie or tart at Whitsun and green berries may be picked for cooking throughout the rest of the summer. Ripe berries may be eaten for dessert in late July and August. They make good jam, and ripe but still firm, berries may be frozen whole or first made into purée.

The ripe berries are either green, yellow, near-white or red, according to variety, and all varieties are self-fertile.

Gooseberries may be grown as bushes or as cordons or fans.

Site Full sun is preferable but partial shade is acceptable. Gooseberries are less prone to having their flowers damaged by frost than either blackcurrants or strawberries, but their tiny fruitlets are vulnerable and the proper pollination of the blossom may be prevented by cold winds which deter insects from flying. So avoid a frost pocket if you can.

Soil Provided they have quite free drainage, gooseberries are very tolerant of different soils and will even succeed in slightly alkaline conditions. The ideal, however, is a slightly acid deep loam. Light, thin soils are least suitable and should be improved by digging in all the rotted organic matter you can spare.

Gooseberries are great potash lovers and this mineral is most likely to be deficient on light land. When preparing all light soil, after digging in farmyard manure, garden compost, leafmould and so on, rake a 35g per sq m (1oz per sq yd) dressing of sulphate of potash into the surface. Alternatively, unless your soil is chalky, you can use wood ashes at the rate of 270g per sq m (8oz per sq yd). (These must have been stored in a dry place, or the rain will have washed out much of the potash.)

Planting You can plant at any time in the dormant season, between October and March, provided the soil is freely workable.

Buy two or three-year-old bushes and plant them 1.5m (5ft) apart, firmly but no deeper than they were in the nursery, as indicated by the soil mark on the stem. If you buy single cordons, each requires a lateral space of 40cm (15in), and if you grow them in rows allow 1.5m (5ft) between each. Fans need a spread of at least 1.8m (6ft).

After planting, mulch 5cm (2in) deep with manure or compost.

Staking Bushes need no stakes but canes should be provided for the central stem of a cordon and for each rib of a fan.

Pruning BUSH GOOSEBERRIES are grown on a short, clear, main stem or 'leg' and are shaped rather like a miniature apple tree. The fruit is produced on year-old shoots and older spurs. Give the first pruning during the winter of planting. Select the strongest six to eight branches for retention, cutting back to half way the previous season's new growth at the end of each branch. Cut back laterals to the third or fourth bud, and trim off unwanted weak growths flush with the stem.

The branches of some varieties (notably those of Leveller and Careless) droop towards the end and this undesirable tendency can be counteracted by pruning to buds pointing upwards.

In some gardens great havoc is done to gooseberry bushes in the winter by birds which peck out the buds. Either prevent this entirely by netting, or make life more difficult for the birds by deferring pruning until late winter, or even March when the leaves are beginning to open. This enables you to make sure you prune to a live bud.

In the second and subsequent winters let your pruning be guided more by the strength of growth during the previous summer. Cut back branch leaders (the new extension growth on each) by a half if vigorous, by two-thirds if weak. Cut back the new growth on laterals to about 7.5cm (3in) if vigorous, to 2.5cm (1in) if weak.

With the passage of time, perhaps after the first three years, the pruning of branch leaders can be less severe but some branches will have to be shortened drastically to an outward or upward pointing bud, to prevent overcrowding. Some may have to be cut out entirely. Similar surgery may have to be performed on branches drooping down to the ground. Prune branch leaders more heavily when vigour needs stimulating.

Below: to prune a gooseberry, cut the previous season's new growth back to half and shorten laterals to the third or fourth bud.

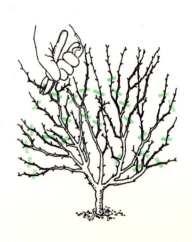

In addition to the winter pruning, near the end of June or in early July cut back all new sideshoot growth to the fifth leaf.

Prune the central stem of a single CORDON back in winter by a third, leaving two-thirds of its new growth. Repeat this each winter but never leave more than 25cm (10in) of new leader. Then in summer, towards the end of June, cut back new lateral growths, each to its fifth leaf. In winter further cut these summer-pruned shoots to three buds. Thus the sideshoots will grow by the space between three leaves each year. When they become too long for the space available or droop unduly, cut them back to an upward pointing bud.

The branches of a FAN are pruned as if each were a single cordon.

Cultivation Deep digging close to gooseberry bushes is likely to damage near-surface roots, but weeds must be kept down. Hoe shallowly or hand-weed. Mulching will help to suppress weeds.

Never let the soil dry out completely, and water when necessary. This is particularly important in the early summer when the berries are swelling rapidly. When you do water, give plenty, at least 25 litres per sq m ($4\frac{1}{2}$gal per sq yd).

Feeding A winter mulch of well-rotted farmyard manure or garden compost will usually supply nitrogen needs but this should be supplemented with a winter or early spring dressing of sulphate of potash raked in gently at the rate of 27g per sq m ($\frac{3}{4}$oz per sq yd), particularly on light sandy soils, or 270g per sq m (8oz per sq yd) bonemeal. Lightly rake the rotted mulch into the surface soil in autumn.

Should the leaves exhibit a scorched appearance at the edges in summer, and possibly also fall prematurely, this indicates potash deficiency. Give an immediate small dose of sulphate of potash, half the normal winter dressing, and increase the winter application by half.

Harvesting You can start picking gooseberries while they are still green, as soon as they are large enough to be worth cooking. Do not strip whole branches but take a berry here and there – this has the effect of thinning the crop so that the remaining fruit will grow all the bigger.

The dessert varieties will not develop their full sweetness until absolutely ripe, but long before this take care to net them against birds.

Troubles DISEASES Undoubtedly, the most serious disease is American gooseberry mildew, all too prevalent these days. This fungus appears as a white powdery mildew on leaves, shoots and berries in spring or early summer. Later in the season this mildew turns brown and becomes felt-like. It spoils the crop and distorts and inhibits growth.

You should cut out the tips of badly affected shoots but prevention is better than cure. Well-pruned bushes grown in the open are less likely to be infected, as are those which have not been given too much nitrogen (which leads to weak sappy growth). If the disease is prevalent in your area, spray with dinocap, or with a mixture of $\frac{1}{4}$kg ($\frac{1}{2}$lb) of soft soap and 1kg (2lb) of washing soda in 45 litres (10gal) of water (double the amount of soft soap if your water is hard). Spray when the first flowers open, repeating this three times at intervals of a fortnight.

Leaf spot, the same disease which may attack blackcurrants, can cause leaf disfigurement and premature fall. Treat as for blackcurrants.

PESTS Apart from birds which peck the buds in winter and the fruit in summer, the green-black larvae of the gooseberry sawfly are the pest most likely to be troublesome. They may have eaten holes in many of the leaves or even stripped them completely before you notice their presence in May or later. Hand-pick or spray with derris or pyrethrum (or with fenitrothion or malathion). Do not spray while the blossom is open before sunset, to avoid killing bees and other pollinating insects.

Aphids may also attack your gooseberries. Spray at once with derris or pyrethrum or with dimethoate or malathion but not within 48 hours of picking. Winter-washing with tar-oil during the dormant season will often do much to lessen the chance of aphid attack.

Propagation You can increase your stock of gooseberries by taking cuttings in late September or October. Cut off shoots of the current year's growth and trim off the unripened wood towards the tip, leaving the cutting between 30 and 38cm (12 and 15in) long. Rooting will be more certain if you dip the lower cut end in hormone rooting powder.

Remove no buds, contrary to old-fashioned practice, and set about 15cm (6in) deep and the same distance apart in a shallow slit-trench which has been lined with a little washed river sand, as for blackcurrant cuttings. Return the soil and make it firm. Inspect the cuttings occasionally and refirm them if frost has loosened them.

Where growth is good, the cuttings may be lifted in just over a year's time, during the dormant season (autumn and winter), and transferred to their permanent quarters. Otherwise leave the new plants undisturbed for another year. When you do dig them up cut off flush with the stem any shoots which have grown out from buried buds and any sideshoots less than 15cm (6in) above soil level, thus giving the new bush a clean leg.

GRAPES (*Vitis vinifera*)

Grapes Outdoors

In the last few years the growing of grapes (*Vitis vinifera*) in the open has become far more popular and many vines have been planted for wine-making. With greater experience and the import of varieties more suited to our climate it has become apparent that reasonable crops of outdoor grapes may be obtained in areas not formerly thought suitable.

Site It used to be thought that outdoor grapes would only succeed in the most favoured parts of the south but they have been found to grow well in many places south of a line drawn from Milford Haven in South-west Wales to the Wash.

The important thing is that the outdoor grapevine should receive all the available sunshine and also be sheltered from cold winds. In gardens north of the line mentioned above and in the more exposed areas it is advisable to grow the vines against a south-facing wall or to protect them with cloches or lights. Also, in such less favoured areas only the early varieties should be attempted.

Soil It has been found that grapes are tolerant of a wider range of soil conditions than was previously imagined. A slightly acid soil is preferable, but grapes will tolerate slight alkalinity (up to pH 8.0) and a soil more acid than pH 6.5 should have lime applied to reduce the acidity. Good drainage is vital and if you are in doubt plant on a bed raised some 23 to 30cm (9 to 12in) above the surroundings. Heavy clay must be lightened with grit or sand and organic matter.

That outdoor grapes need poor soil is another fallacy which has now been exposed. Poor or light soils should be improved by digging in liberal quantities of well-rotted manure or garden compost.

Planting Planting is possible at any time between October and early April, but because of the risk of frost damage to the thin shoots of a very young vine it is safer to delay until March.

As a single vine may bear, on the average, between $2\frac{1}{4}$ and $3\frac{1}{2}$kg (5 to 8lb) of fruit and it takes nearly 1kg ($2\frac{1}{4}$lb) of grapes to produce only one bottle of wine, those who aspire to a home vintage will need to plant a number of vines. If the training is to be on the dwarf double Guyot system recommended below, the vines should be 1.5m (5ft) apart in rows 1m (3ft) apart.

Make a hole somewhat larger than the natural spread of the roots so that the vine will be at the same depth, when firmed in, as it was in the nursery. See that no manure comes in contact with the roots and return the soil over them, firming as you proceed. Water immediately after planting.

Staking Whether free-standing in the open garden or grown against a wall or fence, vines will require a system of horizontal wires to support them. Old telephone wire (with its insulation covering still on) is best, but galvanized wire (3.15mm gauge) will serve instead. Provide a 1.5m (5ft) high stake for each plant, allowing an extra 60cm (2ft) to be buried in a light soil, or 45cm ($1\frac{1}{2}$ft) in a heavy one.

Then provide two horizontal support wires at heights of 30cm (1ft) and 75cm ($2\frac{1}{2}$ft).

Training and Pruning Allow only one shoot to grow the first summer, pinching out all others as soon as you see them. Tie the one shoot loosely to the support post as necessary. Some new vines are slow to start and may show no sign of life until high summer; so have patience.

In November following planting, give the vine its first annual winter pruning, cutting it down to the third bud. During the following summer three shoots will grow up. If any more appear, pinch them out.

In the second November tie two of the three shoots down to the lower horizontal wire and shorten each to about 75cm ($2\frac{1}{2}$ft). Prune the third shoot to three buds which in turn will provide three new vertical shoots the next summer. Pinch out any laterals from these at one leaf.

The two tied down, horizontal growths will each produce vertical laterals during the summer. Allow three or four to grow on each side. Bunches of grapes may now appear but in the first year you should content yourself with only two per vine. Pinch out any others.

In August clip off all the growth from the fruiting laterals above the top wire, to which they should be loosely tied. Do not cut the three replacement shoots at the centre.

Each autumn, as soon as the leaves have fallen, repeat the pruning cycle, cutting out the two fruit-bearing arms, tying in a replacement on either side and pruning back the third replacement shoot to three buds.

Vines planted against walls and fences should be trained and pruned in precisely the same way (see diagram overleaf).

Cultivation Watering in dry weather will be necessary and is particularly important in the first few months after planting.

Keep down weeds by light hoeing or hand-pulling. A 7.5cm (3in) mulch of peat, really well-rotted manure or garden compost spread over the soil surface to a width of 30cm (1ft) on either side of the row will help to suppress weeds and conserve moisture.

It is unnecessary to thin the grapes on the bunches if they are intended for wine-making. For dessert, however, larger individual berries are desirable and thinning will be essential (see under GREENHOUSE GRAPES, page 321).

Keep replacement shoots loosely tied to the stakes and the laterals from the horizontal arms tied to the upper wire as they reach it.

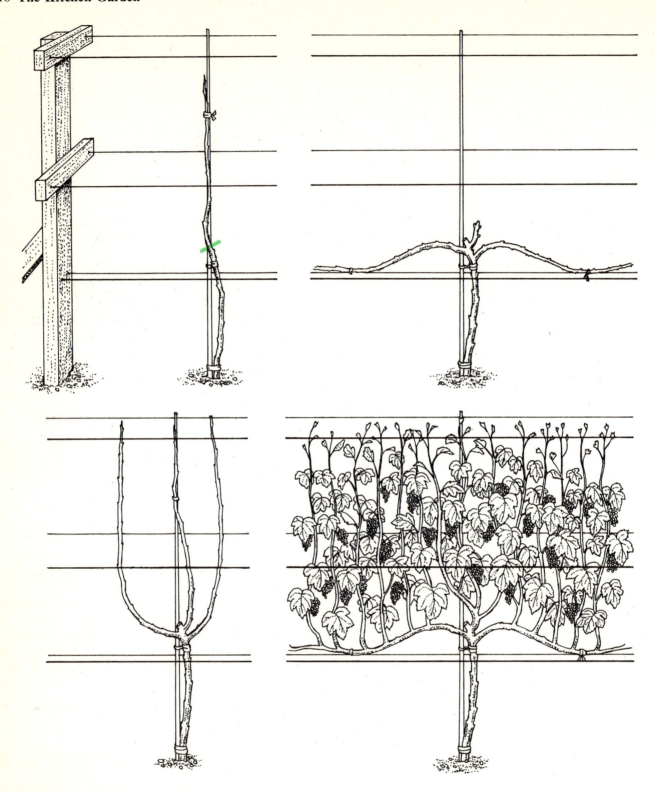

Cloches may be used to give protection in less favoured districts but most designs now available are unsuitable. It is necessary for the ridge to open to allow the vertical shoots to escape, the fruiting laterals being protected below. The best solution is to improvise your own frames, erecting a permanent support framework against which Dutch lights may be leant and secured, with a gap at the ridge.

Feeding Give an annual dressing in January of a mixed general garden fertilizer at the rate of 70g per sq m (2oz per sq yd) plus 35g per sq m (1oz per sq yd) of sulphate of potash. In spring put down a mulch

Facing page, top left: a vine at the end of the first year's growth. Make the pruning cut as indicated by the solid line, leaving three buds.
Below left: at the end of the second year's growth.
Top right: cut back the central cane and tie the two side canes to the horizontal wires at right and left.
Below right: the first fruiting summer. In the autumn, cut back the two horizontal fruiting canes and tie in the two replacement canes.

7.5cm (3in) deep of well-rotted manure, old mushroom compost or garden compost which will supply additional nourishment while deterring weed growth. Spread both fertilizer and mulch over a 30cm (1ft) strip on either side of the vine row.

Where the grapes are being grown for dessert, you should also provide fortnightly applications of liquid manure while the berries are swelling. Stop as they show signs of ripening.

Harvesting Harvest grapes on a dry, sunny day, if possible and cut each bunch with scissors or secateurs – never try to tear it off the vine. Cut with about 5cm (2in) of lateral stem attached. Grapes for wine-making should be left on the vine as long as possible so that they contain as much sugar as possible.

Troubles DISEASES Two types of mildew can be troublesome with outdoor vines but both can be prevented by dusting when the first shoots are some 5cm (2in) long with a half and half mixture of ground sulphur powder and Bordeaux mixture, repeating at fortnightly intervals. Prevention is better than attempting a cure when the trouble is seen and much damage may already have been done.

PESTS Insect pests are seldom a worry, except for wasps which may attack the earliest ripening fruit. Netting is essential against birds.

Propagation You can increase your stock of vines by heeling in pieces of ripened wood when you prune in early winter and planting these out in February as cuttings. Each cutting should be from 20 to 30cm (8 to 12in) long and possess four sound growth buds. Insert them in the ground to half their length.

Alternatively propagate from single buds, known as eyes. In February cut pieces of well ripened wood each about 2.5cm (1in) long with one growth bud at the centre and plant in pots of John Innes No 1 potting compost. Press the pieces horizontally into the soil surface so that just the bud is uncovered.

Water and stand the pots in a greenhouse or propagator and keep them at 21°C (70°F) until new growth shows. Then reduce the temperature to 16°C (60°F).

Below: propagating grapes from single buds. Cut prunings into pieces each carrying one bud (or eye) and press into the surface of a pot of compost.

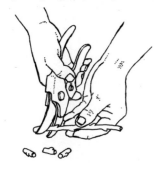

Grapes under glass

Giving grapes the protection of a greenhouse makes the cultivation of this delicious fruit possible in districts unfavourable for outdoor vines, and it also widens the range of varieties which is possible. In particular, it enables one to grow the better quality dessert grapes, some of which can only succeed if at least some artificial warmth is available. It is hardly an economic proposition to grow wine grapes in a greenhouse, although of course any surplus can be made into wine if desired. The crop will be ready from August to October according to variety.

Site and Soil The greenhouse grapevine can either be planted in the open, immediately alongside the greenhouse, and its stem led into the house through a hole in the base, or it may be planted in a border in the house. In either case the soil needs to be reasonably rich and must be very well-drained and either the greenhouse glass should come down to ground level or the side wall should be no higher than 60cm (2ft).

Ideally the vine border should be some 1.5m (5ft) wide and prepared to a depth of 90cm (3ft). Fill the bottom of the border with about 15–25cm (6–9in) of rubble covered with turves to ensure good drainage. Try to obtain some well-rotted stable or farmyard manure and mix this into three times the quantity of good loam.

Planting Nurseries usually raise their grapevines in containers and so theoretically they can be planted at any time. The spring is often recommended, but if you plant in early autumn you can then give the vine its first pruning before the middle of January, after which time any cutting should be avoided because of the risk of the sap bleeding.

Before planting, remove the vine from its container and carefully open up the ball of roots which will probably be rather close-packed. Plant so that the roots are covered by 7.5cm (3in) of soil and make the plant quite firm, treading the soil in with your foot. The single-rod or cordon system of training is the easiest and most commonly followed. If you plant more than one vine, set them 1.2m (4ft) apart and, in the greenhouse border, about 45cm (1½ft) from the glass.

Training and Pruning Before mid-January, while the newly-planted vine is dormant, cut it back to the second bud (if inside) and to the second bud on the stem inside the house if the vine is planted outside. In the latter case rub off any buds on the stem outside.

Allow only one stem to grow up, choosing the stronger if two appear, and pinch out all unwanted shoots at the second leaf.

The house should be equipped with horizontal support wires at intervals of about 30cm (1ft), and 45cm (1½ft) from the glass. As the growing 'rod', or main stem, passes these wires tie it in with soft string. Remove any blossom buds which appear.

In the second winter, and before mid-January, cut the young rod back to half its length. This is continued annually, cutting back the new extension growth by a half each year, until the limit of space is reached. The vine rod may grow vertically up to the greenhouse roof and should then be trained on further horizontal wires 45cm (1½ft) from the glass.

In the second January untie the rod and allow it to arch over. This will encourage an even growth from all buds. Retie in February. During the second summer, permit laterals to grow at intervals of about 18 to 20cm (7 to 8in) and alternately on either side of the rod. Rub out unwanted shoots as they appear.

The first bunch or two may be allowed to swell in this second summer. Pinch out the bearing shoots two leaves beyond the bunch. Tie in all laterals to the horizontal wires and pinch out any sub-laterals immediately after the second leaf.

In the next and subsequent winters, cut back each of the laterals to two buds but allow only the stronger shoot to develop. Year by year more bunches may be allowed to swell and eventually the vine will be strong enough for the laterals to bear two or three bunches each. Always stop two leaves beyond the last bunch to be permitted and pinch out non-fruiting laterals at the fourth leaf.

After the leaves fall, greenhouse grapes require a three-month dormant period with free ventilation.

Where heat is available, growth may be started in February by closing the ventilators and turning on the warmth. Give the border a thorough soaking. Water again when the flowers show.

At first, aim at a temperature of about 7°C (45°F) and then open the ventilators if the sun raises it higher. When the flowers open, try to keep the temperature over 10°C (50°F) and later, when they have set, aim at 18°C (65°F) to 21°C (70°F).

With an unheated greenhouse, you will have to wait for growth to start naturally in March and then raise the temperature by closing ventilators.

Grapes are self-fertile, but pollination will be aided by keeping the atmosphere on the dry side and tapping the rods around midday to disperse the pollen.

For dessert use, grapes must be thinned. Start when the berries are quite tiny, about 2.5mm ($\frac{1}{10}$in) across, and use pointed scissors. Hold the stalks out with a little forked stick so that you do not rub the bloom off the grapes with your fingers. Thin again when the berries have reached the size of peas, and this time reduce their number until they are about 2.5cm (1in) apart.

Feeding Buy some special vine food at a garden shop and dress the border with this at a rate of 70g per sq m (2oz per sq yd), as soon as the flowers have set. Mulch the border afterwards.

Harvesting See under GRAPES OUTDOORS, on page 316.

Troubles DISEASES Powdery mildew can affect young shoots in spring and spoil berries in autumn. It is encouraged by overcrowded foliage, so avoid this by proper thinning. As a precaution against this disease, you can spray with benomyl, dinocap or thiophanate methyl when the first shoots are 5 to 7.5cm (2 to 3in) long, or fumigate the whole greenhouse with a dinocap smoke. Repeat at fortnightly intervals. This treatment will also help to prevent grey mould (botrytis) which may attack the berries in early autumn, and is particularly likely in muggy weather. A little heat and a dry atmosphere will also check the latter trouble.

Shanking, when the berries shrivel, is a physiological trouble due to unsatisfactory soil conditions, either dryness or waterlogging.

PESTS Red spider mites are sometimes troublesome in heated houses, though seldom in unheated ones. They are encouraged by very dry conditions. Fumigate the house with an azobenzene smoke.

Propagation As for GRAPES OUTDOORS: see page 316.

LOGANBERRIES AND OTHER HYBRID BERRIES (*Rubus loganobaccus*)

Loganberries are reputed to be a cross between a blackberry and an American raspberry. Although most people find them too sour for eating raw, cooking brings out their fine flavour and these large berries are justifiably popular. They are easy to grow but more susceptible to winter frost damage than blackberries (although the roots usually survive) and are somewhat more particular as to soil. They do best in a good medium soil or in a light soil which has been enriched with plenty of organic matter. As with blackberries, there is now a thornless version.

Of the various other raspberry-blackberry hybrids, perhaps the best is the thornless Boysenberry, but this is less hardy than the loganberry.

Loganberries and the other hybrids are grown in the same way as blackberries, the canes being trained to horizontal wires and the fruited canes cut out when picking finishes. Propagation is by tip layering.

Troubles Loganberries are rather more susceptible to disease and to the various raspberry pests than are blackberries.

DISEASES Cane spot is a fungus disease causing small purple spots on leaves and greyish purple-edged patches on stems. The fruit may be deformed. Cut out and burn badly infected canes and spray the rest with Bordeaux mixture. In future years, if there is further infection, spray with benomyl or thiophanate-methyl when the buds are 13mm ($\frac{1}{2}$in) long and repeat fortnightly until flowering finishes.

Spur blight is a rather similar disease, causing purple patches near leaf joints which later turn silver. This ends in buds dying and 'die-back' setting in (the infection moves back along the cane until it is killed). Cut out badly affected canes and burn. Prevent by spraying with Bordeaux mixture or benomyl soon after new canes appear and repeat three times at fortnightly intervals.

Virus disease may also attack loganberries, as with blackberries. There is no cure; badly infected canes must be dug up and burnt. Aphids may spread this trouble: protect as for raspberries.
PESTS Raspberry beetle may attack the berries. Treat as for blackberries.

Loganberries and the other hybrids must usually be netted against birds.

MELONS (*Cucumis melo*)

The melon is an ever-popular dessert but whether it should be classed as a soft fruit is debatable, as it has a hard skin or rind. It certainly is not a tree fruit, however, and its cultivation is much like that of the cucumber, to which vegetable it is closely related.

The melon is not hardy and the seedlings need warmth and protection. They may be grown on in heated greenhouses, unheated houses, cold frames or under cloches. One variety at least will fruit outdoors in favourable districts.

Sowing Where a minimum night temperature of 16°C (60°F) can be guaranteed in the greenhouse, melons may be sown for greenhouse culture in January. In many greenhouses it will be necessary to wait until later in the year before this temperature can be maintained.

If you intend to grow the plants in a cool greenhouse, you may sow (in heat) in March but for those to be grown in an unheated greenhouse, cold frame or under cloches, crop sowing should be delayed until early April. Where no heat at all is available, it is possible in the more favoured parts of the country to sow an appropriate variety in late April for planting out in June when all risk of frost has passed.

Fill 7.5cm (3in) pots with a soilless sowing compost or with John Innes seed compost and water lightly. When the pots have drained, sow one seed in each, on its side and pressed in to a depth of 2cm ($\frac{3}{4}$in). If you can provide it, a temperature of 18–21°C (65–70°F) is ideal until germination takes place. Lay a sheet of glass over the pots, to retain the moisture, and cover this with newspaper to keep out light. Remove both as soon as germination occurs and stand the pots in a very light place.

Planting When each seedling has made four rough-edged true leaves in addition to the two seed-leaves, it is ready to be transplanted.

In a greenhouse of glass-to-ground design, prepare a border of rich soil, digging a bucketful or two of rotted manure into each sq m (or sq yd). Then make up more rich soil into 23cm (9in) high planting mounds at 90cm (3ft) intervals along the border.

In solid-walled greenhouses with staging you can fill boxes, which should measure at least 30cm (1ft) deep and 45cm (18in) across, with rich soil or John Innes No 3 potting compost and grow the melons in these on the staging. Again, plant on mounds.

In the cold frame, make up a rich bed and form two mounds, in diagonally opposite corners of each light. For cloches, again prepare a rich bed and put the cloches in position a fortnight before planting, from mid-May to the end of the month according to district. Draw the soil up in shallow mounds about 7.5cm (3in) high and at 90cm (3ft) intervals along the row.

Training In the greenhouse allow a single shoot to grow up, fastening it to a vertical cane or to horizontal wires placed at intervals. When this shoot is 1.8m (6ft) tall, pinch out its growing point. Laterals will now develop and should be supported by tying them loosely with soft string to horizontal wires. When each of these growths has made five leaves, pinch off the tip. Flower-bearing sub-laterals will now develop and should be pinched out two leaves beyond any swelling fruit.

In the cold frame pinch out the first main growth when it has made five leaves. Laterals will then form. Choose the two strongest and pinch out the tips of any others. These two chosen laterals should be directed along the ground on two sides of the frame, and when they are 40cm (16in) long, they should be pinched out. Now fruiting sub-laterals will develop.

Under cloches you follow the same training procedure as in cold frames but directing one main lateral in either direction along the cloches.

Pollination Melons produce male (pollen-bearing) flowers and female flowers (each with its embryo melon visible just behind the petals). For the fruit to swell, the female flower must be fertilized with the male pollen. If more than one female flower appears, the first to be fertilized will swell at the expense of the others. The art of melon-growing is therefore to see that as many female flowers as are required to bear fruit (that is two on a frame or cloche plant, several on a greenhouse cordon) are pollinated on the same day.

In the open, or in freely ventilated frames or cloches, pollination may be carried out by insects, but this is much less likely in the greenhouse. In all cases it is safer to do the job yourself, stripping the petals from a ripe male flower (one in which the pollen tends to fall off) and thrusting it successively into the centre of female flowers.

Other Cultivation Details Give plenty of water at first, but once the fruits begin to swell keep the plants a little drier, though of course you must never deprive them of moisture.

No special feeding is necessary, but mulch the soil surface with a fifty-fifty mixture of well-rotted manure and soil if roots begin to show.

In the greenhouse the swelling fruits need supporting on pieces of netting attached to the training wires. Elsewhere the fruits should be kept clear of the soil on tiles or pieces of slate.

Harvesting Test for ripeness by gently pressing with your thumb the skin at the end opposite the stalk, which becomes soft when the fruit is ready. Small cracks will also appear on the fruit around its stalk.

Troubles DISEASES Powdery mildew is the disease most likely to appear, covering the leaves with a whitish powder and weakening growth. If it appears, cut off the worst affected shoots. Spray with benomyl, dinocap or thiophanate-methyl to prevent the trouble.

Foot or collar rot will attack the base of the stem (the 'collar') if it is allowed to become very wet. It is to prevent this trouble that you plant melons on mounds. Keep mulches from contact with the stem, too.

PESTS Red spider mites are likely to attack greenhouse or frame melons, if they are kept too dry. A humid atmosphere (achieved by spraying with cold water in hot, dry conditions) deters these pests, which cause the leaves to become mottled with grey-brown spots. In bad attacks, the whole plant may wilt; spray with derris or malathion in such cases.

RASPBERRIES (*Rubus idaeus*)

Raspberries are popular because they will succeed in most districts, they give a fairly high yield in relation to the area occupied, they are a favourite dessert fruit, also excellent for cooking and jam-making, and

are generally regarded as the most rewarding fruit for home freezing.
There are two main types, the summer-fruiters and the autumn-fruiters.
Their cultivation is similar except for the time of pruning.

Site and Soil For preference, raspberries should be given a site sheltered
from wind. They will tolerate partial shade quite well.

This fruit does best in a well-drained, slightly acid soil. Alkaline soils
are the only unsuitable ones. A high humus content is desirable to
retain moisture during the summer and they like plenty of potash, which
is often deficient in light soils.

Where the plot needs to be improved by digging in manure take out a
trench 60 to 90cm (2 to 3ft) wide and one spade blade's depth where
each row is to be. Now spread well-rotted manure liberally in this
trench and fork it in. Raspberries root deeply as well as shallowly.
Where manure cannot be obtained use garden compost. See that every
perennial weed root is eliminated as you proceed. It is worth treating
raspberries well initially because they will occupy the same site for a
good number of years.

Support Although not essential, it is easier to erect supports of posts
and wires before planting rather than after. Normally posts 1.5m (5ft)
high are used, with an extra 45cm (1½ft) buried in heavy soil, or 60cm
(2ft) in light soil. Vigorous varieties need an extra height of 30cm (1ft)
and if the raspberries are not to grow inside a permanent fruit cage it is a
good idea to have posts 60cm (2ft) higher still so that a top wire can be
run clear of the raspberry canes to support an anti-bird net. The end
posts will need diagonal struts pointing down the row to take the strain
when the wires are tightened.

Three horizontal wires are now fixed to the posts at heights of 60cm
(2ft), 1.05m (3½ft) and 1.5m (5ft); each wire should be 30cm (1ft) higher
for vigorous varieties. Galvanized wire of 2.00mm (14 gauge) may be
used or, even better, old insulated telephone wire (which is advertised in
most gardening magazines). At the end of each length of wire
incorporate a wire strainer to keep the wire taut.

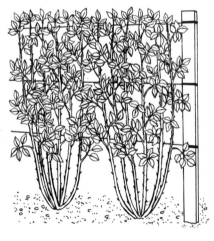

Planting It is possible to plant at any time between November and April
but early autumn planting is by far preferable. Plant so that the roots
are well spread out and the top ones about 7.5cm (3in) below the
surface. Make the canes quite firm. Allow 1.8m (6ft) between rows, and
45cm (1½ft) between plants in the row. Some weak-growing varieties
(notably Malling Jewel) can be planted closer in the row or two canes
put in each hole.

Immediately after planting cut the canes down to 25cm (10in) from
the ground.

Pruning Summer-Fruiting Varieties During the first summer, new canes
will grow up and these require no pruning during their first winter. In
the second year they will fruit, and immediately you have finished picking,
they should be pruned. Cut all the old canes down almost to ground
level. Each summer new canes are produced which fruit the next summer.
At the annual pruning look over the new canes and remove the weaker
ones, keeping only the six strongest. At the end of February just tip the
ends of the canes, cutting them back to 15cm (6in) above the top wire.

Pruning Autumn-Fruiting Varieties These kinds differ in their habit of
growth in that the new canes grow up during the summer and bear fruit
in the autumn of the same year. Defer their pruning until the end of
February and then cut down all of them almost to ground level. If new
growth becomes dense, during early summer cut out the weaker canes,

reducing the number to about eight canes per stool.

Training The canes of the summer-fruiting varieties will need to be secured to their horizontal wires, partly to prevent bunching and allow each cane its fair share of sun and air, partly to prevent wind damage. The best way to do this is to tie each raspberry cane separately with soft string as it reaches each support wire in turn.

A less time-consuming method, but not quite so effective, is to use a running string fastened at one end of the row and then passed round a raspberry cane, over the wire, back past the cane and under the wire, so holding the cane in a loop of string which then travels on to the next cane.

A still easier method of support, reasonably effective in well sheltered sites, is to fix double wires to the posts, held about 23cm (9in) apart by crosspieces. Guide the canes up between these wires as they grow.

The autumn-fruiting varieties are less vigorous and do not grow as tall. A double wire at a height of about 60 to 90cm (2 to 3ft) will usually give sufficient support.

Other Cultivation Details Raspberries thrive in a cool, moist soil and so each spring, when the new canes are growing well, put down a good mulch of well-rotted manure or garden compost.

In spite of the mulch, water will have to be given in dry periods and this is particularly important in the first season and early in the summer when new canes are growing fast and berries swelling. When you do give water, be generous and direct it at the soil rather than the foliage. Weeds must be kept down. Shallow hoeing will help but do not hoe at all close to the canes or you will damage the shallow roots. Hand-pick the weeds near the canes instead.

Feeding In addition to the spring mulch of manure or compost (put down about mid-April) you can give a March dressing of 27g per sq m ($\frac{3}{4}$oz per sq yd) of sulphate of potash, though this will not be necessary unless cane production is poor. Spread it down the row and over a strip about 90cm (3ft) wide on each side and lightly rake into the surface.

Where no manure or garden compost is available for mulching, use peat, after giving an additional March dressing of sulphate of ammonia at 70g per sq m (2oz per sq yd). Also give the sulphate of ammonia to boost growth where this has previously been disappointing.

Harvesting Try to pick when the berries are dry, using two hands for the

Growing and pruning raspberries. A support system for raspberries (left) should have wires placed at 60cm (2ft), 1.07m (3½ft) and 1.5m (5ft), or higher for vigorous varieties. In the autumn tie in the six strongest new canes to the supporting wires at each level (below left), after cutting old canes right back. In spring, prune back the unripened tips (below right) to 15cm (6in) above the top wire.

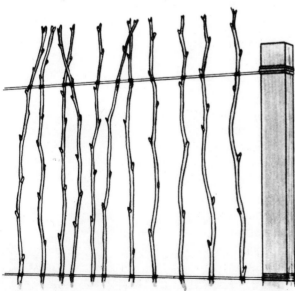

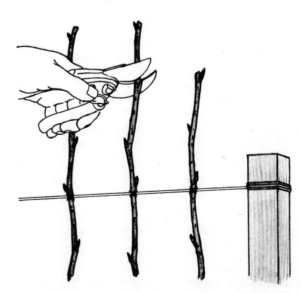

job, holding the shoot with one hand and gently pulling the fruit off with the other, leaving the core or 'hull' of the berry still on the plant.

Troubles DISEASES Virus diseases can be airborne by aphids or soil-borne by eelworms. These serious diseases cause distortion or yellow mottling of the leaves and ultimately reduce cropping severely. There is no cure and affected canes should be dug up and burned. Do not replant on the same site.

Do not confuse virus symptoms with the yellowing between leaf veins brought on by a deficiency of iron, common on alkaline soils. The remedy here is to try to make the soil more acid by using acid fertilizers such as sulphate or ammonia and avoiding all lime. In extreme cases you can water with iron sequestrene according to the maker's directions but this is expensive. Instead, try applying flowers of sulphur in midwinter at a rate of 135g per sq m (4oz per sq yd).

Raspberries also suffer from cane spot and spur blight which attacks loganberries. Symptoms and treatment are similar, so see under LOGANBERRIES (page 321).

PESTS Raspberry beetle grubs may damage ripening fruit. See under BLACKBERRIES (page 308) for treatment.

Aphids are a menace not only for their debilitating effect but because they spread serious virus disease. They will be kept down if you spray the dormant canes with a 5 per cent tar-oil wash in midwinter and also with pyrethrum, derris or malathion just before the blossom opens.

Birds will attack all summer raspberries, which should be netted.

Propagation You can always increase your stock of raspberries by digging up suckers, with some roots, and replanting them in a bed of their own. Because of the great risk of virus disease in this crop the procedure is not recommended unless the parents are absolutely healthy.

RED AND WHITE CURRANTS *(Ribes sativum)*

Red currants are popular in tarts, pies and summer puddings but when fully ripe can also be eaten raw for dessert with sugar and cream. White currants are sweeter and of better flavour and, while not having quite the same eye-appeal, are far better for dessert. Red currant jelly is the traditional accompaniment to roast lamb but excellent jelly can be made from a half and half mixture of the two types.

White currants are simply an albino type of red currant and are grown in exactly the same way.

Both types are usually grown as bushes but are amenable to training.

Site While full sun will give the best results, partial shade is tolerated but naturally delays ripening. These currants may be grown against a north wall. Shelter from cold winds is necessary and in exposed gardens red and white currants must be protected from gales from any quarter.

Soil Good drainage is essential and the best results are obtained on the lighter soils. Red currants do not require as much nitrogen as black currants and they are less tolerant than gooseberries of extremes of acidity and alkalinity. They require plenty of potash.

In preparing a site all perennial weed roots must be eliminated and if your supply of manure or garden compost is limited give first preference to the blackcurrants. Nevertheless, thin, sandy soil must be given body to hold moisture through the growing season and if well-rotted manure or good garden compost cannot be spared, then dig in peat, leafmould or bark fibre. On very light soils, too, complete the preparation of the bed by scattering over the surface 27g per sq m (¾oz per sq yd) of sulphate of potash and rake it in. Never give potash to red and white currants in the form of kainit or muriate of potash (potassium chloride).

Planting The planting season extends from October until the end of February, but autumn planting is much to be preferred.

Allow 1.5m (5ft) each way between bushes as a minimum, 1.8m (6ft) on rich soil, and 38cm (15in) between single cordons. Allow proportionally more room for double or triple cordons and if the cordons are in rows, 1.5m (5ft) between rows. Set them at least 23cm (9in) away from the foot of a wall.

Plant at the same depth as the currants were in the nursery.

Staking Cordons must be staked, one vertical cane for each main stem, which is tied in with soft string. The canes may be supported by horizontal wires and at least one such is essential if the row is free-standing in the open. Against walls or fences the canes may, if desired, be sloped backwards and secured to the wall or fence.

It is not essential to stake bushes but in more exposed gardens it is advisable to provide a few stakes in earlier years to support the main branches. These are easily broken by the wind and it can take years before they are satisfactorily replaced and their proper shape restored.

Pruning Bushes The habit of growth is quite unlike that of the blackcurrant and more like that of the gooseberry. They fruit on spurs on the old wood and at the base of the new wood.

The first pruning should be given during the winter of planting, but in gardens where birds cause much damage by bud-pecking in winter, defer pruning until just before growth is about to begin.

A one-year-old bush will consist of three or four branches, arising from a 'leg', or main stem, about 25cm (10in) high. Cut each branch hard back to the third or fourth bud, which should point outwards.

For the next two or three years, each winter cut back the new extension growth of each main branch by a half, always to outward-pointing buds so as to give the bush a goblet shape.

In the first of these years (i.e. the second year) each main branch can be allowed again to branch making a total of from six to eight branches. The year after they can double again. After that keep each branch to a single extension growth and treat all others as laterals.

For the bush's first three or four years the leaders should be cut back by half each winter; after that let the state of growth govern your pruning, merely tipping leaders if growth is vigorous, but cutting back up to a half if it is weak.

Now deal with the laterals: cut each back to the fifth leaf in June and then in winter prune even harder back, to the second bud.

Pruning Cordons With cordons, shorten the upward extension growth of the main stem or stems by a third each winter, but where growth has been good, never leave more than 25cm (10in) of new wood. Prune all sideshoots to the fifth leaf in June just before the currants start to colour and then, in the dormant period, cut back to the second bud.

Feeding In April spread a mulch of well-rotted farmyard manure or garden compost around and between the bushes. No further feeding is necessary on good soil but on very light or poor soil give a February supplement of bonemeal at 135g per sq m (4oz per sq yd) or sulphate of potash at 27g per sq m (¾oz per sq yd) or wood ash at 250gm per sq m (8oz per sq yd).

Where farmyard manure or garden compost is scarce, mulch with peat or bark fibre after giving a March dressing of sulphate of ammonia

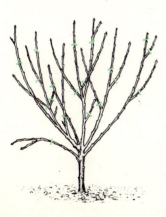

Below: when pruning a mature red or white currant bush, cut back the main branches (leaders) to strengthen them, and cut back each side-shoot to the second bud from the junction with the main branch.

at 35g to the sq m (1oz per sq yd) plus a similar amount of superphosphate. Rake the fertilizers into the surface.

Harvesting The currants ripen between June and early August. Red currants are rather deceptive; although they may look quite red, they often need several more days to develop their full flavour and sweetness. As with blackcurrants, pick off the little bunches complete.

Troubles DISEASES Die-back caused by botrytis fungus (grey mould) sometimes affects red and white currant shoots. It usually enters through pruning wounds, so prune cleanly and paint the larger wounds with protective bituminous tree paint. Cut off and burn infected branches.

Coral spot is a disease in which shoots wilt and shrivel during summer and develop coral-red spots. Prevention is as for die-back. PESTS Red and white currants are subject to all the pests that attack blackcurrants. The methods of control are the same. In the case of gall mites the attacked buds do not swell abnormally but shrivel and drop.

The caterpillars of the gooseberry sawfly may attack. See under GOOSEBERRY on page 313 for symptoms and control.

Propagation Raise new plants in the same way as for gooseberries except that you should rub off all the buds except the top four.

In the November of the next year the cuttings should be ready to transfer to their permanent quarters. Plant them 5cm (2in) deeper than they were in the cutting bed.

STRAWBERRIES (*Fragaria* hybrids and *F. vesca*)

Believed by many to be the most popular fruit of all, strawberries need no introduction. They are ideal for garden cultivation and, apart possibly from melons, will give the quickest results.

There are two main classes of large-fruited strawberries, the summer fruiting kinds, which bear their main crop during June and early July (some varieties sometimes producing a second crop in autumn), and the perpetual, or remontant, strawberries, which start fruiting in June or early July and then crop in a series of flushes until frost brings the season to an end. In addition there are the small-berried alpine strawberries (*Fragaria vesca*). These are dealt with on page 331.

It is most important to start with healthy stock, so buy your plants from a reputable nursery which has its stock certified as disease-free.

Site Although of woodland origin, strawberries do best in full sun, apart from alpine strawberries, which thrive in partial shade. As they occupy the ground for only three or four years, after which they should always be given a fresh site, it is most convenient to allot them a place in the kitchen garden and work them in with the vegetable crop rotation.

Soil Most soils will produce good strawberries but the crop does best on a fairly rich soil well supplied with moisture-holding organic matter.

The ground should be dug deeply in preparation, for the roots will penetrate far if encouraged. Both heavy and light soils will be improved by working in plenty of well-rotted farmyard manure or garden compost. As much as 8.4kg per sq m (15lb per sq yd), approximately equivalent to one garden wheelbarrow load per 1.6sq m or 2sq yd, is not too much. All manure should be well dug in so that none is left visible on the surface: this only encourages botrytis disease.

If neither manure nor compost is available, dig in moist peat or rotted leafmould at the same rate and rake in a mixture of sterilized bonemeal, hoof and horn meal and sulphate of potash, 70g per sq m (2oz per sq yd) of each. On light land, or wherever potash is known to

be deficient, add an extra 18g per sq m ($\frac{1}{2}$oz per sq yd) of sulphate
of potash.

A month or so later, the new strawberry bed will be ready.
Planting Early planting is best. If summer-fruiting kinds can be planted
in late July or August, they will give quite a reasonable crop in their
maiden year. Planting is possible in September and in spring but these
plants are best deblossomed during their first summer to give their root
systems a chance to develop first.

Perpetual-fruiting varieties are not available for planting so early. If
the soil is of good texture and not over-wet, autumn planting is quite
permissible but more often it is preferable to wait until the spring, as
planting is possible even into May. Whenever you decide to plant
perpetuals, the first batch of flowers should always be removed, but
provided this is done a first crop can be expected in late summer or
early autumn from perpetuals, even when they were planted in May.

Allow 45cm (1$\frac{1}{2}$ft) between plants in the row and 75cm (2$\frac{1}{2}$ft) between
rows, for both summer and perpetual varieties. Some less vigorous
varieties (Elista and Pantagruella are two) may be set closer, at 23cm
(9in) apart in the row. Alpine strawberries should be set 30cm (1ft)
apart each way.

Firm planting is vital but at the same time it is important not to plant
too deeply so that the crown, or rootstock, of the plant (where the stem
joins the roots) is covered, nor too shallowly so that the neck of the
plant is exposed. The crown should be just at soil level after planting.

Use a trowel to make the planting hole and if the plant has not been
grown in a pot, make a little hump at the centre of the hole and set the
plant on this with its roots freely spread out to their full length all
round. Where the plants have just come out of pots there is no point in
disturbing the roots more than is necessary and if they are in peat pots
they should be planted in these, not removed, but they are best first
soaked in water for ten minutes.

Cultivation When planting on a hot July or August day it is helpful to
give the plants temporary shade for a few days. Water in dry weather
and particularly during the berry-swelling period, but try not to wet the
leaves more than can be helped. Hand-weed close to the plants.

If summer-fruiting varieties are deblossomed their first year, they will
give a heavier crop in the second than the first-year and second-year
crops combined of non-deblossomed plants. Some gardeners remove the
first batch of flowers on perpetual varieties every year so as to avoid
overlap with summer-fruiters and secure a heavier yield later.

Strawberry plants propagate themselves vegetatively by throwing out
runners which produce roots at joints occurring at intervals. Unless
these runners are required for producing new stock (see below), they are
an unnecessary drain on the plant's resources and are best cut off as
soon as you notice them.

When the berries have started to swell and are heavy enough to begin
to weigh the trusses down towards the soil, protective measures should
be taken to keep them clean and free from soil splashing.

The traditional method is to spread straw (barley straw is best, next
wheat) down the rows but straw is not so easy to obtain today. If you
can get straw, do not put it down too early or it may delay ripening.

Alternatively, use the strawberry mats sold by garden shops or lay
down strips of black polythene, making slits from the edge to the
middle opposite the plants. Tuck the polythene under the fruit trusses

and draw a little soil over the outer edges to prevent wind penetrating beneath. Make sure that there are no depressions near the plants which will collect puddles of rainwater. Before putting down any of these soil covers it is advisable to set slug traps if slugs are a problem.

Another way of keeping the fruit clean is to lift the trusses on small pieces of galvanized wire, bent in a U-shape to support the stem.

Birds are very fond of strawberries and protection by netting is imperative. If the bed is not in a fruit cage, you can improvise a low cage by stretching wire taut between 1.2m (4ft) high posts and throwing a lightweight plastic net over all. Make sure you can lift the netting easily for picking, but peg down the edges if mice or squirrels are a nuisance in your district, and net the crop early.

Harvesting Pick with the stalk intact and handle very carefully by the stalk to avoid bruising the fruit. Harvest regularly and do not leave over-ripe fruits on the plant or they will rot and succumb to diseases.

As soon as the picking of summer-fruiting strawberries has been completed, cut off all the old foliage with shears, leaving only the new leaves already showing at the centres of plants. In the case of perpetual varieties remove the old leaves in early winter when the last berry has ripened.

Feeding Special feeding is not normally necessary with outdoor strawberries except for an annual dose of sulphate of potash at a rate of 18g per sq m (½oz per sq yd), twice as much on light soil. Spread this immediately after cutting down old leaves and removing all weeds. An organic alternative is 135g per sq m (4oz per sq yd) of bonemeal.

Propagation It is very easy to raise new strawberry plants by rooting runners but this should only be done if the parents are productive and absolutely free of disease and aphids. Even then, the risk of virus disease is so great you should not chance your luck in this way for more than two or three years before buying in new stock.

Choose as parents plants which are blossoming well but then remove the flowers or newly set berries. As the runners form, peg the joints down into the surface of compost contained in small pots sunk at convenient points almost rim-deep in the ground. The pots should be filled with either John Innes No. 1 potting compost or a soilless potting compost. Use for pegs lengths of galvanized wire bent to a U-shape.

Pinch out the end of the runners beyond the rooting tuft of leaves, but do not sever them from the parent plant until they are well rooted in about four to six weeks' time. Then cut the runners and a week later set out the new plants in their bed.

Greenhouse Cultivation Extra early crops can be obtained by growing strawberries in pots in a heated greenhouse (known as 'forcing' them). For this, very early rooted runners are required and this may necessitate rooting your own. As soon as you can buy plants in July or your home-layered runners have rooted well in small pots, plant them in 15cm (6in) pots using John Innes potting compost No. 3.

Stand these pots in a sheltered place outdoors, water as necessary and using clean, dry straw or some other litter protect them from frost which may shatter the pots. In January move the pots into an unheated greenhouse and keep them on a shelf close to the roof glass in full light.

Heat is not essential but will secure an earlier crop. If when after a fortnight or so some growth is apparent, a little warmth is given and gradually increased, fruit may ripen early in May. Aim at a temperature of 7°C (45°F) to 10°C (50°F) at first. Increase this slowly to 15°C (60°F)

Above: propagating strawberries is done by pegging the runners into small pots of compost set into the ground.

when blossom opens. After the fruit have set the temperature may be raised to 18°C (65°F); it will be higher, of course, on sunny days.

Hand-pollinate all the flowers, transferring pollen on a paintbrush.

Cloches and Tunnels Crops can also be advanced by a fortnight or more by covering outdoor rows of first-year plants with cloches or plastic tunnels. Put these over the plants in late February in the south, and in mid-March in the north.

During the daytime, when the protected strawberries are in flower, the cloches must be either opened, if their design permits this, or spaced apart a little, to admit pollinating insects. The tunnels should also be opened.

Ventilate similarly, and freely, on hot sunny days. Excessive temperatures will harm the plants. Once berries begin to ripen, opened cloches or tunnels must be covered with lengths of netting to keep out birds and, possibly, squirrels.

Perpetual varieties may be similarly protected in early September to extend their season into November.

Troubles DISEASES Strawberries are very prone to a number of virus diseases which stunt or distort growth and reduce cropping, sometimes even to zero. The symptoms are dwarfing or crinkling of foliage, yellow edges to leaves, or yellow or purple blotches. There is no cure and affected plants should therefore be burned. These troubles are spread by eelworms, hence the need always for a fresh site, and by aphids, which must be rigorously controlled.

Another common trouble in wet seasons is botrytis or grey mould disease. A furry greyish mould grows over affected berries, spreading rapidly. Remove and burn mouldy berries and dust the plants with flowers of sulphur or, if the fruit is to be frozen, with benomyl or thiophanate-methyl according to the manufacturer's instructions, repeating twice at fortnightly intervals.

Powdery mildew sometimes attacks and should not be confused with a virus disease for it causes leaves to turn purple and curl upwards. The undersides of the leaves look greyish. Powdery mildew may appear on the fruits. Control with sulphur (or with benomyl or thiophanate-methyl) when first flowers open and repeat at fortnightly intervals.

PESTS Aphids or greenfly weaken growth and spread virus diseases. In serious attacks leaves may curl and turn yellow. Spray in April before blossom opens with derris or pyrethrum. Repeat later if many live aphids are seen.

Protection is also essential against slugs, birds and, in some areas, squirrels.

Alpine Strawberries These are raised from seed sown from January to March under glass. A temperature of between 10 and 16°C (50 to 60°F) is preferable. As the seedlings develop their first rough leaves, prick them off separately into another seed-tray. Where no heat is available sow in April or outdoors in May. Early-raised seedlings may be planted in their fruiting quarters at the end of May or early June, 30cm (1ft) apart each way. They like rich soil and partial shade. Otherwise, cultivation is the same as for summer-fruiting strawberries, except that the fruit do not need to be 'strawed' as they should not touch the soil and protection against birds is unlikely to be needed, as they do not often eat alpines. These strawberries, however, do have a low resistance to virus diseases, and so should never be planted near to summer or perpetual fruiting strawberry beds.

TREE FRUIT (TOP FRUIT)

APPLES *(Malus pumila)*

Of all fruits, the one most often found in British gardens is the apple. It gives a good return for the initial cost and effort expended on it, in many cases beginning to crop only two or three years after planting.

It is best to avoid standard and half-standard trees, also bush-type trees on vigorous rootstocks, because all of these grow too big for the majority of gardens and are too high for easy picking and pruning, and make protection from birds and spraying with normal garden equipment impossible. The best forms for the garden are the dwarf bush, which gives the highest yield per tree, followed by the dwarf pyramid. Where space is really at a premium, the oblique cordon comes into its own and in some gardens the espalier or horizontally trained tree is convenient.

Most apples require to be pollinated by another variety and this must be borne in mind when deciding what to choose and is an added reason for growing small types of trees for which there will be space to plant more kinds and so improve cross-pollination prospects.

Site Apples will grow in most districts but they do least well close to the coast, at over 180m (600ft), or where the annual rainfall exceeds 1m (40in).

Apples tolerate some shade, but full sunshine improves fruit quality.

Soil Apples will grow well in a wide range of soils, always provided the land is reasonably well drained and not too alkaline. A very few varieties succeed in rather chalky soils, but most need at least a neutral soil and do best in slightly acid conditions. If there is chalk present it should be at least 45cm (1½ft) below the surface.

Generally speaking, the cookers need more nitrogen than the dessert varieties and so can do with a slightly richer soil. As a rule, garden soil which has been previously cultivated will be quite good enough for apples without further preparation than deep digging (see page 56).

The danger is most likely to be that ex-vegetable-plot soil is too rich, thus causing overlush growth and delaying the start of fruiting and predisposing the trees to canker disease (as does also too much moisture and poor drainage). Very rich soil can be 'tamed' by postponing apple planting for a year and growing green vegetable crops in the interval without further manuring.

Planting The planting season begins in October and continues until growth begins in March or April, but autumn planting is preferable.

When ordering your trees patronize a nursery, if you can, which raises its trees from East Malling Research Station virus-tested mother trees. Besides deciding on the form of tree most appropriate to your circumstances and the varieties of your choice, you must also check that you choose trees grafted on appropriate rootstocks.

The most dwarfing rootstock is M 9 (Malling 9) and this is popular for garden planting because it makes the smallest trees, which start to fruit soonest. As a corollary of being dwarfing, the root growth of this stock is poor and trees on it will need to be staked all their lives. If the soil is also poor, a more vigorous rootstock should be chosen. A still more dwarfing rootstock, M 27, will be available in the near future.

M 26 is slightly more vigorous than M 9 and is appropriate for poor soils, weak-growing varieties and where a slightly larger tree is desired. MM 106 is another slightly more vigorous rootstock which may be used in preference to M 9 on poor soils (MM stands for 'Malling Merton', the latter being another fruit research station). M 7 is semi-dwarfing.

Below: types of trained apple trees include (top to bottom) half-standard, pyramid, and bush.

Other rootstocks are M 25, MM 104 and MM 111, which are more vigorous and used for standards and half-standards and large bush-type trees. Trees on these rootstocks take longer to come into bearing and are too big for most gardens but on a poor soil M 25 and MM 111 will produce only medium-sized trees.

The nursery may offer you maiden (one-year-old) trees. These are cheaper and give you the full satisfaction of being able to form the shape of your tree yourself from the outset. Maiden trees can be moved with less root damage than older specimens but take longer to start bearing. More often two or three-year-old trees are sold.

Bush apple trees on vigorous rootstocks need to be 5.5m (18ft) apart each way, those on semi-dwarfing rootstocks, or vigorous rootstocks on very poor soil, should be 3.6m (12ft) apart. Plant dwarf bush trees 3m (10ft) apart on good soil, but only 2.4m (8ft) on poor soil.

Dwarf pyramids on good soil should be 1.2m (4ft) apart with 2.1m (7ft) between rows, and 1m (3½ft) between trees in the row on poor soil.

Oblique cordons should be spaced 90cm (3ft) apart in good soil, and 75cm (2½ft) apart in poor soil; the rows should be 1.8m (6ft) apart.

Espaliers need a spread of at least 3m (10ft), but preferably 4.5m (15ft).

When planting, dig a hole wide enough for all the roots to be spread to their full extent and deep enough for the tree to be at exactly the same depth as it was in the nursery when the planting is complete and the tree firmed in.

Mound the soil up slightly at the centre of the planting hole and sit the tree on this. An assistant to hold the tree is invaluable. Next, drive in the stake and return the soil gradually around and over the roots, firming as you proceed. A few handfuls of peat scattered immediately under and among the roots will aid rapid re-rooting. Never let any manure come into direct contact with the roots but if the soil is definitely poor, after covering the roots, scatter a double handful of sterilized bonemeal over the soil still to be returned.

When planting oblique cordons, try to arrange for the row to run north and south, with the trees pointing to the north, for maximum sunshine. See that the tree is so turned that at the union between rootstock and top part (scion), the latter is uppermost (see diagram), or it may break, and plant at an angle of 45°.

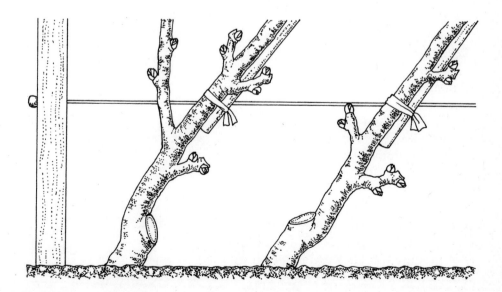

Right: the right and wrong methods of planting oblique apple cordons. The cordon with the scion below the rootstock (far right) will always be in danger of cracking open at the point of their union, thus being exposed to fungus disease. The cordon on the left is planted correctly.

After planting, fasten the tree to its stake with an adjustable tree-tie, but be prepared to adjust this after a month or two when the soil has settled. Also refirm the soil if it is loosened by frost. Before spring comes, cover the ground around the tree to a distance of about a metre (or yard) with a mulch about 5cm (2in) deep of well-rotted manure, garden compost or moist peat to conserve soil moisture. Keep this mulch away from actual contact with the stem of the tree or it may induce rooting from above the union and so nullify the influence of the rootstock.

See that newly planted trees never want for water.

Pruning BUSH TREES The first pruning of an apple tree will depend on its age when planted.

Cut a maiden (one-year) tree down soon after planting to a bud between 50cm (20in) and 60cm (24in) above soil level, choosing one which has three or four others evenly spaced beneath it. Badly placed buds should be rubbed out so that the buds left to grow will produce main branches at regular intervals round the trunk.

If the maiden has any sideshoots (known in this context as 'feathers') below the bud to which you cut, cut these back to four buds and pinch back any growth from them in summer to the sixth leaf.

In the second winter select four or five of the sturdiest shoots to form main branches and cut these back by half their length if growth has been vigorous, or by two-thirds if rather weak. Prune to buds pointing outwards to keep the centre of the tree open and give it a goblet shape. Again cut back all growths you do not require as branches to the fourth bud and to the sixth leaf in the summer following.

By the third winter the tree will have anything from six to a dozen good branches. This time, cut the new extension growth on each branch back a little less drastically, by a third if strong, or a half if weak. Shoots not required as branches should be left unpruned if less than 15cm (6in); otherwise cut to the fourth bud.

In the fourth winter the laterals pruned back to the fourth bud should have produced fruit buds and new shoots. Cut this new growth back to its first bud. Cut back branch leaders by a third if growth is strong, or by a half if weak. Remember that winter pruning stimulates growth.

From now on you continue in this way, gradually pruning less and less as the tree reaches maturity but always taking out damaged branches or misplaced ones which cross others.

Prune new growth on the laterals to one bud, but with time these fruiting spurs will become crowded and you may be well advised to shorten some, or even cut out a few completely.

The method of pruning laterals described above is known as 'spur-pruning'. Some varieties of apple, however, do not respond well to this because they produce a high proportion of their fruits from buds at the end of shoots and are hence known as 'tip-bearers'. Spur-pruning would remove all these shoot ends. A method known as 'renewal pruning' should be adopted with these varieties.

In renewal pruning about a third of all laterals should be left unpruned so that they can develop fruit buds at their tips. The others are cut back to one bud to make new growth. The aim is to secure a balance between fruit and wood production so that there is a steady renewal each year of fruit-bearing laterals.

Well-known apple varieties which fruit at their tips are Beauty of Bath, Bramley's Seedling, Edward VII, Ellison's Orange, Laxton's

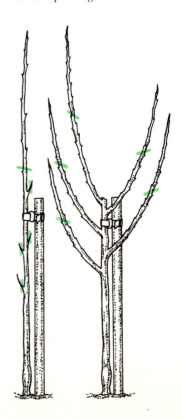

Below: pruning a bush tree. In the first winter after planting, cut the main stem back to between 50cm (20in) and 60cm (24in) and rub out badly placed buds as shown by the lines marked (left). In the second winter retain four or five of the strongest shoots to form leaders (right), and cut these back by a half to two-thirds, making the cuts to outward-pointing buds.

Fortune, Laxton's Superb, Tydeman's Early Worcester, Winston and Worcester Pearmain.

PYRAMID TREES The pyramid tree owes its name to its conical shape resulting from the branches being in layers, the first formed being longest and the top ones the shortest, all springing from a vertical central stem.

If you start with a maiden, cut it down to a bud about 50cm (20in) above the ground. This bud will produce a vertical shoot. Rub out the second bud to avoid a competitor developing and select three or four buds evenly spaced around the stem. These will form the first layer or tier of branches and badly placed buds should be rubbed out.

To stimulate the lowest of your selected branch-making buds to grow out, cut out just above each a little half-moon notch of bark.

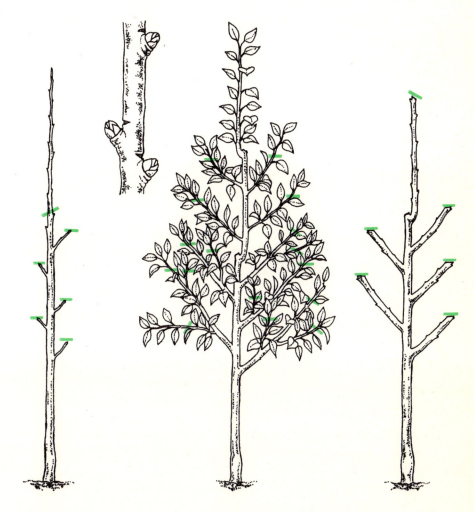

Right: pruning a pyramid. When the maiden is planted (left), cut the stem back to 50cm (20in) and shorten any side growths, making notches immediately above each of the lowest shoots to stimulate growth, as shown (centre left). In the second year cut back the new growth of the vertical leader to a bud 20 to 25cm (8 to 10in) above the previous cut on the other side of the stem (right). Shorten the laterals. In succeeding summers shorten the side growths and laterals as shown (centre).

Each winter, repeat this procedure, cutting back the new growth of the vertical leader to a bud 20 to 25cm (8 to 10in) above the previous cut and on the opposite side of the stem. Again choose well placed buds below for the next tier of branches and notch just above the two lowest.

Continue in this way until the tree reaches a convenient maximum height, about 2m (7ft). That year, wait until May and cut the new leader growth back by half; then, subsequently, each May cut the new upward growth of the central leader to one bud only. Treat branch leaders in a similar way when they overlap those of their neighbours.

In the second winter cut back the first-formed branches to 15 to 20cm (6 to 8in), cutting to downward or outward-pointing buds. The next summer, and in subsequent summers, wait until the new growth has matured and become stiff and woody at the base, the leaves are a deep green colour and these new shoots have reached at least 23cm (9in) long, usually in the second half of July. Then cut back each branch leader to the fifth leaf or sixth, counting from the basal cluster, whichever will result in upward-pointing extension growth. At the same time, prune mature new laterals to three leaves and the mature new season's growth on laterals pruned in previous years to one leaf, in each case counting the leaves after the basal cluster. If, in winter, when you come to prune the central leader, you find there has been secondary growth, from the pruned laterals and branch leaders, cut this back to one bud. This is more common in wet seasons.

CORDONS Cordons of spur-bearing varieties need no pruning immediately after planting, but with a tip-bearing variety cut back the central stem, if a maiden, or the previous season's new extension growth in the case of an older tree, by one quarter of its length. Cut any sideshoots on a maiden cordon which are longer than 10cm (4in) back to the third bud.

Most of the cordon pruning is done in summer, when the new growth

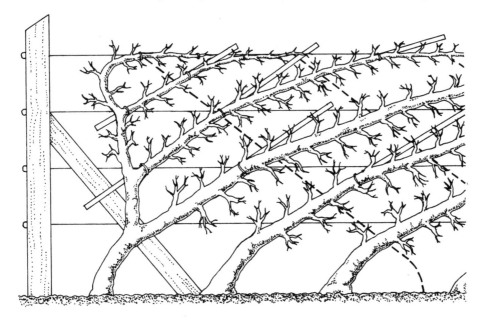

Left: training oblique cordons involves refastening their supports as they grow, and lowering each main stem gradually so that it is horizontal to the ground by the time it reaches the top wire. A second row may be grown in the opposite direction on the other side of the wires, as indicated by the dotted lines.

is mature as described above for pyramids, the sideshoots on a cordon being treated just like those along the branches of pyramids. Shoots still immature at the July or early August pruning should be shortened in mid-September.

The central leader of the spur-bearing cordon needs no winter pruning unless growth has been weak. It can then be stimulated by cutting back what new leader growth there is by a third. Merely prune the tips of the leaders of tip-bearing varieties so that they continue growing rather than produce blossom buds.

When the cordons pass their top wire, you can untie their support canes and refasten at a slightly lower angle. This gives space for a little more extension growth which, by this time, is in any case slowing down. Sometimes it is possible to lower the canes on two or three occasions. When there is room for no more extension, cut back in May.

As the cordons are planted at an angle of 45°, there will be a triangle of blank space above the first tree in the row. Fill this by allowing two laterals to grow up vertically, treating each as an individual cordon.

ESPALIERS Espaliers need a horizontal support wire for each tier of branches. These branches are pruned as if each were a cordon.

If you want to train an espalier from scratch, plant a maiden and cut it down to a bud between 30 and 45cm (1–1½ft) from the ground and having two buds close beneath it on opposite sides of the stem, and pointing along the row. Rub out inappropriately placed buds near the top. Cut a notch above the lowest bud of the three selected buds, as described under PYRAMIDS above.

Allow the three shoots from these three buds to grow, rubbing out any others which start. With soft string, tie the top shoot to a vertical cane and the other two to canes fastened at 45° to the vertical. Equalize growth between the two lower shoots by slightly lowering the cane supporting the stronger one to check it.

At the end of the summer growing season, lower the two arms to the horizontal and thereafter treat as cordons.

If you want to produce another tier, treat the central vertical shoot in the same way as the original maiden but allow a spacing of about 30cm (1ft).

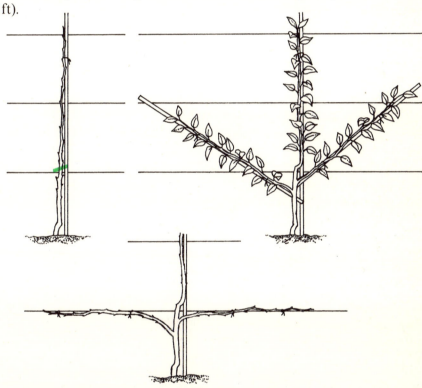

Right: pruning an espalier-trained tree. Cut the stem of a maiden (left) down to a bud between 30 and 45cm (1–1½ft) from the ground, and above the first wire. Choose a bud which has two buds close beneath it on opposite sides of the stem, pointing along the wire. Train the resulting shoots as shown (right) and in the winter lower the two arms to the horizontal wire. Repeat the pruning procedure of the first year in the following winters, until the required number of tiers has been produced.

Cultivation Apples require little attention. Watering may well be necessary in early years before the roots have penetrated deeply. Regular annual mulching will help to conserve moisture. Keep the soil around the tree clean and cultivated for the first few years but if the tree grows too vigorously, it can be checked by allowing grass to grow around it. Nevertheless always keep the soil clear close to the trunk: long grass there may stimulate scion-rooting, harbour mice or encourage you to mow too close and thereby injure the bark.

Overcropping should be avoided. This will result in undersized apples and may cause 'biennial bearing' (cropping properly only once every two years instead of annually). Some varieties are much more prone to this than others. To prevent biennial bearing, the best way to reduce the crop is to rub out some of the blossom buds before they open. Once the habit has begun, do this in the 'on' years when a good crop is expected.

Where an extra-heavy crop has set, start thinning before the natural 'June drop' of fruitlets occurs. Use thin pointed scissors and start by cutting out the 'king' apple, the central one of each cluster and often the largest. Then remove any misshapen or pest-damaged specimens. Continue until they are all spaced some 10 to 15cm (4 to 6in) apart.

It may sometimes be advisable to arrange props to support very heavily-laden branches.

Feeding Annually, in late February, scatter over the soil surface for a little farther than the branches extend 35g per sq m (1oz per sq yd) of sulphate of ammonia and 18g per sq m ($\frac{1}{2}$oz per sq yd) of sulphate of potash and gently rake it in. With cordons and espaliers, scatter the fertilizers over a strip at least 1.8m (6ft) wide on either side of the row. Allow cooking varieties a little more than these quantities of sulphate of ammonia, and trees growing among grass half as much again.

Potash is important for apples, and on light soils likely to be deficient in this plant food, increase the dose of sulphate of potash by a half and if scorch symptoms have appeared at leaf edges (indicating definite deficiency) give up to 70g per sq m (2oz per sq yd).

Every other year also give superphosphate at the rate of 35g per sq m (1oz per sq yd).

Harvesting Do not pick apples until they will part company from the tree quite easily when you lift one in the palm of the hand and give it the gentlest possible twist. The stalk should remain on the apple.

Although an apple may be ready to pick, it is not necessarily yet at its best for eating. The early varieties may be ready at the end of July or during August and, in general, are best eaten immediately. Some varieties will keep reasonably well for two or three weeks.

The mid-season varieties may be ready to pick in August or September and some will keep up to a couple of months or so and may be kept in normal larder conditions.

The keeping varieties are usually not ready to pick until late September or October; some are best left even into November. Properly stored, these may keep right through the winter, possibly until March or April, or even later. This long season is one of the reasons for the apple's popularity.

Spread out the apples under cover to sweat for a few days before storing them.

Storage The ideal conditions for successful keeping are darkness, slight dampness and a low temperature, which should be kept at a steady 1.7°C to 5.6°C (35°F–42°F) – conditions which are difficult for the amateur to provide. If you have a well-ventilated cellar or an old concrete air-raid shelter, you are indeed lucky. Attics and spare bedrooms are too dry and garages and sheds too smelly, for apples will readily pick up taints from petrol, paraffin or onions. Absolute freedom from frost is not vital, but do not handle the fruit when the temperature is below freezing point.

Shelves made from wooden battens spaced about 2.5cm (1in) apart are excellent for apple storage. Set out the apples carefully so that they do not quite touch. Better still, wrap each apple in an oiled apple wrap (bought from a garden shop) or a square of newspaper. Fold opposite corners over the apple, repeat with the other corners and place the apple with the folds beneath. Make no attempt to screw the ends of the paper together: let the weight of the apple keep the folds in place. If a wrapped apple does become mouldy it will not infect its neighbours.

Another way to store apples, and useful where a large crop is concerned, is to store them in polythene bags. Do not put more than 1.8kg (4lb) in each bag, and do not mix varieties. Seal with a metal twist and snip a small corner off each end of the bottom to provide a little but necessary, ventilation. Keep the filled bags in a dark, cool place.

Troubles DISEASES Scab disease used to be a scourge of apples, quite spoiling the fruit with black scabs and fissures. It is worse in the damper areas of high rainfall. It should be no great problem today, however, if you spray at the bud burst stage, when you can first see green at the centre of the swelling blossom buds, with Burgundy mixture or with a systemic fungicide, such as thiophanate-methyl or benomyl. Repeat at the green bud stage, again at the pink bud stage, when the blossom petals have fallen and finally when the fruitlets reach the size of peas.

Powdery mildew is a fungus disease which overwinters on the buds and in spring produces a white powdery deposit over leaves and shoots. Spraying with thiophanate-methyl at the pink bud stage for scab will also control this trouble.

Canker is a fungus disease entering through pruning cuts and is worse where the drainage is defective. It causes the bark to flake and die, and sunken patches appear. If shoots are girdled by canker, they will die, as will the whole tree if the trunk is seriously affected. Cut out diseased tissue and pare it clean; then cover with canker paint. Spraying with Bordeaux mixture in autumn just before the leaves fall, again when half have dropped and once more in early spring when the buds start swelling will also help to control this disease.

PESTS Aphids are a serious menace to apples, causing leaves, particularly those near shoot tips, to curl and distorting growth. Spray at the pink bud stage and again when blossom petals have fallen with derris (or malathion). If you want to combine the insecticide spray with a fungicide spray, be guided by the maker's directions. Winter washing with tar-oil in the dormant season will destroy aphid eggs, but only do this once every three or four years if aphids are a problem, as this washing also kills the predators of red spider mites which may then increase.

Red spider mites make leaves turn yellow or brown in summer. Spray in mid-June with derris, pyrethrum mixture (or malathion).

Woolly aphis (or American blight) is not to be confused with powdery mildew. This is a pest which covers itself with a protective coat looking like tufts of cotton wool: you can find the insect beneath. Remove by hand; if the attack is severe, paint the patches with a spray-strength derris (or malathion), or brush with methylated spirits. If there are patches you cannot reach, give a drenching spray of insecticide, but never before sunset when the blossom is open or you will kill many pollinating insects such as bees.

Two kinds of insect larvae feed inside apples and spoil them. The first to attack is the apple sawfly maggot. The hole where the white grub entered the fruit is visible and often a ribbon-like scar is produced. The fruit falls prematurely. Spray with derris (or malathion or fenitrothion) immediately after petal fall.

The other larva, which is the more serious pest, is the caterpillar of the codling moth. This brown-headed creature tunnels into the fruit, leaving a hole, and feeds near the core: it may still be at home when you come to eat the apple. Control is difficult as it needs precise timing. Reduce attacks by spraying with derris (or fenitrothion or malathion) four weeks after petal fall, repeating in three weeks. Burn fallen fruit.

APPLE VARIETIES

Pollinators The best pollinator is another variety in the same group, failing that the group on either side. Thus, a variety in group F is best pollinated by another in F but the flowering period of a variety in group E or group G will probably overlap sufficiently.

Some varieties produce no fertile pollen and so need another variety to pollinate them but will not reciprocate. Thus a third variety is required to pollinate the pollinator. These varieties without good pollen are indicated by an asterisk. The months given are the fruiting season.

Dessert Apples

SEASON AND NAME	POLLINATION GROUP	COMMENTS
Aug George Cave	D	Regular cropper. Slightly aromatic flavour. Bears on spurs and tips.
Aug–Sept Discovery	E	Very slow to start bearing. Ripens to bright red in sun. Bears on spurs and tips.
Aug–Sept Epicure	E	Heavy, regular cropper. Excellent flavour if eaten immediately.
Aug–Sept Tydeman's Early Worcester	E	Worcester Pearmain type but earlier and better quality fruit. Bears on spurs and tips.
Sept–Oct Worcester Pearmain	E	Reliable old favourite. Does well in north. Tip-bearing.
Sept–Oct James Grieve	D	Crops well. Soft flesh, good flavour, best eaten straight from tree.
Sept–Oct Fortune	D	Excellent flavour. May tend to crop biennially.
Sept–Oct St Edmund's Pippin	C	Golden russet, richly flavoured. Heavy cropper.
Sept–Oct Merton Worcester	E	Worcester Pearmain type but slightly later and juicier, better flavour.
Sept–Oct Ellison's Orange	F Self fertile	Good flavour, with strong aniseed scent when ripe. Tends to biennial bearing.
Sept–Oct Merton Beauty	G	Large fruit of Ellison's Orange type. Pleasant flavour.
Sept–Nov Merton Charm	C	Very good flavour. Starts cropping early but rather weak growing.
Sept–Nov Lord Lambourne	D	Good flavour. Regular and heavy cropper.
Oct–Dec American Mother	G	Distinctive aromatic flavour. Moderate cropper.
Oct–Dec Egremont Russet	C	Very good flavour. Juicy. Good cropper.
Oct–Dec Gravenstein	A*	Outstanding flavour, strongly aromatic. Not a heavy cropper and unsuitable for cordon or pyramid culture.
Oct–Dec Golden Delicious	F	The popular continental apple. A very heavy cropper but needs plenty of sun to finish well.
Oct–Jan Margil	E	Very good flavour. Medium cropper.
Oct–Jan Ribston Pippin	D*	Very rich, aromatic flavour. Crops well.
Nov–Dec Sunset	D	Often recommended as a substitute for Cox's Orange Pippin. Easier to grow and crops regularly.
Nov–Dec Suntan	F	Recent introduction. Cox type. Good flavour, improving into January. Golden Delicious and Malling Kent are suitable pollinators. Can

		fruit on one-year-old wood.	Dec–Feb Claygate Pearmain	F	Good flavour but moderate cropper.
Nov–Jan Kidd's Orange Red	F	Pleasant flavour but only moderately juicy. Regular cropper. Will not pollinate Cox and vice versa.	Dec–Feb Crispin	E*	Good flavour, not unlike Golden Delicious. Bears on spurs and tips. Not pollinated by Golden Delicious.
Nov–Jan Cox's Orange Pippin	E	A famous apple with a very fine flavour, but difficult to grow well. Very prone to disease.	Dec–April Tydeman's Late Orange	F	Cox-like flavour. Keeps well. Tends to biennial bearing.
Nov–Jan Christmas Pearmain	B	Cox type fruit but larger. Very vigorous.	Jan–Mar Duke of Devonshire	E	Good flavour but not very juicy. Good cropper.
Nov–Jan Holstein	E*	Not pollinated by Cox. Rich flavour but bears biennially.	Jan–April Sturmer Pippin	E	Good flavour. Juicy. Needs a warm, sunny garden. Defer picking as late as possible, even into December.
Nov–Jan Orleans Reinette	H	Very good flavour but only moderate cropper.			
Nov–Jan Spartan	F	Unusual dull purple colour. Pleasant flavour.			
Nov–Jan Chivers' Delight	E	Recent introduction. Cox type. Good flavour but not equal to Cox. Excellent cropper.			
Nov–Feb Laxton's Superb	F	Excellent flavour. Very sweet. Crops well but persistently biennial.			
Nov–Feb Merton Prolific	E	Tremendous cropper, usually needs drastic thinning to secure size. Only moderate flavour.			
Nov–Feb Malling Kent	E	Recent introduction. Cox type but better cropper. Keeps well. Discovery, Worcester Pearmain and Golden Delicious would be good pollinators. Can fruit on one-year-old wood.			
Dec–Feb Ashmead's Kernel	G	Superb flavour but erratic and very moderate cropper.			

Dual-purpose Apples

Sept–Oct George Neal	C	Crisp, slightly acid for dessert. Cooks well. Regular cropper.
Nov–Jan Blenheim Orange	E*	An old favourite for its flavour. Bears erratically in earlier years. Makes a spreading tree.
Nov–Mar Newton Wonder	G	A good cooker but rather too sour for dessert for some people, until after the New Year. Persistent biennial bearer but blossom thinning can correct this.
Dec–Feb Crawley Beauty	Self fertile	Sweet and also quite a good cooker. Flowers very late but pollinates itself.
Dec–April Idared	C	Not very juicy. Not unlike Wagener but better flavour and more regular cropper.
Jan–April Wagener	C	Superseded by Idared Inclined to biennial bearing.

Cooking Apples

July–Aug Emneth Early (Early Victoria)	E	Good cooker; crops early but bears biennially.
Aug–Sept Grenadier	E	Cooks to a froth. Reliable, heavy cropper.
Sept–Nov Rev. W. Wilks	C	Cooks to pale yellow froth. Crops heavily but irregularly. Biennial bearing can be corrected by blossom thinning.
Sept–Jan Golden Noble	H	Cooks to golden froth. Reliable.
Oct–Nov Arthur Turner	D	Not a first-class cooker but produces large fruit and some can be used as early as July.
Oct–Dec Warner's King	C*	Cooks to froth. Reliable.
Nov–Feb Howgate Wonder	F	Size is its chief distinction. Regular, heavy cropper.
Nov–Feb Monarch	E	Good cooker but inclined to biennial bearing.
Nov–Mar Bramley's Seedling	F*	Best of all cookers but too vigorous for most gardens. Does not take kindly to training. A tip-bearer.
Nov–Mar Lane's Prince Albert	F	By contrast with Bramley's, a compact grower, suitable for smaller gardens. Very prolific.
Nov–Mar Wellington (Dumelow's Seedling)	G	Reputation as *the* apple for mincemeat. Tends to slight biennial bearing.
Dec–April Edward VII	J	Cooks to a rich red. Flowers late and so may escape frost. American Mother and Crawley Beauty will pollinate it.
Dec–June Annie Elizabeth	Self fertile	Good cooker, useful for its long season, though fruit tends to drop prematurely.

CHERRIES
Sweet Cherries *(Prunus avium)*
These are not often grown in gardens today because they make large trees, difficult to tend and protect from birds. Even as wall-trained fans they need a spread of 5.5 to 7.5m (18 to 24ft) and a height of at least 2.4m (8ft). It used also to be necessary to grow at least two varieties to secure cross-pollination, but a self-fertile variety, Stella, is available.

Site, Soil and Feeding Sweet cherries will flourish on any warm, sheltered site, and on any good, deep soil provided it is well-drained and does not lie in a frost-prone area. They do best in a dry, sunny climate. They should be manured while growing, to maintain a fairly high nitrogen level and provide plenty of potash.

Training fans Fans may be built up in the same way as peaches (see page 353) and must never be pruned in autumn or winter because of the risk of bacterial canker and silver leaf disease infection. Rub out any shoots growing directly towards or away from the wall as soon as they appear. Other shoots not needed to fill vacant wall space should be stopped when five or six leaves have been made. When main branch leaders reach the top of the wall or the outward limit of space, shorten each one to a weak-growing lateral.

In early autumn cut back the previously pinched shoots to three or four buds. Remove any dead wood and tie in growths as necessary.

Harvesting Several pickings will be necessary, as the fruit do not ripen together. Remove the fruit carefully, leaving the stalks still attached to it. Cut the stalks with scissors to avoid damaging the stems.

Troubles PESTS Cherry fruit moth caterpillars (small and green with brown heads) may feed on the blossom and developing fruitlets in spring and early summer; spray with derris just before bud burst and again 10 days later. Cherry black fly, which are aphids, may stunt the young shoots or cause the leaves to twist and curl up. Control this pest by killing the eggs with a winter tar-oil wash.

DISEASES Bacterial canker is the most serious, entering through a pruning cut or other wound in autumn or winter and infecting the leaves the following spring, making them turn yellow and curl up, and finally killing them. It also results in cracks in the bark of trunks and branches out of which may ooze a reddish gum. Do not prune in autumn or winter, and apply anti-canker paint to all wounds, including pruning cuts. You can also spray with a weak solution of Bordeaux mixture in August, September and November.

Sour Cherries *(Prunus cerasus)*
Sour varieties are more suitable for garden cultivation than the sweet for they make smaller trees, whether bushes or fan-trained. They have similar soil requirements to the sweet cherries but are a little hardier and, flowering a few days later, that much less liable to frost damage. Fan-trained trees may be planted against walls facing any direction, including north. They have similar needs for manure to plums.

The variety most often grown is Morello which is self-fertile. The cherries are dark red, almost black, when ripe. They must be protected from birds, which otherwise may strip the trees of fruit.

Pruning Bush Trees Nurseries usually offer two or three-year-old bush trees but maidens can sometimes be purchased. Pruning for the first few years is as for a plum, the head being formed on a 60 to 90cm (2 to 3ft) leg.

Sour cherries fruit mostly on wood made the previous year, and to stimulate a continuing supply of new growth a proportion of branches should be cut back, annually, in spring after growth has started, to two, three or four-year-old wood. Paint all cut surfaces with protective bitumen paint.

Pruning Fans This can follow the same lines as for a peach fan (see page 355). Where long bare shoots develop, however, they should be cut hard back to 5.0 to 7.5cm (2 to 3in) to stimulate new growth.

Harvesting As for sweet cherries.

Troubles As for sweet cherries.

FIGS *(Ficus carica)*

Figs like plenty of warmth and therefore are most likely to succeed outdoors in the southern half of the country, fan-trained against a south wall. The varieties grown in this country produce fruit without pollination and so they are seedless. They try to produce two crops in a year but the second, formed in late autumn, is always killed by our winter weather and this immature fruit should be picked off in November so that they cannot attract mildew.

Soil Figs do best on a well-drained, comparatively poor, shallow soil. On rich ground they produce much lush growth, and few fruits, if any. In average garden soil it is better to restrict rootspread by constructing an underground box against the wall. This box, of concrete or brickwork, should be about 1.2m (4ft) wide, 90cm (3ft) from front to back and 90cm (3ft) deep. The bottom should consist of a 30cm (1ft) deep layer of brickbats or chalk lumps to ensure good drainage. Fill the box with ordinary garden soil.

Planting Plant in spring and mulch around the tree with about 4.0cm (1½in) of well-rotted manure or garden compost.

Pruning No pruning is necessary directly after planting but in subsequent springs form and train the fan in the same way as a peach (see page 355). Figs are prone to fungus disease, so pruning should not be done until March and all dead shoots should be cut back into healthy wood, until no dark stain can be seen in the central tissue.

As figs crop towards the end of their shoots, a few branches should be cut back each spring to short stubs from which shoots will emerge.

Harvesting Figs are ripe when they droop and crack slightly; a drop of moisture should also appear at the 'eye' in the base of the fruit opposite the stalk. Pick and handle them very gently, as they are easily bruised.

Greenhouse cultivation Two crops are possible per year in a heated greenhouse, though only one is likely in an unheated house. Keep the temperature above 10°C (50°F) in winter; figs can withstand a good deal of heat in summer. Water the plants more often and prune as for outdoor figs, except that you should not remove the embryo figs of the second crop in a heated house.

Varieties Only three varieties suitable for outdoor culture are generally offered: White Marseilles, the earliest, with greenish-white fruit; Brunswick, with the biggest fruit, brownish-purple; and Brown Turkey, the latest, less vigorous and therefore the easiest to manage.

These three varieties can also be grown in a greenhouse. Two varieties that should be raised under glass only are Bourjassotte Grise, a late variety with dark reddish-blue skin, and Negro Largo, mid-season, black skinned with red flesh.

Troubles Figs are generally pest and disease-free, frost damage being a much greater danger.

Above: to encourage fruit production, a fig tree's roots should be restricted. Plant in an underground brick or concrete box against a wall, with a drainage layer of brickbats or chalk lumps at the bottom.

Facing page: 'Ellison's Orange'

This page: above left, strawberries grown in a pot; above, a crop of apricots in full bearing; left, 'Doyenné du Comice', which has the finest flavour of all pears
Facing page: the mouth-watering produce of a fruit garden

*Above left: nectarine
'Pitmaston Orange'; above
right: 'Laxton's Cropper, a
heavy-bearing plum; below
right: 'Warwickshire Drooper',
a self-fertile plum*

Above left: 'Seyve Villard', a grape used for making wine; below left: 'Louise Bonne of Jersey', an early-flowering dessert pear

This page: above, 'James Grieve'; above left, 'Ellison's Orange' trained as an espalier; left, 'Egremont Russet' Facing page: above, an espaliered pear tree; below, 'Conference', the best-known of all pears

PESTS The most common fig pests are scale insects, which appear as small brown legless domes. The insect beneath each dome sucks the sap from the leaves and bark and secretes sticky honeydew, on which a black, sooty mould may subsequently grow. Control scale insects by hand-picking or, for a serious attack, by brushing with white spirit (or spraying with malathion, giving two further sprays at 10-day intervals).

DISEASES Coral Spot fungus is seen as pinkish spots on branches, but by the time these appear, the branches will have been killed and should be cut out and burned. This fungus enters the tree through pruning cuts and other wounds. Prevention is far better than cure, so, in addition to cutting out all dead wood, paint wounds with a wound-sealing paint.

MEDLARS *(Mespilus germanica)*

Its crooked habit of growth gives the medlar a picturesque appearance. It starts fruiting early and grows slowly, but its eventual size, up to 7.5m (25ft) makes it too large for smaller gardens. It will grow in most soils if they are well-drained.

Pruning Little pruning should be necessary. Train standard trees by cutting all laterals back to two or three leaves between October and March. Pinch out the leading shoot when the tree has reached its desired height. Remove weak and crossing branches in March.

Harvesting The fruit is ready for harvesting when hard and green late in October or early November, but not for eating until it has been stored in the dry until soft and brown, two or three weeks later. It is not to everyone's taste, but the cheese and jelly made from it is popular.

Varieties The variety Dutch has the largest fruits and a rather weeping habit. Nottingham is the first to start fruiting.

Troubles These should be few, though aphids or caterpillars may attack the leaves and apple mildew may be a problem in spring on the emerging buds: see APPLES, page 332.

MULBERRIES *(Morus nigra)*

Mulberries are slow-growing, long-lived trees and a feature of many old gardens. It is the black mulberry (*Morus nigra*) which produces the pleasant, juicy, rather tart, berries.

Whether grown as a bush or a standard tree, the mulberry is rather large for many modern gardens, eventually reaching 6.0 to 9.0m (20 to 30ft) and probably spreading even more.

Mulberries like the sun and do best in southern Britain, on a deep, moist but well-drained soil.

The deep purple, almost black berries may be harvested in August and September by shaking the branches over a sheet of plastic spread on the ground.

Mulberry trees are usually completely free of pests or diseases.

PEACHES, NECTARINES AND APRICOTS

Peaches *Prunus persica* are one of the real luxury fruits we can grow in our gardens. Nectarines are simply a smooth-skinned type, or 'sport', of peach, just as delicious, grown in the same way except that they do not grow well as bushes and they need watering more frequently while the fruit is swelling. Apricots *Prunus armeniaca* are a closely related fruit, delicious raw (as long as they are really ripe), cooked, or made into jam. All varieties are self-fertile, except for the peach Hale's Early which succeeds better if it has a mate. All are grown in much the same way.

Facing page: above left, the peach 'Rochester' which does best against a wall; above right, blackberry 'Bedford Giant'; below left, 'Merton Glory', a variety of sweet cherry; below right, Cox's Orange Pippin', an apple of superb quality

Peaches, apricots and fan-trained nectarines flourish best in south-eastern Britain, including the London area. This does not mean that they are not worth growing in other areas but they are more difficult in regions of high rainfall. In such places, it is worth trying to restrict the amount of rain reaching the roots: two ways of doing this are to grow the tree against a wall and to pave the path in front.

In the North, choose varieties which ripen by the middle of August and give them the protection of a south-facing wall. Even in the South, the best outdoor peaches are grown against walls. Early varieties may be grown against walls facing West.

Fan-trained peaches, nectarines and apricots may also be grown in greenhouses, fastened to a trellis or against the back wall of a lean-to house. They should not be coddled; ventilate well to keep the air moving and do not allow the soil to become too dry. Hand-pollination of the flowers is necessary for greenhouse crops. Use a soft brush.

Soil Peaches, nectarines and apricots are usually grafted on plum rootstocks (St Julien A being the best for garden planting) and therefore any soil which will grow plums is suitable. Add lime if the soil is very acid but avoid a high lime content as this causes iron deficiency, indicated by chlorosis (yellowing) of the leaves.

Planting Planting is possible from autumn to early spring, but always plant in autumn if possible, as growth begins early in the year.

Plant firmly at the same depth as in the nursery and mulch over the roots to conserve moisture.

If you have room for more than one, plant bush peaches or nectarines 5.5m (18ft) apart; fan-trained trees should be twice as far apart as the distance they will be allowed to extend upwards. Thus against a wall 1.8m (6ft) high, the fans should be 3.5m (12ft) apart.

Staking Bush trees do not need to be staked, but the fan-ribs of a trained tree must be fastened with soft string to canes which in turn are securely tied to horizontal wires at 15cm (6in) intervals.

Pruning BUSH TREES Prune in late April or early May when the buds have begun to grow. Early pruning is directed towards building a framework of sturdy branches, and is similar to the early pruning of a bush apple. If you start with a maiden, cut it back to suitably placed buds (rubbing out misplaced buds) 45 to 60cm ($1\frac{1}{2}$ to 2ft) above soil level. The next spring you can roughly double the number of branches by cutting back each main shoot to about 30cm (1ft) of new wood. Repeat the following year.

If you start by planting a two or three-year-old tree, do not let it bear fruit the first summer and so rub off all blossom buds.

Peaches and nectarines fruit only on wood of the previous year's growth and so pruning should be directed towards producing a continuing supply of new laterals, generally achieved by cutting out about one in three laterals each spring.

Also remove crossing or damaged shoots and when older branches bow down to the ground, cut them out and replace with new branches at a higher level.

FAN TREES Fans may be purchased ready-trained, the price varying according to the number of arms or ribs. These should start to bear after two years. It is cheaper and a fascinating pastime to train your own fan, however, starting with a maiden. It is also more satisfactory because the home-produced fan will be more easily manageable than the nursery tree, usually produced by a short-cut pruning method.

*Right: fan-training a tree.
When the maiden tree starts
developing side-shoots in
spring, select two of the
strongest to form the first two
main branches of the fan (top
left). Rub out all other shoots
and cut out the central stem.
At the end of the following
winter cut each branch back to
a bud between 30 and 45cm (1
to 1½ft) from its point of origin
(top right). Allow four shoots
to develop from each branch:
one at the tip, two on the
upper side, and one on the
lower side (below).*

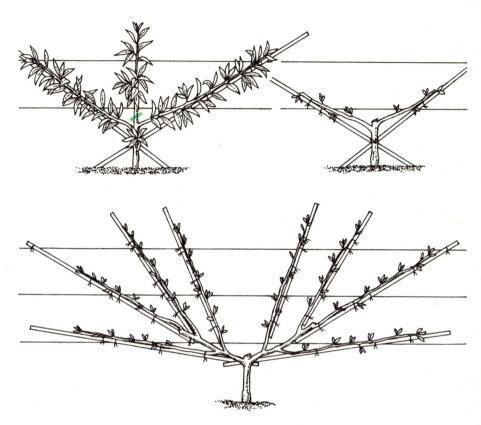

Although fan-training is most common with nectarines, peaches and apricots, the method of producing the tree may also be followed with apples, cherries, pears and plums.

Just before growth starts in early spring, cut the maiden tree down to a lateral or bud about 60cm (2ft) above soil level. Cut out any laterals below this flush with the stem. When shoots develop in spring, select two of these to form the first two main branches of the fan, one on each side of the stem between 23 and 30cm (9 and 12in) high; and so placed that they will grow out parallel with the wall, or nearly so. Rub out all other shoots. As the two chosen shoots grow, tie them loosely with soft string to canes fastened to the horizontal wires at an angle of 45°, at the same time cutting out the one lateral or vertical shoot which grew from the top bud. Paint the wound with bitumen tree paint.

To equalize the rate of growth of the two arms, temporarily depress the angle of the more vigorous one.

At the end of the second winter cut each arm back to a bud 30 to 45cm (1 to 1½ft) from its point of origin. As the shoot grows from the bud nearest the tip of each branch tie it in to the cane. Also look out for two more shoots on the upper side of the branch and one from the underside. When long enough tie these to new canes fastened to the horizontal wires so that all, including the shoot from under the branch, slope upwards. Rub out all other shoots.

Repeat this procedure each February until the available space is filled.

That is how the framework of the fan is developed. When pruning of the fruit-bearing sideshoots from the branches, you must remember that the peach only fruits on wood made the previous year. Allow laterals parallel with the wall to grow at 10 to 15cm (4 to 6in) intervals, tying them in when long enough. Pinch out all other shoots just beyond the second leaf. Pinch out the growing tip of the selected laterals when 45cm ($1\frac{1}{2}$ft) long.

These laterals should bear blossom, and subsequently fruit, the next summer and will produce more laterals. Select one well-placed lateral near the base of the fruiting shoot to act as a replacement when the fruit has been picked. Allow one more to develop about half way along: this will draw the sap and act as a reserve. Allow the new shoot nearest the tip to grow until it has made six leaves, then pinch out. Rub out all other shoots, spreading this over a couple of weeks or so.

If an unwanted shoot develops from a point on the lateral where there is a fruit, do not try to rub it out but pinch it out when two leaves have formed.

After harvesting the last fruit, cut back the old laterals to their replacements. Untie the latter and refasten, spreading them out evenly.

Apricots bear most of their fruit on two- or three-year-old shoots, so there is less need for the extensive pruning and rubbing out performed on the peach; however, the basic principles of fan-training are exactly the same. The important point is not to prune an apricot too hard, or you will end up with a smaller crop.

After harvesting the last fruit, cut back the old laterals to their replacements. Untie the latter and refasten, spreading them out evenly.

Cultivation While in wet districts peaches, nectarines and apricots may have too much rain, the trees must never be allowed to be too dry. Spring mulching helps to conserve soil moisture.

Hang old curtaining, tablecloths or sacking over wall trees in blossom to protect them from spring frost.

Do not be greedy: fruit thinning will ensure larger individual fruits and more regular cropping. When the fruits are the size of walnuts, start thinning by removing those fruits at the back of wall-trained branches, then reducing pairs to singles. Continue over three weeks until the fruit left to ripen are about 23cm (9in) apart for peaches and nectarines and 12.5cm (5in) apart for apricots.

Feeding Do not feed until regular cropping is established beyond laying down a 3.8cm ($1\frac{1}{2}$in) mulch of well-rotted manure or garden compost in May. Too much nitrogen causes excessive growth at the expense of fruiting.

Harvesting The fruit are ready when they feel soft to gentle finger pressure at the stalk end; pick them carefully without pulling and handle very gently.

Troubles DISEASES Peach leaf curl is a common fungus disease of outdoor peaches and nectarines, causing leaves to curl, blister and turn red before dying and falling prematurely. As a routine measure, spray all outdoor peaches and nectarines with Bordeaux mixture, liquid copper or 3 per cent lime-sulphur in January, before the buds start to swell. Repeat in ten days' time and, if the disease appears, again in autumn as soon as the leaves have fallen. Apricots rarely suffer from leaf curl.

PESTS Aphids often attack peaches, nectarines and apricots in spring. Spray liberally, one winter in three, with a tar-oil wash in December. Just before the blossom opens spray annually with derris (or dimethoate or malathion), repeating after blossoming and in summer if necessary.

The glasshouse red spider mite may infest trees growing on walls; these tiny pests thrive in dry conditions. They cause bronzing, speckling or greying of the leaves, which may eventually die. The leaves and stems may also be covered with pale, silvery webs. Spray with derris or malathion, and under glass maintain a more humid atmosphere. Spraying with a strong but very fine jet of water may deter these pests, too.

PEARS *(Pyrus communis)*

Pears are not quite as easy to grow in this country as apples but their treatment is similar. They are less popular than apples as a cooked fruit but for dessert they have similar virtues of a long season and simple storage. As with apples, standards and half-standards are too large for most gardens and so, too, are large bush-type trees. Dwarf bushes, pyramids and cordons are best for the average garden. They may take a little longer than apples to start bearing.

Site Because pears flower earlier than apples, they are more susceptible to frost damage, so plant in a sunny, sheltered position.

Soil Pears will flourish in any medium soil and they tolerate a heavy soil better than apples, always provided it is well drained. They do not do well on very light land.

Planting Planting and staking method is as for apples.

Quince rootstocks are best for garden pears because they give the dwarfest trees and the earliest crops. Quince C is the dwarfest, with the earliest cropping, but at present unobtainable because of virus troubles. Quince A is the next best.

Unfortunately, some pear varieties do not unite well with quince and these have to be worked with a variety that is compatible and the desired variety grafted on that. This is known as double-working; the nurseryman will attend to this.

Cross-pollination also needs thought as most varieties must be pollinated by another variety which produces fertile pollen.

A bush pear tree needs to be at least 3.5m (12ft) from its neighbours, preferably 4.5m (15ft) away, particularly on good soil. Dwarf bushes can be planted a little closer, from 3.0 to 4.3m (10 to 14ft). Pyramids can be 1m (3½ft) apart in rows 2.1m (7ft) apart. Cordons may be planted only 60cm (2ft) apart, or 90cm (3ft) in good soil, with at least 1.8m (6ft) between rows. An espalier pear may eventually have a total branch spread of from 3.5 to 6.0m (12 to 20ft).

Pruning The pruning of pears is as for apples, except that it should be a little lighter for bush pears than for apples in the early years. When the tree is cropping regularly it should then be a little more drastic. In the course of time spurs are more likely to become crowded than with apples, and some should be shortened, others cut out completely.

Cordons, pyramids and espaliers are pruned in just the same way as apples, but because growth starts earlier, it will mature and be ready for summer pruning a week or two earlier.

Fruit-thinning Pears are less subject to biennial bearing than apples; nevertheless, to secure regular good crops, overcropping should be avoided. Timely thinning will also improve fruit size. Start thinning when the fruitlets begin to hang downwards and are 2.5cm (1in) long.

Feeding The feeding programme recommended for apples is also suitable for pears, but as the latter require somewhat more nitrogen than apples, it is advisable to supplement the fertilizer feeds with an annual spring mulch of well-rotted farmyard manure or garden compost spread over the soil surface for a little more than the branches extend, at a rate of one wheelbarrow-load per 7sq m (8sq yd).

Harvesting The pears should be ready for picking when their 'ground colour' (the basic colour of the skin) begins to turn yellow or pale. Do not wait for them to feel soft. As with apples, pick by lifting to the horizontal in the palm of the hand and twisting very gently. Early varieties may be ready late in July or in August, mid-season varieties in September, and December and 'New Year' varieties not until October.

Storage Pears need rather drier storage conditions than apples, and they should not be wrapped or bagged. Bring them out of store a few days before they are required for eating and let them ripen in a living room where the temperature ranges around 16–18°C (60–65°F).

Troubles DISEASES Scab disease, as with apples, can be serious and the disfigurement it causes is similar. Control, too, is the same, spraying with Burgundy mixture or a systemic fungicide at bud burst, green bud and at the white bud stage, again at petal fall and the fruitlet stage. As with apples, clearing away dead leaves in autumn and composting or burning them helps greatly to prevent this disease.

Fireblight is a very serious bacterial pear disease, and must be notified immediately to the Ministry of Agriculture. The symptoms are blackening and shrivelling of flowers, die-back of shoots; also, the leaves turn brown and wither, but do not fall. Your local Ministry of Agriculture representative will advise you about treatment.

PESTS Aphids attack pears as well as apples and their control is similar. Give the first spraying of derris or malathion at the white bud stage and the second when the petals have fallen. Use a winter wash once in three or four years.

The anti-aphid spray will also deal with the pear midge which is responsible for maggots which eat into the fruits.

PLUMS

Plums and gages (*Prunus domestica*) and damsons (*P. damascena*) are very closely related and all grown in the same way. Gages are simply a type of plum with a characteristic flavour which many consider superior to that of other plums. The ordinary plums may be cooking varieties, excellent for stewing or bottling, dessert varieties, or dual-purpose ones, like the well-known Victoria. Damsons are too sharp-tasting for dessert but popular for cooking and the making of damson 'cheese' or preserve.

As trees, plums grow rather tall, even as bush-type trees, and the fruit are particularly attractive to birds. As the size of trees or bushes makes protection difficult, as well as pruning, spraying and picking, plums are best grown in the small garden either as pyramids or fan-trained. The St Julien A rootstock is the best for this purpose.

Some plum varieties are self-fertile, as are most damsons, but others need pollinators.

Site Because they flower earlier, plums are more susceptible to spring frosts even than pears. It is not worth the risk of growing plums in gardens lying in frost-pockets and areas prone to severe frosts. They do best in full sun.

Any plum may be fan-trained but the most favoured situations, against a south or west-facing wall, are best given to the highest quality gages which prefer rather warmer conditions than the others.

Soil A deep medium loam is best but plums will succeed in a clay soil, provided it is well-drained. Trees on very chalky soils are apt to show signs of iron deficiency. A neutral or very slightly acid soil is best, but soils more acid than pH 6.0 should be limed.

Plums need more nitrogen than either apples or pears, and so a site on an old vegetable plot previously well-manured will be to their liking. Soils naturally deficient in food and those which have not been well manured in recent years should have plenty of rotted farmyard manure or garden compost dug in.

Planting The planting season extends from autumn to spring but because growth begins early, autumn planting is always preferable.

Plant very firmly, stamping the soil back around the stem with your foot, at the same depth as in the nursery. Then mulch to retain moisture, keeping the mulch from actual contact with the stem.

Lifting and replanting on the same spot a year later is a mild form of root-pruning and is worth while for bush trees and pyramids to stimulate earlier fruiting.

Set fans 15 to 23cm (6 to 9in) away from the foot of a wall and incline the tree slightly towards the wall.

Bush plums, gages and damsons should be set at least 3.5m (12ft) apart, each way, or 4.5m (15ft) apart in rich soil. Pyramids may be planted a little closer, 3.0 to 3.5m (10–12ft) and fans need a branch spread of at least 3.5m (12ft), preferably of 5.5m (18ft).

Staking Bush trees and maidens destined for pyramid training should be staked at planting time, before the roots are covered with soil.

For bush trees, if you can provide a tall pole, higher than the tree will grow, this can be used to form a maypole-like support in later years for taking the weight of heavily-laden branches.

Fan-trained trees need a support system of horizontal wires spaced at 15cm (6in) intervals. A cane should be provided for each rib of the fan, this being tied securely to the wires and the tree fastened more loosely to the cane with soft string.

Pruning Bush trees The early forming of a bush plum follows similar lines to the early pruning of bush apples except that, because of the danger of silver leaf disease infection, all pruning is best carried out just as growth begins in spring. At this time wounds heal most quickly. Larger cuts should always be painted over with a bitumen tree paint.

If you plant a maiden, cut it down the first spring to about 90cm (3ft), cutting immediately above three or four buds which will throw out shoots evenly spaced around the tree. Rub out misplaced buds. Leave any sideshoots below this for two or three years, but shorten each to the fourth leaf in midsummer.

If you plant an older tree, leave it unpruned for one or two years to gain strength.

At the first pruning of branches, in the second year if a maiden was planted, cut each branch back by a half. The next year branch ends should be shortened slightly.

Mature plum trees need very little pruning and this should be carried out either in midsummer, when silver leaf infection is least probable, or immediately after the crop is picked. Only remove damaged or broken branches and those which cross others and may be causing chafing.

Root-pruning Should a plum tree grow vigorously without fruiting, never imagine you can improve matters by hard branch-pruning: this will only make matters worse. Root-pruning is the remedy.

Young trees may be given simple root-pruning by simply lifting them and then replanting them in the same spot. For larger trees, dig out a semi-circular trench, halfway round the tree, about 90cm (3ft) away from the trunk. Dig down 60cm (2ft), and cut or saw through all thick

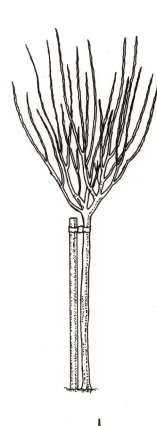

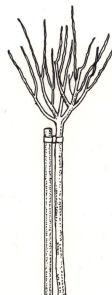

Above: established plums require little pruning, but young trees should have their branches shortened by half at the first pruning, in the second or third year.

roots encountered. Do *not* cut the delicate fibrous roots, and take care not to damage them at all.

Do this in November when the leaves have fallen and a year later repeat the treatment for the roots on the other side. Always check that newly root-pruned trees are securely staked.

Pyramids For this very satisfactory method of training plum trees in a garden you cannot buy ready-made pyramids: instead, you have to start from scratch with a maiden on St Julien A rootstock.

Early in April cut back the central stem of the maiden to a height of 1.5m (5ft). Cut off flush with the stem any sideshoots nearer to the ground than 45cm (1½ft), and shorten the remainder to half their length.

In about the third week of July, when new shoot growth has ceased, cut the new extension growth on each branch back to 20cm (8in), always cutting immediately after a bud pointing downwards. Then shorten any sideshoots from the branches to 15cm (6in). Repeat annually.

Leave the central vertical stem alone in summer but in April cut off two-thirds of the new growth made the previous year. Continue in this way until a height of 2.7m (9ft) is reached and then defer pruning until May and cut back the new growth to 2.5cm (1in) at the most.

Should another strong vertical shoot develop, challenging the leader, cut it out.

Fan trees Fan-trained trees are usually purchased ready-trained with anything from 5 to 12 ribs already formed, and priced accordingly, but if you want to plant a maiden and make your own fan, follow the same procedure as for a peach.

When fans reach the fruiting stage, however, the method of pruning has to differ from that of the peach because the habit of the tree is different.

As soon as growth starts in the spring begin controlling the fan plum by rubbing out any shoots pointing at the wall or directly away from it. Allow other shoots to grow but pinch out their tips when six or seven leaves have been made. Immediately the fruit has been picked, cut back the already pinched-out shoots to half their length.

You can allow new laterals to grow, refraining from pinching them out, to make new shoots to fill vacant places, but never let one grow up vertically as it will weaken all other branches.

Cultivation Plums need plenty of moisture during the growing season. Thus on lighter soils particularly, and in the early years, they may need watering liberally during dry summer periods.

Keep weeds down by shallow hoeing or hand-weeding. Do not fork the soil near plums as this may stimulate undesirable sucker growth. If suckers do appear, try to pull them up rather than cut them, or more will appear.

Plums can sometimes produce over-prolific crops and fruit-thinning is then necessary to improve fruit size and flavour and prevent branch breakage, which is dangerous because it gives silver leaf disease a chance to enter.

Thin in two stages, starting in early June and completing the work when the stones have formed. Remove fruits until each is 5 to 7.5cm (2 to 3in) from its neighbour.

Feeding In early February, dress the soil a little farther than the branches extend with 18 to 27g per sq m (½ to ¾oz per sq yd) sulphate of ammonia and 18g per sq m (½oz per sq yd) sulphate of potash and gently rake in. Once every two or three years also give 53 to 70g per sq m ($1\frac{1}{2}$ to 2oz per sq yd) superphosphate. Where trees are growing vigorously, give the lesser amounts mentioned above. Then in April put down a light surface mulch of well-rotted manure or garden compost.

Harvesting For cooking, bottling or jam-making, pick plums while still slightly unripe. For dessert, plums should be left as long as possible, but in wet weather some varieties are prone to split, and it may be wise to sacrifice some flavour by picking a little early.

Troubles DISEASES The most common plum disease is silver leaf, so named because the infected leaves assume a silvery or leaden sheen. Peaches, nectarines, apricots, almonds, cherries, hawthorns, blackthorn, roses and Portugal laurel can also be attacked by this fungus, but this does not often happen.

The edges of the infected leaves later turn brown and the branch dies. Red spider mite attack and certain physiological disorders can cause rather similar symptoms of leaf silvering, but the diagnosis can be confirmed by cutting through the wood below the silvered leaves: where the disease is present, the inner tissues are stained brown.

Remove and burn all diseased branches, cutting back until no stain is found inside the wood. Seal the wounds with a coat of protective tree paint.

To prevent the disease, prune during the growing season, stop heavily-laden branches from breaking by supporting them, cut off any broken branches immediately, and seal all wounds with protective paint.

Plum pox is an aphid-borne disease new to this country but now causing wide concern. There is no cure, and outbreaks must be notified to the Ministry of Agriculture.

The symptoms include leaf discoloration but this is often inconspicuous and the next sign is the premature fall of the fruit, two to three weeks before normal ripening. There may be dark-coloured bands or rings on the fruits.

PESTS Aphids frequently infest plums, curling leaves and coating them with a sticky substance, also twisting shoots and stunting growth. Spray with tar-oil winter wash in December and January to destroy eggs and then with derris or dimethoate before the blossom opens, at the white bud stage. Repeat later, after blossoming, if any signs of aphids are seen.

QUINCES (*Cydonia oblonga* or *vulgaris*)

Although commonly used as rootstocks for pears, quinces are not much grown for their fruit these days. However, the strongly aromatic fruits do make excellent jam, jelly and cheese, and in small quantities may be included in apple pies to impart an extra tangy flavour.

Any soil which grows pears will suit quinces and, like pears, they do best in warm situations. Plant them 3.5m (12ft) apart and grow as bush trees in the south, or as a wall-trained fan or espalier in colder areas. Once the framework has been formed, bush trees need little pruning.

After harvesting in late October, store the fruits separate from any other kinds of fruit, on account of their strong aroma. They will keep for two or three months.

Champion is an apple-shaped variety, said to be the hardiest. Portugal has big, oblong fruit which turn red on cooking. It is slow to crop. Meech's Prolific, pear-shaped, crops the soonest.

Quinces are rarely attacked by pests or diseases.

THE
HANDYMAN
GARDENER

Construction in the Garden

Fortunately, even a newcomer to gardening can make a sound and attractive job of laying out paths or patios, building low walls in stone or concrete blocks, or of putting up fences, screens and pergolas. The skills required are easily learned, and few jobs are so satisfying.

The necessary tools are few and inexpensive. Modern materials, ready cut and shaped, are designed for rapid and easy arrangement. From simple beginnings, anyone with a little patience can progress from laying a few slabs on sand as a kitchen-garden path, to the building of a fine flight of stone steps or a lovely, flower-studded dry stone wall.

Nor need the work be heavy. It is true that some jobs, the preparation of foundations for example, call for a good deal of concrete mixing, but this can be greatly eased by the hiring of a power mixer for a weekend. Building blocks of concrete are rarely large, and the skill needed lies mainly in taking meticulous care to get them level.

With professional labour today being so expensive, hard to obtain, and often dubious in skill, the do-it-yourself amateur can save a great deal of cost and disappointment by tackling the jobs with his family. In this section we show how jobs are best done, the tools required and the choice of materials for most of the jobs a newcomer is likely to tackle.

Basic Skills

Mortar and concrete Cement is used in two forms in garden building; mixed with sand to form mortar or with both sand and gravel to make concrete.

MORTAR is used to join building blocks, bricks or stones together; to fill up cracks and holes; and as support immediately under paving slabs.
CONCRETE is used to give solid and powerful support in the foundations of walls; under paths and drives bearing heavy traffic; and under buildings.

In both cases the mixtures may vary in their proportions. For example, mortar usually consists of one part cement to three parts of sand, but for work not under great strain, up to five parts of sand may be allowed, so lowering the cost. Note specially that builders' SOFT SAND is used. There is also SHARP SAND (or CONCRETING SAND) which does not make a very adhesive mixture, and is used mainly in concrete. Concrete proportions vary also, commonly being one part of cement, two parts of concreting sand and three parts of gravel. For other purposes a higher proportion of sand and gravel may be allowed.
CEMENT is bought in 20kg (44lb) or 50kg (110lb) sacks. It is vital to keep it in a dry place and to use it within a few weeks of purchase. Stored cement, even if it remains powdery, loses much of its efficiency.
SAND is best bought in bulk from a builders' merchant. To get the best price, take large plastic bags and fill them yourself from his heaps.

You can also buy ready prepared DRY MIXTURES of sand and cement, ready for the simple addition of water. These certainly save a good deal of effort in mixing and ensure accuracy of proportions. The very small packs, though, are expensive for their weight. It is better to buy big sacks of mix from professional builders' suppliers.

Mixing mortar and concrete One golden rule applies always. Mix the dry materials thoroughly *before* adding water. Failure to make a thoroughly even mix will cause pockets of weakness in your work. A good method is to heap up the sand, spill over it the dry cement and then shovel the whole lot to one side. Next, shift the pile back to its original position. 'Turn' the heap in this way five times and you should have a perfect mix, which is even in colour and texture. At this point you can also add colour dyes if you wish to avoid the rather stark grey of plain concrete in your garden. However, do be cautious with your colours. Startling blues, reds and yellows are not attractive. Experiment first with soft, restrained pale browns.

To the dry mix, water is now added. For MORTAR, open a hole in the top of the heap like a volcano crater. Fill this hole with water and use a shovel to work the crater sides down into the water, chopping and stirring. Prevent liquid from overflowing down the heap sides. Once the first water is absorbed, repeat until the whole heap can at last be shovelled together into a smooth but, if anything, rather dry, paste.

(The commonest amateur mistake is to get mortar or concrete *too wet*. It is far better to keep it on the dry side.) Do not mix up more mortar than can be used within an hour. Small mixes, freshly prepared, give much better results and make for easier working.

CONCRETE mixes should have water added from a spray hose or watering can. Sprinkle over the heap, but do not allow any part of this to become flooded. Slowly turn in the dampened parts, continuing as with mortar till the whole heap is moist without being saturated. (When chopped with a shovel, the gash made should only close slowly and without filling up with water. Too much free water will weaken concrete by up to 80 per cent.)

Concrete can be mixed in large batches but lay it as quickly as you can, within an hour if possible, especially in hot weather. Protect the moist mixture from hot sun or heavy rain.

The process of setting is a chemical one, not a simple matter of drying out. Indeed, a covering of damp sacks over new work will help to make sure that the setting process does not go on too fast. Remember, fast setting usually means weakness. Once laid in place, leave concrete to set for at least a week before use. Most concrete actually takes four weeks to reach its full strength, though it is commonly usable for most purposes after ten days.

If for any reason you must have a swift-setting concrete or mortar, try the special high speed cement or rapid setting accelerators from builders' merchants. Follow the directions given implicitly or you may get *too* rapid results!

Shuttering This is a word you will certainly come across in building. It simply means any structure, of wood or metal, that is erected around concrete to hold it in place until it sets. For example, two 15cm (6in) wide planks set on edge, supported by posts about 60cm (2ft) apart, will support the edges of a concrete garden path till the mixture sets. Then after a day or two the shuttering is removed.

CASTING YOUR OWN BLOCKS This shuttering is similar to a MOULD, which is a shaped box within which concrete is poured and allowed to set in the shape of blocks, slabs and so on. You can make your own garden WALL BLOCKS quite easily, using home-made or commercial moulds, though SLABS for paving need rather more careful mixing and setting conditions than building blocks in order to be completely successful. In any case, always store home-cast materials for at least two months before attempting to use them.

Foundations and drainage More structural failures, amateur or professional, are caused by poor foundations than by any other single cause. Paths that bear any regular traffic, and of course motor drives, need foundations that can take a heavy load consistently, day after day, for years without cracking, crumbling or flaking. Even small garden paths will soon subside into unpleasant soggy tracks if their foundations are poor. Garden walls need, if anything, still greater strength below because, besides their greater and more concentrated weight per unit area, they often must withstand sideways pressures and these can exert enormous leverage.

Concrete is by far the best foundation material, but whether a concrete foundation is strictly necessary depends first of all on the kind of soil in your garden. Broadly speaking, clay soils expand and contract a lot throughout the year, taking up water and swelling in winter, drying out and shrinking in the heat of summer. Here, you need deep and strong foundations. A medium loam is less variable. It is often possible, provided the site is well drained, to make do with lighter support and shallower foundations. Gravelly sand shifts very little except on extremely dry sites and may need quite light foundations.

Because of these variations nobody can tell you exactly in every case how deep foundations should be, but in the guides later some idea is given and if in doubt, do give a little greater depth, not less.

Besides concrete, broken brick and stone spread and rammed into a trench from which the soft topsoil has been removed also makes a good foundation. With this a certain amount of concrete is usually spread and rammed amongst the lumps, building up to an unbroken skin from 5–7.5cm (2–3in) thick.

Paving foundations reach to the edge of the area covered, but wall foundations should always be *wider* than the wall itself, so making a little platform on which the wall is built. This greatly increases the wall's initial strength and helps it to resist the attacks of plant roots and the tendency to be pushed over.

When preparing foundations of any type, do so as far in advance as possible before starting the actual building work. With a house drive or a path bearing heavy traffic, do the excavation and scatter stones, broken bricks and gravel, etc. within it and then let the mass settle and be crushed by traffic for as long as possible – several months is not too long. As the inevitable holes and hollows appear, fill them up with more similar material rammed into place. Care taken at this stage will add years to the life of path and wall and reduce later maintenance.

Drainage Drainage – or lack of it – is often a source of problems in garden building. If water cannot drain away freely it will make the soil sodden and airless, spoiling your plants, and undermining your walls, paths and buildings till it finds a way out.

Paving, of course, must have a surface which soon dries and does not retain puddles of water. This sort of drainage is easy to arrange either by giving the path a gentle slope or by making it higher in the middle than at its edges. Remember, though, that paving laid next to a house must drain away from it otherwise your house foundations will suffer. Take care too that the layout of your paths does not anywhere form an enclosure like a rectangle with a lawn or flower bed in the middle. Deep

Right: cut a shallow chisel scratch round both sides and edges of the slab.

Centre: upend the slab and strike along the line of the scratch with a heavy hammer, until the slab splits apart.

Far right: to cut through a block, draw a line round all four edges before starting to trim in the same way as for slabs.

foundations would then act rather like a dam forcing water either to stagnate in a muddy pool or to worm its way out by undermining the paths. This can easily be prevented by fitting lengths of clay or plastic drainpipe crossways through the foundations before the paths are built.

Walls, too, must be watched for this problem and suitable passages allowed at the construction stage.

Block and slab shaping Finally, before starting on actual building you ought really to know how to cut blocks, stones and slabs to shape. Fortunately, extreme accuracy is rarely needed and straightforward cuts are easy. You will need a 1kg (2lb) hammer and a broad stone chisel. A 'mason's hammer' with a chisel back makes the job quicker, especially in stone trimming, but is not essential.

First – slab cutting. Stone or concrete is cut in the same way but concrete is easier as it is even in texture and so less likely to flake off in irregular splits. The procedure is simple. First mark the line of cut on both sides of the slab. Then cut a shallow chisel scratch round both sides and edges. Finally upend the slab and strike along the length of the scratch with your hammer, as shown below. Use firm but not violent blows. After a few strokes the typical ringing sound will deaden to a soft thud as the slab splits along the line and falls apart. Minor remaining irregularities are then trimmed with a chisel or hammer back.

Block cutting usually involves halving a brick or other lump, or else shaping an irregular stone into a rectangular block. Cross cutting is done as with slabs, by making a notch with a chisel and then striking a

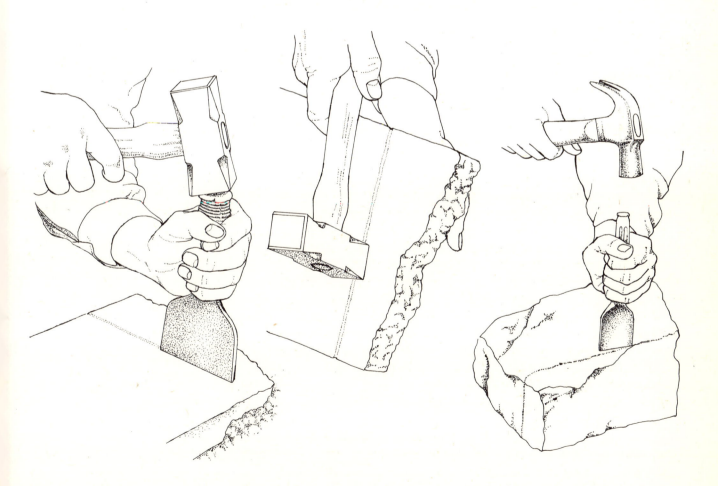

firm blow along the marked line. Shaping stone is more delicate, needing a good eye and a sharp mason's hammer and chisel. Draw a line round the best face of your stone block before starting to trim and work round all four edges to give a roughly rectangular face, as shown on page 367. Practise first before starting on important work!

Paved Areas – Paths, Patios and Terraces

All paving is laid in the same general way, whether it be a narrow path, a broader motor drive, a level patio 9m (30yd) across, or a series of terraces stepped up a hillside. The only real difference lies in the skill of levelling, making sure that the slabs of concrete or stone form an even surface without humps or hollows.

A newcomer to garden building should start with a path, preferably a businesslike path in concrete slabs, such as may be used for the kitchen garden. As experience is gained the slightly more tricky random slab or stone path can be tried until finally a broad area for a patio will seem no trouble at all.

The first rule has already been emphasized. Make good foundations, remembering to slope them evenly and gently (about one in twenty will do) away from any adjacent building. Ram the stones, gravel and earth well. You will need a long builder's level to get the job finally straight, but quite a cheap one will do provided it is at least 60cm (2ft) long.

Slabs on sand This is the simplest method of all and requires very little mortar. It can be easily altered as years go by and the garden plans develop. Its surface soon dries, since there is free drainage between the slabs. Yet it is quite strong enough for normal garden use as a path or patio, though it is not strong enough for motor drives.

Start by spreading a layer of sharp concreting sand, 5cm (2in) deep, over the foundations and tread it down firmly. Make sure that you get this sand smoothly level. A good way of doing this is to make a number of 30cm (1ft) long wooden pegs and drive these in at roughly 1.5m (5ft) intervals over the surface. Now use a long straight board to bridge the gaps between the pegs. Rest your spirit level on top of the board and adjust your pegs till all of them are level with each other. Now you will find it easy to rake the sand beneath so that all the pegs protrude an equal amount from its surface.

It is not quite so easy to lay a SLOPING BED of sand but you can adjust your spirit level for this purpose. For a 1-in-20 slope, use a block of wood which is $\frac{1}{20}$th of the length of your spirit level in thickness. That is, if your spirit level is 50cm (20in) long, the block should be 2.5cm (1in) thick. If it is 80cm (30in) long it should be 4cm ($1\frac{1}{2}$in) thick and so on. Tape the block to one end of the level as illustrated on the previous page.

Proceed as before, laying your long strip of wood over the pegs and the spirit level with its block on top of it. Now if you adjust the pegs until the tool shows level the board will be at the correct 1-in-20 slope. A moment's practice with this soon gives you the hang of it.

LAYING THE SLABS Once the sand bed has been laid, the placing of the slabs follows quickly and easily. Start near one edge, particularly any edge which is near a building. The object is to lower the slabs onto the sand while disturbing this as little as possible.

Tap each slab down using a wooden or rubber-headed hammer or a short length of timber. It will often be found that the slab rocks slightly. Lift it again and scoop out a little of the sand from beneath the middle

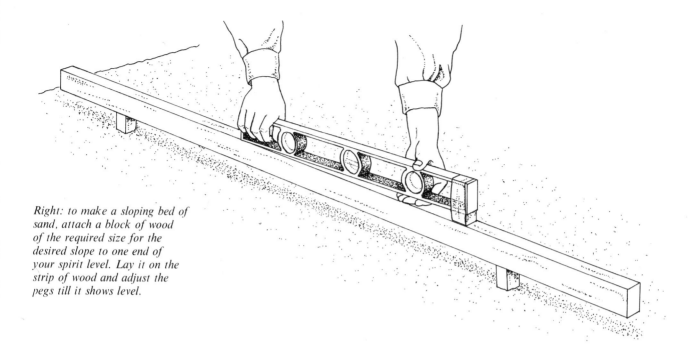

Right: to make a sloping bed of sand, attach a block of wood of the required size for the desired slope to one end of your spirit level. Lay it on the strip of wood and adjust the pegs till it shows level.

of the slab. Then lower it again so that it is supported round the edges rather than at its middle.

Use your spirit level frequently to make sure that all the slabs are accurately placed. Care at this stage will make the final job much better.

Mortar is only used at positions under considerable stress such as the outer edges of a patio. Use a mixture of one part cement to three parts of sand and spread this along the outer edge of the sand foundation.

Tap the slabs gently down into this. Heavy blows at this stage may crack the slabs, so take care.

Use more mortar to smooth up the outer side edges of the path, joining them with a continuous strip of mortar. This will greatly strengthen them later.

Finally fill up all the joints by scattering plain sand over the whole surface. Brush this well down into all the joints, flooding the surface with water. Repeat until the joints remain full of sand.

Slabs on mortar Where there is to be greater traffic, a stronger job can be made by laying the slabs on supporting 'points' of mortar under all joints instead of merely under the outer edges of the paving. As before, first spread a 5cm (2in) sand bed, treading and raking it level.

When making square or rectangular patios outline the area in string and at the corners use two pegs driven in as shown overleaf, so that the corner is clearly outlined.

Start laying the slabs from one such corner. Drop four blobs of mortar onto the sand where the corners of the slab itself will rest (a mix of one part of cement to four parts of soft sand will do).

Lower the slab into place and tap it down with the wooden handle of a heavy hammer. Align the slab edges exactly along the two guide strings. Check its level with a long spirit level.

Smooth away the cement which has squeezed out from beneath the slabs' *outer* edges but let any surplus mortar remain that squeezes out from its inner edges. In this way the edges of adjacent slabs will rest on

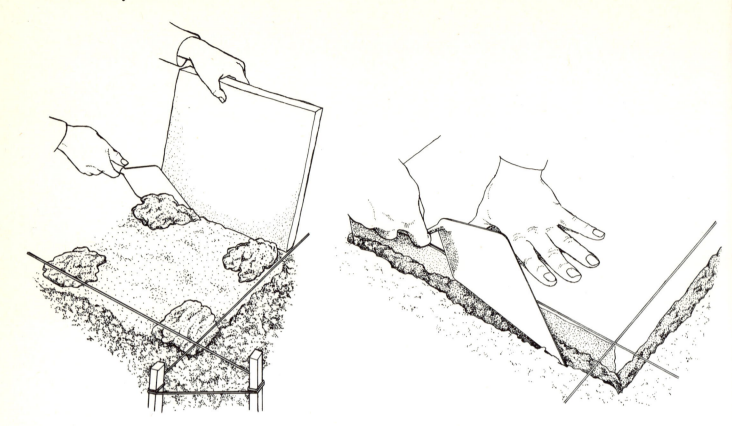

the same mortar blobs and lock the surface together (see above).

The edges of the first slab now act as guides for the rapid laying of the rest. Use a long straight board to assist in checking that each additional slab is level with its neighbours.

Remember too to check diagonally or you may produce a hollow in the middle of the paving which would cause puddles after rain.

Once the cement has set (after four or five days) scatter coarse sand over the entire surface and brush this well down into the joints, flooding with water as necessary.

Solid concrete paths and drives For the strongest garden path or motor drive, solid cast concrete is undoubtedly the most hard-wearing of materials. It is, however, rather harsh in appearance, although this can be improved by applying a soft, sandy coloured dye, or at greater cost by inlaying into the surface different kinds of natural stones.

For path and drive work, a concrete mixture of roughly two parts of sand to three parts gravel and only one part of cement will give a satisfactory result.

To support the concrete until it sets you will need shuttering of rough planking. First dig out the path foundation at least 15cm (6in) deep and drive in along the sides several posts roughly 45cm (18in) long and 3.8cm (1½in) square.

The shuttering planks themselves must be strong but need not be of new wood. You can sometimes hire suitable boards from builders.

Nail the shuttering to the pegs. Hold a stone or heavy hammer behind the pegs as the nails are driven, to take the shocks (as shown, right).

Align the top edges of the boards to the exact height of the concrete path. Use a spirit level to check that they are level crossways. Allow broad paths to slope slightly to one side or the other.

Between the boards lay a foundation of broken bricks and stone about 10cm (4in) deep. Pack these stones carefully together solidly.

Above left: outline the corners of patios with string and two pegs as shown, and start laying the slabs from one such corner, dropping a blob of mortar where each corner of the slab will rest.

Above: smooth away only the cement which oozes from the slabs' outer edges.

Below: for concrete paths and drives, use shuttering planks nailed to pegs driven in along the edge of the foundations.

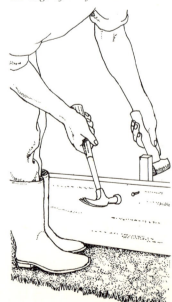

Ram the foundations with a heavy baulk of timber. If possible leave the stones to settle for several weeks, walking and driving on them to pack the stones down.

You can buy the concrete ready mixed, which is best if the job is a large one, or mix it yourself, preferably with the help of a hired concrete mixer. Wheelbarrow it into place and shovel it down between the boards, working it well with a chopping motion of the shovel.

Overfill the space and rake off any surplus approximately level but about 2.5cm (1in) above the top edges of the boards.

Beat the wet concrete surface flat with a length of timber held across the shuttering boards. This beating will bring to the surface a creamy liquid cement which will set to give a slightly rough surface ideal for most garden purposes and for drives.

Above: ram the foundations with a heavy baulk of timber, and leave them to settle for several weeks, walking over them as much as possible.

Above right: after laying the concrete between the shuttering planks, beat the surface flat with a length of timber held across it, as shown.

A smoother finish can be made by using a rectangular float trowel but this is a fairly skilled job and the amateur often produces an overworked surface which flakes and becomes powdery.

Cloudy, cool and moist weather is best for concrete work so always protect newly laid concrete against heavy rain and too hot sun. Several layers of polythene or wet sacking will serve. Hold these down with bricks for about five days until the concrete has initially set.

Inlaid stone surfacing Probably the strongest and most attractive of garden paths is where natural stone is inlaid into solid concrete. This is relatively easy to do but rather expensive. Thin slabs of sandstone or limestone are best. The procedure is straightforward enough. As each metre (yard) or so of the path is filled up with moist concrete, rake this out slightly below the top of the shuttering. The exact amount below depends on the thickness of stone you are using. Now tap the stone pieces gently down into the moist concrete using the wooden shaft of a heavy hammer. The concrete will rise up between the stones and can be smoothed off with the trowel. Take care, though, to prevent so far as possible cement liquid getting on to the surfaces of the stones. If this does happen, wipe it immediately with a wet cloth or sponge, or the marking may become permanent.

Finally, smooth off the cement between the stones with the tip of a trowel. This will give a path which has an upper surface of natural stone but the strength and permanence of the thick concrete beneath.

Variations on the themes Upon these basic methods of laying slabs on pure sand, mortar supports or solid concrete you can develop a number of attractive alternatives.

CRAZY PAVING in natural stone is most attractive, and where traffic is light the pure sand-bed method will serve. This is obviously much cheaper than inlaying the slabs in concrete. The art lies in choosing pieces to make an attractive pattern. Keep big stones to the path edges (laid first) and fill in with smaller pieces. Mortar under really small bits will help them to remain in place. A great advantage of this type of path is that small creeping plants and mosses can be established to spread attractively amongst the stones, as shown below.

BRICK PATHS can also be laid on pure sand. Always use weathered secondhand bricks rather than new ones if possible. A 'crowned' path (with the middle higher than its edges) is made by using a prepared curved wooden gauge to keep the crown regular (bottom left). Again, plants can be allowed to creep between the bricks. Many patterns are possible or bricks and concrete blocks can be combined.

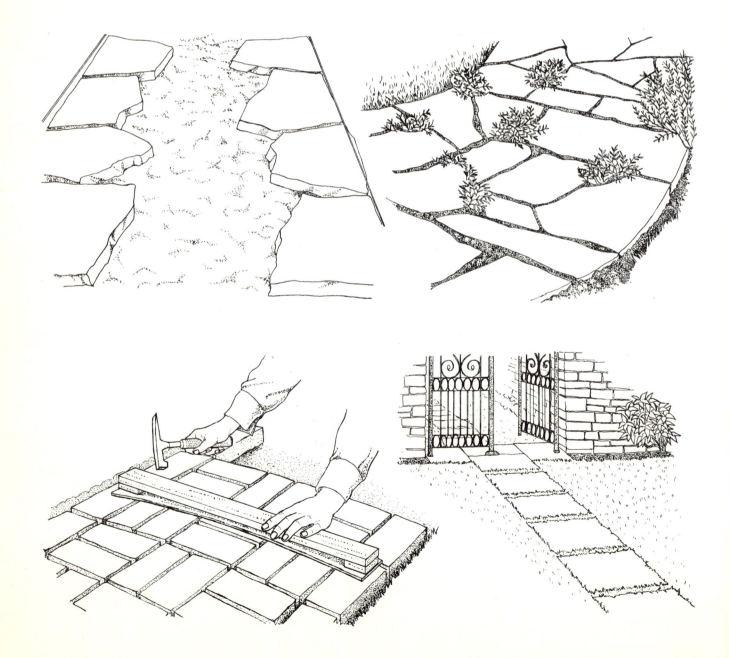

INLAID SLABS in lawns are also attractive. Scoop out 5cm (2in) deeper than your slab thickness and bed each stone solidly down on sand so that its top edge is just below lawn level, for easy mowing (bottom right).

Two further distinct path types can also be made in gardens, using GRAVEL and ASPHALT. They are very similar in methods and particularly lend themselves to curved outlines.

With both it is vital to have solid foundations of broken bricks and stones as well as supporting kerbs on either side to hold the surfacing material into place.

Kerbing can be of wood, stone, brick or concrete. Wood is simply planks of timber, heavily rot-proofed by soaking in preservative, and supported on substantial short posts, rather like shuttering.

Brick, stone or concrete kerbs (these last precast in thin slabs to be set on edge) are embedded in soft mortar well supported at both sides to withstand the pressure of the gravel or asphalt.

GRAVEL for paths is of two types:

Shingle is fine broken pebbles raked out level and rolled. It never forms a completely solid surface, but is easily maintained. Though it often allows easy foothold for weeds, it is equally easy to rake these out and a thin additional topping of gravel can renew an old path.

Ballast or *self-setting gravel* includes fine particles of sand and grit as well as small stones, and if put down wet – with a texture rather like stiff concrete – makes a reasonably solid surface.

ASPHALT is also of two types, either laid *hot* or *cold*, but no amateur should try using hot asphalt. Instead, buy ready-to-lay bags of cold asphalt available in black or several other colours. This material is simply tipped into place, raked out evenly level and carefully rolled flat. A scattering of pebbles in a contrasting colour rolled in last enables different effects to be produced. Occasional rerolling, especially in hot weather, may be needed over the first few weeks.

Motor drives Building a full-size, full-strength drive is not technically difficult, preferably after some practice with smaller items, but will call for a fair amount of manpower. Concrete will be the usual and best choice for strength, durability and easy maintenance. Even a small drive, though, will call for several tons of materials to be mixed, spread, worked down and levelled, quite apart from the erection of shuttering. The best procedure is to gather together friends and neighbours to help with a single load of ready-mixed concrete.

The procedure is exactly the same as laying a concrete path. The only problem to watch out for is the *expansion* of the completed work which may result in strain cracks. All concrete expands and contracts with the seasons and to absorb this, large areas are laid out as several separated panels rather than as a single block. These sections are separated by 1.5–2.5cm ($\frac{1}{2}$–1in) thick lengths of wood (part of the original shuttering left in place), flush with the surface. Note that these 'expansion boards' must be full depth, completely separating each panel of concrete from its neighbour. An expansion board for each 2m (6ft) of drive is usually enough.

Building Walls

Walls in a garden are primarily for decoration. It takes a good deal of building skill to produce high quality brick walls for any other purpose, for example the walls of sheds or greenhouses. The usual garden materials are solid concrete blocks, roughly squared stones and the open

Far left: when laying crazy paving, first lay the big stones along the path edges, then fill in with smaller pieces of stone.

Left: this type of path laid on a sand bed enables plants to be established between the stones.

Far left: use a curved wooden gauge to make a 'crowned' brick path.

Left: slabs laid in a lawn should be just below lawn level for easy mowing.

delicate castings often called screen blocks. The simplest of all to build is certainly the decorative dry stone wall where soil is used instead of cement between the pieces. This soil can be planted with small creepers and rock plants to make a most attractive garden feature.

Making a dry stone wall These walls can be very attractive when clothed in flowers and creeper. Try to fit them into your garden plan in some unexpected way. The wall shown, for example, can be used as a seat.

Almost any type of flat stone can be used, the easiest being slabs of sandstone or limestone. Wide, flat stones are much easier to build with than thick or irregularly-shaped kinds. You can even use broken concrete slabs with the broken edges outwards.

Unlike most kinds of wall, a low decorative dry stone wall does not require deep foundations. It is enough as a rule to tread the soil really well underneath where the wall is to be built.

All dry stone walls must be built thinner at the top than at the bottom. This helps to keep them secure. Getting this taper correct is easiest if you make a pair of wooden guides nailed together as shown and erected at each end. Then choose your thickest stones for the base and arrange the first with their best edges facing outwards along the bottom line of the wall. Lay the front and back rows and give all the stones a slight inward tilt to make sure that rainwater finds its way into the wall instead of tending to run out from it. Next spread a thin layer of fine soil over the slabs you have laid and lay onto them a further pair of rows (see illustration, right).

Continue to build upwards with alternate soil and stone, using the guides to give you a regular taper.

Small pieces of stone are used to fill the gaps in the middle. You can also use more soil at this point. This soil will accommodate small plants which can be planted as the work progresses.

Broad rectangular slabs, though often expensive to buy, make an attractive capping. Bed them solidly and check that they are either dead level or with a very slight slope to give good surface drainage. Walls such as this require practically no attention apart from weeding and will last for many years.

Cemented stone walls Cemented walls in stone are built in roughly the same way as dry stone walls but using a four to one sand/cement mortar instead of soil between the blocks. Always keep the mortar liquid from the exposed surfaces of the stones. Concrete blocks coloured and shaped to look like natural stone are nowadays often cheaper and very much easier to build with and should be the first choice for a

Above: using a pair of wooden guides which taper at the top, lay the rows of stones with a slightly inward tilt, with a thin layer of soil between each row.

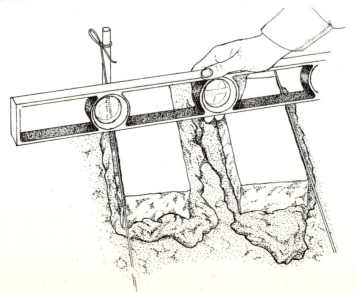

Left: using guide strings to indicate the width of the wall, build a cemented stone wall with care, checking that the two faces of the wall are parallel and level with each other.

Right: join screen blocks with two narrow strips of mortar rather than one thick spread.

newcomer to garden building. This type of wall does need reasonably solid foundations, preferably a smooth layer 10cm (4in) thick of well rammed stones and concrete. Make sure that this is as level as possible.

This particular wall is a simple double-faced kind with a good appearance on both sides. Commence building using guide strings set the wall thickness apart. With the normal mortar (one part cement to three parts of soft sand mixed not too wet) lay a strip of mortar along one side of the wall foundation rather longer than a block length.

Press the first block firmly down in line with the string. Adjust the height of the string to run exactly along the top edge of the block. Then lay a second block at the other end of the wall in the same way.

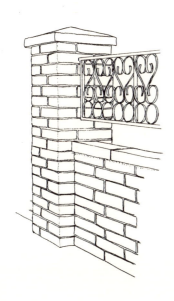

Right: when the first row of each wall face is completed, lay a dry block and a 1cm (⅜in) thick piece of wood across both ends of the rows, and lift the guide strings on top of them. Then lay the next and succeeding rows.

Below: pillars may be built as part of cemented stone walls. Success depends on accurate vertical building.

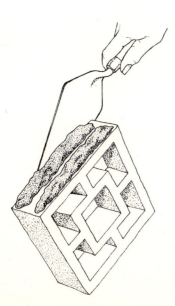

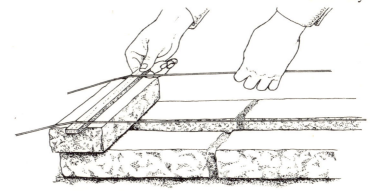

Start the other face of the wall similarly and use a spirit level bridged between to check that the two blocks are parallel to and level with each other. The small gap between the block ends is filled with an offcut of broken block.

After the first blocks have been laid, work inwards along the line of strings from each end. For each added block lay a mortar bed as before and apply more mortar to its end. You will find that practice is needed as well as the right mortar consistency to get it to stick on well.

Press each block down into its bed and against its neighbour.

The last block in the middle may require shortening. Blocks that are irregular in length are least conspicuous towards the middle of a wall. If you have to cut one this is easy with a hammer and chisel or a chisel-backed mason's hammer. Simply cut a shallow scratch across both the top and bottom of the block. Then a final, firm blow will usually split the block cleanly to length.

Next, lay a *dry* block across both ends of the rows and lift the guide strings on top of it. Slip also a 1cm (⅜in) thick piece of wood under the strings to raise them by the thickness of a mortar bed (as shown above). These raised strings act as guides to laying the next and succeeding rows. Ensure that the joints between the blocks are staggered. They must not be directly above each other. Instead, every block of the second row must bridge a joint in the row below. To complete such rows you will need to cut half blocks.

Check each row for level as you go along, using a long timber. This is most important. Also, keep the wall faces vertical as they rise.

Finally, for the wall top you can use wide concrete slabs on a mortar bed. Get a size that will overhang about 4cm (1½in) over the front and back of the wall. A final cleaning with a stiff brush to remove crumbs of adhering mortar and the wall is complete, ready to give years of service.

Pillars With a little practice, you can also build pillars in blocks either at the ends of or along the length of simple walls. Always work out beforehand the exact placing of each block and cut the lengths necessary. Stand them together 'dry' to make sure that you have the correct number. Then build carefully using the level vertically. Accurate vertical building is essential for all types of pillars.

Screen blocks These openwork blocks used either alone or in combination with bricks or other blocks are most popular in gardens today. They are also remarkably easy to use, since they are large and light. The principles are the same as with solid blocks. You will find, though, that it is easiest to use two narrow sausages of mortar on the joining sides of the blocks rather than one thick spread. Then, as the blocks are slid together, a smooth and relatively thin joint is made full of mortar. Be sure to keep any surplus mortar off the faces of the blocks as, if this is allowed to dry, it may mark them permanently.

Retaining walls Retaining walls to hold back soil are tricky to build until you have had a good deal of practice with simpler kinds. The pressures behind them can be immense, especially on heavy wet land. The rules for building such walls are:

1. Never build a retaining wall higher than three feet.

2. Always dig deep and broad foundations, using plenty of concrete in them. These foundations must be much wider than the wall itself.

3. Always give such walls a pronounced backward slope to lean them against the soil that they are supporting.

4. Always provide drain holes through the wall both near the bottom and scattered across its base so that water is never trapped behind it.

5. Build carefully, packing the space behind the wall with stones and gravel.

6. In general it is often stronger, simpler and more attractive to support a bank with a rockery rather than with a wall. The cost of rough rockery stone is less, and the chance of collapse much reduced.

7. Build such supporting rockeries from the base of the slope, digging in there your largest stones. Try to avoid too straight and wall-like an appearance but pack them tightly. Spread soil over this first layer and add a second row stepped back a little. It is not unlike the dry wall building described earlier but using bigger stones – the bigger the better.

8. Another attractive method with sloping ground is to lay heavy paving exactly as described earlier but at an angle up the slope. This must not be done if the angle is steeper than about one in two or it may become unstable. Always use plenty of cement between the joints of the

Below left: to make steps in the garden, dig out foundations and fill the bottom hole with stones.

Below: spread mortar across the treads and up each side of the excavation. Embed stones along the sides first, to stop soil falling in on the treads.

sloping paving but leave 'weeping holes' through the paving at intervals to allow water behind to escape.

Steps in the Garden

No amateur should tackle building steps except after a good deal of practice with simpler stone work. However, in many parts of the garden a flight of stone or block steps can then be a real asset in both appearance and utility. The first thing is to decide on the actual size of the steps. This is worked out by a simple method. For comfortable use the breadth of each step added to twice its height should total 66cm (26in). For example, if a step tread is 30cm (12in) broad its height should be 18cm (7in). A 36cm (14in) broad step should be 15cm (6in) high, and so on.

The actual building combines the skills of paving and wall building. Start at the bottom of the steps and dig out foundations, ramming broken stones into the hole to a depth of at least 10–12.5cm (4–5in). It is the bottom tread which takes the most wear.

Always use mortar under the treads. Spread a layer about 2.5cm (1in) thick across the tread and up the sides of the excavation. Embed stones along the sides first to support the soil and prevent it falling inwards.

Right: having laid the first tread, spread more mortar along the back of it, and in this embed the riser blocks.

Far right: with the first riser complete, spread a second layer of mortar over the tread above it, before laying the slabs. Work up the flight in this way.

Right: finally, squeeze soft mortar into any joint not completely filled.

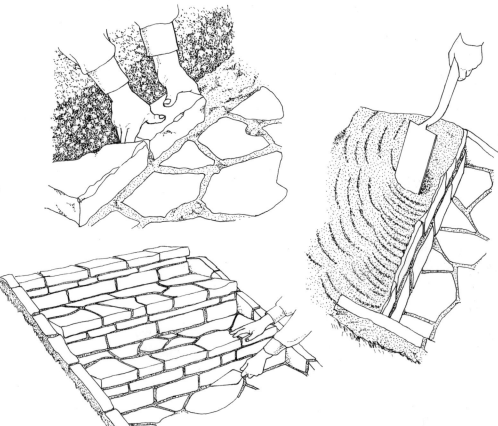

Now lay the treads exactly as for the slabs on mortar paving described earlier. At the back of each tread spread a further layer of mortar in which to embed the riser blocks. These should be square and regular for ease of building. Embed them in the wet mortar and pack behind them smaller pieces of stone (see illustration above).

With the riser complete, the second layer of mortar to support the tread above can now be laid. This tread should project about 2cm ($\frac{3}{4}$in) over the front face of the riser beneath to form a lip.

Continue up the flight and finally squeeze soft mortar into any joint that is not completely filled. Tidy the work up with a brush and remove any traces of spilled cement from the stone or it will mark this permanently.

The strongest steps of all For maximum wear nothing is the equal of concrete for garden steps. They do not look very delicate, but they are safe and strong. Use them wherever a steep or dangerous slope is to be traversed which will have continual wear. You can improve the appearance a little by using cement dye and by leaving the surface rough in texture instead of smoothing it off. Making solid concrete steps is relatively simple if you take care in setting up the shuttering. Always measure, check and adjust this before laying any concrete, for you will not find it easy to alter the finished job.

Make the shuttering with two side planks joined together by cross planks at the position of each step. Support the side planks with posts outside, or the pressure of the wet concrete may force them apart. The cross planks must be vertical and with the upper edge of each one exactly level with the lower edge of the one above it. Note that you leave a gap below each plank at least 5cm (2in) deep so that the concrete when poured in will set into a continuous solid mass.

Make the concrete in the usual way and chop it thoroughly down till it is level with the top of each cross plank. Beat the surface smooth with a straight edge of timber and work rapidly up the flight so that each step is joined to the one beneath whilst the concrete is still wet. Leave the steps to harden for at least ten days before using them or you may find that the sharp edge of the step is broken away by the traffic. The shuttering however can be removed earlier than this and any defects in the cement face trimmed up with a little smooth mortar.

Fences, Screens and Pergolas

No matter what else may differ in fences, pergolas, screens or archways, one thing is common to all and vital for a good job. The posts *must* be strongly held in the ground and resist both strain and rot.

Given strong posts, you can then add horizontal rails to make 'ranch style' fencing, rails and vertical strips to give cottage palings, or overlap planking. You can apply panels of different types, netting in wire or plastic or expanded wooden trellis. When erecting GATES the need for strong posts is even greater.

Posts may be of wood, concrete or, sometimes, steel. Wood rots, steel rusts, concrete survives. If at all possible, use concrete posts, even for an otherwise wooden fence. Even if you use wooden posts above ground you can still bolt these at their bases to short concrete 'mini-posts' that you can buy from builders' merchants.

Unfortunately the higher cost of concrete posts may prevent their use. Still, wood can be preserved to give a reasonably long life and there is even one timber – cedarwood – which is practically rot-proof even when sunk in the soil. All other woods need preservative treatment and the methods are, in order of effectiveness:

1. Commercial pressure impregnation with chemical preservative.
2. Repeated immersion of the posts in a bath of wood preservative.

Never use creosote or ordinary wood preservatives where plants are to be grown near a fence or trained on a trellis or pergola. Use a special horticultural preservative, such as Cuprinol Green, which will not harm the plants.

3. Several coats of brush-applied preservative.

4. Charring the posts' bases black over a slow fire.

The best support method for posts is undoubtedly to embed their bases up to soil level in solid cast concrete. Dig a hole at least 60cm (2ft) deep and put in a 15cm (6in) layer of broken stones. Cover this with concrete mix and push the posts down into it whilst it is still wet. Rapidly work more concrete round and ram this hard. Continue the concrete up the sides of the posts to just above soil level. It is at this point that they rot most readily, so it is best to bring the concrete up about 10cm (4in). Smooth the concrete off so that it slopes away from the post, to prevent water being trapped against the wood. Support the posts until the concrete sets; this takes at least a week, so do not add further parts to the fence, such as rails or panels, until the concrete has become fully hard.

This all takes effort and costs money but is certainly worth it in the long run, especially for important boundary fences, for example, or tall structures such as pergolas. For low fences up to only 1.2m (4ft) tall and not exposed to strong winds, posts set in rammed stone alone will serve, especially in heavy soil. In general, embed these posts to either 45cm (1½ft) or one-third of the total fence height, whichever is greater.

Finally, do protect the *tops* of wooden posts. Water can easily get in to any exposed end grain and cause rot. Caps of wood or tin are good and greatly lengthen the post's life.

GATEPOSTS need special treatment. A garden gate that sags soon becomes difficult to open. To prevent this always embed both gate posts in concrete and make sure that this concrete itself is in one solid block. First dig out a trench 30cm (1ft) wide across the whole width of the gate. At the ends the hole must be 45cm (1½ft) deep to accept the posts but at the centre 25cm (9in) deep is enough. Next, assemble the gate to both its posts including hinges. Hold the gate and posts together with temporary struts nailed across. Now place one or two shovelfuls of concrete at the bottom of the trench ends and lower the posts into place. Support the fence with temporary bracing and then fill up around the posts and across the entire trench with concrete rammed down. Now, simply leave the gate-post foundations to set hard. Do not remove the bracing for at least ten days. Indeed, since concrete becomes stronger and stronger over a period of four weeks it is best to leave the concrete undisturbed, if you can, for this length of time.

Fences Fence posts are always erected in the same way. Variety in fencing comes from the different manner in which wood, metal or plastic can be applied to them. Here is a summary of the main types. (The exact size of planking, spacing and shape can be varied to give an immense range of patterns.)

RANCH STYLE Screw broad, horizontal planks to the faces of the posts, spaced a little apart. This type is very attractive if painted in white.

COTTAGE PALINGS Screw two or three horizontal rails to the posts and then fix vertical, identical planks spaced evenly apart. This type is attractive in white or dark colours as well as the natural wood.

HORIZONTAL OVERLAP Starting at ground level, screw broad planks to the posts, overlapping each one on to the plank beneath. You can get 'feather edge' planks with one thin and one thick edge for this.

VERTICAL OVERLAP Similar to horizontal but the vertical planks are fixed to cross rails behind.

TRELLIS AND NETTING Fix two or three horizontal rails to the posts then apply expanding trellis, or plastic or wire netting.

PANEL FENCING *Method A* Space the post centres exactly to panel length and then screw these to the fronts of the posts so that the panel ends meet each other closely. This is the easier method. Posts can be erected and the concrete allowed to set before the panels are fixed.

Method B Make the gaps between the posts exactly panel length so that these fit between, the posts being visible on completion.

Rustic Pergolas and Archways Work to a prearranged pattern of some pleasing design and avoid complexities. Use 'triangular' designs to give extra rigidity. The top rail and one other longitudinal rail are best kept continuous to give lengthways strength. Treat all sawn surfaces with horticultural wood preservative before fixing the pieces together.

Garden Buildings

Many gardeners buy either a garden shed or a greenhouse, or both. There is of course an enormous range of types, sizes and patterns but all will have certain common requirements regarding the choice and preparation of the site and the erection of the building.

Choosing the Site Soggy, wet ground is useless for building. Any site must be well drained. Quite apart from the discomfort of getting to the shed or working in a soaking wet greenhouse, continuous ground damp will rot timber. Avoid sites in hollows; a gentle slope is ideal. If possible raise any garden buildings slightly above the surrounding soil level on foundations of brick or concrete blocks.

Laying Foundations For best results give your building foundations of solid concrete or pre-cast blocks laid out rather like very narrow paths. Let these rise a little above soil level and simply sit your structure on them. The extra labour will be well worthwhile in the long run. A skilful worker can embed bolts in the soft concrete which will accept the bottom rail of shed or greenhouse but the spacing is critical. An amateur will probably find it easier to borrow a power drill and a masonry bit to cut holes into the solidified concrete later and place in these holes expanding plugs such as Rawlbolts.

Erecting the Building The erection of sheds or greenhouses is usually straightforward enough. The general rules are:

1. Study the plans and parts carefully first. Do not rush into the job. Check the sections and label them clearly, looking out for small but important differences, left or right hand pieces, etc.

2. If possible erect the main parts together temporarily with ropes or wire to make sure that they do fit, that the bolt holes match, and that the parts face the right way, not inwards instead of outwards.

3. Now erect the sides and use the recommended method of fixing down. Do not rely upon the building's weight alone to hold it in place on your foundation. Have help available to manoeuvre the pieces.

4. Check frequently that the sides and ends form a true rectangle and that the parts themselves are accurately rectangular or square. To do this, measure across the diagonals of the frames. Both diagonals will be exactly the same length if the frame is square. If the diagonals are not equal it means that the frame has been warped into a diamond shape.

5. Wear gloves when putting in panes of glass. Do not force these into place. Failure to fit usually means either the wrong piece is being tried, or that the frame has been twisted out of square.

6. If you want electricity installed, do get a professional to do the job. Many amateur installations are potential death traps.

Gardening Calendar

In drawing up a calendar of jobs in the garden that is to stretch for the full twelve months, it is important to realize that its accuracy will vary from year to year. No amount of foresight can take account of the most unpredictable feature of gardening in this country: the weather. Added to this, it must be remembered that the climate, in particular the temperature, varies with the region.

The job of this monthly guide, therefore, is to give an indication of the work that would normally need doing at that time of the year in warmer gardens in the south and extreme western part of the country. Add between two and four weeks to these dates for spring sowings and plantings and subtract two to four weeks for autumn operations. Experience and the advice of other local gardeners is, however, the best guide.

With this in mind, we shall review the gardening year month by month under the headings VEGETABLES, LAWNS, ORNAMENTAL PLANTS, FRUIT and THE GREENHOUSE.

January

Vegetables One of the most important jobs this month is to make sure that hardy vegetables already growing in the garden, such as cabbages and Brussels sprouts, are allowed to grow without being eaten by birds, particularly pigeons. If pigeons are a menace, cover the crops with a net. You do not need an elaborate arrangement; quite cheap plastic nets are readily available in most garden shops.

Stored root vegetables, such as carrots, beetroot and potatoes, will also need attention. Remove any that are beginning to go rotten; if left, this damage will quickly spread to others.

This is a good time to order seed. The sooner you send your order off, the quicker your seeds will arrive. Never leave it until the last minute, as delays in sowing will then be inevitable.

Lawns Make sure that any dead leaves are cleared off regularly. These can smother the grass, turn it yellow and encourage disease.

This is a good time to overhaul the mower and, if necessary, have it sharpened and checked professionally, and to check all other tools.

If you are planning to make a new lawn in the spring, the ground should be dug over as soon as possible to allow it to weather and settle naturally.

Ornamental Plants As with vegetables, this is the time to choose varieties and order your seeds. If you are a newcomer to gardening, you should be careful as some of the plants and varieties you may fancy could require conditions for raising and growing that you will not be able to provide.

Freezing winds can play havoc with many shrubs. Clear polythene sheeting or sacking draped over them during the worst weather may look unattractive, but is preferable to having them damaged or killed.

Fruit So long as you avoid frosty weather, pruning may continue. During prolonged spells of harsh weather, birds, particularly house sparrows and bullfinches, may peck out and feed on the blossom buds. Protect trees and bushes from this by netting the smaller ones and those against walls, and spraying the rest with a proprietary bird repellent.

If you have not done so already, apply a tar-oil winter wash to trees, bushes and canes, if you have had serious trouble with caterpillars, aphids and other pests, to kill their overwintering eggs or the caterpillars or pupae.

The Greenhouse Plan how you are going to use your greenhouse this year and order all the necessary seeds. Give overwintering plants as much light as is available by putting them close to the glass and keep the glass clean at all times to allow maximum light entry.

Ventilate the house whenever possible; fungal diseases thrive in a stagnant atmosphere. The watering of pot plants should be kept to a minimum.

February

Vegetables Be sure to pick up all leaves that drop off cabbages, broccoli and other Brassicas to reduce the risk of slug damage. In addition, prepare slug traps baited with beer or sweetened milk, or use the other methods described on page 36.

Prepare the ground for peas and runner beans by filling trenches with well-rotted farmyard manure, straw or garden compost. Cover this with soil and allow it to settle.

If you want early potatoes, buy the seed tubers now. Stand them in wooden fruit trays, seed boxes, or egg-trays, with their eyes facing upwards, in a cool, well-lit and well-ventilated place so that short and sturdy sprouts develop.

Lawns Earthworms may start to become active again with the approach of spring. During dry weather, the casts should be brushed away. If allowed to remain, they can be the start of a take-over by moss and weeds. Use a potassium permanganate solution or a derris wormkiller.

Top-dressing the lawn with a good compost can be carried out towards the end of the month. This should consist of approximately two parts sifted loam and one part each of sharp sand and lawn peat. See the chapter on LAWNS for rate at which to apply it.

Ornamental Plants In favoured districts, gladioli corms can be planted in a sheltered position towards the end of the month and, so long as the soil is workable, herbaceous plants can be split up and replanted. Only the strong growths towards the outside of the clumps should be used, the worn-out centre being discarded.

Snow should be shaken off trees and shrubs to prevent the branches from being broken by its weight.

Fruit Pruning should finish this month.

If Peach Leaf Curl was a problem last year, be ready to spray the trees with a copper fungicide, before the buds start to swell.

Feed all trees and bushes with fertilizers fairly rich in potash, to encourage fruit production. Gooseberries, particularly, need plenty of potash, which can be supplied by adding dried seaweed manure at the rate of 90g per sq m (3oz per sq yd).

The Greenhouse Be sure that all electrical gadgets and automatic watering systems are in working order, or you may be faced with disasters as soon as the growing season gets under way.

Any potted bulbs that have passed the winter outside in a peat bed should be brought into gentle heat when you notice that growth is progressing nicely.

Where sufficient heat is available, begonia and gloxinia corms can be started into growth by placing them in boxes of seed compost.

For the exhibitor or any gardener who wants a particularly early crop, onions may be sown under glass now for planting out in May. Early varieties of cabbage and cauliflower should also be sown now, if weather conditions permit.

March

Vegetables When the soil is in good condition, the seeds of the following vegetables may be sown outdoors: broad beans, Brussels sprouts, cabbages (summer cabbage, under cloches unless mild), carrots (towards the end of the month, or earlier in frames or under cloches), leeks, lettuces, onions, parships, peas (earlies), spinach (under cloches if cold).

Potatoes (earlies only) and onion sets may now be planted, but only if the soil is beginning to warm up.

Autumn-sown lettuces that have spent the winter in a greenhouse or cold frame can be transplanted into the open garden.

Lawns Mowing can start this month. Set the blades high, at about 2.5cm (1in) above the lawn surface. Cutting too short this early in the year may damage the grass.

Roll the lawn very lightly to settle it after winter frosts. Do this using the lawn-mower with the blades tilted up out of the way.

If the weather is milder by the end of the month, grass seed can be sown to make a new lawn; if you are planning for autumn sowing instead, the site should be dug thoroughly and it is not too early to start now, for a really fine lawn.

Ornamental Plants This is the main month for sowing hardy annuals outdoors. The area should be marked off into sections for the different plants and, for best results, each group should be arranged in bold drifts.

Any winter-flowering shrubs that have finished blooming should be pruned now to ensure the maximum period of growth before they flower again next winter.

The main pruning job, though, will be on the roses; read the section on pruning in the ROSES chapter (pages 94–95).

The Greenhouse The following seeds of half-hardy flowers may be sown in seed-trays under glass for planting out in late May once the risk of frosts is over: *Ageratum*, *Alyssum*, *Antirrhinum*, Asters, Begonias, Dahlias (from seed), *Helichrysum*, Lobelias, French and African Marigolds, *Mesembryanthemum*, *Nemesia*, Petunias, Salvias, Stocks and Zinnias.

Likewise, you can sow the following vegetables, although some varieties of those marked (G) will have to be grown under glass throughout as they are too tender to be transplanted outdoors: aubergines (G), calabrese, celery, cucumbers (G), French beans, some herbs, marrows (including courgettes), peppers (G), sweet corn and tomatoes (G).

Melons can also be sown now under glass; most will need to remain protected.

Except for the beans, cucumbers, marrows, melons and sweet corn which can be sown singly in pots or peat pots, all the other seeds should be sown thinly in pots or seed trays.

Pot plants, both here and in the house, can now be watered and fed more frequently and any that require it should be moved into larger pots.

April

Vegetables The following may be sown outdoors. Some of them will have appeared in the March list, but a second mention here indicates that another sowing can be made to give a succession of crops: Broad Beans, Beetroot, Brussels Sprouts, Cabbage (Autumn and Winter Cabbage), Carrots, Kale, Leeks, Lettuces, Onions, Peas, Parsnips, Radishes, Savoys, Spinach, Sprouting Broccoli and Turnips.

Once Brassicas such as winter cabbage and Brussels sprouts have finished cropping and begun to go to seed, they should be pulled up and added to the compost heap, as long as they are not infected with pests or diseases. Dig the ground they occupied in readiness for other vegetables.

When peas are 10–15cm (4–6in) high they should be supported. If this is left too late, it will be a difficult job and the crop may well be spoiled.

Protect potato haulms (leaves) with cloches, dry straw or bracken, to prevent frost damage.

Lawns As the frequency of mowing increases, the height of cut should be reduced a little at a time. Reseed any bare patches.

The lawn can also have its first feed of the year now. Choose a lawn fertilizer high in nitrogen.

A new lawn can be sown as soon as the weather has settled and the soil is drying out nicely. See the chapter on LAWNS, page 150, for details of different mixtures and amounts of seeds to use.

Leatherjackets and the fungal disease *Fusarium* may create problems this month. Prevention and control are described on page 164.

Ornamental Plants Once the hardy annuals sown last month are large enough to handle, they should be singled out to the correct distances (which you will find on the back of the seed packet). There is always a temptation to leave them closer but this will only lead to overcrowding and a poor performance.

Prune flowering shrubs once they have finished blooming. This is also a good month for planting evergreens and conifers; they will have started growing by now and the check to their development will be minimal.

Control aphids as early as possible, by hand-picking or spraying with water or a 'safe' pesticide (described on page 35) to prevent large numbers building up.

Do not neglect bulbs that have flowered; over the next few weeks they will still be growing and storing up energy for next year. A light dressing of a fertilizer such as bonemeal, watered in, will work wonders.

Fruit Keep a look-out for aphids and other pests. You may not expect frost to be a danger now, but sunny days are often followed by still, clear nights, during which frost can be surprisingly severe for the time of year. Frost will damage fruit coming into blossom. Small trees and bushes can be protected quite adequately by covering them with an old sheet, some sacking or clear polythene sheeting.

The Greenhouse As soon as any seedlings are large enough to handle, they should be pricked out into boxes of potting compost. Two dozen to a standard seed tray is a convenient number as they fit in neatly as four rows of six plants each, which still leaves them with plenty of room.

Seed of runner beans and marrows (including courgettes) may now be sown singly in pots for planting out after the frosts.

Open ventilators in warm weather during the middle part of the day, but close them again by late afternoon.

May

Vegetables If you could not raise them in a greenhouse, runner beans and sweet corn can be sown outdoors and, towards the end of the month, marrows (including courgettes) and ridge cucumbers too.

Canes or netting for the runner beans can be put up at the same time as sowing to save work later on and avoid damaging the roots of the plants.

Start earthing up potatoes when the haulms are 10cm (4in) high; this will help produce heavier crops, and prevents the tubers turning green and poisonous on exposure to light.

Carrots, lettuces, onions and parsnips sown in March should be thinned to the correct distance, and Brussels sprouts, summer and autumn cabbages and savoys can be planted in their final positions.

Sow more lettuces, radishes and peas, also maincrop and Australian varieties of cauliflower and winter cabbages.

Lawns The mower blades can be lowered to the final desired height now but, except on the finest lawns, this should not be less than 1.9cm ($\frac{3}{4}$in).

Be ready to water recently-sown lawns and continue preparations for September sowing.

Conditions will be ideal this month for killing any lawn weeds, as described in LAWNS, page 150.

Ornamental Plants Once the spring bedding plants are nearly over they should be pulled up and the ground thoroughly dug and prepared for the summer ones. Any tulips or other bulbs that were with them should be lifted, dried off and stored ready for planting out again in the autumn.

The ground for dahlias should be well enriched with well-rotted farmyard manure or garden compost. The sprouted tubers can be planted towards the end of the month, remembering to put in the supporting stake at the same time.

Window boxes, tubs and hanging baskets can now be planted up.

Stakes or other supports for tall herbaceous plants should be put in place whilst the shoots are still small. Twiggy pea sticks are ideal for this as they will be unobtrusive once the plants have grown their full height.

Sow wallflowers and other biennials for flowering next year, and examine roses for black spot.

Fruit Keep a sharp watch for the following pests and diseases.

Top fruit: greenfly, caterpillars, sawfly and mildew (apples).

Bush fruit: greenfly, caterpillars, capsids, big bud mite (blackcurrants) and mildew (gooseberries).

Strawberries: greenfly, grey mould (botrytis).

Take precautions against night frosts; fruit is at its most vulnerable when in blossom.

The Greenhouse This is the time to harden off half-hardy plants for planting outside. This can be done by moving them outside every morning and bringing them in at night. By the end of the month, they should be left outside the whole time except when a frost is expected. To save all this work, make yourself a cold frame outside, put all the pots and boxes in it and give them progressively less protection by opening the light wider, finally removing it altogether.

Greenhouse tomatoes and cucumbers should be in their final positions by now.

Give as much ventilation as possible on sunny days; the temperature can rise alarmingly quickly. It is also a good idea to be ready to provide some form of shading.

June

Vegetables The half-hardy vegetables sown in the greenhouse in March and April can safely be planted out now after being hardened off as described under THE GREENHOUSE for May. These include French beans, calabrese, cauliflowers, various herbs, peppers, tomatoes and sweet corn. The first week of the month is also a good time to buy seedlings of any of these for planting directly into their final positions. Leeks and other plants still in the seedling rows should also be planted out as soon as they are ready.

Before planting out any vegetables, though, the soil must be properly prepared and fed if necessary. Water the soil or planting hole if it is at all dry just before planting, and water the plants well after planting.

Sow more lettuces, radishes and peas but try to plan a gap in the cropping if you intend to be away on holiday later on.

Learn to distinguish between harmful and beneficial insects in the garden and encourage and protect the latter, so that dealing with the former is less of a problem.

Lawns This is still a good time for controlling weeds if you did not manage to do the job in May. A problem this month is the appearance of grass flower stalks, sometimes called 'soldiers' or 'bents'. Regular mowing should keep them to a minimum but, if they have become too numerous, a side-wheel or a rotary mower will get rid of them.

Raise the height of cut during periods of drought, because the grass is under enough stress then without adding to it. Water an established lawn only in prolonged dry weather (though new lawns may need more watering). Do so in the cool of the evening, applying plenty of water with a sprinkler if possible, and spike the lawn beforehand to help the water penetrate.

Ornamental Plants As soon as you can, plant out all the hardened-off, greenhouse-raised, half-hardy annuals. They should be in flower by now and will give an instant display. Plant them at the closest recommended spacing, remembering however that they will grow further, and give them a really thorough soaking once they are in place. Make sure that they have plenty of water in their first two or three weeks.

Any plants that have finished flowering should have the dead flower heads removed so that they do not set seed and weaken the plant. This applies particularly to roses. Keep hoeing amongst hardy annuals to kill any weeds.

Fruit Strawberries will need attention this month, apart from routine pest and disease control. Straw should be spread between the rows and beneath the plants to keep the fruit off the ground. This will prevent them from being splashed with mud and will reduce the risk of grey mould (botrytis). Runners should be removed.

Spray apples with derris against codling moth this month to avoid maggoty fruit, if this is a problem in your area. Spray once at the beginning of the month, again two weeks later, and finally at the end of the month.

The Greenhouse Once tomato fruits start to form, the plants should be fed regularly with one of the proprietary liquid tomato fertilizers. These are rich in potash to encourage flowering and fruiting. To make sure that the flowers set fruit, tap the plants gently at least once a day; a moist atmosphere will also help, so spray with water if the air is markedly dry.

Give as much ventilation as possible. If necessary, shade the glass.

July

Vegetables The final sowings of peas should be made early in the month if they are to mature properly.

In less favoured districts, spring cabbages for next year can be sown towards the end of this month. This will allow them plenty of time to build up strength before the winter. Continue to sow lettuces and radishes.

Pea and bean plants should not be kept short of moisture in dry weather, and any runner beans coming into flower will benefit from spraying with a fine mist of water when it is hot and dry, directed both above and below the leaves; this will help the flowers to be pollinated. Maincrop potatoes should have their final earthing-up.

Lawns Regular mowing should be done at least once a week; remember to raise the height of cut a fraction during periods of drought.

Try to kill all lawn weeds before the end of the month. Once they are in flower, they are far harder to control and will, of course, spread seed.

Any lawn food applied should be watered in well to avoid the possibility of scorch and to carry it down to the roots.

Ornamental Plants The first flush of roses will be over during July. Be sure to remove all dead heads to encourage further blooms. This is also another time to feed roses so that the second flush of flowers is good.

If you want to grow herbaceous perennials from seed, this is a good time to sow most of them.

So long as the lawn has not been treated with a weedkiller, the mowings will make a good mulch amongst shrubs, helping to retain moisture, suppress weeds and keep soil temperature more constant. Never apply a mulch to dry soil.

Fruit Mature plum trees should be pruned now. Bear in mind that they are very susceptible to silver leaf disease, caused by a fungus which releases its spores during the winter. These enter through pruning cuts and other wounds, so cut cleanly and paint all cuts more than 2.5cm (1in) in diameter with wound-sealing paint.

Once strawberries have finished fruiting, cut off the leaves with shears and rake them up carefully along with the straw that you placed beneath the fruit last month. Burn the rakings immediately to reduce the risk of diseases and pests.

The Greenhouse Ventilate at all times, even if it is cool and cloudy. A stagnant atmosphere in the greenhouse encourages diseases.

Watering should be attended to daily and liquid feeding about once a week for many plants.

Winter-flowering stocks for the house can be sown now; 'Beauty of Nice' is one of the best varieties.

August

Vegetables This month is the time for final sowings of lettuces and radishes to mature this year. Late in the month, sow spring lettuce in a sheltered position.

White Lisbon onions may also be sown for a spring harvest, along with the Japanese varieties of bulb onions. In milder southern gardens, sow spring cabbages, too, at the beginning of the month.

Pick all peas and beans when they are still young. They taste much better and the plants will continue cropping for a longer time.

Lift onions gently with a fork and if it is dry, lay the bulbs on soil or on sacking to ripen. If it is wet, raise them on a platform of wire netting, moving it into the shed if the wet weather persists. Do not store onions until they are thoroughly dry.

Lawns Make the final preparations for a new lawn and sow towards the end of the month. Once sown, never allow the new lawn to dry out.

Continue regular mowing and remember to vary the direction of cutting to avoid damaging the grass. Give the last summer feed at the end of the month.

Ornamental Plants Before it is too late, make a note of any plants you would like to move. Once they have died down, you will forget where and what they were.

This is the month for ordering spring-flowering bulbs. Send your orders in early to avoid disappointment. In addition, it is the best month for planting daffodils and narcissi.

Pay some attention to plants trained up walls and fences. They will have made a lot of growth by now and this should all be tied in with soft fillis string or raffia to prevent wind damage. Prune and tie in the new shoots of rambler roses after they have flowered.

Take cuttings of bedding geraniums (pelargoniums). Put them into a seed or cutting compost and avoid overwatering.

Fruit Once raspberries and loganberries have fruited, the old canes should be cut down to the ground and the new ones tied into position. Immediately after doing so, remove and burn the old canes to lessen the risk of disease.

If you can buy certified disease-free plants, this is the time to plant new rows of summer-fruiting strawberries. They should give a good crop next summer.

The Greenhouse Arrange for the watering to be done if you are on holiday. Although bulbs prepared for Christmas flowering may not be available yet, others can be planted in pots and bowls. Put them outdoors in the coolest place you can find and cover them with moist peat.

Pinch out the tops of tomato plants now so that all the plants' resources go into developing and ripening the existing fruit.

Single-flowered chrysanthemums should be disbudded to leave just the main flower bud on each stem. Remove any shading towards the end of the month, unless it is exceptionally hot and sunny.

September

Vegetables Winter lettuces, such as Arctic King, should be sown in the warmest position possible or where they can be protected with cloches. Turnips for winter use can also be sown now.

Lift maincrop potatoes, and store in hessian or paper bags (not plastic ones) or straw-lined boxes in a frost-free shed, or in a clamp outdoors, as described on page 276. You can start planting out spring cabbages as soon as they have four or five leaves; in colder, northern gardens it may be better to leave the young plants in the seedbed throughout winter, transplanting them in early spring.

As soon as crops have finished, remove all plant remains and dig the ground. This will discourage slugs. Hand-pick any Cabbage White caterpillars you see, before they can do any damage.

Lawns New lawns can still be sown early in the month. If you do not wish to grow your lawn from seed, turf may be laid for new lawns from now until April except during severe winter weather.

Mowing will not be needed quite so often now and you should start raising the height of cut to strengthen the grass.

Ornamental Plants All spring-flowering bulbs should be planted before the end of the month to give them time to become established.

Several hardy annuals can be sown in September; they will give good ground cover for the winter and will flower a lot earlier next year than the spring-sown ones. Remove faded flower heads from herbaceous plants.

This is a good month for planting evergreen shrubs and conifers; they will have time to settle in before the winter. Always give them plenty of water after planting.

Fruit Beware of September gales and protect fruit trees if necessary. Many varieties of apple and pear will need picking; some varieties of apples and most of pears should be used soon after harvesting, but many apples can be stored for a long time.

Order all fruit trees, bushes and canes as early as possible, so that you are at the top of the list when it comes to sending them out. Much sought-after varieties of some fruit are often sold out early.

Look out for wasps when picking fruit. Jam pots half-filled with watery jam and sealed with paper with a hole in it make good traps if placed near the trees.

The Greenhouse Give plenty of air still. This is the time that grey mould (botrytis) and tomato leaf mould can be most troublesome.

Pot up prepared bulbs for Christmas flowering. Keep the glass spotlessly clean, to make the best use of the failing sunlight. Remove any shading that remains, for the same reason.

October

Vegetables Lift and store beetroots and carrots. These need to be kept moist to prevent them from shrivelling, so damp peat or sand are the best materials to put them in.

The winter lettuce sown last month should be thinned to reduce the risk of disease. Earth up leeks to produce a long, white, blanched stem.

Autumn cauliflowers can be protected from frost by breaking off a leaf and placing it over the 'curd', or head.

Onions must be stored in a dry, airy, frost-proof place.

Lawns This is the main time for autumn maintenance. The lawn should be briskly raked twice, the second time at right angles to the first, and mowed after each raking. This will remove all stringy and dead growth and reduce clover. Follow this by a thorough spiking to improve drainage and correct compaction.

Apply a good autumn lawn food; you can finish off with a top dressing as described under February.

Take action against leatherjackets if small brown patches appear and starlings are paying particular attention to the lawn (see page 164).

Ornamental Plants The summer bedding plants will be dying off by now. Pull them up and dig the beds, thoroughly incorporating well-rotted farmyard manure or garden compost. Tread it down and set out plants such as wallflowers, forget-me-nots and Darwin tulips. These will make a fine show next spring.

Between now and November is the best time to cut down herbaceous perennials and split up the clumps for replanting. Do this every three years or so to keep them young and strong.

Late-flowering pot-grown chrysanthemums should be brought under cover before they are caught by the frost.

Fruit Most of the later varieties of apples and pears should be picked now before the birds discover them. Always lift the fruit off gently; never drag it away with a piece of twig. Handle it carefully at all times; bruises and wounds quickly rot in store.

Each fruit should then be wrapped in newspaper or in special oiled wraps and placed in slatted boxes for storage in a cool but frost-free shed. Stored in this way, varieties such as 'Winston' and 'Bramley's Seedling' will keep in good condition until April or even May.

The Greenhouse Tomatoes will need attention now. All remaining fruit should be picked off; the small green ones can be used to make chutney. The rest will usually ripen quite well if placed in a warm, dark place indoors.

If the greenhouse can be cleared of all plants you want to keep, it is a good plan to burn a sulphur candle in it before removing the spent tomato plants. This will kill all pests, diseases and weeds.

November

Vegetables Tall plants, such as Brussels sprouts and purple-sprouting broccoli, should be earthed up around the base of the stem to encourage new roots and to carry water away from the neck. They should also be tied to canes to prevent them from being blown about.

Cut down and put on the compost heap all vegetables that have been killed by the frost, as long as they are pest and disease-free.

A sowing can be made early in the month of Aquadulce-type broad beans and a round-seeded variety of pea, such as 'Feltham First'. Although they are often only marginally earlier than spring-sown ones, they stand up to early summer droughts much better.

Dig any vacant land and leave it to stand rough over the winter. The frost and rain will improve the structure, particularly of clay soils. Lime can also be added now, but must not be added at the same time as manure (see page 24).

Lawns Broken edges should be repaired. Cut out the damaged section and turn it round so that the clean cut forms the new edge. A small piece of turf will make good the damage. The laying of a new lawn from turf can continue providing the weather is not very wet or frosty.

Fallen leaves will damage the lawn if allowed to remain on it, so brush them off regularly. Try to avoid walking on a frosty lawn; you will crush the grass, which may remain in poor condition for some weeks.

Ornamental Plants This is a good month for planting roses and other deciduous trees and shrubs, but good ground preparation is essential; they are going to be there for a long time.

Established roses may need to be cut back in readiness for the winter; by shortening any extra-long stems, they will not be rocked about nearly so much. Proper pruning must wait until March.

Lift, dry off and store dahlias and gladioli in a frost-free but cool place.

Fruit This is one of the best times to plant tree, bush and cane fruits. If stakes are required for support, put these in once the hole is dug but before you plant the tree; this avoids root damage.

Start pruning as soon as the leaves have fallen; make sure you know exactly what you should do before you pick up the secateurs.

The Greenhouse A good way to cut down heat loss is to line the greenhouse with polythene. On particularly cold nights, sheets of newspaper placed over the plants will give added protection.

Never overwater. It can rot the roots and lead to diseases.

December

Vegetables Winter cauliflowers can become discoloured if the sun strikes the heads when they are still frozen. Prevent this by gently lifting them with a fork and leaning them over to face North.

Make sure that rats and mice cannot get at stored root vegetables. Small quantities can go on a shelf and larger amounts should be covered with small mesh wire netting.

Continue digging the vegetable plot as long as it is not wet or frozen.

Lawns Make a note of where water lies on the lawn following heavy rain so that the areas can later be spiked or built up.

You may still turf a new lawn whenever the soil is in good condition.

If overacidity is indicated by the presence of the weed Sheep's Sorrel and certain species of moss, dress the lawn with ground chalk.

Brush off dead leaves and other debris regularly.

Ornamental Plants Many deciduous trees and shrubs can still be planted during suitable weather.

Re-firm any plants that have been loosened by wind or frost. A puddle collecting in a hollow at the base of the stem can lead to collar rot – an additional reason for re-firming. Check stakes and ties.

Tidy up the herbaceous beds or borders. Allowing dead or dying plants to remain in the soil will simply encourage slugs, snails and other pests as well as helping to harbour diseases.

Fruit Stone fruit (plums, peaches, nectarines, apricots and cherries) should be given a tar-oil winter wash this month if aphids, scale insects, or other insect pests were a serious problem the previous summer. In a mild year, stone fruit can start growing very early in the year, when spraying would harm them. Bush and cane fruits may be similarly treated; but only if necessary, as the wash destroys many predators of the pests, too.

Continue pruning but avoid doing so during frosty weather as the wounds can be damaged.

At the same time, remove any 'suckers' of plums or raspberries that have grown from the roots. These should be dug away and pulled out and not simply cut off or new suckers will soon grow up (see ROSES, page 95).

The Greenhouse The end of the year brings a good opportunity to have a really thorough clean-up. Remove all rubbish and scrub down the inside of the house with a sterilizing solution such as Jeyes Fluid, to kill pests and diseases.

Give ventilation whenever possible to reduce the risk of diseases. Keep all cuttings only as moist as they need to be to avoid wilting.

Glossary

Acid: see the chapter on SOIL, page 17.
Adventitious Aerial roots that arise from stems.
Alkaline: see the chapter on SOIL, page 17.
Alpines Plants native to high altitudes and others grown in the rock garden.
Annual A plant that grows, flowers and sets seed in one growing season, and then dies.
Aquatic A plant with roots submerged in water producing leaves and flowers in or on the water.
Axil The angle between the leaf or leaf stalk and the stem from which it arises.
Beard The fleshy hairs on the upper surface of the FALLS of some iris flowers.
Bedding An association of hardy or tender flowering and/or foliage plants.
Berry: see FRUIT.
Biennial A plant that grows one year, flowers and sets seed the next, and then dies.
Blindness Death of the growing point or flower buds.
Blanching Growing stems or leaves of vegetables in darkness to make them white and improve their flavour and tenderness.

Bleeding Sap oozing from a cut surface.
Bolting The premature development of flowers.
Bottom heat Heat applied to plants from below; used to forward crops and speed the rooting of cuttings.
Bracts Modified leaves sometimes resembling petals.
Break An axillary bud starting into growth.
Bud An embryo shoot, flower or flower-cluster.
Budding: see ROSES, page 77.
Bulb A plant storage organ consisting of a swollen underground bud surrounded by fleshy scales (enlarged leaf bases) which store food during a resting period.
Bulbil Small bulb-like structures formed in the leaf axils of some plants, such as the Tiger Lily.
Bush tree Height 2–3m (7–10ft), width 2–3m (7–10ft), trunk less than 1m (2–3ft).
Calcifuge Plants that hate lime and flourish only in acid soil.
Callus Tissues produced by the plant to protect wounds.
Canes Stems that are hollow or pithy.
Catch crop Quick-maturing crops grown and harvested on a plot reserved for a later

main crop.
Catkin Unisexual flowers without petals, often pendulous.
Chimaera: see MUTANT.
Chlorophyll The green colouring matter in plants which enables them to manufacture their own food from water, carbon dioxide and sunlight energy.
Chlorosis A physiological disorder in which chlorophyll production in the leaves is inhibited, so that they turn yellow.
Clamp Winter store for root crops.
Cloche Glass or plastic structures used for crop protection.
Compost 1. Mixtures of loam, sand, peat or leafmould for plants grown in containers – these are seed or potting composts.
2. Vegetable matter allowed to rot down with the help of a nitrogen-containing activator to form a substance rich in plant-food and humus that can be used as a substitute for animal manure. Always referred to as 'garden compost' in this book.
Conifer Primitive tree producing its seeds within protective cones.
Cordon Trees kept to a single stem and grown at an angle of about 40

degrees to the ground.
Corm Stem base swollen with food reserves producing a bud at its apex.
Corolla: see PETALS.
Corona In daffodils, the circular outgrowth of the petals (also known as the crown, trumpet or cup).
Cotyledons Seed leaves, which appear before the true, 'adult' leaves.
Crocks Broken pieces of pot placed at the base of plant pots or trays to ensure good drainage.
Crown This word has a number of meanings in horticulture:
1. The basal part of a herbaceous perennial from which the shoots grow (e.g. in chrysanthemum, asparagus or rhubarb).
2. It is often used in a looser sense to refer to the whole rootstock, as in rhubarb or asparagus.
Cultivar Cultivated varieties of plants produced by plant breeders.
Curd White immature flower buds forming the head of a cauliflower.
Cutting: see the chapter on PROPAGATION, page

Damping off The collective name for a group of fungus diseases that attack seedlings, causing them to rot near soil level and topple over.

Damping down Soaking the floor and staging in a greenhouse with water to create a humid growing atmosphere.

Dead-heading Removing dead flowers (see ROSES, page 77).

Deciduous Plants that lose their leaves in autumn.

Dibber or Dibble A tool with a blunt point used for making planting holes when transplanting seedlings or cuttings.

Dicotyledon Plant having seedlings with two seed-leaves, or cotyledons.

Dormancy Period of rest, usually in winter.

Double or semi-double Flowers with more than the usual number of petals for the species.

Dot plant Plants conspicuously different used to break the monotony of bedding schemes.

Drawn Describing spindly growth induced by overcrowding.

Drill Straight furrow drawn in the soil for seed sowing.

Dwarf pyramid Fruit tree 1–2m (3–6ft) across and 2–3m (6–9ft) tall.

Earthing up Drawing soil up around plant stems to exclude light, as with celery or potatoes, or to prevent winds dislodging tall-growing plants.

Espalier Fruit tree grown flat, often against a wall, with branches trained horizontally in pairs in opposite directions.

Etiolated Describing spindly, pale growth made by plants when light is withheld.

Evergreen Plant that retains its leaves throughout winter.

Eye 1. Bud.
2. The centre of a flower when it contrasts with the colour of the petals.

F₁ Hybrid Plants produced by crossing two varieties or two pure-bred selections of one kind of plant; they are the first generation of such a cross. The symbol 'F₁' stands for 'first filial'. F₁ hybrids usually produce larger, more vigorous and healthier plants, or improved crops. They do not breed true. Producing F₁ hybrids is a costly process, so seed of these plants is more expensive than that of ordinary varieties.

Fan Fruit tree trained against a wall, with branches radiating in a fan-shaped pattern from the central stem.

Falls The three pendulous outer petals of an iris flower.

Fastigiate Erect, columnar habit of growth.

Feathers 1. Short shoots growing out of the main stem of young fruit trees, or 'MAIDENS'; these are described as 'well-feathered' if they have many such growths.
2. The term feathered is used to describe the markings on some kinds of tulip.

Fertilization Union of the male pollen-grain nucleus with the female embryo in the ovule to produce a seed capable of growing into a new plant.

Fertilizers: see the chapter on manures and fertilizers, PLANT FOOD, page 24.

Flore-pleno: the same as DOUBLE OR SEMI-DOUBLE, in referring to flowers.

Floret Individual flowers that together constitutes a flower-head, as of daisies or chrysanthemums.

Flower That part of the plant adapted for sexual reproduction and seed production.

Forcing Hastening the growth of plants by the use of heat.

Friable Soil in a good physical state for growing plants – crumbly, neither too moist nor too dry, and easily cultivated.

Fruit Structures in or on which seed is developed.

Fumigate To control pests or diseases by means of poisonous smoke or fumes; usually used in a tightly-closed greenhouse.

Fungicide Chemical for controlling fungus diseases of plants.

Germination Process in which a seed breaks into life, thrusting a tiny root downwards into the soil and a shoot upwards through it into the air.

Glaucous Grey-blue; used to describe leaves or stems of some plants.

Grafting The union of a cultivated variety (the 'scion') onto a more vigorous root (the 'stock' or 'rootstock'). See also the chapter on PROPAGATION, page 40.

Half-hardy Plants that will not survive the average British winter.

Half standard Trees grown on a bare stem about 1.4m (4½ft) high.

Hardening off Acclimatizing plants raised under glass to cooler conditions before planting them out in the open.

Hardy Any plant that will flourish outdoors in Britain.

Haulm The unproductive stems and leaves of some vegetable crops, such as potatoes, peas and‘ beans.

Heel: see the chapter on PROPAGATION, page 40.

Hep or hip Fruits of a rose.

Herbaceous: see the chapter on HERBACEOUS PERENNIALS, page 132.

Herbicide Chemicals used for weed control.

Hoary Describing leaves or stems densely covered with hair.

Hormones Chemical messengers that control growth and other processes in plants; similar substances are now produced synthetically and are used for several purposes, such as assisting the rooting of cuttings, killing broad-leaved weeds and encouraging the setting of fruit.

Hose in hose One flower enclosing another.

Humus Final stage in the decomposition of animal or vegetable matter. See also the chapters on SOIL and PLANT FOOD, pages 17 and 24.

Incurved Flowers with incurving petals.

Inflorescence That part of the plant producing flowers.

Inorganic Not derived from animal or vegetable sources.

Insecticide Chemicals used for control of insect pests.

Intercrop Quick-maturing crops grown between others that are slower-growing, e.g. rows of lettuces between rows of cabbages.

Internode The length of stem between two leaf joints or nodes.

Joint (node) In most plants, the point where the leaf joins the stem.

John Innes A banker whose legacy was used to found a horticultural research institute at which the first standardized composts were named in his honour. These John Innes composts are often referred to simply by the abbreviation ‘JI’. JIP1, JIP2 and JIP3 are abbreviations used to describe the different types of potting compost.

Juvenile Describing the leaves of some trees when young, having a different shape from the mature leaves.

Layer: see the chapter on PROPAGATION, page 40.

Leaching Loss of nutrients from the soil when they are washed away by rain.

Leader(s) The most prominent shoot(s): the leading or terminal shoot at the end of a branch.

Leafmould Brown, flaky substance rich in humus and plant foods formed by the decomposition of leaves.

Lime White calcium-containing compound which is capable of reducing soil acidity.

Loam Soil which is an ideal blend of clay, sand, silt and humus.

Maiden Fruit tree with one season’s growth after grafting.

Manures: see the chapter on MANURES AND FERTILIZERS, page 24.

Monocotyledon Plants whose seedlings have only one seed leaf.

Mulch Organic matter placed in a layer around plants.

Mutant Shoots or plants that arise spontaneously with a different habit of growth.

Naturalizing: see WILD GARDEN.

Neutral Soil midway between acid and alkaline (pH 7).

Node: see JOINT.

Offset A young plant produced naturally on a short lateral stem, as in houseleeks, or from many types of bulbs; these provide a means of propagation in many cases, producing plants identical to the parent.

Organic Substances derived from or belonging to the animal or vegetable kingdoms.

Oxygenating Used to describe plants liberating oxygen from leaves growing under water.

Pan 1. Saucer-like container for seed germination.
2. Layer of compacted lower soil.
3. Crust on the soil surface after rain.

Peat Partly decomposed organic matter.

Perennial: see the chapter on HERBACEOUS PERENNIALS, page 132.

Petals Modified leaves protecting the sexual organs of the flower and attracting pollinating insects.

pH Scale used to indicate degrees of soil acidity (see chapter on SOIL AND COMPOSTS, page 17).

Pinching out The removal of the growing point. Also known as STOPPING.

Plunge To sink plants

in containers in beds of sand or peat to conserve moisture.

Pollen Male cells released from the stamens in the flower.

Pollination Transfer of pollen from the stamens to the female stigma which contains the ovule in the ovary (see FERTILIZATION).

Potting 1. 'Potting-up' is placing a plant in a pot of compost.
2. 'Potting-on' is moving a plant from a smaller pot into a larger one.
3. 'Repotting' is using the same pot but replacing spent compost with fresh.

Pricking out Moving seedlings into larger containers.

Pruning Removing dead or overgrown shoots.

Remontant Repeat-flowering as in some roses; repeat-fruiting, as in some strawberries: also known as 'perpetual'.

Rhizome Creeping, thickened, underground stem.

Rogue: see MUTANT.

Rootstock: see GRAFTING and the chapter on HARDY HERBACEOUS PERENNIALS, page 132.

Runner Elongated, prostrate stem; also known as a stolon.

Produced by many plants, such as strawberries.

Scion: see GRAFTING. and the chapter on PROPAGATION, page 40.

Seedling 1. Any plant, regardless of age, raised from seed.
2. Small plants soon after germination.

Self-coloured Flowers of a single colour.

Self-fertile Plants that set seed with their own pollen.

Self-sterile Plants that will not set seed with their own pollen.

Sphagnum Kind of moss found in bogs; a constituent of one type of good-quality peat.

Specimen Any plant, but usually a tree or shrub, grown so that it can be viewed on its own from all angles.

Spit Term used in digging to refer to a spade's depth of soil, between 25 and 30cm (10–12in) deep.

Sport: same as MUTANT.

Spur 1. Short woody shoot.
2. Tubular outgrowth from sepals or petals which produces nectar, as in columbines, delphiniums and violets.

Stamen Male pollen-bearing organ.

Standard 1. Tree grown on a bare stem about 2m (6ft) high.

2. The uppermost petal of sweet-pea flowers and other plants of the pea family.
3. One of the three erect inner petals in an iris flower.

Sterile Describing plants failing to set seed.

Stigma Top of the pistil, the female organ of the flower.

Stock: same as ROOTSTOCK; see under GRAFTING.

Stolon: see RUNNER.

Stool Persistent woody rootstock which produces shoots used for propagation by taking cuttings, as in chrysanthemums.

Stopping: see PINCHING.

Strain A selected race of plants.

Stratification Mixing fleshy fruits with sand and exposing them to cold to break their dormancy prior to seed sowing and so speed up germination.

Succulent Plants that have developed swollen, fleshy leaves or stems, which store water, as an adaptation to living in very dry conditions, e.g. cacti, houseleeks and stonecrops.

Sucker Underground shoot originating from a root.

Synonym Redundant name for a plant; in

this book prefaced by the sign =, e.g. *Filipendula ulmaria* (= *Spiraea ulmaria*).

Tender Used to describe any plant liable to frost damage.

Tendrils Modified leaves or stems enabling plants to cling, as on peas.

Tilth Soil with a fine, crumbly structure.

Top dressing Surface application of fertilizer or manure.

Transpiration Loss of water vapour through the leaves.

Transplanting Moving plants, usually to give them more room.

Truss Cluster of flowers or fruit.

Tuber Thickened, fleshy root or underground stem, which serves as a storage organ as of dahlias (root tubers) and potatoes (stem tubers).

Type The true species, as opposed to the naturally arising or cultivated varieties.

Variegated Patterned with a contrasting colour.

Vernalization Treatment of seed to break dormancy and assist germination.

Wild garden Planting informally; simulating nature. Plants so grown are said to be 'naturalized'.

Index

Acknowledgements

The publishers would like to thank the following individuals and organizations for their kind permission to reproduce the photographs in this book:

A–Z Collection: 290 above, 290 below, (Brian Furner), 255 above left, 255 above right, 255 below left, 255 below right, 292 above left, 292 above right, 292 below left, 292 below right; Bernard Alfieri Photo Library: 250 above left; Rex Bamber: 254 below; Pat Brindley: 250–1 above, 251 above right; Peter Coates: half-title, introduction 6–7; Valerie Finnis: 44, 45, 46, 47, 99, 100, 102, 104, 159, 194, 200; The Iris Hardwick Photographic Library: 294 below; House Beautiful: 43; George E. Hyde: 291; D.F. Merrett: 197; John Rigby: 256 below right, end papers; Harry Smith Horticultural Photographic Collection: contents 4–5, 8, 41, 42, 97, 103, 153, 154, 155, 156, 157, 158, 160, 193, 195, 196, 198, 199, 348 below, 348–9 above, 349 above, 349 below (R.H.M. Robinson), 249 above left, 249 above right, 249 below, 250 below left, 250 below right, 251 below left, 251 below right, 252 above, 252 below left, 252 below right, 254 above, 256 above, 256 below left, 256 centre, 289 above, 289 below, 293 above, 293 below left, 293 below right, 294 above, 294–5 below, 295 above, 295 below right, 296 above left, 296 above right, 296 below left, 296 below right, 346 above left, 346 below, 346–7 above, 347 above right, 347 below, 348 above, 350 below, 352 above left, 352 above right, 352 below left, 352 below right (Downward and Crowson), 98, 345; Pamla Toler: 2–3; Linda Yang: 48

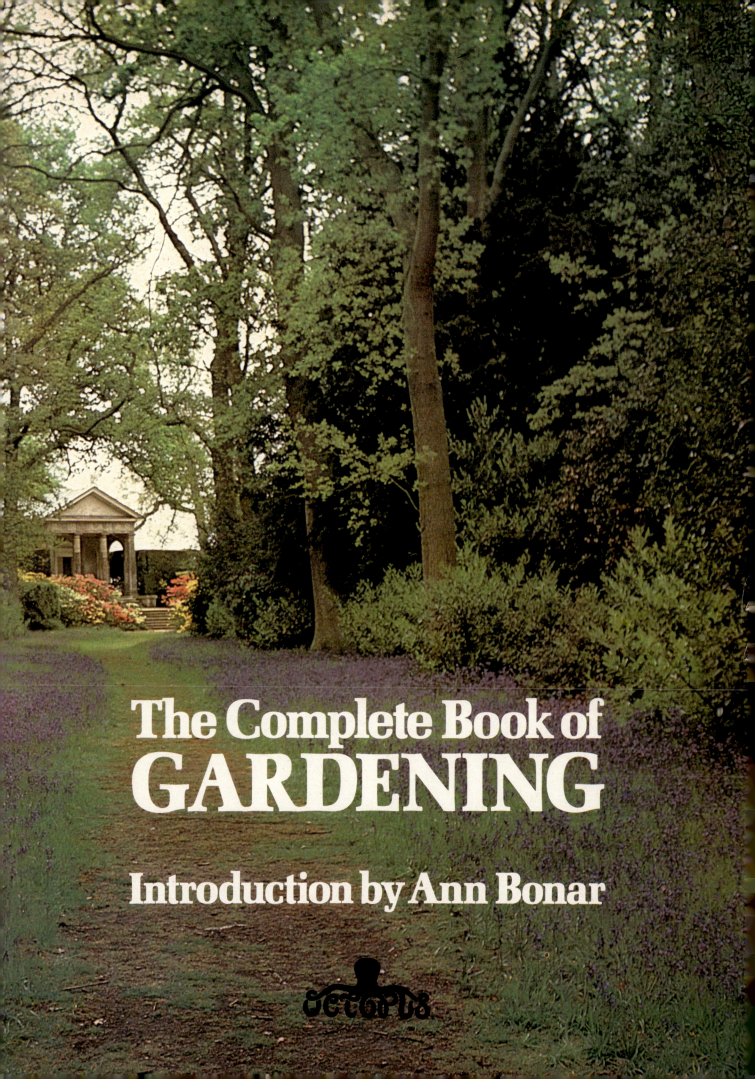

The Complete Book of
GARDENING

Introduction by Ann Bonar

octopus